Media and Glocal Change

Oscar Hemer
& Thomas Tufte
[editors]

Media and Glocal Change : Rethinking Communication for Development /
  Thomas Hylland Eriksen...[et.al.]. ; edición literaria a cargo de:
  Oscar Hemer y Thomas Tufte - 1a ed. - Buenos Aires : Consejo
  Latinoamericano de Ciencias Sociales - CLACSO ; Suecia: Nordicom, 2005.
  496 p. ; 23x16 cm.

  ISBN 987-1183-26-7

  1. Cambio Social y Comunicación I. Hemer, Oscar, ed. lit. II. Tufte, Thomas, ed.
lit. III. Título
  CDD 303.483 3.

Other indexing terms (descriptors) assigned by the Virtual Library of CLACSO:
  Development Communication; Globalization; Social Change; Local Change;
  Information and Communication Technologies; Mass Media; Cultural Change;
  Social Development; Communication Policy; International Cooperation

Otros descriptores asignados por la Biblioteca Virtual de CLACSO:
  Comunicación para el Desarrollo; Globalización; Cambio Social; Cambio Local;
  Tecnologías de Información y Comunicación; Medios de Comunicación de
  Masas; Cambio Cultural; Desarrollo Social; Política de Comunicación;
  Cooperación Internacional

Media and Glocal Change

Rethinking Communication
for Development

Oscar Hemer
& Thomas Tufte
[editors]

Thomas Hylland Eriksen
Kevin Robins
Asu Aksoy
Oscar Hemer
Silvio Waisbord
Jan Servaes
Patchanee Malikhao
Thomas Tufte
Nancy Morris
Maria Celeste Cadiz
James Deane
Ulla Carlsson
Tim Allen
Nicole Stremlau
Rafael Obregon
Mario Mosquera
Paolo Mefalopulos
Karin Gwinn Wilkins
Madanmohan Rao

Manne Granqvist
Sarat Maharaj
Gilane Tawadros
Alfonso Gumucio-Dagron
Ullamaija Kivikuru
Kemal Kurspahic
Gordon Adam
Clemencia Rodríguez
Minou Fuglesang
Kate Winskell
Daniel Enger
Ricardo Ramírez
Arvind Singhal
Peer J. Svenkerud
Prashant Malaviya
Everett M. Rogers
Vijay Krishna
Christopher Kamlongera

 norden

CLACSO

Consejo Latinoamericano
de Ciencias Sociales **CLACSO** Conselho Latino-americano
de Ciências Sociais

Colección del Programa de Edición y Distribución Cooperativa de CLACSO

Director de la Colección: Atilio A. Boron - Secretario Ejecutivo de CLACSO

Área de Difusión y Producción Editorial de CLACSO
Coordinador: Jorge Fraga
Edición: Florencia Enghel
Diseño Editorial: Miguel A. Santángelo / Lorena Taibo
Revisión de pruebas: Mariana Enghel / Ivana Brighenti
Logística y Distribución: Marcelo F. Rodriguez
Sebastián Amenta / Daniel Aranda

Arte de Tapa: Miguel A. Santángelo

Impresión: Gráficas y Servicios SRL

Primera edición en inglés
Media and Glocal Change. Rethinking Communication for Development
(Buenos Aires: CLACSO, septiembre 2005)

CLACSO
Consejo Latinoamericano de Ciencias Sociales
Conselho Latino-americano de Ciências Sociais
Latin American Council of Social Sciences
Av. Callao 875, piso 3º C1023AAB Ciudad de Buenos Aires, Argentina
Tel: (54-11) 4811-6588 / 4814-2301 - Fax: (54-11) 4812-8459
e-mail: clacso@clacso.edu.ar - http://www.clacso.org

NORDICOM
Nordic Information Centre for Media and Communication Research
Göteborg University
Box 713 Sprängkullsgatan 19, SE 405 30 Göteborg, Sweden
Telephone +46 31 773 10 00 (switchboard) - Telefax +46 31 773 46 55
e-mail: nordicom@nordicom.gu.se - http://www.nordicom.gu.se

Table of contents

Foreword

"The villager can't eat communication". Chris Kamlongera from Malawi
made that statement at a seminar in Italy a few years ago –capturing at once the
essence and the dilemma of communication for development. This book is about
exploring both the potential and the limits of communication –of using communication both as a tool and as a way of articulating processes of development and
social change, improving everyday lives, and empowering people to influence
their own lives and those of their fellow community members. The essence is
communication; the dilemma is that communication will not solve every problem,
although it can contribute in some ways to problem-solving –we just need to get
better at knowing how! The discipline of communication for development is currently at a crossroads, and the approaches that have been taken over the last few
decades require serious rethinking. Technologies are evolving, societies are changing, globalization is impacting on everything –and communication for development is evolving and changing, too: as a tool, as an approach and as a scientific
sub-discipline of communication concerned with debates and issues relating to
development and change in society. The aim of this book is to contribute to the
critical reflection about how communication works in processes of change within
the contexts of globalization. Or, to rephrase the opening statement, this book
asks: how *can* the villager –and city dweller– use communication?

It would be relevant at this point to say a couple of words about how
the book project emerged. It has grown out of the collaboration built up since
2000 in the distance education Master programme in communication for develop-

ment ComDev at Malmö University in southern Sweden. Oscar Hemer has been the coordinator since the programme's inception in 2000, and Thomas Tufte is one of the lecturers, coming over from Copenhagen to teach and supervise. Every year, some 30 new MA students in communication for development from every corner of the world experience our search for appropriate teaching materials. We spent a lot of time identifying relevant books, putting together collections of articles, and tracing the best course material. This book emerged out of the need to have a starting point for course materials in a single coherent format. Now, almost three years after the initial idea for the book, the present volume is the final product.

We would like to thank all the many people who have helped to make this project happen. We would also like to thank our two publishers for agreeing to take on the book: Ulla Carlsson and her team at NORDICOM in Gothenburg, and Atilio Boron, Jorge Fraga, and Florencia Enghel, all at CLACSO, Buenos Aires. Florencia played the important bridging role between Scandinavia and Argentina, having just graduated from the ComDev Master programme at Malmö University; she also came up with the brilliant idea of a joint project between NORDICOM and CLACSO. Many thanks also to DANIDA and Malmö University for financial support for the project. All 36 contributors from all the corners of the world –each in their own way dealing with communication for development– also deserve special thanks for their contributing articles, for showing patience through the editorial processes, and for contributing to this rethinking of communication for development. A special note goes to Everett Rogers who sadly passed away in October 2004, before the publication of his co-authored contribution. Ev Rogers was one of the pioneers in the field, having spent half a century thinking about how to use –and using– communication for development. His capacity for continuously assessing and critically reassessing his own perspectives on communication for development is the spirit this book seeks to capture. Lastly, thanks go to all those people –villagers or city dwellers– who have directly or indirectly participated in, inspired, and served in focus groups and alike –and whose concerns and lives this book hopes to address.

Oscar Hemer   Thomas Tufte

Hagestad, Sweden, and Dyssegård, Denmark, June 21, 2005

Introduction

The challenge of the glocal
Oscar Hemer & Thomas Tufte

A spectre is haunting the world –the spectre of globalization. All
the powers of old academia have entered into a holy alliance to
exorcise this spectre: social scientists (especially economists) worry
about whether markets and deregulation produce greater wealth
at the price of increased inequality. Political scientists worry that
their field might vanish along with their favourite object, the
nation-state, if globalization truly creates a 'world without
borders'. Cultural theorists, especially Marxists, worry that in spite
of its conformity with everything they already knew about capital,
there may be some embarrassing new opportunities for equity
hidden in its workings. Historians, ever worried about the problem
of the new, realize that globalization may not be a member of the
familiar archive of large-scale historical shifts. And everyone in
academia is anxious to avoid seeming to be a mere publicist of the
gigantic corporate machineries that celebrate globalization.

The above travesty of the first sentences of *The Communist Manifesto*, combined with the opening reflections on 'anxieties of the global' in Indian anthropologist Arjun Appadurai's introduction to the anthology *Globalization* (2001), gives a fair view of our current predicament, not only or even primarily in the academic world. Whether we like it or not, we are bound to relate to the phenomenon demonized –and exorcized– as globalization. First introduced in the field of cultural sociology to analyse changes in global cultural flows (Robertson, 1992), it has increasingly attained a purely economic definition, as the on-going reorganization and consolidation of global capitalism since the fall of the Soviet empire and the end of communism as a global competitor to Western liberal democracy. But defined so narrowly, globalization is but *one* aspect —albeit a fundamental one— of the more general transformational process which Catalan sociologist Manuel Castells has described and analysed as "the rise of the Network Society" (Castells, 1996, 1997, 1998).

According to Castells we are truly witnessing something new and never before experienced. The network society has evolved, not by historical determinism as an orthodox Marxist analysis would have it, but rather by coincidence, through the synergy of a couple of circumstances that happened to coincide:

» the new Information and Communication Technology (ICT), and the integration of the world into global computer networks;

» the shrinking costs of communications in a more material sense (transports), making global migration feasible;

» the fall of the Berlin wall and the restructuring of global capitalism;

» the new social movements —women's rights, the environment, human rights, etc.— that have evolved since the 1960s.

Whether we share Castells' notion of a 'qualitative leap' or regard globalization as merely the culmination of a process which has been under way for at least 150 years, we can all agree that the rapid global changes in the last few decades, illustrated by the two symbolic landmarks of the crumbling Berlin wall and the tumbling Twin Towers of the World Trade Center, face practically all sectors of human society with new challenges, not least the field of communication in a development context.

This field is currently undergoing a series of changes and innovations. New information and communication technologies (ICTs) are setting a new scene for access, content, formats and interactivity. Economic globalization is producing wealth in former less-developed areas and providing potentially powerful means for poverty alleviation, while at the same time leading to increased social and economic marginalization. HIV/AIDS is posing one of the biggest communication challenges in the history of communication for development, while important new areas such as conflict resolution are emerging and demanding attention. Altogether, this situation is articulating the required move towards not only increasingly thinking of and advocating social change objectives when practising strategic communication, but also rethinking and redefining some of the fundamental assumptions.

Reconstructing development

'Development', to start with, has been under scrutiny for some time. The grand paradigms of the 1960s (modernization) and '70s (dependency) were followed in the '80s and '90s by a multiplicity of generally less assuming approaches, some of which radically questioned the very concept of development. As Dutch sociologist

Jan Nederveen Pieterse (2001) has pointed out, there is an unholy alliance between the strong neoliberal perspective, associated with economic globalization and structural adjustment, and the radical post-development perspective, proposing local de-linking and resistance to globalization, in their common repudiation of 'development' as discourse and politics. But following the deconstruction of development, we can now witness its gradually emerging reconstruction as *world development*. Development is no longer a process reserved for 'developing countries'; all societies are developing as part of a global process, making the dichotomy of 'first' and 'third' worlds obsolete –at least in the geopolitical sense. The entire world is 'in transition' and development must therefore be rethought as a regional, transnational, global project (Pieterse, 2001: 45).

The paradigms of communication for development have to some extent been corollaries to the paradigms of development theory and politics, with a move from top-down diffusion to empowering participation –the latter corresponding to what Jan Servaes has called "the multiplicity paradigm" (chapter 5). But the relation between development thinking and the theory and practice of development communication calls for new reflection in the light of Nederveen Pietserse's suggested *critical globalist* perspective.

Informatization for social change?

The Internet is the backbone of the network society and globalization is intrinsically involved in the parallel processes of virtualization and *informatization* (as corresponding to industrialization). Yet, the so-called digital revolution has mainly been portrayed as an exclusive concern of the wealthy nations. The booming literature on cyberspace and the new techno-culture in the '90s showed little, if any, interest in the developing countries. ICT has, however, quickly established its own niche within development cooperation. Two diametrically opposing and equally justified opinions can be identified where the implications of ICT for development are concerned:

» it strengthens and further widens the divide between developed and developing countries;

» it is a shortcut to prosperity without the need for polluting industrialization or resource-consuming investments in heavy infrastructure.

In Castells' analysis, ICT has a privileged position, also in a development context:

> The fundamental digital divide is not measured by the number of connections to the Internet, but by the consequences of both connection and lack of connection. Because the Internet is not just a technology. It is the technological tool and organizational form that distributes information power, knowledge generation, and networking capacity in all realms of activity. Thus, developing countries are caught in a tangled web. On the one hand, being disconnected, or superficially connected, to the Internet is tantamount to marginalization in the global, networked system. Development

without the Internet would be the equivalent of industrialization without electricity in the industrial era. That is why the often-heard statement concerning the need to start with 'the real problems of the Third World' –meaning health, education, water, electricity, and the like– before coming to the Internet reveals a profound misunderstanding of the current issues in development. Because, without an Internet-based economy and management system, there is little chance for any country to generate the resources necessary to cover its developmental needs, on a sustainable ground –meaning economically sustainable, socially sustainable, and environmentally sustainable (Castells, 2001: 269).

India's 'communication revolution' (Singhal and Rogers, 2001) is an interesting example of *informatization* as a development strategy. What has always been regarded as India's major set-back –its huge population– has suddenly become its great comparative advantage. Some 100,000 qualified computer engineers graduate every year, and have turned India into the world's 'outsourcing centre'. India's advantage over the other giant, China, is of course the language –English being a national language and lingua franca. India's change since the mid 1990s has been dramatic. Yet it remains at the bottom of the Human Development Index (HDI) list, with one of the highest illiteracy rates in the world. And it is precisely the combination of low HDI and high ICT capacity that makes India a pilot case in efforts to open new frontiers for informatization as a tool for economic *and* social change.

The cultural turn

'Transnationalism', as defined by Kevin Robins and Asu Aksoy (chapter 2), is another fundamental challenge to development communication strategies, which are still to a large extent formulated and implemented within the framework of the nation-state, or the (culturally) bounded local community. Global migration and TV satellites have resulted in big, new, globally scattered diasporic cultures linked in transnational public spheres, which are undermining the 'imagined communities' of the national media.

Among the main potential new agents of social change in a global context, as part of what Appadurai calls 'grassroots globalization' or 'globalization from below' (1996, 2001), are the *transnational advocacy networks*, or TANs, which form an increasingly important part of the NGO world that in turn plays an increasingly crucial role in international development cooperation.

Transnationalization may reinforce cultural (and national) identities, but *transcultural* processes are also a central feature of reflexive global modernity, expressed as 'creolization' or 'cultural hybridity' and analysed by post-colonial theorists such as Appadurai and Homi K Bhabha. 'Culture' is, however, a problematic concept in a development context.

The social engineers of the modernization model regarded it as at best a colourful yet insignificant vestige of the past which would eventually fade away, like religion. At worst, and not without reason, (cultural) tradition was seen as a major obstacle to social and economic development. Culture was not a major concern of the opposing dependency school either –except as an expression of political resistance to (cultural) imperialism. Cultural differences, which could have explained why a group of East Asian economies in the decades that followed were apparently to refute the dependency theory, were still not considered to be of any significance.

But in the '90s –proclaimed by the UN as the Decade of Culture– the tables were turned and culture suddenly became the key word in development discourse. In 1995, the World Commission on Culture and Development presented its report *Our Creative Diversity*, introducing the notion of 'cultural freedom' as "the right of a group of people to follow a way of life of its choice". The World Commission was followed by an *Action Plan on Cultural Policies for Development* (1998) and the UNESCO declaration on *Cultural Diversity* (2001), intended to be a supplement to the better-known Agenda 21.

The cultural turn in development discourse coincides with a general trend in the social sciences. Moreover, it happens at a time when 'culture', as a consequence of globalization, tends to become synonymous with 'identity' –national, religious or ethnic. Cultural policies are increasingly taking the form of identity politics that are often militant, as discussed in depth by Thomas Hylland Eriksen in chapter 1. The 'right to culture' has thus tended to create an antagonism between (individual human) rights and culture, understood as a bounded group identity. Cultural freedom as opposed to individual freedom seems to reflect the classical opposition between relativism and universalism.

In his constructive critique of *Our Creative Diversity,* Eriksen (2001) even suggests that we should abandon the word culture in a development context:

> There is no need for a concept of culture in order to respect local conditions in development work: it is sufficient to be sensitive to the fact that local realities are always locally constructed, whether one works in inner-city Chicago or in the Kenyan countryside. One cannot meaningfully rank one locality as more authentic than another. What is at stake in development work is not cultural authenticity or purity, but people's ability to gain control over their own lives[1].

Yet insistence on respect for local circumstances remains fundamental, and support for local arts and the preservation of historical environments are becoming increasingly important features of international development cooperation. Whether we like the term 'cultural heritage' or not, it is one of the emerging areas within the field of communication for development.

1 The full text is available on Eriksen's webpage, <http://folk.uio.no/geirthe/UNESCO.html>.

18 | Media and communication in development cooperation

'Coherence' is becoming a buzz-word in the jargon of development policy-makers, indicating a growing awareness of the inter-relatedness of different, often opposing policies. For example, the sum of development aid from North to South is minuscule compared with subsidies to agricultural production in the donor countries, and exports from the South are effectively hindered by trade barriers and import restrictions in the North. The divide between rhetoric and reality seems abysmal. Nevertheless, the very formulation of the UN Millennium Goals, with poverty alleviation as their prime objective, and the adoption of 'coherent' policies for international development cooperation –such as Sweden's recently ratified 'policy for global development'– may be important steps towards a truly globalist development perspective.

However, the fundamental role of media and communication in promoting global change is remarkably absent in almost all the declarations. In spite of the focus on democracy and human rights, the seemingly obvious means to achieve these goals –plural media and functional public spheres– still occupy a peripheral position in bilateral as well as multilateral programmes. Moreover, there is often a sharp divide within the development agencies, between 'media support' on the one hand and 'strategic communication' on the other, as if media and communication were opposed and even conflicting entities.

Media support, mostly in the form of training in journalism and financial aid to 'free' media, represents an insignificant proportion of development budgets, and strategic communication even less –if indeed it is even defined as a separate objective. Few development agencies have yet bothered to formulate a communication policy.

This situation is slowly but steadily changing. Primarily this is due to the imminent challenge of the HIV/AIDS epidemic and the evident need for coordinated health communication measures. Secondly it is a consequence of the new patterns of global and local conflicts and the no less urgent need for conflict prevention and resolution. Rwanda and the former Yugoslavia are but two examples of the media's disastrous ability to instigate violence and even genocide. Bosnia after the Dayton agreement provides a single example of failed media efforts with a peace-building pretext, but there are other, albeit few and less well-known, cases which demonstrate the media's peace-breaking potential.

There may, however, be a conflict of interest here, between liberal ideals of freedom and plurality, on the one hand, and the prevention of incitement to violence and ethnic strife and the protection of vulnerable groups, on the other. This emerging conflict bears some resemblance to the once divisive controversy over the 'New World Information and Communication Order', which may appear distant and long since refuted today, yet is well worth re-examining in the light of current tendencies in the global media landscape.

The holistic approach

One of the common conclusions found throughout this inventory of the field is the call for a holistic approach. Health communication will surely remain the single most important area within the field of communication for social change, with conflict resolution as the runner-up. But these are of course intimately linked vis-à-vis the overall goal of poverty alleviation and the equally emphasized objectives of democracy and human rights. The environment, including the man-made environment and heritage, is another area of increasing importance. Sustainable development does not only concern the natural environment and the rural poor, but also the cultural heritage in urban environments. The socio-cultural dimension of sustainability is fundamental from a development communication perspective, with the potential to promote social inclusion and participatory democratic citizenship.

The successful use of narrative and fiction is perhaps the most striking feature when it comes to actually mediating social change. *Edutainment* (Entertainment-Education) has become the favoured medium for HIV/AIDS communication, with success stories such as HIP Femina in Tanzania, Puntos de Encuentro in Nicaragua and the often evoked Soul City of South Africa. Not only culture in general, but art –*the arts*– is becoming a particularly important player in the field, with equally interesting implications for artistic imagination and investigation.

The current ComDev debate

The debate about communication for social change is currently being articulated by a range of major international initiatives within the development business.

» Since 1997 the Rockefeller Foundation has hosted a range of meetings and seminars seeking to articulate a global dialogue upon key challenges in the field, and calling for a stronger social change agenda in many development challenges (Rockefeller Foundation, 1991 and 1999). This has raised substantial debate on the fundamental question of how to define social change. From 2004 the Communication for Social Change Consortium has continued this series of meetings and seminars. Recent meetings in this forum have debated the key competencies required and drafted what may become a generic Master programme in communication for social change <www.communicationforsocialchange.org>.

» Based on global consultations in 1998-2000 with practitioners and scholars, UNAIDS came up with an HIV/AIDS communication framework (Makinwa, B., Airhihenbuwa, C., and Obregon R., 1999). This sparked a lot of debate but had some difficulty in linking up with practice. The WHO and especially PAHO have, with USAID support, pursued some of the ideas and are working on curricular design in the Latin American region in particular.

» The International Roundtables on Communication for Development, having met regularly since 1988, had their eighth roundtable in Managua, Nicaragua, in November 2001, discussing these issues along three lines of debate: behaviour change communication, advocacy communication and communication for social change (Roundtable Declaration, November 26th 2001).

A lot of debate is thus taking place on the issue of communication for social change, but having participated in some of the debates outlined above, we the editors of this book have realized that there is a tremendous need for more systematic reflection upon where the field is heading. There is also an outspoken need for a clearer understanding of the key components in such a field of research and practice, for discussion of the epistemologies, the theories, the methods and the successful cases, all in an integrated manner. And such an integrated discussion should be set in the context of globalization in all the aspects –economic, political and not least cultural– which are setting the agendas. With the field of communication and development booming, there is also a clear need for greater professionalism amongst media and communication practitioners in the development business.

Moreover, recent theoretical and methodological developments in the broad field of communication research –and not least audience research– have still been incorporated on only a very limited scale into current practices in communication for development. This missing link must be challenged. There also exists a wide range of successful practices that deserve attention for feeding back into academic reflection in the field.

Lastly, but most crucially: there is a need to link all these issues to provide efficient responses to the burning societal challenges, for example that of HIV/AIDS. This book therefore wishes to integrate reflection on epistemology, theory, methodology and successful case studies in order to move the field towards a new phase, enabling media and communication practitioners to respond better to the realities of a *glocalized* world. We have chosen the term 'glocal' –derived from American sociologist Roland Robertson's notion of 'glocalization'– to stress the dual character of the globalization process, as being 'globalization' and 'localization' simultaneously. Glocal change means social change in a global *and* local context. It implies rethinking the discourses of both 'development' and 'communication' in the light of a third discourse which provides the general frame: that is, globalization.

Our ambition is thus to try to delineate the characteristics of what might be understood as an emerging interdisciplinary communication discipline, committed to development and to social change, and for that purpose seeking to bridge the best of traditionally separate communication paradigms, and drawing on successful experience.

Previous and parallel publications

The general subject of media and globalization has seen a number of publications in the last decade, such as the reader *Media in Global Context* (1997) and the more recent anthologies *News in a Globalized Society* (2001) and *Global Encounters: Media and Cultural Transformation* (2002). An attempt at globalizing the field of media studies is made in *De-Westernizing Media Studies* (2000) and media case studies form a significant part of *Culture and Global Change* (1999), both anthologies published by Routledge, which has also issued a series of working papers on *Transnationalism*, with a degree of focus on media and communications, at the website Transnational Communities[2]. *Globalization* (2001), with Arjun Appadurai's explicit call for new forms of pedagogy and collaborative research on (grassroots) globalization, could also easily be enlisted for our purposes here.

The closest more recent material in the specific field of Communication for Development is the anthology *Approaches to Development Communication*, edited by Jan Servaes and published by UNESCO in 2002. Servaes' previous work (1999; Servaes, Jacobson and White, eds., 1996) provides examples of related material. However, these publications focus more specifically on participatory communication, as in White (ed., 1999), for example. A two-volume anthology is in the pipeline (Gumucio Dagron and Tufte, eds., forthcoming), and will be published by the Communication for Social Change Consortium. However, this publication's focus is on gathering key classics –texts that have played a key role over the history of the field, especially in conceptual development of its thinking and practice.

In the field of entertainment-education a major publication has just been published (Singhal et al, 2004). However, as with the work of Servaes or White, it only deals with one specific aspect of communication for development.

New publications are being issued in each thematic area mentioned in this book, but many have a very specialized focus (such as those mentioned above, or also Downing, 2001 or Bouman, 1999) or remain on the practitioner's level (which includes many UN publications on radio, video or on the use of specific methodologies and tools). A sound contribution to the field was McKee et al, (2000), which dealt with all relevant aspects of designing, implementing and monitoring social sector programmes and using communication in that respect. However, this focuses on methodologies, has no in-depth presentation of cases, and does not offer the overall societal framework that we suggest. Substantial case presentations are found in Gumucio-Dagron's report *Making Waves* (2000), but they remain case presentations.

What has been lacking to date is a comprehensive contemporary presentation of the whole field of communication for development, broadening the perspective, bridging the existing paradigms, providing the development context, and offering an introduction to what is increasingly becoming a new field of research and communication practice. The ambition of this anthology, gathering leading contemporary theorists and practitioners in the present field and adding important authors from closely connected areas of research and practice, is therefore to present an integral reflection upon where the still-emerging field of communication for development is coming from and, particularly, where we believe it should be heading.

The book is organized in three parts, with the first part setting and redefining the general framework (epistemology, theory and methodology), the second mapping the new field, and the third providing some exemplary case studies linked to the chosen sub-areas of the field.

Editing an anthology like this is always a hazardous and somewhat random task. We are aware that some areas have received more attention than others and that important new subjects within this dynamic field may be missing altogether. But this anthology should of course be regarded as our contribution to an ongoing process.

Part I

Globalization, media and culture

Chapter 1

How can the global be local?

Islam, the West and the globalisation of identity politics

Thomas Hylland Eriksen

In an important sense, the present human world is more tightly integrated than at any earlier point in history. In the age of the jet plane and satellite dish, the age of global capitalism, the age of ubiquitous markets and global mass media, various commentators have claimed that the world is rapidly becoming a single place. Although this slightly exaggerated description has an important point to make, an even more striking development of the post-cold war world is the emergence –seemingly everywhere– of identity politics whose explicit aim is the restoration of rooted tradition, religious fervour and/or commitment to ethnic or national identities, majoritarian and minoritarian. As I write from my home in Oslo, Norway has just celebrated its Constitution Day (17 May), and never before has there been as many folk costumes in town as this year. More than 90% of the population celebrate 17 May, and more than half of the women wear folk dresses (*bunader*). The number of men, although much lower, is also on the rise. In my childhood, three decades ago, which unfolded in a less intensely globalised world, folk dresses were rarely seen in the urban centres of south-eastern Norway. Now, consider the fact that only a few months earlier, Norwegians had, like other West Europeans, been debating the question of whether or not to legislate against the use of headscarves (*hijabs*) among Muslim immigrant women. Again, a couple of decades ago, *hijabs* were hardly ever seen among Muslim immigrant women in Europe. Even today, many young Muslim women wear the *hijab* against their father's wish.

     In all likelihood, few of the very many women (and men) sporting neo-traditionalist garb on Constitution Day would have reflected on the parallel between the rise of visible identity markers among minorities and in the majority. And one would have to be a social scientist interested in globalisation to see these markers of difference not as a "natural" expression of a "natural" identity, nor as a simple reaction against globalisation, but as *one of its most common forms*. If anything, globalisation at the level of social identity is tantamount to a re-negotiation of social identities, their boundaries and symbolic content. Nobody is quite certain as to what it means to be a Berliner, a Malaysian or a Norwegian any more, but this does not necessarily mean that these identities are going away. Some of them are in fact strengthened, with new or old symbolic content; some wane to the benefit of others; some are enlarged or shrunk as to social compass. Just as a fish is totally uninterested in water as long as it swims happily around –it is even unlikely to be aware of the existence of water– most people don't think twice about those of their identities that can be taken for granted. But the moment you drag the poor creature out of the sea, be it on a hook or in a net, it immediately develops an intense interest in water; what the water means to it, how it is essential for its survival, and –not least– the peculiar nature of water. Had fish been equipped with an ability to ponder, a great number of short-lived (and doubtless post-structuralist) theories about water would have been sketched in haste, in maritime surroundings, every day. In the case of humans, not only are the national, regional and local identities contested and challenged, but it is becoming increasingly difficult to defend absolutist views of gender and kinship identities as well. Place, that is to say a fixed, stable, meaningful space, is becoming a scarce and flexible resource. Maintaining a predictable and secure group identity is hard work these days.

Globalisation as annihilation of distance

It cannot be contested that globalisation in all its forms –political, cultural, economic, military…– is a pervasive tendency influencing the lives of people everywhere –from the Amazon rainforest to Japanese cities. The concept has recently become a fashionable one in social and cultural studies, and as a result, its meaning has become fuzzy. I would propose, therefore, a view of globalisation as *all the sociocultural processes that contribute to making distance irrelevant*. It has important economic, political and cultural dimensions, as well as equally important ethical implications. Truly global processes affect the conditions of people living in particular localities, creating new opportunities and new forms of vulnerability. Risks are globally shared in the era of the nuclear bomb, transnational terrorism and potential ecological disasters. On the same note, the economic conditions in particular localities frequently (some would say always) depend on events taking place elsewhere in the global system. If there is an industrial boom in Taiwan, towns in the English Midlands will be affected. If oil prices rise, that means salvation for the oil-exporting Trinidadian economy and disaster for the oil-importing, neighbouring Barbadian one.

Patterns of consumption also seem to merge in certain respects; people nearly everywhere desire similar goods, from cellphones to readymade garments. Now, a precondition for this to happen is the more or less successful implementation of certain institutional dimensions of modernity, notably that of a monetary economy –if not necessarily evenly distributed wagework and literacy. The ever-increasing transnational flow of commodities, be they material or immaterial, creates a set of common cultural denominators which appear to eradicate local distinctions. The hot-dog (*halal* or not, as the case may be), the pizza and the hamburger (or, in India, the lamburger) are truly parts of world cuisine; identical pop songs are played in identical discotheques in Costa Rica and Thailand; the same Coca-Cola commercials are shown with minimal local variations at cinemas all over the world, Harry Potter volumes are ubiquitous wherever books are sold, and so on. Investment capital, military power and world literature are being disembedded from the constraints of space; they no longer belong to a particular locality. With the development of the jet plane, the satellite dish and more recently, the Internet, distance no longer seems a limiting factor for the flow of influence, investments and cultural meaning.

Globalisation is, in other words, not merely another word for the growing transnational economy. It is true that it is largely driven by technology and economic interests, but it must be kept in mind that it encompasses a wide range of regular events that are not in themselves technological or economic. Take the human rights discourse, for example: in the course of the second half of the twentieth century, the ideas and values associated with human rights have spread from educated elites worldwide (and not just in the West) to villagers and farmers in areas which until recently seemed both remote and exotic to the Western eye. The rapid dissemination of human rights ideas is, in fact, probably one of the most spectacular successes of globalisation.

Identity politics as globalisation

At the same time, we have in recent years witnessed the growth, in very many societies in all continents, of political movements seeking to strengthen the collective sense of uniqueness, often targeting globalisation processes, which are seen as a threat to local distinctiveness and self-determination. A European example with tragic consequences is the rise of ethnic nationalism in Croatia and Serbia from the 1980s, but even in the more prosperous and stable European Union strong ethnic and nationalist movements grew during the 1990s, ranging from Scottish separatism to the anti-immigration Front National in France and nationalist populism in countries like Austria, Denmark and the Netherlands. In Asia, two of the most powerful examples from recent history were the rise of the Taliban to power in Afghanistan and the meteoric success of the Hindu nationalist BJP (Bharatiya Janata Party, "Party of the Indian People") in India; and many African countries have also seen a strong ethnification of their politics during the last decade-and-a-half, as well as the rise of political Islam in the Sahel and the north. In the Americas, various minority movements, from indigenous groups to African Americans, have with increasing success demanded cultural recognition and equal rights. In sum, politics around the turn of the millennium has to a great extent meant identity politics.

This new political scene, difficult to fit into the old left–right divide, is interpreted in very different ways by the many academics and journalists who have studied them. This is partly because identity politics comes in many flavours: some are separatist nationalist movements; some represent historically oppressed minorities which demand equal rights; some are dominant groups trying to prevent minorities from gaining access to national resources; some are religious, some are ethnic, and some are regional. Many writers see identity politics in general as an anti-modern counterreaction to the individualism and freedom embodied by globalisation, while others see it as the defence of the weak against foreign dominance, or even as a concealed strategy of modernisation. Some emphasize the psychological dimension of identity politics, seeing it as nostalgic attempts to retain dignity and a sense of rootedness in an era of rapid change; others focus on competition for scarce resources between groups; some see identity politics as a strategy of exclusion and an ideology of hatred, while yet others see it as the true-born child of socialism, as an expression of the collective strivings of the underdog.

Neither of these interpretations and judgments tells the whole story, both because the concrete movements in question differ and because the phenomenon of identity politics is too complex for a simple explanation to suffice. What is clear, however, is that the centripetal or unifying forces of globalisation and the centrifugal or fragmenting forces of identity politics are two sides of the same coin, two complementary tendencies which must be understood well for anyone wishing to make sense of the global scene at the turn of the millennium.

For a variety of reasons, globalisation creates the conditions for *localisation*, that is various kinds of attempts at creating bounded entities –countries (nationalism or separatism), faith systems (religious revitalisation), cultures (linguistic or cultural movements) or interest groups (ethnicity). For this reason, a more apt term, coined by Roland Robertson (1992), could be *glocalisation*. Let me now move to a general description of some features that the "glocal" identity movements of the turn of the millennium seem to have in common –the rudiments of a grammar of identity politics[1].

First, identity politics always entails *competition over scarce resources*. Successful mobilisation on the basis of collective identities presupposes a widespread belief that resources are unequally distributed along group lines. "Resources" should be interpreted in the widest sense possible, and could in principle be taken to mean economic wealth or political power, recognition or symbolic power. What is at stake can be economic or political resources, but the *recognition of others* has been an underestimated, scarce resource, as well as meaningful social attachments where one is in command of one's own life to an acceptable degree.

1 For a fuller analysis, see Eriksen, T. H.; "Ethnic identity, national identity and intergroup conflict: The significance of personal experiences" in Ashmore et al (2001).

Secondly, *modernisation and globalisation actualize differences and trigger conflict*. When formerly discrete groups are integrated into shared economic and political systems, inequalities are made visible, since direct comparison between the groups becomes possible. Friction occurs frequently. In a certain sense, ethnicity can be described as the process of making cultural differences comparable, and to that extent, it is a modern phenomenon boosted by the intensified contact entailed by globalisation. You do not envy your neighbour if you are unaware of his existence.

Thirdly, *similarity overrules equality ideologically*. Ethnic nationalism, politicized religion and indigenous movements all depict the in-group as homogeneous, as people "of the same kind". Internal differences are glossed over, and for this reason, it can often be argued that identity politics serves the interests of the privileged segments of the group, even if the group as a whole is underprivileged, since it conceals internal class differences.

Fourthly, *images of past suffering and injustice are invoked*. To mention a few examples: in the 1990s, Serbs bemoaned the defeat at the hands of the Turks in Kosovo in 1389; leaders of the Hindu BJP have taken great pains to depict Mughal (Muslim) rule in India from the 1500s as bloody and authoritarian; and the African American movement draws extensively on the history of slavery. Even spokesmen for clearly privileged groups, such as anti-immigrant politicians in Western Europe, may argue along these lines.

Fifthly, *the political symbolism and rhetoric evokes personal experiences*. This is perhaps the most important ideological feature of identity politics in general. Using myths, cultural symbols and kinship terminology in addressing their supporters, promoters of identity politics try to downplay the difference between personal experiences and group history. In this way, it becomes perfectly sensible for a Serb to talk about the legendary battle of Kosovo in the first person ("*We* lost in 1389"), and the logic of revenge is extended to include metaphorical kin, in many cases millions of people. The intimate experiences associated with locality and family are thereby projected onto a national screen.

Sixthly, *first-comers are contrasted with invaders*. Although this ideological feature is by no means universal in identity politics, it tends to be invoked whenever possible, and in the process, historical facts are frequently stretched.

Finally, *the actual social complexity in society is reduced to a set of simple contrasts*. As Adolf Hitler already wrote in *Mein Kampf*, the truly national leader concentrates the attention of his people on one enemy at the time. Since cross-cutting ties reduce the chances of violent conflict, the collective identity must be based on relatively unambiguous criteria (such as place, religion, mothertongue, kinship). Again, internal differences are undercommunicated in the act of delineating boundaries towards the frequently demonized Other.

Identity politics is a true-born child of globalisation. The more similar we become, the more different we try to be. Paradoxically, however, the more different we try to be, the more similar we become –since most of us try to be different in roughly the same ways worldwide, as I have suggested.

Against the view that identity politics is somehow anachronistic, it has been argued many times, always correctly, that although it tends to be dressed in traditional garb, beneath the surface it is a product of modernity and its associated dilemmas of identity. The strong emotions associated with a tradition, a culture or a religion can never be mobilized unless people feel that it is under siege. We are, in this sense, like fish.

Viewed in this way, the collective emotions that identity politics depend on reveal themselves to be deeply modern emotions associated with the sense of loss experienced in situations of rapid change. The need for security, belonging and enduring social ties based on trust is universal and cannot be wished away. Ethnic nationalism, minority movements and politicized religion offer a larger share of the cake as well as a positive sense of self, and like it or not, these movements will remain influential in most parts of the world until something better comes along.

The case of "the West" and "Islam"

The single most discussed field of tension involving identity politics is doubtless the relationship between "the West" and "Islam". Since the Salman Rushdie affair from 1988, but especially after 11 September 2001, this presumed opposition has been subject to an enormous amount of attention, both among secularised North Atlantic peoples, Muslims and everybody else. Drawing on the presupposition that identity politics, which is often antagonistic in nature, is a main form of globalisation, I now proceed to analysing some aspects of this assumed conflict as a trueborn child of globalisation. But first, a short detour.

The perhaps most influential organic intellectuals of the current regime in Washington are Francis Fukuyama and Samuel Huntington. Both are authors of widely distributed books about the "new world order", and both are keenly listened to in circles near the White House. However, they seem to be saying opposite things. Fukuyama (1993) has argued that Western democracy is the only game in town worthy of the name, and that global politics nowadays simply consists in attempts, by the less unfortunate nations, to achieve the same levels of consumption and liberal rights as those enjoyed by Americans. In this context, he also argues that the quest for recognition is fundamental and accounts for various forms of identity politics. Huntington (1996), on the other hand, has argued that current and future conflicts take place not between ideologies, but between "civilisations", that is related clusters of cultures, such as the West, Islam, Hinduism and Eastern Christianity. Both Fukuyama and Huntington have been severely criticised by academics and other intellectuals, and this is not the place to repeat all the criticisms. On the contrary, I would argue that they are both partly right. Fukuyama is right to assume that recognition by others is a notoriously scarce resource in the contemporary world, but he is wrong in believing that recognition can only be achieved through the successful adoption of Western values and ways of life. Huntington is correct in saying that cultural differences are important, but he is hopelessly off the mark when he tries to map out those differences –his concept of civilisations is theoretically inconsistent and empirically misleading– and there is also no reason to assume that such differences necessarily lead to conflict. In fact, it has been shown that *none* of the armed conflicts of the 1990s conformed with Huntington's predictions[2].

We must nonetheless concede that these conservative American thinkers correctly claim that recognition and respect are important, and that cultural differences matter. Where does this lead us?

It seems to lead us in the general direction of postcolonial theory. According to writers such as Frantz Fanon, Ngugi wa Thiong'o and Edward Said, the most difficult form of decolonisation consists in decolonising the mind; in developing a self, and an identity, and a self-consciousness which is not based on the categories of the colonisers. In giving the people of the world the choice of being either with the US or with the terrorists (as he did in a speech delivered in autumn 2001), Bush II refuses to acknowledge any position which is developed out of other concerns than the US–"terrorists" axis.

Human rights and the means of communication

In the context of the current crisis, this starting-point implies certain preliminary conclusions: effective human rights activism requires at least a minimal knowledge about local contexts and, particularly, about local conflicts. For poor countries to give wholehearted support to notions of the inalienable rights of the individual, more is required than decisions to cut aid to countries which are not yet committed to a free press and multi-party parliamentary democracy. What is needed are social reforms which give people increased control over their own existence –literacy programmes, land reforms, new job opportunities and so on. As an implication, a global policy is needed where both big power (state, geopolitics) and small power (family, community) are more equitably distributed. This struggle, moreover, is as much about the means of communication as about the means of production. As the late Algerian author Rachid Mimouni put it, what ought to be required of the Europeans is "rather an attempt to understand than material aid. What can democracy mean in a country like Ethiopia, where dozens die of starvation every day?" (1992: 156). There are, in other words, serious problems which are not solved by a formulaic introduction of human rights, and there are people who for perfectly understandable reasons see talk about the freedom of expression as a diversion from the real issues. One may by all means argue that Muslim men should give their wives the same rights and opportunities as, say, Scandinavian women have (opinions are free), but it would

2 Fox, Jonathan, "Clash of Civilizations or Clash of Religions: Which is a More Important Determinant of Ethnic Conflict?", *Ethnicities*, 1(3): 295-366.

be silly to assume that they think in the same way as we do. If one does so –promoting human rights with the subtlety of a bulldozer– one implicitly says, as missionaries and foreign aid aristocrats have done for years, that the experiences of others have no value, and that the others had better become like ourselves before we bother to listen to them. One actually says that they *do not exist* until they have become similar to ourselves. Respecting other life-worlds is, it must be emphasised, not the same as ethical relativism, but on the contrary a recognition of the need for a dialogue to go both ways, since the alternative is monologue or worse: the sound from one hand clapping[3].

The very conceptual pair "The West" and "Islam" is deeply problematic. "The West" is a vague geographic term, including the EU, the USA and their richest satellites (Canada, Norway, etc.), as well as two of the easternmost countries in the world, Australia and New Zealand. Islam is a universalistic religion with adherents in every country, including all the Western ones. Could "The West and the East" have been used instead, as a more consistent dichotomy, or perhaps "Christianity and Islam" as in the old days? Hardly. All such dichotomies are Trojan horses concealing the hidden agenda of overstating the importance of one particular boundary at the expense of neglecting all the others.

There is little to indicate that religion as such can be a source of conflict. A Christian fundamentalist has more in common with a Muslim fundamentalist, at the level of basic values, than each of them has with non-religious persons. The forms of religiosity and the expressions of respect for al-Lah (or God, as we say in English), are similar in both cases. Hundreds, possibly thousands, of European Muslims have discovered this and have thus joined Christian Democratic parties. Moreover, there are important ecumenical dialogues taking place across "religious divides" in many places, including a major Islamic conference in Cairo in 1995, where central Muslim leaders condemned all forms of terrorism on Islamic grounds, calling for extensive dialogue with the other monotheistic religions originating in West Asia. At a more everyday level, it is easy to see that folk religiosity on either side of the Mediterranean, for example, has many similarities –saints, prayers, beliefs in the evil eye, and so on. Following the attacks of 11 September, one should also keep in mind, all Muslim heads of state except Saddam Hussain and the Taliban condemned the mass murder. Already on the same evening, the *Tehran Times* stated that Islam forbids suicide and that a murder of an innocent, according to the Koran, is tantamount to a murder of all humanity.

Malaysia's then prime minister Mahathir offered to negotiate between the USA and its adversaries in the autumn of 2001, and this might have been a fruitful move: Malaysia is an overwhelmingly Muslim country, but it is also committed to Western notions of modernity. The USA did not take the offer up, and

3 An excellent contribution to this dialogue was the volume *Pour Rushdie*, co-edited by a Jew and a Muslim (both women and both anonymous), including texts by a hundred Arab and Muslim intellectuals (Paris: La Découverte, 1993).

during a visit a month after the bombing had begun, I heard of no Malays who defended the terrorist attacks, but a lot of them seemed to admire Osama. Wrong address, no doubt, but the Castro effect no less.

If Malaysia's "moderate Islam" had been granted its place in the sun, fewer Malays would have looked up to Osama bin Laden, and more Westerners would have discovered the similarities between the three great West Asian religions. Seen from a Hindu or East Asian point of view, the three religions appear as virtually identical. Even from the inside, the parallels are striking. The Muslims who have joined Christian Democratic parties in European countries have done so because Christians and Muslims have shared interests in fighting phenomena such as religious slackness, secularisation, birth control and divorces. During another Cairo conference, in the autumn of 1994, the Catholic Church and Muslim clerics joined forces to make a joint statement condemning abortion. Moreover, many –anthropologists, journalists and others– relentlessly show the absurdity of lumping together Indonesian rice farmers with Turkish merchants under the umbrella of "Islam"; just as intellectuals in Muslim countries are perfectly well aware that "the West" contains something close to a billion individuals with a variety of values, societies and ways of life.

Polarisation

The current trend is that of growing polarisation. The relationship between the West and Islam, as it has developed since the Gulf War, is beginning to resemble the armaments race between the USA and the Soviet Union –a schismogenetic process par excellence. In the end, both superpowers had enough nuclear weapons to annihilate humanity many times over. These days, self-proclaimed representatives of both Islam and the West compete –not over the number of warheads, but over the souls of unattached individuals, in rhetorical attacks on each other. In research on ethnic relations, this kind of mechanism is sometimes called *dichotomisation*, that is the mutual defining of the other as the opposite of oneself –as that which one does not want to be. Enemy images always depend on this kind of simplistic, stereotypical depictions of the other. Realistic, nuanced descriptions contain too many shades of grey and too much complexity to be of ideological use in creating hatred and implacability. Seen from the north-west, Muslims, or "Islam", may thus appear as undemocratic, sexist, illiberal, underdeveloped, brutal and culturally stagnated. The enemy image, incidentally, is adjusted as its proponents change historically. While the generalised Muslim woman today is depicted as an oppressed, intimidated and powerless person, it was common in Victorian times to depict her as a profoundly erotic, mystical and seductive character.

Seen from the south-east, the Europeans, or the people of the West, may appear as cold individualists, as normless, immoral, arrogant, brutal, decadent and insensitive. These dichotomisations owe little to objective differences between Islam and Christianity, but to power relations feeding into assumptions about cultural differences. Roughly the same stereotypes that are now commonly used about Muslims have been used variously to describe South Europeans, North Norwegians, blacks and "Hindoos" in the past. They are responses to a need in the population where the stereotypes are formed rather than expressions of characteristics in the stereotyped population.

Muslim stereotypes of "the West" would themselves have been worthy of a book-length treatment[4]; suffice it here to say that they are no less simplistic and no less antithetical to openness and dialogue than the Western images of Islam and Muslims. For a recent example, it has been shown how the Pakistani press, in the months following the attacks, contributed to strengthening mutual stereotyping through portraying the "clash of civilizations" perspective as the only Western view of the matter (Ali, 2002).

Beyond cultural stereotypes is the language of undiluted bigotry and chauvinism, as in certain forms of war reporting. During the Gulf War, the Western press wrote of the US-led forces as "lionhearts, professional, heroes, daring, loyal, resolute, brave", while Iraqi soldiers were described as "brainwashed, paper tigers, cowardlike, desperate, the bastards from Baghdad, mad dogs, unscrupulous, fanatical"[5]. More recently, Bush II spoke of the suicide pilots of 11 September notoriously as "cowards". As Susan Sontag pointed out shortly afterwards[6], many strong words may be used to describe these madmen (such as, for example, brainwashed or psychotic), but cowards they were definitely not. Similarly, it is difficult to say that the US pilots, who dropped their cluster bombs on Afghanistan from a comfortable height before returning for breakfast, were exceptionally courageous.

Important things are at stake. If the perverse idea of a civilizational conflict between the West and Islam catches on, which it may well do notwithstanding the insistence to the contrary by Western leaders, the result is likely to be escalating violence on both sides. In Gregory Bateson's system theory, this kind of self-reinforcing process is known as *schismogenesis*[7]. Bateson, a versatile and original thinker, applied the concept of schismogenesis to as diverse phenomena as alcoholism, gang violence and arms races. Convinced that the cause of schismogenesis was an error in the dominant Western mode of thought –the error of individualism– Bateson wrote that if, for example, boasting is an element in the relationship between group A and group B, then "it is likely, if boasting is a response to boasting, that each group will drive the other to an exaggerated emphasis on this pattern, a process which –if it is not checked– only can lead to more and more extreme rivalry and, in the final instance, to enmity and break-

4 See, however, Lewis, Bernard (1982) *The Muslim Discovery of Europe* (London: Weidenfeld and Nicholson) and Carrier, James, ed. (1995) *Occidentalism: Images of the West* (Oxford: Oxford University Press) for two very different approaches to this subject.

5 Quoted from Ottosen, Rune (1994) *Mediestrategier og fiendebilder i internasjonale konflikter* (Media strategies and enemy images in international conflicts). Oslo: Universitetsforlaget, p. 42.

6 *Frankfurter Allgemeine*, 15 September 2001.

7 "Culture contact and schismogenesis" (1935), reprinted in Bateson (1972).

down in the entire system" (Bateson, 1972:68). In his model of schismogenesis, moreover, the only way the self-reinforcing circuits could be changed would be through the interference of a third agent (or network node) leading to a new framing of the issue. Translated into poststructuralist language, the discursive hegemony putting "the West" against "Islam" in a deadly embrace can only be broken through the intrusion of one or several counterdiscourses framing the world in different terms. These counterdiscourses have been abundantly available both before and after 11 September. However, politicians and a majority of influential media commentators seem to accept that the conflict has something to do with the West and Islam, even if they usually concede that Islam is complex and that most Muslims are naturally peaceful. In the Muslim part of the world, where the media are less liberal and the political leadership by and large less attuned to the population, the situation has been different. While the political leaders have supported the US against the Taliban/Al-Qaeda, the media have generally not offered a very nuanced picture of the West, portraying the "clash of civilizations" view as representative of "Westerners" (Ali, 2002). In spite of important cracks in the mutual enemy images, therefore, there are clear indications that they have been strengthened after 11 September. The anti-immigrant new right in the politics of several European countries experienced a healthy growth after the attacks, and in countries like the Netherlands and Denmark they currently have considerable political power. Public debates about minorities in several European countries have been redefined from a dominant focus on discrimination and labour market issues to a less charitable focus on enforced marriages, sexual mutilation and *hijabs*. Condolezza Rice is on record as having explained to a concerned citizen that the reason "they" hate "us" so much is that "we elect our leaders" and that "you and I [meaning women] are allowed to work". In Muslim countries, Gilles Kepel quotes religious leaders who worry that the attacks have led to a deep setback in the ongoing, and in many ways progressing intellectual dialogue between Muslims and Westerners (Kepel, 2002).

There are some exceptions. A few influential commentators and politicians saw the terrorist attacks and the retaliation of the USA in the same light. In an address to the summit of the Organisation of Islamic Countries in February 2002, Malaysia's prime minister Mahathir defined a terrorist as "someone who attacks civilians", thereby seeing the suicide pilots and the US Air Force over Afghanistan as the same kind of actors.

Single horrors such as the deliberate bombing of the Mazar-i-Sharaf prison and the accidental killing of more than forty Afghanis on their way to a wedding in 2002, or new routine forms of punishment witnessed in the provisional, but already long-standing Guantanamo prison where inmates are neither considered criminals nor prisoners of war and therefore deprived of all their rights, would have raised an international storm of protest had the perpetrator been any other country than the post-11 September USA. The complacent and indifferent reactions from the White House, even after the violent transgressions in the Abu-Ghraib prison in Iraq (2004) can only be understood as an indication that the regime in the USA sees it as necessary to bracket democratic rights, at least temporarily. The recent withdrawal of the USA from various forms of international cooperation, including international courts of justice and environmental treaties, suggests that global dialogue may have to proceed without the participation of the USA in the near future.

The postcolonial perspective and global identity politics

Arguments involving respect of others and recognition of cultural differences tend to lead to accusations of cultural and moral relativism. Let us therefore consider these objections. On the one hand, practically every intellectual and politician in the rich countries supports a set of universal values ratified by the United Nations (particularly the *Universal Charter* of 1948); that all individuals should have the same rights and liberties. On the other hand, nobody can deny that these rights and liberties are unevenly distributed in the world, that many are denied rights deemed essential in the West; and moreover, that people who live in different social environments inevitably experience and interpret the world in different ways.

Many historians and social scientists have in recent years shown how both past and present change according to shifting circumstances[8]. The history of India will not be the same if it is written in New Delhi as if it is written in London: both versions may be true, but historical truth is always partial. Similarly, both women and ethnic minorities have in recent decades demanded that their versions of past and present should be granted their rightful place in education and public spheres, so that e.g. metropolitan French children learn about slavery just as Guadeloupean children learn about the Gauls, or that American children learn about the brutality of the European invasion of North America just as they learn about George Washington and the cherry tree.

It is difficult to contest the assumption that such a relativisation of the past makes it possible to tell historical narratives with improved accuracy. It has nevertheless also been said that this kind of relativism, perhaps particularly in the field of literature, can also degenerate into "political correctness" and downright nihilism, where the classic values of truth, beauty and virtue are not produced through a shared process of evaluation, but through political decisions based on ideas of equity between groups. Conservative thinkers like Alain Finkielkraut (1987) and Fukuyama's mentor Allan Bloom (1987) warned against these tendencies in the 1980s and both defended universal (or, it might be objected, hegemonic) criteria for aesthetic and moral norms. Not surprisingly, both were accused of acting as spokesmen for a kind of white man's burden which by default would consider all non-European cultural expressions as inferior, since the standards were set by the likes of Plato and Shakespeare. There is no easy response to this objection.

8 See e.g. Fernandez-Armesto (1996) or Wallerstein (1991).

Already in the 16th century, Michel de Montaigne ventured to suggest that cannibalism might be no less rational than customs taken for granted by his French countrymen. A century later, another famous Frenchman, Blaise Pascal, wrote that truth is another on the other side of the Pyrenees. Both accepted the relativity of truth and value as a fact which could not easily be overcome. In the 18th century, the founder of the early Romantic *Sturm und Drang* movement in Germany, Johann Gottlieb von Herder, wrote somewhat more systematically on cultural differences. He insisted, against the Enlightenment philosophers, on each people's right to its distinct cultural and linguistic identity. The so-called universalism of the likes of Voltaire he discarded as a form of provincialism: Voltaire might believe that he sought to disseminate a universal form of civilization, but what he was really engaged in was –to use a more recent term– French cultural imperialism. The role of France in 18th century Europe may in some respects be compared to the role of the USA in the contemporary world. French language, manners and fashions were *à la mode* from St. Petersburg to Boston, and it was not surprising that the strongest anti-French reactions came from their closest neighbours and oldest enemies, the Germans. The parallel with the contemporary situation confronting the USA with Muslims is tempting to draw.

Respect and fascination for the customs of other peoples has in practice been easy (and completely free of charge) so long as they were far away. Tensions develop more easily in the contemporary world. Thanks to accelerated globalisation and migration, we now live in a truly global society where everyone is in the same boat in terms of ecology, military power, economics and politics. We have all been brought closer to each other in this stage of modernity, and the problem of relativism has moved from the confines of literary speculation and academic research to the forefront of politics. Although globalisation clearly reduces cultural differences –the monetary economy, mass media, human rights thinking and state interventions are everywhere, to mention a few examples– it has increased the attention given to cultural differences many times over. Partly this is simply a result of increased contact: it is through contact with others that one becomes aware of oneself, and the presence of others may seem a threat to one's own culture and customs. Partly the intensified interest in cultural difference is a product of nostalgia and alienation: identity politics tends to glorify a mythical past when "our way of life" was still intact and undisturbed by the disruptive forces of global modernity; it draws much of its emotional energy from a sense of loss caused by change. It could thus be said, as a general principle, that the more similar people become, the more different they try to be.

In this kind of situation, cultural rights become a coveted resource and a feature of political life that needs to be taken seriously. American Indians are no longer far away in their reservations, and they cannot simply be assimilated into the melting-pot of US modernity: they demand both territory, compensation, quotas in the educational system and influence over reading lists. Muslims are no longer colonised peoples under European military control, but highly articulate and audible voices in the global public sphere –whether they are based in Bradford or in Peshawar– and they demand respect and equity. After 11 September, the violence is no longer even mainly unilateral. As Osama bin Laden said in his famous al-Jazeera interview, he wishes to make it clear that Americans can no longer sleep safely in their beds.

Dangerous cultural relativism?

Minority rights issues and political Islam cannot simply be lumped together; there are important differences. But they have one thing in common, as do all identity politics, namely the demand for a more democratic, more just global regime of communication. Although the methods of fundamentalists like Osama bin Laden are frightening, their demands are perfectly comprehensible and even, to many, reasonable. It would be ridiculous to claim, as certain extreme relativists do, that alien perspectives on the world are impossible to fathom. To anyone but autists, psychopaths and brainwashed fanatics, it is perfectly possible to understand, for example, ecological, religious, neoliberal or ethnic fundamentalism, but such an understanding requires that one makes an effort to put oneself in the other's place. Doing this does not necessarily mean that you "lose yourself". As Clifford Geertz (1983) puts it: "You don't have to be one to know one". Making an effort to understand the local experiences and cultural judgements that underpin practices such as female circumcision, arranged marriages, Premier League football or sati (widow-burning) is not the same as lending support to them. If one is to understand a text, one has to be aware of one's own pre-understanding and one's own prejudices to give it justice. This also applies to meetings between people with different values, experiences and horizons.

If understanding across boundaries and translation between cultural worlds is possible, then, it may also perhaps be argued that it is possible to establish shared standards of beauty, truth and virtue. This is probably true, but it will not happen through authoritarian imposition of values from a hegemonic power; only through equitable dialogue and mutual empathy. In such an ideal situation of communication (which the world has not seen), it cannot be taken for granted that Beethoven will be judged superior to Indian ragas. This position, which posits the essential unity of humanity, differs from the multiculturalist position, which takes as its premiss that cultures are bounded, and assumes that the best one can hope for is coexistence side by side.

An important distinction has to be made between cultural relativism as *method* (in order to understand) and as *world-view* (in order to act and make judgements). The first variety is the only alternative to crude and authoritarian dismissals of alternative views, while the second variety is a recipe for confusion and nihilism. Cultural relativist method is a necessity (everything has to be understood within its proper context), while cultural relativist morals are a tragedy. Understanding is not the same as defending.

In a truly dialogic democracy, participants would have to demonstrate knowledge of others before moving on to critical or condescending statements about them. Having established the necessary knowledge, each individual would be free to choose his or her side, for one does not necessarily become a Nazi by reading and understanding *Mein Kampf*. It would, in other words, not be acceptable to oppose Islam without knowing what Islam is. If this simple principle had been established in public debate and politics, it would have improved the quality of many interventions considerably.

If, instead of dialogic democracy, one chooses ignorance since understanding the other ostensibly leads to dangerous relativism, there are only three alternatives: violence, silence or the language of power.

Dialogue is more urgently needed today than in earlier periods, when non-white, non-Christian peoples were forcibly muted and Europeans largely dealt with them as servants, negative cultural stereotypes and research objects. "The others" have in every way homed in on us. Thanks to the globalisation of information flows, a statement made in Tehran may in a matter of few moments lead to a heightened temperature in Trinidad; and a sudden catastrophe in Manhattan may immediately put the entire world on an edge.

Advice to the new hegemons

Allow me to end this chapter with some personal reflections of a general character, which have nothing to do with Islam as such, but which concern the role of "the West", and particularly the USA, in global society. Europeans and North Americans of predominantly European origin have now dominated the world for more than five hundred years. It may perhaps be about time that this long hegemony comes to an end, whether it happens indirectly through migration, violently through self-destructive entrenchment against a foe which is generated from within (terrorism), or simply through shifts in the dynamic of the global economy[9]. One may only hope, if this happens in the century that has just begun, that the new hegemons will continue to absorb, renew and develop the genuine contributions of European and North American society to global civilization, such as the respect (at least in principle) for human life and integrity, impartial bureaucracy and, especially, the capacity for doubt and ambivalence which has been a trademark quality of European culture (if not of European power politics) since the Renaissance. It may also be hoped that the new hegemons are able to learn the right lessons from the mistakes of Europe and the West: the fanatical technological optimism, the lack of community and solidarity, the class divisions and indifference, the fundamentalist arrogance in relation to others, the stressful way of life under careerist regimes of work, growing street crime, racism and discrimination, the lack of consideration for the environment... Looking back on the last

9 It is time and again argued that the economic powerhouse of the world moved from the Atlantic to the Pacific basin decades ago, but that most Europeans still have not caught up with this.

centuries –let us say the period that began with Columbus' landing on 12 October 1492 and the subsequent expulsion of Muslims and Jews from Spain a few weeks later– the chances are good that the networked, decentralised world which may now be emerging, can turn out to be more humane than five hundred years of European hegemony have been. It will not happen with the help of Osama bin Laden and Taliban-like networks, but it won't happen with the help of American bomber planes either. One has to be blind and deaf in order to believe that this is the "best of all possible worlds", a world where every person has the same values and where opportunities are equally distributed. The currencies of the global society are dollars and bombs, and this society speaks business English with an American accent. Nobody ought to be surprised if some of those who are overwhelmed, or overrun, by this power react like greenhouse plants are supposed to react to heavy metal: by rolling up into small, hard balls.

No matter where power and dominance may be concentrated –now and in twenty years– this period, when the world is probably about to be re-moulded, is a good period for a renewal of world-views. The old, dominant world-view presented a hierarchical world composed of peoples, civilizations and nations that were clearly delineated in relation to each other, geographically and culturally speaking; they had their own history, their own values and their own customs, as it were. Europe and the West, according to this view, represented reason and progress, even if others had also contributed bits and pieces. This image is now about to be replaced by a world characterised by exile, flows, intensified contacts, creolisation, hybridisation and all forms of mixing; where no boundaries are absolute notwithstanding attempts to build ever taller walls; but where people continue to have different experiences because they live under varying circumstances. Territorial power is faltering and is being challenged everywhere –Microsoft to al-Qaeda– by the more flexible power of networks. If the demands for justice, respect and recognition from Muslims and others are not now met by another response than condescending arrogance, this world will almost certainly catch fire. In the old world, injustice and rage could be "contained". Not so in the network world.

This is a world of impurities, grey zones, uncertainties and ambiguities, where the belief in progress is being replaced by ambivalence, where self-confidence is being replaced by anxiety, where trust is threatened by suspicion, and where the ability to listen has become a more important faculty than ever before in history.

Chapter 2

New complexities of transnational media cultures

Kevin Robins & Asu Aksoy

Until quite recently, what prevailed in European media culture was the system
of public service broadcasting, involving the provision of mixed programming
–with strict controls on the amount of foreign material shown– on national channels available to all. The principle that governed the regulation of broadcasting
was that of national 'public interest'. Broadcasting should contribute to the political and cultural life of the nation –it was intended to help in constructing a sense
of national unity. Thus, in Britain, during the earliest days of the BBC, the medium
of radio was consciously employed "to forge a link between the dispersed and
disparate listeners and the symbolic heartland of national life" (Cardiff and
Scannell, 1987: 157). And, in the postwar years, as the media historian, Paddy
Scannell, has demonstrated, both radio and television "brought into being a culture in common to whole populations and a shared public life of a quite new
kind" (Scannell, 1989: 138). Historically, then, broadcasting assumed a dual role,
serving both as the public sphere of the nation state and as the focus for national cultural identification. We can say that broadcasting has been one of the key
institutions through which people –as listeners and viewers– have come to imagine themselves as members of the national community.

Over the past twenty years or so, however, things have changed, and
changed in quite significant ways. From the mid-1980s, dramatic upheavals took
place in the media industries, laying the basis for what must be seen as a new
kind of media order. Two factors have been identified as being particularly significant in this transformation. First was the decisive shift in media regulatory princi-

ples: from regulation in the national public interest to a new regulatory regime –sometimes erroneously described as 'deregulation'– primarily driven by economic and entrepreneurial imperatives. Second was the proliferation of new, or alternative, distribution technologies, and particularly satellite television, which made it possible –maybe inevitable– for new transborder broadcasting systems to develop –bringing about, as a consequence, the formation of new transnational and global audiovisual markets. Driving these developments were new commercial and entrepreneurial ambitions in the media sector. And what was particularly significant here was the strong expansionist tendency at work in these ambitions, pushing all the time toward the construction of enlarged audiovisual spaces and markets. The objective and the great ideal in the new order –among media entrepreneurs and policy makers alike– was to achieve the 'free flow of television'. The fundamental imperative was to break down the old boundaries and frontiers of national communities, which had come to be seen as restricting the free flow of products and services in communications markets. There was consequently a logic in play whereby the new audiovisual spaces became detached from the symbolic spaces of national communities and cultures.

Discussions of these developments have tended to be seen in terms of the shift from one historical epoch or era to another –the transition from the public service era to that of global markets. In this metaphor of epochal shift, there is a tendency to overemphasize the contrast between the two epochs, and also to oversimplify the nature of each period. What we want to suggest is the use of a different metaphor to grasp the nature of the transformations that have been occurring. We would suggest that change is more akin the process of geological layering. What has happened is that the new audiovisual spaces and markets have come to settle across the old national landscape. Public service broadcasting continues to exist at the same time that new kinds of audiovisual markets and spaces have come into existence. Also important to emphasize, we believe, is that both 'public service' and 'global' are fluid and changing categories. In Europe, through the 1990s, for example, the idea of public service shifted in important ways to include provision of programming for minorities and also the recognition of cultural rights in the European regions. We should be clear as well that global broadcasting has developed in such a way as to include transnational and diasporic broadcasters like Roj TV (formerly MED TV) and Al-Jazeera, as well as giants like Disney and Time Warner. If we consider the European continent now, what should be apparent is the extreme diversity and complexity of audiovisual spaces –national, local-regional, and transnational. Viewers may tune in to the services of public service providers like RAI, ZDF, to local Welsh or Basque channels, to CNN or Sky, and also to Zee TV or TRT-INT. And through these new transnational developments, we maintain, the nature of the European cultural landscape and European public culture is being significantly reconfigured.

In the following discussion, what we want to explore is how new transnational cultures and new forms of transnational experience are being initiated through the consumption of transnational media. What is happening –what might happen–, we ask, when it is possible to tune in to the new channels from anywhere and everywhere else? What is it that might be different and distinctive about transnational media cultures? What is their relation to, and what are their implications for, the older national broadcasting order? Our interest is in the mundane, everyday experience of transnational viewing. We pursue these questions through an analysis of the use of transnational satellite broadcasting by migrants living in Europe. Migrant audiences are particularly avid consumers of satellite television, and their viewing experiences can, therefore, provide a particularly good way into understanding the significance of the new transnational media. How, we shall ask, do migrant audiences relate to the different national media systems that they have access to? And what new kinds of transnational experience might be opening up for them?

In order to ground our inquiry, we focus on a particular case study, that of Turkish-speaking migrants living in Europe. All across the European space now, Turkish-speaking populations are tuning in to the numerous (more than forty –the exact number is in constant flux) satellite channels that are broadcasting programs from Ankara and Istanbul. Just like other migrant groups –Maghrebis, Arabs, Chinese, Indians, Afro-Caribbeans, and many more– they are now able to make use of transnational communications to gain access to media services from the country of origin (or elsewhere). This has been a very important development, a development of the last decade, which has very significant implications for how migrants experience their lives, and for how they think and feel about their experiences. What, then, is this significance? What is the nature of migrants' engagement with the new transnational media? What precisely is the difference that satellite television makes for those who live in transnational contexts? These are key questions that we want to pose.

To address these questions we draw on research that we have been undertaking amongst the Turkish-speaking populations in London (see Aksoy and Robins, 2000, 2003; Robins and Aksoy, 2001, 2004). In order to see how it is that ordinary Turkish people are relating to the new transnational media, what it is that they are doing with television, then we have to listen to Turkish people talking about their responses and reactions to it. Trying to make sense of what they have to say will therefore be a primary aim of this chapter. What we then have to recognize, however, is that the interpretation of what they are telling us is far from being a straightforward matter. It is not straightforward because so much clearly depends on the conceptual and theoretical framework in terms of which one seeks to make sense of the responses and accounts of Turkish viewers. In the following section, we shall argue that the currently prevailing framework –which has been mainly concerned with how transnational satellite broadcasting systems sustain new kinds of 'global diasporic cultures' or 'long-distance imagined communities'– is deeply problematical, essentially because it seeks to understand transnational developments through what are categories of the national imaginary, and is consequently blind to whatever it is that might be new and different about emerging transnational media cultures. We will then proceed to develop our own approach, which seeks to move beyond the taken-for-grantedness of the national mentality and its fundamental categories (those of 'community', 'identity' and 'belonging') in order to explore alternative possibilities of transnationalism. What we will actually describe, through our analysis of focus group discussions with Turkish viewers, is a new cultural situation in which national and transnational dispositions interact. It is a situation in which the national mentality may be disrupted, creating a space for new transnational perspectives to emerge.

Beyond diasporic cultural studies

A key endeavour of this chapter, then, is to open up an agenda concerning the appropriate categories for understanding what is happening –actually, what might unexpectedly be happening– in transnational cultural experience. Let us first briefly indicate why we distance ourselves from the growing body of work on transnational communications functioning within the framework of what we might call diasporic cultural studies. Here it is generally argued that new media technologies are making it possible to transcend the distances that have separated 'diasporic communities' around the world from their 'communities of origin'. 'Diasporic media' are said to be providing new means to promote transnational bonding, and thereby sustain (ethnic, national or religious) identities and cultures at-a-distance. They are being thought about in terms of possibilities they offer for dislocated belonging among migrant communities anxious to maintain their identification with the 'homeland' (and the basic premise is that this kind of belonging must be the primary aspiration of any and every such 'community').

Now, of course we can recognize a certain kind of truth in this argument. From our own work on Turkish migrants in London, it is clear that access to Turkish-language media can, indeed, be important for overcoming the migrant's experience of cultural separation. But if there is some kind of truth here, we would say that it is only a very partial truth. The problem with diasporic media studies is that its interests and concern generally come to an end at this point. The inquiry is brought to a premature halt, with the ready acceptance that transnational broadcasting does in fact, and quite unproblematically, support the long-distance cohesion of transnational 'imagined communities' –and without ever confronting what it is that might be new and distinctive about the experience of transnational broadcasting. Because it has been principally concerned with acts of bonding and belonging, the diasporic agenda has generally been blind to what else might be happening when migrants are, apparently, connecting in to the 'homeland' culture. The limits of diasporic media studies come from the readiness to believe and accept that migrant audiences are all behaving as the conventional and conforming members of 'diasporic communities'.

The root problem is simply that the theoretical categories available to diasporic media and cultural studies make it difficult to see anything other than diasporic forms of behaviour. Individuals are derived from the social orders to which they 'belong'; they amount to little more than their membership of, and participation in, any particular 'imagined community'. This is clearly an example of the kind of social theory that is powerfully criticised by Anthony Cohen, an approach that treats society as an ontology "which somehow becomes independent of its own members, and assumes that the self is required continuously to adjust to it" (1994: 21). In this kind of approach there is no place for self-awareness and self-consciousness –and, as Cohen argues, by neglecting self-consciousness, "we inevitably perpetrate fictions in our descriptions of other people" (1994: 191). To see anything more than diasporic behaviour in migrant audiences, it is necessary to introduce the category of the self-conscious individual, who is "someone who can reflect on her or his experience of and position in society, of 'being oneself'" (1994: 65).

As Cohen says, the imperative should be "to elicit and describe the thoughts and sentiments of individuals which we otherwise gloss over in the generalisations we derive from collective social categories" (1994: 4). The crucial point is that individuals are endowed with the capacity for both emotion (feelings, moods) and thought (reflecting, comparing, interpreting, judging, and so on). We should be concerned, then, with their minds and sensibilities, and not their cultures or identities –with how they think, rather than how they belong.

In the present discussion, we do not want to enter directly into a theoretical discussion of the categories of culture and identity that are being proposed in these analyses of so-called diasporic communities. Our critique will take a more oblique form, moving the argument into an empirical frame, via an exploration of certain new developments in migration that cannot be made sense of within this diasporic cultural agenda (and that may actually be affecting the conditions of possibility of the diasporic imaginary). We want to consider new practices that seem to open up alternative, and potentially more productive, dimensions of migrant experience. We are concerned with the kind of developments described by Alejandro Portes and his colleagues, in which "a growing number of persons… live dual lives: speaking two languages, having homes in two countries, and making a living through continuous regular contact across national borders" (Portes et al, 1999: 217). Through a "thick web of regular instantaneous communication and easy personal travel" (1999: 227), it is argued, migrants are now routinely able to establish transnational communities that exist across two, or more, cultural spaces. In what follows, then, we want to look at how these new kinds of transnational networks and mobilities may now be changing the nature of migrant experience and thinking. We shall be concerned with the cultural potential that may be inherent in these transnational developments as they occur at the level of everyday experience. And we shall be particularly attentive to the possibilities that these new connections may be creating for moving beyond the agenda of national identity and the frame of imagined community.

Contradictory experiences of transnational television

It is in the terms set out by Anthony Cohen that we now want to reflect on the experiences of Turkish migrants living in London. What do they think and feel about Turkish channels and programming? What is the difference that transnational television has made for London Turks? What we may say is that transnational television has introduced entirely new dynamics into the management of distance and separation. Let us start from this crucial question of distance –from the idea that the new media systems can now work to bridge global or transnational distances. And let us do so by reflecting on what this seemingly straightforward idea might actually mean in reality. In the frame of diasporic cultural studies, we suggest, the agenda is about the maintenance of at-a-distance ties; it is about the supposed capacity of transnational media to connect migrant communities back to the cultural space of their distant 'homelands'. On the basis of our own research, we would characterise what is happening somewhat differently: in terms of how –in the case of our informants– transnational media can now bring Turkish cultural products and services to them in London, and of how 'Turkey' is consequently brought closer to them. As one focus group participant puts it,

> [I]t gives you more freedom, because you don't feel so far away, because it's only six foot away from you, you don't feel so far away from it. Cyprus is like one switch of a button away, or Turkey even, mainland Turkey, you are there, aren't you? (Focus group, Enfield, 21 April 2000).

Even a young woman who migrated when she was quite young, and who is therefore not really familiar with the country, has this sense of greater proximity to the actuality of Turkey. She thinks that it is very good to be able to watch satellite television

> because you too can see what's been going on in Turkey, the news... I used to think that Turkey was a different kind of place [başka bir yer]. It's bringing it [Turkey] closer [yakinlaştiriyor] (Focus group, Islington, London, 29 March 1999).

Television makes a difference because it seems to be in its nature –in the nature of television as a medium– to bring things closer to its viewers.

In one of our group discussions, two women tell us of how satellite television now allows them to be synchronised with Turkish realities. 'Most certainly [Turkish] television is useful for us', says one. 'It's almost as if we're living in Turkey, as if nothing has really changed for us'. The other confirmed this, saying that

> When you're home, you feel as if you are in Turkey. Our homes are already decorated Turkish style, everything about me is Turkish, and when I'm watching television too... (Focus group, Hackney, London, 7 December 1999).

The key issue here is to do with the meaning of this feeling of 'as if nothing has really changed for us'. In the context of the diasporic cultural studies agenda, this feeling of synchronisation would be thought of in terms of long-distance bonding with the 'homeland', the maintenance of at-a-distance links with a faraway 'somewhere else'. For us, in contrast, it is simply about the availability in London of imported things from Turkey –where we might regard the availability of television programmes as being on a continuum with the (equally common nowadays) availability of food, clothes or furnishings from Turkey. 'Nothing has really changed' does not refer to ethno-cultural re-connection to some imagined 'homeland', but simply to the possibility of having access in London now to Turkish consumer goods and the world of Turkish consumer culture. It is 'almost as if we're living in Turkey' in that sense –being Turkish in London, that is to say, and not at all in the sense of 'being taken back home'.

Television brings the everyday, banal reality of Turkish life to the migrants living in London. The key to understanding transnational Turkish television is its relation to banality. Vladimir Jankélévitch has noted how people who are in exile can imagine they are living double lives, carrying around within them "inner voices... the voices of the past and of the distant city", whilst at the same time submitting to "the banal and turbulent life of everyday action" (1974: 346). This is the mechanism of psychic splitting –where the banality of the 'here and now' provides the stimulus for nostalgic dreams and fantasies about the 'there and then'. Now, what we regard as significant about transnational television is that, as a consequence of bringing the mundane, everyday reality of Turkey 'closer', it is progressively undermining this false polarizing logic. The 'here and now' reality of Turkish media culture disturbs the imagination of a 'there and then' Turkey –thereby working against the romance of diaspora-as-exile, against the tendency to false idealisation of the 'homeland'. We might say, then, that transnational Turkish television is an agent of cultural de-mythologisation.

This process of de-mythologisation can work in different ways. Here we will give two examples of how television can be used as a kind of reality-testing device. The first comes from an interview with an active member of London's Turkish-Cypriot population, a man in his forties who has been settled in Britain for many years. We find ourselves discussing the question of young people, relationships and the family, and he expresses quite critical opinions about what he clearly regards as the out-of-date morality of the Turkish-Cypriot community. In many ways, he says,

> you become almost frozen in your understanding of where your community is. The longer you are here the more you are likely to have views and attitudes that are more conservative and out of date. I've seen people my age and even younger, expecting things of their children that they have rebelled against.

He then moves on to suggest that transnational television could actually play a positive role in countering this migrant conservatism. 'In many ways', he comments,

I wish they would watch more Turkish television. Some of their attitudes
are far behind what the messages are. You turn on the Turkish television,
and some of it is refreshingly modern. It's quite normal to watch people
having affairs, or who are having relationships, who aren't married, on
Turkish television. You would never have had that twenty years ago. But
some of the mind set is relating to that. The first time a girl is having a relationship is when they get married –you see that with second-generation
people. They don't get that from satellite. They get it from their parents
(Interview, Camden, London, 20 April 2000).

What he is arguing is that television programmes and images that show how life
and morals are in Turkey now can serve as a valuable corrective to migrant attitudes that, he believes, have become stuck in some ideal and timeless image of
Turkish-Cypriotness.

The second example comes from a young woman of eighteen, we
shall call her Hülya, who migrated to Britain from eastern Turkey when she was
seven years old. At one point, towards the end of our discussion, she tells us how
much she likes watching old Turkish movies on television, 'especially the love
films', which she likes to watch 'to see the old Turkey. [...] It gives you a very
sweet sense'. But earlier she had spoken about a very different experience of
watching Turkish television:

We have one TV set, and this is why we have arguments, because I'm irritated by the news. I find it bad for my health. You might find it funny but,
really, you sit in front of the television, you are going to watch the news,
you are relaxed, everybody is curious about what's happening in Turkey;
and then it says, 'Good evening viewers, today four cars crashed into each
other'. God bless them. They show these things, people covered in blood.
People who know nothing about rescuing, trying to drag these people out,
they pull them, and in front of your eyes people die. I am a very sensitive
person. Somebody dies in front of you, and they show this, and they don't
do anything. For me, this is like torture. For them maybe it is not like torture, but for me it is. Two or three years ago, I was *very* upset, when this
guy was killed because he had a tattoo saying 'Allah' on his back. Then, I
don't know this person, but I was so touched that I cried. And I called
Ahmet Taner Kişlali [a famous journalist]. These kinds of events make me
very sad, because I'm delicate, and they wear me out, so for that reason I
don't watch (Focus group, Hackney, London, 3 November 1999).

What is made apparent here is television's great capacity for conveying harsh and
cruel aspects of the Turkish reality –Turkish news programmes are far more explicit than British ones in showing images of violence and bloodshed. For a great part
of Turkish viewers, news programmes are very disturbing (the often intense dis-
comfort of watching the news was an issue that ran through practically all of our
focus groups). In some parts of its schedules, then, television may nourish warm

and nostalgic feelings. But at news time, especially, the principle of reality will always return, through images of Turkey that frequently provoke and shock. The news can be profoundly unsettling for migrant viewers. As Hülya says of her own experience, it 'creates a psychological disorder' [psikolojik durum yaratıyor].

What is important here is the evidential nature of television (which may be constructive, as in our first example, but also disturbing, as our second example makes clear). What we want to emphasize here is the capacity of the reality dimension of television to undercut the abstract nostalgia of the diasporic imagination. Turkish viewers come to participate in the mundane and banal world of everyday television. It is this aspect of television culture that goes against the idea that the proliferation of Turkish transnational media is now associated with an ethnicisation of media cultures and markets in western Europe (for such an argument see Becker, 2001). In our own work, we have not found this to be the case. We are inclined to agree with Marisca Milikowski when she argues that it is, on the contrary, associated with a process of de-ethnicisation. As she says, Turkish satellite television "helps Turkish migrants, and in particular their children, to liberate themselves from certain outdated and culturally imprisoning notions of Turkishness, which had survived in the isolation of migration" (Milikowski, 2000: 444). The world of Turkish television is an ordinary world, and its significance resides, we suggest, in its ordinary, banal and everyday qualities –which are qualities it has in common with countless other TV worlds.

Turkish audiences look to the ordinariness of Turkish television. Like any other viewers of broadcast television, they look for "the familiar –familiar sights, familiar faces, familiar voices", as Thomas Elsaesser (1994: 7) puts it, "television that respects and knows who they are, where they are, and what time it is". And, to a large extent, we may say that they are able to find what they are looking for. And yet, at the same time, there is still something that is wrong, something that does not quite work properly with transnational Turkish television. At the same time as they can enjoy them, migrants can also find Turkish channels disturbing, unsettling, frustrating. This is apparent in a very dramatic fashion in Hülya's abrupt shift from feeling relaxed in front of the television to feeling worn out by what she saw on it. Many, many other people expressed these kinds of affronted and disgruntled feelings about the programmes they were watching. In one group, a woman objects to the production standards of Turkish television.

> We perceive Turkish television as being of poor quality, and rather sensationalist, and unedited, so it's a bit crude... I mean, it will show you things in an unedited way, whether it's blood and guts, or violence or whatever.

And she adds, in a joking tone,

> I can't take it seriously if it's Burt Lancaster with a Turkish accent –doesn't really appeal (Focus group, Haringey, London, 22 November 1999).

There is something about Turkish television that presents itself as in some way inadequate, deficient, often unacceptable. The experience of watching transnational television is ordinary, but never straightforwardly.

When Turkish people talk about what frustrates them, they point to the images, the programmes, the scheduling, or the nature of particular channels. But, somehow, it seems to us, this doesn't really get at what is 'wrong' with watching television from Turkey. There is something more that is disconcerting about watching transnational television, an elusive something else. We can perhaps get at what this something might be from a passing observation that was made by Hülya. We were talking about Muslim festivals, and about the sense that she and her friends had that the significance of religious holidays was diminishing in the London context. We asked whether Turkish television helps to remind people of the traditional holidays, and to create the festival atmosphere that seemed to have been lost. 'How could that help?', says one young woman sceptically. And Hülya says

> It's coming from a distance… It's coming from too far. It loses its significance. I mean, it could have significance, but it's coming from too far.

Later, when asked whether the availability of satellite television had implications for her identity and her relation to Turkish culture, she picks up on the same idea. 'No', she says,

> it can't, because it's too distant. Imagine that you were talking to me from I don't know how many thousand miles away. How much would this affect me? (Focus group, Hackney, London, 3 November 1999).

Perhaps we can make sense of this by referring back to Thomas Elsaesser's observation that the audiences of broadcast television want television programs that know who they are, where they are, and what time it is. Is it that television from Turkey doesn't seem to know its transnational audiences in this way? Is Hülya pointing to something that is new or different about the working of transnational television? Is she signalling something that might actually make transnational cultural interactions distinctive?

Transnational media experience and television theory

Turkish migrants clearly have quite complex thoughts and sentiments about the television channels and programmes that they are watching. And what is also clear is that they have a critical engagement with the new transnational television culture.

What they say demonstrates considerable awareness and thoughtfulness about different aspects of this culture, from the aesthetic and production values of particular programmes, through to the overall impact of the new services on the quality of their lives in Britain. What we now want to do is to go on and reflect on these complex attitudes and relations of Turkish migrants towards transnational television. We want to try to make sense of what Turkish people are telling us in the context of more general ideas about the role and significance of media in modern life (which Turks are as much a part of as any other group).

For the most part, as we have suggested above, transnational media of the kind we are concerned with here have been considered in the special context of 'diasporic culture' and identity politics. Migrant audiences have been seen as, in some way, different; and the study of their supposedly different dispositions and preoccupations has seemed to belong to the specialized domain of ethnic and migration research. We ourselves believe that their media activities should be looked at with the very same media theories that have been applied to 'ordinary' (i.e. national, sedentary) audiences. Marisca Milikowski (2000: 460) is quite right to insist that we should look at migrant viewing from the point of view of "ordinary uses and gratifications" –for, as she observes, "non-ideological and non-political gratifications usually go a long way to explain a certain popular interest..." This we regard as an important principle of methodological democracy and justice. We should reflect on what is happening through transnationalisation of Turkish media culture in the light of media theory concerned with ordinary uses of, and gratifications from, everyday television.

Here, we think that the work of Paddy Scannell (1989, 1996, 2000; Cardiff and Scannel, 1987) –whom we referred to above as a leading historian of public service broadcasting– can serve as a particularly useful and productive point of reference. We have reservations, we must say, about certain aspects of Scannell's overall project –it is very national in its orientation, and often seems to be treating British broadcasting as an ideal-type model (for critical observations on the politics of Scannell's agenda, see Morley, 2000: ch. 5). But we do think that there is a great deal to be learned from his detailed analysis of the emergence of distinctive modes of address in national broadcasting cultures –how broadcasters learned to address listeners and viewers in appropriate ways (ways in which they would wish to be addressed). Scannell's work alerts us to the significance of the particular rhetorical structures that have come to mediate the relation of producers and consumers of broadcasting services. What he provides us with is a sustained account of the communicative structures and ethos that have made broadcasting culture work for its audiences. It is, moreover, a historically situated account, showing how the specific communicative forms of radio and television developed and functioned in the particular and specific context of national broadcasting systems. Scannell's concern is with how, at a particular historical moment, broadcasting media came to develop communicative forms that functioned as arguably the primary mediation between the private domain of everyday life and the public life of the nation state.

It seems to us that these communicative and rhetorical aspects of programming and scheduling are absolutely crucial for our own exploration of transnational Turkish television and its audiences. Of course, the codes that have evolved in the Turkish context differ somewhat from those of Scannell's British case

–the state broadcaster, TRT, has always had an 'official' tone, and it was only in the 1990s, through the development of private channels, that more informal modes of address came to be elaborated (Aksoy and Robins, 1997). But we may say that they have functioned in the integrative way, working to mediate the relation between private and public spheres of life in Turkey. And what seems to us to be a key issue, in the context of our own present concern with Turkish satellite broadcasting in the European space, is what happens to these nationally-forged communicative structures in the changed circumstances of transnationalisation. The point about Scannell's analysis is that it is essentially a phenomenology of national broadcasting –or perhaps, more accurately, a national phenomenology of broadcasting. It assumes that there is something universal and timeless about the way in which national broadcasting cultures have worked. What we observe is that there are likely difficulties when communicative structures that have worked more or less well in a national context are then made to do service in new transnational contexts. We are concerned with the communicative limits of structures that have served to mediate between the private and public lives of the nation.

There are two (closely related) arguments that we want to make here. The first is straightforward, emerging directly from our previous discussion, and can be made quite briefly. Scannell is concerned with what he calls the "care-structures" of radio and television, by which he means the practices that "produce and deliver an all-day everyday service that is ready-to-hand and available always anytime at the turn of a switch or the press of a button" (1996: 145-146). What this means, he says, is "making programmes so that they 'work' every time", and in such a way that viewers or listeners come to regard them as "a natural, ordinary, unremarkable, everyday entitlement" (1996: 145-146). In considering these care structures, Scannell has put particular emphasis on the temporality of broadcasting, on what he calls its "dailiness". "This dailiness yields", he says, "the sense we all have of the ordinariness, the familiarity and obviousness of radio and television. It establishes their taken for granted, 'seen but unnoticed' character" (2000: 19). And what Scannell wants us to recognize and acknowledge is the immense pleasure that this mundane quality of broadcasting has had for viewers –the pleasure that comes from the combination of familiarity, confirmation, entitlement and effortlessness.

And what we want to emphasize is that this particular pleasure principle is, of course, also present in Turkish broadcasting culture. Turkish broadcasting culture also exists as an ordinary and mundane culture. And the appeal of Turkish television, as with other broadcasting cultures, is equally the appeal of its ordinariness. Through it, Turks living in Europe have access to, or can extend their access to, what Jostein Gripsrud (1999) calls the domain of "common knowledge". They can be part of the great domain of "anonymous discourse" that broadcasting has brought into existence, the banal domain of "inattentive attention" (Brune, 1993: 37). What we are arguing, then, is that migrant viewers are looking to find what the national television culture has always provided. Like any other

Kevin Robins & Asu Aksoy

viewers, Turkish-speaking viewers in Europe are also in search of broadcast television that is meaningfully and effortlessly available. They are also wanting –and to
a quite large extent finding– the pleasures of familiarity and confirmation. And
our point is that the desire for such an engagement with Turkish television is
entirely *social*, and not at all ethno-cultural or 'diasporic', in its motivation.
Migrant viewers are in search of ordinary social gratifications, precisely the kinds
of gratification that Scannell is concerned with.

Our second argument is more complex, and takes us back to what
Hülya said about Turkish television seeming to come from a distance and, consequently, losing its significance. What we want to get at is the particular feeling of
ambivalence that very many Turkish people have about transnational television
(which is more than the routine ambivalence that we all seem to have). They
enjoy and appreciate the programmes they see; and yet, at the same time, watching them can frequently cause frustration and provoke resentment. Sometimes, it
seems, transnational engagement with Turkish television culture doesn't 'work'.
In Scannell's terms, we may say that the care structures of television break down.
And what we want to suggest, as an explanation for this, is that, whilst considerable gratification may be got from everyday television, there are particular difficulties with its "sociable dimension", which Scannell regards as "the most fundamental characteristic of broadcasting's communicative ethos" (1996: 23). Put
simply, Turkish television often seems to its transnational viewers to be failing or
lacking in its sociable aspect.

Scannell draws our attention to the remarkable capacity of broadcasting
to generate a sense of "we-ness", through the creation of "a public, shared and
sociable world-in-common between human beings" (2000: 12). What Scannell
means when he talks about the creation of a "world in common" is, of course, a
national world in common; what is at issue is the contribution of broadcasting to
the institution of the 'imagined community'. His account is often extremely idealis-
tic, but what we think Scannell usefully brings out is the way in which television and
radio have worked to create a public world with "an ordered, orderly, familiar,
knowable appearance" (1996: 153). It is a world in which television and radio contribute to "the shaping of our sense of days" (1996: 149). The dailiness of broadcast media gives rise to the sense of "*our* time –generational time– the time of *our*
being with one another in the world" (1996: 174). The broadcasting calendar "creates a horizon of expectations, a mood of anticipation, a directedness towards that
which is to come, thereby giving substance and structure (a 'texture of relevances')
to everyday life" (1996: 155). According to this ideal-type scenario, broadcasting
produces a "common world –a shareable, accessible, available public world": what
it does is "to create and to allow ways of being-in-public for absent listeners and
viewers" (1996: 166, 168). It connects "everyone's my-world" to the "great
world", which is "a world in common, a world we share" (1996: 172, 174).

And what we are arguing here is that it is this sociable functioning of
broadcasting that doesn't 'work' properly for migrants watching Turkish televi-

sion in Europe. Transnational viewers are often disconcerted because, on very many occasions, they cannot relate to Turkish programmes as a natural, ordinary, unremarkable, everyday entitlement. In the case of news this is particularly apparent. If, as Scannell argues, "the care structures of news are designed to routinise eventfulness" (1996: 160), then we may say that in our Turkish case, at least, these care structures do not function well across distance. In the transnational context, there is a problem with the mode of address. Broadcasting works on the basis of what Scannell calls a "for-anyone-as-someone" structure of address: it is addressing a mass audience, and yet appears to be addressing the members of that audience personally, as individuals. "The for-anyone-as-someone structure expresses and embodies that which is between the impersonal third person and the personal first person, namely the second person (the me-and-you)", says Scannell (2000: 9). "The for-anyone-as-someone structure expresses "we-ness". It articulates human social sociable life". In the Turkish case, it seems that viewers may often be made to feel like no one in particular. The conditions no longer exist for feeling at home in the 'we-ness' of Turkish broadcasting culture.

Why does the 'my world' of Turkish migrants no longer resonate properly with a Turkish world in common? Why are there problems with the mode of address in the case of transnational broadcasting? Why are the care structures of broadcasting disrupted? The reasons are to do with the context of consumption. As we have said, transnational broadcasting is not about magically transporting migrant viewers back to a distant homeland. It is about broadcasting services being delivered to them in their new locations –in the case of the Turks we have been discussing, it is in London. What this means is that the world of broadcasting is not seamlessly connected to the world of the street outside, as it would be for viewers watching in Turkey. Migrant viewers cannot move routinely between the media space and the 'outside' space of everyday Turkish reality. And since so much of what broadcasting is about has to do with connecting viewers to the life and rhythms of the real world of the nation, there are bound to be difficulties with the dislocated kind of viewing that migrancy enforces. Turkish migrants will often protest that Turkish television exaggerates. 'When you see these things you naturally believe them', one man said to us.

> But I've been back from Turkey for two weeks, and it's nothing like that really. It's nothing like how it's shown. Turkey is the same Turkey. Of course, there are scandals, and there are people who live through them. But television doesn't reflect things as they are (Focus group, Hackney, London, 16 December 1999).

Migrants tend to forget that exaggeration is an integral part of television rhetoric in Turkey, and it is only when they go back for a visit that they recognize the discrepancy between screen reality and street reality (whereas viewers in Turkey are checking out this discrepancy on a continuous basis). We may say that the decontextualisation of the migrant viewing situation often results in a kind of interference in the reception of cultural signals from Turkey.

A further consequence of the dislocated context of consumption is that migrant viewers can never be in a position to watch Turkish television naively or innocently. We must be aware that they actually operate in and across two cultural spaces (at least) –Turkish and British. As well as watching Turkish channels, most of them are very familiar with British television. And they will often make comparisons between the two broadcasting cultures (concerning, for example, programme quality, scheduling, bias, censorship). We may say that there is a constant implicit comparison going on, and very often the comparisons are explicit –Turkish programmes are always watched and thought about with an awareness of British television in mind. As one man put it to us,

> We have the opportunity to compare things we see with what happens here. Before, we didn't know what it was like here (Focus group, Hackney, London, 16 December 1999).

When we say that Turkish migrants cannot watch Turkish television innocently, we mean that they can no longer watch it from the inside, as it were. They cannot recover the simple perspective of monocultural (national) vision. They are compelled to think about Turkish culture in the light of other cultural experiences and possibilities.

We have said that watching transnational Turkish television can be a frustrating and often disillusioning experience. What we want to emphasize in conclusion is that this disillusionment can also be a very productive experience. Through their engagement with Turkish (alongside British) media culture, Turkish migrants develop a comparative and critical attitude, and may become more reflexively aware of the arbitrariness and provisionality of cultural orders. In the present argument, we have been principally concerned with how the ordinary world of broadcast television can work to undermine the diasporic imagination. What should also have become apparent in the course of our argument, however, is the potential that exists, too, for working against the grain of the national imagination, against the confining mentality of imagined community.

Conclusion: transnational experience and media policy

In this discussion, we have been critical of diasporic cultural studies and the agenda centred on 'diasporic media'. Our objection has been to what we regard as a basic wrong assumption made by its exponents: that the people who watch transnational satellite television do so as mere ciphers of the 'imagined communities' to which they are said to belong. What we call into question is the idea that migrants function principally in terms of the categories of collective attachment and identification. As Roger Rouse has observed, "the discourse of identity suggests that social collectivities are aggregates of atomised and autonomous elements, either individuals or sub-groups, that are fundamentally equivalent by virtue of the common possession of a given social property" (1995: 358). Human individuals are reduced to the status of being the poor representatives of whatever imagined community they happen to have once been aggregated into. Rouse points to the socio-cultural efficacy of this logic of identity. We may consider it, he says, in terms of "hegemonic efforts to make ideas about identity frame the ways in which people understand what it is to be a person, the kinds of collectivities in which they are involved, the nature of the problems that they face, and the means by which these problems can be tackled" (1995: 356). Our problem with the project of diasporic cultural studies is that, in the end, it contributes to the extension and perpetuation of these hegemonic efforts in the context of contemporary global change. Ultimately, everything remains predicated on the logic of national identity and a national, or national-style, cultural frame.

We have felt it necessary to go against the grain of the prevailing culturalism, and to take greater account of human consciousness and self-consciousness –to recognize that the minds of Turkish migrants may provide a more significant and interesting research focus than their identities. This means moving our agenda away from the 'problem' of migrant culture and identity, to consider how it is that migrants experience migration, and how they think and talk about and make sense of their experiences. The point about identities is that they require simplicity. In the case of minds and consciousness, what is important is always their complexity. And what we suggest is that transnational experiences may now be helping to foster more plural, and also more complex, intellectual and imaginative perspectives. At the beginning of this discussion, we mobilised a geological metaphor to characterise the complexity of contemporary developments in the media landscape in Europe. Across the old order of national audiovisual spaces, we suggested, we have come to see the subsequent layering of regional spaces and of global and transnational spaces. Now, at our discussion's concluding point, what we are invoking is actually the mental space equivalent of this new geographical complexity. We might also apply the geological metaphor to the minds of our Turkish interviewees. Turkish viewers take in the diversity of media cultures that we have referred to. They are watching a whole range of Turkish-language channels, and some would watch Kurdish TV; they also watch the British channels, as well as global channels such as CNN or MTV; and they are also reading local Turkish newspapers and listening to local Turkish (and Kurdish), as well as British, radio. They have to find ways to accommodate differences of view and perspective. They have to accommodate the new cultural complexity that emerges out of the contemporary encounter between national and transnational cultures spaces.

Turkish viewers are inevitably caught up in a process of constant comparison between the different (national) cultures they consume. And this process necessarily involves a certain distantiation from (national) cultural codes and rhetorics. Thus, in the migrant context, where the ideal rhetorical situation of Turkish national television is significantly undermined, there may be possibilities for a more reflexive and critical engagement with television from the 'homeland'. What we have tried to suggest is that, in the Turkish case at least, transnational television might actually be working to subvert the diasporic imagination and its imperatives of identification and belonging. What emerges from our discussion of Turkish migrant experiences is the possibility –it is by no means a necessity or an inevitability– that transnational cultural developments might open up new possibilities for mental space: perspectives beyond the national imagination. "It all depends on the rifts and leaps in a person", Elias Canetti (1991: 20) once observed, "on the distance from the one to the other *within himself*". Transnational experience is surely about developing –and putting a positive value on– this capacity to travel the distance from the one to the other within oneself.

Our discussion here has focused exclusively on Turkish migrants. But is it possible, you might ask, to generalise from it? We do not want to make more general and abstract claims about migrant experience. As a result of a number of factors –the geographical proximity of Turkey and Western Europe; the particular historical trajectory of Turkish migration; the working out of Turkish identity politics in recent years– there are important specificities in the Turkish case. We believe it is crucial to be attentive to these specificities. But this does not mean that our argument is only a narrow and limited one. We do believe that what we have been describing has relevance for other migratory experiences. The point, however, is that, because each migrant population, in each locale, has its own specificities, nothing can be directly read off from one set of findings. It is not possible to generalise from any individual case study, then. But what is possible is to use the particular resonances of a case study to throw light on the distinctiveness of other migrant experiences –Iranians in the United States, for example, or Koreans in Latin America. Our Turkish case study can surely be evocative for the understanding of different migrant cultures.

We conclude our discussion by making the point that the emergence of the new transnational cultural spaces and of new cultural experiences of the kind we have been describing must have considerable implications for cultural and media policy. Or perhaps it is more accurate, at this point, to say that the emergence of these spaces *should* have such implications. For, if it is clear that developments in transnational broadcasting are raising important new issues for audiovisual policymakers, it is the case there is at present no constituency or agency for discussing what the policy implications of these new developments might be. We may say there are now possibilities for the institution of what could be an interestingly –and productively– new transnational European cultural map. And yet media policy remains predominantly and stubbornly national in its scope and concerns, and has not really begun to consider the implications of a situation in which migrant populations are now watching a complex new array of transnational programming –programming from across the world. No agenda –and, perhaps more seriously, no imagination– has yet emerged to deal with the new challenges arising as a consequence of the new other-than-national dynamics in media industries and cultures.

As a consequence of the proliferation of transnational television channels of all kinds, we have been seeing a fragmentation of the national media space. The relationship between audiences and the national public sphere once mediated by public service broadcasters has now changed in a significant way. Migrant audiences are no longer dependent on the provision of minority programming in their country of residence, and are no longer necessarily loyal to, and held by, the public service channels and broadcasters. The audiences within any particular national territory now constitute different publics, not necessarily sharing in the common knowledge pool or the reference point of the nation. These are developments that raise important questions. What are the cultural implications when sizeable migrant communities cease to watch the national channels of their 'host' country for cultural diversity strategies and policies? Does the concept of 'minority' programming cease to be adequate for addressing audiences that have, until now, been categorized in this way? How should cultural diversity policies in broadcasting be re-invented in the age of transnational broadcasting? What is the significance of the new transnational media for public-service ideals, nationally but also increasingly at the transnational scale? How should public broadcasters be responding to the increasing penetration of transnational broadcasters into the mainstream audiences? What are the appropriate scales of intervention for media policy agencies now, given the transnationalisation process?

The processes of media transnationalism are posing a whole new set of questions with respect to public culture in the European space. Important new issues are being opened up concerning cultural provision, cultural diversity, and public culture, on a basis that now exceeds the national framework. What is called for is a new political and cultural geography for media policy and regulation.

Chapter 3

Writing the world

Oscar Hemer

The discourse of cultural globalization has a parallel in post-colonial thought, but there has been surprisingly little contact between these seemingly closely related traditions. In this chapter I will propose a dialogue between the two, and suggest that the arts, and especially literature, may provide suitable common ground. Taking Paulo Freire's notion of 'writing the world' as a starting-point, I base my argument on a comparative discussion of three main writing practices (journalistic, academic and literary), drawing on my own experience as a writer and journalist and the 'transgressing' examples of Caryl Phillips, Flemming Røgilds and Antjie Krog. I end up with a discussion on the specific role of fiction in communication for social change, primarily as a means of investigation and secondly as a vehicle for empowerment.

The global and the post-colonial

It may be worthwhile recalling that globalization is a quite recent concept, i.e. only some twenty years old. And when it was introduced, by Roland Robertson[1], it had quite different connotations from those it has since attained. Robertson's discussion of globalization was actually an offspring of the cultural debate of the '80s on the

1 The term is usually attributed to Robertson although he makes no claims for having coined it. It appears as early as 1985 in an article in the magazine *Theory, Culture & Society*, "Modernization, globalization and the problem of culture in world-systems theory", and is systematically discussed and defined in *Globalization - social theory and global culture* (1992). Robertson is also the father of 'glocalization', which he picked up in Japanese business jargon and gave his own interpretation.

modern and the post-modern, and the G-word was originally an attempt to better describe 'the post-modern condition' by putting this general, all-encompassing, yet intriguing and somewhat obscure feature of contemporary culture in a global perspective. Robertson, Michael Featherstone, Scott Lash and other cultural sociologists involved in the magazine *Theory, Culture & Society* opposed the common notion of 'cultural imperialism' and pointed to the fact that global cultural flows were not just going in one direction, spreading Western (American commercial) culture to every corner of the world, as the analysts and opponents of 'McDonaldization' claimed and many of today's anti-globalization activists still take for granted.

In the arts, and at the time especially in literature and music, impulses were increasingly going from 'periphery' to 'centre'. *The Empire Writes Back* is the witty title of an influential textbook from 1989 by three Australian researchers in comparative literature, Bill Ashcroft, Gareth Griffiths and Helen Tiffin, analysing the current literary revival in the Commonwealth, which seemed to almost exclusively involve writers originating from either the former colonies in the Caribbean, Africa, Asia and Australia, or minority groups in the metropolitan centre (London). What has been labelled 'post-colonial literature' is no doubt the most important global tendency in literature in recent decades, giving the very notion of *world literature* an updated relevance and new meaning, albeit perhaps not in the same sense as 'world music'[2].

The post-colonial is mainly attributed to the two principal powers of the late colonial era, the British and French empires, but post-colonial literature found its ground-breaking predecessor in the Latin American literary 'boom' of the 1970s. The influence of 'magical realism' and especially Gabriel García Márquez' masterpiece *Cien años de soledad* (A Hundred Years of Solitude) has, for good and for bad, been enormous among writers all over the world, not least in the former British colonies. Salman Rushdie, the iconic figure of the post-colonial literary boom, has often declared his debt to García Márquez for the conception of his twice Booker Prize-awarded first novel, *Midnight's Children*[3]. Latin American writers' main contribution to world literature was not only their syncretistic fusion of myth and history but, more importantly, their *incorporation of the colonial other* into the scheme of the (European) modern novel –not only as an ornamental figure, as in the abundant existing colonial literature, but as a subject[4].

---

2 'World music', originally coined to describe western rock music with elements of popular music from Africa, Latin America and Asia, has become increasingly synonymous with the category 'ethnic music'; that is, any non-western music, traditional or modern, produced and distributed by the global music industry. Traditional European popular music is often also included in the diluted definition. 'World literature', going back to Goethe's definition from 1830, has of course other connotations but tends to attain a similar meaning as 'literature in one of the European colonial languages –in reality only English– by writers with a mixed or non-western origin'.

3 When the prestigious Booker Prize, given to prose fiction from the Commonwealth, celebrated its 30th anniversary in 1998, *Midnight's Children* was elected 'Booker of the Bookers'.

4 I have written several articles and essays about the Latin American contribution to world literature and its role as a 'missing link' to post-colonialism. See for example "Från dualism till pluralism. Carlos Fuentes och det latinamerikanska bidraget till romankonsten" (From dualism to pluralism. Carlos Fuentes and the

If we define post-colonial literature as literature which –explicitly or not– deals with questions of cultural identity and the remaining colonial structures of the post-colonial world[5], it has its theoretical parallel in post-colonial thought, which mainly started as *post-colonial reading* of literary and scientific works, anthropological accounts, historical records, etc. in order to reveal and demonstrate the contradiction between the underlying assumptions and the (often unwitting) colonialist ideologies (Ashcroft, et al 2000)[6].

The development of 'post-colonial thought' –eventually leading to the very specialized and quite marginalized academic discipline of today– runs parallel in time to the discussion on the post-modern, part of which developed into a discourse on cultural globalization, as indicated above. Yet, in spite of the obvious parallels and potential connections, there has, with a few but important exceptions, been surprisingly little dialogue.

The lack of communication can to some extent be explained by political and cultural differences, but the main obstacle has probably been academic specialization. The globalization of culture was typically a concern of (British and American) cultural sociologists and anthropologists, while the post-colonial theorists were mainly (Asian and African) historians or scholars of comparative literature. One of the 'connectors', with a natural foothold in both discourses, is Arjun Appadurai, whose exploration of the transnational public sphere (1996) has contributed a very useful theoretical framework for the study of media and globalization. Another exceptional example of concretely applied post-colonial theory, with direct relevance to our purpose here, is Indian historian Dipesh Chakrabarty's profound critique of historicism –the basis of prevailing evolutionist development thinking, with its deep roots in colonial notions of Western supremacy (Chakrabarty, 2000).

If we are to address global modernity –or rather *modernities* in the plural– and imagine global change, I would argue that the post-colonial dimension is a necessary supplement and corrective to post-national globalization discourse. Re-focusing on modernity certainly does not imply a return to the modernization paradigm, which equated modernization and westernization. Cultural globalization in the sense proposed here could rather be defined as the de-westernization of modernity, what Chakrabarty means by *provincializing Europe* –that is, the task of exploring how European thought, which is now everybody's heritage and affects the whole world, may be renewed from and for the margins (2000: 16). I further suggest that the arts may be the common ground where

Latin American contribution to novel writing) in *Peninsula* (1989) and "El Boom Revisited" in the Norwegian magazine *Marginal* # 3 (1994).

5 Actual power relations as well as more subtle mental figures, not only in the former colonial empires but also in countries like Sweden, which were not formally part of the colonial system.

6 An early example of post-colonial reading is Eric Williams' *British Historians and The West Indies* (1966). Edward Said's *Orientalism* (1978), often regarded as the foundation stone of post-colonial thought as a discipline, is also basically a post-colonial reading of significant works in British and French literature from the colonial era.

these different yet perfectly compatible discourses can best communicate. As demonstrated by the evidence of post-colonial literature, global modernity took on a plural form in art before being articulated in theory.

Writing practices

English, rich as it is in vocabulary, lacks a proper word for what in German is called *gestaltung*. The suggested translation 'design' is not quite accurate. 'Designing the world' is not what I have in mind here. Hence, for lack of a proper alternative, I stick to the verb 'writing'. And the 'surrogate' is actually even more appropriate, since it offers an unforeseen association with Brazilian liberation pedagogue Paulo Freire's work. Reading the word, he says, is dependent upon reading the world. Literacy, according to Freire, is that which enables us to more fully read and transform the world *–to write the world* (1987).

Appadurai also addresses the relation between word and world, which he considers to be the subject matter of cultural studies. In his wide understanding, "*Word* can encompass all forms of textualized expression and *world* can mean anything from the means of production and the organization of life-worlds to the globalized relations of cultural reproduction". Today, the tension between word and world is translated to a "complex negotiation" and the task of ethnography becomes "the unraveling of a conundrum":

> What is the nature of locality as a lived experience in a globalized, deterritorialized world? (1996: 52)

I shall not go into further detail on Appadurai's analysis of "the role of imagination in social life", but his reflections on "ethnographic writing" certainly have relevance for the other forms of writing, not least fiction, which I shall discuss at greater length here.

There is, of course, an immense variety of writing practices, but I will concentrate on three main forms, or rather norms, and especially their inter-relations. We are all more or less familiar with each of them –as readers, if not as writers. Let us call them the *literary*, the *journalistic* and the *academic* norm and illustrate their relationships using an equilateral triangle.

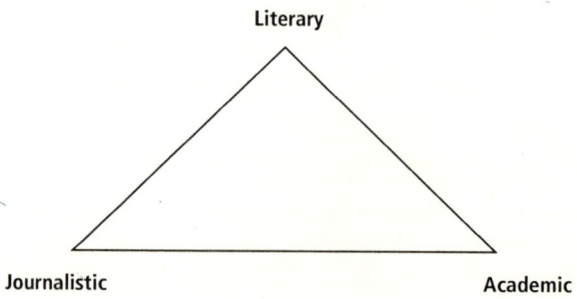

I have, for practical reasons, chosen a two-dimensional geometric figure, but in reality there are of course no such absolute categories as Literature, Journalism and Academia. They are all mixed and interrelated practices with more or less blurred borderlines. Yet they represent different approaches and perspectives, and are distinguished by certain clearly defined normative conventions. The model is not hierarchical; the three sides are equal and it does not really matter which position is where. There is, however, a reason, which I will explain later, why the literary norm is put on top of the others.

Unlearning to learn

So, let us start at the base and look at the relation between journalism and academia –apparently the two least compatible and most contradictory norms.

The academic way of writing is one that we all learn in its modest form at primary and secondary school –the *composition*. At university level it is refined as the *paper* and, in its most advanced form, the *thesis* or *dissertation*. The academic disposition follows a strict linear formula, containing the following elements: introduction, discussion, conclusion and summary. You can possibly leave out the summary, but none of the others as they are all essential for the understanding of the thesis. You must specify your research material and declare what theories and methods you have applied. You must build up your argument in order to draw your conclusion; this has to be solid, founded on previous research and according to specific scientific conventions. It takes time to write –and to read. It demands attention all the way. It is, by definition, a slow practice.

The journalistic norm represents, in most respects, the very opposite. When you come as a student to a School of Journalism, or as an apprentice to a newspaper or radio station, the first thing you are taught is to forget everything you learned in school –to turn the conventional writing formula upside down or the other way around: skip the introduction and get to the core immediately! I studied at Stockholm's School of Journalism in the mid '70s, before computers, and we were instructed to simply put the paper in the typewriter and start writing. Hand-written drafts, or even key-word dispositions, were strictly forbidden.

Now I am, of course, talking about the extreme journalistic norm –the one of news reporting.

> *World Trade Center leveled to ground in terrorist attack. Over 3000 dead.*

Only after giving the core information –the actual event– in one or two sentences, can the news reporter give the background and go into detail. The principle is simple: the essential facts first, then additional information of gradually decreasing importance, so that the editor can cut from the end without losing consistency.

According to a common myth, this formula of reporting dates back to the American Civil War of the 1860s, when the telegraph network was vulnerable to sabotage and thus unreliable. There is, however, little evidence of the 'inverted pyramid' being used during the war (Campbell, 2004). Nonetheless, it has been the ruling norm of news journalism in Western media since the late 19th century. News became an industry and journalism basically an industrial form of writing –*text production*. The inverted pyramid also lives on even without any practical reasons, although the Internet and new forms of multimedia journalism are now transforming the conditions of information access and distribution.

News journalism may not be our main concern here, but what I am hinting at is the journalistic approach, which can be applied to all journalistic genres, including arts and feature journalism. As a journalist working in the media, you are in a tough competitive situation. You simply have to get to the core and/or find a clue that catches the attention of your audience, in order to get your message across. Otherwise, all your creative efforts are in vain. You never get a second chance to make a first impression.

The journalistic norm would certainly make an interesting subject for post-colonial deconstruction. It is formulated by liberal ideals of freedom and transparency, while at the same time dictated by the industrial production process of the media industry and –most important– market forces.

Journalism has always been conditioned by the market more or less, but global integration of the media and entertainment industries makes commercialization of the media a prime driving force, blurring the formerly well-protected borderline separating 'news' from 'entertainment' (Sreberny-Mohammadi et al, 1997; McChesney, 1999; Hjarvard, 2001). What always applied to the tabloid press and commercial radio and TV stations is increasingly spilling over into morning newspapers and public service channels (this tendency towards market dictatorship, which may be a constituting aspect of globalization, strongly affects the publishing industry and thereby literature as well).

Investigative journalism

Academic writing is a *primary* practice, in the sense that it actually (ideally, at least) makes a scientific contribution. It is, from the journalistic point of view, *news*, i.e. the matter that journalism is supposed to feed on. Accordingly, the journalistic practice is mainly a *secondary* one; it reports and reflects on a primary source –an event, a commissioned report, a work of art, a dissertation. Journalism would then, ideally, be the art of summarizing, synthesizing and, thus, explaining a subject.

But journalism is also a form of investigation, and as a research method it has a lot in common with academic research, although this is never, or rarely, explicitly acknowledged. *Investigative journalism*, or muck-raking as it is commonly called among journalists, had its big break-through after *Washington Post* reporters Bill Woodward and Carl Bernstein's disclosure of the

Watergate scandal, which eventually led to the impeachment of US President Richard Nixon in 1974.

In the aftermath of Watergate, all self-respecting major Western media appointed investigative reporters and many still keep an elite staff of journalists with special privileges. But even these few star journalists have, from an academic point of view, ridiculously little time at their disposal. The standard would be a week or two –at the maximum a month– to do a major investigation into, say, the trafficking of women from the former Soviet Union and its links with global crime networks. What is more, while doing this research these investigative journalists would still be supposed to do at least some of the regular routine reporting on the side (as a regular reporter you work in a one-day perspective; if a commissioned report is handed out at 10 a.m. you are expected to deliver the article by 3 p.m.).

I worked for many years for the arts section of *Sydsvenska Dagladet*, the main daily newspaper of southern Sweden, edited in Malmö. Apart from literary reviews and chronicles and day-to-day commentaries, I specialized during the '90s in a form of essayistic travel writing from the world outside Europe, mainly Latin America and Africa[7]. I was not a foreign correspondent and I never wrote reports while travelling. I gathered my material and my impressions, and wrote the articles when I came home. Overall, this would be a process involving at least one month and at most three months of research, travel and writing.

From the employer's point of view, of course, this meant quite high costs for what was considered to be very exclusive material. They could send out a regular reporter and a photographer to fill the same amount of editorial space in less than a week. And they would not note any qualitative difference. Or worse: they would note the difference and prefer the latter news-oriented and presumably more easily digested reading. The well-researched (literary) reportage has become a very rare genre, at least in the news media.

Judging by current tendencies in the media, the gap between journalistic and academic practices is definitely widening. But although their positions are by definition contradictory and conflicting, they are also no doubt complementary and can perfectly well be combined. Many academic writers could certainly use a more journalistic approach.

Journalistic literature, literary journalism

The relation between the journalistic and the literary norm is perhaps even more antagonistic, or dialectical, but in a more subtle manner. According to a common saying, all journalists are frustrated novelists. In fact, few journalists dream of an academic career. There is even an explicit anti-academic sentiment in the media, stronger among journalists than in most other intellectual professions, while

---

7 Some of these articles are gathered in the books *Andra städer. 3 essäreportage från Syd* (1993) and *Kuba & Kina. 2 postkommunistiska reportage* (1996).

many journalists *aspire* to become fiction writers. Sweden's commercially most successful novelists in the last few decades have, with but a few exceptions, all been former journalists[8]. And among the great majority of economically non-independent writers, quite a few make their living as (part-time) journalists. Not only do practitioners mingle, but the distinction between the forms is often difficult to draw; there are all kinds of mixed genres along the scale, from Norman Mailer's detailed documentary novels about the moon landing or mass murderer Gary Gilmore to the personal columns and semi-literary causeries which have boomed in the media lately.

New Journalism, launched by American novelist and non-fiction writer Tom Wolfe in the 1970s[9], is a prime example of deliberately fused writing practices. One of Wolfe's own sources of inspiration was novelist Truman Capote's true crime story *In Cold Blood* (1966), an exposition of a multiple murder in Kansas, USA, in 1959. New journalism could be seen as journalism gone literary or documentary literature. However, as the term indicates, it sticks strictly to journalistic standards in terms of accuracy and factual detail. The 'new journalist' is free to use literary forms of expression and to voice his own subjective feelings and reflections, but he is certainly not allowed to add (fictitious) characters or events to his story. The writer of documentary or historical *fiction*, on the other hand, may make the same claims regarding *realism* but yet feel obliged to fill in the narrative gaps, with the excuse of providing an interpretation. This distinction is subtle but crucial, and I will come back to it later.

Yet the relationship is hardly an equal one. Like the academic, the literary writer tends to look down on journalism as an ephemeral and popular (even vulgar) form of writing. The traditional divide between 'high literature' and popular culture is still there, although the barrier is being broken down, not least thanks to post-colonial writing; one of the latter's most important features has been the incorporation of popular cultural forms and mythologies, and it often manages to reach a wide readership without compromising its artistic integrity.

Mutual respect

Literature and academia, finally, seem to enjoy the most harmonious relationship, partly because it is the least developed one. The fusions along this axis are not as abundant as other mixed genres and often meet with suspicion from both sides. In Scandinavia –and, to a lesser extent, in Anglo-Saxon culture– 'academic' connotes 'anemic' with regard to literature and 'essayistic' is not a positive characteristic when it comes to science (latin cultures show greater acceptance for transgressions along these lines and subsequently boast a prominent tradi-

8 Marianne Fredriksson and Jan Guillou, to name two of the internationally most renowned.
9 It was codified in 1973 in a collection of writing co-edited with E.W. Thompson called *The New Journalism*.

tion of what we might call 'high-brow' essay writing). Yet, and precisely because the positions are clearly defined, there is also a sense of mutual respect between these two primary practices.

The construction of a novel is certainly different from the construction of a doctoral thesis, but in some cases, at least, they may both demand corresponding amounts of effort. Writers are of course more vulnerable (and sensitive) to market forces than academic researchers, but both are more or less dependent on subsidies and grants. As forms of investigation, the one is supposedly 'freer', the other more constricted by rigid (scientific) standards. In fact, literary standards may be just as constricting and inhibiting, but in a different manner.

The subject matter

So far I have been reasoning uni-dimensionally, looking at these three positions two by two, as a set of different dichotomies. Now let us look at all three at a time in a more bi-dimensional way. Let us try to identify some genres that are actually fusions of the three approaches. The most obvious are the review and the essay.

There are all kinds of reviews, from the brief commentary in a daily newspaper to the comprehensive critique in an annual academic journal. The newspaper critic, whether an employee or not, is in a sense a journalist, but his standards are more academic than journalistic. However, they are not academic in the strict sense either, since they contain an important element of *subjectivity*. There is no established standard for the critique of a work of art. The critic is sometimes accused of being a 'judge of taste' and his critique random, merely a matter of taste. It is not, of course. There are several, mostly implicit, qualitative criteria, but these are not as easily detectable as those by which a scientific work is validated. In examining a dissertation one can use a check-list to ensure that this or that satisfies the minimum requirements. When reviewing a work of art one is actually examining another person's –the artist's– subjective expression. The subject matter is the subject itself.

The good review is faithful to its object, if not to the writer. My own experience as a writer is that the critic at best discovers aspects of my own work that I have not consciously perceived myself. The critic can thus be a co-creative interpreter, and the review a kind of extension of the reviewed work of art –literally a re-view, from a different angle.

The essay can be an extended review. But the essayist does not have to be a critic, and should in any case be *more* than a critic. He speaks in his own right and may also base his reflections on his own prime experience, as a researcher, reporter or human being (travel writing is another genre containing elements of all three practices, which can be approached from any apex of the triangle). What I am getting at is, once again, the element of *subjectivity* –the vertical axis of my figure and the reason why I put the literary norm on top.

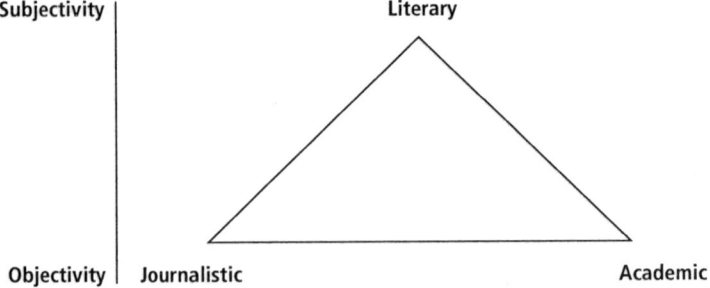

Subjectivity

Literary

Objectivity | Journalistic

Academic

'Objective' and 'subjective' correspond in this figure to the related yet not identical 'fact' and 'fiction', and both these dichotomies serve in defining the literary practice vis-à-vis the other two. But the tension between the objective and the subjective applies to both journalism and academia. There is neither a linear, gradual move from fact to fiction nor, necessarily, an exclusion process of 'either –or'. I offer three examples.

The Atlantic home

Caryl Phillips was born in St. Kitts in the Caribbean in 1959, moved with his parents to England in the early sixties and is now living part-time in London, part-time in New York –a typical post-colonial exile trajectory. As a black immigrant from the colonial periphery, growing up in dismal Leeds, he constantly faced racism and discrimination and naturally became concerned with issues of cultural identity and belonging. 'Home' is an essential concept in all his work, which comprises novels, essays and drama. Other themes that he always comes back to are the historical legacy of slavery and 'the burden of race'. He would probably consider himself to be mainly a fiction writer (his fifth novel *Crossing the River* was short-listed for the Booker Prize in 1993) but he is also a prominent critic.

The work I have in mind here is categorized as one of his non-fiction works, although he himself calls *The Atlantic Sound* (2000) a reportage novel. The title's 'sound' has a double meaning, but should mainly be understood in its geographical sense of the Atlantic as an inner sea, the inner sea of Phillips' own biography but also of modernity. The slave trade, trafficking in 'black gold', was the dark fundament of rising global capitalism, of embryonic globalization, if you will.

So it is a personal history, starting with the same Atlantic crossing that he did as a four-month-old baby, from St. Kitts to Dover, and now as a 40-year-old receptive reporter, while all the time referring to the primordial journey. But it also becomes a general history of the Atlantic, from this personal post-colonial point of view. Phillips continues his journey to some carefully chosen ports on both sides of the basin: Liverpool, Accra and Charleston, South Carolina, 'the Ellis Island of Afro-Americans'. He travels as an observant and sensitive reporter, recreating his impressions with poignant detail and great sensuality, and intelligently commenting on them in a way that never stands in the way of the reader's own reflection. It is travel writing at its best.

But in the midst of these episodic travelogues, he suddenly puts in a historical short story from the late 19th century: the sad tale of an ambitious native palm oil producer from the Gold Coast who is cheated by his British associates. This character wants to buy his own steamship and sends the money to Liverpool in good faith and waits for the ship, which of course never arrives. So he sends his son to Liverpool, still in good faith, to find out what happened. The short story tells us about the son's wide-eyed impressions of Liverpool and his struggle for justice (he finally wins the case and sends his father's associate to prison, but loses the money).

This exemplary piece of post-colonial historical fiction is juxtaposed against Phillips' own visit to late 20th century Liverpool, which is clearly finding difficulties in dealing with its shameful past as a financial centre of the slave trade. From modern Liverpool the journey goes on to modern Ghana, the former Gold Coast. And so on. By moving between time layers and mixing genres correspondingly, Caryl Phillips makes the one perspective shed new light on the other. *The Atlantic Sound* is neither fiction nor non-fiction but novel, essay and reportage all in one. And above all, perhaps, it marks a home-coming, symbolically and literally. As Phillips remarks in the essay selection *A New World Order* (2001):

> After thirteen years of compulsive itinerancy, I know my Atlantic 'home' to be triangular in shape with Britain at one apex, the west coast of Africa at another, and the new world of North America (including the Caribbean) forming the third point of the triangle (…) Across the centuries, countless millions have traversed this water, and unlike myself, these people have not always had the luxury of choice (…) These are the people that I have written about during the course of the past twenty years, and as one book has led to another, I have grown to understand that I am, of course, writing about myself in some oblique, though not entirely unpredictable, way (2001: 305).

The alienation effect

My second example, Danish poet and freelance sociologist Flemming Røgilds, is one of the few academic researchers that have deliberately approached a fictional form and method. Since the early '80s Røgilds has been doing extensive research on youth culture, especially among second-generation immigrants, in Great Britain and in his native Denmark. Like Caryl Phillips, he has been concerned with 'race' and 'roots', but from the (white) sociologist's point of view. In his books, based on participant observation and in-depth interviews, he always uses his own diary as part of the raw material. But in *Charlie Nielsens Rejse* (Charlie Nielsen's Journey, 2000), subtitled 'Travels in multicultural landscapes', he takes a step further, turning himself as a researcher into a fictitious character. The year is 1997 and Charlie Nielsen, the writer's alter ego, a Danish cultural sociologist of late middle age, (re)visits two European metropolises which can be con-strued in some ways as each other's opposites: London and Berlin.

Through the fictionalized form, Røgilds tries to achieve a *verfremme-dung* effect in German playwright Bertolt Brecht's sense, thus taking an 'objec-tive' view of his own educational process during his sometimes bewildering excursions into the urban twilight zone. Charlie Nielsen takes us to parts of London and Berlin unknown to most of us, introducing us to scholars and intel-lectuals who help him understand what he is seeing. The book consists mainly of their analytical conversations, at a high level of abstraction yet firmly anchored in the surrounding reality, which raises questions for Charlie Nielsen such as what it means to be white, what the actual heritage of fascism is and in what way racism and nationalism are interrelated.

In Røgilds/Nielsen's analysis Britain and Germany respectively represent the heritage of empire and extreme nationalism in Europe today, and his travels turn into a journey of discovery into the complexity of our present age which, in Røgilds' own words

> bridges the gap between innocence and experience at a specific point in European history which puts one in mind of the decline of the West.

However, it is not a sense of doom that stays with the reader, but rather the quiet confidence that Charlie Nielsen feels in London about the African Diaspora, where he has found a 'home away from home'.

The parallels with Caryl Phillips are obvious. Røgilds' fictionalized soci-ological documentary and Phillips' 'reportage novel' approach the same funda-mental questions from different angles of my triangle, with corresponding amounts of personal risk-taking and involvement.

Guilt and truth

My final example is South African journalist/poet Antjie Krog's personal account of her country's Truth and Reconciliation Commission, *Country of My Skull* (1999)[10]. The Commission, headed by Bishop Desmond Tutu, was set up soon after the first free elections in 1994. Its aim was to establish a picture of the gross human rights violations committed between 1960 and 1993, during the apartheid regime. From 1996 and over the next two years South Africans were exposed almost daily to the horrific testimonies of both victims and perpetrators. Antjie Krog –herself an Afrikaner, a descendant of the original Dutch settlers whose racist ideology and nationalist policy formed the apartheid system– cov-ered the Commission's work for the South African radio. The search for 'truth and reconciliation' touched her own sense of guilt; it was a process in which she came to terms with her own history and heritage.

10 The first South African edition was published in 1998, but I refer to the British edition, with an added epilogue.

But *Country of My Skull* is more than her account of the hearings. Rather, it is her reflections upon her professional experience as a radio reporter and her personal (human) responsibility as an Afrikaner and South African. When she looks back at her work she realizes that there was something more, something which journalism (alone) could not cover. So she goes back to the records and tells the story all over again, but in a semi-fictitious way, in a kind of meta-journalism linked to the very core of the issue, the very concepts of truth and reconciliation.

In one of the chapters, exemplary of her method and style, she delves into the story –or, rather, the diverging stories– of the killing of black policeman Richard Mutase and his wife in November 1987. This was one of the innumerable violations committed by the regime's death squads. The three murderers entered the house, took the wife to a back room and waited for the victim's arrival. When he came they assaulted him and shot him in the head. Before leaving they also killed the wife, but left the couple's six-year-old son, sleeping in another room, to wake up and find his parents mutilated and murdered. It is not clear, from the three testimonies, whether the killing of the woman and sparing of the child were intended or not. It is not even clear who actually shot Irene Mutase, since two of the squad members put the blame on each other. Antjie Krog gives us transcripts of the three oral testimonies and a fourth, fictionalized account of the event, by writer John Miles[11]. And she analyses them, she detects the imprints of the narrators, the "remembered core phrases and images that carry the distillation of the entire story". But even if the core elements overlap and give a seemingly objective view of what happened, one crucial question remains:

> Either Hechter or Mamasela killed Irene Mutase. The truth does not lie in
> between. There cannot be a compromise between the two versions.
> Is the truth known only to the dead?
> Between the bodies, the child Tshidiso remains. Which truth does he inher-
> it? It is for him that the truth must be found.
> And so, if the truth is to be believed in this country, it must perhaps be
> written by those who bear the consequences of the past (1999: 135).

So, how can we pursue the truth? Aren't we always stuck with a patchwork of subjective truths (and lies)? Don't we have to make more or less random selections and interpretations all the time? Of course, and to Antjie Krog this is an argument for using fiction in order to 'distill' reality. When confronted about her method she makes the following declaration:

> I'm not reporting or keeping minutes. I'm telling. (…) I cut and paste the
> upper layer, in order to get the second layer told, which is actually the story
> I want to tell. I change some people's names when I think they might be
> annoyed or might not understand the distortions.

---

11 John Miles's novel *Kroniek uit die doofpot* was based on documentation that was given to him in a Checkers packet by the dead Richard Mutase's lawyer.

But then you're not busy with the truth!

I am busy with the truth … *my* truth. Of course, it's quilted together from hundreds of stories that we've experienced or heard about in the past two years. Seen from my perspective, shaped by my state of mind at the time and now also by the audience I'm telling the story to. In every story there is hearsay, there is a grouping together of things that didn't necessarily happen together, there are assumptions, there are exaggerations to bring home the enormities of situations, there is downplaying to confirm innocence. And all of this together makes up the whole country's truth. So also the lies. And the stories that date from earlier times.

And the affair that you describe in here. Is that true?

No, but I had to bring a relationship into the story so that I could verbalize certain personal reactions to the hearings. I had to create a new character who could not only bring in new information but also express the psychological underpinnings of the Commission. Surely I can't describe how I eavesdropped and spied on others? What gives a story its real character is the need to entertain –to make the listener hang on your lips (256).

Most journalists would probably buy the first part of the argument. After all, journalism could be just another word for "cutting and pasting the upper layer, in order to get the second layer told". But they would most certainly object to the second part –the bringing in of a fictitious character. This is where *Country of My Skull* crosses the line.

Antjie Krog met harsh criticism, especially from some of her journalist colleagues, for supposedly confusing journalism and fiction. That would have been a relevant objection if she had not openly declared and discussed her method. As it is a relevant objection to many other hybrid forms of journalism and fiction, such as Norwegian reporter Åsne Seierstad's much debated 'documentary novel' *The Bookseller of Kabul* (2003), where there is no discussion and apparently no awareness of the hazards in fusing genres and practices[12].

The three examples above are chosen precisely because they are consciously crossing genre-lines, not in order to confuse them but to deliberately let the different perspectives and norms illuminate one another. You can only do that if you master both –or all three– practices. And you will have to be anchored in one perspective, from which you approach the others. The very centre of the triangle is –and should probably remain– empty.

Fiction and social change

Fiction, like myth, is part of the conceptual repertoire of contemporary societies. Readers of novels and poems can be moved to intense action (as

12 For an interesting critique of Seierstad's doubtful claims on 'truth', see Terje Tvedt "The native strikes back. Om budbringere og verdensbeskrivelser" in *Samtiden* 4-2004.

with *The Satanic Verses* of Salman Rushdie), and their authors often contribute to the construction of social and moral maps for their readers
(Appadurai, 1996: 58).

As my examples above indicate, fiction has a privileged position in relation to
other writing practices when it comes to communication for social change.
Dramatized fiction, especially, in the form of live theatre, film or broadcast soap
operas, are potentially very powerful tools which should be handled with care.

Literature played a key-role in the formation of nation-states and the
construction of national identity, in Europe as well as in the newly independent
former colonies of Africa and Asia. Many post-colonial writers actively contributed to the nation-building process, providing mythology and epics for identification. Literature has served a similar, (nationally) modernizing and vitalizing
function in Ireland, Norway and Iceland as it has in India and Nigeria. One important difference, though, is that the literature of the developing world is mainly
written in the European colonial languages –English, French and Portuguese. The
major exceptions are the non-European world languages, Arabic and Chinese,
and the Spanish and Portuguese of Latin America, which are usually not regarded
as colonial languages in the same sense as English and French. But translation
into one of the European world languages –in reality English– is a prerequisite for
recognition and incorporation into 'world literature'[13].

If literature –prose and poetry– played a crucial role in building the
imagined communities of both colonial empires and nation-states, post-colonial
writing –not only literature but other forms of mediated fiction and non-fiction as
well– may serve as an important means of deconstructing the same mythologies
and mental figures and, possibly, foster the building of new transnational and
glocal communities.

The role of the writing I have pictured here as a transgressive practice
is dual. It is primarily a means of investigation and discovery, secondly a vehicle for
identification and empowerment. There is a conflict between these two objectives and my point is that the second must always be subordinated to the first.
Writing which merely aims at behaviour change may or may not use fiction, but it
is certainly neither literature nor journalism. It is, at best, social marketing and
may have limited effect as such, more or less like commercial advertising –and like
commercials it will have to be repeated incessantly. Lasting global change requires
(the formation of) a global public sphere –or, rather, several over-lapping transnational or glocal public spheres. Writing and thus transforming the world, in
Freire's sense, is a complex process of collaborative teaching and learning.

---

13 This was a matter of heated discussion among some of the early post-colonial writers. The most radical position was held by John Ngugi from Kenya, who argued for the importance of a 'decolonialization
of the mind' and decided to turn his back on his colonial up-bringing. He changed his name to Ngugi wa
Thiong'o and started writing in his mother tongue, kikuyu. Whether he succeeded or not is difficult for
an outsider to judge. But from an intellectual, if not artistic, point of view, such 'de-linking' strategies
seem to be dead-end streets.

74 | Whether we are writers of fiction, journalists or social scientists, one first step would be to re-examine our own professional practices, whose conventions we too often take for granted, and, to quote Appadurai (2001), seriously consider the problems of the global everyday.

Communication and social change

Chapter 4

Five key ideas: coincidences and challenges in development communication

Silvio Waisbord

The field of development communication has come a long way since its begin- | 77
nings in the 1950s. Back then, it was mainly associated with a systems model of
communication, functioning as 'a science to produce effective messages' as an
add-on to agricultural extension programs, and was conceived primarily as a tool
of top-down development programs. These days, however, it is more theoretically
diversified and strategically nuanced. It has become an umbrella term for a wide
range of communication programs and research (Waisbord, 2000).

Evidence of this diversity is the alphabet soup of approaches and interventions that commonly fall under 'development communication', such as communication for development, communication for social change, information, education and communication, behavior change communication, social mobilization,
media advocacy, strategic communication, social marketing, participatory communication, strategic participatory communication, and so on. Given this conceptual
cacophony, no wonder there is maddening confusion and persistent questions
about similarities and differences. The proliferation of labels, approaches and theories is grounded in several factors: the aspirations of donors and agencies to have
signature projects; the efforts of NGOs and agencies to strengthen expertise in
specific approaches; academic trends and debates; the diversity of disciplinary traditions and professional backgrounds among practitioners and scholars; and the
ambivalent attitude vis-à-vis Western theories and strategies around the world.

There have been many attempts to clarify this persistent confusion
and sort out the differences and similarities among theories and approaches (see

Galway, 2002; Melkote and Steeves, 2001). This is a useful exercise of interest primarily to academics rather than to practitioners. At the field level, distinctions among approaches are less significant and pragmatic concerns more important. Disregarding theoretical lineages, different strategies and tools are blended and used simultaneously.

My goal in this paper is to argue that, lost in the linguistic labyrinth, there are important agreements on programmatic and strategic issues. To continue to discuss 'what theory and approach is better' is valuable as an exercise in the sociology of knowledge, and in examining unsolved epistemological contradictions in theories that inform practices. The problem is the tendency to relapse into tired polemics that prevent us from understanding that debates over 'best theories' fundamentally deal with different questions than the field as a whole is trying to tackle. It is worth attempting to solve the conceptual complexity that is inherent to the field, but it remains unclear what benefits this will bring to communication practice.

Five key ideas

While well-entrenched and seemingly irreconcilable differences characterized the field in the past, there is a budding consensus around a handful of key ideas. Such consensus cannot be understood as a paradigm shift: the old paradigm may have passed, as Everett Rogers famously stated back in the mid-1970s, but no single paradigm has replaced it.

There is growing consensus around five ideas in thinking and practicing development communication: the centrality of power, the integration of top-down and bottom-up approaches, the need to use a communication 'tool-kit' approach, the articulation of interpersonal and mass communication, and the incorporation of personal and contextual factors.

First, the centrality of power. While in early work power was absent or only tangentially addressed, particularly in programs based on informational and diffusion premises, current thinking is that power should be at the forefront. Power is present in the idea that community empowerment should be the main goal of interventions. Individuals and communities become empowered by gaining knowledge about specific issues, communicating about issues of common concern, making decisions for themselves, and negotiating power relations.

Such thinking reflects the influence of participatory communication thinking that emerged in response to the failure of traditional development approaches in the 1970s. Since then, participatory theories have successfully changed the terms of the debate and become part of the vernacular in the development field. The agenda of major donors and agencies, from the World Bank to many private foundations, shows that community participation is the watchword of the day. We could argue about whether the presence of participatory language in the programs of development institutions is mere pro-forma or a genuine commitment to community empowerment. However, it is hardly disputed that, whatever the issue at stake, the purpose of development initiatives is to contribute to processes by which communities gain more control over their lives. There is less agreement, however, on how empowerment is defined and measured or which strategies need to be implemented. Often, 'empowerment' is used loosely, without considering that it is not an issue in which 'everybody wins', but rather, a political struggle through which communities and individuals negotiate and wrestle power away from others.

A second key idea is that 'top-down' and 'bottom-up' approaches need to be integrated. Having been dominant during the 1950s decolonization era, the top-down model that puts governments and a network of Western experts at the helm of development programs has been discredited. There has been a widely shared sentiment that this model was responsible for the disastrous record of the 'first wave' of development. A 'bottom-up' approach gained support in different quarters as a way to remedy, if not all, at least some of the key problems of 'top-down' development. It was concluded that Northern concerns and policies drove development initiatives, and that Southern expectations and needs were relegated.

After the pendulum swung from government-led to community-based approaches in the development community in the 1970s and '80s, there has been a growing realization that top-down and bottom-up communication strategies are necessary to tackle a host of problems successfully. Ideas about community mobilization and participation provided a much-needed antidote to a mentality that approached development as a matter for governments and international donor agencies. Moreover, the increasing support for decentralization (in areas such as health, environment, and education) in developing countries made community-based approaches necessary.

However, the focus on community empowerment should not lead us to underestimate the role of governments. Whether a government decides that a given issue is a priority substantially affects the prospects of development work, a point forcefully demonstrated in recent programs on infectious diseases. One lesson is that the earlier a government gives priority to HIV/AIDS, the more likely it is that communication interventions will be successful. By contrast, the lack of interest among governments in putting tuberculosis at the top of their agenda accounts for why the disease still ravages over big swaths of the developing world (WHO, 1999). The different positions and actions that governments took vis-à-vis polio eradication have proven to be tremendously important in achieving results (USAID, 2000). What we learn from these experiences is that commitment from central and local governments to specific development issues has proven to be indispensable, particularly for scaling-up successful projects at the national level (Borgdorff, Floyd and Broekmans, 2002).

Recent communication scholarship has not examined this issue carefully enough. Arguably, this is the result of a position that flatly rejected government actions and paid almost exclusive attention to the role of civil society at both the national and global levels. It is unquestionably important to recognize the importance of civic institutions in addressing and tackling development problems, especially given the persistent shortcomings of states and the private sector, coupled with the consolidation of global forms of participation. We cannot underestimate, however, the fact that governments continue to play a big part in development programs, basically because their action (and inaction) affects the lives of millions of people, particularly marginalized and poor populations. For better or worse, the presence of the state can be beneficial or detrimental. States carried considerable responsibility for the many catastrophes in development aid projects from the 1950s onwards. Let us not forget, however, that they were not the only culprits. In the context of Cold-War *realpolitik*, an entire system of international aid that supported corrupt and tyrannical states in the developing world, despite their obvious transgressions and failures, was equally to blame for the many disastrous results.

To conclude that governments are inherently antithetical to development, as some of the literature on global civil society suggests, leads dangerously to a downplaying of the reality of world governance in which states still matter (Morris and Waisbord, 2001). Curiously, such anti-state conclusions offered by progressive and liberal analysts fall into a sort of neo-conservative position that demonizes states without offering proposals for democratizing and strengthening them in ways that would serve development goals. Alternatives to help improve governments' contributions are equally necessary. From facilitating and coordinating actions, or putting obstacles to and undermining developing programs, governments have an important presence. Such presence is contingent on multiple factors, such as the political and personal interests of current administrations and officials, the past record of governments in local communities and so on. States still matter in development for a number of reasons: official health and educational systems reach a large percentage of the population in many developing countries (such as in the majority of Latin American countries), national governments are important linchpins in international agreements and programs, official positions set the tone and the stage for development initiatives, international aid projects that leapfrog domestic authorities often run into all kinds of political and logistical difficulties, etc.

A third key idea is the need to have a 'tool-kit' approach to communication (see FAO, 2002). Practitioners have recognized the need for a multiplicity of communication strategies to improve the quality of life in communities. Different techniques in different contexts might be necessary to deal with specific problems and priorities. For example, conventional educational and media interventions might be recommended in critical situations such as epidemics, when a large number of people need to be reached in a short period of time. Social marketing has proven useful in addressing certain issues (for example, to raise immunization rates), but may not be adequate to promote community participation and underlying, long-term problems. Social mobilization of a vast array of organizations offers a way to deal with the multiple dimensions of certain issues such as education, sanitation, nutrition, family planning, respiratory problems, AIDS, and child survival. Media advocacy is advisable in certain contexts where a significant proportion of the population gets information from a variety of media programming. Popular media (drama, community radio, singing groups) have proven to be effective in generating dialogue in small communities.

A fourth key idea is the need to combine interpersonal communication and multimedia activities. A number of successful interventions suggest that media channels and interpersonal communication should be integrated (see Fraser and Restrepo-Estrada, 1998). The media are extremely important in raising awareness and knowledge about a given problem. They are able to expose large numbers of people to messages and generate conversation among audiences and others who were not exposed. Because social learning and decision-making are not limited to the consideration of media messages but also involve listening and exchanging opinions with a number of different sources, interventions cannot solely resort to the mass media. Although television, radio and other media are important in disseminating messages, social networks are responsible for the diffusion of new ideas (Rogers and Kincaid, 1981; Valente et al, 1994). Entertainment-education programming is one way, for example, of activating social networks and peer communication in the diffusion of information. Nothing replaces community involvement and education in the effective dissemination of information. Media-centered models are insufficient to achieve behavior change. The most successful strategies in family planning, HIV/AIDS, nutritional and diarrhea programs have involved multiple channels, including strong, community-based programming, networks, peer counseling, and government and NGO field workers (McKee, 1994). Similar conclusions are found in the recent UNAIDS (1999) communications framework, which recommends the integration of multimedia and interpersonal communication. The media have powerful effects only indirectly, by stimulating peer communication and making it possible for messages to enter social networks and become part of everyday interactions. Interpersonal communication is fundamental in persuading people about specific beliefs and practices such as mothers' decisions to vaccinate their children, adopt hygiene practices, and keep communities clean.

The fifth key idea is the incorporation of approaches that focus on individual and environmental factors in understanding the role of behavior change communication (see HealthCom, 1992). Changes in behavior and social conditions cannot be addressed only by targeting personal or contextual factors but, rather, need to be sensitive to both in order to understand problems and design solutions (Hornik, 1990; Smith and Elder, 1998; Soul City, 2000). This idea has been particularly relevant in behavior change programs which have gradually moved away from individual-centered approaches to a multi-prong approach that considers environmental factors that are affecting individual behavior (Hornik, 2002). Because environmental factors affect behavior (in terms of both initiation and maintenance),

Media and Glocal Change

they need to be addressed. What constitute environmental/contextual factors is debatable. It is not obvious which factors are 'external' and which 'internal' to individuals' action. For example, behavioral scientists typically assume that gender and culture are contextual; by contrast, anthropologists and sociologists approach them as constitutive of individual identity. Consider the cases in which Muslim mothers refuse to allow all-male non-Muslim teams to vaccinate their children (because they are prohibited from talking to men other than their husbands), or Quechua-speaking mothers are reluctant to give birth at official health posts in Peru (because health workers are disrespectful of their child-birthing traditions). Are gender and culture contextual or constitutive of individual behavior? This point reflects larger epistemological and disciplinary differences concerning the main unit of analysis in development work.

Further examination of the relations between individual behavior and contextual factors (such as policy, law, systems) is necessary. On the one hand, the presence of contextual factors does influence behavior. Water systems, vaccination distribution systems, and garbage removal systems, are important determinants of specific behaviors (hand-washing, vaccination rates, and garbage disposal, respectively). On the other hand, the availability of institutional and contextual conditions that are, in principle, conducive to specific behaviors, does not always result in the desired social and healthy behavior. 'Build systems and they will come' does not always work. The existence of health posts in rural areas does not guarantee that mothers will choose institutional childbirth. Easier access to condoms does not necessarily lead to any increase in condom use with different partners across age groups. The availability of mosquito nets in malaria-stricken regions does not automatically mean that people will use them. Interdisciplinary dialogue and work on these issues between behavioral and social scientists is crucial in producing studies that adequately consider the multiple levels that affect individual and social behavior.

Why consensus?

Considering that bitter polemic has characterized the field, the emerging consensus on five ideas is remarkable. Certainly, old disputes and preferences for specific strategies have not disappeared. Identifying the existence of a growing consensus does not mean that donors, governments, non-government organizations and other stakeholders have amicably resolved all their differences. There are still different communication agendas and priorities. Differences in ideological and theoretical sympathies, in the expertise of cooperating agencies and NGOs in approaches decided on, and in donors' goals and expectations continue to shape communication strategies. Considering the diversity and the richness of interests and interdisciplinary backgrounds in the field of development communication, it would be unrealistic to expect complete agreement. However, there has been a tendency to move away from 'one-model-fits-all' solutions to the belief that inclusive approaches and openness to a diversity of programmatic insights and strategies is required.

It is important to emphasize that the consensus around those five
ideas forms at the practical more than at the theoretical level. Pragmatic needs have encouraged the integration of concepts that theoretically remain separated. It is not unusual for community mobilization and peer network activities to be part of the same program, yet few efforts have been made to explore where participatory theory and social network theory meet (or if they meet at all). Behavior change interventions are increasingly more sensitive to the need to integrate policies and individual decisions* that affect specific behaviors (e.g. smoking, institutional childbirth, vaccination), but communication policy and interpersonal communication theories still remain strangers to each other.

Particularly in the light of the gap between theory and practice, it is worth discussing the factors responsible for the convergence. First, there is an increasing interest in finding solutions to specific problems. This shift suggests an encouraging trend in the field: the propensity to engage in love affairs with specific ideas is giving way to a more eclectic and open disposition, less attached to theoretical orthodoxies and more interested in blending approaches. The evolution of the thinking about information-diffusion approaches, new technologies, and participatory models expresses this shift, namely, the move from uncritical support to a growing skepticism about reductionist positions.

The excitement about the possibilities of the information-diffusion approaches which dominated the field in its early days has receded. Because the diagnosis stated that lack of information and traditional norms prevented development, as the modernization tradition concluded, communication was assigned the role of disseminating 'the right knowledge' to facilitate cultural change. These days, however, the notion that communication equals information, or that development problems are reduced to citizens' 'lack of information', have been discredited. Some critics pointed out that its simplistic model of information-transmission, largely derived from systems theory and mathematical and engineering models, was inadequate for understanding the complexities of communication. Sometimes communication, not information, is the issue at stake. Others argued that 'diffusionism' failed to make a nuanced distinction between knowledge, attitudes and behavior. Influenced by 'powerful media effects' theories, it ignored the fact that the path from information to attitude to practice does not run straight.

Likewise, the enthusiasm for 'new information technologies' has receded in favor of more nuanced recommendations. Almost inevitably, at any critical juncture of 'the rise of new technologies', the field has experienced techno-hype about the prospects for the latest gizmos in development work. Transistor radio, television, cable television, satellite television, portable tape recorders, video, personal computers, the Internet, wind-up and solar radio have all been hailed as revolutionary, indispensable tools for redressing socio-economic and political conditions, promoting dialogue and participation, reaching all populations, etc. It would be silly to dismiss the relevance of information technologies in development efforts. They are potentially helpful in creating opportunities for debate, exchange of ideas, and participation, but they need to be ana-lyzed within specific institutional contexts and political-economic conditions (Chetney, 2001).

There has also been considerable enthusiasm about participatory approaches. It is indisputable that the issue of participatory citizenship is and should be central to development efforts. In insisting on this point, participatory approaches offer an important critique of top-down interventions (Thomas, 1994). They correctly charge government-centered, donor-led, and expert-designed models of development with neither consulting communities nor put-ting them at the center. The poor record of development interventions is rooted in the fact that communities did not become empowered as a result of massive investments. The reason was that communities were understood as passive actors, the presumed 'beneficiaries' of the actions of governments and donors rather than the central actors in development.

Having successfully challenged old conventions, participatory approaches have not devoted sufficient time to the consideration of several ques-tions. Under what conditions is participation possible? What happens when par-ticipatory ideals run counter to community norms or are rejected by local author-itarian practices? How is participation possible at different stages of development programs (e.g. funding, planning, instrumentation, evaluation, sustainability)? How is community empowerment and participation measured? (Chetley, 2002) Important efforts are being made to address these questions in a critical manner, but much remains to be done (Cooke and Kothari, 2001; Estrella, 2000; Heeks, 1999; Oakley and Clayton, 2000).

Another reason for growing consensus is the growing interest in 'what works' rather than in 'what we believe'. Donors seem more inclined to know the results of their investments and, as recent programs in immunization and HIV/AIDS suggest, to cooperate with other donors in finding common approach-es. This need is particularly tangible among government donors, which need to demonstrate results to their policymakers. In turn, this need is passed on to NGOs and other organizations that implement programs. In the competitive world of development aid and funding, showing positive results has become increasingly more important in demonstrating expertise and capacity vis-à-vis various audi-ences (Edwards, Hulme and Wallace, 2000; Roche, 2000). This 'strategic thinking' attests to a renewed urgency in finding practical solutions, whether to promote grassroots participation or achieve behavior change.

A third reason for convergence is that recent experiences show that integrated, multiple strategies work. Consider the cases of Uganda, Thailand and Brazil, countries whose efforts in fighting the HIV/AIDS epidemic have been gen-erally applauded. In those countries, a combination of different actions is widely seen as responsible for important successes (Hogle, Green, Nantulya, Stoneburner and Stover, 2002). Governments played a fundamental role by encouraging discussion of problems and solutions, putting HIV at the top of the

Silvio Waisbord

agenda, and making public commitments that acknowledged, first and foremost, | 85
that HIV/AIDS was an important public issue. Several stakeholders and organizations worked in many ways towards a common objective. Communication strategies used interpersonal and mass communication interventions. Many media
organizations offered opportunities for open debate. Out of these experiences,
one important lesson has emerged: a combination of actions by governments
and civil society is crucial in confronting HIV in particular, and more generally, in
tackling development issues (Scalway, 2002; UNAIDS, 1999).

There is increasing sensitivity to the problems of applying universally
strategies that have been successful in specific contexts. In countries where political and cultural factors limit participation and maintain hierarchical relationships, participatory approaches might be difficult to implement, as they require a
long-term and political process of transformation. This does not mean that participation should be abandoned as a desirable goal, but that interventions that
aim to mobilize communities need to adopt different characteristics in different
circumstances.

Communication and social change

If the convergence of several disciplinary and theoretical traditions in development
communication is partly responsible for perennial conceptual confusion, it is also
the source of disciplinary and theoretical cross-pollination. Scholars, professionals
and activists working in forms of development communication have been trained
in a variety of disciplines (communication studies, cognitive psychology, journalism,
anthropology, sociology, behavioral sciences, public health, information systems,
education). Until recently, the possibility of cross-disciplinary collaboration and
influence was insufficiently exploited, and seemed to be a problem rather than an
advantage, a source of proprietary, defensive arguments about 'best practices'.
The convergence around 'five key ideas' suggests, if not a complete reversal, certainly a positive trend of integrating ideas from various disciplines.

There are many recent examples of this trend. Witness the interest in
'social capital' and 'social networks', concepts which, while having a distinct
theoretical DNA, currently straddle disciplinary boundaries. Likewise, the use of
political and media advocacy also reflects an interest in exploring different
paths to bring about social change that recognizes both the strengths and
weaknesses of the media. Ongoing efforts to search for a common theoretical
and programmatic ground, such as recent work by the Rockefeller Foundation
and Johns Hopkins University, are also testimony to this trend (Figueroa,
Kincaid, Rani and Lewis, 2002).

Perhaps one of the most promising attempts to find commonalities is
the idea that social change is the ultimate goal of development communication
(Servaes, Jacobson and White, 1996; Wilkins, 2000). 'Social change' serves as an
umbrella term for a variety of communication initiatives and actions that set social
transformations in motion. 'Social change' allows analysts and practitioners from

a variety of disciplines to find common ground and articulate efforts toward a common vocabulary. Of course, this is not an entirely new idea, but it has slowly moved toward the top of donor and agency agendas. The debate focuses less on defining 'best practices' for 'information-education-communication' or channeling community participation, issues that had long occupied the field, and instead takes a broader position on how communication contributes to social change.

Disagreement persists on a number of important issues: who determines improvement? What indicators of social change are considered? What role do different actors play in enabling social change? How can individual and social change be integrated? How does social change happen? Is it the result of the sum of individual changes, as psychologists affirm? Is it the consequence of social processes that are not the sum of individual changes, but rather the result of structural, macro-social changes, as sociologists conclude? What is the role of communication in processes of collective action and social change?

To think in terms of how communication contributes to social change also seems useful to avoid getting embroiled in well-worn debate about the meaning of 'communication' in 'development communication'. Given the diversity of disciplinary and professional backgrounds, it is wishful thinking to imagine that it is possible to formulate a single definition that would satisfy all the parties, once and forever. Nor is it clear what purpose this should serve. Trying to find the 'real' definition of 'communication' and to police disciplinary borders is a red herring, particularly considering other more pressing and interesting challenges and tasks. Moreover, it would be misplaced to expect such efforts to achieve a theoretical synthesis. To produce an unambiguous definition of 'communication' seems a tall order. Since the field first originated, the notion has lacked a single definition. There have been important attempts to clarify its meanings, but no canonical definition has ever been generated.

The fact that 'communication' and 'communications' are still used indistinctly reflects this elusive conceptual ambiguity. For some, communication means community empowerment and social mobilization; for others, the work of media and other information technologies; and for others, public relations and publications. There is little chance of settling the debate, and the eventual benefits of reaching conceptual consensus are unclear. The issue cannot be resolved because communication scholars and practitioners seek to answer related but different questions. How is cultural change promoted? How are information and innovations spread? How does communication contribute to community empowerment? How do citizens mobilize to take over ownership of their lives? How does communication affect behavior change?

The divide has persisted in the field. On the one hand, communication is understood as an instrument helping development projects to achieve specific goals, mainly through the dissemination of information. Thus, if the goal is to reduce infant mortality, teach new farming methods, and promote specific environmental policies, communication involves methodologies and tools for spreading information and changing behavior in order to achieve the development results. From this perspective, communication is conceived as 'strategic communication', a link in the 'information-education-communication' chain, a component in comprehensive initiatives to engender transformations in health, political, environmental, education and other issues. Communication intends to maximize the delivery and effectiveness of messages. It is a branch of the information sciences and commercial practices such as public relations, marketing, and advertising.

On the other hand, communication is defined as the goal of development, as stated in the mission of programs and institutions such as UNESCO and UNICEF (which defines communication as a 'right'). Development should aim to improve the dialogic capacity of communities, particularly in poor areas of the world. The lack of access to communication and information is one of the most tangible problems in the developing world. Efforts should be directed at enhancing the opportunities for communities to talk and listen to others, identifying problems, determining goals, deciding courses of action, and assigning responsibilities. Communication is about building the community rather than transmitting information. Media technologies are instruments in facilitating the communication process rather than vehicles for exchanging information. Communication is understood as citizenship, as a way to comprehend membership and action in political communities. So, for example, community radio is conceived as a mechanism for people to voice their opinions about specific issues and a resource to mobilize citizenship into action.

Given the conceptual duality of communication, it comes to no surprise that theories and strategies have given answers to some, but not all, questions. The issue at stake is not the lack of robust explanations or perceptive insights, but rather, the need to clarify questions and goals. Like the discipline of communication at large, development communication deals with a number of related yet separate problems (Nair and White, 1993). Stimulating participation, changing media policies, contributing to behavior change, increasing access to media, and expanding opportunities for getting information have all been proposed as the goals of interventions in development communication. What is needed is to further discuss the problems that the field addresses, and to examine ways to reach goals rather than to offer predetermined solutions (Wilkins and Mody, 2001).

The next challenges

Development communication faces two sets of challenges. The first set of challenges deals with two critical aspects of development projects: scale and sustainability. After more than five decades of experience in development communication, we seem to know what works (Morris, 2001). Because there are persuasive explanations and findings about 'what works' in small-scale, community projects, yet a shortage of convincing results at the national level, 'scaling up' projects has become an important concern, particularly for donors. Results from community empowerment and participation projects can't be easily 'trickled up'. How can successes in community projects concerning environmental protection and infectious diseases be replicated on a larger scale? Are lessons directly applicable to programs that target larger groups? (DFID, 2002; International HIV Alliance, 1998; WHO, 2002).

Another preoccupation is the sustainability of development projects. 'Sustainable development' features prominently on the agenda of donors and agencies, referring to development actions that put communities at the center and have long-lasting impact (United Nations, 2002). The concern for the duration of development work (and results) derives from a sense that projects show results as long as donors regularly inject funds and make a long-term commitment. As Michael Edwards (1999: 83) eloquently puts it, "Winning short-term gains on the basis of heavy external inputs is not difficult; what is difficult is sustaining them against the background of weak politics, fragile economies, and limited capacities for implementation". This lack of continuity is problematic, among other reasons, because such practice makes community interventions dependent on donors' agendas, which are prone to change due to several factors (from policy shifts to personnel changes) (Bräutigam, 2000). Rather than helping to generate community ownership, funding patterns intensify a sense that projects 'belong' to the donors. When the future of projects hinges on donors' priorities, it is illusory to expect that communities will acquire a sense of ownership and maintain their accomplishments. In other words, the problem is to avoid foreign-induced development that follows the needs and expectations of Northern actors and, rather, to stimulate development that responds to Southern, internal priorities.

A second set of challenges deals with issues specific to communication. One is bridging the divide between 'small' and 'big' media. Although one may argue that this distinction is becoming obsolete as new technologies erase old boundaries between 'narrowcasting' and 'broadcasting', it is important to pay attention to both kinds of media. The Internet and other hybrid communication technologies are increasingly eliminating that distinction and certainly offer new opportunities, but for the vast majority of people in the developing world, 'small' and 'big' media remain the most accessible.

Typically, communication studies pay exclusive attention either to commercial, large-scale media or to community-based media. While it is unquestionable that the mass media are important, given their reach and popularity, we should not lose sight of the relevance of 'small' media. Plenty of experiences attest to the importance of citizens' media in mobilizing communities and nurturing citizenship in the developing world (Gumucio-Dagron, 2001; Mody, 1991; Rodríguez, 2000). However, it is dangerous to fall into a romantic position that sees grassroots media as the only spaces where citizens can voice opinions, get information, and redress social conditions, while ignoring the fact that large-scale media institutions are of tremendous importance in people's everyday lives. There are plenty of reasons for the extensive suspicion felt in development circles about the role of the big media: throughout the developing world, they largely function according to principles (political benefit and economic profit) that do not promote democratic and development goals. However, such distrust informs a 'small-is-beautiful' mentality that brushes aside the potential of mainstream media for contributing to development goals. Media experiences that aimed to foster a dialogue about 'taboo' issues such as HIV and female genital cutting suggest that the mass media are crucial in generating public discussion among citizens and commitment from political authorities. In specific circumstances, they provide important information that makes a difference in controlling epidemics, create a 'buzz' around development initiatives, put issues in the national agenda, and mobilize populations.

Another important matter that deserves further attention is the connection between communication and cultural change. The relationship between communication and culture lies at the core of development. Certainly, pioneering projects in the field have examined it, but from a 'white man's burden', modernist perspective that, explicitly or implicitly, proposed 'Western' culture as the model to be followed while denigrating other cultures. Today, *pace* multiculturalism and feminism, this kind of perspective, if not completely debunked, is less influential in development circles than in the past. Much remains to be discussed, however.

One of the most troubling issues is the relation between development communication and cultural change. Some projects aim to preserve and strengthen local beliefs and practices, while others aim to eliminate them. While cultural diversity is at times cherished and encouraged, it is also seen as an obstacle to development goals. Local cultures are seen as what should be changed: patriarchy prevents women from making healthier decisions, homophobia perpetuates stigma, traditional sexual arrangements contribute to HIV transmission, certain funerary rituals spread disease, religious and magical beliefs dispute scientific research about the effects of vaccinations. Also, local cultures are seen as providing valuable and necessary resources for promoting development/social goals: community networks are crucial in disseminating information, and the support of religious leaders is crucial in reaching populations. These tensions raise a number of issues about development and cultural rights which are rarely confronted head-on, particularly from a communication perspective. Who had the right to determine which cultural practices are desirable and need to be preserved? This gap is surprising, particularly considering how extensively development communication scholarship has criticized the impact of global flows of information on cultural diversity; however, it has not sufficiently explored certain dilemmas central to cultural change.

One of the most important sets of questions deals with the cultural ethics of development communication. When is universalism defensible? Does relativism always trump universalistic principles? What if communities invoke cultural sovereignty to defend practices that are widely contrary to other people's (particularly Northern) norms? In many cases, there is an unmistakably Western, individualistic conception, full of do-good intentions, that aims to promote cultural change based on ideals articulated in international human rights documents. Consider the ongoing debate on female genital cutting. As defined by donors and NGOs, the goal is to achieve cultural change ('the elimination of the practice'), and the challenge is to find effective mechanisms for changing deep-seated cultural norms and practices (Population Reference Bureau, 2001). Clearly, those who perform the ritual (traditional healers, medical professionals) benefit from the existing power system that informs FGC and call upon 'cultural traditions' to defend their positions. Development organizations criticize them by waving the flag of international human rights as the basis for building a common, humane world and promoting a rights-based approach to development. Similar dilemmas are also present in other development interventions, such as safe motherhood, family planning, and HIV prevention. How can we reconcile local knowledge and practices with Western-styled conceptions of safe childbirth? Upon what grounds should we defend cultural identity while aiming to change sexual and marriage practices rooted in paternalistic cultures? How is it possible to draw a distinction between cultural relativity and the search for a common political and ethical ground? What can communication say about these dilemmas? While ethicists and international law scholars have made interesting inroads into these questions, communication analysts still need to grapple with them.

My objective in this article was to issue a call that would transcend debate in the field of development communication by suggesting areas of convergence and future directions. The most challenging research and practical questions are no longer whether 'transfer of knowledge' or 'participation' should be the end goal of communication, a debate that, like polyester pants and disco music, is reminiscent of 1970s fashion. Some scholars and professionals certainly continue to believe that perfecting the arts of knowledge-transference or tapping the potential of new information technologies should be communication's sole preoccupation and contribution to development. There will always be those who believe that communication's role in development means producing materials (at best, ubiquitous, culturally-sensitive posters), resorting to communication as the cure-all solution when everything else has failed, or consider communication an optional line in their budgets. Changing these views and defending why communication matters in development are worthy efforts, particularly for program officers whose jobs depend on communication's achieving recognition as a fundamental component in development programs. Those goals should not be the only concerns, however. If the field is to remain an important space for debate and reference in development theory and practice, it needs to tackle questions that are central to both *development* and *communication*.

Chapter 5

Participatory communication: the new paradigm?

Jan Servaes
& Patchanee Malikhao

Participatory communication requires *first of all* changes in the thinking of 'communicators'. The needles, targets, and audiences of communication and development
models, combined with self-righteousness, titles, and insecurities, perhaps sprinkled
with a dash of misdirected benevolence, often render 'experts' a bit too verbose and
pushy. Perhaps this is because it requires much more imagination, preparation and
hard work to have dialogical learning. It is far easier to prepare and give lectures.

However, there is possibly a valid reason why we have two ears, but
only one mouth. Communication between people thrives not on the ability to
talk fast, but the ability to *listen* well. People are 'voiceless' not because they have
nothing to say, but because nobody cares to listen to them. Authentic listening
fosters trust much more than incessant talking.

Participation, which necessitates listening, and moreover, trust, will
help reduce the social distance between communicators and receivers, between
teachers and learners, between leaders and followers as well as facilitate a more
equitable exchange of ideas, knowledge and experiences. However, the need to
listen is not limited to those at the receiving end. It must involve the governments
as well as the citizens, the poor as well as the rich, the planners and administrators as well as their targets.

In this chapter we present:

» an historical overview of the debate on development in general, and
development communication in particular, since its emergence on the
political agenda in the fifties;

» the differences between a so-called diffusionist or top-down communication model versus a participatory or bottom-up communication model;

» two general differences in approach within the participatory model, which lead to different 'types' of participatory communication projects, especially at the community media level;

» by way of conclusion we identify eleven changes within the communication for social change field which will, in our opinion, further condition and complicate the future of the field.

From modernization, over dependency, to multiplicity

Development communication in the 1950s and 1960s was generally greeted with enthusiasm and optimism. Building on the American scholar Daniel Lerner's influential 1958 study of communication and development in the Middle East and Wilbur Schramm's 1964 study on the role of media for national development, communication researchers assumed that the introduction of media and certain types of educational, political, and economic information into a social system could transform individuals and societies from traditional to modern.

This optimism was in line with the 'Zeitgeist' after the Second World War and the fall of Nazism and fascism. The founding of the United nations stimulated relations among sovereign states, especially the North Atlantic Nations and the developing nations, including the new states emerging out of a colonial past. Though the 'cold war' clouded this stage of enthusiasm, the superpowers –the United States and the former Soviet Union– tried to expand their own interests to the developing countries. They both started to promote opposite versions of 'modern futures' to the so-called Third World.

In fact, the USA was defining development and social change as the replica of its own political-economic system and opening the way for the transnational corporations. At the same time, the developing countries saw the 'welfare state' of the North Atlantic nations as the ultimate goal of development. These nations were attracted by the new technology transfer and the model of a centralized state with careful economic planning and centrally directed development bureaucracies for agriculture, education and health as the most effective strategies to catch up with those industrialized countries.

This mainly economic-oriented view, characterized by endogenism and evolutionism, ultimately resulted in the *modernization and growth* theory. It sees development as an unilinear, evolutionary process and defines the state of underdevelopment in terms of observable quantitative differences between so-called poor and rich countries on the one hand, and traditional and modern societies on the other hand.

As a result of the general intellectual 'revolution' that took place in the mid '60s, this Euro- or ethnocentric perspective on development was challenged by Latin American social scientists, and a theory dealing with *dependency and underdevelopment* was born. This dependency approach formed part of a general structuralist re-orientation in the social sciences. The 'dependistas' were primarily concerned with the effects of dependency in peripheral countries, but implicit in their analysis was the idea that development and underdevelopment must be understood in the context of the world system.

This dependency paradigm played an important role in the movement for a New World Information and Communication Order from the late 1960s to the early 1980s. At that time, the new states in Africa, Asia and the success of socialist and popular movements in Cuba, China, Chile and other countries provided the goals for political, economic and cultural self-determination within the international community of nations. These new nations shared the ideas of being independent from the superpowers and moved to form the Non-Aligned nations. The Non-Aligned Movement defined development as political struggle.

Since the demarcation of the First, Second and Third Worlds has broken down and the cross-over centre-periphery can be found in every region, there is a need for a new concept of development which emphasizes *cultural identity and multidimensionality*. The present-day 'global' world, in general as well as in its distinct regional and national entities, is confronted with multifaceted crises. Apart from the obvious economic and financial crisis, one could also refer to social, ideological, moral, political, ethnic, ecological and security crises. In other words, the previously held dependency perspective has become more difficult to support because of the growing interdependency of regions, nations and communities in our globalized world.

From the criticism of the two paradigms above, particularly that of the dependency approach, a new viewpoint on development and social change has come to the forefront. The common starting point here is the examination of the changes from 'bottom-up', from the self-development of the local community. The basic assumption is that there are no countries or communities that function completely autonomously and that are completely self-sufficient, nor are there any nations whose development is exclusively determined by external factors. Every society is dependent in one way or another, both in form and in degree. Thus, a framework was sought within which both the centre and the periphery could be studied separately and in their mutual relationship, both at global, national and local levels.

More attention is also being paid to the content of development, which implies a more normative approach. Another development questions whether 'developed' countries are in fact developed and whether this genre of progress is sustainable or desirable. It favours a multiplicity of approaches based on the context and the basic, felt needs, and the empowerment of the most oppressed sectors of various societies at divergent levels. A main thesis is that change must be structural and occur at multiple levels in order to achieve these ends.

Diffusion versus participatory communication

The above general typology of the so-called development paradigms (for more details, see Servaes, 1999, 2003) can also be found at the communications and culture level. The communication media are, in the context of development, generally used to support development initiatives by the dissemination of messages that encourage the public to support development-oriented projects. Although development strategies in developing countries diverge widely, the usual pattern for broadcasting and the press has been predominantly the same: informing the population about projects, illustrating the advantages of these projects, and recommending that they be supported. A typical example of such a strategy is situated in the area of family planning, where communication means like posters, pamphlets, radio, and television attempt to persuade the public to accept birth control methods. Similar strategies are used on campaigns regarding health and nutrition, agricultural projects, education, and so on.

This model sees the communication process mainly as a message going from a sender to a receiver. This hierarchic view on communication can be summarized in Laswell's classic formula, –'Who says What through Which channel to Whom with What effect?'–, and dates back to (mainly American) research on campaigns and diffusions in the late '40s and '50s.

The American scholar Everett Rogers (1983) is said to be the person who introduced this diffusion theory in the context of development. Modernization is here conceived as a process of diffusion whereby individuals move from a traditional way of life to a different, more technically developed and more rapidly changing way of life. Building primarily on sociological research in agrarian societies, Rogers stressed the adoption and diffusion processes of cultural innovation. This approach is therefore concerned with the *process of diffusion and adoption of innovations* in a more systematic and planned way. Mass media are important in spreading awareness of new possibilities and practices, but at the stage where decisions are being made about whether to adopt or not to adopt, personal communication is far more likely to be influential. Therefore, the general conclusion of this line of thought is that *mass communication is less likely than personal influence to have a direct effect on social behaviour.*

Newer perspectives on development communication claim that this is a limited view of development communication. They argue that this diffusion model is a vertical or one-way perspective on communication, and that development will accelerate mainly through active involvement in the process of the communication itself. Research has shown that, while groups of the public can obtain information from impersonal sources like radio and television, this information has relatively little effect on behavioural changes. And development envisions precisely such change. Similar research has led to the conclusion that more is learned from interpersonal contacts and from mass communication techniques that are based on them. On the lowest level, before people can discuss and resolve problems, they must be informed of the facts, information that the media provide nationally as well as regionally and locally. At the same time, the public, if the media are sufficiently accessible, can make its information needs known.

Communication theories such as the 'diffusion of innovations', the 'two-step-flow', or the 'extension' approaches are quite congruent with the above modernization theory. The elitist, *vertical or top-down orientation* of the diffusion model is obvious.

The *participatory model*, on the other hand, incorporates the concepts in the framework of multiplicity. It stresses the importance of cultural identity of local communities and of *democratisation and participation at all levels* –international, national, local and individual. It points to a strategy, not merely inclusive of, but largely emanating from, the traditional 'receivers'. Paulo Freire (1983: 76) refers to this as the right of all people to individually and collectively speak their word:

> This is not the privilege of some few men, but the right of every (wo)man. Consequently, no one can say a true word alone –nor can he say it for another, in a prescriptive act which robs others of their words.

In order to share information, knowledge, trust, commitment, and a right attitude in development projects participation is very important in any decision-making process for development. Therefore, the International Commission for the Study of Communication Problems, chaired by the late Sean MacBride, argued that "this calls for a new attitude for overcoming stereotyped thinking and to promote more understanding of diversity and plurality, with full respect for the dignity and equality of peoples living in different conditions and acting in different ways" (MacBride, 1980: 254). This model stresses reciprocal collaboration throughout all levels of participation.

Also, these newer approaches argue, the *point of departure must be the community*. It is at the community level that the problems of living conditions are discussed, and interactions with other communities are elicited. The most developed form of participation is self-management. This principle implies the right to participation in the planning and production of media content. However, not everyone wants to or must be involved in its practical implementation. More important is that participation is made possible in the decision-making regarding the subjects treated in the messages and regarding the selection procedures. One of the fundamental hindrances to the decision to adopt the participation strategy is that it threatens existing hierarchies. Nevertheless, participation does not imply that there is no longer a role for development specialists, planners, and institutional leaders. It only means that the viewpoint of the local groups of the public is considered before the resources for development projects are allocated and distributed, and that suggestions for changes in the policy are taken into consideration.

Two major approaches to participatory communication

There are two major approaches to participatory communication that everybody today accepts as common sense. The first is the dialogical pedagogy of Paulo

Freire (1970, 1973, 1983, 1994), and the second involves the ideas of access, participation and self-management articulated in the UNESCO debates of the 1970s (Berrigan, 1977, 1979). Every communication project that calls itself participatory accepts these principles of democratic communication. Nonetheless there exists today a wide variety of practical experiences and intentions. Before moving on to explore these differences it is useful to briefly review the common ground.

The *Freirian argument* works by a dual theoretical strategy. He insists that subjugated peoples must be treated as fully human subjects in any political process. This implies dialogical communication. Although inspired to some extent by Sartre's existentialism –a respect for the autonomous personhood of each human being–, the more important source is a theology that demands respect for otherness –in this case that of another human being. The second strategy is a moment of utopian hope derived from the early Marx that the human species has a destiny which is more than life as a fulfilment of material needs. Also from Marx is an insistence on collective solutions. Individual opportunity, Freire stresses, is no solution to general situations of poverty and cultural subjugation.

These ideas are deeply unpopular with elites, including elites in the Third World, but there is nonetheless widespread acceptance of Freire's notion of dialogic communication as a normative theory of participatory communication. One problem with Freire is that his theory of dialogical communication is based on group dialogue rather than such amplifying media as radio, print and television. Freire also gives little attention to the language or form of communication, devoting most of his discussion to the intentions of communication actions.

The second discourse about participatory communication is the UNESCO language about *self-management, access and participation* from the 1977 meeting in Belgrade, the former Yugoslavia. The final report of that meeting defines the terms in the following way.

» Access refers to the use of media for public service. It may be defined in terms of the opportunities available to the public to choose varied and relevant programs and to have a means of feedback to transmit its reactions and demands to production organizations.

» Participation implies a higher level of public involvement in communication systems. It includes the involvement of the public in the production process, and also in the management and planning of communication systems.

» Participation may be no more than representation and consultation of the public in decision-making.

» On the other hand, self-management is the most advanced form of participation. In this case, the public exercises the power of decision-making within communication enterprises and is also fully involved in the formulation of communication policies and plans.

Access by the community and participation of the community are to be consid- | 97
ered key defining factors, as Berrigan eloquently summarizes: "[Community
media] are media to which members of the community have access, for information, education, entertainment, when they want access. They are media in which
the community participates, as planners, producers, and performers. They are the
means of expression of the community, rather than for the community"
(Berrigan, 1979: 8). Referring to the 1977 meeting in Belgrade, Berrigan (1979:
18) (partially) links access to the reception of information, education, and entertainment considered relevant by/for the community:

> [Access] may be defined in terms of the opportunities available to the pub-
> lic to choose varied and relevant programs, and to have a means of feed-
> back to transmit its reactions and demands to production organizations.

Others limit access to mass media and see it as 'the processes that permit users to
provide relatively open and unedited input to the mass media' (Lewis, 1993: 12)
or as 'the relation to the public and the established broadcasting institutions'
(Prehn, 1991: 259). Both the production and reception approaches of 'access' can
be considered relevant for an understanding of 'community media'.

These ideas are important and widely accepted as a normative theory
of participatory communication: it must involve access and participation
(Pateman, 1972). However, one should note some differences from Freire. The
UNESCO discourse includes the idea of a gradual progression. Some amount of
access may be allowed, but self-management may be postponed until some time
in the future. Freire's theory allows for no such compromise. One either respects
the culture of the other or falls back into domination and the 'banking' mode of
imposed education. The UNESCO discourse talks in neutral terms about 'the public'. Freire talked about 'the oppressed'. Finally, the UNESCO discourse puts the
main focus on the institution. Participatory or community radio means a radio station that is self-managed by those participating in it.

Participatory communication for social change

Participation involves the more equitable sharing of both political and economic
power, which often decreases the advantage of certain groups. Structural change
involves the redistribution of power. In mass communication areas, many communication experts agree that structural change should occur first in order to establish participatory communication policies. Mowlana and Wilson (1987: 143), for
instance, state:

> Communications policies are basically derivatives of the political, cultural
> and economic conditions and institutions under which they operate. They
> tend to legitimize the existing power relations in society, and therefore, they
> cannot be substantially changed unless there are fundamental structural
> changes in society that can alter these power relationships themselves.

Therefore, the development of a participatory communication model has to take place in relation with overall societal emancipation processes at local, national as well as international levels. Several authors have been trying to summarize the criteria for such a communication model. The Latin American scholar Juan Somavia (1977, 1981) sums up the following (slightly adapted) components as essential for it:

(a) *Communication is a human need:* the satisfaction of the need for communication is just as important for a society as the concern for health, nutrition, housing, education and labour. Together with all the other social needs, communication must enable the citizens to emancipate themselves completely. The right to inform and to be informed, and the right to communicate, are thus essential human rights and this both individually and collectively.

(b) *Communication is a delegated human right*: within its own cultural, political, economic and historical context, each society has to be able to define independently the concrete form in which it wants to organize its social communication process. Because there are a variety of cultures, there can therefore also arise various organizational structures. But whatever the form in which the social communication function is embodied, priority must be given to the principles of participation and accessibility.

(c) *Communication is a facet of the societal conscientization, emancipation and liberation process.* The social responsibility of the media in the process of social change is very large. Indeed, after the period of formal education, the media are the most important educational and socialization agents. They are capable of informing or disinforming, exposing or concealing important facts, interpreting events positively or negatively, and so on.

(d) *The communication task involves rights and responsibilities/obligations.* Since the media in fact provide a public service, they must carry it out in a framework of social and juridical responsibility that reflects the social consensus of the society. In other words, there are no rights without obligation.

The freedom and right to communicate, therefore, must be approached from a threefold perspective: *first,* it is necessary for the public to participate effectively in the communication field; *secondly,* there is the design of a framework in which this can take place; and, *thirdly,* the media must enjoy professional autonomy, free of economic, political or whatever pressure.

In sum, participatory communication for social change sees people as the nucleus of development. Development means lifting up the spirits of a local community to take pride in its own culture, intellect and environment. Development aims to educate and stimulate people to be active in self and communal improvements while maintaining a balanced ecology. Authentic participation, though widely espoused in the literature, is not in everyone's interest. Due to their local concentration, participatory programmes are, in fact, not easily implemented, nor are they highly predictable or readily controlled.

Different 'types' of participatory communication projects

In spite of the widespread acceptance of the ideas of Freire and UNESCO by development organizations and communication researchers, there is still a very wide range of projects calling themselves 'participatory communication projects'. There is an evident need for clarification in descriptive and normative theories of participatory media. What does it mean to be participatory? It is necessary to make further distinctions and arguments to deal with a wide variety of actually existing experiences and political intentions.

A review of the literature turns up the following *types* (Berrigan, 1979; Berque, Foy and Girard, 1993; Fraser and Restrepo, 2000; Girard, 1992; Lewis, 1993; O'Connor, 1988; O'Sullivan, 1979):

(1) participatory media are internally organized on democratic lines (as worker co-operatives or collectives);

(2) participatory media are recognized by their opposition to cultural industries dominated by multinational corporations;

(3) participatory media may be traced to the liberation of linguistic and ethnic groups following a major social transformation;

(4) the strong existence of participatory media may be explained in terms of class struggle within the society;

(5) participatory media may be identified as "molecular" rather than "molar" (a collectivity of individual autonomous units rather than one that is homogenized and one-dimensional);

(6) participatory media (like the montage of Eisenstein and the theatre of Brecht) by design requires a creative and varied reception from its audience.

Reyes Matta (1986) argues that participatory communication is first and foremost an alternative to media dominated by transnational corporations. This is the context in which any alternative must operate. To succeed is to have won against the culture industries that are dominated by multinational corporations. The line of thought developed by CINCO (1987) is a development of this because it involves above all a structural analysis of communicative institutions. For the CINCO researchers media are alternative if they have a democratic institutional structure. Here the issue is one of ownership and control that is external to the community against access and participation in the media organization.

Legitimacy and political credibility can be fostered by the establishment of what is called *participatory democracy*, the building in of actual participation from the public. This is only possible when the communication system is decentralized. The control over communication and information may not be monopolized by one or a few segments of the society. Unfortunately, most of the time structural aspects stand in the way of the ideal of democracy. In most developing countries, the first stone for bridging the gap between the ruling elite and the masses has still to be laid. For the establishment of participatory democracy, therefore, dialogue must be made possible between the authorities and the public, nationally, regionally, and locally. In the political sector, this can be done through political parties, pressure groups, civil action groups, environmental movements, and the like. Thus political credibility as well as social and cultural identity of the population and an awareness and support of the development goals are needed.

The concept of Community Media (CM) has shown to be, in its long theoretical and empirical tradition, highly elusive. The multiplicity of media organizations that carry this name has caused most mono-theoretical approaches to focus on certain characteristics, while ignoring other aspects of the identity of community media. This theoretical problem necessitates the use of different approaches towards the definition of community media (Table 1), which will allow for a complementary emphasis on different aspects of the identity of community media (for an elaboration, see Carpentier, Lie and Servaes, 1991). For a more elaborate description of the different domains of alternative/participatory media, see Lewis (1993: 12).

Table 1: Positioning the four theoretical approaches on Community Media (CM)

	Media-centred	Society-centred
Autonomous identity of CM (essentialist)	Approach I: Serving the community	Approach III: Part of civil society
Identity of CM in relation to other identities (relationalist)	Approach II: An alternative to mainstream	Approach IV: Rhizome

By way of summary

The above-described changes in the field of communication for development could be summarized as follows.

1. The growth of a deeper understanding of the nature of communication

The perspective on communication has changed. Early models in the '50s and '60s saw the communication process simply as a message going from a sender to a receiver (that is, Laswell's classic S-M-R model). The emphasis was mainly sender- and media-centric; the stress laid on the freedom of the press, the absence of censorship, and so on. Since the '70s, communication has become more receiver- and message-centric.

The emphasis now is more on the process of communication (that is, the exchange of meaning) *and on the significance of this process* (that is, the social relationships created by communication and the social institutions and context which result from such relationships). As a result, the focus has moved from a 'communicator' to a more 'receiver-centric' orientation, with the resultant *emphasis on meaning sought and ascribed rather than information transmitted.*

2. A new understanding of communication as a two-way process

With this shift in focus, one is no longer attempting to create a need for the information one is disseminating, but one is rather *disseminating information for which there is a need.* The emphasis is on information exchange rather than on the persuasion in the diffusion model.

The 'oligarchic' view of communication implied that freedom of information was a one-way right from a higher to a lower level, from the centre to the periphery, from an institution to an individual, from a communication-rich nation to a communication-poor one, and so on. Today, the interactive nature of communication is increasingly recognized. It is seen as fundamentally two-way rather than one-way, interactive and participatory rather than linear.

3. A new understanding of culture

The cultural perspective has become central to the debate on communication for development. Culture is not only the visible, non-natural environment of a person, but primarily his/her normative context. Consequently, one has moved away from a more traditional mechanistic approach that emphasized economic and materialistic criteria to a more *multiple appreciation of holistic and complex perspectives.*

4. The trend towards participatory democracy

The end of the colonial era has seen the rise of many independent states and the spread of democratic principles, even if only at the level of lip service. Though often ignored in practice, democracy is honoured in theory. Governments and/or powerful private interests still largely control the world's communication media, but they are more attuned to and aware of the democratic ideals than previously. At the same time, literacy levels have increased, and there has been a remarkable improvement in people's ability to handle and use communication technology. As a consequence, *more and more people can use communication media and can no longer be denied access to and participation in communication processes for the lack of communication and technical skills.*

5. Recognition of the imbalance in communication resources or the digital divide

The disparity in communication resources between different parts of the world is increasingly recognized as a cause of concern. As the centre nations develop their resources, the gap between centre and periphery becomes greater. *The plea for a more balanced and equal distribution of communication resources can only be discussed in terms of power at local, national and international levels.* The attempt by local power-elites to totally control the modern communication channels –press, broadcasting, education, and bureaucracy– does no longer ensure control of all the communication networks in a given society. Nor does control of the mass media ensure support for the controlling forces, nor for any mobilization around their objectives, nor for the effective repression of opposition.

Some may argue that thanks to the new ICTs, especially the Internet and www, one has to re-address the debate on the digital divide; however, others remain sceptical and less optimistic.

6. The growing sense of globalization and cultural hybridity

Perhaps the greatest impetus towards a new formulation of communication freedoms and the need for realistic communication policies and planning have come from the realization that the international flow of communication has become the main carrier of cultural globalization. This cultural hybridity can take place without perceptible dependent relationships.

7. A new understanding of what is happening within the boundaries of the nation-state

One has to accept that "internal" and "external" factors inhibiting development do not exist independently of each other. Thus, in order to understand and develop a proper strategy one must have an understanding of the class relationships of any particular peripheral social formation and the ways in which these structures articulate with the centre on the one hand, and the producing classes in the Third World on the other. To dismiss Third World ruling classes, for example, as mere puppets whose interests are always mechanically synonymous with those of the centre, is to ignore the realities of a much more complex relationship. The very unevenness and contradictory nature of the capitalist development process necessarily produces *a constantly changing relationship*.

8. Recognition of the 'impact' of communication technology

Some communication systems (e.g., audio- and video-taping, copying, radio broadcasting, and especially the Internet) have become *cheap* and so simple that the rationale for regulating and controlling them centrally, as well as the ability to do so, is no longer relevant. However, other systems (for instance, satellites, remote sensing, transborder data flows) remain *very expensive*. They are beyond the means of smaller countries and 'have-nots'. Moreover, they may not be 'suitable' to local environments.

9. From an information society to knowledge societies

Information has been seen as the leading growth sector in society, especially in advanced industrial economies. Its three strands –computing, telecommunications and broadcasting– have evolved historically as three separate sectors, and by means of digitization these sectors are now converging.

Throughout the past decade a gradual shift can be observed away from a technological in favour of more socio-economic and cultural definitions of the Information Society. The term Knowledge Societies (in plural as there are many roads) better coins this shift in emphasis from ICTs as 'drivers' of change to a perspective where these technologies are regarded as tools which may provide a new potential for combining the information embedded in ICT systems with the creative potential and knowledge embodied in people: "These technologies do not create the transformations in society by themselves; they are designed and implemented by people in their social, economic, and technological contexts" (Mansell & When, 1998: 12).

True knowledge is more than information. Knowledge is the sense or meaning that people make of information. *Meaning is not something that is delivered to people, people create/interpret it themselves.* If knowledge is to be effectively employed to help people, it needs to be interpreted and evaluated by those it is designed to help. That requires people to have access to information on the issues that affect their lives, and the capacity to make their own contributions to policy-making processes. Understanding the context in which knowledge moves –factors of control, selection, purpose, power, and capacity– is essential for understanding how societies can become better able to learn, generate and act on knowledge.

10. A new understanding towards integration of distinct means of communication

Modern mass media and alternate or parallel networks of folk media or interpersonal communication channels are not mutually exclusive by definition. Contrary to the beliefs of diffusion theorists, they are *more effective if appropriately used in an integrated fashion, according to the needs and constraints of the local context.* The modern mass media, having been mechanically transplanted from abroad into Third World societies, enjoy varying and limited rates of penetration. They are seldom truly integrated into institutional structures, as occurs in some Western societies. However, they can be effectively combined, provided a functional division of labour is established between them, and provided the limits of the communication media are recognized.

11. The recognition of dualistic or parallel communication structures

No longer governments or rulers are able to operate effectively, to control, censor, or to play the role of gatekeeper with regard to all communications networks at all times in a given society. Both alternate and parallel networks, which may not always be active, often function through political, socio-cultural, religious or class structures or can be based upon secular, cultural, artistic, or folkloric channels. These networks feature a highly participatory character, high rates of credibility, and a strong organic integration with other institutions deeply rooted in a given society.

Chapter 6

Communicating for what?

How globalisation and HIV/AIDS push the ComDev agenda

Thomas Tufte

Prologue: youth essays from Grahamstown, South Africa...

Close by to my house there is a little girl who is HIV positive. At her home it's only her sister who knows about the young girl's status. They are both scared that if they tell their parents, they will chase her away from home. Her sister told me, and asked if I could keep it a secret.

In clinics people who are HIV positive are being treated badly. Even if you ask them to get you some water, they will shout at you for no reason. Even if you are in too bad a condition to be discharged, they will tell you that you need to go home because there's no place for you here. You can just go home and die there. If your family knows your status they won't take you to the doctor or hospital, only when your situation is worsened they will take you to TEMBA SANTA HOSPITAL (TB Hospital) and say you have TB. Even at your funeral they will just say you died of TB. I think if we can learn to be more open about AIDS, we can defeat it (NB9-Female).

I'm quite sure that most cases of aids take place in underprivileged communities where life isn't the same as those of the more privileged communities. By this I mean that drugs, alcohol abuse, etc ... play a major role in HIV/AIDS. The lesser fortunate people have no goals to achieve in life and often have many problems early on in their lives so they turn to drugs, alcohol, sex! I feel that this above is what takes place right here in

Grahamstown, in our own community and us who are more fortunate shouldn't just say 'well they will die sooner or later so we don't need to worry' (K9-Male).

I believe that AIDS is a sad thing and can be overcome. The community needs to start acknowledging the fact that AIDS is everywhere at anytime and at any place. I believe that AIDS can most definitely be overcome if we stand together and break down this destructive disease known as AIDS (MW20-Male).

The lack of results

The history of HIV/AIDS communication and prevention is close to disastrous in the lack of results obtained, especially with regard to combating HIV/AIDS in developing countries. Some people and organisations do, with reason, flag show-cases as Senegal, Uganda or Thailand for having responded with some noteworthy impact upon the pandemic. However, on a global scale, the hard facts make the case quite clear: no developing country with serious HIV/AIDS pandemics is anywhere near finding a solution, and has achieved only limited impact by using communication in preventing the further spread of the pandemic.

The above testimonials from essays by 16-18 year olds in Grahamstown, South Africa, as part of a research project on HIV/AIDS communication for prevention, indicate some of the current problems experienced by young South Africans. One of the main problems with HIV/AIDS is that of stigma. According to the Collins English Dictionary, stigma is 'a distinguishing mark of social disgrace'. Sadly, the myths and misunderstandings surrounding this mark of disgrace, the fear of meeting this mark, and the denial of having this mark, the HIV virus, altogether create the very difficult situation to tackle.

The young girl's situation exposed above indicates this. Stigma results in ill treatment in hospitals, in the silence or gossip in the community, and it is leading to avoiding confirmation of their own HIV status. It's a situation that is locked, and where communication possibly and hopefully can have a stronger role to play as facilitator of opening up this tightly locked situation in so many communities. The current high emphasis on rolling out anti-retroviral treatment (ARV) is changing the current emphasis from focus on prevention or integrated approaches to an almost complete focus on HIV treatment. Having treatment centrally on the AIDS agenda is in many ways crucial –it creates a strong incentive for people to know their status, it also catalyses action on stigma and it creates the focus for political activism on HIV/AIDS.

However, as stated by the UN Millennium Project's working group on HIV/AIDS, there is a strong need to invigorate HIV prevention, and treatment can assist prevention in important ways. But treatment alone will not bring the epidemic under control (UN Millennium Project, Working Group on HIV/AIDS, January 17 2005). Thus, ARV is still a dream for the large majority. Young people living in AIDS-struck societies feel their identities are at risk. As one young boy in Grahamstown stated, "The word AIDS or HIV gives me shivers every time I hear it. The reason for this is that there were a lot of people that I know that had the virus, but almost all of them passed away" (G16-M). Young people who are, by definition, the most energetic, the most optimistic, the invincible generation with their future ahead of them, are increasingly feeling at risk. As another young man wrote in his essay, "If you get the HIV virus, your future gets stuck!" You become part of a real 'no future' generation. That's at least the perception many young Africans have due to the lack of a cure to AIDS.

Feeling at risk again results in states of denial and situations of stress where many young people develop an attitude signalling 'they don't care'! Some of them deny that they are at risk, and most often they blame the spread of the virus on somebody else –some groups of 'others'– be it the opposite sex, be it marginal groups as prostitutes, be it those in another neighbourhood or be it simply 'others'! HIV/AIDS is, in that respect, dividing societies far more than it is promoting unity or the degree of collectivism required for confronting the problem.

HIV/AIDS is obviously a problem of poverty and unequal power relations in society. It is a pandemic which is blossoming in societies with gender inequity. It is a pandemic which travels with human trafficking or with migrant labour. And it is a pandemic which strikes hardest amongst those that cannot afford any form of treatment. HIV/AIDS is a symptom of social and economic injustice, and should be combated accordingly. It is not just about changing individual behaviour, to abstain from sex or using a condom. That's just treating the symptoms, and not the actual causes.

New conditions of instability

The situation with HIV/AIDS affecting young people raises a number of questions. Why have the outcomes of past experiences been so limited? What has been erroneous about the strategies used, and how can this be changed in the future? A key problem, which has been raised increasingly, has been the lack of attention to the root causes of HIV/AIDS (Panos, 2001; UNAIDS, 1999). This chapter draws attention to some fundamental development challenges that are at the core of the matter: the challenges of economic and cultural globalisation. I will argue that one of the consequences of the current economic and cultural globalisation is the emergence of what Arjun Appadurai has termed "new conditions of instability in the production of modern subjectivities" (Appadurai, 1996: 4).

Appadurai highlights two key issues that characterise the current transformation of society. They are *mass migration* and *electronic mediation*. In the process of transformation, with mass migration and mass mediation, the consequence for many individuals is the articulation of ontological *in*security. This idea is the reverse of a concept put forth by Anthony Giddens. On the other side of the coin, impacting not least amongst broad populations in developing countries, but also in, for example, Eastern Europe, economic and cultural globalisation is resulting in social marginalization and disempowerment. With such consequences follows a growing sense of instability in the production of modern subjectivities. People feel unsure about and don't understand current processes of development. It often transcends clashes between tradition and modernity and has more to do with the ability or not to control the conditions of ones own everyday life.

The argument in this chapter is that a critical review of HIV/AIDS communication is required in the context of this (too) briefly sketched downside of current development processes. The hypothesis is that many of the root causes of HIV/AIDS, be it gender inequality, unemployment, or poverty, are intrinsically tied to the processes of globalisation in a complex cause-effect relationship. Thus, the spread of HIV/AIDS and processes of globalisation are interlinked. Developing efficient responses to HIV/AIDS requires more than conveying a clear message about sexual behaviour. It requires broader strategies to empower the audiences to handle difficult conditions of everyday life, beyond tradition versus modernity, and facing the multiple dimensions and consequences of globalisation. It requires tackling the overarching condition of everyday life experienced by many, not least marginalized groups in developing countries: instability in the production of each and everyone's 'modern subjectivity'. For many of these audiences, HIV/AIDS communication that works will be communication for social change.

Two key objectives

My first aim with this chapter is to assess the key challenges of HIV/AIDS communication and prevention within the overarching context of economic and cultural globalisation. Firstly, clarification is required in problem identification. Without a precise problem identification as how to conceive of HIV/AIDS –be it either as a health problem, a question related to cultural practice or as an overall development problem– we cannot start to formulate precise solutions. I will argue that HIV/AIDS must be approached as a development problem, which is both caused by, and impacts upon contemporary processes of globalisation, including issues such as migration, new economy and consumer culture.

The second aim is to analyse what consequences the issues of interdependency between HIV/AIDS and globalisation will have for the practice of HIV/AIDS communication. If we assume a fundamental and possibly growing societal 'order of instability in the production of modern subjectivities', how should we then tackle the problem of HIV/AIDS from a communication perspective? Arguing for HIV/AIDS communication that empowers and promotes social integration is abstract academic discourse until concrete pathways ahead are suggested. Step one, I argue, is a paradigmatic shift in most of the existing communication practices in HIV/AIDS prevention work. A fundamental rethinking is required, moving beyond the often very taken for granted or 'common sense'-like understanding of communication present in many institutions working in HIV/AIDS prevention. In a second step, trust must be created. Only then will the audiences engage in the media text and flow of communication. Thirdly, relevance and recognition must be sought –in media texts, programs and discourses that move beyond the simple epidemic and into the broader contexts of everyday life. Linked to this is the fourth issue: methods and strategies must be identified whereby some of the outlined root causes can be dealt with in the concrete strategy development.

To pursue objective two, a stronger recognition of how different communication paradigms result in different communication practices with different expected outcomes may well help focus the problem-solving strategy.

Although we are more than 20 years into the epidemic, we have not yet properly addressed the root causes of HIV/AIDS. More, and especially better responses –recognizing the complexity of HIV/AIDS– are obviously required to counter the pandemic (Skuse, 2003).

The history of and response to HIV/AIDS

Providing a brief retrospective shows that the HIV/AIDS epidemic has continuously grown and spread since the first cases were identified in the early 1980s. Today more than 40 million people are infected with HIV and more than 20 million people have died of AIDS (UNAIDS, 2003). Southern and Eastern Africa is most severely struck, with approximately 40% of women between the ages of 15-49 in Botswana HIV positive. Almost every fourth adult in South Africa is HIV positive. India has the largest HIV+ population in the world when considering in absolute numbers. China is a ticking bomb, with no confident figures to really tell us the magnitude of the problem. Epidemiological curves from the Caribbean show several countries with exponential growth of the epidemic, which is also the case in Central America (UNAIDS, 2003).

Europe and USA managed in the late 1980s to curb the epidemiological curves. Large campaigns, political support and focused interventions amongst the most vulnerable groups of the population had impact. However, today, Europe is again threatened, with dramatic rises in the number of HIV positive cases in many Eastern European countries. Ukraine is most severely struck with approximately 1% of the 15-49 year olds being HIV positive (Amon et al, 2003). Epidemiologists indicate 1% being the crucial limit between epidemics that still are predominantly in vulnerable populations and thus easier to control, and epidemics that are spreading into the general population and growing beyond control. Thus, considering labour migration and general interaction between East and West Europe, there is a risk that HIV/AIDS may re-emerge as a serious problem also in Western Europe.

Communication-wise and campaign-wise there have been phases of more or less attention attributed to this issue. Anthropologist and Project Director Barbara Zalduondo from the USAID-financed Synergy Project has termed current developments in HIV/AIDS communication as the second generation of HIV/AIDS communication (Zalduondo, 2001). USA has since 2001 taken substantial steps ahead, partly in their conceptual approach, but in practice mostly in financial terms. Hence, USAID has, especially from 2002 and onwards, radically increased their support to the combating HIV/AIDS.

In the NGO world, one of the centres of excellence is the Centre for Communication Programs, an independent institution at Johns Hopkins University in Baltimore. Researchers there have worked with family planning, reproductive health and HIV/AIDS prevention in approximately 40 countries worldwide. A rapidly growing number of NGOs work with HIV/AIDS, in prevention, care, support and treatment –but a minimum of these organisations possess the competencies and resources to develop well researched, monitored and evaluated communication interventions, not to mention long-term interventions. At the government level, many countries have been slow in recognizing the magnitude of the problem in their countries. Only within the last 6-8 years have many governments set up high-level national HIV/AIDS committees. While many governments are increasingly seeking to coordinate and take the lead in the national response mechanisms, NGOs continue to hold an important role in combating HIV/AIDS, tackling the most pressing issues in countries struck by governmental denial and low priority, or struck by mere lack of funds.

Internationally, the debate about how to combat HIV/AIDS gained new momentum in the late 1990s. In 1997 UNAIDS initiated a global consultative process which led to the development of the UNAIDS Communication Framework (UNAIDS, 1999). Following this process, and recognizing the dramatic magnitude and severity of the HIV/AIDS pandemic, today there is a vivid and continuous debate on how to use communication in the struggle against HIV/AIDS. A central part of this debate is taking place on the web-site <www.comminit.com>, which belongs to the international network The Communication Initiative, established in 1997 by a broad range of inter- and non-governmental entities and organisations.

Defining the problem of HIV/AIDS

The first issue to address is how the development of HIV/AIDS connects to the processes of especially economic and cultural globalisation. This begs the question: how do we define HIV/AIDS? Is it a health problem, a cultural problem, a socio-economic problem or something else? Obviously, it is a bit of each, but first and foremost my argument is that HIV/AIDS must be considered a development problem, including dimensions of gender, culture, spirituality, policy and socio-economic conditions.

In some regions of the world, the problem is of such a magnitude that it transcends all traditional sectors of development, be it agriculture, education, transport, industry or health. This effort to clearly define how we conceive the problem of HIV/AIDS is crucial because it has implications for the manner by which the problem solving is organized and focused: what sector institutions shall be involved in the response? What actions and activities are important? Who are the target audiences? What is the time perspective?

For many years, HIV/AIDS has been considered a health problem, where problem-solving was limited to biomedical and public health solutions dealing with access to health services, voluntary counselling and testing, treatment, care and support. WHO was for the first many years the leading international organisation (lead agency in UN), and many of the early national HIV/AIDS committees were set up at middle range political levels, almost always within ministries of health and guided by WHO. The main issue in the early years of the pandemic was to define priorities between prevention and treatment. Today, this discussion has become more nuanced. More holistic approaches have developed, recognizing the need to deal with prevention, care and support (Zalduondo, 2001; Morris, 2003). Today, there is an increasingly strong movement towards the promotion of mass treatment. WHO, as the key UN agency, and Medecins Sans Frontière as the key international NGO, have lead roles in this movement. In terms of problem identification, many practitioners still tend to approach HIV/AIDS as a health problem where the main issue is to avoid getting the virus, learning to live with it or, most importantly, treat it. The broader socio-economic aspects of the HIV/AIDS problem are still not incorporated into many programs, and the challenges for HIV/AIDS programs influenced by the dynamics and conditions of globalisation remain to be better understood.

Culture, gender and sexual practices

Another approach has been to understand HIV/AIDS as a cultural problem. In this context, the focus has long been to view culture as a barrier to safe sexual behaviour (UNAIDS/Airhihenbuwa et al, 1999). HIV/AIDS is largely a sexually transmitted disease, and the bulk of previous and current HIV/AIDS prevention communication deals with changing exactly that: sexual behaviour. Such campaigns have addressed initiation rituals, sugar-daddy practices, prostitution, child abuse, negotiation of sexual practices and gender inequality, among other issues. Often sexual practices have been seen and interpreted mainly as cultural practices that hindered safe sex and therefore had to change. Tribal systems of social organisation, patriarchal structures and polygamy have been seen as key socio-cultural barriers. Stated bluntly, traditional ways of life have often been seen as mainly problematic to the advancement of safe sex and ultimately preventing the spread of HIV. In more recent years, such approaches are less frequent. The issue of culture and cultural practices is increasingly being framed within the conditions of a rapidly changing world, where many people are caught in conflicts between tradition and modernity and between patriarchy and gender equality. Culture is increasingly understood as a required context of action rather than simply an obstacle. Culture can be viewed as a resource in the combat of HIV/AIDS. What still remains to elaborate and analyse are the dynamics between local cultural practices and the global cultural discourses articulated in, for example, media flows, be it in radio or TV soap operas, musical genres or talk shows.

HIV/AIDS as a development problem

Today, despite the strong treatment focus currently in force, there is increasing recognition of viewing HIV/AIDS as a development problem. Thus, there is a gradual but slow mainstreaming of HIV/AIDS components into sector programs of governmental development agencies as SIDA, DANIDA, DFID and USAID. However, the broader integral analysis of development and globalisation is still very much an academic discourse. It has, to some extent, found its way into some development policy documents. This is the case in the DANIDA policy document from 2001, which expressed the philosophy upon which DANIDA's development strategy was subsequently formulated (Danida Analysedokument, <www.um.dk>).

As for the specific problem of HIV/AIDS, broader societal perspectives are seldom analysed in any depth or brought in any significant manner into the problem identification and into the development of response models[1]. Obviously, you might well give up hope and become disillusioned if you recognize the magnitude and levels of complexity surrounding HIV/AIDS. However, without this recognition, many of the root causes may well persist, and HIV/AIDS prevention and communication remain Sisyphus' work.

HIV/AIDS and globalisation

When I argue that the spread of HIV/AIDS is linked to processes of globalisation, it must be seen both as a product and cause of globalisation (Altman, 2001: 69ff). The complex cause-effect relation between the spread of HIV/AIDS and globalisation can be spelt out into many sub-components, of which the following are just a few.

New economy

Although HIV/AIDS can strike anybody no matter their social status, it is an epidemic that first and foremost strikes against the socially marginalized groups in our contemporary, globalised world. The nations with the highest prevalence rates are, without exception, low-income countries. As such, the rise and spread of HIV/AIDS can arguably be seen as a consequence of the negative social implications the free market and new economy have on the world society. As the Polish sociologist Zygmunt Bauman states, when reflecting upon globalisation:

---

1 I base this judgement on my experience as a consultant to *Danida* in HIV/AIDS communication and prevention. Thus, participating in the development of different sector programmes in Mozambique, Zambia and Central America, I experienced what one might call 'the pragmatics of development practice' where institutional, financial and also conceptual constraints hindered any elaborate analysis of how responses to the HIV/AIDS pandemic could be tied to larger cross-sectoral development challenges in contexts of for example globalisation and regional development. *Danida* did, during the previous government, establish an International HIV/AIDS Think Tank in which I participated. During the 3-4 meetings held in its one year of existence (2001-2002), a range of further-reaching conceptual issues were debated. However, the link to the practitioners did not evolve far.

> A particular cause of worry is the progressive breakdown in communica-
> tion between the increasingly global and extraterritorial elites and the ever
> more 'localized' rest. The centres of meaning-and-value production are
> today exterritorial and emancipated from local constraints –this does not
> apply, though, to the human condition which such values and meanings
> are to inform and make sense of (Bauman, 1998).

A communicative disconnection is occurring between the elite cosmopolitans and the more 'localized' rest, and HIV/AIDS strikes the worst amongst the localized rest. What has happened with HIV/AIDS significantly supersedes the otherwise similar development occurring with the development of cholera in Latin America in the early 1990s. Generally, it is seen that unsustainable development processes pave the way for epidemics to flourish. In the 1980s the following was seen in Latin America: "increased national debt, rapid urbanisation, environmental degradation and inequitable access to health services, and reduced public expenditure on public health infrastructure. Cholera then arrived in 1991, spreading rapidly across the continent in an epidemic of 1.4 million cases and more than ten thousand deaths in nineteen countries" (Lee and Dodgon in Altman, 2001: 72).

Linked to such unfortunate structural adjustments and general development processes, there is a strong irony in how the World Bank's structural adjustment programs in several developing countries weakened the health structures which, in subsequent years, could have helped prevent the spread of HIV (Altman, 2001: 72).

The porosity of national borders

Another aspect of the globalisation-HIV/AIDS relationship lies in the transnational character of the epidemic. In its essence it is a travelling epidemic that moves, without distinction, across borders. As a virus, HIV travels with humans carrying it by any means of transport to any part of the globe. Any human mobility carries the risk of transporting the HIV virus. Consequently, the recent mushrooming of high level national HIV/AIDS committees will only make sense to the degree that migratory trends both within and beyond national borders are contemplated into the programmes these national committees develop.

One aspect of this transnational character of HIV/AIDS is reflected in the growing internationalisation of trade in both sex and drugs, leading to a rapid spread of HIV in for example Southeast Asia (Altman, 2001: 71) and Europe (Amon et al, 2003). With large prevalence rates in the general populations of many places, the epidemic spreads through different kinds of motion or 'travel', for example, seasonal workers, migration, etc. For example in Denmark, one of the most significant aspects of the moderate rise in HIV prevalence seen in recent years originates from immigrants from some African countries who have arrived HIV positive the country.

Global response mechanisms

Today, the World Bank and the Global Fund are among the key players in the global combat of HIV/AIDS. The globalisation of human welfare reflects a strong broadening in how the HIV/AIDS epidemic is conceived, and what responses are proposed. The first global response mechanism was the global AIDS program established by WHO in 1986, focusing on health and biomedical aspects of the struggle against HIV/AIDS. In 1995 UNAIDS was established, co-sponsored by seven of the large UN-agencies (including UNICEF, UNDP, WHO, UNESCO and the World Bank). Although constrained by a very limited budget, UNAIDS has been instrumental in contributing to the international HIV/AIDS debate, and has been innovative in the field of communication, suggesting a communications framework which seeks to deliver the argument on how to situate HIV/AIDS programmes in five contexts: government policies, socio-economic conditions, gender, culture and spirituality. This has led to a rich debate and many subsequent contributions, not least from the Rockefeller Foundation (1999), DFID (Skuse, 2003) and from the PANOS Institute (2001).

In 2001 the Global Fund for the Combat of HIV/AIDS, Malaria and Tuberculosis was established, following the extraordinary UN General Assembly in June 2001. This has contributed to the raising of additional funds. Finally, USAID is now heavily prioritising the combat of HIV/AIDS through the ambitious PEPFAR-program of the Bush administration. However, the focus is on treatment, and there is growing criticism of the way in which PEPFAR is emphasizing abstinence as the key solution, thus undermining many years of social marketing of condoms. Despite UNAIDS and the Global Fund being significant intergovernmental organisations, the global response remains a minefield of differing national, organisational, professional and personal interests, resulting in problems of lack of coordination, duplication of efforts, contradicting messages and efforts.

Furthermore, what many HIV programs still often overlook is the problem of integrating very different epistemological frameworks and understandings of illness (Altman, 2001: 73). UNAIDS' conceptual framework already in 1999 highlighted the need to recognize and contemplate such different health belief systems.

Cultural globalization

Beyond the emphasis of UNAIDS' conceptual framework indicating multiple contexts to take into consideration, the nature of the HIV/AIDS problem and the rise and ravage caused by HIV/AIDS are, on the overall level, closely linked to the cultural dimension of globalisation. Arjun Appadurai, in formulating his *theory of rupture*, explores the relation between globalisation and modernity. In this exercise he emphasizes two issues characteristic of the ongoing rupture –or transformation– in society: mass migration and electronic mediation. He sees these two

phenomena as interconnected and both affecting the "work of the imagination" | 115
as a constitutive feature of modern subjectivity (Appadurai, 1996: 3). Appadurai
argues that the electronic media "offer new resources and new disciplines for the
construction of imagined selves and imagined worlds". Juxtaposed with the both
voluntary and forced mass migrations, the result, he argues, is "a new order of
instability in the production of modern subjectivities" (ibid: 4).

It is this 'new order of instability', articulated by these forces of mediation and motion, to which HIV/AIDS has a connection. First of all, HIV/AIDS
impacts on and is impacted by the electronic mediation and physical motion.
With migration, AIDS travels. With the electronic media, American, national and
international representations of sexuality, love, and relationships travel the
globe, reaching also the high prevalence countries of Southern and Eastern
Africa. The new order of instability is, on one hand, affected by the existence of
HIV/AIDS, a lethal and existential threat to each and everyone, threatened in
their most intimate of actions –that of sexual practices. Dealing heavily with
issues as sexuality, love, and relationships, substantial parts of the media flow
consist of discursive representations of these issues –discourses that interact
with their audience and contribute to the articulation of modern subjectivities.
The work of the imagination, thus coloured by everyday life *and* by mediated
symbolic worlds, spins a sophisticated thread of mixed feelings, merged lived
and mediated experiences, and becomes a filter on today's processes of cultural
globalisation. The young boys and girls in Grahamstown, South Africa, are living
their lives in this context.

It is in this context that the workings of the imagination, and in particular the role of entertainment, become factors to include when designing
responses to HIV/AIDS. It is *de facto* an issue which many newer strategies are
working with: how to explore the popularity of international genres as soap
operas, talk shows and musical programs, aiming to educate, inform about and
mobilize against HIV/AIDS. Innovative strategies can be seen in the work of the
NGO *Puntos de Encuentro* in Nicaragua (see chapter 23 in this volume), with
Soul City in South Africa (<www.soulcity.za>, see chapter 9 in this volume) and
in the *Femina Health Information Project* in Tanzania (see chapter 24 in this volume). However, a critical aspect to analyse much further is how the genres –popular and explored in the HIV/AIDS combat– represent issues of relationships,
love, and sexuality. Possibly, these discourses most often impact negatively on
the 'new order of instability', which people are living and experiencing.
However, a groundbreaking example of televised entertainment education is the
South Africa TV soap opera *Tsha-Tsha* which is based on Paulo Freire's philosophy of *conscientização*[2].

2 Personal conversation with Kevin Kelly in Grahamstown, South Africa, October 2002.

116 | Paradigms in HIV/AIDS communication

> *Communication strategies can help stop the epidemic, and*
> *certainly, they can slow it down. A fundamental step is to realize*
> *that the HIV/AIDS epidemic is not just a biomedical and health*
> *problem. It represents a political problem, a cultural problem, and*
> *a socio-economic problem, one which behaviour change*
> *communication can help address, and possibly solve. (...)*
> *what is really needed to change the world is an integration of*
> *biomedically based scientific findings with communication-*
> *science-based interventions and advocacy. The 2002 Barcelona*
> *Conference marked the emergence of intervention and policy*
> *from the shadows of biomedical science. Only 14 biannual*
> *international AIDS conferences were required to reach this*
> *obvious conclusion. Once the worldwide epidemic is redefined*
> *more accurately, then its solution can be realized.*
>
> Singhal and Rogers (2003: 388-389)

In their book *Combating AIDS – Communication Strategies in Action*, Arvind Singhal and the late Everett Rogers have made a thorough analysis of a broad range of communication strategies that have been implemented in countries around the world. Their quote above indicates two points from their concluding chapter. Firstly, the quote highlights the point that HIV/AIDS needs to be better understood, beyond just a health problem. Secondly, it emphasizes the relevance of communication strategies based on behaviour change communication. The first point supports the case I make in this chapter, placing the discussion of HIV/AIDS within a discussion of globalisation –considering the nature and characteristics of economic, cultural, and political aspects of globalisation.

Singhal and Rogers' plea for behaviour change communication (BCC) strikes the core of my second issue to be raised in this chapter, that of communication paradigms: what communication approach should inform our problem-solving strategy in HIV/AIDS prevention efforts? Within the experiences to date, two main competing paradigms have dominated the field of HIV/AIDS communication. As such HIV/AIDS communication can be seen as a sub-field of the more encompassing field of communication for development. A lot of HIV/AIDS communication publications have also emerged within the field of health communication more specifically. A joint characteristic of these writings has been their use of communication models originating in the diffusion paradigm. Drawing on Everett Roger's classical book from 1962, *Diffusion of Innovations*, what I call the diffusion paradigm draws on psychological and psychosocial theories, persuasive communication theory, social learning theory, and play theory. For example, social marketing and early entertainment-education, both used extensively in HIV/AIDS communication, draw heavily on this paradigm (Tufte, 2001). This communication paradigm emphasizes individual behavioural change.

On the other hand, we have the participatory paradigm. This has origins in Paulo Freire's theory of dialogical communication and liberating pedagogy

(Freire, 1970) and refers to the alternative communication practice seen in grass-root and social movements and NGOs. This communication paradigm is based more on the principle of dialogue. It is community oriented and understands participatory process as empowering per se, and as end goals to pursue in communicative practices (for more elaborate presentations of both of these paradigms see chapters 7 and 9 of this volume).

In many cases, institutions have taken a stand on how to address the problem, oriented towards one of these paradigms. For example, the Centre for Communication Programs at Johns Hopkins University is predominantly oriented towards BCC, while the PANOS Institute is predominantly oriented towards the participatory paradigm.

Communication for social change

At the International Roundtable on Communication for Development in Managua, November 2001, key UN-agencies, NGOs and scholars were gathered to discuss HIV/AIDS communication. At this meeting, PANOS had, in a back-ground document, structured their discussions around three major approaches to HIV/AIDS communication: 1. behaviour change communication; 2. advocacy communication, and 3. communication for social change.

This international debate, along with several subsequent debates, has in recent years centred discussions around three different approaches to HIV/AIDS communication. These are *behaviour change communication (BCC), advocacy communication,* and *communication for social change.* Behaviour change communication has traditionally been the approach in HIV/AIDS communication, focusing on individual behaviour change and often grounded in an understanding of the problem as being lack of information. Based on theories of diffusion, these initiatives are often large scale media campaigns that spread information in hope that knowing more, people change behaviour. Experiences in many countries show, however, that people have increasingly high levels of factual knowledge on HIV/AIDS, but the knowledge is not leading to behavioural change. Thus, the debate is increasingly focusing on two other approaches: advocacy communication and communication for social change. *Advocacy communication* deals with the specific objective of advocating the rights and problems of HIV/AIDS, for example the rights of PLWHAs, or of orphans and abused children. *Communication for social change* is the term used whereby the underlying causes of HIV/AIDS are being recognised: poverty, gender inequality, unemployment, etc. Following this principle, HIV/AIDS communication must address the structural determinants that lead to these situations, and is often rooted in participatory processes where issues of empowerment and human rights are at the centre of concern.

What the Managua Roundtable demonstrated was a number of unre-solved issues. Firstly, there was a clear *discursive consensus* around the terminology –everybody speaking of the need for participatory approaches. However, scratching the surface, a lack of conceptual clarity and clear definitions was evident: what definitions should be given to participation, social change, mobilisation, and other key concepts. Secondly, there were *no uniform, immediate objectives* when speaking about combating HIV/AIDS through communication. Obviously, reducing HIV/AIDS was the long-term objective everyone agreed upon, but should this require deeper social change, individual behaviour change, political change or other forms of change (cultural, legal, economical, etc.)? In this chapter, I have argued that HIV/AIDS and the negative social impacts of globalization are pushing the agenda of strategic communication towards a more elaborate social change agenda.

Lastly, the Managua Roundtable demonstrated that very *differing methodologies* were applied in the communication strategies presented, reflecting the broad diversity of approaches to HIV/AIDS communication and prevention (see <www.comminit.com> for the Roundtable declaration).

A key gap, which is apparent in the field of communication practices, is the weak link between the practices of development communication (under which HIV/AIDS communication pertains) and advances in communication theory. The conceptual and methodological insights generated within qualitative audience analysis from the mid 1980s and onwards are, for example, not connected to the HIV/AIDS communication practices. In this context, the development of cultural studies as an interdisciplinary field in academia still has limited resonance within communication practise, despite the increased recognition of culture as a determining factor. The interdisciplinary nature of cultural studies, the understanding of audience reception practices and the integrated approaches of political economy with cultural studies are all fields which could well contribute to redefining the field of HIV/AIDS communication within the framework of a social change agenda.

Finally, as mentioned previously, the growing bibliography exploring the role of media and communication in the process of cultural globalisation is also a body of knowledge still disconnected from problem-identification and problem-solving in the fight against HIV/AIDS. A closer relationship between theory and practice should be promoted. Drawing the past many years' experience with qualitative audience reception analysis and audience ethnography into the field of communication for development can help move the focus of communication practitioners from the narrow text-audience relationship often seen to the broader interdisciplinary analysis of the dynamic relation between media and communication with social and cultural practices –and behaviours– in everyday life.

Narrating instability?

Many organisations and experts have argued for the contextualisation of HIV/AIDS communication as a means to improve the impact of the interventions. Likewise, many organisations and experts have called for the need for better research, formative and summative research in communication for development in general, and in HIV/AIDS communication more specifically. However, this article

has pointed at a deeper-lying challenge for HIV/AIDS communication: to explore
the consequences of globalisation upon modern subjectivities and analyse how this impacts upon the ontological security amongst target audiences. Consequently, the challenge is also to redefine the communication paradigm upon which to base concrete strategy development. What people, communities, organisations, governments and international agencies should also be discussing when dealing with HIV/AIDS are issues that reach deeper and beyond the simple sexual behaviours of people, whereby the HIV virus is physically transmitted.

The Latin American scholar of communication and culture, Jesus Martin-Barbero, has reflected upon how modern identities are articulated, and has made a point which is relevant for the case I make in this article; that success stories (communication) about HIV/AIDS are only possible if they strike the identity and cultural strings of the audience. As phrased by Martin-Barbero:

> The modern identities –contrary to those attributed to a pre-existing structure as nobility or working class– are constructed in the recognition of others (…). In order for the plurality of the world's culture to be taken politically into consideration, it is indispensable that the diversity of identities can be told, narrated. This relation between narration and identity is constitutive: there is no cultural identity, which is not narrated (Martin-Barbero, 2002).

Consequently, the current instability of modern subjectivities, and the conditions of this instability, must be captured and narrated –this is the contemporary condition of identity work from which human behaviour departs. As such it is one of the most important, if not the most important communication challenge in the fight against HIV/AIDS.

Methodology

Chapter 7

The diffusion and participatory models: a comparative analysis[1 and 2]

Nancy Morris[3]

Communication is a key component of many overseas aid programs. Efforts to | 123
improve living conditions in the world's poorer areas through social service and
infrastructure development are often accompanied by communication campaigns
aimed at the general populace. Development communication has been defined
as "the strategic application of communication technologies and processes to
promote social change" (Wilkins, 2000: 197). The field of development communication is dominated by two conceptual models: diffusion and participation.
These models have distinct intellectual roots and differing emphases in terms of
program designs and goals. Comparing the objectives and outcomes of projects
based on these models and querying the extent of the gap and the overlap
between them is the central focus of this chapter. It examines published studies
and working papers that report on specific interventions –commonly termed

1 A version of this chapter appeared as Morris, Nancy, "A Comparative Analysis of the Diffusion and
Participatory Models in Development Communication", *Communication Theory*, 2003, 13(2), pp. 225-
248. Used by permission of Oxford University Press.

2 This research was made possible through support provided by the Global Office of Health and Nutrition
G/PHN, Bureau for Global Programs, Field Support and Research, U.S. Agency for International
Development, under the terms of Cooperative Agreement No. HRN-A-00-98-00044-00 (the CHANGE
project), with the Academy for Educational Development and its subcontractor, the Manoff Group, Inc.
The opinions expressed herein are those of the author and do not necessarily reflect the views of the U.S.
Agency for International Development.

3 The author would like to acknowledge the contributions of Robert Hornik, Sandy Kyrish, Judith A.
McDivitt, Tom Polcari, Silvio Waisbord and Karin Wilkins.

"campaigns" or programs[4]. Development projects have many goals, including educational, environmental, and economic improvement. This chapter focuses on –but is not strictly limited to– interventions concerning health, particularly infant health, HIV/AIDS, family planning, and general health promotion. It favors studies published in the last decade, and interventions carried out in what has come to be called the developing world –Africa, Latin America, and the less-industrialized countries of Asia.

The stated aims of these projects fall largely into categories that derive specifically from differences in the diffusion and participatory approaches. The diffusion model –named for Everett M. Rogers' (1962) diffusion of innovations theory– focuses on knowledge transfer leading to behavior change. The participatory model –based on ideas from Paulo Freire's (1970) *Pedagogy of the Oppressed* focuses on community involvement and dialogue as a catalyst for individual and community empowerment. Interventions based on any variety of the diffusion model center on mass media. Participatory campaigns concern interpersonal channels almost exclusively: group meetings, workshops, and sometimes localized "small media" such as community theater (Boeren, 1992: 47; Kalipeni and Kamlongera, 1996) or interactive posters (Laverack et al, 1997). Figure 1 summarizes the two approaches.

Figure 1. Summaries of diffusion and participatory approaches

Diffusion model

Definition of communication: information transfer - vertical
Definition of development communication: information dissemination via mass media

   Problem: lack of information
   Solution: information transfer: knowledge **»** attitudes **»** practice
   Goal: outcome oriented: behavior change

Frameworks	*Types of interventions*
Modernization	Social marketing
Diffusion of innovations	Entertainment-education

Participatory model

Definition of communication: information exchange/dialogue - horizontal
Definition of development communication: grassroots participation via group interaction

   Problem: structural inequalities/local knowledge ignored
   Solution: information exchange/participation
   Goal: process-oriented: empowerment, equity, community

Frameworks	*Types of interventions*
Social change/praxis (Freire)	Empowerment education
Social mobilization/activism	Participatory Action Research (PAR)
	Rapid Participatory Appraisal (RPA)
	Community Involvement in Health (CIH)

4 Although Eisele et al (2000) argue that there is a distinction between the meanings of "intervention" and "program", the terms will be used interchangeably here.

Although participatory communication is often defined in contrast to the more traditional diffusion model, the two are not polar opposites. The diffusion model has evolved in a participatory direction since its initial formulation, and participatory projects necessarily involve some element of information transfer. Nonetheless, most development communication projects tend to identify themselves quite clearly as belonging in one or the other category.

The studies included in this chapter were selected on the basis of the following criteria: each was an empirical study of one or more communication interventions that included information on the objectives and nature of the intervention, the method of evaluation, and the outcomes. Some studies that do not meet these criteria are referred to, but this review is based on studies for which that information is provided. All of the studies, regardless of their framework, were examined for evidence of outcomes identified with the diffusion model –that is, changes in knowledge, attitudes and practices– and outcomes identified with the participatory model –that is, empowerment, community building, and social equity. Figures 2.1 and 2.2 chart the objectives, methods, and reported outcomes of the same set of studies, grouped according to whether they are categorized as diffusion or participatory interventions. As exercises in data reduction, these figures are necessarily oversimplified and interpretive.

The studies included in this chapter comprise an opportunistic sample of working papers and published studies on development interventions. They were found through keyword searches for such terms as "health communication", "public health", "participatory research", and "community participation" on the ProQuest, First Search Sociological Abstracts, and other databases, as well as by tracing bibliographical and Internet references. Although the 45 projects examined do not constitute an exhaustive collection of relevant material, the inclusion of more studies seems unlikely to produce patterns undetected from this partial review.

While some projects' evaluations were manifestly more rigorous than others, for the most part researchers' assessments of outcomes are accepted at face value. There are several reasons for not delving into issues of research methods, reliability and validity, or justifications for claims about results. These reasons concern the amount of detail reported for each study, the pitfalls of trying to compare different types of outcomes, and the varying requirements of the journals in which these studies appear.

First, many of the studies reviewed here contain insufficient detail about how the evidence was gathered to gauge the quality of their conclusions. Some quantitative studies specify how their samples may or may not represent the population of interest, but not all of the articles include this information. Most of the survey-based studies do not include copies of the questionnaires used or verbatim transcriptions of key questions. The absence of explicit information on sampling procedures and questionnaire content impedes assessment of survey validity. Likewise, the studies based on qualitative methods –the prevailing approach for evaluating participatory projects– generally provide few details of their procedures. Evidence for claims of community empowerment comes in the form of brief excerpts from interviews or meetings, or descriptions of interactions. At times no evidence is provided; the researchers simply assert that empowerment has occurred. These problems are exemplified by the author of a participatory study who flatly rejects standard evaluation norms, and then makes a claim about results:

> This presentation of findings neither evaluates the project nor establishes cause-and-effect relationships between specific project activities and certain participatory outcomes. Notwithstanding, some relationships are evident... The data show that, over time, the [subjects] thrived as individuals and as a group and became known and respected in the community (Dickson, 2000: 195).

Without extensive descriptions of contexts, interactions and other bases for researchers' interpretations of events, it is difficult to assess claims based on ethnographic methods such as participant observation.

A lack of methodological exposition is not unique to this body of material. A team of researchers reviewing write-ups of community action health programs found that none of the 17 articles they looked at provided sufficient information on "sampling and control procedures, reliability and validity of instruments, analysis techniques, and specification of details of the intervention" to allow "rigorous scientific evaluation" of the studies (Hancock et al, 1997: 229). A review of nutrition education projects similarly found that "[d]etailed descriptive information about the program setting or context and the communication or education strategy are commonly lacking" (Cerqueira and Olson, 1995: 57), and a review of 41 articles about HIV/AIDS prevention campaigns concluded that "conceptual and methodological rigor in reporting fundamental communication components can be improved" (Myhre and Flora, 2000: 41).

The second reason that this chapter does not deeply scrutinize methods is that there is a question of comparable measurability. Participatory outcomes of empowerment and equity do not have agreed-upon conceptual or operational definitions, and consequently are less amenable to measurement than such outcomes as the percent change in vaccinations before and after a campaign or even slippery hypotheticals such as the intention to use contraception in the future. As Eng Briscoe and Cunningham say, "Participation is not an objective that exists in specific quantities or that can be measured in particular units to be compared over time", nor is it "simply a yes-no variable that is either present or absent" (1990: 1350). Laverack et al (1997: 26) put this more starkly: "it is not very clear what measures of outcome can be used for demonstrating that an individual or group has become 'empowered'".

Finally, although most published articles have been subject to peer review, studies written up in different types of journals focus on different aspects of the research process and supply varying depth of detail. To compare the participatory and diffusion frameworks, the studies must be taken seriously, not rejected out-of-hand for providing insufficient evidence to support their claims. For all of these reasons, the studies discussed here are for the most part examined and evaluated on their own terms[5].

Outcomes - diffusion framework

Many development interventions are in effect advertising campaigns for such "products" as contraception or immunizations. The use of established advertising techniques to promote development goals via media such as TV, radio, newspapers and billboards is termed social marketing (Kotler and Roberto, 1989: 24). Social marketing has adopted not only the forms of marketing, but also its tools: consumer research, pretesting, and audience segmentation (Backer, Rogers and Sopory, 1992: 32). Most media-based development projects can be placed into the social marketing category.

Social marketing campaigns have produced varying degrees of success. At one end of the range of outcomes are studies that found little or no effect for mass media interventions. For example, a childhood immunization campaign in Zaire that included print and radio material and the training of health workers found that while radio listening did lead to increased knowledge about immunization among poorer, less-educated people, this knowledge was not extended into practice: "no evidence was found that radio spots or programs about immunization influenced people to have their children immunized" (Yoder, Zheng and Zhou, 1991: 38). A study of a campaign to distribute Vitamin A to children in Central Java found increased use of the vitamin, but statistical analysis of survey data showed that this was not attributable to the media campaign (McDivitt and McDowell, 1991). A study of a Nigerian media campaign promoting immunizations found a limited correlation between radio exposure and knowledge about whooping cough (Ogundimu, 1994: 236).

Other studies found some effects traceable to mass media. Results of a Bolivian family planning campaign featuring 11 TV and radio spots showed campaign exposure associated with increased knowledge, positive attitudes, and, to a lesser extent, increased adoption of contraception (Valente and Saba, 1998).

Two family planning campaigns —one in The Gambia and the other in Mali— combined social marketing and entertainment-education techniques, with interestingly contrasting results. The campaign in The Gambia resulted in improved knowledge, attitudes and practices in people with no education who heard the campaign's radio drama (Valente et al, 1994: 98). This association was reversed in Mali. Evaluators of a multimedia campaign found that uneducated

---

5 For critiques of development communication research see Yoder, Hornik and Chirwa (1996); Sherry (1997); McKillip (1989); Servaes (1999: 95-117). Freedman's (1997) critique discusses selection bias; Westoff and Rodríguez (1995) discuss problems of inferring causal direction.

respondents were not affected by campaign exposure, while those with some schooling were (Kane et al, 1998: 320).

Other projects have claimed broad success with social marketing techniques. A media campaign in the Philippines had clearly positive effects: "The evidence suggests that the mass media information campaign was largely responsible for the improvement in vaccination coverage" (McDivitt, Zimicki and Hornik, 1997: 111). Also in the Philippines, an evaluation of a TV-based social marketing campaign to decrease fertility found an increase in modern contraceptive use, judged to be a significant direct effect of the communication intervention (Kincaid, 2000). Data from a project in Nigeria "suggest very strongly that mass media interventions can play a major role in promoting family planning use in certain situations" (Piotrow et al, 1990: 272). An analysis of Demographic and Health Survey data in Kenya found that "mass media can have an important effect on reproductive behavior" (Westoff and Rodríguez, 1995: 31). A study of a family planning campaign in Tanzania asked whether a message gained effectiveness by being carried in a variety of media. The researchers concluded that multiple exposure to a message via different media "had an incremental effect on contraceptive use". That is, the more media sources a woman was exposed to, the more likely she was to adopt contraception (Jato et al, 1999: 65-6.)

A subset of social marketing is entertainment-education, which has been defined by leading U.S. proponents in classic diffusion terms as "the process of purposely designing and implementing a media message to both entertain and educate, in order to increase audience knowledge about an educational issue, create favorable attitudes, and change overt behavior" (Singhal and Rogers, 1999: xii). Entertainment education messages may be carried by, for example, a soap opera or popular song specifically written for that purpose, or in vignettes inserted into variety shows. The key characteristic is that the media fare is not presented in an overtly didactic way; it is presented and meant to be consumed as entertainment.

Big claims have been made about the power of the entertainment-education strategy. For instance, "[e]ntertainment –through television, radio and music– is one of the most effective communication strategies for reaching the public to promote family planning and other public health issues" (Singhal and Rogers, 1989: 39). Yet an examination of empirical studies reveals that not all interventions have achieved the desired effect. Researchers in India, for example, found that while exposure to a prosocial soap opera did elicit viewer involvement with the characters, it did not achieve its central aim: "a single TV series did not significantly affect viewers' awareness of beliefs that promote womens' status" (Brown and Cody, 1991: 135). An examination of a radio soap opera in Zambia designed to disseminate information about AIDS found changes over time in some behaviors, but "little credible evidence... that exposure [to the radio drama] produced effects on risky behavior related to AIDS or on knowledge or other outcomes" (Yoder, Hornik and Chirwa, 1996: 200). A meticulous review of the reported outcomes of 20 entertainment-education soap operas led John Sherry to conclude that "the best-designed research using powerful statistical controls suggests no significant effects on knowledge, attitudes or behaviour which can be attributed to the soap operas" (Sherry, 1997: 93).

Nonetheless, many entertainment-education projects have been judged to be successful. A group of researchers studied radio soap operas promoting family planning in four African countries. They found it difficult to separate out the effects of radio drama from other factors but concluded that "the evidence strongly suggests that the soap operas do motivate many listeners to adopt modern contraceptive methods" in Ghana (Lettenmaier et al, 1993: 9). Another finding of positive effects comes from Piotrow et al, who state that entertainment-education material inserted into popular TV programs "influenced knowledge about clinic services and contributed to increased clinic attendance" in a family planning campaign in Nigeria (Piotrow et al, 1990: 269). Everett Rogers and his collaborators conducted a field experiment to examine the effects of an entertainment-education radio soap opera meant to encourage family planning in Tanzania. One area of the country received radio broadcasts; another did not. Using a variety of measures, they found that the soap opera had "strong behavioral effects on family planning adoption" (Rogers et al, 1999: 193). Douglas Storey et al (1999) attribute a direct effect on Nepali family planning attitudes and use of contraception to a radio drama.

Entertainment-education has been enthusiastically embraced by many development communication practitioners (Singhal and Rogers, 1999; Lettenmaier et al, 1993; Piotrow et al, 1990). Entertainment-education television and radio programs tend to be highly popular with audiences (Singhal and Rogers, 1989; Brown, 1991: 118; Lettenmaier, 1993: 7; Ume-Nwagbo, 1986: 161). Their generally high production values may be a factor in their popularity, but, crucially, the programs are produced in local languages, and feature local settings and situations. It is increasingly recognized in media studies that audiences favor local content when it is available (Hoskins, McFadyen and Finn, 1997: 32-5; Straubhaar 1991). Perhaps some of the enthusiasm among practitioners for entertainment-education interventions is due to the indubitable popularity of the shows, which would be evident to researchers in the field. But popularity is not equal to efficacy. Their popularity indicates that these shows entertain; the mixed results of these studies suggest that they do not always educate.

The projects discussed above relied on mass media as the agent of message diffusion. But an aspect of development campaigns that shows up in study after study is the contribution of interpersonal communication to behavior change. The link between media messages and interpersonal communication has been highlighted by communications researchers dating back as far as Lazarsfeld, Berelson and Gaudet's classic formulation of the two-step flow process (1944) and Everett Rogers' *Diffusion of Innovations* (1962).

Kathleen K. Reardon and Everett M. Rogers stated in 1988 that "almost every diffusion study finds that peer networks play an especially crucial role in decisions to adopt a new idea" (1988: 295). This observation led them to term the academic divide between interpersonal and mass communication a "false dichotomy". Substantiating this claim, many studies reviewed here noted the role of media in sparking interpersonal communication, which in turn leads to changes in behavior. While some campaign planners deliberately sought to encourage interpersonal communication, others were surprised to discover that post-campaign evaluations revealed a significant role for interpersonal communication.

One channel of interpersonal communication is the health system. When health promotion campaigns attempt to stimulate demand –for contraceptives, immunizations or other health services– contact with health system personnel becomes a source of information. Evaluations of several development communication interventions explicitly examined interpersonal communication through the formal channel of the health system.

As with other types of interventions, these have had mixed results. Some showed media to be more influential than interpersonal communication. A family planning campaign in Zimbabwe used an entertainment-education soap opera, print material and "motivational talks" to encourage men to take a more active role in family planning. In this case, the interpersonal channel was not judged effective; researchers found that "[b]ecause of radio's extensive reach, the soap opera was responsible for changing the behaviour of more than four times as many men as the pamphlets and motivational talks combined" (Lettenmaier et al, 1993: 9). Similarly, an evaluation of an immunization campaign in the Philippines found that exposure to campaign messages through mass media, not through contact with health workers, resulted in increased knowledge, which led to increased practice. The researchers do not mention the role of informal interpersonal channels, but focusing on the Philippine health care system, they establish that "contact with or information from organized interpersonal channels did not contribute to the change in vaccination knowledge" (McDivitt, Zimicki, and Hornik, 1997: 111).

Some campaigns have shown the converse, with formal interpersonal communication proving the key to behavior change. A study of a media-based immunization campaign in Nigeria found the vast majority of respondents naming the clinic or health personnel as the most important source of vaccination information with a far smaller percentage of respondents citing radio messages as their information source (Ogundimu, 1994: 233). In Zaire, formal interpersonal communication channels in a child health campaign accounted for an improvement in practice. Radio messages had scant coverage, and some print materials were not distributed. Thus the bulk of this campaign was interpersonal. Researchers attributed improved health behaviors to the training of health workers and volunteers and suggest that "intense interpersonal training may produce changes in behavior among a small number of people in a short amount of time" (Yoder, Zheng and Zhou, 1991: 13).

Clearly, interaction with health service workers can be significant in development campaigns. But, as much research has indicated, a salient factor in many people's decision-making is informal interpersonal communication with friends, family, peers, and other potential opinion leaders, innovators, or early adopters. Mass communication can trigger such interpersonal communication.

A study of a family planning campaign in The Gambia found that exposure to an entertainment-education radio drama "was associated with inter-personal communication about contraceptives with partners or friends" and that these discussions, rather than the radio programs directly, led to increased clinic visits (Valente et al, 1994: 99). A family planning campaign in Ghana (Hindin et al, 1994), and family planning and AIDS campaigns in Tanzania (Rogers et al, 1999; Vaughan et al, 2000) report similar findings.

Patil and Kincaid (2000) examined an AIDS education social marketing campaign in the Philippines. They found that the campaign did not affect knowl-edge about AIDS, which was already at a high level in the country. Practice –con-dom use– did improve, however. Statistical analysis of survey data uncovered an unanticipated relationship. Campaign messages and either the intention to use condoms or current use of condoms were not, as the researchers had expected, directly related. Rather,

> [t]hese analyses reveal that there are myriad indirect paths for information to process from a campaign to behavior change and condom use through interpersonal communication and perception of peer use of condoms. In fact, it is the indirect exposure not direct exposure that creates the path from the campaign to the desired behavior (Patil and Kincaid, 2000: 17).

The researchers' collapsing of responses indicating intention to use condoms and current use of condoms together into the "behavior" category might be questioned, but that does not affect the issue under examination here: the dis-tinction between direct campaign exposure and indirect exposure through inter-personal channels.

While Patil and Kincaid reported an unforeseen finding of the impor-tance of interpersonal communication, some communications interventions rely on this channel. Family planning campaigns are often designed to encourage spousal communication about contraception, which has been shown to be asso-ciated with contraceptive adoption (Rogers et al, 1999). Storey et al evaluated a campaign that used entertainment-education, health worker education and other tools to promote family planning in Nepal. Among the explicit means of doing so was promoting husband-wife discussions of contraception. The researchers found significant effects of the campaign "primarily through its effects on interpersonal communication about family planning" with health per-sonnel and spouses (1999: 290).

Several studies posed research questions about the relative merits of interpersonal and mass media channels in achieving behavior change. Valente and Saba (1998) explicitly sought to compare the influence of mass media and interpersonal communication in a family planning campaign in Bolivia. They found that media exposure led to increased knowledge and attitude change, and to interpersonal communication itself, which was more strongly associated with behavior change. They also found that media could, in effect, substitute for personal contact by providing information to those respondents who did not have contact with contraceptive users (1998: 114-16). A media and interpersonal communication campaign to improve children's nutrition in Bangladesh signaled the importance of interpersonal communication aspects of the campaign, particularly in lower SES households (Hussain, Aarø and Kvåle, 1997: 108). Employing multiple research methods to evaluate an entertainment-education and health worker training family planning campaign in Nepal, Storey et al found that interpersonal and mass communication interacted in significant ways to promote behavior change (Storey et al, 1999; Boulay, Storey and Sood, 2000).

Outcomes - participatory framework

The evaluation of participatory campaigns has a dual focus, because these campaigns have two sets of goals. They seek to achieve some specific development end –referred to as an outcome and evaluated by "outcome indicators"– and also to empower communities via participation –referred to as process and evaluated by "process indicators". Evaluation of outcomes can be undertaken by observation of results such as clinic records. Evaluation of processes, empirically a less straightforward undertaking, was often a greater focus in the studies reviewed here. This is complex territory, in great part because the lack of agreed-upon definitions of community, empowerment, or participation (Manderson, 1992: 9; Gumucio-Dagron, 2001: 8).

This "conceptual fuzziness" (Huesca, 2000: 75) notwithstanding, researchers involved in participatory projects found evidence of success in their case studies. Dickson examined a Canadian health promotion project for older Aboriginal women. The women participated in meetings, planning committees, workshops, and consultations with government organizations concerning health education and services. Dickson's case study focused on process indicators. Citing as evidence brief excerpts from gatherings, she found: "many examples of the [subjects] reaching out and establishing external community connections, relationships, and partnerships; learning more about and critically analyzing community issues that are important to them; becoming activists, speaking out on issues and being involved in decision-making; and being recognized and honored by the community at large" (Dickson, 2000: 207).

Purdey et al report on participatory projects in Nepal that were part of a Canadian initiative to support community-based participatory development. The participatory aspect of this project began with community members choosing the projects to be supported. One project concerned irrigation. Villagers' attempts to build a reservoir had not succeeded, and the outside facilitator worked with them "to enhance the reservoir group's interaction skills and confidence", to encourage "everyone, regardless of caste or gender to participate and have their say", and to promote liaison with government agencies. As outcomes, the researchers report that reservoir was near completion when the article was written, and the group "gained confidence in their ability to work together and influence agencies... [and] overcome not only physical, bureaucratic and interpersonal difficulties but also the dependency attitude unwittingly created by outside development agencies" (Purdey et al, 1994: 334).

A write-up of another project supported by the same agency similarly concluded with a list of "empowerment outcomes" noted by the researchers: "a strong sense of community identity, an open decision-making structure, many people with recognized leadership skills... increased sensitivity toward gender and social equality, heightened self confidence in dealing with local issues, better two-way awareness of/interaction with resource agencies" (Purdey et al, 1994: 342).

Wallerstein, Sanchez-Merki and Dow describe a project to reduce morbidity and mortality among high-risk adolescents in New Mexico. This high school-based intervention was meant to facilitate community activism through "empowerment education". The program consisted of 7-week intensive workshops with at-risk youth. In this case, the participatory aspect of the project consisted of group discussions of possible "action strategies to make healthier choices for themselves and their communities" followed by work in a peer-education program or a community action project. To evaluate the program, in addition to observation and interviews, the researchers administered a questionnaire to participating students and control students. They found that youths who participated in the intervention showed a statistically-significant increase in "socially responsible efficacies" compared to the control population (Wallerstein, Sanchez-Merki and Dow, 1997: 196-7, 206).

Another type of participatory project was a "healthy lifestyle" project in Australia. The intervention was designed to encourage health behavior to prevent obesity, diabetes and cardiovascular disease in an Aboriginal population susceptible to these conditions. This program was participatory because community members worked with a nurse-educator to identify factors contributing to the high level of diabetes in the community and then designed a program of diet and activity changes. Aboriginal health workers were employed by the project, which included education and exercise sessions.

Program outcomes were evaluated through interviews and the analysis of clinical data. In terms of outcome measures, tracking four years after the start of the program showed a significantly reduced percentage of sedentary people and a significantly greater proportion of people reporting attempts to lower their fat and sugar consumption, but no decrease in diabetes prevalence in the community. Program participants showed some improvement in some clinical measures. In terms of process measures, six years after its inception the program was still in operation, had community support, and was run by community members. This, state the reseachers, is "in our opinion, a measure of success in itself" (Rowley et al, 2000).

In some cases, researchers noted that participatory goals may have been overambitious. Laverack et al evaluated a child health education campaign in Ghana. The participatory aspect of the campaign took the form of community workshops to develop health education materials for use in schools and clinics. The materials included such things as interactive posters and other materials designed to contribute to participatory learning. The outcome variable analyzed was simply whether the materials were used –that is, whether people in the target audiences had been exposed to and liked the materials. The researchers found that for various reasons, the materials were not being used as extensively as the campaign planners had envisioned. Looking at the process, the researchers comment, "situational factors posed genuine problems to the wider use of empowerment approaches and we often had to resort to a 'semi-participatory' approach" (Laverack et al,1997: 25).

The planners of a Navajo breastfeeding project in New Mexico also found that the reach of their empowerment goal exceeded their grasp: "the initial goal of community empowerment with reference to infant feeding and health was clearly beyond the scope and time frame of this project, and required skills and connections beyond those already present... it was necessary to scale down this goal" (Wright et al, 1997: 637).

Sarri and Sarri point out that "work and daily survival requirements constrained participation" in participatory projects they were involved with (1992: 118). Rifkin has suggested that participatory interventions, whether rooted in target or empowerment frames, have set "unrealistic expectations". Reviewing several community health worker projects, she concludes that community participation is an elusive concept and that health and social service professionals have been unable "to manipulate social change in the direction of their own preconceived notions of progress and development" (1996: 84-9).

A different sort of criticism of the empowerment model comes from Brunt, Lindsey and Hopkinson who ponder "the dilemma posed when the world-views of one culture are juxtaposed with those of another" (1997: 19). Getting away from such top-down imposition was part of the initial impetus for the participatory model. Yet, working with the rural ethnic Hutterites –a traditional religious sect in Canada– the researchers found themselves

> challenged by the prospect of working with a culture in which an emancipatory, grassroots approach runs counter to community norms, expectations, and desires. For example, the approach of holding forums open to all members of a community is consistent with the process of empowerment... However,... [the Hutterite] deference to hierarchy rendered the grassroots approach, which is ideally predicated on widespread community participation, largely ineffective (1997: 25).

Criticizing "the ethnocentricity of empowerment", Brunt, Lindsey and Hopkinson conclude that the imposition of this model "may unwittingly undermine Hutterite cultural and spiritual values" (1997: 25-6).

Ends/means

Diffusion and participatory interventions tend to define their objectives in terms of diffusion and participatory ends. Few studies mention outcomes related to the other framework. Part of this disjuncture derives from the different methods of data-gathering favored by each approach. Certain sorts of results are amenable to certain sorts of measurement. Researchers are unlikely to find what they are not looking for and unlikely to look for what they do not believe they can measure. Nevertheless, there is some overlap not only in the aims but also in the outcomes of projects based on each of these frameworks.

Participatory communication interventions necessarily have goals beyond the primary Freirian ones of empowerment, equity, and community-building. Each project has a specific focus. While most participatory studies examined here claim at least some success in achieving participatory goals, some, though not all, also discuss the behavior changes that are the underlying rationale for the interventions. Some studies include little information on these. For example, Dickson (2000) concentrates her discussion on the empowerment outcomes of a health program for Aboriginal Canadian elderly women, mentioning but not detailing "knowledge and skills developed in some areas" (2000: 212). Hildebrant (1994) outlines a scale of "process criteria" for judging interventions but does not detail either process or outcome results.

Studies that do note outcomes as indicated by ethnographic measures include Purdey (1994), Sarri and Sarri (1992), and Wallerstein, Sanchez-Merki and Dow (1997), all of which claim that community members became increasingly empowered over the course of the projects. Other participatory studies measured outcome indicators with clinic statistics. Rowley (2000) found some health behavior change in an Aboriginal Australian community, Wright (1997) found improved breastfeeding practices in Navajo mothers. These types of outcomes are typical of those sought in projects based on the diffusion model. Notably, both of these outcomes are demonstrated by statistical analysis of clinic data, which allows findings characteristic of diffusion studies.

Few diffusion studies explicitly mention the types of outcomes typically sought in participatory projects. Nonetheless, diffusion campaigns may well reduce social inequality, an outcome consistent with goals of participatory interventions, by extending health care to all levels of society. Just such a finding was made in Ecuador's broad-based child immunization campaign. Asking whether the campaign's effects were "equitably distributed across the socioeconomic spectrum", evaluators found that compared to previous immunization efforts, which had resulted in much greater immunization coverage in higher socioeconomic strata, the increases in immunization coverage "were shared at least equally among social groups and possibly were relatively larger among the worse-off groups" (Hornik et al, 1991: 4).

Other diffusion studies that mention participatory ends include a radio-based family planning campaign in The Gambia that was felt to have "an empowering influence" on uneducated respondents because "other forms of education rarely reach these women directly" (Valente et al, 1994: 100), and an entertainment-education soap opera in Tanzania, which was found to produce the empowering outcome of increasing "listeners' sense of self-efficacy with respect to family-size determination" (Rogers, 1999: 205).

Combinations of participatory and diffusion approaches

The studies described so far are clearly self-identified as diffusion or participatory in approach. Several studies straddle the approaches in interesting ways.

A literature search produced only one study that explicitly tested participatory and diffusion approaches to health communication against one another. Krishnatray and Melkote (1998) designed an experiment to compare condensed versions of two existing programs in India that sought to further the treatment of leprosy by destigmatizing the disease. Subjects from three villages were assigned to either a diffusion group, a participatory group or a control group, with approximately 90 subjects per group. Each subject attended a one-day health education camp. The diffusion group was exposed to clinical information via video and slides; the participatory group engaged in dialogue with leprosy patients and health workers. Statistical analysis of pretest and posttest surveys showed that the participatory treatment was more effective than the diffusion treatment in effecting destigmatization. While they acknowledge the limitations of the laboratory setting, the researchers do not address other methodological matters such as how subjects were recruited or the comparability of the three villages. Moreover, this study might be better categorized as a comparison of teaching methods than of participatory and diffusion approaches. It does not meet the participatory criterion of some sort of community input into an intervention[6].

Two other studies merit examination for the ways they link participatory and diffusion approaches and for their insightful analyses. Both of these studies describe process indicators related to the participatory aspects of the projects, and use quantitative measures as evidence for their conclusions about the outcome indicators –health behaviors.

A campaign to promote breastfeeding on the Navajo reservation in Arizona used techniques drawn from both social marketing and participatory frameworks. It began with an ethnographic study of Navajo perceptions about breastfeeding, carried out by Navajo researchers. Using the findings from this formative research, the intervention was designed to address barriers to breastfeeding. At the level of the health system, the program educated health care workers. At the community level, the intervention took the form of a social marketing campaign. At the individual level, education materials were produced for new mothers. A layer of interpersonal communication was built in to the project:

---

6 As has been noted, some other interventions that bill themselves as participatory projects are similarly lacking in grassroots input (e.g. Antunes, 1997; Díaz, 1999; Pribadi, 1986).

an elderly volunteer visited the maternity ward of the Indian health service hospital to talk with mothers about the benefits and procedures of breastfeeding. The participatory aspects of the program consisted of the collaboration with community members in the initial research and the preparation of materials, and "numerous attempts… to facilitate local discussion of the issues involved in infant feeding" (Wright et al, 1997: 631).

The program was evaluated through examination of medical records for all babies born the year before and the year after the intervention. These data showed statistically significant improvement in breastfeeding practices, including initiation, duration, and age at which formula was introduced, following the intervention.

This program doubtless owes its success to its carefully targeted intervention, its multiple message channels, and the cultural awareness embodied in its design and execution. Its clean evaluation is due in part to unusual characteristics that made it possible to study the entire community: most Navajos use free Indian health service facilities, and standardized medical forms include information about infant feeding practices (Wright et al, 1997: 636). These factors allowed the straightforward assessment of the intervention's success in achieving its outcome goals. Its process goals, however, were judged to have been less successfully met and were scaled down during the course of the project (Wright et al, 1997: 637).

A second study linking participatory and diffusion frameworks employed quite a different research method. Eng, Briscoe and Cunningham set out to discover whether there existed a relationship between community participation in water supply projects and participation in other primary health care activities. To answer this question they compared villages in two countries that had community-based water supply projects funded by the U.S. Agency for International Development. Togo and Indonesia were selected as having the best-matched sets of communities. For each country the researchers collected data from 30 villages: 10 with participatory water supply projects, 10 with non-participatory water supply projects, and 10 with no water supply projects.

As a gauge of community participation in other primary health care activities, the researchers selected participation in an immunization program –an activity that is not directly influenced by water supply, and for which detailed data are available. Analyzing immunization records, they found that villages with participatory water supply projects had consistently higher immunization rates on the immunization series selected as a measure than had the other two sets of villages. The researchers convincingly ruled out the possible alternative explanation that the findings were due to pre-existing differences between the types of villages that were chosen for participatory water projects. They thus demonstrated that immunization –a goal typically addressed by diffusion programs– can be achieved as a spillover effect of community participation in another social realm (Eng, Briscoe and Cunningham, 1990).

138 | Problems of measurement

The examples discussed so far suggest that the difficulties of assessing what works and of comparing the two frameworks are exacerbated by measurement issues, particularly the gulf between the types of measurement typically used in diffusion and participatory research. In some sense comparing these two models is a question of apples and oranges. Participation and diffusion approaches have differing underlying frameworks. Although both approaches share the objective of improving health or other social conditions, participatory studies tend to focus more on the goals related to the empowerment ends than the behavior change ends. Program strategies differ: interventions in diffusion studies are centered on mass media; in participatory studies they are centered on interpersonal interaction.

Measurement tools also differ. Most diffusion studies are based on quantitative survey data; most participatory studies are based on participant-observation and other qualitative ethnographic methods. It is difficult to compare results obtained by such disparate means. This, too, has been found to be the case in other research reviews. Researchers evaluating literature on AIDS/HIV prevention campaigns encountered "many conceptual and measurement inconsistencies across studies" that hampered comparisons (Myhre and Flora, 2000: 41). A group of specialists assessing the evaluation of malaria intervention projects in Africa found it difficult to compare study results because the studies did not have a common set of "standardized outcome indicators" for gauging outcomes (Eisele et al, 2000: 3). It might be too much to ask diffusion and participatory studies to share "standardized outcome indicators" but even within the category of participatory studies, "there is little consistency in how community participation is conceptualized and subsequently measured" (Eng, Briscoe and Cunningham, 1990: 1350).

For these reasons it seems pointless to try to compare these studies as if they were apples and apples. What can be said is that many studies claim some success and that few studies claim complete success for the projects they evaluate. It should further be noted that this review of research may be overstating the achievements of development communication interventions; as research analysts have pointed out, published studies are biased towards successful campaigns (Hornik, 1997: 53; Bauman, 1997: 667).

Crossover

The sometimes-vast philosophical differences between diffusion and participatory practitioners, added to the differences in campaign strategies and measurement methods, may exaggerate the apparent gap between the approaches. Comments from studies lodged in each of these frameworks acknowledge the need for elements of the other framework.

Many diffusion studies conclude that community participation is important in development interventions. While it has been noted that these days development projects must at least give lip-service to the notion of participation (White, 1994: 16), some diffusion evaluations evince thoughtful reflection about the value of community participation. Evaluators of a project to encourage child spacing in Jordan acknowledged that the resources put into creating the campaign were wasted because the topic was considered too sensitive to be promoted in that country. Evaluators concluded with a hallmark of the participatory approach: "one lesson to be learned form this experience is the importance of local participation in the choice of topics to be addressed" (McDivitt, 1991: 3).

Correspondingly, a researcher criticized some family planning efforts in India, not, in this case, because of the nature of the topic, but again because outsiders' standards were imposed; campaign materials were based on United Nations-defined motives for adopting family planning that were shown to be irrelevant to the intended audience. "The reliance on international motives to reach local minds invites distortion and rejection of messages", commented William J. Starosta, who appealed for participatory communication: "The client must be given greater voice in defining his own needs... communication materials should reflect the input of... groups of villagers" (Starosta, 1994: 257-9).

Similarly, a critique of an immunization campaign in Nigeria criticized its top down approach and failure to conduct adequate research into the local context (Ogundimu, 1994). The success of a family planning intervention in Nigeria was attributed precisely to such research: "involving health workers and members of the intended audience in the process of message development proved invaluable", remark the evaluators, continuing with a statement straight out of the participatory communication canon:

> This process not only resulted in improved materials but also generated a sense of involvement in the process among health workers. Such involvement should be standard procedure in all communication projects, which need to emphasize that communication is a process, not a product (Piotrow et al, 1990: 266, 272).

While many diffusion researchers recognize the value of community participation, there also exists crossover in the other direction. Although participatory communication is often defined against the traditional diffusion model (Rockefeller Foundation, 1991; Cornwall and Jewkes, 1995; Laverack et al, 1997; Huesca, 2000: 74), evaluators of some participatory studies call for activities that fit clearly within the diffusion model of knowledge transfer.

One example of this is a Rockefeller Foundation report on communication for social change. Communication for social change is defined in participatory terms as "a process of public and private dialogue through which people define who they are, what they want and how they can get it... [it] empowers individuals and communities, it engages people in making decisions that enhance their lives..." (Rockefeller Foundation, 1999: 8, 18). Yet the report poses questions couched clearly in diffusion terms:

can we create a 'transfer of knowledge' or type of curriculum that can be exported worldwide easily and economically? What's in such a curriculum? Who are the trainers?… How do we reach people in those areas of the world most in need of this knowledge but who have the smallest number of resources to access such training? (Rockefeller Foundation, 1999: 24).

Hildebrant explained the expansion of community participation and the consequent reduction in involvement of researchers and other outsiders in a South African health project in terms that suggest the diffusion model: "The amount and level of activity of the two groups varied inversely as expertise and organizational abilities of the outside people were transferred to the community people" (Hildebrant, 1994: 284).

Another evocation of diffusion principles appears in a summary of community-based participatory efforts at malaria control: "Health education plays an important role in predisposing a community to intervention", says the researcher. Communities whose understanding of the causes and prevention of disease is not "in concordance with biomedical understanding" need "new information about disease transmission and vector control prior to the introduction of an intervention" (Manderson, 1992: 13).

These comments illustrate, if such an illustration is needed, the folly of trying to rigidly isolate these approaches from one another. Laverack et al, noting that participatory and diffusion methods "are often presented as mutually exclusive", make a case for combining them: "a suitable strategy for many programmes will probably be a pragmatic mix of both approaches", a combination they term "semi participatory" (1997: 26).

The generalized goal of community participation is not just a reflection of contemporary views concerning respect for all cultures. It is also increasingly recognized by diffusion-oriented policymakers as a means to enhance the effectiveness of development programs. On the other hand, even in the most grassroots-level participatory efforts, information does need to be passed along; people need to learn skills and gain knowledge to better take control of their lives. This possibly troubling aspect of participatory programs was noted by some authors:

> The analysis also… provides… evidence that that shows that successful community-based programs require a substantial, sustained input from properly-trained external collaborators in the planning, execution and operation phases of a project (Eng, Briscoe and Cunningham 1990: 1358).

Participatory communication activist and scholar Jan Servaes echoes this point.

> Participation does not imply that there is no longer a role for development specialists, planners, and institutional leaders. It only means that the viewpoint of the local public groups is considered before the resources for development projects are allocated and distributed and that suggestions for changes in the policy are taken into consideration (Servaes, 1999: 157).

Such comments and examination of the studies reviewed here suggest | **141** that, like the claim made by Reardon and Rogers (1988) about the spurious distinction between interpersonal and mass communication, the distinction between participatory and diffusion approaches may be justifiably described as a false dichotomy.

Conclusion

This analysis has reviewed development communication projects for evidence of successful outcomes linked to the goals of diffusion and participatory approaches. Examination of many studies shows that many types of interventions produce at least some of the desired results, but under different conditions they produce different results, some more successfully than others.

One reason that it is difficult to discover a pattern of successful techniques is that most campaigns use some combination of strategies, but they do not use the same combination. Strategies vary depending on local needs, resources and politics, and program aims. It can be difficult, then, to sort through and attribute change to one or another piece of an overall campaign or to a certain combination of factors.

The Rockefeller Foundation report on communication for social change makes this case in terms of participatory projects: "Because dialogue and debate are the immediate objectives and are difficult to measure or attribute to any particular intervention, and because it is recognized that social change is likely to take a long time, this work is very difficult to assess and evaluate" (1999: 19). Concerning projects based on diffusion principles, Storey et al (1999: 272) similarly state: "the causes of any given health behavior change can be highly complex, so it is unlikely that any one message or act of communication will consistently produce action".

Certainly, the foregoing has revealed no clear pattern of success in development communication interventions. Interventions based on different theoretical models, communication strategies, measurement tools, and goals have met varying degrees of success at different times and in different places.

In the end, this chapter has been not so much about whether diffusion and participatory-based development campaigns achieve their goals but about why it's difficult to generalize about what works, or, stated in terms of the scientific method, what can be replicated. But the prospect of generalizability and replicability of development communication campaigns seemingly remains out of reach.

Jan Servaes makes a virtue of this lack of replicability: "each society must attempt to delineate its own strategy to development, based on its own ecology and culture. Therefore, it should not attempt to blindly imitate program and strategies of other countries with a totally different historical and cultural background" (Servaes, 1990: 38). It is not possible, maintains another scholar, "to identify a single solution to a complex set of problems which do not share a common history of creation" (Rifkin, 1996: 90).

One of the basic discoveries of the globalization of commerce is that blanket multinational strategies for selling products do not work. Instead, marketers are adopting local strategies based on research into the specificities of local cultures (Maxwell, 1997). In this case development communication practitioners, who have long employed techniques of research and message diffusion drawn from marketing, again echo the marketers, and perhaps even anticipated this fundamental tenet. Participatory communication analyst Susan B. Rifkin could be addressing a corporate boardroom when she asserts "community participation can be seen as a set of views and activities which reflect a solution to a specific set of circumstances. The process under which solutions develop might have some universal characteristics but the solution itself will be local" (Rifkin, 1996: 89). Even in the developed world, argue Hancock et al, interventions must be localized: "standard interventions may not be acceptable within the community setting. A standardized approach that includes flexibility to individual community variability may be more appropriate" (Hancock et al, 1997: 236).

Development communication researchers, like their marketing counterparts, have argued that foreign models and assumptions don't work (McDivitt, 1991; Starosta, 1994; Ogindimu, 1994; Brunt, Lindsey and Hopkinson, 1997) and that successful campaigns owe their success, at least in part, to their incorporation of local norms, vocabulary and understandings, not to mention participation (Wright et al, 1997; Marmo da Silva and Chagas Guimarães, 2000).

This may seem discouraging to campaign planners seeking a globally efficacious intervention template, but it is important to be aware that local communities retain their unique characteristics and expectations. Here, too, is a page from the marketers' book. For better or worse, Nike, Coke and Ford are finding that solid research into local norms and values enhances their ability to turn a profit by shaping products and advertising to specific audiences. As has been suggested by researchers from both participatory and diffusion schools of thought, such research and its skilled application can also enhance the ability of development communication practitioners to achieve their ends.

The gap between diffusion and participatory approaches is being bridged by proponents of both models, who knowingly or unknowingly have borrowed elements from one another. What will work in the local environment is not a question of which is the superior approach. It is a question of shaping project goals to community needs and finding the most appropriate means to pursue those goals.

Figure 2.1. Studies reviewed - diffusion framework | 143

AUTHOR(S)	FRAMEWORK				OBJECTIVES									MEASUREMENT									REPORTED OUTCOMES							
	media: entertainment-education	media: social marketing	media + interpers	participatory	infant health	family planning	AIDS/HIV	other-health	other	empowerment	equity	democratization-community decis mkg	build ldrshp/organizational capacity	pre-post survey	pre-post panel	post survey	quasi/field experiment	focus groups/ interviews	participant-observation	clinic data	other qualitative	other quantitative	improved K	improved A	improved P	empowerment	equity	democratization-community decis mkg	build ldrshp/organizational capacity	collaboration with govt/other orgs
Bertrand et al. (3 sites)		X	X			X								X		X		X					X	X	X					
Boulay, Storey & Sood		X				X										X							X	X						
Brown & Cody	X								X							X							X							
Hindin et al.		X				X										X								X						
Hornik et al.		X	X		X									X				X						X				X		
Kane et al.	X	X				X								X									X	X	X					
Kincaid		X				X										X								X						
Kincaid et al.		X				X												X			X		X	X						
Lettenmaier et al.	X					X								X					X		X		X	X	X					
McCombie & Hornik			X				X							X				X					X	X	X					
McDivitt		X			X									X				X					X							
McDivitt & McDowell		X	X		X													X	X	X			X		X					
McDivitt, Zimicki & Hornik		X			X				X					X									X		X					
Ogundimu		X			X													X			X	X	X							
Patil & Kincaid		X					X								X									X						
Piotrow et al. Nigeria - a		X				X												X						X						
Piotrow et al. Nigeria - b	X					X										X		X						X						
Piotrow et al. Nigeria - c	X	X				X										X		X						X						
Piotrow et al. - Zimbabwe	X		X			X								X									X	X	X					
Rogers et al.	X					X								X				X		X	X	X		X	X	X	("self-efficacy")			
Storey et al.	X	X				X								X	X			X		X	X	X		X	X	X				
Valente & Saba		X				X								X	X								X	X	X					
Valente et al.	X	X				X								X					X				X	X	X	X				
Vaughan et al.	X						X							X				X				X	X	X	X	("self-efficacy")				
Westoff & Rodriguez	X	X				X																X	X	X						
Yoder, Hornik & Chirwa	X						X							X									X	(not causal)	X					
Yoder, Zheng & Zhou		X			X									X									X	X						

Figure 2.2. Studies reviewed - participatory framework

AUTHOR(S)	media: entertainment-education	media: social marketing	media + interpers	participatory	infant health	family planning	AIDS/HIV	other-health	other	empowerment	equity	democratization-community decis mkg	build ldrshp/organizational capacity	pre-post survey	pre-post panel	post survey	quasi/field experiment	focus groups/ interviews	participant-observation	clinic data	other qualitative	other quantitative	improved K	improved A	improved P	empowerment	equity	democratization-community decis mkg	build ldrshp/organizational capacity	collaboration with gov/other orgs
	FRAMEWORK				OBJECTIVES									MEASUREMENT									REPORTED OUTCOMES							
Antunes et al.				X		X			X					X											X					
Diaz				X	X								X					X	X	X					X			X		X
Dickson				X				X		X	X		X						X	X								X	X	X
Eng, Brisco & Cunningham			X	X	X													X	X		X				X					
Hildebrant				X				X		X											X				X	X				X
Hussain, Aaro & Kvale		X	X	X	X												X						X		X					
Kalipeni & Kamlongera				X				X		X		X							X	X		X	X	X	X	X		X		
Laverack, Sakyi & Hubley				X				X		X			X				X		X						X					
Purdey et al.- irrigation				X						X	X	X							X							X		X	X	X
Purdey et al.- stoves				X						X	X	X	X						X							X		X	X	X
Rowley et al.				X				X		X		X		X						X			X		X	X				X
Sarri & Sarri - Bolivia				X				X				X							X						X			X	X	X
Sarri & Sarri - Detroit				X			X		X										X						X			X	X	X
Wallerstein, Sanchez-Merki & Dow				X			X	X	X		X			X				X	X						X			X		
Wang & Burris				X	X		X		X		X							X	X						X					X
Wright et al.	X			X	X				X											X	X				X					

Chapter 8

Communication for empowerment
The practice of participatory communication in development[1]

Maria Celeste H. Cadiz

Back in 1993, when I was leading the transfer of a project to a new site, I found myself trying to explain to town and village officials about 120 km southwest of Manila that our project was aiming for people empowerment. "The project aims to empower the villagers", I explained sincerely and with comfort that I was mouthing a previously threatening phrase that was by that time already associated with the establishment[2]. "This is if you will permit us to carry out our project in the village under your jurisdiction". We were met with reflective silence and polite questions.

It was several months later when our partners in the village disclosed their impressions as we, in our own words, attempted to woo them to grant permission to undertake a foreign-funded project coordinated by a national agency in their village.

To the town mayor and village officials, we were suspect. Coming from a state university sometimes notorious for producing insurgents with strong communist and socialist leanings and mouthing these words, these people must be leftists, they thought, which they later admitted to us. This was 1993, seven years after the decline of martial rule in the Philippines under the term of its sec-

---

1 Key reflections in this article were originally drawn out in discussions with colleagues Ma. Ciejay J. Calara and Ma. Teresita B. Osalla based on their and the author's involvement in development communication projects. They were first presented in a Lecture Series and subsequently published in Rola & Foronda (2003) p. 301-315.

2 Then President of the Philippines Fidel V. Ramos used the phrase as his election campaign slogan, and kept repeating the slogan in advocating his programs while in office.

ond post-martial law president. The then president of the republic was mouthing "people empowerment" as a slogan and I felt it safe and acceptable to echo a development paradigm I believed with conviction.

Defining participatory communication for development

How does participatory communication for development work, which capitalizes first and foremost on empowered partners? Why the emphasis on participatory approaches and empowerment? In answer to these questions, I would like to excerpt from a synthesis I recently posted in a web-based forum on participatory development communication (PDC) in community-based natural resource management (CBNRM):

> Being participatory for the sake of being participatory is not the important issue –rather, the real issue is the reason behind why an NRM (or development) initiative should involve the people in community– so that they feel ownership of the NRM (or development) research or action project; so that it truly addresses their needs from their own perspective; and as such, so that they will commit to see the NRM (or development) initiative through until it is completed. Participation of the people enables us to devote our efforts and resources to concerns that they share and consider important. It builds up people's confidence and capabilities to undertake or again involve themselves in future initiatives to address other NRM and development concerns. In short, the NRM (or development) initiatives become sustainable" (parentheses supplied).

Bessette (2004) defines participatory development communication as "a planned activity, based on the one hand on participatory processes, and on the other hand on media and interpersonal communication, which facilitates a dialogue among different stakeholders, around a common development problem or goal, with the objective of developing and implementing a set of activities to contribute to its solution, or its realization, and which supports and accompanies this initiative".

Servaes (2003) elaborates participatory communication for development as where the point of departure must be the community:

> It is at the community level that the problems of living conditions are discussed, and interactions with other communities are elicited. The most developed form of participation is self-management. This principle implies the right to participation in the planning and production of media content. However, not everyone wants to or must be involved in its practical implementation. More important is that participation is made possible in the decision-making regarding the subjects treated in the messages and regarding the selection procedures.

Beyond the micro or community/local level, participatory communication in development also applies at the international, national, as well as project management (organizational) and individual level. Its foundation is in Freire's (1970) basic model of the dialogue, originally asserted in the context of educating the underdeveloped sectors of society, now considered an important development communication model.

Fig.1. Freire's dialogue

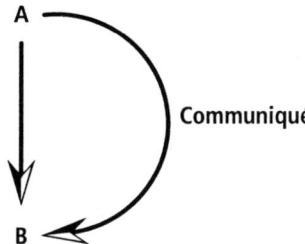

Five characteristics of Freire's dialogue

A closer study of Freire's model informs us on how best to proceed with participatory communication in development. Practitioners should mind that five interrelated attributes or qualifiers of the dialogue are in place if they are to employ participatory approaches in development.

1. Communication between equals. First, the model emphasizes equality between the change agent and the development partner. "Teacher" and "student", "extensionist" and "farmer", "expert" and "user", "communicator" and "audience", and "sender" and "receiver" interchange roles in a mutually beneficial two-way interaction. The redundancy in the preceding statement is intentional for purposes of emphasis. Our paradigm shifts from a view of our counterparts as development "beneficiaries" ("objects") to that of development "partners" and "colleagues" (fellow "subjects"). Freire thus differentiated his dialogue, which in the translation of his work was labeled "intercommunication", from a communiqué or top-down directive or memo where one party assumes a superior role and his/her counterpart is ascribed the subordinate role.

In the same vein, Servaes (2003) observed that participatory communication stresses reciprocal collaboration throughout all its levels, citing MacBride et al's (1980) argument promoting "more understanding of diversity and plurality, with full respect for the dignity and equality of peoples living in different conditions and acting in different ways".

2. Problem-posing. Freire likewise qualifies his model as a *problem-posing* dialogue, contrasted to a "banking-type" of education where teachers, trainers, extensionists, or development communicators merely "deposit knowledge", expecting the development "object" (in contrast to a self-determining "subject") to be able to "withdraw" these when the need arises. On the other hand, a problem-posing dialogue or participatory communication draws from the learner's or people's stock knowledge, experiences, and insights, eliciting these by raising relevant thought-provoking questions rather than merely presenting prescriptive solutions to development problems. In this sense, Freire's educational philosophy does not depart much from that of ancient Greek philosopher Socrates, who emphasized dialectic reasoning through question and answer.

The model shifts the role of development communicators from just serving as transmitters, conveyors, translators, and disseminators of relevant information, to that of facilitators of a process of social change capitalizing on human learning at the individual level and in community. This shift in paradigm places lesser burden on the communication specialist to single-handedly choose and provide needed answers to fill information gaps associated with development needs and problems. On the other hand, this view of the communicator as facilitator adheres to the notion of development as a self-determined and self-initiated process best sustained when it is not artificially imposed from outside the community.

The communicator can best perform his/her role in development as facilitator, consensus-builder, mediator (Quebral, 2001), and conflict negotiator if guided closely by Freire's dialogic method. A communication theory patterned after the Freire model is Kincaid's (1979) convergence model, which presupposes the goal of communication to be mutual understanding.

3. Praxis, a cycle of action and reflection. Translated into communication practice in development, a change agent refrains from lecturing and recommending development solutions without first drawing out from users their needs, own analysis of the development problem and its possible solutions, and requests for technical information. Instead, s/he adopts the adult education approach of capitalizing on the people's experiences, an inductive approach to teaching that first analyses practice, then by reflection draws from such analysis theories and generalizations in the form of lessons learned.

In his most influential book *Pedagogy of the Oppressed*, Freire (1970) expounds on knowledge (which the book's English translation labeled as "the word") being the result of praxis or the cycle of action and reflection. Action is the practical application of knowledge while reflection corresponds to abstraction and theorizing. In practical terms, knowledge is incomplete without one or the other, but is richer when theory and practice are highly integrated. Tungpalan and Bulsara (1981) as cited by Cadiz (1994) noted that too much action and too little reflection is activism, while too much reflection and too little action, verbalism.

Development work thus involves engaging in action with partners, in the process learning with them in alternating activities and evaluations or reviews of actions taken. Participatory development communication is thus best studied and theorized in action, perhaps from a critical perspective.

4. *Conscientizing.* Freire expounds on conscientization, a process of advancing critical consciousness. In a dialogue, development partners, as deliberate, construing, and goal-seeking participants, grow in understanding human, social and development processes. In this process, participants increase their willingness to take risks. They become a party to or stakeholders of social change, based on a conscious decision to engage in such change, uncomfortable as conditions brought about by change may be, and based on a deeper understanding of their realities. In praxis, therefore, conscientization takes place.

A good measure of whether participatory development communication proceeds fruitfully is when development partners' conscientization becomes evident. A challenge for researchers and practitioners is coming up with indicators or evidences of conscientization, often seen not in individual behaviors but in mechanisms and systems collectively put up by people in community. This is aligned with Chu's (1987) recommendation for development communication research and evaluation to direct its attention less on individual behavior and psychological variables to "institutional effects". I call them "system level" effects from a systems perspective. For example, did the community set up its own version of a communication center or library? Did the village officials institute a new policy or regulation providing a mechanism for people's participation in their deliberations?

Further, conscientization is not only for development partners in community. As active participants in a dialogue between equals, it should also be evident in the change agent and development sponsors, managers, and facilitators coming from international, government, and nongovernment agencies, and the academe. For example, have administrative procedures been revised to allow a certain degree of flexibility accommodating people's agendas?

5. *Five values.* Finally but not the least, Freire explicitly states that the "true" dialogue happens in a context of five overriding values: love, humility, hope, faith in development partners' capability, and critical thinking –values that a classical and empirical social scientist would rather avoid for their "vagueness" and "subjectivity". True to the qualitative researcher's ontological assumption of multiple realities, however, followers of Freire's dialogic approach to development openly claim this subjectivity and leaning in favor of resource poor partners. These values can be translated into interpersonal communication protocols such as giving priority to active and non-judgemental listening over expressing oneself, much akin to Covey's (1989) habit no. 5 of highly effective people, "seek first to understand, then to be understood". Hope is related to Covey's habit no. 4, the win-win mindset or the abundance mentality.

Elements of communication for empowerment

In initiatives in communication for development that I and colleagues at the College of Development Communication, University of the Philippines, Los Baños,

have participated in, common practical elements in communication for empowerment are present, as follows:

1   *Provision of access to information.* Based on the traditional view of
development communication as a means to disseminate technical information towards productivity, food security, and environmental conservation, this is often the primary justification for a communication component in development programs. In a project that organized rural communities to operate their own low-powered radio stations, people living
in remote areas were given access to information that would not normally be readily available to them. This is the same emphasis of communication centers in rural Philippines and telecenters in India. In our university town rich in scientific and academic information and knowledge,
a community cable television program provided information on current
events and on the community itself, aiming to contribute to a community mindset in the municipality. A mechanism to circulate such community information was previously lacking in the town.

2   *Putting users/beneficiaries and local people in control.* The essence
of empowerment is control, where local people's control spells
faithfulness to Freire's participatory approach. This element is exemplified by projects that equip local people to manage and oversee
appropriate media facilities such as community public address systems, low-powered radio stations, and simple communication centers and telecenters.

3   *Building local people's capabilities in communication.* A prerequisite of
putting local people in control of development processes where communication is an integral component is the building up of local people's capabilities. Training of local people or cooperators in communication skills, such as in community broadcasting, community or village
journalism, computer skills, and Internet surfing; as well as in discern-
ment of the relevance of information and their proper use/application,
are necessary. Often, what are overlooked are interpersonal communication skills including personal empowerment and value reaffirmation,
which are more basic requirements in participatory communication.
Likewise, managerial skills such as problem-solving and decision-making skills are fundamental. Conflict resolution and negotiation skills
are similarly important.

4   *Emphasis on small and appropriate media.* Low-powered radio transmitters that allow local broadcasting are examples of small media
appropriate for rural communities. So are wall newspapers and black-
board or bulletin board news, as well as audiocassettes, puppetry, and
youth theatre. "Small is beautiful" because small is often simpler, easier, and requires less resources to use.

5 *Learning with partners.* Participatory communication for development $\quad\mid\quad$ **151**
is a joint learning experience between equals where knowledge-build-
ing in it is integral. New approaches, best practices, and insights
evolve out of the joint efforts of partners, thereby enriching the discipline grounded on praxis.

6 *Working as a collective.* Development happens at the community
rather than at the individual level. A requisite of participatory development is that beneficiaries or partners should be organized. People are
better able to make change happen when their decisions are made as
a community or collective.

7 *Capitalizing and building on felt needs.* Obviously, people will not pay
attention to messages that they find irrelevant to their realities.

8 *Making it enjoyable.* People pay attention and participate in activities
that give them satisfaction. Entertainment as a reinforcement is simply
the application of learning theory toward behavior change.

9 *Giving them hands-on experience.* Development means change,
change requires learning, and learning by doing is rich and meaningful.

10 *Sharing resources.* Often, there is only so much of people, funds,
materials, machines and time available. But putting what we respectively do best together brings about synergy of efforts. Development
as a collective effort also springs from various stakeholders becoming
more as *shareholders.*

The process

Communication for empowerment is a deliberate and systematic process. Just as
Servaes (2003) emphasizes the framework of multiplicity, there is no best, single
approach or strategy or communication channel for empowering people.
Communication for empowerment is a process rather than a technique. The basic
questions we ask ourselves when we engage in such an initiative are:

» How do we start?

» How do we proceed?

» What are the signposts we should watch out for?

» What milestones should we aim for?

» What next?

» What is our ultimate aim?

However, we do not need to embark on such an undertaking without any guidelines in the hope of learning through trial and error or "learning by ear". We proceed through the usual project management cycle of pre-planning, planning,
implementation, evaluation and re-planning. Five generic steps synthesizing elab-

orate models like FAO's Development Support Communication (DSC), USAID's Communication for Technology Transfer in Agriculture (CTTA), FAO's Strategic Extension Campaigns (SEC) (Oliveira, 1993), and Johns Hopkins University's strategic communication and social marketing are as follows:

1   Assessment (development investigation)

2   Planning (strategy development)

3   Materials preparation and message delivery

4   Implementation

5   Evaluation

6   Planning for continuity

Simple as the listing of the above steps seems, there is much in *how* we proceed with each step that can make the process empowering and its impact sustainable. The five characteristics of Freire's dialogue, translated into the practical elements of communication for empowerment above, can spell the difference.

Selected participatory approaches

Relevant participatory approaches, most of which are directly grounded on Freire's model and educational philosophy, include community organizing (CO), action research, participatory action research (PAR) or participatory research (PR), and social mobilization (socmob) with its components advocacy and networking.

Community organizing (CO) is a problem-solving approach whereby the community is empowered with the knowledge and skills to identify and prioritize its needs and problems, harness its resources to deal with these problems and take action collectively (Patron, 1987 cited by Cadiz, 1994). A community organizer plays a key role in facilitating the process.

CO proceeds in three stages with eight, four and two steps respectively, as follows:

1   Awakening - a) area selection, b) entry into the community, c) social investigation/community study, d) integration, e) contact-building and spotting of potential leaders, f) core group formation, g) core training and mobilization, and h) formation of community organization;

2   Empowerment - a) program planning, b) project planning, c) implementation, and d) evaluation; and

3   Restructuring - a) phase-out and b) establishment of a new system of work relationship (Lucas, 1991 cited by Cadiz, 1999).

Cadiz (1999) further noted:

> In a community where people are passive recipients of changes in wider society and are locked up in dehumanizing poverty and other social ills,

community organizing is an intensive process of awakening people's critical consciousness and developing their leadership capabilities to take
action on their development problems.

Many communities in the Philippines had gone past the awakening stage, where
the arduous task of conscientization can now be bypassed and the people's
involvement in the project management cycle in the empowerment stage is the
main concern (Cadiz, 1999).

Action research, which is more of an approach to undertaking and
studying communication in development, is defined as a type of applied social
research differing from other varieties in the immediacy of the researcher's
involvement in the action process (Rapoport as cited by Foster, 1972). It aims to
contribute both to the practical concerns of people in an immediate problematic situation and to the goals of social science by joint collaboration with a mutually acceptable ethical framework. Both the people and the researcher intend to
be involved in a process of changing the system itself. Action research proceeds
logically in six systematic steps, namely, 1) analysis, 2) fact-finding, 3) conceptualization, 4) planning, 5) execution, and 6) more fact-finding/ evaluation, in a
spiraling circle. In essence, action research is the application of the scientific
method in dealing with social problems, with the aim of promoting people's liberation and growth.

I commented in 1999,

In my view, development communication is best studied in action, or as
action research. The urgency of the need to take action, often innovative in
nature, on development problems and issues makes action research the
most relevant approach to the practice and study of development communication. Not only can action research in development communication contribute to knowledge-building in the field, it likewise enables testing and
refinement of initiatives that can create immediately-needed development
impact (Cadiz 1999).

Participatory action research (PAR) or participatory research (PR) is a form of action
research, taking its questions from the perceptions of practitioners within local
contexts and building description and theories within the practice context itself
and tests them there. Its only difference from action research is that in PAR or PR,
practitioners are subjects as well as co-researchers (Argyris and Schon 1985).

PAR has three dimensions as 1) a method of social investigation, 2) an
educational process, and 3) a means of taking action for development (Ferrer and
Pagaduan, 1981 as cited by Cadiz, 1994) where the role of the professional
researcher is primarily to complement people's initiative and efforts. Among
PAR/PR and community organizing advocates in the Philippines, PAR/PR and CO
are often used interchangeably. However, PAR/PR seems to place greater emphasis on the component of social research in action than CO, while the latter is oriented more towards action and problem/issue solving.

Social mobilization is the process of bringing together all feasible and practical intersectoral and social allies to raise people's awareness of and demand for a particular development program, to assist in the delivery of resources and services and to strengthen community participation for sustainability and self-reliance (McKee, 1992). The UNICEF characterized social mobilization as a self-sustaining process; a multilevel approach that is both bottom-up and top-down; based on an in-depth and comprehensive understanding of a country's socio-cultural and politico-economic contexts; carefully planned and costed for feasibility so as to ensure that demand created in the mobilizing process is met; intensified programming at selected pressure points; a dynamic process requiring a fast-moving support response. Social mobilization uses the five approaches of political mobilization, government mobilization, community mobilization, corporate mobilization, and beneficiary mobilization (McKee, 1992).

Advocacy is the organization of information into argument to be communicated through various interpersonal and media channels with a view to gaining political and social leadership acceptance and preparing a society for a particular development program (McKee, 1992). As the term implies, it is per-suasive communication for or against an issue or concern. The major audiences of advocacy are leaders and funding agencies –decision-makers who have the say as to how resources are allocated. Thus, the main purpose of advocacy is to generate support for a project in terms of funding allocation or some commit-ment of resources. Wide acceptance of a project or its cause is also an impor-tant goal of advocacy, because political leaders will support a cause that has popular backing. Interpersonal communication plays a key role in advocacy ini-tiatives, where mediated communication is often used as supplement and as message reinforcement.

Networking and alliance-building with other organizations, sectors or communities is a strategy of community organizing aimed to enhance the strength of one's position most especially in advocating a cause or socially-desir-able action or program. In social mobilization, we need to identify our allies, or other persons, organizations or movements having similar interests and programs as ours (Cadiz, 1999).

A program can form alliances or networks with a wide variety of organizations and entities, such as different types of nongovernment organiza-tions including civic organizations, private voluntary organizations, nonprofit foundations, cooperatives, church-related associations and the church, among others. Likewise, government agencies with which a program may link with include line agencies, research and development agencies, service providers, local governments and their units, among others. Influential private individuals and political leaders can also be powerful allies, as well as local, national and interna-tional funding agencies (Cadiz, 1999).

In a society or community where development goals converge, alliance-building is a strategic move to produce desired impact in such a society or community. It provides for resource sharing and synergy of efforts among various sectors toward common goals. The following concerns in society are those where various sectors' goals are often seen to easily converge: environmental conservation, health and sanitation, moral and cultural upliftment, poverty alleviation, and disaster and crisis assistance and management (Cadiz, 1999).

Components of communication for empowerment

In communication initiatives toward empowering people for development, we now recommend the inclusion of the following components, not necessarily in their order of priority or chronology:

1 *Communication training.* Development communicators must remember that they cannot monopolize nor accomplish all the devcom work that needs to be done. Because communication is intrinsic in all human processes and therefore a key in development initiatives, all persons and entities involved need to be equipped with better communication skills. It is better if these are *development communication* skills, or communication skills infused with a clear vision of and bias for development.

2 *Communication planning and strategizing.* We recommend postponing the identification of a specific communication channel or technique until a communication plan is made. This planning process should adhere to the process described above, with proper consideration of the context in which they will be used and preferably participated in by partners and beneficiaries.

3 *Communication media design and production.* Often, development communication is perceived to be solely focused on media materials design and production. However, this aspect ought to be properly placed within an overall communication plan arrived at in a rational manner and mindful of a participatory development process.

4 *Communication technology.* Beyond the design and production of devcom materials is a need for the application and even further innovation of appropriate communication technology. Here, convergence among technologies is observed to be a contemporary phenomenon and needs to be anticipated and incorporated.

5 *Communication utilization center.* Access to information is a key to empowerment, and so is the availability of options. Agencies and organizations of various natures and persuasion produce many different communication materials, and often all that is needed is for users and information-seekers to have access to them.

6 *Communication archiving/data banking.* As information and knowledge mounts in this information age, what is needed is the manage-

ment of information to enable users to sift through and select those that are useful. Knowledge management applied in development is an emerging concern in development communication.

7 *Communication evaluation.* Because development communication is best studied in action, evaluation ought to be built in every stage from preplanning to post-implementation.

All these communication components will be uniquely configured as they would be closely tied with the specific development subject matter or concern in question, with its unique set of stakeholders, be it in food security, natural resource management, health, child rights, poverty alleviation and livelihoods, land reform, and so on.

Some lessons in communication for empowerment

The following lessons are drawn from reflections on successes, difficulties, and frustrations in my and colleagues' involvement in participatory development communication projects. Many who engage in development work already know or at least have a sense of many of these lessons. Thus, it is more appropriate to label these as "lessons reinforced" rather than "lessons learned":

1 If we are to carry out approaches toward empowering people, we should start with a clear definition or set of indicators of empowerment. From our experience, communication empowerment includes the following dimensions.

   a Participants can fulfill their basic needs (food, shelter, peace).

   b Participants have high self-esteem and foster such in others.

   c Participants can or are enabled to exercise their power to choose because:

      » They have or can access information needed in making decisions.

      » They have the know-how needed to be able to make sound decisions and address problems (application of scientific method, decision analysis skills).

      » They are free to decide, unhampered by inequitable cultural, social, religious, ethnic, gender, physical and political factors.

   d Participants exercise their choice in order to fulfill their human potential (not to destroy themselves).

   e Participants have a community or collective mindset.

2 Central in the enabling process of people empowerment is value formation or reinforcement. We have seen how many development programs have fallen short of their expectations largely due to the lack of values among participants.

3 Paradigms and mindsets may need to be shifted first in embarking on action for empowerment. Empowerment is a different paradigm or

mindset to development altogether compared to delivery and diffusion of services, information and other benefits. It produces a more sustainable impact but it works with a different set of assumptions. Many times, the shift in mindset is needed foremost in the advocate or sponsor of development –we ourselves, our researchers, our institutions, our extensionists and partners in the countryside.

4 Building of leadership qualities and communication know-how is also essential; hence these competencies should always be incorporated in technical capability building. Technical capability can be cancelled out by the lack of leadership and communication competence, but produce impact a hundredfold coupled with these qualities.

5 Communication for empowerment involves more listening and facilitation of dialogue than delivering information, more learning together than teaching the other.

6 In nurturing a spirit of voluntarism, burnout can be a common consequence. Many of our partners in development fall out in their participation because they need to attend to the realities of their more immediate, basic needs –food, clothing, shelter, and education of the children. Or, our partners can become over-committed with the various aspects of voluntary work.

7 Local politics and religion can contradict and cancel out communication efforts toward people empowerment. Factionalism can be detrimental to development initiatives, and differences in political and religious persuasions are common sources of such division in a community.

8 Who you enroll as partners and their personal characteristics count a lot in determining the success or failure of empowerment efforts. There are times when it is simply tough luck for us to find out later that we chose the wrong cooperators or the wrong community because we were unable to carefully screen them for absorptive capacity for empowering initiatives. Personality traits, such as diligence, trustworthiness, commitment, service-orientation and dedication, especially of leaders, play a big role in the potential success of a development project.

9 An indication that empowerment has been achieved is that new projects are initiated and sustained in the locality. Sad to say, this indicator is often not observed within the duration of a project, but some time after its termination. This impact often takes more time to gel than a specified duration of a project.

10 All partners need to appreciate the role of communication in their development –a large part of development communication practice should include development communication advocacy. Communication is integral as a planning, implementing and evaluation mechanism in all devel-

opment projects, whether or not its proponents recognize this. Development communication specialists cannot do all the communication work for development. Their role should be to empower all stakeholders in development with communication skills coupled with a clear vision of and orientation for development.

11 Project failure is often rooted in poor project management, not in inadequacies of the project environment.

The call for evidences

A nagging question that funding agencies are concerned with is: does participatory communication really spell a difference in development initiatives? Is investment in this human dimension of development worth it?

Thus our challenge is in showing how participatory approaches work well compared with initiatives without participation. Funding agencies' language of success is spelled in dollars and cents, and their decision-makers similarly seek hard (quantitative) evidences of "better" development. Evaluation and research need to present such hard evidences in their language, albeit grounded on a single view of reality.

On the other hand, the multiplicity framework raises the validity of subjective, qualitative evidences of people's conscientization, empowerment, and well-being, as well as of the sustainability of initiatives. Participatory development advocates themselves need to assert the validity of its qualitative, multifaceted dimensions and further develop appropriate monitoring and evaluation models, indicators, and methods. Aligned with this is the need for deliberate knowledge-building as we continue to learn, refine, and evolve our participatory development communication approaches while their environment and the context of development continuously change.

Chapter 9

Entertainment-education in development communication

Between marketing behaviours and empowering people

Thomas Tufte

Prologue

A. In 1937 a statue of Popeye was erected in the American spinach capital, Crystal City, in Texas, USA. The first cartoon character ever to be immortalized in public sculpture, Popeye and his 'father', E.C. Segar, were credited by the spinach growers. Sales were up 33% and Popeye had saved an industry in the crisis-torn US of the 1930s. The marketing of spinach via Popeye's spinach-eating had worked. But more than a commercial success, Popeye had become a role model for many children in the US who had changed eating habits and begun eating more vegetables, spinach in particular. Popeye thereby became an early experience of what later was developed and came to be known as entertainment-education: "the process of purposively designing and implementing a mediating communication form with the potential of entertaining and educating people, in order to enhance and facilitate different stages of pro-social (behaviour) change" (Bouman, 1999: 25).

B. In 1996 the Brazilian telenovela *Rei do Gado* (The Cattle King) brought a very polemical issue to the screen, that of agrarian reform and the social movement of the landless peasants in Brazil (the SEM TERRA movement). The issue was raised in the midst of serious land conflicts in Brazil. Nineteen landless peasants were killed in a conflict with landowners shortly before the telenovela went on air. The narrative –telling the story of a rich landowner who falls in love with a poor landless woman who was part of a group that occupies part of the rich landowner's estate– becomes a direct comment to the contemporary conflict in Brazil. The fictitious senator fighting for an agrarian reform in Congress became a 'true' spokesman of the landless in Brazil, and achieved –acting as senator– twice to meet in real life with Brazil's President Cardoso. This fictitious 'senator' had obviously gained clout and negotiation power. When he was killed in the telenovela, supposedly by the landowner's contract killers, two real senators participated, acting themselves, in the fictitious burial of the fictitious senator. *Rei do Gado* thus visibilized a growing social struggle, making the problem an issue of public knowledge, debate and concern. It portrayed key characters legitimizing this particular social struggle as a political struggle. It had tremendous effect, significantly increasing public attention, both the media attention and the political attention –attributed to the real SEM TERRA movement (Tufte, 1998).

Both of these examples are drawn from the margins of entertainment-education, but they are brought here to illustrate some of the positions and trends in current EE-practice. The Popeye story is a very early example of how entertainment-genres, here a cartoon, have been used for the promotion of individual behavioural change. It pre-dates by decades what later came to be known as EE through social marketing. It is also an early example of how commercial and public health interests can merge in a joint communication effort, creating a win-win situation where both stakeholders –the spinach industry and the public health of the people– gain from the intervention. *Rei do Gado* is an example of how the prime genre in entertainment-education, the serialized TV narratives (be they telenovelas, soap operas or similar genres), can serve the agendas of social movements by making the core problems visible and thereby empowering audiences and putting pressure on politicians.

EE - a contested communication strategy

The use of entertainment-education (EE) as a communication strategy in development work has grown significantly over the past decade (Singhal and Rogers, 2004, 1999; Sabido et al, 2003; Tufte, 2001; Bauman, 1999). The use of EE has for decades been seen in addressing health-related issues as blood pressure, smoking, vaccine promotion and family planning. It has also been used for the past 15 years in HIV/AIDS prevention. EE is also a communication strategy which is being applied increasingly in sectors such as environment, rural development, conflict resolution and peace-building (Skeie, 2004). At the strategic level, the objectives vary: from promoting individual behaviour change to supporting social change; from enhancing social mobilization to articulating peoples participation and empowering minority or marginalized groups to collective action. The main point here is that EE is increasingly being used as a strategic tool with a varying diversity of agendas.

The aim of this article is two-fold. First, it is to provide an introduction to the history and development of the use of entertainment-education in communication for development, from the early experiences in the 1950s and 1960s to the abundance of cases seen today. Second, it is to attempt a categorisation of the different approaches to EE, suggesting three generations of EE-communication; from the social marketing strategies which marked early experiences and continue to exist as a widespread approach, over the more interdisciplinary strategies linking diffusion and marketing with some degree of participation, to the transdisciplinary third generation of approaches. This third category is explicitly oriented toward identification of social problems, power inequalities and their root causes, most often enhancing collective action and structural change.

The EE-communication practice we observe today is a negotiated strategy with epistemological foundations from scholars and strategists rooted in different schools of thought; varying cultural traditions of storytelling; a breadth of organisational traditions, trajectories, priorities and constraints; political agendas; varying media infrastructures and, finally, with the *ad hoc* tool box of communication also playing a crucial role in determining the final outcome of *de facto* developed strategies. In providing a brief history of the development of EE and in outlining the three core generations of EE practice, some of these synergies and characteristics will appear.

Cutting across this article is the aim to deconstruct how and where EE has managed to transcend traditional dichotomies found within both development theory and communication theory –binary thinking of either arguing for diffusion of innovations *or* participatory strategy, either modernisation strategies *or* a dependency strategy, either top-down *or* bottom-up, etc. Thus, in addition to providing some categorisation of the different existing EE-strategies, the aim is also to provide some degree of substance to conceptually developing a more critical strand of EE, the third generation of EE.

A core element of contestation has been the nature of the impact of EE. Recurrently, critical scholars have questioned the possibilities and limitations of EE. The epistemological aims, theoretical foundations and working methodologies in the actual practice have been questioned. Nancy Morris (in this volume) indicates that popularity is not equal to efficacy. John Sherry (1997: 93), in reviewing 20 EE soap operas, states that "the best-designed research using powerful statistical controls suggests no significant effects on knowledge, attitudes, or behaviour which can be attributed to the soap operas". Lettenmaier et al (1993: 9) indicate that they found it difficult to separate out the effects of radio drama from other factors. Thus, some clarifications are needed in understanding the possibilities and limitations of the three different approaches to EE, for example:

» What aims and objectives drive EE-strategies?
» At what level of society are interventions sought?
» What notion of change informs the strategy?
» What results do EE strategies seek?
» How do EE-strategies work with the genre, and with the actual narratives?

» Who participates in developing the content of the strategy and narrative?

» What is the time line in an EE-strategy?

» How is the impact assessed?

There is an abundance and diversity in current EE communication practice. There is also a growing number of recent works contributing to a furthering of the thinking around EE (Bauman, 1999; Fuenzalida, 2005; Gao, 2005; McKee et al, 2004; Parker, 2005; Skeie, 2005; Singhal and Rogers, 2004; Storey, 1999). Together, this is contributing to a gradual broadening in epistemological, theoretical and methodological foundations. It is a breadth that can sustain the argument that EE is not just one uniform communication strategy, that of social marketing conceived as far back as in the days of young Popeye in the 1930s. It is much more. My suggestion for a broad definition EE is thus:

> Entertainment-education is the use of entertainment as a communicative practice crafted to strategically communicate about development issues in a manner and with a purpose that can range from the more narrowly defined social marketing of individual behaviours to the liberating and citizen-driven articulation of social change agendas.

From Mexican telenovelas to South African TV-series

If we make a brief retrospective into the history and development of EE as a sub-field of study within communication for development, the first characteristic to highlight is that, in many ways, it has followed the key theoretical and methodological trends from communication for development in general. It is reflected in the three generations of EE between which I am distinguishing in this chapter.

One of the first modern examples of EE is *The Archers*, a series produced by the BBC radio drama and broadcast in England in the early 1950s (it still runs!). Since 1951 it has communicated important information to the farmers in England, and in the mid 1950s it was listened to by two out of three adult Englishmen (Fraser and Restrepo-Estrada, 1998). However, from 1972 it gave up its deliberate educational perspective, becoming 'just' an ordinary radio soap opera. It was in the 1970s, however, that EE began to gain some more elaborate theoretical grounding. Social marketing is one of the key origins of today's EE-strategies, and is still at the core of many first generation EE-communication interventions. The use of social marketing developed in the 1970s and was quickly tied up with music, drama and storytelling. Entertainment was particularly linked to mass media-based strategies, especially television and radio. It was also in the 1970s that some of the key theories were developed, including Albert Bandura's theory of social learning (Bandura, 1977).

One of the pioneers in the use of TV-fiction for pro-social behaviour change was Mexican Miguel Sabido. Between 1975 and 1985, Sabido produced

a total of seven soap operas with built-in social messages. They were broadcast at
Mexico's largest television network, Televisa, and were large audience successes.
In countries such as India, Kenya, Tanzania and Brazil the use of television and
radio and the explicit use of fictional genres gradually developed and became
building stones in the continuous development of EE communication strategies
(Singhal and Rogers, 1999; Sherry, 1998; Japhet, 1999; Tufte, 2000).

First generation EE - marketing behavior

Several issues characterized the growing use of telenovelas in strategic communication with the development of EE strategies. Firstly, with the work of Miguel
Sabido, *a particular development of the genre* was developed, where mass education and behavior change via the media grew as a concern and ambition.
Telenovelas, which had traditionally been conceived of as entertainment, were
increasingly ascribed an educational potential as a tool both for dissemination
of information and for awareness raising and behavior change. Social marketing, as the first generation of EE, dealt with the marketing of social behaviors,
most often health related behaviors –to individuals watching the programs. EE
communication interventions have diversified in scope and aim, thereby also
changing the content of the genre. Where many of the social marketing driven
radio and television dramas have worked systematically to explore how best
and most accurately to convey messages and promote individual behavioural
change, more recent initiatives –reflected in the second and third generation EE
interventions– have had a stronger focus on communicating structural inequalities, representing and working with power relations and social conflict in the
everyday life of the characters, and by representation of such problems stimulating debate and collective action. The key distinguishing feature lies in varying
definitions of the problem to be addressed. Social marketing strategies define
the key problem as a lack of information, while the second and third generations of EE define the problem as societal problems such as structural inequality and unequal power relations.

Second generation EE - bridging of paradigms

The second generation of EE was characterized by introducing new theoretical
and methodological perspectives to the first generation EE. Stated bluntly,
what happened in the mid and late 1990s was an acknowledgement that marketing of individual behavioural change often constituted a limitation in scope
with the sole focus of securing sustainable improvement in the area of the
identified problem, be it health, as it often was, or education, rural development, etc. With a growing recognition of complexity in the social, health, and
other developmental problems to be addressed, a furthering of the conceptual basis was required, beyond the exclusive focus on individual behavioural
change. It resulted first and foremost in the introduction of participatory

approaches into many EE-communication strategies, although in an instrumental manner.

While EE from its inception has maintained a focus on individual behavioural change, social change agendas began to emerge in the 1990s as a key goal for many EE-strategies. Alongside the individual as a unit of change, there grew an increased attention towards structural elements as equally important focal points. Society as a unit of change began to be addressed. Critical social theory has been increasingly incorporated into the theoretical debates about EE, challenging more behaviorist cause-and-effect understandings of communication. This is where both participatory communication and also more recent reception theory have become relevant, suggesting more nuanced and complex understandings of the process of interpretation, meaning making, and change.

This second generation of EE was still growing out of the historical roots of EE, thus not discarding nor social marketing as a strategy, individual behavior change as a goal, or social learning theory as a basis. It sought, however, to bridge this practice, originating in a modernization-oriented diffusionist paradigm of development with elements from the participatory development paradigm.

It is only in the most recent years that a more fundamental critique of EE has grown to what I, in this article, call a third generation EE. It is represented by not only a radical shift in definition of the key type of problem to be addressed, but also a changed understanding in the notions of entertainment, of culture, of education, and of change. Whereas the second generation EE marks a more interdisciplinary and inclusive furthering of the strategies known from the first generation EE, there is now a growing voice of critique, marking the emergence of a fundamentally different way of approaching EE as a communication practice. It is an approach which is in line with some of the post-colonial critiques of the dominating paradigms of development.

However, before engaging with the most recent third generation EE, a key innovator in the second generation of EE communication practice should be highlighted. It is the South African NGO Soul City. Soul City has increasingly pledged multimethodological strategies, combining several media, promoting partnerships to civil society and grassroot activities as well as to formal educations institutions.

Soul City - a cyclical communication strategy

The pioneers of the Soul City project are two medical doctors, Shereen Usdin and Garth Japhet. During the early 1990s, Garth Japhet, executive director of Soul City, worked in clinics among poor groups in the city as well as in the countryside:

> In the early 1990s I worked both in the rural areas of Zulu land and in the townships of Soweto and Alexandra in Johannesburg. Here I realized that I despite my training as a doctor had no real influence on the basic problems (Japhet, 1999).

Japhet and his colleague Shereen Usdin realized the need for health training on basic issues such as childcare, contraception, and AIDS. The overall objective, according to Japhet, was to develop an on-going vehicle that could promote social change. From the outset, the media were considered the vehicles whereby information had been and continued to be made accessible, real, and appropriate to the audience. Through formative research, the audiences played a crucial role in the overall message development process and were ultimately the agents of change, deciding for themselves how and if to use the information provided. Soul City developed an inclusive vehicle where the core agents of change were the audiences. The unit of change transcended the individual viewers, listeners and readers, and was, instead, the broad society.

The guiding communication strategy for Soul City is *edutainment*, or, their denomination of entertainment-education. Japhet argues for a *cyclical communication strategy*, where a number of inputs are fed into the media vehicle. The outcome of the evaluation then results in a number of outputs. The overall process and the outputs in particular are then evaluated which in turn serves as a key input into the next phase of the on-going vehicle (Japhet, 1999).

As for inputs, there are two key inputs: *the audience and expert centered research process*, the formative research, and *the partnerships* established with civil society, government, private sector, international partners, and others. In a very participatory process, messages are developed and worked into the creative products, the media narratives, including TV, radio, and print. Soul City emphasizes that the model is generic, and that any narrative form can be applied in the media vehicle. It could also be popular theatre, music or any other form of popular cultural narrative. Soul City has had the opportunity to work in prime time and with the mass media and firmly believes in the efficiency of this process. However, if those opportunities are not available, the medium may well be another. The media vehicle produces two key types of output: *the direct output* (changes in knowledge, attitude, social norms and intermediate and direct practices as well as the development of a supportive environment favoring these mentioned changes); and *the development of potential opportunities*. These potential opportunities, made possible through media intervention, include a number of interesting opportunities, some of which Soul City has come far in making use of. Others are still being developed. These include educational packages, advocacy at both community and national level, and the development and use of Soul City's brand name.

Soul City has been active since 1994 and has constantly and closely evaluated the outcomes of the ongoing communication interventions. It lies beyond this article to reveal the findings, except to state that the Soul City EE-vehicle has secured changes and results both by changing individual behaviour and by influencing more profound social change processes. The heavy emphasis Soul City puts on monitoring and evaluating its communication strategy has contributed to making it an international show case which has inspired many other

EE focused communication strategies world-wide including Latin America (<www.soulcity.org.za>; Tufte, 2001).

Soul City represented a major methodological break-through in EE praxis when it initiated activities in the early 1990s. As such, it spearheaded the effort to bridge traditions of social marketing and health promotion with participatory strategies of involving the audiences in all stages of the communication strategies. It has been recognized internationally as a key innovator in the 1990s EE-initiatives, spearheading what I've called the second generation of EE-interventions.

Third generation EE - empowerment and structural change

Very recently, a new wave of initiatives is being seen in the field of EE. These are EE-initiatives which have moved beyond the 'either diffusion or participation' duality of previous initiatives. They differ conceptually, discursively, in practice, and in the manner in which issues are conveyed in the mass media. Previously, the focus was on correct and possibly culture-sensitive messages conveyed via the mass media. The focus today is on problem identification, social critique, and articulation of debate, challenging power relations and advocating social change. There is a strong recognition that a deficit of information is not at the core of the problem. Instead the core problem lies in a power imbalance, in structural inequality, and in deeper societal problems. Solutions are sought by strengthening people's *ability to identify* the problems in everyday life, and their ability to act –collectively as well as individually– upon them. Empowerment is the keyword of the third generation EE.

Because social and structural inequality lie at the core of the problem, the EE-initiative will advocate for social change –not excluding but often in addition to individual behavioral change– in order to find solutions. From a communications perspective, communication for social change is emerging as the key concept (<www.communicationforsocialchange.org>; Rockefeller Foundation, 1997; see also chapter 6 in this volume).

The most successful case of using TV fiction for social change purposes in Latin America is a genuine 'home-grown' case from Nicaragua. It is the case of the NGO *Puntos de Encuentro* that has succeeded not only in producing the first Nicaraguan telenovela ever, but also in putting a broad range of social issues on the agenda for large youth populations in Nicaragua. The telenovela is called *El Sexto Sentido* (The Sixth Sense). It included 36 episodes in the first series, transmitted in 2001, and 26 episodes in the second series, from 2004. The most innovative pro-social use of telenovelas in Latin America is currently growing in a small country with no tradition for domestic production of telenovelas. *El Sexto Sentido* was a tremendous success –the most popular TV program for the youth audience at all (see chapter 23 in this volume). Significant for this, as an example of the third generation of EE, is the strong community based approach. *Puntos de Encuentro* had a decade-long trajectory in community-based participatory work

with women. From that experience, the need grew to develop a media vehicle
that could provide voice and visibility in pursuit of their social change objectives.

Learning how? From marketing and persuasion to participation and liberating pedagogy

Inherent in ascription to EE is the understanding that entertainment genres are used
for educational purposes. However, what are the notions of education applied in
these different EE-generations? Questions of how and to what degree audiences
are influenced by what they see has led to controversy regarding the *educational*
value of such strategies. This is reflected in the different approaches that exist within EE where strategies range from media-borne social marketing strategies to
empowerment strategies as Augusto Boal's liberating theatre (Boal, 1979).
Fundamentally, these different approaches are more than mere differences in communication tools. They reflect epistemological differences in how to conceive learning and education, how to conceive audiences as either passive recipients or active
participants in the communication process, and they ultimately reflect different
aims, objectives and understandings regarding development and change.

The epistemological differences within one or the other EE approach
reflect similar differences within the overall field of communication for development. While social marketing strategies traditionally focus on individual behavior
change, there has been a growing concern for the need to develop community-
based strategies as a means to involve the audiences or target groups more effectively. Thus, the traditions of participatory communication –known for many
decades from the field of grassroot communication, alternative communication,
and citizen media initiatives– are finding their way into mass media borne EE
strategies. This has led to a resurgence of the Brazilian adult educator Paulo
Freire's dialogical pedagogy as a central perspective to second generation EE
strategies (Freire, 1967, 1968). These EE strategies range from Boal's theatre for
development strategies to JHU/PCS more recent strategic thinking that makes at
least some initial mention of Freire and his principles of community involvement,
dialogue and process-orientation (Figueroa et al ,2002).

Paulo Freire himself had no deep understanding of, or interest in, the
mass media, as he made plain in an interview that I conducted with him in 1990
(Tufte, 1990). His main orientation was to face-to-face communication and small-
scale group interaction. However, Freire had a clear understanding of the need to
deal with the power structures of society, and the need for the marginalized sectors
of society to struggle to conquer a space for their critical reflection and dialogue. A
previous interview with Freire identified a clear strategic aspect required for social
change communication: the need to conquer space, to challenge normative, moral,
and social borderlines, and to arrange a critical dialogue on pertinent issues as a
pathway towards social change (Tufte et al, 1987). Freire's *conscientização* (consciousness-raising) could be utilized to secure community involvement in EE strategies. This pathway –if followed consequently– offers a means through which EE

interventions can be connected to the questions of power, inequality and human rights. While used only in a limited manner in the second generation EE, these are the principles guiding the third generation of EE communication practice.

Breaking the silence: the forces of narratives, emotion and popular culture

Having now outlined the brief history of entertainment-education and provided some notion of the characteristics of the three main lines of EE communication practices, some reflection is required as to what the main genre in EE, radio and TV soap operas, actually consist of in terms of content, dramaturgy, and other entry points that help explain why it has become such an attractive genre in communication for development.

One of the key issues is that the genre connects so very well –in dramaturgical rhythm and in content– with the everyday lives of many people. Thus, the format is very appropriate in order to reach to large audiences. Secondly, it is a genre which has a documented ability to articulate debate. People engage, identify and involve themselves strongly with the stories told in radio and TV drama. When this is explored strategically, it may well contain the potential to articulate debate around difficult-to-talk-about issues. HIV/AIDS is the case in point. With Freire's thinking increasingly incorporated into the conceptual basis of the second and third generations of EE-communication practice, a conceptual approach has been applied which helps break this widespread silence around HIV/AIDS and also the 'silence of poverty' experienced in many countries. In his most recent book (2002), Jesus Martin-Barbero mentions the 'culture of silence' that characterises large sections of the marginalized segments of (Latin American) societies in their response to dominating social classes. Martin-Barbero brings this concept forward, originally developed by Paulo Freire (Freire, 1967: 111). It is central to understand the need for strategies to break silence. Thus, it can very well be used in current discussions about HIV/AIDS and the far too widespread silence with which the epidemic is being accepted –by the victims as well as by the populations and opinion leaders of the developed countries.

The 'culture of silence' can be explained both in the history of some of the peoples (colonialism, the masses not having the strength and opportunity to go up against the root causes of the health problems they are faced with today) as well as in them not having the indignation and energized rage with which to demand changes and better conditions of life. The result is an internalized acceptance of the 'status quo'. However, today there are increasing numbers of minority and marginalized voices that –through electronic media– have gained access and are making their cases visible and voices heard. They are achieving advocacy communication, articulating a strong, powerful, and well-founded process of communication for social change. Although it is not always easy, and many voices are still silenced, what can be documented is the use of Freirean liberating pedagogy in identifying problems and in seeking to understand the mech-

anisms of the 'culture of silence'. Freire's liberating pedagogy becomes a communication practice in the development of solutions.

The force of fiction

Why then melodrama? Why telenovelas? Why these genres as the chosen form in
entertainment-education strategies? To answer these questions, we must look
closer at what this form of narrative offers audiences. Drawing on my own
research upon Brazilian telenovelas, and recalling the example of *Rei do Gado*
which I used in the prologue to this article, there are a series of elements in the
narrative construction, and in the relationship between such narratives and their
audiences, that make the genre attractive for strategic communication.

The field of tension created in the quotidian mixtures of dramatic love
stories and subtle class conflicts has been, and continues to be, the main recipe
stimulating what I have called socio-emotional reactions of the viewers, and in
multiple ways articulating the cultural and social practices of everyday life among
the audience (Tufte, 2000). On one hand, the love drama, being central in all
telenovelas, enables the identification and engagement. For example, the concern with and responsibility for the family is central. It is present in the audience's
identification with the often conflict-oriented relations between parents and children, men and women, brothers and sisters. Values such as unity, love, and mutual understanding are emphasized, when the women are asked to give reviews of
favourite telenovelas and when asked to highlight positive elements. Negative
elements present in their discourses include issues of disrespect, betrayal, and
personal ruptures of various sorts, reflecting –as with the positive elements–
dimensions of their own social reality and personal experience.

Along with the love story, social mobility of the principal female character is often a central element in the narrative, stimulating identification among
low income women. Most of the women interviewed possessed this ambivalence
between dreaming about an easier life and focusing on the positive elements
among themselves and their associates.

Despite a clear class discourse in the readings, the physical portraits of
the lower social classes in telenovelas tend not to be as physically explicit as in real
life. Slums are seldom seen, and worker's boroughs are always built almost beyond
recognition, being cleaner, more beautiful, and always more bountiful and richer
than in real life. Nevertheless, the reader clearly comprehends who are the 'rich'
and who are the 'poor'. So, despite a particular aesthetic that avoids the exposure
of social inequality, a social interpretation of the narrative is clearly perceived in the
language the women use in reference to the characters and the narrative in general. All of them use expressions as 'to rise in life', 'up there-down here', 'fight to get
there', 'rise-fall', and 'ascend-descend'. There are many other similar expressions,
internalized proverbs saying that 'you must not give up', 'keep your head up high',
'there is a reason for it all', 'keep going', etc. These expressions seem to reflect an
understanding of the social inequality among the persons of the narrative, but the

expressions also reflect a reasoning and interpretation whereby social inequality can be explained, although not justified, and secondly, giving room for hope and aspiration for social change and ascent. The struggle not to give up and to maintain their personal pride despite social misery becomes essential.

It is this fundamental struggle that telenovelas in some way recognize, and in which *Rei do Gado* is no exception. The poor landless woman, whose shelter is burnt to the ground, happens to marry the rich landowner, maintaining the hope and aspiration of the audience –some would say the delusion of the audience– for social change and ascent.

However, telenovelas also make visible (Thompson, 1995) and consider quotidian problems (and pleasures, I would add), as Brazilian media scholar Carlos Eduardo Lins da Silva at one point called them (Da Silva, 1985: 114), problems that everybody has and fights with in their day-to-day life –relationship problems with family and friends, economic problems, personal dramas, etc. Despite portraying a material world often far from the viewers' own lives, the telenovelas strike some everyday experiences which are recognizable for the viewers, thereby sparking identification and feelings of satisfaction and pleasure. This recognition promotes a sense of social and cultural membership, counterbalancing the many processes of socio-cultural and political-economic marginalization experienced by many low income citizens in the world.

In addition to the symbolic order of everyday life constructed and reconstructed in these melodramatic narratives, telenovelas offer viewers a socio-cultural and often also political framework of reference. Altogether, the social and cultural particularities of the constructed roles and relations in the narrative are often very recognizable to the audience. These particularities are a product of, and referent to, a particular history, culture, and socio-economic situation that the members of the audience have in common. These processes of identification and recognition with "persons, problems and situations in common" contribute to and generate a sense of belonging, a sense often being of national belonging (Thompson, 1995). Thus, telenovelas emotionally enrich everyday life of the viewers, articulating and reinforcing particular social and cultural practices, thereby contributing to a particular symbolic construct of the country in question, and simultaneously articulating a feeling of member of a national collectivity (Tufte, 1998).

Because of their narrative structures and relevant content, telenovelas can promote a strong feeling of audience membership, especially into the imagined community of the nation, thereby creating the 'cultural connection', or a link, between the stories told in the telenovela and the viewers' struggles and concerns as citizens in society. It is in this perspective that telenovelas in Latin America, and similar entertainment and fiction genres in other countries, should constantly be revisited. The social and cultural role of television fiction in everyday life should increasingly be analysed, in order to understand the significance the audience give to them, and to understand how telenovelas –along with other cultural rituals of everyday life– make visible issues and struggles of common concern.

Swim in the cultural waters

Paulo Freire once said "you must swim in the cultural waters of the people", paraphrased from an article comparing Freire and N.F.S. Grundtvig (Tufte, 1987). One of the problems in early forms of EE, and in many of the media-borne campaigns, has been the lack of connection to 'the cultural waters' –and the life experiences– of the people.

Paulo Freire's ideas –developed from the 1950s into the 1970s– have regained momentum and force, amongst both scholars reflecting upon EE and a growing number of practitioners. Many of the ideas he launched and many of the analyses he conducted about how to articulate processes of *conscientização* have equal power today. Not least the fight against HIV/AIDS seems to carry the potential for policy makers, organisations, social movements and ordinary people in their communities, to come together and fight against this threat to human kind.

Freire's thoughts are today the epistemological centre of many of the efforts to combat HIV/AIDS, be it in the work of theatre groups where Augusto Boal's Freire-based methodology flourishes or large-scale media-heavy campaigns as the CADRE-run campaign Tsha-Tsha in South Africa (Kelly, 2002). In the academic writing around EE, Freire's thoughts are coming forth after many years away (Singhal, 2004; Tufte, 2003a). As Andrew Skuse points out, instead of focusing on behaviour, community dialogue is crucial (Skuse, 2003). Even the ideas of theology of liberation from the church movements of Latin America in the 1980s resonate well with the type of social critique which drives this third generation of EE. The problem is not merely one of lacking information. The problem has to do with the structural violence in society.

What is characterising the third generation of EE-strategies is a conceptual basis that moves beyond integration of diffusionist and participatory approaches. The epistemological drive is a commitment to social change, based on analysis of the structural violence, the unequal power relations and guided by commitments to human rights and social justice. These still emerging third generation EE strategies are, furthermore, combined with a strong orientation towards collective action. *Puntos de Encuentro* with *El Sexto Sentido* is an example of that (see chapter 23 in this volume). EE communication efforts are increasingly seen applied to combat HIV/AIDS, poverty, conflict and thus combat what Skuse calls "the immoral of human action" (Tufte, 2001; Skuse, 2003).

One strategy - three approaches

The growing interest for EE, seen in practice in the cases mentioned above, is confirmed in the theoretical-methodological substantiation of EE as both a theoretical and practical approach to education, development, and social change. It can lead to belief that new strategies are developing to enhance education, development, and social change on the basis of competent and active involvement of the people it is about. The development of EE is seen in many elements; the increased recognition of radio and TV drama as expressions of popular culture, the increased publishing on EE, the institutionalisation of the field as seen with the global EE conferences (1989, 1997, 2000, 2004) in PCI's yearly Soap Summit, and the curricular development represented in the growing number of courses offered in EE. Finally, the epistemological, theoretical, and methodological diversification of EE is not least seen in the work of the new generation of EE scholars, which is characterized by both the critical and fundamental rethinking of EE based on the third generation conceptual basis, as well as bringing EE into new fields of practices, as is, for example, conflict resolution and environmental protection.

Applying EE in accordance with post-colonial, alternative, citizen-oriented and often grassroot-driven development theory and practice is, as I see it, an appreciation of new languages and formats in liberating pedagogy. At the level of communication practices for social change, it is a recognition of the need to move beyond information-driven solutions and towards communication-driven solutions, beyond *logos* alone to *mythos* as well, that is: beyond reason and towards emotion, not in an either-or dualism, but in integrated strategies where learning and awareness-raising is not just about conveying information but about involving people in changing society.

Concerns about citizenship and human rights are at the core of this matter, and when it comes to the use of radio and TV drama in EE strategies, it is also about exercising and recognizing the *cultural citizenship* of the audiences (Tufte, 2000). EE, as an educational strategy, in the language used, content focus, and notion of audience involvement as manifested in the third generation EE, is treading new ground as a strategy of *conscientização* that moves beyond marketing, towards empowerment, and more in sync with the mediated and globalized world of today.

In conclusion, the communication practices of entertainment-education are consolidated into what I view as three different approaches. They are referred to as three generations of EE because of the chronology of the development –the first generation emerging in the 1970s, the second generation emerging in the 1990s, and now, the third generation gaining voice and conceptual basis in the contemporary debate about communication for development. The first generation EE, having existed for longest, is, in many critiques of EE, the key object of criticism (Waisbord, 2001; Morris, 2003 and in this volume). However, some of the voices critical to EE begin now to connect the growing use of EE with the rehabilitation of popular culture as a source of power and change in everyday life (Martin-Barbero, 1993, 2002), exploring the options to formulate critical, post-colonial, post-development (Escobar, 1995), social change oriented uses of EE. This approach represents another way of thinking about development and change, despite drawing on the same genres as in the first and second generation EE. Figure 1 highlights –with the risk of simplification– the key differences.

The definition of the key problem is focused on structural inequalities more than on lacking a specific piece of information. This reflects that the notion

of change differs –the first generation focusing on changing the behaviour and
norms of individuals, while the third generation is oriented towards also addressing the underlying causes influencing and determining individual behaviour. The
notion of how to catalyse a change process differs from it seen as an externally
driven change agent that targets a specific audience (first generation) to the third
generation EE understanding the change process as something catalysed from
within, by the community itself, or by members of the community.

Figure 1: (De-)constructing the field of entertainment-education

Entertainment-Education	First generation	Second generation	Third generation
Definition of Problem	Lack of Information	Lack of Information and Skills Inappropriate Contexts Structural Inequalities	Structural Inequalities Power Relations Social Conflict
Notion of Entertainment	Instrument: Tool for Message Conveying	Dynamic Genre: Tool for Change	Process: Popular Culture Genre as Form of Expression
Notion of Culture	Culture as Barrier	Culture as Ally	Culture as 'Way of Life'
Notion of Catalyst	External Change Agent targeting X	External Catalyst in Partnership with Community	Internal Community Member
Notion of Education	Banking Pedagogy Persuasion	Life Skills, Didactics	Liberating Pedagogy
Notion of Audience	Segments Target Groups Passive	Participants Target Groups Active	Citizens Active
What is Communicated?	Messages	Messages and Situations	Social Issues and Problems
Notion of Change	Individual Behaviour Social Norms	Individual Behaviour Social Norms Structural Conditions	Individual Behaviour Social Norms Power Relations Structural Conditions
Expected Outcome	Change in Norms and Individual Behaviour Numerical Result	Change in Norms and Individual Behaviour Public and Private Debate	Articulation of Social and Political Process Structural Change Collective Action
Duration of Intervention	Short Term	Short and Long Term	Short and Long Term

Finally, it is important to highlight the different notions of education or learning.
Drawing on Freire's distinctions between the depositing of information –the
banking pedagogy of education– and the empowering process of learning
through 'naming the world' in a dialectic process of action-reflection-action –the
liberating pedagogy, a clear parallel can be drawn to the approaches of the first
and third generation EE. The first generation EE seeks to convey messages and

transfer information through mass media in what is similar to the principles of banking pedagogy. The third generation seeks to articulate and to promote the dialectic process of debate and collective action centred on social issues, conflicts, inequalities, and power imbalances in societies. This is in line with the principles of Freire's liberating pedagogy.

It lies beyond the scope of this chapter to spell out the underlying analysis and theoretical-methodological rationale behind each categorization in the above Figure 1. My fundamental argument is that EE is not just one communication strategy. It can be many different approaches that all have in common the use of entertainment as a communicative practice crafted to strategically communicate about development issues in a manner and with a purpose that can range from the more narrowly defined social marketing of individual behaviours and to the liberating and citizen-driven articulation of social change agendas. At this stage, generation one and two have revealed some of the communicative potentials of using entertainment such as storytelling, drama or music. However, through investigation into how to use communication for development, a rethinking of development, as reflected in post-colonial and late modern thought as Escobar (1995), Appadurai (1996), Bauman (1998, 2003) and many others, has the potential to shape a very strong epistemological basis for entertainment-education communication practice based on diversity in voice, human rights, and cultural citizenship.

Part II

Mapping the field

Chapter 10

Media, democracy and the public sphere

James Deane

The relationship between media, democracy and the public sphere has been the subject of intensive and increasing academic debate over the last forty years. The most influential thinking on the concept of what the public sphere is and why it is important has been made by the German philosopher Jürgen Habermas. His conception, first defined and outlined in his *Structural Transformation of the Public Sphere* (1962) and updated by him over the next four decades, provides a starting and reference point for this chapter.

The role of the media has been particularly highlighted by Habermas in forming a crucial constituent and catalyst for the existence of the public sphere. In general, the media have been characterized principally through their perceived evolution from a fourth estate guarding the public interest into media that commodify news and are more interested in people as consumers than as citizens.

This brief discussion will not seek to rehearse these debates —covered exhaustively elsewhere— in detail, but it will attempt to examine the current state of the media in facilitating public debate and underpinning democracy. It will focus particularly but not exclusively on those countries where marginalization from public debate and a lack of voice in democratic decision-making have the most immediate and severe consequences —namely those countries where most or a large minority of people live on less than two dollars a day. It will also seek to focus on what realistically can be done to counter the negative trends identified in the chapter[1].

1 Few of the trends highlighted here are adequately researched or well understood and resources available for tracking these trends are extremely limited. Many of the highlighted trends are based on the

178 | The media and the public sphere in 2004

"The public sphere can best be described as a network of communicating information and points of view" which is "reproduced through communicative action", argued Habermas. The principles of the public sphere, which according to him initially evolved in the 17th and 18th centuries, involved an open discussion of all issues of general concern, where issues relevant to the public good could be subject to informed debate and examination. The public sphere thus presupposed freedoms of speech and assembly, a free press, and the right to freely participate in political debate and decision-making.

The importance of exposing issues of public policy and concern to public debate has been the subject of many other authors, including in the context of development policy –the best known and most influential of whom has been Nobel Prize winning economist Amartya Sen and his analysis that catastrophic but preventable disasters such as famines rarely or never occur in democratic states (Sen, 2001). Partly because of these arguments (and other, as we shall see below) the existence of free and plural media constitutes a major policy platform of much current development policy by bilateral and multilateral organizations, particularly in its role of ensuring good governance and transparency in decision-making.

Much commentary on media in relation to the public sphere over recent years portrays an almost linear process of the erosion of the public sphere and the media's role in creating it. This was already identified by Habermas (1962), as summarized by Douglas Kellner:

> Hence, Habermas describes a transition from the liberal public sphere which originated in the Enlightenment and the American and French Revolution to a media-dominated public sphere in the current era of what he calls "welfare state capitalism and mass democracy". This historical transformation is grounded, as noted, in Horkheimer and Adorno's analysis of the culture industry, in which giant corporations have taken over the public sphere and transformed it from a sphere of rational debate into one of manipulative consumption and passivity. In this transformation, "public opinion" shifts from rational consensus emerging from debate, discussion, and reflection to the manufactured opinion of polls or media experts. Rational debate and consensus has thus been replaced by managed discussion and manipulation by the machinations of advertising and political consulting agencies [...] For Habermas, the functions of the media have thus

author's own exposure of working to support media in developing countries and of communication and development issues over a period of twenty years, particularly his work with the Panos Institute <www.panos.org.uk>. Further analysis of some of these trends can be found in the Global Civil Society Yearbook 2002 published by the London School of Economics <www.lse.ac.uk/Depts/global/Yearbook> and updated more recently in "The other information revolution: media and empowerment in developing countries", by James Deane with Fackson Banda, Kunda Dixit, Njonjo Mue and Silvio Waisbord in *Communicating in the Information Society*, Bruce Girard and Sean O'Siochru (eds.), UNRISD, 2003.

been transformed from facilitating rational discourse and debate within | **179**
the public sphere into shaping, constructing, and limiting public discourse
to those themes validated and approved by media corporations[2].

Particularly over the last decade, the dizzyingly rapid change in the media, not least in resource poor countries, has made it difficult to track both the effects and implications for public policy and the direct impact on ordinary people's lives. Much of this change has been spectacular, and spectacularly positive for the evolution both of democracy and the public sphere. Later in this chapter we will document the growing crisis and shrinking space for public debate, but before doing so we need to acknowledge that the picture is a complex and contradictory one and that in many respects the public sphere has undergone an unprecedented expansion.

For most countries on the planet, the most consistent trend over the last two decades has been the decisive shift from government control to private (and to a much less extent, community) ownership and control of media. Most of the inhabitants of the planet, encompassing the former Soviet Union, China, most of Africa, and large parts of Asia including several democratic countries such as India, were to one degree or another exposed to information that their governments wanted them to be exposed to. In many countries, particularly in Latin America, where government control of media was not exercised through ownership, it was exercised by proxy, particularly where media were controlled in large part by private interests closely linked to government or other elites.

The fall of the Berlin wall in 1989 and the massive political changes that swept much of the world following its collapse led to a transformation of media in most countries. Governments who saw their power base mostly as rural populations initially liberalized the more urban based print media, but often sought to retain control of the broadcast media, particularly radio with its much greater reach to rural populations. Liberalization of radio ended up being the most important and radical change during this period which continues now. There were four main mutually reinforcing and interlocking reasons why governments decided to liberalize media in general, and broadcasting –a key tool through which political control was exercised– in particular.

The first is political, with new governments being swept into power in the wake of the end of the cold war, the accompanying collapse of one party states (many of them the client states of the superpowers) and a wave of democratic elections that followed. New governments were elected, committed to more democratic and open government and explicitly to more open media.

Second was the spread of new communication technologies, which itself had two main consequences. The first was that the Internet and other new technologies made control of information far more difficult, and therefore control of other media more expensive and less worthwhile. Second, economic

2 Kellner, Douglas, "Habermas, the public sphere and democracy: a critical intervention", UCLA. The full text can be downloaded at <www.gseis.ucla.edu/faculty/kellner>.

development was increasingly seen as being dependent on access to new technologies. Liberalization of media went hand in hand with a broader liberalization of communications, based on an assumption that liberalization of ICTs and media were essential for the effective functioning of increasingly liberalized and free market economies.

Third was globalization and the increasing economic pressures to open up markets, and the accompanying trend of freer access to information.

Finally there was a steady increasing pressure from donors on developing countries to liberalize media both as part of a generalized trend to open markets and liberalize industries and as a concerted attempt to invest in good governance, transparency, democratic government and human rights.

These and other trends had, by the early years of the 21st century led to a transformation in media marked by four main consequences.

The first was the widespread *proliferation* of media organizations: a huge increase in the number of newspapers, magazines, radio stations and television stations. In Uganda in 1987 there were two radio stations, one of which was independent of government. Today there are more than 100, almost all of them independent of government. In India there was just one television station in 1990, but following the introduction of CNN (1990), Star TV (1991) and Asia Television Network (1991), soon to be followed by many more, there has been a revolution in the number, content and structure of Indian broadcasting (although the government is one of very few democracies in the world to retain a virtual monopoly of terrestrial broadcasting). Similar patterns can be seen in many other countries.

The second was the *content* of the media transforming largely dull, formulaic programming into engaging, popular high energy programming, with a drive to maximize audiences –or at least audiences with disposable income. Programming has focused principally on capturing high spending, urban based, middle class young audiences, and content has reflected that.

The third is the introduction of *new communication technologies*. New technologies have radically reduced broadcast and print media production costs and revolutionized the delivery platform of media, particularly with the introduction of satellite and cable. More importantly, the spread of the Internet and mobile telephony, together with the rapid fall in the costs of telecommunication following liberalization of those industries, has created a communication environment where communication increasingly happens between people horizontally, rather than being directed to people vertically.

The fourth –largely a consequence of the new technologies– is a fresh *interactivity of media*. In 1926, the German playwrite and author Bertolt Brecht wrote:

> The radio would be the finest possible communication apparatus in public life, a vast network of pipes. That is to say, it would be if it knew how to receive as well as transmit, how to let the listener speak as well as hear, how to bring him into a relationship instead of isolating him. On this prin-

ciple the radio should step out of the supply business and organize its lis- · | **181**
teners as suppliers.

The 1990s saw the dawn of a new radio age, an age where radio did begin to organize its listeners as suppliers, with the flourishing not only of many hundreds of radio stations but many types, and a new era of interactivity for radio broadcasting. For a large minority if not a majority of people on the planet, radio remains the most important communication medium available in terms of its accessibility and reach. During the 1990s, liberalization of radio awakened a long smothered public demand for debate and discussion. Liberalization unleashed a pent up energy both from the private commercial sector, which was responsible for most of the mushrooming of radio, and from a burgeoning community radio sector. The latter, through the commitment of thousands of community organizations (such as AMARC, the World Association of Community Broadcasters) and individuals and the steadily increasing interest of donors, has flourished.

From Kenya to Nepal, Uganda to Sri Lanka, and in dozens of other countries, talk-shows, discussion programs and phone-ins have become some of the most popular programming. Focusing on everything from football to the upcoming national elections, from "Big Brother" to HIV/AIDS, they have sometimes done as much as investigative journalism to shine a light on social and political issues. Even in countries where liberalization has been slow or non existent, there are important examples of talk radio catalyzing major social change. In China for example, the well known radio journalist Xin Ran (2003) has published an internationally best selling account of how her radio talk-show –entitled *Words on the Night Breeze* and principally made up of contributions from women from all over the country– for the first time brought to public attention the appalling accounts of hidden, unnoticed discrimination and abuse. In Uganda, radio stations hold regular *Ekimeeza*, public debates on current issues bringing together perhaps 400 people, the results of which are broadcast. Civil society has enjoyed unprecedented access to the airwaves from radio producers hungry for opinion and perspective. The 1990s and first years of the 21st century saw massive, unprecedented and complex social changes across the world, and much of that was shaped by these new interactive and dynamic media environments.

Such debate and discussion is happening for many reasons in many different media. It is happening first and foremost because it is popular, attracting large audiences and therefore popular with advertisers. Radio talk-show hosts themselves have become well known personalities and have demonstrated real leadership in hosting issues of public concern. It is happening because many of these countries have been starved of spaces for public discussion and debate.

Habermas originally argued that a public sphere, independent of the reigning governments, was established out of a space carved out in the coffee houses of enlightenment Europe. The radio revolution in many developing countries can arguably be seen as a similar phenomenon, where public debate over radio meshes with the billions of informal and interconnecting conversations enabled by the new technologies of mobile telephony and the Internet. Information and communication have become impossible to control, and many countries where information used to be subject to absolute government control have seen unprecedented public debate and the arguable emergence of a fresh kind of public sphere. New spaces have been formed, independent of government.

The spread of more democratic forms of government, the liberalization of media and telecommunication systems, the ensuing proliferation, popularity and interactivity of the media –all of these suggest a substantial expansion of the public sphere for much of humanity.

How public is public?

However, Habermas' original thesis was criticized because those who he posited as first forming a public sphere where independent political debate could take place excluded large parts, if not the majority of populations. They tended to be male, urban based with disposable incomes, educated and literate. The original conception of the public sphere particularly excluded the poor and women.

The same exclusion is not only happening now, but is increasingly happening with much of the world's media. The early energy and dynamism following liberalization, and much of the idealism and hope that accompanied it among journalists, radio talk show hosts and others is declining in the face of a powerful set of trends. Most of these trends are eroding the public sphere and particularly from a development perspective, transforming what were a series of government monopolies into a series of private oligopolies.

When viewed from the perspective of development, a growing crisis may be emerging, a crisis marked by a collapse (or sometimes still birth) of public interest media. A new competitive market among media has brought innovation, dynamism and often greatly enhanced democratic debate, and has in a myriad of cases in many countries brought about profound social change, much of it positive.

But while the proliferation of media in the wake of liberalization in many countries was initially marked by an upsurge of public debate on a whole range of issues, evidence is growing that, as competition intensifies, content is increasingly being shaped by the demands of advertisers and sponsors who pay for the newly liberalized media, and an increasingly intense focus on profitability. The result is more urban biased, consumer oriented media which have diminishing interest in or concern for people living in poverty.

There are four main trends.

Alongside the rapid growth in all forms of media is the growing power of advertising. Unless subsidized by wealthy individuals or political parties, by the state, by donors or by community contributions, media organizations need to make a profit to survive. The vast majority of media organizations which have emerged in the new media landscape are dependent on advertising. Advertisers are obviously interested in those who are likely to buy their products, which is normally a young, middle class audience with disposable income (increasingly a stronger market in media terms in developing countries than the traditional ABC1 market of highly educated high income individuals). Content of most media is increasingly aimed at attracting advertisers and is therefore focused on the main preoccupations of those advertisers want to sell to. Inevitably this means that issues of concern to those in rural areas, the poor and other minorities are not a commercial priority.

The dynamic between media and profit and particularly advertising has been extensively commented on in many countries over many years, but in developing countries the issue takes on an added dimension. For most people, particularly those living in rural areas, the media are often the principal source of information beyond their communities and outside their own informal communication networks. This includes information on everything from political developments to agricultural techniques, from weather to HIV/AIDS prevention and of course a panoply of other issues. Poor people, especially the almost three billion people in the world living on less than two dollars a day, do not constitute a market for advertisers. While media liberalization has had many benefits in terms of opening up new forms and spaces of public debate, there is no incentive for this debate to encompass the concerns of those living in poverty.

As a consequence, those concerns are increasingly being ignored. Editors and journalists increasingly report pressures to focus on a consumer oriented, advertising driven media agenda. This is not a problem in terms of creating spaces for public debate if other media, particularly public service media, are available to fill in the gaps. However, the former state monopoly broadcasters and media organizations, who retain the greatest capacity to reach rural and marginalized populations, are facing intense competition from commercial organizations as governments reduce budgets. As a consequence many are in crisis.

As well as a shift to more commercially and consumer oriented content, there are reports of cutting of language services, particularly in minority languages, and of transmitter capacity. In this sense, the digital divide –a phrase used in relation to the Internet, mobile telephony and other digital technologies– is being reflected in a much broader, deeper and perhaps more fundamental information divide between urban and rural, rich and poor. This is an information divide being shaped by far more than access to technology, it is one shaped by access to content relevant to people's lives, and the capacity of people to have their voices heard in the public domain. In countries where incomes are so low, such access and such capacity to express a voice have much more severe and immediate human consequences than in richer countries.

Journalism as a profession is dramatically changing and concepts such as investigative journalism are arguably under siege. Journalists themselves who want to explore and investigate development stories affecting those from outside the capital, are finding it more and more difficult to get either resources or attention from their editors. Rarely rewarding and always a difficult and dangerous profession, investigative journalism is arguably becoming steadily less attractive and there is little incentive and decreasing inclination among many journalists to focus on development issues since this is a poor career move. With no paying market for poverty related content, incentives for journalists, editors, publishers and owners to prioritize it are declining. Journalism training is also under pressure, particularly that which has a public interest remit, and journalism schools in some developing countries are finding that graduates are as often snapped up by the public relations and advertising industries as they are by news organizations.

Concentration of media ownership

The second trend, linked to this increasing power of advertising, is the growing concentration of media ownership –at the global, regional and national levels. Concentration of media ownership at the global level has been well documented, particularly by Robert McChesney (1999), who argues that there has been an explosion in recent years in corporate media, an explosion which fundamentally undermines public life. Chronicling a wave of mergers and acquisitions during the 1990s McChesney points to a series of fundamentally anti-democratic trends which are eroding the public sphere both at national and global levels.

Much has been written over many years arguing that a cultural imperialism is in play with giant Western media and communication conglomerates determining a set diet of content to be consumed in all corners of the world. The picture is more complex than this with a long catalogue of failures of Western organizations assuming that what is popular in the US will be popular in India, China or Nigeria. India provides the most dramatic example of this where Star TV and other satellite providers had to rewrite their business plans in the 1990s to adapt to consumer demand for indigenous content, content which ended up creating new cultural hybrids meshing influences from many different sources.

> Given the rapid growth of television in India, from two channels to over eighty in a decade, cloning might be one means of coping with the imperative to fill the program hours. Original imported programs run the risk of failing completely in the foreign market or at best catering to a small minority. For example, US or UK programs cater only to those well educated in English and somewhat Anglophile. While cloning offers some hope of achieving a domestic ratings winner, this is by no means guaranteed. The clone in another country could fail utterly, do just as well, or even outstrip the original program's performance in its own country[3].

Nevertheless, this concentration of media ownership is also a globalization of media ownership, with a very small number of giant global corporations owning and controlling media in all parts of the world. If such concentration of media ownership is undermining national public spheres, it is also undermining a global

3 Media Development, Dr. Amos Owen Thomas, School of Marketing & Management, Griffith University.

public sphere. The alternative is a reinvention of public service media which, according to McChesney, need to transform national boundaries.

In the end the goal should be not merely to have a series of national media systems with dominant public service components but to have a global public sphere as well, where people can communicate with each other without having the communication filtered and censored by corporate and commercial interests.

The third trend is the growing reliance for most people on the planet for their news on a small number of increasingly powerful northern based news providers, such as the British Broadcasting Corporation (BBC), Reuters and Cable News Network (CNN). While the costs of equipment and technology for news organizations have decreased, the costs in skills and distribution required for a substantial news gathering operation have increased markedly. Most developing country media are heavily reliant for their coverage of international news stories, including on issues as fundamental to their audiences interests as stories on globalization, trade and international politics. In newly democratic countries in the South, and particularly within civil society, there is a renewed and growing frustration at the southern media's dependence on what are perceived to be partial, biased or at least fundamentally Northern-centric news organizations for international coverage and the setting of news agendas.

There have been important exceptions to this trend, with the emergence of some new major southern based news organizations, such as Al Jazeera, which has rapidly established a greater credibility within the Arab world, particularly following the events of September 11, 2001 –albeit amidst intense controversy. But the emergence of networks such as Al Jazeera have been exceptions to a trend where many services established to provide news from a developing country perspective are facing financial difficulties. While there are important initiatives among southern news organizations (either commercial in the form of large media conglomerates such as the Nation Media Group, or non commercial such as several news exchange projects), none of these look at all like challenging the dominance of the northern news organizations.

From globalization to parochialism

Finally, there is a growing pressure and intimidation of media in the context of the war on terrorism and at a time of global insecurity in the wake of the events of September 11. Never before has communication across boundaries and between cultures been more important in nurturing a global public sphere, and never before has global security depended on the existence of channels that promote such communication. Arguably those channels have rarely been more fragile.

The prevailing context for much development discourse work before September 11 was focused on globalization and the associated interdependence and interconnectedness of all peoples, a process fundamentally dependent on and shaped by increasingly rapid flows of information around the world. The events of and following September 11 heralded a marked shift in international political attention away from globalization, a shift accompanied by an increased parochialism in communication channels.

This was most clearly demonstrated in media reporting of the ensuing conflicts, especially in Iraq. Several major western media organizations (including the New York Times, the Washington Post and CNN) have publicly questioned their own coverage of the run up to the Iraq war. These events saw the increasing credibility of new media players such as Al Jazeera who have, amidst controversy, constituted a major challenge to the dominance of western based news networks. In the US the emergence and rapid popularity of other new players such as Fox TV, explicitly more patriotic in its news values in coverage of the war on Iraq and the war on terror, has reinforced a trend towards a more fragmented media industry. These are among many developments that suggest a growing fragmentation of mainstream media reporting at a time of international crisis. Many countries, such as Uganda, have passed new draconian laws making support for terrorism by media organizations, a capital offence.

At a time when the international community is so divided, these trends might have been expected to prompt an increase in support for organizations seeking to foster informed public discourse and communication at national and international levels. Much evidence suggests that the contrary has happened. At the international level, many of the main international NGOs dedicated to generating perspectives from developing countries and broader information flows across boundaries and cultures have suffered substantial uncertainty in funding. At the national level, decisions by many donor organizations to provide budget support to governments have often resulted in a shift of resources away from civil society organizations, many of them dedicated to fostering informed dialogue in society.

In summary, this is a complex, contradictory revolution marking an extraordinary transformation over little more than a decade. New freedoms, a blossoming of public debate, a resurgent community radio movement, a proliferation of channels and titles across all media, a dynamic interplay between old and new technologies, the increasingly globalized nature of information and communication industries and connectivities, the loosening of government control over information, have all characterized this revolution. So, though, have a growing concentration of media ownership, a marginalization from communication agendas of those who do not constitute a paying market, a continuing, deepening North-South divide in information flows and a new threat of self censorship even among some of the most august news organizations in the world.

What is to be done?

While many of the trends summarized above are new, or are taking on fresh and important complexions, their underlying themes have been the source of discussion and debate for many years. There have been concerted attempts to highlight such trends in the past and put in place strategies to combat them, most notably the MacBride Roundtable and the ensuing debate over the New World Information and Communication Order in the 1980s. Donor organizations have provided funding to projects to encourage public debate and advance the role of the media in holding governments to account, but such funding is woefully inadequate, particularly when held against the vast sums being spent globally.

The nurturing of a global public sphere will depend on four main things happening.

» The first is to develop a better understanding of these trends and their impact on people's lives. Evidence of the link between public debate and development impact is growing, such as for example in the field of HIV/AIDS where evidence strongly suggests that countries where a vibrant public sphere has existed have been far more successful than those where it is limited (Scalway, 2003); and from the introduction of poverty reduction strategies by the World Bank, which are now the central pillar for poverty reduction in many developing countries but where public debate and consultation has been heavily criticized for being too limited and transparent, including within the media. The Power Reduction Strategy Papers (PRSP) process has been seriously undermined as a result (Warnock, 2002). Much more work needs to be done in order to track and understand these changes.

» The second is the successful evolution of an increasingly vibrant and effective alternative media movement. Conferences such as the *Our Media* Conference in Porto Alegre in July 2004[4] and many thousands of other initiatives, demonstrate the vitality and growth of alternative media. A new credibility and hope is attaching to different forms of media, from websites to news and features services as publics become hungry for different forms of news and a growing community media movement worldwide, while desperately under-resourced and fragile, is growing strongly.

» The third is the Internet. A great deal has been written on the potential of the Internet to create a new independent global public sphere, and its potential was perhaps most feverishly captured in the Declaration of Independence of Cyberspace by the Electronic Frontier Foundation in 1996:

> Governments of the Industrial World, you weary giants of flesh and steel, I come from Cyberspace, the new home of Mind. On behalf of the future, I ask you of the past to leave us alone. You are not welcome among us. You have no sovereignty where we gather. We have no elected government, nor are we likely to have one, so I address you with no

4 More details can be found at <http://www.ourmedianet.org>.

greater authority than that with which liberty itself always speaks. I declare the global social space we are building to be naturally independent of the tyrannies you seek to impose on us. You have no moral right to rule us nor do you possess any methods of enforcement we have true reason to fear[5].

Similarly documented has been the steady domination of the Internet by the same media and communication conglomerates that dominate much of the rest of the global communication infrastructure. Despite this, the Internet is the most decentralized, adaptive and interactive technology in existence and its use historically by civil society has been a core component in the growing influence of civil society in recent years. The gender movement, so often routinely excluded from earlier discussions of the public sphere, has in particular succeeded in successfully exploiting the creation of this new independent space.

The Internet also suffers from the same –but far more acute– division in access as the media, with poor, rural and marginalized communities generally those with least access to it, and with content least reflective of their needs.

The fourth, and perhaps most fundamental, is the creation of an environment where these trends and issues can be discussed in ways that command credibility amongst a broad audience. These issues are not and should not be limited to a small number of highly committed social activists, but to a broader swathe of people who are directly and indirectly affected by them (these might include for example mainstream journalists concerned about corporate interference in setting news agendas as well as development and civil society organizations). Very few global fora exist where the relationship between media and the public interest can be debated constructively in a way that can engage a broad spectrum of opinion.

The role of the media in the modern information society received scant attention at the latest World Summit on the Information Society (December 2003) compared to new communication technologies. Debates over the connection between media and poverty seem unlikely to progress substantially within the context of the next phase of the WSIS, and the opportunities of drawing the mainstream media themselves into such a debate appear slim. Before and since the debates over the New World Information and Communication Order in the 1980s, the subject of media content, ownership and relationship to public interest has been a subject of bitter disagreement.

The right to communicate

The long-standing problems associated with the role of the media in relation to development surfaced prominently in the approach to WSIS, as many information and communication NGOs had come together with a central vision "grounded in

5 Barlow, John Perry (1996) *Declaration of Independence of Cyberspace*, distributed via Internet and elsewhere.

the Right to Communicate, as a means to enhance human rights and to strength-
en the social, economic and cultural lives of people and communities".

This grouping, Communication Rights in the Information Society
(CRIS), was highly effective both in assembling a large number of civil society and
media advocacy organizations working on issues of information, and in engaging
positively and highly efficiently in the WSIS preparatory process. However, criticisms were expressed by some media freedom organizations, most notably by the
World Press Freedom Committee and Article XIX, over some articulations of this
right to communicate. They feared that successful establishment of such a right
could lead to the imposition of controls over independent media[6].

The sometimes bitter debates, redolent of those of the New World
Information and Communication Order in the 1980s, exemplified the continuing
challenge of opening up a serious international public debate of the role of the
media in the 21st century. While social advocacy organizations are increasingly
concerned with the power and lack of accountability of concentrated and consumer oriented media, media freedom organizations remain concerned about
any formal attempt to erode hard-won media freedoms.

The intimate connection between public discourse through the media
and poverty has been highlighted for many years, but open and constructive discussion of this and other issues of social concern has often proved difficult. The
rapidly changing communication environments in some of the poorest countries
and the growing importance of communication for alleviating poverty suggest
that new ways of discussing these issues, with the central inclusion of mainstream media and affiliated organizations, is becoming increasingly urgent.
Currently however, credible fora which can bring together mainstream, alternative and social advocacy organizations, as well as government and development
decision-makers on these issues are in short supply. Given the experience over
the years such a debate would almost certainly need to be led by non governmental (particularly media) actors.

A new language and discourse is required which places these issues
firmly within the context of the current challenges facing humanity at the beginning of the 21st century, and within the realities and complexities of the new
communication environment. An attempt was made by the Panos Institute
(involving this author) with the Rockefeller Foundation to reach a level of consensus among those who have so often disagreed on debates of the role of the
media in the public sphere. That meeting drew together media freedom organizations with social activists working on these issues (particularly those advocating
a right to communicate) and sought to reach sufficient agreement that could be
used as a foundation from which a more constructive and broader debate could
be founded. The declaration from that meeting is represented below.

6 Further information can be found at <www.crisinfo.org>, <www.article19.org/docimages/1512.doc>
and a particularly strongly worded attack by the World Press Freedom Committee published on the US
State Department website, <www.state.gov/e/eb/rls/othr/20101.htm>.

If there is to be determined and effective action to reverse the remorseless erosion of the public sphere –principally caused by the growing disinterest of the media in public interest issues– then a basic platform needs to be agreed upon. The Bellagio statement is one potential component of a far more intensive process that should be undertaken.

Bellagio Symposium on Media, Freedom and Poverty Statement

The Bellagio Symposium on Media, Freedom and Poverty came together to explore the links between and develop a better understanding of current media trends and poverty. This meeting was in part an attempt to bridge differences in approach among organisations involved in media freedom, media pluralism and social advocacy. While we have differences in perspective, we agreed on the following points.

We are particularly concerned that in the World Summit on the Information Society some of the measures being considered run counter to freedom of expression; that insufficient attention is being paid to the crucial role of the media, and to the importance of poverty reduction; and that there is inadequate mapping of development objectives against the proposed actions.

We believe that urgent attention needs to be brought to bear on issues of media and poverty in ways that are rooted in the principle of freedom of expression.

1   Freedom of expression, as expressed in Article XIX of the Universal Declaration of Human Rights, is a fundamental right which underpins all other human rights, and enables them to be expressed and realised. The eradication of poverty is essential to the realisation for all peoples of the aspirations in the Universal Declaration of Human Rights.

2   People living in poverty face particular obstacles to achieving freedom of expression and access to the media which are associated with the conditions of poverty. These obstacles include economic, social, educational, logistical, and political factors. Economic obstacles include the cost of equipment for production, distribution and reception, and the costs of licences and operation; social obstacles include gender and language; educational obstacles include literacy and language; logistical obstacles include transport, physical access and electricity; political obstacles include repression and lack of will of many states to allow democratic expression and to give voice to the most marginalised groups, as well as censorship by government, commercial and social interests.

3   The interests and concerns of people living in poverty are not sufficiently exposed in the media. Economic and market pressures on
the media are tending to deprioritise journalistic investigation and
reporting on issues of social and public concern. Because the poor
often do not constitute a viable market, issues of concern to them
are increasingly and particularly marginalised. New strategies, which
address these issues and reinforce freedom of expression, need to
be devised. Threats to media freedom and freedom of expression
continue to come from undue political influence but we are also
concerned about issues of economic control and pressure.

4   We recognise that these obstacles need to be overcome in the interests of society as a whole, and not only because in many societies
poor people are the majority. When people do not have a voice in
the public arena, or access to information on issues that affect their
lives, and where their concerns are not reasonably reflected in the
media, development tends to be undermined and catastrophes
such as famines are less likely to be averted. Lack of access to communication undermines the capacity of the poor to participate in
democratic processes. Frustration and alienation over lack of means
of expression lead to disaffection with the political process resulting
in apathy or violence.

5   Realisation of freedom of expression for people living in poverty
requires: media pluralism and diversity, including diversity of forms
of ownership; more equitable access to communication; support for
cultural and linguistic diversity; and promotion of participation in
democratic decision-making processes.

6   Action points

    i   There is a growing number of initiatives taken by the media, by
people living in poverty and by other actors to address poverty
reduction, including issues of voice, content and access to information and communication. These should be encouraged and actively supported. Best practices should be publicised and exchanged.

    ii Access for the disadvantaged to information and communica-
tion should be an integral part of any strategy to reduce poverty. Such a strategy should include participatory media.

    iii Community media should be specifically encouraged, including
through access to licences and spectrum allocation. Frequencies
should be allocated in a balanced way amongst community, commercial and public service media. Broadcast licensing should be
administered by independent and transparent regulatory bodies.

iv There is a need for increased resources, better coordination and targeting of training programmes; including training journalists in poverty related issues.

v Involvement of media in education, and the development of media literacy, should be promoted.

vi Public service broadcasting mandates should include obligations to provide information and education to address issues of poverty; and to ensure that public service broadcasters provide universal service.

vii National communication policies should be developed that address access to communication for people living in poverty. Such policies should be developed and implemented in a transparent and participatory manner.

viii Professional standards and ethics of journalism, as defined by journalists themselves, should be supported and encouraged. The journalistic ethic should include sensitivity to issues of poverty.

ix Journalists should be provided with living standards and working conditions which enable them to realise these professional standards.

x South-South and South-North exchanges between media and journalists should be encouraged, including personnel, training, equipment and content.

xi Support should be provided for civil society organisations in working with the media.

xii Mechanisms should be encouraged for making newspapers more affordable and more available to the disadvantaged, including measures to cut the price of newsprint and equipment.

xiii The use of ICTs to provide the media with more diversity of information sources should be promoted; together with combinations of traditional and new information technologies to facilitate better access to communication for people living in poverty.

xiv Resources should be provided, including by public authorities, to address shortcomings in communication access for those living in poverty and to remove cost and other barriers, in ways that do not compromise freedom of expression.

xv More research needs to be undertaken on the implications of current media trends for poverty reduction.

5th October, 2003

Chapter 11

From NWICO to global governance of the information society
Ulla Carlsson

We, the representatives of the peoples of the world, assembled in | **193**
Geneva from 10-12 December 2003 for the first phase of the
World Summit on the Information Society, declare our common
desire and commitment to build a people-centred, inclusive and
development-oriented Information Society, where everyone can
create, access, utilize and share information and knowledge,
enabling individuals, communities and peoples to achieve their
full potential in promoting their sustainable development and
improving their quality of life, premised on the purposes and
principles of the Charter of the United Nations and respecting
fully and upholding the Universal Declaration of Human Rights.

Declaration of Principles, "Building the Information Society: A
Global Challenge in the New Millennium"

These words preface the political plan of action adopted by the World Summit on the Information Society (WSIS) in Geneva in December 2003. This was not the first time the international community had set out to draft policy on information and communication issues in a global arena.

Information and communication have occupied the United Nations system since its early years. In the first years after the war, optimism prevailed: technological advances were seen to hold the promise of enabling all the peoples of the world to exchange and diffuse information at will, thereby promoting knowledge and mutual understanding among peoples and nations. As early as 1946, one year after the UN was founded, the 'free flow of information' principle was agreed on. Two years later, in 1948, the UN summoned its member nations to an International Conference on Freedom of Information; that same year, the UN also adopted a Universal Declaration of Human Rights. The principles were adopted in consensus. The framework for the normative role UNESCO assumed in this period is perhaps best captured in the following excerpts from the two principal documents:

> All states should proclaim policies under which the free flow of information within countries and across frontiers will be protected. The right to seek and transmit information should be insured in order to enable the public to ascertain facts and appraise events... (*Calling of an International Conference on Freedom of Information*, FN resolution 1946-12-14).

> Everyone has the right to freedom of opinion and expression; this right includes freedom to hold opinions without interference and to seek, receive and impart information and ideas through any media and regardless of frontiers (*Universal Declaration of Human Rights*, Article 19, FN 1948-12-10).

It was with the founding of the UN and UNESCO that norm-setting in relation to information and communication was elaborated on an international plane. Otherwise, communication was one of the very first sectors to be subjected to international regulation. The International Telegraph Union (ITU, subsequently International Telecommunication Union), one of the oldest international organizations, was founded in the mid-nineteenth century. In 1947, the ITU was made a specialized agency of the United Nations and charged with regulating and planning telecommunications services throughout the world.

In the beginning, the normative role of the UN and UNESCO was closely aligned with work relating to the protection of human rights, but in the 1960s technological advances in the field of telecommunication introduced a need for international regulation of an entirely new kind, such as rules for the use of space for communications satellites. Consequently, questions concerning information assumed a new political valence or charge, and discussion of them revolved increasingly around the doctrine of free flows of information. The spirit of consensus that had prevailed in 1948 had degenerated into a climate of confrontation and conflict. The debate was to have a crucial influence on the work of UNESCO, which was the main arena for these issues for nearly twenty years, from the late 1960s to the mid-1980s.

Chronic imbalances in international information flows became the focus of attention, and a new doctrine concerning 'the free flow of information' emerged. The situation had its roots in the tumultuous process of national liberation from imperial powers that had swept through Asia and Africa in the preceding decade. The new states demanded recognition of their sovereignty –in politics, economics and the cultural sphere. At the same time, the new nations were in need of aid from the industrialized countries of the North. National and economic development was the first priority, and the mass media were seen to play key roles in the process.

In the Cold War era the newly independent countries of the third world were of strategic importance to both East and West. Development aid was an important factor in 'winning the hearts and minds' of developing nations. New patron-client relationships emerged; old, established ones changed. The successes achieved by the oil-producing countries of OPEC in the 1970s strengthened the position of the third world as a bargaining partner (albeit rising fuel prices had serious impacts on some developing countries). In succeeding years, the third world made its voice heard in international fora as never before, formulating programmes for far-reaching reform. A set of demands that would result in a New International Economic Order was put on the agenda; demands for reform of existing patterns of news and information flows –in short: *a new international information order*– were soon to follow. But a new international information order, in the sense its advocates intended, was not to be. After some brief years of debate, the issue disappeared from international agendas, and discussion of a New World Information and Communication Order (NWICO) also waned in the North –though not in the South.

In the first years of the new millennium, information and communication issues have resurfaced in the global arena in a somewhat different guise: the *World Summit on the Information Society (WSIS)*. The UN, UNESCO and the ITU are all involved in the new arena, where information and communication issues are primarily treated in terms relating to 'global governance'. It is these most recent developments that form the starting point for the present chapter, which analyses the rise and fall of the NWICO with particular attention to structural and institutional aspects of the media and communication system and the actions of various actors in the arena of international politics[1]. With the NWICO as a backdrop, a discussion then follows of the information order of today in relation to processes of globalization, media developments in third world countries and, ultimately, our understanding of 'development'. The chapter concludes with a few remarks concerning the efforts being made within the framework of the WSIS to apply a governance perspective to fundamental issues relating to information and communication in the world today.

The international media system

The principal complaints that the third world voiced in the 1970s, and which subsequently evolved into the demand for a new international information order, concerned the imbalance of information flows (in the case of news vir-

---

1 The findings of the study are reported in full in Ulla Carlsson, *Frågan om en ny internationell informationsordning; en studie i internationell mediepolitik* (The issue of a New World and Information Order; a study in media politics), Göteborg: Göteborg University, Dept. of Journalism and Mass Communication, 1998. See also Ulla Carlsson, "The Rise and Fall of NWICO. From a Vision of International Regulation to a Reality of Multilevel Governance", *Nordicom Review* (2003) 2, pp. 31-68.

tually a 'one-way flow'); the general disrespect for third world peoples' cultural identities that the imbalance reflected; the hegemony of transnational communications companies (perceived as a threat to the nations' independence) and the inequitable distribution of communications resources among regions of the world.

A rich body of research confirmed the validity of the complaints. The studies documented the imbalance of flows between developed and developing countries, between North and South. The international system of communications was designed to serve the needs of the industrialized countries. A small number of transnational companies controlled the markets for news and for communications technology. Developing countries had no choice but to make use of the structures created by and for the industrialized regions of the world. National media systems in the third world remained poorly developed; many were state-controlled. Poorly developed and economically weak, mass media were unable to report news events in their own countries or to report world events to their national audiences. As a consequence, they were heavily dependent on international news agencies. The material these agencies carried was strongly event-oriented and superficial, personifying and dramatizing events of the day (Bishop, 1975; Boyd-Barrett, 1977; Harris, 1976; Höhne, 1977; Nordenstreng and Varis, 1974; Tunstall, 1977; Schramm, 1980; Varis, 1977).

Mass media in the development process: ideology and strategy

The two main focal points in the issue of a new international information order were the role of the media and mass communication in the development of society and the relationship between industrialized and developing countries.

The development process was strategically important in the industrialized countries' contest for the third world. The emergence of new media technology highlighted the role of the media in this process. Scholars who studied national development in the postwar era through the 1960s identified phenomena in the development process that formed the nuclei of two separate paradigms: the paradigm of modernization and the paradigm of dependence, the latter a reaction to the former. Whereas the modernization paradigm saw the problems of developing countries as consequences of historical factors, the dependency paradigm pointed to contemporary causes: underdevelopment as a consequence of capitalism, expressed as colonialism and imperialism.

The 'free flow of information' concept was formulated in the USA in the final throes of the Second World War. No national frontiers should be allowed to hinder the flow of information between countries. Even while the war was still raging, it was apparent that the USA would emerge from it as a world power. The Americans saw before them a world without colonial ties, a world that lay open to a robust, expansive American economy. The information sector was a key factor in paving the way for economic expansion. People everywhere were tired of the propaganda and censorship that were part of the war effort and welcomed the thought of 'free flows' warmly. The idea of a 'free flow of information' was spread over the world. It was particularly important to win support for the concept in the United Nations and especially its specialized agency, UNESCO (United Nations Educational, Scientific and Cultural Organisation). Thus, UNESCO came to be the main arena in which information and communication issues were debated in the postwar period.

UNESCO had two prime roles: it provided assistance and it established norms. The first of these roles related directly to the development effort and 'modernization'. But when, in the 1960s, proponents of the dependency paradigm called the concept of modernization into question and demanded reform, it was the first of what came to be known as the 'wars of ideas'. The ideological components of the two paradigms provided the terms for the will to reform represented in the call for a new international information order, and UNESCO's norm-setting role was to become the portal through which the third world's demands made their way onto the international agenda (cf. Eek, 1979).

The rise of the NWICO

The non-aligned countries introduced the demand for a new international information order in the mid-1970s as an extension of already voiced demands for a new world economic order. Although the non-aligned countries could hardly be considered a unit in terms of ideology or political-economic systems, and as a group had leanings toward both of the major blocs, they maintained a remarkably united front on the issue of a new international information order (cf. Sing and Gross, 1984). That the demand for reform of the international communications system arose out of the non-aligned camp was hardly sheer chance (Hamelink, 1979). A prime factor was the tumultuous change that was taking place in the world oil market. The 'OPEC Crisis' or 'fuel crisis' of 1973 broke a position of near-total dominance that the USA had enjoyed for over a century and won the non-aligned countries an unprecedented bargaining position.

After 1973, the issue was no longer a question of national liberation in a strictly political, juridical sense but ambitions extended into the economic and cultural spheres as well, which, of course, sharply challenged prevailing power relationships. The new international information order rested on four cornerstones, the 'four Ds': democratization of the flows of information between countries; decolonialization, i.e. self-determination, national independence and cultural identity; demonopolization, i.e. setting limits on the activities of transnational communications companies; and development, i.e. national communication policy, strengthening of infrastructure, journalism education, and regional cooperation (cf. Nordenstreng, 1984). The media, particularly news flows, were central. A new way of looking at development was evident; its ingredients were tenets arguing that development presumes self-determination and cultural identity, and recipient countries should control the aid received. Add to this an international perspective, and a commitment to regional cooperation.

The third world's complaints and the demands for a new international information order that were raised in UNESCO developed into a bitter struggle that came to a head in the work on a 'declaration on the media' in the period 1974-1978[2]. But it was issues relating to satellite communication and the need to regulate the new technology which portended a change in climate within UNESCO. The General Conference of 1972 adopted a resolution put forward by the Soviet Union that set out principles for how satellites might be used for the exchange of news, information and cultural expressions[3]. The vote was 55 for, 7 against, with 22 abstentions. Astoundingly, the USA had been outvoted. In the ensuing years, the West frequently found itself in the minority as third world countries tended to vote with the Eastern bloc.

The MacBride Commission

Just as the strife surrounding the Declaration on the Media was culminating in 1976, a commission was appointed with the brief of analysing existing problems relating to communication in the world and suggesting principles that might guide work towards a new world information order[4] –from 1978 'a new world information and communication order', or NWICO[5]. The commission, chaired by the Irish politician, diplomat and Nobel Laureate Sean MacBride, submitted its final report, *Many Voices, One World. Communication and Society, Today and Tomorrow*, to Amadou-Mahtar M'Bow, Director-General of UNESCO, just before the 1980 General Conference. The sharp differences that had characterized the discussions throughout the 1970s were also present in the MacBride Commission. Considering that it consisted of 16 members representing different ideologies, different political, economic and cultural systems, and different geographical areas, it was no small achievement for the Commission to manage to reach agreement on as many points as it did. Sean MacBride comments in his Foreword to *Many Voices, One World* that the members "reached what I consider a surprising measure of agreement on major issues, upon which opinions

2 The UNESCO Declaration on Fundamental Principles Concerning the Contribution of the Mass Media to Strengthen Peace and International Understanding to the Promotion of Human Rights and to Countering Racialism, Apartheid and the Incitement of War (1978). The Declaration may be seen as an attempt to formulate fundamental guidelines for the role of mass media in the international system.

3 Guiding principles on the use of satellite broadcasting for the free flow of information, the spread of education and greater cultural exchange.

4 The International Commission for the Study of Communication Problems, or MacBride Commission, was appointed in 1976. One of its principal tasks was to "analyse communication problems, in their different aspects, within the perspective of the establishment of a new international economic order and of the measures to be taken to foster the institution of a 'new world information order'" (UNESCO Work Plan for 1977-1978, 19C/5 Approved, §4155).

5 UNESCO used the concept of a 'new world information order' for only two years. In the final version of the mass media declaration adopted in 1978 the phrasing is: "...a new, more just and effective world information and communication order". The change may be seen as a further adaptation to the position of the West, and as a retreat from a new order to improvements in the status quo.

heretofore had seemed irreconcilable" (xviii). Due to differences in the group, the | 199
report does not offer any specific proposals regarding communication policy principles. On the other hand, it does offer a good number of recommendations and
suggestions aiming to bring about a "more just and more efficient world information and communication order". A majority of those who commented on the
report, including many who were essentially critical, agreed that *Many Voices,
One World* was the most thoroughgoing document of its kind on communication
to have been produced in UNESCO's name (cf. Hamelink, 1980).

The Commission report stressed that it concerned not only developing countries, but the whole of humanity, because unless the necessary
changes were made in all parts of the world, it would not be possible to attain
freedom, reciprocity or independence in the exchange of information worldwide. The Commission confirmed the persistence of imbalances in news and
information flows between countries and of marked inequalities in the distribution of communication resources. The Commission were agreed as to the
necessity for change and that the current situation was "unacceptable to all"
(xviii), but its members were unable to agree on a definition of the concept of
a 'new world information and communication order' (NWICO), nor were they
able to specify the link with a new international economic order, as they had
been asked to do.

Above all, the Commission sought solutions whereby third world
countries would develop and strengthen their independence, self-determination
and cultural identity. They also explored ways to improve international news
reporting and the conditions under which journalists operate. Several central proposals focused on the democratization of communication, i.e. issues relating to
access and participation, and "the right to communicate" –actually a cluster of
rights: "the right to be informed, the right to inform, the right to privacy, the
right to participate in public communication" at all levels, international, national,
local and individual, was strongly emphasized (265, 173).

Although its mandate embraced all forms of communication, the principal focus of the MacBride Commission rested on the mass media. The mobilizing capacity of the media was emphasized in relation to issues of national development, while the media's role as a source of continuity was emphasized in relation to cultural identity. The Commission described the media's contributions to
social change and the preservation of national cultural identity. Thus, we find
expressions of both change and integration perspectives. But in contrast to the
international perspective of the third world countries, the approach of the
MacBride Commission was decidedly national.

Overall, the Commission applied a development perspective to conditions in the third world. Most calls for action were addressed to the developing
countries, whereas the role of the industrialized world was largely confined to
that of donor. Although the Commission's recommendations were far more concrete than is common in UNESCO, only seldom did they refer to actors by name.

That is to say, the recommendations were strategic in nature rather than action-oriented, which, it should be noted, were necessary if agreement was to be reached on the principles for a NWICO. With regard to commercialization of the mass media and measures to limit the activities of transnational companies, the Commission's recommendations were elevated to the systems level and formulated in very general terms. Thus, the report offered nothing in the way of a blue-print for change, which was a disappointment to many. On the other hand, the Commission did support many of the demands that the third world countries had formulated in 'the four Ds'.

When the time came for the work of the MacBride Commission to be debated at UNESCO's General Conference in 1980, it became apparent that Director-General M'Bow had changed his position. Previously a proponent of the third world countries' demands, he now assumed a role of mediator. The recommendations of the MacBride Commission were conspicuously absent from the agenda. Nonetheless, they were frequently referred to in the debate and influenced the formulation of what was to be known as 'the MacBride Resolution' that was the outcome of the Conference. For the first time, a UNESCO resolution set out the foundations of a new world information and communication order, or NWICO. It contained paragraphs on measures to remove hindrances and remedy other negative effects (monopolization and concentration), to promote freedom of information and freedom of the press, to provide for journalists' freedom and responsibility and to ensure a diversity of sources, to help preserve cultural identity, and to ensure the right to participate in information flows and access to information sources. All these elements were present, albeit in a more diluted form than in the MacBride report, not to mention the third world countries' demands for reform.

Of the focal themes in *Many Voices, One World*, only cultural identity is included in the resolution text. It proved impossible to reach agreement on independence, self-determination and the 'right to communicate'. The most far-reaching of the Commission's recommendations, those relating to democratization of communication, were reflected in three clauses on the right to participate in information flows and processes and to have a 'right to communicate'. The text was a grave disappointment to the non-aligned countries. The most concrete sections of the resolution had to do with development and aid. These emphases were further reinforced by the institution of an International Programme for Communication Development (IPDC), another indirect fruit of the MacBride Commission.

The UNESCO 1980 General Conference: a turning-point?

The 1980 General Conference approached amidst mounting uncertainty about the future of UNESCO. The third world's demands for radical reform of the prevailing information order were perceived by some in the West as a threat to the 'free world', i.e. as "freedom under attack" (Fascell, 1979). Many Western countries perceived the movement as an "effort by the Soviet Union and some Third

World countries to foster government control of media under the guise of a New World and Communication Order" (Goddard-Power, 1981: 142).

Meanwhile, fatigue was widespread within UNESCO, and many delegates felt that some change was necessary if the organization were to live on in keeping with its statutes. Media issues had dominated UNESCO's agenda for most of the 1970s, with wars of words and ideas being waged on two front lines: East vs. West and North vs. South. Towards the end of the decade there were even public doubts that UNESCO could be fully functional if the inflamed debate on communications media continued for much longer. Both the USA and Great Britain threatened to leave UNESCO on repeated occasions. Media issues were not the sole cause of this turmoil; the leadership style of Director-General M'Bow was also highly controversial and contributed to the deadlock (Gerbner, Mowlana and Nordenstreng, 1993).

By 1980 there was a general will, both among the countries of the Eastern and the Western blocs and within the third world, to reach some kind of a modus vivendi on media issues so that the atmosphere within UNESCO might normalize. Even the Soviet delegation showed signs of a willingness to compromise, a change in attitude deriving from the political repercussions of the country's invasion of Afghanistan the year before. It came as a surprise to many when UNESCO members at the 1980 meeting managed to agree on both a first draft of a NWICO and a development program (IPDC). In addition, third world countries met with much more support for their demands than ever before in a UNESCO document, even though the MacBride Commission's recommendations had been struck from the agenda. The work of the Commission had, however, cleared the path, which benefited the third world countries in several respects. The ideas of the non-aligned countries had won recognition. UNESCO members were able to agree on several fundaments for a new world information and communication order, several of which corresponded with the intentions of the non-aligned countries. Surprisingly, even a clause on monopolization and concentration of the media won approval. The industrialized countries promised aid to help to build and develop communication systems in developing countries. One can take this as evidence that the third world advanced its position and that the NWICO concept had won some measure of acceptance. At the same time, the West put development and aid issues squarely on the agenda and managed to turn the focus away from their own roles and onto conditions in the third world countries. The international dimension was diluted, as it had been in the MacBride Commission's work. In this we can perceive a crossroads for UNESCO on the horizon, a point at which the organization would have to choose between continued work on a new information order and a more decided focus on development and aid issues.

From regulation to international aid

After 1980, UNESCO's General Conference adopted one international agreement having bearing on the information and communication sector (Right to

Communicate, 1983). Otherwise, the only resolutions emanating from UNESCO related to the communication program, IPDC. These were clear indications of a different climate and different power relationships from those of the preceding decade, in which UNESCO produced no fewer than eight international agreements on information and communication. The bitter debates of the period over issues like freedom of information, social responsibility of the media, the free flow of information, news imperialism and, ultimately, a world information and communication order form a parenthesis in UNESCO's history to date. The NWICO question was dead, 'history', and practical development assistance moved to centre stage. The factors behind the change can be summarized in four points.

» First, the MacBride Commission made a significant contribution by structuring the problem area, which made it possible to raise the intellectual level of the debate. The issues were made concrete through the solutions the Commission proposed. The Commission's emphasis on development was also a step in the direction of change.

» Secondly, the institution of the IPDC became a symbol of the new emphasis on development and practical action, an emphasis that was to grow successively stronger during the 1980s as the development program progressed. Development aid was once again the prime focus. The Western countries were enthusiastic about the IPDC and considered it their work. There were very likely tactical motives behind their standpoint; an emphasis on practical assistance might serve to modify the demands of third world countries and reduce the severity of the ideological conflicts (Garbo, 1984; Goddard-Power, 1984; Harley, 1984; Nordenstreng, 1984). But were it not for the MacBride Commission's focus on development issues, it is not likely that the programme would have seen the light of day.

» Third, the change in posture of UNESCO's Director-General in response to widespread criticism of his ineffective leadership and favouring of the developing countries was important in this context. The preoccupation with issues relating to the mass media had, what is more, nearly paralysed UNESCO. The survival and proper functioning of the organization required a change and forced the Director-General to modify his policy by, for example, striking the 82 recommendations of the MacBride report from the agenda in 1980, assuming instead the role of mediator.

» Fourth, and finally, the friction subsided when the USA and Great Britain first threatened to leave and then left UNESCO in 1984 and 1985, respectively. The USA pointed to the work on the NWICO as one of its reasons for leaving the organization. After the 1980 meeting, the USA and other Western countries launched an anti-NWICO campaign. A document known as the Talloire Declaration, adopted by an international conference arranged by the World Press Freedom Committee et alii in 1981, exemplifies the critique. UNESCO was also criticized for inefficiency and for having become 'politicized'. The prominence and influence of third world countries in UNESCO in the early 1980s, a result of Director-General M'Bow's policies, was a source of constant irritation (Bartelson and Ringmar, 1985). The USA had additional complaints, as well. The foreign policy of the newly installed Reagan Administration differed markedly from that of the Carter Administration (Gerbner, 1993; Levin, 1984). The exit of two major powers dealt a hard blow to UNESCO's finances, which resulted in a shift in the power constellation within the organization. The position of the Director-General was weakened, the Western countries advanced their position at the expense of third world countries, and the Eastern bloc was relatively passive.

Even after 1985, the third world countries continued their campaign for a NWICO, but to no avail. Their influence had been reduced, partly due to the fact that OPEC no longer wielded the same degree of influence on the oil market. Armed conflicts between several of the OPEC countries meant that the non-aligned countries could not muster a united front as they had in the 1970s. It was impossible for individual countries both to campaign for a NWICO and to seek more assistance from the countries that opposed it. As a consequence, at the 1989 General Conference NWICO was taken off the agenda once and for all, leaving the stage open for 'free flow' to make its comeback (cf. MacBride and Roach, 1993).

Full circle

The efforts of third world countries to bring about thoroughgoing reform of the information and communication order within the framework of UNESCO, the principal norm-setting international forum in this area, failed. A political idea had to be sacrificed for the sake of development assistance. The successively narrowing focus on aid issues in the 1980s represents a reversion to the thinking of the 1960s. In retrospect, one might say that policy came full circle with the institution of the IPDC communication programme in 1989. UNESCO's role vis-á-vis the developing countries was once again that of aid donor.

Thus, the issue of a new world information and communication order (NWICO) was apparently an expression of the spirit of the times, an era of ideological debate and conflict, a period in which power relationships on international markets were challenged and changed. The issue of a NWICO, as formulated in the 1970s within UNESCO, was an outgrowth of the two development paradigms and its ideological components. In a longer perspective, we also see that the 1970s formed a period of transition, from politics and ideology to market solutions.

The 1950s and '60s were, overall, optimistic. Wealthy countries prospered, poor countries gained their independence. People had faith in political solutions, believed in the promise of new technology and economic growth. But in the 1970s this faith weakened; ideological conflicts surfaced, the status quo was questioned, and collective solutions were advanced. The 1980s, then, saw the disintegration of many of the very institutions that had inspired optimism twenty and thirty years earlier. Deregulation, commercialization, consumerism and individualism became watchwords. The change was clearly linked to the advance of technology-driven globalization. Whereas a new economic world order could be discerned as early as the 1970s, it was only in the following decade that a new political world order emerged. The driving forces behind this latter metamorphosis were quite beyond the reach of the international political system; they were also, ideologically speaking, quite contrary to the thinking behind the NWICO concept.

Globalization in the media sector

Mass media play a decisive part in what we call the globalization process. Without the media and modern information technology, globalization as we know it today would not be possible. Access to various media, to telephony and to digital services, is often held to be crucial to our political, economic and cultural development. Free and independent media are also vital to the survival and development of democracy. Meanwhile, a good proportion of the people of the world lack electricity and access to telecommunications and are thereby condemned to marginalization.

The development of innovative information technologies and the ongoing processes of deregulation and concentration of ownership have spurred the pace of globalization. Specifically communications satellites and digitalization –not least the Internet– have had an enormous impact. These innovations have opened up worldwide markets for media products such as television programmes, films, news, games and advertising. They have been a *sine qua non* for the formation and proper functioning of global enterprises and flows of information across national frontiers. The production and distribution of media products are highly concentrated branches, with respect to both content and ownership. Meanwhile, traditional distinctions, between information and entertainment, between hardware and software, between product and distribution, are blurring.

Much of what could be discerned only vaguely on the horizon back in the 1970s is now upon us in full force. The volume of information we have at our disposal has multiplied many times over; it is available via many new players and many new channels in 'the new information society'. The relationships between the wealthy countries and the poor countries of the world that the MacBride Commission described at the end of the 1970s still seem to prevail, essentially unchanged, albeit some of the terminology is new. Today we speak of 'the digital divide', which, as Secretary-General Kofi Annan points out, actually consists of several 'divides': a *technological divide* in terms of existing infrastructure; a *content divide* in the sense that much of the information available on the web lacks all relevance to people's real needs, while it also presumes fluency in English; a *gender divide*, in that women and girls generally have poorer access to information than men and boys; and a *commercial divide*, whereby electronic trading tends to strengthen the links between some countries, with the risk that others will be increasingly marginalized[6].

Global actors in the media market

Much of the debate about a NWICO in the 1970s revolved around news flows across national frontiers. Studies made in the 1970s confirmed a decided imbalance in the flows between North and South. One of the main demands regarding a NWICO was the call for a more equitable and democratic flow of information; initially, this mainly meant flows of news.

The objects of the non-aligned countries' criticism were mainly the major wire services that operated worldwide: AP, AFP, dpa, Reuters and UPI. Because of their dominance they were held responsible for the 'one-way flow' of news and other information between North and South.

The international wire services were pioneers in the development of a global network. Having started up in the early 1850s, they were the first transnational media systems, products of modernity. They defined political and economic news, thereby creating a product that was sold, in different packaging, to political and economic elites, either directly or via the mass media, at home and in other parts of the world. The wire services developed information technologies in order to improve the global communications networks. Today, they distinguish themselves from other actors on the global market in that they both contribute to globalization and consolidate their own countries (Hjarvard, 2001).

Contemporary news flows differ from those in the 1970s in their much larger volume and greater diversification. But interest in using sources other than the major wire services is limited, so they have retained their privilege of defining what constitutes news. Particularly the market leaders AP and Reuters also supply Internet services with news copy. Here there is a natural link with the main sources of news film. The news market today is highly diversified and segmented into a number of subgenres –business news, sports news, entertainment news, medical news– and the Internet facilitates further development, in terms of both geographical extent and volume. But the content the services carry does not seem to have evolved to any notable extent. When CNN 'stole' a sizable share of the global market in the mid-1990s, the dominance of the USA in news reporting worldwide was the target of criticism, and researchers found that "the news seen on World Report is the same old news of the world" (Fluornoy and Stewart, 1997: 23).

6 Address by UN Secretary-General Annan to the World Summit on the Information Society, Geneva, December 10, 2003.

Some collaboration between established news agencies (EBU) and news agencies in the third world was established in the 1980s as a direct consequence of the NWICO debate. Danish media scholar Stig Hjarvard, who has studied the exchange of news footage within Eurovision, found that Asia (Asiavision) is the only region where the EBU regularly gathered news in the 1990s. Otherwise, use of third world sources was no more than sporadic. Less than 4% of the material carried by EBU's news exchange, EVN, in 1991 originated in regional collaboration with third world news organizations. To some extent, the sparse representation may be attributed to a scarcity of material that is of relevance to EBU's viewers. Hjarvard analysed the obstacles and disinterest that collaboration had met on the national level and commented that it seemed to occur despite, rather than as a result of, national policy. Interest resides among journalists, not governments (Hjarvard, 1995: 505).

But even if regional collaboration has not brought about any major changes, regionalization of news reporting has developed, particularly in the Arab world. The news service *Al jazeera* is a case in point. But this is not to say that *Al jazeera* is a major news source outside the Arab world.

An examination of the structure of the production and distribution of media products does not turn up any thoroughgoing changes since the 1970s as far as news flows are concerned. Researcher Oliver Boyd-Barrett presumes that nothing has changed and points out that the most problematic aspect today resides not so much in the skew geopolitical pattern of news diffusion, as in the effects of the very narrow range of news content carried, the focus on elites and conventional Western news values, conflict rather than stability, and events rather than processes (Boyd-Barrett, 1997). This is so despite the fact that, thanks to the Internet, many more different news sources around the world are available than was even conceivable 20-30 years ago. That is to say, there is an unprecedented potential for both more diverse and more extensive news flows.

Transnational media companies grow even bigger

Critics of the status quo in the 1970s took the concentration in the media sector and the threat to diversity that it posed as cause for demanding some form of international regulation of media markets. Since then, media corporations have grown considerably. Back in the 1970s, the objects of concern were the major wire services and, above all, film studios that operated on the international market, such as Columbia, Warner Brothers, Twentieth Century-Fox and United Artists –all based in the USA. Indeed, it is among these companies that we find the germ of many of the transnational corporations (TNC) that dominate the media market today. Some of these companies have taken advantage of deregulation and privatization over vast regions of the world and have purchased and fused with other companies to become global media conglomerates.

The TNCs operate on multiple levels, global channels spread the same message (in the same language), regional channels in local languages are established, and technical systems are made available. A few transnational media companies, most of which are based in the USA or Europe, dominate the spread of media products. Their cultural presence is considerable on virtually every continent. Lately, they have begun to establish themselves in the developing countries. Together with the World Wide Web, the expansion of media TNCs has also increased the paramount status of English.

Table 1. The largest media corporations in the world by media sales volume in 2003 (USD billions)

1. AOL Time Warner	40	USA
2. News Corporation	19	Australia
3. Viacom Inc	19	USA
4. Walt Disney Comp.	18	USA
5. Vivendi Universal	18	France
6. Bertelsmann AG	15	Germany
7. Sony Corporation	12	Japan
8. Reed Elsevier	8	The Netherlands/Great Britain
9. ARD	7	Germany
10. NBC	7	USA

Source: Nordicom 2004.

Most of these companies are primarily involved in television and entertainment, but several also deal in news gathering and distribution. All control more than one medium and are thus able to advertise and sell their products in one medium or across others.

Both of the two transnational corporations in the third world are to be found in Latin America. They are *Globo* in Brazil and *Televisa* in Mexico, with volumes of roughly USD 2-3 billion each (*Variety* Aug 26-Sep 1, 2002 and Sep 15-21, 2003). Having started out in the newspaper branch, the two companies have now expanded into television, pay-TV, music publishing and book publishing.

The media have become increasingly commercialized over the past few decades. Market shares are worth a great deal of money. How economic transactions are organized and the degree of concentration of economic power in various branches play a decisive role in the globalization process. A country's place in the global pecking order is a function of its ability to compete on the world market. Competitive strength is not only a question of efficiency or economic rationality; many factors –political, social and economic– are involved. Samir Amin points out five different monopolies that the dominant actors make use of to maintain and strengthen their hold on the market and that together form the framework in which globalization takes place. The five monopolies relate to technology, finance, natural resources, media and communications, and weapons of mass destruction. In the case of the media and communications, Amin gives the following motives:

...[The media and communications] not only lead to uniformity of culture but also open up new means of political manipulation. The expansion of the modern media market is already one of the major components in the erosion of democratic practices in the West itself (Amin, 1997: 5).

The media situation in the third world: status quo?

The issues of cultural identity and the right to participate in international flows of information are related to both national media structures in the developing countries and the countries' links with the global system. The only concrete political result of the work on a NWICO within UNESCO was a focus on the development of national media in the third world through, among other things, increased development assistance.

Several countries in the third world still lack an adequate infrastructure for modern mass media. This hinders their development, while it also blocks their access to the international news and media system. The lack of electricity and telecommunications over much of the developing countries' territory is one key problem. Other hindrances reside in the realm of national media policy. Those who can change the situation are not always motivated to do so; those who want to change the situation are not always in a position to do so.

An examination of existing international statistics in the communications sector shows some improvement in third world countries since the 1970s, though in some more than others. For example, the density of radio and television receivers has risen, as has newspaper circulation. The broadcast media have expanded particularly markedly. In the mid-1960s UNESCO recommended that each country should have at least 20 TV sets, 50 radio receivers and 100 newspaper copies per thousand inhabitants. In 1980, the MacBride report notes that 100 countries in Africa, Asia and Latin America had not reached these minimum standards by the mid-1970s. Ten years later, five countries were still below the three standards, and an additional 55 were below at least one of them. African countries predominated among these least developed countries with respect to the media (Beam, 1992). Ten years down the line, the figures have improved further –though only in some countries, and not others. Again, the poorest countries of Africa lag behind. In several developing countries, the pace of progress in the media sector has been quite slow, particularly in rural areas, where a majority of the people live.

Table 2. Media densities in the world, 1970 and 1997,
Units per thousand inhabitants

	Daily newspapers		Radio receivers		TV sets	
	1970	1996	1970	1997	1970	1997
The world, total	107	96	245	418	81	240
Africa	12	16	93	216	4.6	60
America	170	141	698	1,017	209	429
Asia	49	66	81	255	20	190
Europe	281	261	465	729	205	446
Oceania	269	227	779	1,071	188	427
Developing countries	29	60	90	245	9.9	157
Sub-Saharan Africa	10	12	83	202	1.5	48
Arab states	17	36	131	269	21	119
Latin America & Caribbean	76	101	196	412	57	205
Eastern Asia & Oceania	26	56	97	306	3.3	253
Southern Asia	12	33	34	118	0.9	54
Least developed countries	4.5	8	56	142	0.5	23
Developed countries	292	226	643	1,061	263	548

Source: UNESCO 2003 <http://www.uis.unesco.org>.

In the world as a whole, it is estimated that there are about 250 television sets per thousand inhabitants, a considerably higher figure than for those who have a telephone (Human Development Report, 2002). In less than a decade from the mid-1980s to the mid 1990s, the number of television channels in the world doubled, as did average viewing time and the number of TV sets in households. Satellite television is accessible worldwide; transnational satellite channels have vastly increased the volume of programming available to viewers, and numerous niche channels carry specialized content to various target audiences –not least young viewers. In developing countries, which have experienced rapid deregulation, many Western-style radio and television channels now serve urban areas. Feature films, serial drama, talk shows and music predominate. Still, not everyone has access to television. In the poorest countries the estimated density of television sets per thousand people is only 23.

Radio is still the medium that reaches the most people. The fact that a good share of the third world still lacks electricity makes radio crucially important outside urban areas. Between 1970 and 1997, the density of radio receivers in developing countries increased from 90 to 245 per thousand inhabitants.

In the interval 1970-1997, newspaper circulation in the developing countries doubled, from 29 to 60 per thousand. Circulation nearly doubled in the least developed countries as well: from 4.5 per thousand in 1970 to 8 per thousand in 1997. This is still far below the UNESCO recommendations in the mid-1960s (100 per 1,000 inhabitants).

The Internet is generally considered the cardinal example of 'the digital revolution'. In 2003, an estimated 11% of the world's population had access to the Internet (ITU, 2004). More than three-quarters of today's Internet users are to be found in the wealthiest (OECD) countries, which have 14% of the world population. Only 1-2% are located in Africa. Thus, we find a huge gap between different parts of the world –'the digital divide' is as wide today as it ever was. Most prognosticators say that the new information technology will make a tremendous difference in the future, but that a majority of the world's population will not have access to the net. The lack of telecommunications infrastructure in regions of Africa, Asia and Latin America will keep many people in the margins.

Table 3. Internet users and telephone subscribers per 100 inhabitants, 2003

	Internet users	Tele subscribers
Africa	2	9
Asia	7	29
America (North)	53	111
America (South)	8	40
Europe (East)	17	74
Europe (West)	40	144
Oceania	38	95

Source: ITU 2004 <http://www.itu.int/ITU-D/ict/statistics/>.

The Internet is known to be the younger generation's medium par excellence. But in Africa, South America and a good part of Asia, the proportion of children and young people who have Internet access is only a couple of per cent. Meanwhile, roughly 90% of Swedish children have Internet access at home. Children and young people in the wealthiest countries of the world are a truly multimedia generation, whereas for many of the children in the world television is out of reach, and books are in short supply.

The IPDC was inaugurated to accelerate expansion of the mass media in the third world. But even after twenty years, the results of the programme are modest, to say the least. In some instances, support made possible through the IPDC has significantly contributed to regional news exchanges, and to some extent it may be credited with having facilitated news gathering. But all too often, national media policy has stood in the way of international news exchange and news gathering across national frontiers.

IPDC operations have been criticized widely, and in 1995 reforms designed to make the programme more efficient got under way. But at the same time it is difficult to see how the IPDC can help to create functional media structures. The establishment of a modern communications infrastructure is much too costly for any one development programme. Deregulation in the third world has opened the door to competition, privatization and foreign ownership, but this route to development often implies new dependency relationships.

The conditions found in the third world in the 1970s are largely unchanged in the 100-odd countries that have experienced a slow pace of development and are still politically and economically dependent on other countries. In these countries, the situation described in the MacBride Commission's report still applies.

A third development paradigm

The new world information order, as formulated by the non-aligned countries, was clearly linked to the dependency paradigm, particularly the elements decolonization and demonopolization. But the documents also contained an indication of a new position in the countries' quest for their own paths toward development and communication; this had to do with independence, self-determination and cultural identity. The demand for a new international information order may be seen as a reaction to the modernization paradigm.

The MacBride Commission was clearly influenced by the non-aligned states' ideas. *Self-reliance* and *cultural identity* were key principles in the Commission's recommendations. Concepts like *access* and *participation* were made explicit. The Commission also introduced the local level and horizontal communication into thinking about development. There was also a hint of the idea that the causes of underdevelopment might be found in the developed and the developing countries alike. This 'new' view was also expressed in the IPDC resolution of 1980.

The MacBride Commission's recommendations were hardly unequivocal, however. The ambiguities were particularly apparent in the Commission's treatment of communication technology and technological development. Here, the Commission's thinking alternated between the modernization and dependency paradigms; the concept of neocolonialism confronted decolonialization. But, above all, the recommendations suggested a third, alternative concept of development.

In the early 1980s, some scholars and development experts began speaking of 'another development', a term first coined in 1978 in *Development Dialogue*, the journal published by the Dag Hammarskjöld Foundation. Here, key concepts are *cultural identity* and *self-reliance,* and *access* and *participation*. This third approach may be characterized as a reaction to both the modernization and dependency paradigms. Universal models, which of necessity are always simplistic, were rejected in favour of an emphasis on the characteristics and needs of each individual country and the conviction that development efforts must start with specific conditions and needs. Social, economic, cultural and religious components of development were identified; and the focus rested more often on local conditions than on the nation or international relations. This is not to say that relationships of international interdependency were ignored. An oft-cited phrase was "Global problems, local solutions". Adherents of this approach also regarded traditional values as an important factor in fostering a sense of identity and meaning and a source of continuity in the face of social change. At the same time, democratic processes and regard for human rights were kept in focus (Hedebro, 1982; Kothari, 1984; Jayaweera, 1987; Kumar, 1994; Mowlana, 1988; Servaes, 1989; Yoon, 1996).

Most recently, much of the work with 'another development' has focused on the concept of *multiplicity*, introduced by Jan Servaes in the late 1980s. The focus on multiplicity has also entailed a focus on participatory communication for social change. The approach is normative. The researchers and field workers who subscribe to this school of thought often work on local projects to create the preconditions for new communicative situations, often on a 'grassroots' level.

The links between this third paradigm of development and the NWICO debate and the ideas implicit in the MacBride resolution are obvious. Concepts like self-reliance and cultural identity took their place on the international agenda and thus won political acceptance on the conceptual level. The MacBride Commission involved social scientists –sociologists, political scientists, educationalists, media scholars, and so forth– and other experts from all parts of the world, which ensured the inclusion of many of the concepts that were to recur in both theory and practice in ensuing decades. It is difficult, however, to distinguish cause from effect. In all probability the present position can be put down to the mutual exchanges between regions, academic disciplines, experts, politicians, etc., that the discussion of a NWICO and, not least, the MacBride Commission broke ground for.

In conclusion

The issue of a New World Information and Communication Order that occupied the UNESCO agenda in the 1970s is unique in that for once, international diplomacy and policy-makers acknowledged the international character of the media, their structures, world-views and markets.

Some of the developments during this past decade could be discerned on the horizon even when efforts were being made to create a NWICO. Indeed, increasing concentration of media ownership, monopolization of markets, and a decline in diversity were among the complaints that the third world countries and others raised. However, it was quite impossible to envisage the breadth and depth of what was to come in the closing decades of the century. The globalization in the media system, spurred by deregulation and privatization, concentration, commercialization and, not least, new information technology, could not be foreseen in its manifold entirety. It was these developments that ultimately sealed the fate of the NWICO as an issue.

The globalization of the media has accelerated and the digital divide has widened in recent years, and international information and mèdia issues are once again in focus on the international agenda. Even if the points of departure and terms of reference used today are quite different from those in the 1970s, 'development' is still bound up with the modernist project of the Western world. Today, however, solutions to the problems and issues are not sought in top-down steering and regulations on an international scale. Contemporary society is far too complex for that, and discourages the thought of 'a new international order' of the sort envisaged in the 1970s. We now see an era of multilevel governance of the media and communication system –an interplay between many different actors, public and private, on multiple levels, from the local to the global.

One of the main items on the global agenda today is the *World Summit on the Information Society, WSIS*. Arranged by the International Telecommunication Union (ITU) in partnership with, among others, UNESCO, under the high patronage of the UN Secretary-General, its anticipated outcome is "to develop and foster a clear statement of political will and a concrete plan of action for achieving the goals of the Information Society, while fully reflecting all the different interests at stake"[7]. Among the fundamental ideas behind the WSIS is an ambition to create a more inclusive Information Society and to bridge the digital divide in a North-South perspective.

Many have expressed concern that the WSIS has come to apply an increasingly technical perspective to issues relating to telecommunication and the Internet. Many voices, not least within the civil society, have called for more attention to the media, human rights and communication rights in the final document; that is to say, the Universal Declaration of Human Rights, and not least its Article 19, which emphasizes freedom of expression, and the principles of a free flow of information, a free circulation of ideas, freedom of the press, participation in the communication process, the right to communicate, cultural diversity, and so forth, are once again in focus. Critics have also seen a danger in marginalizing traditional media, as the WSIS has tended to do. They point to negative consequences, particularly in the poorest countries, not least relating to the advancement of human rights.

When the final WSIS document is adopted in 2005, 25 years will have passed since the MacBride Commission submitted its report to UNESCO. Like the MacBride Commission in 1985, the WSIS has identified important issues and problem areas with regard to global information and communication. Regardless

7 <www.itu.int/wsis/basic/about>.

of one's overall judgement, the WSIS also must be credited with new thinking with respect to how information and communication issues may be handled in the global arena; the governance perspective is truly something new. However, it will require hard work to ensure that the information society, or the knowledge society in UNESCO's parlance, stands for the attainment of basic economic, social and political rights for people around the world. The significance of the WSIS will depend on the extent to which national governments, the private sector, the civil society and other relevant stakeholders are brought into the continued work towards these goals.

Chapter 12

Media policy, peace and state reconstruction

Tim Allen & Nicole Stremlau

On 28 March 2004 US troops in Baghdad padlocked the door of *Al-Hawza*, a
popular Shiite newspaper. Paul Bremer, the Administrator of the Coalition
Provisional Authority (CPA), had ordered the paper to be closed for allegedly incit-
ing violence against coalition troops. It was asserted that continuing to allow the
flow of inaccurate anti-American rumours was hindering the possibility of promoting peace and unity. The decision was taken against the advice of the CPA's
Media Development Director, Simon Haselock, and was met by angry cries of
"where is democracy now". The Vice Chairman of the Committee of Concerned
Journalists argued that the move was a step backward, noting that,

> ...it's hard for me to see how the suppression of information, even false
> information, is going to help our cause[1].

The Council for Islamic Revolution in Iraq declared that,

> punishing the paper will only increase the passion for those who speak out
> against the Americans[2].

In July, Iraq's interim Prime Minister, Iyad Allawi, issued a decree allowing the
paper to reopen, apparently to show his "absolute belief in the freedom of the
press". Himself a Shiite, this was seen by some as a way of currying favour with

---

1 Gettleman, Jeffrey (29 March 2004) "G.I.'s Padlock Baghdad Paper Accused of Lies", *The New York
Times*, <http://www.nytimes.com/2004/03/29/international/worldspecial/29PRES.html>.
2 Ibid.

the radicals. If so, they were not impressed[3]. Soon afterwards his own concerns about critical media coverage were highlighted when his government closed down the Iraq office of the well-known Arabic-language media organisation, *Al-Jazeera*. Allawi explained:

> We have asked an independent committee to monitor Al-Jazeera for the last four weeks... to see what kind of violence they are advocating, inciting hatred and problems and racial tensions... This is a decision taken by the national security committee to protect the people of Iraq, in the interests of the Iraqi people[4].

These events are indicative of the complexities and competing interests that drive media[5] policy in environments affected by violent conflict, and they draw attention to a conundrum that is not unique to Iraq. Should media freedom be an essential aspect of peace building, or does peace building necessitate the restriction of dissent –in other words, censorship? Particularly since the end of the Cold War, the 'international community', i.e. the vague entity which is primarily made up of rich-country governments, Non Governmental Organisations (NGOs), International Finance Institutions (IFIs) and the United Nations (UN) system, has tended to stress accountable governance as a centrepiece of both peace-building initiatives and programmes for social and economic development. There is, of course, a great deal of rhetoric and hypocrisy in this. Also as Simon Haselock has noted during his work in Iraq,

> the 'International Community' is a multi-headed hydra and the heads are all looking at each other and all the time arguing amongst each other[6].

Nevertheless, this liberal agenda has tended to drive media policy. Open media are seen as a 'good thing', and have been promoted even in somewhat extreme circumstances, such as those that have prevailed in Afghanistan following the US-lead invasion. Here we ask if such a strategy is really appropriate.

Establishing a political framework is vital to peace building, and the crucial underlying aspect of this is the issue of security. Peace requires the acceptance of certain hierarchies and the prevention of violence, based on some semblance of the rule of law. In such circumstances, a degree of censorship may be essential. When Rwandan President Paul Kagame publicly states that his country

3 El-Tablawy, Tarek (July 19, 2004) "Controversial Iraqi Newspaper Reopened", Editor and Publisher (<http://www.editorandpublisher.com> accessed 20.09.04).

4 Agence France Presse (August 8, 2004) "Iraq Orders Al-Jazeera Office in Baghdad to Close" (<http://www.commondreams.org/headlines04/0808-02.htm> accessed 21.09.04).

5 When addressing issues of the media we are primarily referring to the local news media and similarly when referring to media policy we are addressing strategies towards local media. Such media are usually at the centre of debates regarding free expression and are often the most threatening form of media during times of peace building.

6 Simon Haselock, "Media, the Law and Peace building: From Bosnia and Kosovo to Iraq", The Alistair Berkley Memorial Lecture at the London School of Economics (21 May 2004) <http://www.crisisstates.com/News/berkley.htm>.

is not ready for an entirely free media environment, he has a point. Local media, most notoriously the government radio station *Mille Collines*, undoubtedly played a significant role in the genocide. In the aftermath of social upheaval, the crucial short-term issue is not how to promote freedom of speech but rather how controls on expressing dissent should be exercised.

The chapter will begin by identifying and discussing the current prevailing liberal policy towards the media's role in peace-making and peace-building[7]. We will then proceed to assess whether this has been an effective or ineffective approach and conclude by suggesting ways in which the debate can be reframed or expanded. In brief, we will argue that laissez-faire policies towards media development in societies that are in the process of resolving violent conflicts are unlikely to be the best option. While recognizing that proposing censorship is problematic and controversial, we argue that there have to be restrictions on material that is divisive and inflammatory -although this inevitably raises questions of who should decide what is unacceptable and on what basis.

The media, violent conflict and peace

Despite a large and growing literature relating to peace initiatives, it is remarkable how the role of the media has often been ignored. The capability of the media to inflame hatred and promote violence has been relatively well documented from early studies of the role of the radio in Nazi propaganda campaigns to the more recent examples of Rwanda and the former Yugoslavia –see, for example, Mark Thompson's *Forging War* (1994) and the various contributions to Allen and Seaton's *The Media of Conflict* (1999).

This literature has highlighted the need to prevent the media from being used to mobilize populations for mass slaughter, and various strategies for intervening have been proposed by international agencies, policy-makers and analysts for what has been termed 'information intervention'[8]. Nevertheless, ways in which a media environment can be either constructed or regulated to promote peace have yet to be sufficiently explored[9].

---

7 By the term *media* we are essentially referring to news media although the points made also relate to other forms of communication. *Peace-making* and *peace-building* are terms that are widely used but rarely defined. We take peace-making to mean the pushing forward of the project of peace sometimes through military intervention and sometimes through negotiation. Peace building will often involve peace-making but also suggests the establishing of institutions that will allow peace to become self-sustaining.

8 Jamie Metzl coined the term "Information Intervention" in a 1997 *Foreign Affairs* article. Metzl, Jamie F. (1997) "Information Intervention: when switching channels isn't enough", *Foreign Affairs*, vol. 76, no. 6, November/December 1997, pp. 15-20.

9 As Gadi Wolfsfeld notes, "Why is there so much research about the role of news media in political conflict and war and so little concerning media and peace? [...] There is not one major study which has looked at the role of the news media in an ongoing peace process... Even the most casual observer cannot fail to be impressed with the ability of the news media to serve an either constructive or deconstructive role in the promotion of peace". Wolfsfeld, Gadi (1998) "Promoting Peace through the News Media. Some Initial Lessons from Oslo Peace Process", in Tamar Liebes and James Curran (eds.), *Media Ritual and Identity*, London: Routledge, p. 219.

One recent attempt to do so is *Forging Peace* (2002) edited by Monroe Price and Mark Thompson –a follow-up to Thompson's *Forging War*. The text offers many useful insights, notably with respect to legally grounded preventive and intervention measures, but its focus is actually quite limited. The questions it poses and the conclusions reached are indicative of most of the literature; how the 'international community' can use media policy to simultaneously promote 'market democracy'[10] and peace. The assumption is that these projects are interlinked or even synonymous with one another. But the majority of war and post-war situations do not involve international reconstruction efforts of significant energy and resources to warrant such emphasis. In violently disturbed zones in Africa, for example, market democracy is not likely to be a possibility for a long time.

The *Forging Peace* approach nevertheless reflects the dominant liberal agendas of international organisations, most rich-country governments, and the main international news organisations that claim to be unified behind a policy of minimal media regulation. The World Bank has recently argued in a book entitled *The Right to Tell* that this will lead to economic development by increasing transparency. Staff at the Bank would probably nowadays accept that free and vibrant media, as with all liberal programmes, actually require a relatively strong state including, for example, a well-functioning legal system to protect individuals against libel or racist abuse. Yet, when it comes to war zones, the 'received wisdom' seems to be that the best way to counter divisive speech is to allow for more speech, so that multiple perspectives are available, rather than to impose restrictions. Along these lines, Ross Howard, Director of the Institute for Media Policy and Civil Society (IMPACS)[11], argues that the media are an imperative component for peace-building because:

> At its best, [the media] is the safeguard of democratic governance. At its best means accurate and balanced reporting which fairly represents a diversity of views sufficient for the public to make well-informed choices. Reliable and diverse media that can express themselves freely provide early warning of potential outbreaks of conflict. They serve as watchdogs over leaders and officials and hold them accountable. They monitor human rights. Their presence is essential to the functioning of other civil society actors. In less optimal environments, the media can still foster stability by providing essential information about humanitarian initiatives[12].

As with so much of the literature, the starting point here is the benefits of the media at 'optimal performance'- i.e. in rich democracies[13]. From the perspective

10 Market democracy is a term that eludes exact definition, but it evokes a combination of liberal economic policies with systems of accountable governance emphasising individual freedom, constraints on state power, human rights and some form of democracy.

11 A Canadian charitable organization that can be found at <www.impacs.org>.

12 Howard, Ross (2002), "An Operational Framework for Media and Peace building", *IMPACS*, January, p. 4.

13 Even in places where the media have the characteristics that Howard refers to, there are grounds for scepticism about his assertions. The news media in the US, for example, have sometimes been important

of Iraq, Rwanda or Afghanistan, Howard's comment about 'less optimal environments' seems rather naïve. In such places, the media may not be restrained by the kinds of institutionalised legal and other mechanisms available in the US or the UK. Certainly the media can, and often do, have a much more significant impact than just providing 'information about humanitarian initiatives' –one that is just as likely to be detrimental as positive. The Rwandan government's Milles Collines radio station was after all partly a product of an internationally supported peace and democratisation project[14]. Yet, in almost all of Howard's 'less optimal environments' proponents of free expression are deeply reluctant to concede situations where restricting the media may be appropriate except in the most blatant or dire of circumstances.

In the aftermath of the genocide in Rwanda, there has been discussion about the warning signs and signals that might provide enough evidence to warrant disruption of broadcasters or the shutting down of a printing press before violence breaks out or immediately after. But much discussion remains focused on opening the media and encouraging more voices to counteract the offender, thereby promoting a 'marketplace of ideas'(a term that goes back to a US court case of 1919 when Justice Holmes argued that ideas will compete against one another and that truth will prevail in this 'marketplace'[15]). Not only does censorship disrupt natural media competition but it encourages elites to exploit information flows in their own interests. As Index on Censorship stresses, limiting free expression only leaves room for protecting the ideas or prejudices that those in power approve or do not find threatening.[16] This line of argument has prompted several international donors to intervene in war-damaged places by funding opposition voices. Some agencies, such as USAID, have been known to subsidize anti-government papers that are barely comprehendible for the sole reason they are anti-government or have encouraged ethnic-related media outlets to proliferate. These policies are made with the idea that they will contribute to a variety of perspectives and thus promote understanding and peace.

in safeguarding democratic governance, but have also failed to do so on numerous occasions. At the time of writing, President Bush has won a second term in office, in spite of the fact that his administration has systematically provided misleading information about the situation in Iraq, and has manifestly violated human rights at the prison at Guantanamo Bay. It has been noted by several analysts that the US administrations are generally good at weathering press criticism, so long as a policy is maintained. After a while, the press moves on to another issue. The 'CNN effect' only seems to work when an administration's policies are unclear or subject to change.

14 The signing of the Arusha accords in 1993 enacted a power sharing agreement between the Hutus and Tutsis supervised by the United Nations. High on the agenda for the transition was the integration of the armies, the return of refugees and the development of free media, all of which would culminate in the 1995 multi-party elections.

15 In the case Abrahms vs. The United States, Holmes drew upon John Milton's "Areopagitica" (1644) and John Stuart Mill's "On Liberty" (1859), and argued in his Abrams dissent: "But when men have realized that time has upset many fighting faiths, they may come to believe even more than they believe the very foundations of their own conduct that the ultimate good desired is better reached by free trade in ideas –that the best test of truth is the power of the thought to get itself accepted in the competition of the market… That at any rate is the theory of our Constitution. It is an experiment, as all life is an experiment".

16 See for example <www.indexonline.org>.

Not surprisingly, feelings run particularly high on the issue of media freedom amongst many journalists. But it is worth bearing in mind that like other actors in the peace industry, journalists themselves are not immune to conflicts of interest. After all, whatever the integrity of their staff, global media networks obviously have self-serving motives. Press freedom in poor countries is a market into which they can expand and increase the use of their services. US economist R. H. Coase, amongst others, has drawn attention to these kinds of ulterior motives.

> The press is, of course, the most stalwart defender of the doctrine of freedom of press, an act of public service to the performance of which it has been led, as it were, by an invisible hand. If we examine the actions and views of the press, they are consistent in only one respect: they are always consistent with the self-interest of the press[17].

Other conflicts of interest and disagreements about how to encourage press freedom help explain why current media policy in Iraq has ended up being so confused- as indicated by the closing down of the Al-Hawza newspaper against Simon Haselock's advice. On the one hand, the United States policy has been to create an environment in which multiple voices can be heard as an antidote to the Baathist regime's propaganda or perhaps more importantly as an indicator of democratic governance or respect for 'human rights'. It is for this reason that the US government has made so much capital out of the fact that there are now an estimated 300 newspapers in Baghdad. On the other hand, the US government has reacted aggressively to what it regards as inaccurate or inflammatory reporting. There are, in addition, serious tensions between the occupying allies as to what is considered an appropriate strategy. The UK approach to developing viable media is based upon its own experience with a state funded public broadcaster. Simon Haselock describes this problem:

> In the US the notion of public broadcasting is synonymous with state and state broadcasting is synonymous with the sorts of things which used to happen in these centralist regimes. It is extremely difficult to get people to understand that what public broadcasting gives you is the ability to require a broadcaster not to be controlled but to deliver certain services and have the funding necessary to be able to do it[18].

Haselock has had to push for a public broadcasting mechanism in Iraq against US doubts. In his view there was no choice.

> We could not build an information mechanism in Iraq, or Iraqis could not build an information mechanism in Iraq if they had to rely on the basis of a commercial investor. They may only, for instance, want to provide a service

---

17 Coase, R. H. (1974), "The Market for Goods and the Market for Ideas", *The American Economic Review*, May, Vol. 64, No. 2, p. 386.
18 Haselock, Simon. Alistair Berkley Memorial Lecture.

which targets a particular section of the community or a particular region
of a community of where they are most likely to get advertising revenues[19].

However, like the Americans, the Iraqis too have found a state funded yet editori-
ally independent broadcasting instrument a difficult concept to grapple with.
Also the incoming Iraqi government is much more concerned about controlling
and constraining the flow of news through a new Ministry of Information (which
is headed by a former Baathist intelligence officer) than grappling with the complexities of establishing an effective public broadcaster.

What has been happening in Iraq highlights the need to put the
prevalent emphasis on press freedom and political openness into a context of
what is actually going on, rather than linking it to an invocation of what would
be ideal. Media freedom and responsibility in post war environments arise in
what Roland Paris describes as an enormous experiment in social engineering
that seeks to transplant specific economic, political and social models in war
shattered states in order to control civil conflict: in other words, pacification
through political and economic liberalization[20]. Experience has shown that this is
highly problematic.

States emerging from violent conflict tend to lack institutional mechanisms for any kind of sudden transition to market democracy. Attempts to develop these institutions quickly during a peacekeeping mission by individuals and
organizations that may not be entirely familiar with local dynamics can actually
hinder attempts towards long-term peace. After political liberalization, for example, Angola was struck by an increase in violence while premature elections in
Bosnia hindered reconciliation by reaffirming the separation of parties[21]. Similarly,
critics of the UN mission in Cambodia have argued that economic liberalization
has promoted growing inequalities between the cities and countryside while
political liberalization has exacerbated factionalism and has essentially encouraged the development of two separate but parallel governments fraught with
tension[22]. Here (and as we are currently witnessing in Iraq and Afghanistan) the
political concerns of external actors take precedence over the realities on the
ground. There is a strong desire by the rich countries that have been actively
involved to have a 'victory' –be it by establishing a media environment with 300
competing newspapers or facilitating elections in a short time frame.

Rwanda is perhaps the most extreme case and has quickly become the
textbook example. A peace process was linked to one of the worst genocides of
the twentieth century. There is strong evidence that a drive towards political liberalization with international support helped create the political environment which
allowed the killing. In particular, Snyder and Ballentine have persuasively argued

19 Ibid.

20 Paris, Roland (1997), "Peace building and the Limits of Liberal Internationalism", *International Security*, Autumn, Vol. 22, No. 2 p. 56.

21 Ibid.

22 Ibid, p. 65.

that the conflict was intensified by greater press freedom. Rapid liberalisation of the media was part of the Arusha peace accords[23]. It immediately spawned numerous news media outlets, largely dominated by opposition voices. Highly inaccurate and overtly biased editorials became prevalent. As Gerard Prunier puts it:

> A vibrant press had been born almost overnight –in terrible bad faith[24].

The Hutu elite, already feeling threatened by the potential loss of power they were to face, did not take these developments lightly. One reaction were the radio broadcasts of the government's *Milles Collines*.

In the wake of the genocide some international organizations, notably Human Rights Watch, continued to promote democratic accountability and take the position that free media could have helped avoid the tragedy. Snyder and Ballentine argue that it was "precisely the threat of such accountability that provoked the slaughter"[25]. In retrospect, most now agree that it would have been appropriate to clamp down on the hate speech of *Milles Collines*. Even Reporters Sans Frontières has warned in regards to Rwanda's neighbour Burundi, that the error committed in Rwanda of applying the rule of laissez-fare in the name of the principle of liberty of the press must not be repeated[26].

In Burundi, a new law on freedom of information has been enacted, and neither the 'international community' nor the government is restricting the hate speech that is presently being broadcast. Instead, they are relying on two radio stations based in the Democratic Republic of Congo to provide alternative points of view[27]. After what happened in Rwanda, once again relying on a marketplace of ideas in a precarious environment appears to some analysts as very risky. Such concerns are a reason why there have been initiatives by groups such as BBC Monitoring to establish systems to identify warning signs of impending violence, based on media content analysis. This inevitably has methodological limitations. The same kinds of extreme or misleading statements may be widely dismissed by one population as nonsense, but widely accepted by another as 'facts'. It all depends on the specific political processes at work. Nonetheless, as we will discuss in the next section with reference to South Africa, media monitoring of this kind is surely a positive development. At the very least it may highlight cir-

23 In the Arusha accords in August of 1993 the 'international community' pushed forward a peace deal between the Rwandan government and the RPF. Under the new UNAMIR (United Nations Assistance Mission for Rwanda) the UN was sent in to monitor the ceasefire and oversee the political transition. Canadian General Romeo Dallaire, backed by then Secretary General Boutros-Boutros Gali, argued that at least 5,000 UN troops were required to keep the peace. The US in the wake of the debacle in Somalia argued for 500 troops, a compromise was reached with 2,500.

24 Gerard Prunier as quoted in Snyder, Jack and Karen Ballentine (1996) "Nationalism and the Marketplace of Ideas", *International Security*, Autumn, Vol. 21, No. 2, p. 32.

25 Snyder and Ballentine, p. 33.

26 RSF as quoted in Snyder and Ballentine, p. 33.

27 Some NGOs disagree with this philosophy suggesting it pollutes objective journalism. As the IMPACS study suggests, "Under no circumstances, however, is the promotion of biased information or viewpoints masquerading as journalism a valid approach" (IMPACS, 4).

cumstances that require closer investigation, and it makes it a little more difficult for strategically unimportant parts of the world to be simply ignored.

Overall, there has yet to be a consensus on what should comprise best practice in peace-building media policy. The ideal of press freedom continues to be promoted in a simplistic way, but on the ground there is a great deal of 'hand-to-mouth' improvisation and often there are manifestly contradictory strategies. There is as much evidence that internationally supported initiatives have exacerbated local circumstances as that that they have contributed to political stability. The record, in so far as one has been kept, is very mixed. Old formulas, such as the US example or even the British public broadcasting model, may be largely irrelevant. At the very least, circumstances are very different from one country to another.

The media and state reconstruction

We now turn to situations in which international media-assistance interventions have been less overt or significant than in the instances mentioned above. We comment briefly on various developments in Ethiopia, Uganda and South Africa[28]. In all three countries, efforts have been made to move beyond the simplistic free/unfree dichotomy of so much of the debate, and local governments have sought out alternative ways of conceptualising relationships between the media and state during complex transitions. In focusing on them we do not intend to suggest that they should become 'ideal types' to be emulated elsewhere nor that they are the only countries grappling with these issues –we could have just as easily drawn on numerous other cases. They nevertheless raise important issues of broad applicability and that should have a much more central part in discussions about the roles of media in peace building than is usually the case.

Africa's so-called 'New Leaders', notably President Museveni of Uganda, Prime Minister Meles Zenawi of Ethiopia and President Kagami of Rwanda, have forcefully put forward an argument that they are pursuing a democratization strategy that will minimize the potential for divisive violent conflict. Not surprisingly they have provoked a critical response from human rights organisations. Human Rights Watch, for example, argues that Museveni's development strategy, referred to as a "movement system", is nothing more than "old wine in new bottles"[29]. Similarly the progressive federalist constitutional structure Meles has crafted in Ethiopia has been described by critics as the façade of an authoritarian and bureaucratic regime[30].

28 We have chosen these three countries largely because of our own interests and experience. We just as easily could have used many other cases, including Ghana, where the media have been instrumental in shaping the political environment.

29 This argument is laid out in Human Rights Watch's book, *Hostile to Democracy: The Movement System and Political Repression in Uganda*, New York: Human Rights Watch, 1999.

30 John Harbeson (2000) "A Bureaucratic Authoritarian Regime", *Journal of Democracy*, Johns Hopkins, p. 65.

These leaders doubtless have their own ulterior motives; nevertheless their argument should be taken seriously. Supporters, for example, have argued that the Ethiopian People's Revolutionary Democratic Front (EPRDF) has been relatively successful in holding the country together while also allowing space for the expression of ethnic diversity. They commend the relative success of the current leadership, pointing out that 'there are few precedents in today's world for transforming a deeply traditional, authoritarian, underdeveloped and severely damaged country'. The case may be instructive, as it challenges us to re-think exactly what we mean by media development and what an appropriate trajectory might look like.

The conflict between the Ethiopian state under Meles Zenawi and the Ethiopian press has sometimes been intense. Certainly the government is not above persecuting individual journalists and newspapers. It has generally failed to cooperate with the independent media, normally excluding their journalists from official events- within the last 10 years the private press has yet to be invited to one of Meles's press conferences. In 2000, Ethiopia had more imprisoned journalists than any other African country (an achievement that has subsequently been eclipsed by its neighbour Eritrea). Reporters Sans Frontiers has claimed that Meles is a "predator of press freedom". In May 2004 Ethiopia's Ministry of Information released the latest and likely final version of a draft *Proclamation to Provide for Freedom of the Press*[31]. Amnesty International, Article 19 and Human Rights Watch along with both local and international journalists have been deeply critical, arguing that it will further restrict the media and that it is indicative of a broader trend of deteriorating human rights conditions[32].

However, it is quite possible to put a more positive spin on what has occurred. It could be argued that Meles' Ethiopia is pursuing a path of media development consistent with the agenda proclaimed by the 'New Leaders'. His government has combined aggressive constraint procedures with provision of relatively considerable space for dissent. It is striking that the text of the recent *Proclamation* has not ignored inputs by various local organisations and journalists. Many free-media activists think that the law is too restrictive, but they have to concede that some of their concerns have been taken into account, and in several instances they have seen changes addressing their points in the various drafts. Moreover, despite Ethiopia's low rating for press tolerance, there is a considerable amount of open discussion –some of it highly charged and vociferous. The government's harsh attitude towards the independent

31 Essentially, the draft proclamation is part of an effort by the government to develop a regulatory framework that will concern itself not only with freedom of expression issues but freedom of information issues making Ethiopia one of a handful of countries in Africa that have developed a legal framework for freedom of information. The South African group *Resolve* has been contracted by the Ministry of Capacity Building to consult on how to draft and implement these laws while the Ministry of Information has been focusing on the draft press laws.

32 See for example Article 19s "Briefing Note on The Draft Ethiopian Proclamation to Provide for the Freedom of the Press" (London, June 2004).

media[33] has been matched by an equally aggressive response. Indeed, the majority of Ethiopian newspapers make the indecencies of the UK's tabloid press seem mild. Even the Ethiopian Free Press Journalists Association has noted that alarmist and false reporting is very prevalent, as well as stories that lack sufficient evidence to substantiate their assertions. For many of the papers, it would appear that their sole purpose has been to try to de-legitimise the government or to antagonise particular groups. While the effects of the *Proclamation to Provide for Freedom of the Press* have yet to be properly assessed, the debate the government has facilitated about media responsibilities and the limits to what is acceptable to say, may not be misplaced. It may indicate that things are less simple than has been asserted, and that this government is struggling to come to terms with a free media environment by trying to create a viable framework in which it can operate, without undermining the overarching agenda of re-invigorating the Ethiopian state.

A particular aspect of Ethiopia's *Proclamation* that has been criticised by organisations promoting press freedom is the clauses that mention the illegality of false accusations. Article 19, in a briefing on the draft of the *Proclamation* explained the basis of its reservations:

> ARTICLE 19 is opposed in principle to legal measures that prescribe the working methods of the media, or legal provisions requiring all news to be truthful. The media should be free to organise its internal working arrangements. Furthermore, goals of publications should not be prescribed, as this may be open to abuse on the grounds that a publication did not have these goals. Similarly, legal requirements requiring media to check the truthfulness of what they seek to publish are inappropriate. These matters are properly addressed in professional guidelines. In any event, it is well established that the nature of the newsgathering process means that the media may make mistakes[34].

Article 19 has expressed similar views with respect to developments in Uganda. Here the organisation can claim some credit for influencing the February 2004 decision of the Uganda Supreme Court to declare that the offence of 'publishing false news' was incompatible with the right to freedom of expression. This relates to the court case between Charles Onyango-Obbo and Andrew Mujini Mwenda versus The Attorney General of Uganda. The written comments on the case, submitted by Article 19, exemplify the prevailing 'international' approach to many of the issues we have been discussing.

The Article 19 commentary opens by summarising the case in which two journalists were charged with publishing false news suggesting that late

---

33 In Ethiopia the print media (ie. newspapers) are a mix of government and private. The radio and television remain almost entirely controlled by the government.

34 Article 19s' "Briefing Note on The Draft Ethiopian Proclamation to Provide for the Freedom of the Press" (London, June 2004).

President Kabilia gave a large amount of gold to Uganda. However, no comments are made about the specific details.

Obviously the intention was not to address the particular case but rather use it as an opportunity to attack Section 50 of Uganda's Penal Code. This states that "any person who publishes any false statement, rumour or report which is likely to cause fear and alarm to the public or to disturb the peace is guilty of a misdemeanour"[35]. No attempt is made to assess the local context in which this code might operate. Rather, Article 19 makes its argument on the basis of principle, asserting that the false news provision is inconsistent with international and constitutional guarantees of freedom of expression and cannot be regarded as either 'reasonable' or 'justifiable' restrictions as allowed in instances of speech that may be threatening[36]. The legal cases cited are all from outside the African continent from either Europe or America. Indeed, the brief reads as though the author merely cut and pasted various segments from a report that may have initially been created for another purpose.

The position put forward by Article 19 is an interesting example of an international organisation using local legal mechanisms to prevent an African government from constraining press freedom. Doubtless many readers will think this was an entirely credible intervention. It is probably the case that 'false information' laws are more likely to be exploited by governments than more specific provisions on incitement to violence, which most African governments have on their statute books[37]. However, one immediate consequence of striking off Section 50 of the Penal Code is that it removes a legal instrument through which the government of Uganda might try to contain hate speech.

Perhaps more importantly, the case illustrates a 'human rights' strategy that is unable to adjust to the specific context in which it is operating. As Jon Lunn has noted, there is a prevailing "international legal absolutism" evident among organisations such as Article 19. Specific historical or political considerations, that might be required to address the particular local realities of countries in complex transitions, are subordinated to the "global justice agenda"[38]. It seems reasonable to ask whether this strategy is appropriate for countries whose primary goal is peace and state-reconstruction.

---

35 There is a following provision that the accused can offer defence by proving that he took measures "to verify the accuracy of such statement, rumour or report as to lead him reasonably to believe that it was true". Article 19 report, Onyango-Obbo and Mwenda vs. Uganda Attorney General.

36 Their brief suggested that Section 50 of the Penal Code that states: "(1) Any person who publishes any false statement, rumor or report which is likely to cause fear and alarm to the public or to disturb the public peace is guilty of a misdemeanor and (2) It shall be a defense to a charge under subsection (1) if the accused proves that, prior to publication, he took such measures to verify the accuracy of such statement, rumor or report as to lead him reasonably to believe that it was true" is in contradiction with Section 29 of the Ugandan Constitution stating "(1) Every person shall have the right to- (a) freedom of speech and expression, which shall include freedom of the press and other media".

37 In Uganda, part of the Constitution states that "no person shall prejudice the fundamental or other human rights and freedoms of others or the public interest".

38 Jon Lunn, "The power of justice/justice as power: observations on the trajectory of the international human rights movement", unpublished paper, January 2003 (available on request from Jon Lunn at <j.lunn@lse.ac.uk>).

President Museveni of Uganda shares many of Meles's perspectives on state reconstruction and political development; indeed he has probably been something of a model for Meles to emulate. Ugandan journalists have not always had an easy time, and there is no doubt that some have faced outright persecution. Nevertheless, as in Ethiopia, the parameters within which various kinds of media have been allowed to develop have been greater than most Uganda watchers would have thought possible in the mid 1980s. Visitors to the country are often amazed at the dynamism and critical qualities of the county's newspapers and radio stations. Not surprisingly, the independent newspapers are the more outspoken, but the government-owned *New Vision* is no mere propaganda device[39]. News media have been allowed to be openly hostile to government policies, and have frequently been able to take powerful individuals to task in much the same ways as journalists have done in post-transition South Africa.

In South Africa, the use of news media by politicians has had almost the opposite effects to those that occurred in Rwanda. The media were critical on details of government actions and policies –often very critical indeed, but were broadly supportive of the national reconciliation and state-building project. What has occurred in South Africa illustrates how a government's media policies may clash with the 'global justice' movement, and be bitterly opposed by many journalists, yet contribute substantially to essential political processes. At the time of the transition from apartheid to democracy there was the distinct possibility of the country being engulfed by civil war and political turmoil. Astute use of the available news media resources helped stop this from happening. One decisive example occurred after Chris Hani, a charismatic black leader who was popular in the townships, was gunned down in his driveway. President Mandela appealed for calm through the South African Broadcasting Corporation (SABC), pointing out that the woman who identified the perpetrators was a white Afrikaner woman. His action is widely assessed to have played a key role in diffusing a potentially explosive situation.

The relationship between government and news media has not been an easy one, however. After coming to power the ANC attempted to influence the SABC for its own purposes, prompting fierce debate within the country as to what the relationship between the new government and the public broadcaster should be. The SABC has had to fiercely defend its relative independence. A particular arena of tension has been a consequence of the government's determination to eradicate all forms of hate-speech, including subtle racial biases. For obvious reasons there has been determination to push this policy to the limit and systematic efforts have been made to ensure that all established media organisations are accountable on the issue. The South African Human Rights Commission even

---

39 To give just a couple of examples from 1998: *New Vision* reported embezzlement of monies intended for fuel "for military operations against Joseph Kony rebels in northern Uganda, and the diversion of supplies, including medicines from the army to the LRA rebels" (*New Vision*, 6 April 1998, "UPDF officer charged"; *New Vision*, 11 April 1998, "Two Kony bodyguards held in Kampala").

went so far as to subpoena editors of some of the most liberal and progressive newspapers, an action which was hugely controversial with journalists and human rights organisations. What ensued was a year-long investigation into identifying and defining racism in the media, and a great deal of debate about what should be done to prevent it[40].

At one level the inquiry failed, in that it was unable to carry out the task it assigned itself (i.e. identifying subtle racism), but it facilitated an important discussion across society. It forced journalists and editors to step back and reflect upon the role they should play during the important transition period, and helped create a situation in which they became acutely aware of the unconscious ways in which they might be promoting counterproductive stereotypes. It has led to a considerable amount of unregulated self-censorship: there are many things now that just cannot be said. In the fragile circumstances of post-apartheid South Africa, this has surely been valuable —even if it has limited a journalist's capacity to tell the truth as she or he sees it.

It is also important to note that these pressures and constraints have not incapacitated the South African news media. Far from it, if anything it has increased their importance and made them more of a voice for the population as a whole than they ever were in the past. By and large, they have been vigorously outspoken, frequently launching exposes of politicians and sometimes even the government itself. Given the relative weakness of opposition parties in the country, the press has to a large extent taken on the role of holding the ANC to account.

In this respect, it must be recognised that the post-apartheid media in South Africa were still operating in an established and recognized legal system —the broader structural institutions were in place to provide recourse when due. This marks a critical difference from many other countries. In short, there were courts to turn to if someone had to sue for libel, there was a judiciary that remained strong, and executive leadership that worked within the legal framework. There were of course also entrenched hierarchies associated with these broader structural institutions. The Human Rights Commission challenged some of these, but only up to a point. In general, the ANC government has sought to guarantee the rights and safety of political and economic elites. This has been very unpopular with many political activists, not only in South Africa itself, but it is the case that functioning state systems require such hierarchies. As Mandela accepted, to change them overnight would have been catastrophic. Elsewhere, peace-building governments may not inherit similarly institutionalised social stratification. Ideally, this could be avoided —but that is not the way things work. Effectively hierarchies have to be established as part of the state construction process. This is one of the most difficult things for human rights organisations

---

40 While the SAHRC is 'independent' of the government, there are clear and strong links including between Barney Pityana, the former Chairperson of the SAHRC and the current leadership in the ANC.

and development agencies to come to terms with, and lies behind much of the | 229
criticism levelled at the likes of Museveni and Meles.

Conclusion: a case for media manipulation?

As this chapter has argued, the current approach to media policy in countries emerging from violent conflict is problematic and needs to be re-thought. Let us conclude by reviewing the arguments put forth and suggest a possible way forward.

First, it is important to note the impact liberal ideology has had on ways in which media policy is constructed and the need to re-conceptualise the role of the state in media development. In the 1960s, Samuel Huntington suggested that open institutions such as a free press were 'luxuries' transitioning states could ill afford. In short, he argued that the potential disruption of mass public participation was simply a risk that countries struggling to modernise need not take. Such ideas were always controversial, and were understandably seen as discredited by the militarised autocracies of the 1970s. The promise, however, of political and economic liberalisation has proved almost as fruitless in most parts of the world. As this chapter has illustrated, the prevailing approach to media development is indicative of the broader ideological liberal approach to political development and is thus vulnerable to similar criticisms. Developing an open media environment, like other liberal projects, requires the presence of a strong state which includes, among other features, a well functioning legal and judicial environment.

Second, the prevailing approach towards the media in transitioning countries is structured around the experience and impressions of rich countries rather than local realities. While almost everyone is beginning to accept that markets have to be regulated, and that state institutions have to be strong for them to work effectively, the need for checks and balances in transitioning countries continues to be under-emphasised. This is partly because free media continue to be considered by many journalists and NGOs as a human right. Article 19 of the Universal Declaration of Human Rights, however, is about individual and collective rights and liberties, not about the independence of media organisations[41]. Additionally, there is a tendency in rich countries for domestic media environments to be seen as something of an ideal, exemplifying the population's openness and freedoms. As most readers are well aware, the reality is more complicated. Rich countries do not have perfectly competitive marketplaces of ideas. While formal state censorship may be

41 The text of Article 19 is as follows: "Everyone has the right to the freedom of opinion and expression; this right includes freedom to hold opinions without interference and to seek, receive and impart information and ideas through any media and regardless of frontiers". We do note, however, that some of the world's most progressive constitutions, such as South Africa, have provisions for providing for the right to open media. In addition, as certain norms have been accepted as 'standards', we recognise that this may be contested terrain; however, conflating one with the other can be profoundly misleading. It may well be that there are good reasons for a government to want to control media organisations and to put limits on what they can say and how it can be said in order to protect the human rights of their citizens including their right to development.

minimal, there are nevertheless mechanisms and codes of conduct that serve a similar role. In the UK for example, simply by looking at who owns newspapers and funds TV stations one can see that the media market is constrained. Along a similar vein, many in the US media have made clear that they recognise their negligence and failure in the run-up to the war in Iraq when certain ideas that challenged the rationale behind the war were not given a 'fair' and 'equal' voice.

The third argument we have made is that the tendency of journalists and human rights organisations to ignore the local realities and rather push their own 'international justice' agenda may be counter-productive. While the media and human rights organisations have effectively lobbied, particularly in weaker states, against the use of state constraint, they have similarly divorced issues of media liberalisation from the political context. Given the asymmetrical power relations between large human rights organisations with substantial lobbying power in rich countries and poorer countries with leadership that is regarded as weak and semi-autocratic at best, it is easy to see how local initiatives or arguments for slower media liberalisation fall on deaf ears. Thus, foreign 'experts', often in line with rich countries, are increasingly defining and dominating processes such as 'truth' and 'justice'. As John Lunn describes, this approach is unfortunately something we are all familiar with.

> During the colonial period, Africans (and other colonised) were often viewed as children who were not ready yet for self-government. In the modern world, a similar characterisation is creeping back in. Locals are seen as lacking the capacity or maturity to govern themselves. ... new forms of trusteeship are justified on the basis that reactionary and opportunistic local political leaders cannot be trusted to rule justly and fairly[42].

Given the complexity of political transitions and state reconstruction it would be unfortunate if viable local alternatives were not explored or tolerated because they may possibly contradict some of the expectations or standards of rich countries. As we described in this chapter, the controversial approach taken by Africa's 'New Leaders' may present one of these alternative strategies. Accepting such approaches, however, will necessitate some degree of systematic assessment on the nature and intentions of the current government. While such analysis is often difficult, it does clearly warrant further exploration and study.

Fourth, whatever the rhetoric about promoting freedom of expression, the situation on the ground is often muddled, contradictory and sometimes hypocritical. In places like Iraq this has been at least partly because US and other occupying troops from rich countries are themselves vulnerable to attack and have thus been inclined to shut down media outlets. But more generally, concerns about hate speech are supplanted in initiatives to create a space for promoting news

---

42 Jon Lunn, "The power of justice/justice as power: observations on the trajectory of the international human rights movement", unpublished paper, January 2003 (available on request from Jon Lunn at <j.lunn@lse.ac.uk>).

manipulation, ideally without enforcement procedures or explicit controls. In many respects this is, of course, how news media in particular are effectively restrained in rich countries, including the UK and US. Also in Iraq and other war zones, while some international organisations are promoting multiple voices and freedom of speech, others are experimenting with mechanisms to manipulate the marketplace of ideas including efforts to promote peace by funding particular media outlets. This kind of 'peace media' approach has become popular with some donor agencies, such as Oxfam, and also with some large media organisations, such as the BBC. The intention is to make the content of the programmes more interesting and just generally better than the alternatives available. Results have so far been mixed, but such experiments are interesting and clearly have possibilities for development[43]. While peace media are certainly an important initiative that is gaining momentum and popularity, the general approach to media development continues to be dominated by 'one size fits all' laissez faire projects. As this strategy is not likely to be entirely abandoned, there is, however, the potential for slowing it down and concentrating on rebuilding institutions. Doing so would also suggest greater understanding from rich countries of the challenges faced by transitioning governments. It would also reduce charges of hypocrisy –such as those that emerged from Iraq– as it would demonstrate that it is not only rich countries that can be trusted to impose censorship and shape developing media environments.

Fifth, in instances when more institutionalised mechanisms that may exist in rich countries are either not present or functioning properly, explicit constraint may be required. When this is necessary, a crucial issue is: by whom? Just as developing countries have successfully argued at the WTO that they are willing to buy into liberal market economics but they want concessions and safeguards –there are parallel lessons for the media as well. But giving the state too much control may also be a risky proposition, as a long line of African autocrats has clearly taught. An alternative strategy will clearly require some degree of international or regional oversight as well as greater transparency and accountability.

One possibility is the establishment of a United Nations global media watchdog that could serve as a central component to ensure standards and procedures are adhered to and to prevent abuse. Monitoring, however, must be done according to certain accepted principles and undertaken in such a way that is not seen as simply reflecting the values and interests of the world's rich states. The proliferation of Truth and Reconciliation Commissions (TRC) offers a possible analogy for establishing a media oversight body with both local and international

---

43 Oxfam-Quebec, for example, has sponsored a very successful peace programme in Somalia –Radio Galkayo. This programme tackles a variety of issues such as de-mining, concerns of women and peace and reconciliation. It is produced by some young journalists in the area and has been successful at spearheading community projects that have brought together various factions. Not all attempts at peace media are successful and a recent attempt in Somalia by BBC Trust is indicative of just how problematic it may be. The BBC Somali service hosted a drama series to discuss conflict resolution. They however made a grievous error in selecting the choice of actors and one clan regarded the drama as a plot by another clan to attack them. (Adam and Holguin, 2003: 10).

credentials. In Sierra Leone, for example, the TRC is a hybrid of local and international jurists. Independent Media Commissions might adopt this hybrid structure thus allowing for the participation of both local and international media bodies. These Commissions would also serve as an important mechanism for facilitating local dialogue about past media abuses as well as discussions about responsible peace building reporting.

In the case of Africa, another option may be found within the African Peer Review Mechanism (APRM)[44], a central component of Africa's new development initiative –the New Partnership for African Development (NePAD)[45]. Everyone would feel more comfortable with limitations on media freedom if states had to request permission to impose them. Perhaps a system could be established similar to how law enforcement officers must request a search warrant from a court. For example, if states subscribed to the APRM and agreed to be held accountable to prevent abuse, in return they would be allowed greater scope for restricting the media during precarious transitions and more time in which to develop the infrastructure for a free media environment.

These initiatives, however, will require further re-evaluation of the overall peace building agenda as well as some degree of compromise from the NGOs and human rights advocates that so passionately hold to their own perspective. While it is premature to propose a new approach to media in peace building environments, we hope this chapter has succeeded in questioning the underlying assumptions of the liberal approach. There is much research to be had in continuing to sketch out alternative frameworks for thinking about the media's role in transitions. It is our hope that future initiatives will be characterised by a greater focus on holding local strategies to account rather than the continued imposition of rich country strategies.

---

44 The APRM is an instrument that is used for self-monitoring by the participating countries. Both Uganda and Ethiopia are currently on the fifteen-member steering committee. Countries that have agreed to join the APRM submit to periodical peer reviews whose primary purpose is to foster the adoption of certain policies, standards and practices with the intention of achieving political stability and cooperation. For more information visit the African Union's website or the reports from the 2002 meeting where the APRM was established. See for example:
<http://www.au2002.gov.za/docs/summit_council/aprm.htm>.

45 For more information on NePAD see the official website: <www.nepad.org>.

Chapter 13

Participatory and cultural challenges for research and practice in health communication

Rafael Obregon
& Mario Mosquera

Arguably, health communication is one of the most dynamic areas in the field of development communication. In fact, it is one of those areas that often seem to receive greater attention from communication researchers and practitioners, a perception that may have been fueled by the emergence of HIV/AIDS and the critical role of communications to combat the epidemic. By the same token, Latin America has made very important contributions to the field of development communications over the years. The indigenous practice of development and health communication in the region often has taken some distance from dominant approaches to the field, primarily those arising out of the developed world. This is especially true when it comes to the emphasis on participatory approaches in development and health communication in Latin America, which often clashes with the more positivistic, strategic approaches developed by researchers and practitioners in the developed world.

In this chapter we attempt to highlight some of the methodological and research challenges that the practice of health communication brings to the field of development communication. We do so by providing an overview of development communication research and practice and the centrality of participatory approaches to health and development communication with a stronger focus in Latin America, followed by a discussion of the evolution of health communication approaches, and the challenges that researchers and practitioners may want take into account in the near future.

The chapter is divided into three sections. Section one will focus on the participatory, critical and cultural roots of communications in Latin America.

This section seeks to provide readers with a historical and conceptual context of the key transformations that have taken place in the region. It discusses the Latin American response to dominant paradigms in development communications and the movement toward participatory, critical and cultural approaches in the study and practice of communications, which have permeated most of the work in development communication in the region.

Section two deals with the emergence and evolution of health communication including a brief discussion about the main approaches that have influenced the practice of health communication. Drawing from key ideas developed in the previous section, the final section of the chapter focuses on some of the immediate and future challenges that development and health communication practitioners and academics must bring into their practice and analysis. In doing so, there is an attempt to connect the main aspects of the development of health communication in Latin America with some of the broader issues discussed in this book on research and methodological issues in development communication.

Participatory, critical and cultural roots of development communication in Latin America

The 1960s brought several social and political developments in Latin America, which had a profound impact on its socioeconomic landscape. In this volatile context the "revolutionary" and liberating work of Paulo Freire in Brazil provided a new and fresh approach to the implementation of adult education programs which, inadvertently, set many of the principles of communication for development and social change. One of Freire's vital assumptions was the critical capacity of the illiterate. He argued that every human being, no matter how uneducated, is capable of looking at his/her world in a critical manner leading to a dialogical encounter with others (Freire, 1986). This led to the notion of "dialogue of knowledge", in which both teacher and student engage in an exchange of knowledge based upon their realities. In Freire's view, literacy programs would not only teach people how to read and write, but also would help people *conscienticize* (consciousness-raising) of and transform their realities.

Also in the 1960s, the U.S. launched several efforts to modernize Latin America and other regions of the world. A great number of U.S. researchers traveled to Latin America to share their developmental model, which had worked very well in the U.S., but eventually failed to produce similar results in Latin America (Beltran, 1976; Diaz-Bordenave, 1976). Television became the dominant medium, which led to the implementation of several media development programs based on Wilbur Schramm's (1964) ideas on *Mass media and national development*. For instance, with underlying notions of powerful media effects, media development programs were carried out in El Salvador to support formal education initiatives. Similar projects were implemented in Africa, and throughout Latin America. However, many of these projects failed due to a lack of understanding of local conditions and cultural practices (Rogers, 1976; 1987).

The concept of dependency theory emerged and quickly gained serious support. First stated by Andre Gunder Frank (1966), dependency theory viewed development and underdevelopment as necessarily inter-connected (Cardoso and Faletto, 1979). One essential idea was that underdevelopment in the Third World was, to a large extent, caused by unequal trade relations necessary for the development of the First World. Theorists aligned with the dependency paradigm argued that "Latin American economic and political development is structured according to the needs of developed industrialized capitalist states" (Fejes, 1986, p. 247; Cardoso and Faletto, 1979).

Communications research in Latin America quickly developed a strong critical approach (Schwarz and Jaramillo, 1986). Luis Ramiro Beltran, a Bolivian communication scholar, became a strong critic of modernization and diffusion of innovation programs. In his seminal article "Alien premises, objects and methods in Latin American communication research", Beltran (1978) discussed the weaknesses of modernization programs. These programs were based on what Everett Rogers (1976), perhaps the most influential scholar on diffusion of innovations, later defined as the old dominant paradigm: top-down approach, big scale projects, focus on economic growth, capital intensive technology, and centralized planning. Efforts were made to use communication as a development tool in the region, which led to the consolidation of a critical stance to external development models. CIESPAL, a training institution created with UNESCO's support, emerged as an alternative to train media and communication professionals increasingly aware of the social needs of the region. However, by 1973 CIESPAL was gradually forced to reshape its orientation. Political developments in the region (i.e., the establishment of military dictatorships in Peru and Chile, and soon in other nations) led to the adoption of new working frameworks.

The non-democratic context emerging in the region and the increasing power garnered by media organizations in Latin American countries became fertile ground for critical approaches to communications, fueled by the thinking of educators (i.e. Freire), social developers (i.e. Diaz Bordenave), and communicators (i.e., Beltran, Mario Kaplun), amongst others. Development communicators throughout the region played a key role in promoting dialogical and participatory approaches to communications and development. Yet, in many cases this type of work was perceived as too critical or even revolutionary at times, given the current socio-political situation in most countries. Hence, they often operated from the margins.

The '80s brought new critical elements into the study of Latin American communication research, particularly in the area of cultural studies. Unlike previous approaches, the most distinctive feature of this line of research in Latin America was its less political character. O'Connor (1991: 60) argued that:

> The cultural studies that has emerged from Latin America during the last decade is theoretically sophisticated and subtle. But it seems to lack the explicit Marxism and Feminism of the researchers and activists that emerged in the 1970s.

Two of the most relevant figures are Jesus Martin-Barbero and Nestor Garcia-Canclini. Martin-Barbero's major contribution is his analysis of media, mediation, and popular culture, and how media have transformed concepts of culture in Latin America. He argued that "cultures of urban and rural masses are increasingly products of the mass media" (1993: 18). However, by no means is this viewed as a passive relationship. Rather, in Martin-Barbero's view, people constantly re-elaborate, reinterpret, and transform messages offered by the media. Schlessinger (1993: xii) summarizes Martin-Barbero's thinking:

> What Martin-Barbero contends is that we should shift our attention from forms of analysis concerned with the ownership and control of media structures and with messages conceived as hegemonic ideology to modes of reception in the context of wider social relations.

At the root of Martin-Barbero's reasoning is his definition and understanding of popular culture. Martin-Barbero holds that although common wisdom characterizes popular culture as "a homogeneous subject defined either in positive terms as a pole of resistance, or in negative terms as a product of manipulation, a corrupted version of elite culture" (1993: 18), this dichotomy fails to recognize the social, economic and symbolic dimensions of popular culture. Rather, the relationship between popular culture and media brings with it the concept of mediations, in which culture is constantly resisted, negotiated and contextualized, and yet it is provisional.

Similarly, Nestor Garcia-Canclini's contributions are rooted in the analysis of media and culture. One of his fundamental premises is the concept of culture and subcultures created by the media. Media produce new cultural communities without territories that are difficult to define in conventional cultural terms (1992). Garcia-Canclini criticizes the deductivistic and inductivistic approaches in the analysis of popular culture. Deductivistic approaches impose cultural definitions in structural, macroscopic terms from the outside. By contrast, inductivistic notions view individuals as units of a group or community who are culturally labeled with no options for redefining their world (1988). In both cases, Garcia-Canclini argues, the conflictual interaction that takes place between dominant and dominated groups is ignored. He implies that it is this interaction and the interpretation of it what gives meaning to culture. Also central to Garcia-Canclini's thought are the ideas of everyday life, meaning, and cultural mediations.

While taking somewhat different paths, both Garcia-Canclini and Martin-Barbero incorporated notions of resistance, a permanent construction of popular culture removed from the negative connotations of the past, and the constant process of negotiation and transaction in which groups, regardless of their position in society, engage in everyday life. At the root of Martin-Barbero and Garcia-Canclini's work is the role of media, particularly television. A great deal of these negotiations and resistance take place in the world of mass communications, especially with television, which is seen by many as a homogenizing tool that attempts to construct a fixed model of culture. Further, both authors have found *telenovelas* to be a critical genre through which audiences engage in a daily struggle of cultural negotiation.

Despite its less political connotations, Martin-Barbero and Garcia-Canclini's work still conveys a critical flavor. Martin-Barbero's and Garcia-Canclini's views have shaped Latin American communication research, and their thinking is often brought into development communication approaches. Their influences are reflected in the value accorded to culture as an entry point in development communication as well as through a number of audience reception studies of telenovelas and other media genres (see Fadul, 1993; McAnany, 1993; Allen, 1995; Tufte, 1995).

In short, the appearance of critical research and cultural studies in Latin America was the result of the convergence of several social and cultural events, coupled with the failure of developmental models that were transferred to Latin America in several areas, including communications. In retrospect, not only do we see a strong critical and culture-based orientation but also a thrust toward participatory communication, a fundamental assumption in Rogers' new development communication paradigm (1976), a concept that was already present in the works of Paulo Freire back in the '50s and '60s. Thus, a critical view, the role of culture, and participatory communication became central to the theory and practice of development communication in the region.

Conceptual approaches to health communication: from information to social change?

Although health communication has been present in the region since the 1960s and '70s, primarily through family planning programs, it only developed as a field at the beginning of the '80s. Hence, only recently have many of these elements rooted in the communication tradition of Latin America been incorporated into the practice of health communication. The Declaration of Alma Ata (1978) was an important conceptual shift from previous visions of health care and prevention –largely dominated by high technology, hospital-based concepts of health care– towards the search for innovative and flexible approaches that paid greater attention to knowledge already possessed by local people. This was a meaningful shift in the power relationship from what was termed "scientific management" (Pfeffer and Coote, 1991) toward health interventions controlled by lay people. According to MacDonald (1992), the spirit of the Alma Ata declaration was mainly underpinned by communitarian values, which aimed to enhance the democratic distribution of power in decision-making in health.

The community development movement emphasized the importance of involving people in their own development, while the state and its welfare institutions and professionals sought to transfer their responsibilities for health care provision to individuals and families (Sanchez, 1994). This strategy of individual responsibility for self-care assumes that the basic cause of an individual's illness or lack of health is the individual him/herself, not the state or the existing social structures.

Therefore the solution must come primarily from the individual and not from structural changes of the economic or social system (Navarro, 1986). Communication strategies in this context have centered not only in exclusively achieving change in behavior but also in achieving effective communication by producing adequate, persuasive messages that respond to the symbolic universe of the target groups without attempting to create a dialogue for change nor a participatory process.

According to the World Health Organization, health communication is the study and use of communication strategies to inform and influence individual and community decisions to improve people's health. This type of communication is recognized as a necessary element in the efforts to improve personal and public health. Similarly, health communication may contribute in all aspects of disease prevention including physician-patient communication, adherence to treatment, and the design, implementation and evaluation of public health communication campaigns.

Health communication is generally conceived as a strategic process aimed at achieving a rational use of health services, and improving the efficiency and effectiveness of programs directed at disease prevention and health promotion. Research has shown that health communication programs based on solid theory may bring health to the forefront of the public agenda, reinforce sanitary messages, stimulate people to seek more and better information, and in some cases lead towards healthier lifestyles. Four key elements of the communication process are typically used in health communication: source, message, channel, and audience, increasingly coupled with social mobilization and participation components and with rigorous research. It is generally agreed that effective programs in health communication identify and prioritize key behaviors, segment audiences, design messages based on scientific evidence and research, and reach audiences through key channels, while mobilizing communities to become involved in this processes (Piotrow et al, 1997; Freimuth, 1992).

Nevertheless, other authors differ in their approach to the role of communication in health, particularly when it comes to issues of target populations and audience needs. Gumucio-Dagron (2001) argues that communication has often been conceived erroneously either as propaganda or as simple diffusion of information. Accordingly, he adds, many governments, international agencies, and NGOs view communication as an opportunity to gain visibility concentrating their work in the use of mass media and in other activities that, for instance, may impact urban areas, but not necessarily those areas most in need.

Health communication has undergone important conceptual changes over the past decades. Table 1 is an attempt to summarize these changes through the identification of the main approaches that have characterized the implementation of health communication and some key characteristics of each approach. While this table is by no means exhaustive nor does it provide the fullness of how health communication has evolved, it does illustrate some of the key transformations that health communication has experienced over the years.

Table 1. Evolution of health communication approaches

Approach	Strategies	Characteristics	Centrality of...
Information and education	Counseling; health education	Extensionist model, top-down communication	Messages, recommendation of behaviors
Information, education, communication (IEC)	Increasing use of mass and interpersonal communication	Greater articulation of interventions and more strategic character; limitations with complex behaviors (i.e. HIV/AIDS)	Media messages and products, educational materials, planning methodologies, KAP research, focus on changing behaviors
Communication for behavior change (CBC)	Increasing use of multiple communication strategies, linkages with social mobilization interventions and health services	Strong use of social and behavioral psychology and communication theories; more research-driven processes	Focus on behaviors (ideal and attainable), barriers and enablers, focus on behavior change at the individual level, efforts to reach measurable impact
Context-based approaches (UNAIDS's HIV/AIDS Framework)	Integration of various communication strategies and media interventions; use of local media	Contextual domains as areas subject to change through communications (government & policy, socio-economic status, culture, gender, spirituality)	Focus on changing context to facilitate individual and collective behavior change
Communication for social change	Social mobilization, community participation, dialogue-based, alternative media	Greater emphasis on empowerment and local ownership	Focus on changing structural dimensions through communication processes, impact at the individual and collective levels, social norms, rights

Three central themes emerge from this table. First, it may be argued that participatory and dialogical elements were, for the most part, absent in the initial approaches to health communication, while the latter two approaches are certainly characterized by issues of culture and participation. Second, while behavior change –whether individual and/or collective– remains the primary goal in the first three approaches and it is certainly present in the latter two approaches, the way to reach this type of change is what distances each of these approaches as it is explained in the next paragraphs.

Third, IEC and CBC approaches are characterized by two central features: they aim directly at the notion of generating behavior change on individuals, and lately on collectivities; and they are essentially message-centered and rely on the critical role played by carefully designed messages and communication strategies that will eventually lead to behavior change. For instance, IEC focuses on communication activities aimed at preventing disease and at promoting health by strengthening people's capacity to act on their own health and development. Thus, IEC seeks to improve people's knowledge about health issues and to stimulate attitudinal and behavior change through a set of integrated communication strategies. IEC starts with the assessment of people's needs followed by the identification of key communication mechanisms and messages that may lead to changes in behavior and to improvements in the health of the population.

In Communication for Behavior Change (CBC), multiple theories and concepts have been taken from other disciplines (i.e. social psychology) or elaborated to understand why individuals behave in a certain manner with respect to their health, how and when they may use health services, their acquisition of health-related habits, modification of knowledge and attitudes, and ultimately health behaviors. Most variables considered in CBC are derived from a set of widely used psychological theories that have had a strong influence in health communication research such as the health belief model, the theory of reasoned action, and social learning theory. However, there is increasing consensus on the number of contextual variables that need to be considered when predicting or understanding human behaviors.

On the other hand, contextual approaches and communication for social change frameworks take a different route. In essence, both approaches recognize the need to generate change in the contextual and social dimensions of health through communication and other elements as changes on these variables will eventually facilitate and lead to changes in people's behaviors. The UNAIDS' HIV/AIDS communication framework developed out of the growing concern for the perceived lack of effectiveness of existing strategies in containing and/or curbing the HIV/AIDS epidemic. It is stated:

> Seeking to influence behavior alone is insufficient if the underlying social factors that shape the behavior remain unchallenged. Many communications and health promotion programs proceed on the assumption that behavior, alone, needs to be changed, when, in reality, such change is unlikely to be sustainable without incurring in some minimum social change. This necessitates attention to social environmental contexts (UNAIDS, 1999: 15).

The framework called for greater attention to five contextual domains (policy, government, gender, culture, socio-economic, spirituality) that play a central role in determining people's behaviors. Thus, it was argued, there was a need for a greater focus of communication strategies on these domains as a way to generate change in people's behaviors in the context of HIV/AIDS (Airhihenbuwa, Makinwa and Obregon, 2000). For instance, it is generally agreed that condom promotion alone is not sufficient to curb the epidemic and that a shift in the balance of power relations in gender relations is critical to ensure women's empowerment to negotiate condom use.

Lastly, Communication for Social Change (CFSC) focuses on the larger | **241** notion of social development and on the role that communication may play in generating change. It calls for greater participation and control of communities over communication processes and it highlights the need to allow community voices to be heard and become the leading voices of processes of change (Rockefeller Foundation, 1999). The CFSC model describes a process in which "community dialogue" and "collective action" come together to produce social change in a particular social environment to improve the well being, i.e., health, of its members. Social change implies the participation of the community in all processes concerned with the planning, implementation and evaluation of development and health programs[1].

In short, from a historical perspective, there has been a significant shift in health communication thinking, at least conceptually, from approaches mainly centered on effects, individual behavior change, and biomedical thinking, towards an approach in which active participation of people directly affected by the problems as well as culture and social relations are now key references for the design, implementation and evaluation of health communication programs. While IEC and CBC-based projects and initiatives have been implemented widely throughout the world yielding mixed results –depending on the type of health issue at hand (i.e., vaccination and family planning, very successful; HIV/AIDS, little success), the UNAIDS' communication framework and the CFSC model still are in the process of being further operationalized and implemented on different scales in order to provide specific examples and evidence of their application.

However, given their focus on issues of participation, empowerment, dialogue, and culture, these two approaches, the UNAIDS' framework and CFSC, clearly resonate with the background of development communication in Latin America. Similarly, given the increasing attention to issues of culture and participation, models focused on CBC have moved toward hybrid models (Sood, Menard and Witte, 2004). As these approaches are progressively used in health communication with an increasingly central role being played by issues of participation and culture, they bring up a host of methodological and research challenges that are addressed below.

Challenges for the research and practice of health communication

Never before had the work of Paulo Freire been given so much attention in the Western development communication literature as it has been the case over the past five years (i.e., Tufte, 2004; Tufte, 2004a; Singhal, 2004; Richards, Thomas, and Nain, 2001; Servaes, 2001). By the same token, the focus on participation and culture brings up important questions related to issues of planning, evidence, meas-

1 See Gumucio, A. (2001), *Making Waves: Stories of Participatory Communication*, for an anthology of community-based, participatory communication projects around the world.

urements, impact, and indicators amongst other issues. For instance, as Nancy Morris, whose full article appears on this volume, puts it referring to outcomes and evaluation of processes, "the task is complex, in part because of the lack of accepted definitions of community, empowerment, or participation" (2003: 232).

Arguably, the practice of health communication in the region has reflected some sort of co-existence of different models and approaches –IEC, CBC, participatory approaches–, and there is certainly a long way to be covered with regards to the role of participation and culture in health communication. Below we briefly discuss some of the issues that health and development communication practitioners and researchers should consider in the context of participation and culture in health communication.

Issues of participatory planning and evaluation

According to Gumucio (2001), to speak of *planning* in health communication one may compare health programs and communication programs. Assessment, planning, and implementation tend to be vertical, one-way processes. On one side are the organizations and systems that generate preventive or corrective actions, while on the other extreme are the recipients, receptors of these actions. In health communication planning one may frequently find very vertical approaches wherein there is a primary source of decision-making or message-generation, with a receiver who appears to be quite passive. Yet, participatory approaches are increasingly gaining terrain in a new pluralistic socio-economic paradigm, wherein communities must be active protagonists of the changes that affect them directly. If this is so, Gumucio affirms, they should also be responsible for their health, hence their own communication and planning. This participatory planning approach facilitates the process of problem identification, search for solutions, commitment to reach the defined goals, and, more importantly, to assume a monitoring role. As health communication planning incorporates more and more participation and culture as central elements, communities will demand greater control of processes or greater efforts for consensus building, an aspect health communicators must be prepared to deal with.

A second challenge that requires careful analysis is the integration of heavily participatory processes with the required evidence-based data in the health sector. How could evaluation of participatory communication processes contribute to the identification of specific contributions of communication to changes in society and health? The importance of *evidence* in health communication practice and research should be seen in the larger context of discussions on evidence-based medicine taking place throughout the world[2]. Evidence-based approaches in health can be described as health policy and health care delivery driven by systematically collected proof on the effects of health-related interven-

2 For a more detailed discussion see Brownson, R.C., Baker, E.A., Leet, T.L., Gillespie, K.N. (2003) *Evidence-based public health*, Oxford University Press.

tions from the social and health sciences (Speller et al, 1997). During the 1990s, debates on evidence-based medicine have influenced the national and international agendas for health policy and health research. While the debate stems from a fundamental concern with medical and public health practice, it cannot be dismissed as pertinent only to medicine. Health communication is also challenged by this debate. In the industrialized world, health communication practitioners and researchers are urged to base their work on evidence, typically using a full range of quantitative methodologies.

Over the past two decades the focus on reducing disease and behavioural risk factors has placed an overemphasis on the role of health communication in addressing lifestyles, focusing its attention on assessing individual health outcomes in connection with behavioural impact. In attempting to support evidence-based health communication, it is important to understand the underlying values, ideas and interests that are behind how evidence is produced, defined, operationalised, and measured. Therefore, the analysis of evaluation processes has great relevance, starting from the selection process to define the nature of indicators that evaluate the success of an intervention.

In public health and medical practice, wherein the concept of evidence-based is borrowed, evidence is usually produced through highly quantitative randomized trials. Evaluation criteria usually include the use of controls and measurements before and after the intervention. One of the fundamental problems in using randomised controlled trials in health communication research is that where interventions aim to influence populations it may be difficult to randomly allocate units of analysis in social settings, thus quasi-experimental control designs are commonly used. According to Speller et al (1997), one of the major problems with studies employing quasi-experimental design is the "contamination" of the control group. This poses a serious dilemma as the practice of public health relies on that data. The issue here is to assert whether or not the intervention produces a health gain in the experimental group or whether that health gain is produced by cultural factors. This cannot be determined by looking at outcome measures alone. Qualitative research can make significant contributions to assessing the effectiveness of interventions by revealing processes, exploring cultural and social diversity, and developing new approaches. It includes a broad range of methods such as case study, ethnography, participatory action research, participant observation and grounded theory.

Therefore, it is important to ask about the scope and purpose of health communication: is it to change lifestyles, as in the case of communication for behaviour change? Or is it to help people overcome social conditions that affect their health, as posed by the UNAIDS framework and CFSC? The implicit value in each of these questions will guide the type of evidence that may be gathered. A health communication process strongly influenced by a biomedical focus is guided to change high risk attitudes and behaviours on individuals; a health communication focus on social change promotes the participation of people, organisations, and communities towards the goals of increased individual and community control over the determinants of health and disease. The central question of evaluation, therefore, is not simply *does it work?*, but *how does it work, for whom, and in what circumstances?* According to Fetterman (2001), the purpose of the evaluation for empowerment is to understand what is happening in a certain situation, from the perspective of the participants, so much as from the perspective of health personnel and policy makers.

The increasing *integration of qualitative and quantitative methods* to assess impact of interventions constitutes another challenge in health communication. However, social scientists that rely on qualitative approaches face issues of external validity and replicability as international organizations tend to privilege quantitative over qualitative research as a the primary data to assess impact. While qualitative research plays an important role in formative research to inform project design and implementation, the same qualitative methods do not have equal weight when it comes to research for impact evaluation. Health communication practitioners and academics need to explore ways to bring qualitative research into the mix of methods to evaluate impact of interventions. For instance, the Soul City Project, an entertainment-education based health communication intervention in South Africa, has developed a methodological approach that integrates qualitative and quantitative data to assess impact.

Cultural issues

> *"The concept of culture highlights the general potential for human beings to learn through social means, such as interaction with others and through the products of culture"*

Challenges related to culture may be wide-ranging. However, two issues stand up, particularly in connection with the importance ascribed to culture in the communication context and tradition of Latin America. First, the possibility of looking at culture as an entry point for health communication interventions as opposed to exclusively relying on epidemiological and behavioral objectives as points of departure. This aspect is discussed below as interculturality. Second, the need to look at reception studies as an option for the evaluation of media components of health communication interventions, particularly interventions that use entertainment-education vehicles such as drama.

Interculturality starts with the acknowledgement that diverse belief systems related to health, healing and wellness exist, and that the perception of illness and disease and their causes varies by culture. Interculturality implies work on a set of community practices in which meanings relating to habits, behaviours and attitudes are produced, including those that intervene in the social production of health and disease. This approach to communications processes begins with the recognition of the multiple mediations, actors and discourses that take part in the construction of meaning and are built and developed in each community.

Thus, culture becomes the essential element to work with in the context of health. An example of this approach is found in a participatory health communication project undertaken in Malambo, a suburban community in Colombia's Atlantic Coast. Instead of focusing immediately on the epidemiological indicators related to youth and sexual and reproductive health, using elements from Martin-Barbero's thinking, the project has focused on the relationship between sexuality and culture, working on three areas: ways and spaces of socialization and construction of a sexuality environment, language and symbolic codes through which sexuality is expressed, and how youth approach their sexual health. Through a participatory process, youth have defined their own goals and communication strategies, and through a heavily reflective process that has been facilitated by the use of various communication strategies –radio shows, radio dramas, community activities, interaction with other community members– it is expected that important changes in gender and sexual practices will take place (Vega and Suarez, 2003; Suarez, Mendivil and Vega, 2004).

Dramas –whether radio, TV, theater– have turned into a fundamental component of many health communication interventions. The entertainment-education strategy, which makes systematic use of entertainment media to educate and generate behavior change is based on various theories, particularly on Albert Bandura's social learning theory and the power of role modeling to help people see themselves through the content of drama and reflect upon their own lives to eventually adopt certain healthy behaviors. However, the development of cultural studies in Latin America has led to a very rich body of knowledge, particularly through reception studies of television that have analyzed how people make sense of the content of TV dramas often negotiating, resisting, and reassigning meaning to media content.

Although the various audience's readings of media texts in the context of entertainment-education have been noted in the past (Singhal, 1999), health communication research has, for the most part, ignored the potential of reception studies as an alternative to analyze how audiences make sense of health communication messages (Tufte, 2004). Most evaluations are fixed on determining whether a particular message has led to a change in attitude or to a self-reported behavior. Reception studies pay special attention to how people relate to messages and to how they incorporate those messages to their daily life, a process that does not follow a linear pattern. Thus, health communication may benefit tremendously from the possibilities of analysis that reception studies offer. Thomas Tufte has made one of the few efforts that attempt to analyze young people's experiences in the context of health communication interventions from an audience perspective. In his preliminary analysis about his ethnographic work in South Africa, Tufte begins to uncover various issues such as identity, stigma, and denial, which may not come to light using a behavior change perspective.

Filling these gaps in health communication research and practice will require a rich and ongoing dialogue of practitioners and academics over the next years. Some of the steps that may be taken in that direction may include: to build a joint basis for the collection of data about successful experiences with a focus on communication, participation and culture; advance processes of training in search of technical excellence in participatory planning in health communication; identify key elements for the sustainability of health communication programs and their institutionalization; and galvanize greater dialogue and exchange of experiences between South and North through various scenarios with the participation of health communication professionals. In fairness, this closing discussion has raised more questions and challenges than answers or alternatives. However, it is our hope that by raising them we may contribute to further analysis that will eventually lead to new responses and a more robust field of development and health communication.

Chapter 14

Communication for sustainable development: applications and challenges

Paolo Mefalopulos

The way in which communication has been conceptualized and applied in development has already been treated in other sections of this book. Nevertheless, it
might be valuable to reflect in more depth about how communication is being conceived and applied when referred more specifically to sustainable development. This
term is formally associated with the general definition, as it evolved at the Earth
Summit held in Rio de Janeiro in 1992, that expected sustainable development to
"equitably meet development and environmental needs of present and future generations". While such a definition provides a common base of understanding, it
does not grant a precise and consistent conception of what is entailed in practical
terms. Keeping in mind that many organizations do not always share a similar conception, sustainable development is usually considered to embrace two basic
dimensions: the environment and rural development. Some organizations, such as
the World Bank, also include the social dimension as a key area in this respect[1].

Combining the three dimensions mentioned above allows maintenance of a conception capable of embracing a wide range of development issues
while also establishing a direct link between people, and in particular the poorest
and most marginalized sectors of society, and the initiatives aimed at improving
their lives. It is quite evident how rural and environmental issues are closely interrelated with social issues. All are concerned with how people use the available

1 Some organizations explicitly refer to the economic dimension as a key component in sustainable
development, though this can be considered as running across all the dimensions.

resources and, ultimately, they are all about poverty alleviation. Even if it would be wrong to reduce development to the struggle against poverty, there is little doubt that currently this is the main front, as is also reflected in the Millennium Development Goals (MDGs).

Table 1: Millennium Development Goals

1. Eradicate extreme poverty and hunger	2. Achieve universal primary education
3. Promote gender equality and empower women	4. Reduce child mortality
5. Improve maternal health	6. Combat HIV/AIDS, malaria and other diseases
7. Ensure environmental sustainability	8. Develop a global partnership for development

The above goals have been recognized as key indicators of sustainable development (World Bank, 2001) and, though only one goal specifically addresses the environment (i.e. No. 7), the 'sustainability factor' is present in virtually every MDG. Issues related to health, education and gender are pertinent to most aspects of social and rural development, and so are crucial for ensuring sustainability.

Communication, in its wide range of conceptions and applications, is instrumental in dealing effectively with the issues mentioned above. For instance, let us consider three broad categorizations into which development communication can be divided: communication for behaviour change, communication for social change (or participatory communication) and advocacy. The way these approaches are selected and applied usually depends upon the purpose of the intervention. Each of them might be based not only on different functions, but often also on different overall purposes (e.g. to change specific practices or to empower), different communication perspectives (e.g. a linear model for media campaigns or a dialogical model to facilitate mutual understanding and trust building) and different methodological approaches. The fact that these differences at times imply divergent, if not conflicting, positions, should be a cause for concern. The variety of approaches and perspectives is often considered an asset of communication, though unless there is a common, consistent theoretical framework upon which to draw, that richness of approaches and perspectives can actually be considered one of its major weaknesses.

Achieving sustainability in rural development depends largely on the way stakeholders perceive the proposed change and the way they are involved in assessing and deciding about how that change should be achieved. Thus, one of communication's main roles has become to facilitate people's participation, and this is acquiring a rapidly increasing relevance in sustainable development, at least formally. Any intervention, be it in the social, rural or environmental dimension, needs to be based on a participatory model in order to be sustainable. The consensus around this issue seems to be almost universal. Currently, there is no development organization that does not put the notion of participation at the forefront of its overall mission.

Participation and empowerment can be considered the two major pillars of communication for sustainable development. As a concept, participation is highly praised and widely used but, most probably, it is even more widely misused. Research conducted in this area (Mefalopulos, 2003) has confirmed that participation is not only used in ambiguous and often inconsistent ways, but it can also be conceptualized and applied in different ways within the same project or programme. In the operational routines of development projects and programmes, the term participation can be encountered in a number of different contexts, none of which might actually carry the genuine sense of participation, i.e. play an active role in the decision-making process. Defining precisely what is implied by a "genuine application of participation" is certainly a major challenge.

Among the many classifications on the subject, Pretty (Pretty et al, 1995) presents an interesting one, identifying seven different kinds of applications, based on the way development organizations interpret and apply participation in the field. He starts from passive participation, where people are considered to be participating merely by showing up at meetings, and ends up with self-mobilization, where the stakeholders take full control of decisions regarding their lives. In between these two extremes there is a range of possibilities, none of which can be considered to be fully participatory. Hence, the wide formal consensus on the need for including participation in sustainable development is sensibly weakened at the implementation stage by the improper and partial notion that is often used when participation is conceived and applied.

This leads to what can be considered to be the second pillar of communication for sustainable development: empowerment. The rise in the relevance of this concept has occurred more recently than that of participation. Empowerment is another 'charged' term in the context of sustainable development, as it is used in a number of different ways. One of the most referred to is the notion that empowerment is about individuals taking control of decisions regarding their own life or, as Freire (1997) stated, that it is about individuals liberating themselves from structures and relationships of domination. A World Bank publication (Narayan, 2002: 14) gives a definition which is not too far from this conception: "Empowerment is the expansion of assets and capabilities of poor people to participate in, negotiate with, influence, control, and hold accountable institutions that affect their lives".

In the 1990s, a Food and Agriculture Organization (FAO) project supported the establishment of the Centre of Communication for Development under the auspices of the Southern Africa Development Community. Among other activities, the Centre developed an innovative methodology known as Participatory Rural Communication Appraisal, or PRCA. This is a methodology that combines participatory approaches with communication methods aimed at investigating issues, especially in rural settings, while building the capacities of the individuals involved in the process. As the FAO/SADC handbook (Anyaegbunam et al, 1998: 49) states: "Unlike traditional communication research, PRCA does not only reveal the best ways of designing messages for the grassroots. It also helps to identify strategies and materials to enable rural people articulate their own perceptions of community needs, local knowledge, opportunities, problems and solutions…". The articulation of one's own knowledge, perceptions and reality is the key to genuine participation, where stakeholders have the power to shape the decision-making process.

By combining participation and empowerment in the daily practices of communication for development, PRCA allows stakeholders to play an active role in defining their realities and priorities. This strengthened the added value of such an approach for the sustainability of projects, on the one hand, but on the other revealed a number of contradictions or 'disjunctures' between the normative conception and the practical applications, as we discuss in the next section. In the meantime, it should be noted that the process followed in communication for sustainable development does not differ greatly from communication approaches in other sectors, e.g. health. Though at the needs assessment phase more attention might be paid to long-term environmental implications or to issues of particular interest in the rural context, the overall process follows a similar pattern. The proper application of communication for development (i.e. through a horizontal, dialogical model) appears to carry implicitly higher potential for sustainability.

Mapping out disjunctures

Despite the fact that communication is highly praised by virtually every major development stakeholder and decision-maker, communication specialists in this field still complain that it is not applied consistently and effectively (Mefalopulos, 2003). The reasons for this apparent contradiction are numerous, though they most often diverge along the lines of theoretical versus operational considerations. There can be little doubt that the current development conception, even if it is gradually evolving, is still rooted in what can be referred to essentially as the positivist paradigm; i.e. there is only one reality and it can be uncovered only by using the correct, scientific method. On the other hand, the communication model has evolved towards a more participatory and complex dimension of development, which should account for a multiplicity of perspectives as indicated by Servaes (1990, 1999) and others.

The newly emerging paradigm is rooted in constructivism, where it does not matter if there is one or more than one reality, since even if there is a single reality, it could never be fully and objectively accounted for. The ontological, epistemological and methodological implications of this conception are far reaching, as illustrated by Guba (1990). To be consistent with this paradigm, reality can only be conceived as socially constructed, and no single reality can be assumed to be the correct or 'true' one. It follows that communication is essential in defining and comparing the multiplicity of realities and that a traditional, top-down conception of development, where decisions are taken by those 'who know better', should be abandoned altogether in favour of people-centred, endogenous processes of decision-making.

The latter statement might seem quite radical and yet it is simply the logical consequence of what is being said and preached in the development arena by decision-makers and practitioners alike. A communication model based on genuine dialogue would almost automatically produce participation and empowerment (Anyegbunam et al, 1998; Bohm, 1996; Freire, 1997). This carries a number of implications, which are not always easy to comply with, given the current structure of development. For instance, many development projects and programmes are still initiated and planned in cities far away from the affected areas. This constitutes a definite impediment to full participation and correct adoption of communication, as we shall discuss later.

Another obstacle in applying a more genuine participatory approach resides in the timeframe within which most projects and programmes are planned and implemented. There can be little doubt that centralized vertical planning allows for tighter control and accounting of time. It makes it easier to set and meet deadlines since in participatory processes the first challenge often starts from the moment an agreement must be reached about when and where to meet. It is easy to see how such a process could take an unpredictable amount of time, which could not be easily 'controlled' by external agents. Similar considerations can be applied to another crucial phase of development interventions: evaluation.

There are very few examples of impact assessment in which those who are often referred to as 'beneficiaries' have been in control of the objectives, design and outcome of the process, even if they are ultimately those most concerned with assessing the impact of the intervention. In order for this to occur, the overall framework of development would need to be adjusted, taking into account the way initiatives are conceived, managed, implemented and evaluated. Until then, genuine participation approaches might have a hard time in being implemented or might result in causing 'disjunctures' among different project components. The following is an example of such a disjuncture, which occurred in a project carried out in a southern African country.

As part of their hands-on training in participatory communication, a group of extensionists at the Ministry of Agriculture carried out a PRCA in some grassroots communities. The overall scope of the project was to provide horticultural sites, and related training, to promote the adoption of a variety of crops in order to increase the communities' food supply. The exercise revealed that many of the original project's objectives were not well-aligned with the communities' needs and perceptions. The extensionists, who had initially taken a defensive stand supporting the project's perspectives and objectives, spent more time with the villagers in the communities and started to understand their perspectives better and value them more.

The extensionists' attitude towards the peasants gradually changed and it became more 'emphatic' regarding the communities' needs and perceptions. This was considered a success by the facilitators of the training programme, whose main objective was to promote the adoption of participatory communication approaches to strengthen the project's sustainability. Unfortunately, the success of the training programme was counterbalanced by the failure of the project's management to understand and value such an approach. The changes proposed by the extensionists, rooted in their interaction with the farmers, were viewed with suspicion and rejected by the management. As a result, the extensionists felt all the more frustration for having to face both a conflictive situation with their management and the resentment of the villagers, who saw their needs and perspectives being ignored once again.

Applying communication for sustainable development

In September 2004, the Food and Agriculture Organization of the United Nations (FAO) hosted the 9th UN Roundtable on Communication for Sustainable Development in Rome[2]. One of the crucial issues that emerged, and not for the first time, was that in order to guarantee the success and sustainability of development initiatives, participatory communication approaches had to be adopted systematically in all kinds of development interventions. A review of the available data indicates that a significant number of projects and programmes already include communication activities in their operations (Mefalopulos, 2003), and a significant amount of the budget for development initiatives is already devoted to that purpose. If communication is being used increasingly in development projects and programmes, why is there a problem? To put it simply, the difficulty lies in the *when* and the *how*.

The question of how communication can be used to aid development efforts could be answered by presenting a basic typology composed of three cases. Communication can be mainly used to: exchange information and build consensus around specific issues; support the achievement of projects' objectives; and assist in identifying and defining projects' objectives. In the first case, communication is used to inform and/or consult relevant stakeholders about key issues. It usually provides a full picture of a given situation, addressing the identified information gaps and the required changes. An awareness campaign about the causes of AIDS or about the needs for land reform could be examples of this modality. The second case is probably the most frequent, though it is also the least effective, as it usually implies that projects' objectives have already been defined, often in a top-down matter, and communication must help to achieve these objectives no matter how they are perceived by the 'beneficiaries'. The last scenario is more participatory and effective in terms of ensuring a higher degree of sustainability for projects, but as it breaks out of the traditional boundaries of communication, it is not yet widely applied. Here, communication is not about

2 The UN Roundtable meets every two years to examine, discuss and assess current trends in communication for development and to set the priorities for future directions in the field. UNICEF hosted the first roundtable in 1989 in New York, and since then it has become a bi-annual event, dedicated to providing input for development communication programmes and strategic guidance for professionals around the world. The focus of the 2004 Roundtable was on three main themes: natural resources management; research, extension and education; and isolated and marginalized groups.

communicating messages or persuading people to change. It is about building trust, sharing knowledge and experiences, identifying and investigating problems, needs and opportunities and, finally, about defining priorities and solutions.

The participants in the 9th UN Roundtable identified and strongly promoted the idea that communication is a process needed primarily to facilitate dialogue and assess the situation in a participatory manner. The Roundtable final resolution includes a couple of points worth mentioning. First, it should always be remembered that even when we are referring to environmental issues or natural resource management, "communication for development is about people" and, as such, problems cannot be addressed simply by applying a scientific approach without taking into full account the knowledge and perceptions of the people affected by the change. The second point concerns the role of communication, which is considered to be a two-way process aimed at supporting the coming-together of stakeholders, facilitating the assessment of problems and defining strategies leading to change.

Viewed in this way, communication is breaking out of the traditional model, which focused on the transmission of messages. Now, communication is acquiring a more integrated and holistic dimension. It provides a number of approaches, methods and techniques that professional communicators can use to facilitate a social process meant to compare, contrast and construct different perspectives and perceptions, before even attempting to define the objectives of a project. This point was considered so crucial that participants in the 9th Un Roundtable drafted the following proposal in their final recommendations: "Governments, donors and development agencies should require the incorporation of a communication needs assessment in any development initiative (and eventually devote a specific percentage of the budget to this purpose, e.g. 0.5%)."

Development is about change, and if development initiatives of any kind are to be sustainable they should start with mechanisms that ensure broad participation by all those who have some interest in the intended change. Communication, by its very nature, is the essential ingredient in ensuring meaningful participation, capable of resulting in the active exchange of knowledge and perceptions needed to successfully define problems and plan solutions. In this regard, communication goes beyond 'communicating' and enters a sociological dimension where it becomes instrumental in constructing realities or, as Wilkins (1994: 2) noted, in constructing "intersubjective meanings constituting shared realities produced and maintained within social communities". Hence, communication is also needed in understanding, contrasting and sharing the realities of different stakeholders, before even thinking about communicating messages. The multiplicity of realities is a 'fact' that needs to be taken into account, and not a nuisance to be ignored or corrected by trying to impose the proper perspective. Such an assumption (i.e. that there is only one 'correct' reality) has often been identified as one of the major causes of failures in development projects (Anyaegbunam et al, 1998; Mefalopulos, 2003).

An FAO/SADC publication[3] presents an interesting case concerning a water irrigation project initiated by the Ministry of Agriculture of a Southern African country in order to provide food security and more opportunities for a poor rural community in a drought-prone area. One of the major activities of the project was the construction of a dam to allow water for irrigation and better cultivation of the land. The expected results were a wider variety of crops that would ensure not only better nutrition but also additional income revenue for the communities in the area. The Ministry's officers were surprised to see that, as they proceeded with this project, the community reacted with suspicion, if not hostility. When, towards the end of the project, a PRCA[4] was carried out to assess the situation, the results were even more shocking. The perceptions of the community about the project, which the Ministry had envisioned as leading to food security and increased self-confidence, were actually the opposite; i.e. deep insecurity and stress. It is not possible to go into greater detail in this context concerning the causes of this situation. Let us simply state that the divergent views were mainly due to the lack of two-way communication between the project officers and the communities, leading to different conceptions of the project objectives and related activities that were undertaken.

By using dialogue to compare different realities or different perceptions, communication not only plays an instrumental role in building trust among stakeholders but, through the systematic use of dialogue, it also plays a crucial role in problem-analysis and problem-solving. Some institutions are convinced that participation can perform the same functions of communication for development, but this is not the case. The available evidence indicates that participatory approaches, while extremely valuable, are not sufficient to identify and systematically sustain the necessary communication activities and provide the full array of the information needed to effectively assess problems, define objectives, devise strategies and support projects (Mefalopulos, 2003). Moreover, entry points upon which a successful communication strategy could be designed are seldom if ever addressed by participatory assessments, weakening their chance of achieving sustainability. Participatory approaches often suffer from some of the contradictions illustrated above (i.e. partial or improper use of the notion of participation) and there is no guarantee that a participatory assessment will provide precise indications concerning levels of awareness, knowledge or attitudes on a certain topic, or that it will provide an accurate picture of the information and communication system of a community. These and other key issues could be addressed effectively by communication if it were included in the initial phase of development initiatives.

In development, most efforts follow two basic modalities: specific projects, or wider sectoral programmes (e.g. water, agriculture, etc.). Though it

3 Anyaegbunam, C. Mefalopulos, P., and Moetsabi, T. (1998) *PRCA: Starting from the People*, Harare, Zimbabwe: FAO/SADC.

4 Participatory Rural Communication Appraisal, a participatory communication research methodology devised in Southern Africa and mentioned in a previous section.

has been criticized for a number of reasons (Mefalopulos, 2003), the most common mode of operations in development remains 'the project approach', consisting of specific activities designed to address and solve a specific problem or set of problems. Projects are usually managed and operated in a business-like manner, with central planning, and monitoring and evaluation of the activities. The 'project approach' provides a structure that appears to please all the major decision-makers involved in the process or, stated differently (Shepherd, 1998), this approach is still dominant because donors, implementing agencies and recipient countries have a "coincidence of interest around the Project".

Since the project approach is still the most widely used in development operations, it is worth discussing the practices of communication for sustainable development as they relate to the 'project cycle'. This term is defined consistently among development organizations, with certain variations that account for minor differences in the type of categorization rather than for substantial differences (Mefalopulos, 2003). The project cycle can be typically divided into the following phases: 1) identification of area/sector of intervention; 2) research/appraisal; 3) project formulation; 4) planning/strategy design; 5) activities implementation; 6) evaluation (and monitoring). Available data suggest that communication, when included, is often considered in phase four or five, very seldom considered in the project formulation and almost never in the first phase (Mefalopulos, 2003).

The consequences of this delayed inclusion are numerous. First of all, the absence of communication considerations makes it more difficult to involve relevant stakeholders in the decision-making process and account for their perceptions from the beginning, even if participatory tools are adopted at a later stage. The strategic effectiveness of communication is greatly reduced if it has to be incorporated into a project in which decisions regarding objectives and outputs have already been taken and there is little or no room for adjustment. Moreover, regardless of the nature of the communication intervention (e.g. campaign, education, social mobilization, etc.), there are certain information requirements which need to be collected at the very beginning, such as a survey of stakeholders' perceptions (which is as crucial as a scientific study investigating facts), and the identification of influential sources and assessment of the communication/ information system of each group of stakeholders. Moreover, including communication from the very beginning should facilitate the design and inclusion of a baseline, which is essential not only to monitor the process and evaluate the overall impact of the communication intervention, but also very useful in fine-tuning the overall goal and specific objectives of the project.

A baseline based on qualitative inputs, triangulated with quantitative data, would ensure the validity and appropriateness of the intervention proposed. Relevant indicators should be identified from the early stages of the project cycle in order to ensure that the baseline will be effective in guiding and monitoring the project's progress. In the field of communication for sustainable development, a number of institutions are now including specific assessments to account for environmental and rural issues from the early phases of projects. Increasingly, environmental assessments are carried out at the beginning of projects considered to be of high visibility. However, when they are conducted by environmental specialists they run the risk of being focused on the 'scientific reality' of the issues in question, neglecting other social dimensions and issues that, even if not directly involved with the environment *per se*, might affect the overall design of the project.

For instance, an assessment carried out for a project aimed at reducing the air pollution in a crowded Asian city focused mainly on the environmental issues and their implications for the people directly affected by this problem, neglecting other relevant aspects. It failed, for instance, to probe and understand the magnitude of the problem from different perspectives, such as future risks to child health. The communication campaign focusing on the health hazards for commuters did not produce any major results, probably because adults were not so concerned about potential health hazards in the long term (as is also indicated by studies on the effects of tobacco). However, if identified at the beginning, a campaign aimed at highlighting the risks and negative effects on child health might have had a bigger impact (maybe by addressing mothers' concerns and using them as a primary channel to convey the message to the primary audience).

From what has been argued so far, it can be inferred that communication for sustainable development is first and foremost about dialogue, participation and empowerment. These are the core elements in which the current perspective of communication is rooted. Even if there is only a limited amount of quantitative evidence, the failures of projects in past decades and current data both indicate that involving people in the decision-making process concerning change affecting their own life increases the chances of success and sustainability in development projects, as is also indicated by documentation produced by the World Bank (1992) and others (Fraser and Restrepo-Estrada, 1998; Mefalopulos, 2003; Shepherd, 1998). However, promoting the adoption of communication for development should not be based purely, or even mainly, on cost-effectiveness considerations. It is the right of every person to be involved in decisions concerning his/her own life, regardless of how time-consuming this can be or what costs are involved. After all, nobody would argue that if a dictatorship is proved to be a more cost-effective form of government it should replace democracy. Similarly, participatory communication should not be adopted only if proved more cost-effective, but also, and above all because it is the 'right' thing to do, as it allows the genuine participation of all stakeholders in the decision-making process concerning change affecting their own lives.

The added value of communication for sustainable development

As already stated, communication for sustainable development is about 'people first'. Unfortunately, current practices do not always seem to adhere to this notion. Environmental issues might have a major impact on a global level, but the world's poorest citizens cannot demonstrate their full appreciation for those concerns if they have to face a daily struggle for survival. As the oldest villagers in an African rural area said to a group of foreign environmental protectionists trying to convince them to stop hunting protected species: "We agree with you that safeguarding the wildlife is very important, but to us, at the end of the day, being able to feed our people and our children is more important than preserving endangered animals". Sustainability for future generations cannot be achieved unless it also addresses concerns related to the *here* and *now*. Communication can ensure that concerns for the future will be linked with the needs of the present.

The World Bank, one of the major actors in the field of development, has also begun to pay closer attention to this field and in 1998 established a Development Communication Division, or DevComm. The Division's mission is to promote the adoption of strategic communication in all Bank-sponsored projects and programmes. To do this effectively, policy planners and other decision-makers need to be convinced of the value of communication. Ideally, as stated earlier, the ethical value of this approach should be sufficient to incorporate it into the daily routines of development. As this has not been the case, it would be helpful to demonstrate its practical and economical value. Is communication cost-effective? And if so, can how this be proved?

Metaphorically, we could think of communicators as firemen. When called to put out a fire, there is only so much firemen can do, depending on when they were called, how big the fire is, and the resources at their disposal. Calculating the cost of an incident caused by somebody's negligence is not that hard. It can be done by simply calculating the extent of the damage and adding the total cost of the firemen's intervention. By assessing how much has been saved by rapid deployment of the firemen, it is possible to make a precise cost-benefit analysis of their intervention. Now, let us imagine that firemen were asked to participate in an extensive campaign on how to avoid fires caused by domestic negligence. In this case, it would be easy to calculate the cost of the campaign, but how do we calculate the amount of money saved as a result?[5] Similarly, when we are called to address a problem in an on-going project/programme, the communication impact should be calculated keeping in mind that some of the damage has already been done.

If communication had been incorporated from the very beginning of the process, it might have prevented the occurrence of the problems and the related waste of resources. But in such a case, it would be very difficult to assess the cost-effectiveness. How can we measure something that is not there? If communication is properly applied at the beginning, chances are that most problems would be dealt with before they ever occurred. Economists and communication specialists should perhaps sit down together and, rather than assess the cost-

5 A possible way could be a comparative analysis using statistics from previous years, but, in addition to not being very reliable, this would also be impossible in many countries where statistics are not available.

effectiveness of communication, they should assess the cost of, and wasted money involved in, projects and programmes associated with failures due to the lack of proper communication. Putting it another way, if there is a need for an economic perspective on this matter, let us show the added value of communication by highlighting the costs of non-communication!

Conclusions

At this point, let us summarize the main challenges faced by communication in the field of sustainable development and reflect on how we can move forward. Since rural and environmental issues appear to be high on the agenda of development, communication should seize this opportunity to climb the development agenda as a necessary way of supporting people-based change. This can be done by successfully facing three broad challenges, which summarize the issues discussed so far:

1 In sustainable development, the traditional notion of communication based on media and message design is not sufficient to deal with the current challenges of the emerging development framework, based on a strong participatory vision. While development communication specialists seem to be fully aware of this, policy planners and decision-makers appear to be less so. Thus, the latter need to be made to understand that communication is not simply about sending messages, or informing and persuading people in order to change behaviour. Communication professionals must take up the task of 'educating' policy planners and decision-makers about the shifting role of communication. By facilitating mutual understanding and by building trust among stakeholders, communication becomes of critical value in fostering participation and strengthening sustainability. In other words, even before we address practical, operational issues, the purpose and functions of communication, as discussed in this chapter, should be clearly defined and promoted among decision-makers.

2 The next challenge, closely related to the above point, concerns the practices adopted in deciding when to apply communication. Currently, approaches in communication for sustainable development are considered mainly after projects' objectives have been defined, and activities planned. This implies that communication constitutes a stand-alone component supporting these objectives and activities. But to be meaningful and effective, communication should be used strategically as part of the process of investigating key issues, not only matters of communication, and of defining the programmes' and projects' objectives, regardless of their nature. Communication is transversal to any discipline, and applying it from the beginning allows stakeholders to share perceptions, knowledge and practices in a way that facilitates

the identification and design of meaningful programmes, taking into account all the different perceptions, needs and knowledge.

3 The last point concerns the importance of finding ways to assess the impact of communication for sustainable development. This impact should be measured in both quantitative and qualitative terms. To be consistent with the new conception of development, evaluation should also be rooted in a participatory model. This would have major implications for a number of issues, such as what should be measured, which indicators should be adopted and, ultimately, who should be in control of the design related to evaluation. If development is to be based on people's participation, it should follow that the degree of success should also be assessed according to criteria selected by those very same people, i.e. the 'beneficiaries'. For instance, when we assess the impact of a programme aimed at reducing deforestation, the evaluation cannot focus only on progress made in reducing the rate of deforestation, but should also assess how that change has affected people in the area.

In conclusion, it should be reiterated that communication for sustainable development, while being similar in many respects to other communication approaches, is particularly effective in building bridges across various stakeholder groups. It is crucial in filling perception and knowledge gaps that might create problems or hamper chances of success in development efforts. Sustainability presupposes a balance between peoples' present and future needs, which are often related to the environment. Naturally, communication alone cannot always provide solutions to every problem, but it is a highly effective and ethically appropriate approach which can mediate and look for viable solutions, as indicated in the following example that occurred in a Central American country.

The high rate of deforestation in a certain area was drastically reduced when active dialogue between local communities and outside experts brought the realization that there was a market for the resin extracted from the trees. The income generated by selling the resin was comparable to that generated by cutting the trees and selling the wood, but without depleting the resources for future generations.

Certainly, such a perfect solution cannot always be found easily. Nevertheless, to be sustainable, whatever solution or change is identified and agreed upon can only take place with the active involvement of all the relevant stakeholders. Communication for sustainable development is all about that; i.e. the professional application of a set of principles and methods to facilitate the exchange and sharing of knowledge and experiences among the relevant stakeholders. This provides the added value needed to make the assessment, the design, the implementation and the evaluation of development initiatives more effective and more relevant to people, and hence more sustainable.

Chapter 15

Out of focus: gender visibilities in development

Karin Gwinn Wilkins

Women. What are we good for? Absolutely everything. But you would never know it from development work. Within development rhetoric, women have value in terms of our capacities to reproduce and to nurture children, families, communities and nations, our propensity to consume, and our victimisation in violent confrontations. In essence, we breed and feed; we buy and cry. But we do so much more. We create; we console; we connect. Our visibility as dynamic, active participants has been obscured. So how have we achieved this disjuncture?

In the spirit of "mapping the field" I explore, in this chapter, tensions in the field across approaches recognizing women, gender, and feminist concerns. The very visibilities of development issues shift in focus and frame, across historical moment as well as institutional context. The panoptic gaze described by Escobar (1995) illustrates how development institutions with power are able to inscribe their characterizations of women in order to justify their own political and economic agendas. Women not only serve as a prominent "target" within media campaigns, particularly in the areas of population, health, and nutrition, but also function symbolically as nurturers of community and nation, and as victims justifying development, and military, intervention.

Within the context of the broader field of development communication, we can distinguish attention to what development communicates about particular people, problems, and solutions, from well rehearsed discussions of how communication strategies promote development (Wilkins and Mody, 2001). In order to provide an overview of the field, I focus on the shifting visibilities of women and gender within development, the material structures within which these visibilities are articulated, and consider how feminist critiques might contribute to this dialogue.

Communicating women, gender, and feminism in development

Development strategies designed to address women's issues face a paradox: despite more and better programs and research efforts, women's conditions are not improving. Women are more likely than men to suffer from poverty, with their access restricted to critical education, health, employment, and political resources (Neft and Levine, 1997; Steeves, 2000). Clearly, a few isolated, meager development projects are not enough to raise the political, economic, and social status of women on a global scale. However, development programs comprise fundamental strategies implemented toward resolving gender inequities. It is important to critique development discourse in order to build potentially improved models for social intervention: this deconstruction may help us consider how to reconstruct our strategic paths toward social change (Nederveen Pieterse, 2001).

Development discourse communicates assumptions about women, gender, and feminist critique through its articulation of broad programmatic goals as well as of specific project strategies. On the one hand, one can conceptualize the field of development as having moved historically through a period of no attention to women toward a recognition of women's integral roles in the development process (WID), incorporating over time, and in some limited instances, an understanding of the broader gender dynamics that structure men's and women's participation in development processes (GAD). Since the introduction of GAD, feminist critiques have gained more attention, situating issues of gender within other conditions of oppression, such as ethnicity and class, in a global context.

While these contributions can be seen as representing historical shifts in the field (Wilkins, 1999, 2000), it is important to recognize that at present each of these approaches still permeates development discourse. It is not that moving from attention to WID toward a recognition of GAD implies that development work no longer operates within the framework of WID. Rather, each of these approaches works in different ways, guiding project activity and program justification, in different ways. Issues of feminism, gender and women should be seen as intersecting in some instances, while serving different political purposes in other senses through the course of development work.

The movement toward recognizing women's roles in development (WID) in the 1970s reinforced broader attention to women's issues raised by social movements as well as by global conferences on the subject. The 1975 UN conference in Mexico City launched that Year of Women, which then led into the Advancement of Women (1976 until 1985). WID discourse focuses on women's contribution to development through their economic production (Boserup, 1970) and human reproduction (Staudt, 1985). These two roles emphasize women's active contributions, such as through farming, toward their material gain, as well as women's more passive roles, as nurturers for their children and families. The emphasis here is on women as a specific group, irrespective of other conditions, such as class, ethnicity, or urbanity. Instead, projects emphasize the importance of selecting women as beneficiaries or participants, the language depending on the perspective of the project.

An articulation of gender concerns over women's issues is meant to signal recognition of gender roles as being socially constituted. Development programs focusing on "gender" do more than focus on women as subjects and objects of development, but instead attempt to address or at least understand the structural systems of patriarchy and power that inhibit women's and men's potential (Cardinal, Costigan and Heffernan, 1994; Dagenais and Piché, 1994; Parpart, 1995). GAD projects should be addressing more of the social and structural issues of development, in contrast to WID projects that target women as individuals in the process of social change.

Next, feminist scholarship builds on this recognition of the broader systems of power that contribute toward and inhibit gender concerns, adding more complexity and political dimensions. First, issues of gender are recognized as being closely connected with broader experiences of oppression, connected with various conditions of marginality, such as race, ethnicity, and class (Luthra, 1996; Sreberny-Mohammadi, 1996; Chua et al, 2000; Mohanty, 1991a, 1991b). Feminist critiques of the representation of "third world women" as being constructed in monolithic terms as generic others, as passive, traditional, and victimized (Hegde, 1996, 1998; Mohanty, 1991a, 1991b; Shome, 1996), have contributed substantially in this realm. Some (Calás and Smircich, 1996; Hegde, 1998) advocate a more political stance, moving beyond academic research deconstructing development texts, toward strategies addressing experiences of oppression. In addition, a critical feminist approach points us not only toward the concerns raised within local communities, but also toward power dynamics within donor institutions, such as the proportion of women employed and the types of positions held.

Envisioning women in development

In keeping with the dominant mode of development approaches, in this section I consider how women, in particular, become seen through development practice, when considered as targets or participants of projects. Specifically, I comment on the passive and monolithic characterization, particularly in terms of the sexualisation of women through reproductive health and population programmes, the commodification of women as consumers through communication campaigns, and the victimisation of women through emergency aid and military intervention. This discussion then allows for further exploration regarding the extent to which more active roles might be engaged, and gender and feminist concerns might be integrated into development work.

In much of development discourse, particularly in the Women in Development (WID) tradition, women's roles tend to be conceived through their bodies, as motherly nurturers or sexual temptresses (Calás and Smircich, 1996; Chua et al, 2000; Cloud, 2004; Meyer and Prugl, 1999; Mohanty, 1991b; Rodríguez, 2001; Wilkins, 1999). It is particularly worth noting that in many donor organisations financial resources devoted to "women's" issues tend to be channeled through children's health, nutrition, and population programmes. For example, an intervention to address deficiencies in iodine, iron, and vitamin A justified its attention to women of reproductive age in order to improve "pregnancy outcomes and increased productivity" (Smitasiri and Dhannnamitta, 1999: 5).

The sense that women are passively suffering from the burdens of their sexuality and reproductive capacities, as a result of their "traditional" cultures, becomes more pronounced in those regions that are culturally distant from the homes of prominent bilateral donors (Chua et al, 2000; Mohanty, 1991b). An Orientalist approach to development incorporates patriarchal assumptions, which envision "other" women in passive roles requiring "our" assistance. "Helping" women in these culturally distant spaces focuses on women's sexuality, through development programmes focusing on attempts to control women's bodies.

Although reproductive health may be an important issue, development programmes should be faulted for concentrating on this at the expense of a broad range of concerns, and for constructing women as passively responding to interventions instead of as actively engaging in decision making about their own sexuality. But it is not just that development agencies create roles for women as passive victims requiring assistance: these visions of women vary across cultural space, such that cultural "others" are more easily justified as targets for development intervention.

Development communication campaigns also rely on passive characterisations of women, conceived as "targets" for intervention. The underlying model of social marketing assumes that individuals (not policies or structures) are the appropriate targets for change, and that behavior change is an appropriate focus for intervention. While the "product" advocated through social marketing campaigns need not pertain to a material artifact but might also refer to an idea, often the suggested practice, particularly in health and nutrition programmes, involves consumption, such as of ORS packets, vitamins, or other material goods. This is not to discount other campaign issues that do not target tangible products for purchase, such as breastfeeding and exercise, but to draw attention instead to the commercial foundations upon which social marketing campaigns are created. As an extension of a commercial model, social marketing targets individual consumers as passive recipients just waiting to be activated into purchasing the right product, which will somehow improve their lives, as well as the lives of their children and families. Consumption then becomes the appropriate way for individual women to engage in social change.

One of the reasons for the popularity of social marketing in communi- cation projects directed toward women is that this very framework of social change does not question, but instead reinforces a global power structure that privileges global corporations, which require us to engage in practices of consumption. Focusing on individuals as the locus of change also distracts us from recognising the power of a collective group in resisting dominant groups such as corporations. Thus, the potential for women to organise and engage critical social issues is marginalised in favor of women's consumption patterns.

Some approaches to entertainment-education may be subject to similar critiques. In some scripts, women become subject to communication strategies attempting to convince them to "role model" themselves after fictional characters, rather than encouraged to see broader systems of gender dynamics or to engage in collective acts of resistance to consumer culture or to oppressive political systems. Whereas women may not necessarily be targeted as consumers per se as in social marketing, the privatisation of this public interest strategy means that commercial interests compete with socially beneficial purposes. The very structure of many of these programmes involves the "partnership" of private industry with development institutions ostensibly acting in the public interest. This "partnership" limits the potential for communication messages to engage in more controversial subjects and strategies. The integration of commercial products, in the name of the "public good", draws attention away from potentially more environmentally sound and politically responsive solutions.

Women are often used as a justification for development assistance in conflict situations, particularly in discussions of humanitarian and emergency aid. In textual as well as visual references, women crying over death and destruction are used to explain why resources need to be diverted to particular territories. The point here is not that women do not suffer; women do. But so do others. So do men. But women are compelling as victims, largely due to our broader sense of women's subservient role in our society. Playing on these stereotypes, we lose a sense of the humanity of pain and suffering. Instead, women's rights have the potential to become a pretense for development, as well as for military intervention. US rhetoric explaining military intervention in Afghanistan (Cloud, 2004), along with justifications among many development institutions recently investing in this territory, foreground women's concerns as both target and justification.

One of the more politically attractive means of securing fiscal support within the US Agency for International Development (USAID) for women's issues involves leveraging interventions in areas of crisis. The assumption is that emergency relief, to nations such as Sudan, Nigeria and Angola, would be more attractive to American constituents and the US Congress. One way to allocate resources for women then becomes to work with women in crisis territories. For example, a program in Rwanda targets resources directly to women and women's groups to meet their basic needs for food and shelter. The intervention privileges those women who are widows, particularly with children, and those groups with women officers. Funds are allocated for building homes and for establishing women's cooperatives to market their agricultural products. This strategy connects these projects to larger development issues: "assisting Rwandan women to overcome the burdens of genocidal warfare and the barriers of custom, tradition, and law" (USAID, 1999b: 1).

Women, often the subject and target for development intervention, embody more than the sexual, reproductive, consumption, and victim functions typically portrayed in this discourse. In contrast, some projects do envision women in more active roles. For example, the Women and AIDS research program recognizes women as actively engaged, within an inequitable dynamic in which power differences between men and women inhibit safe sexual practices (Weiss and Gupta, 1998). In Morocco, USAID works with NGOs on voter education campaigns targeting women and consulting with female candidates for parliament. In addition, a Danish supported regional program for Women and Law in Southern Africa (WLSA) informs communities of women's legal rights while advocating women's political networks. The Japanese funded TESDA project in the Philippines provides technical training in skills in order to enhance women's positioning in the formal economic sector. Micro-enterprise and agribusiness projects encourage women to become active entrepreneurs through acquiring loans and investing in infrastructure. Micro-enterprise projects tend to focus on integrating women into the commercial private sector. For example, some micro-enterprise programs teach women how to use computer technologies, as a way to market their products across national boundaries. In Afghanistan, USAID supports projects designed to help rural women generate income through dairy and poultry, in addition to attempting to register them to vote. Other projects in the education sector, such as those teaching girls new technologies or women literacy in order to promote women's political rights and economic opportunities, may also be seen as constructing women as more active participants.

These efforts suggest a pluralist model of social change, in which public education stimulates informed dialogue among individual constituents. Key here is the conceptualization of women's involvement in a formal democratic political structure, rather than the mobilization of women in order to advocate for more progressive feminist concerns. Similarly, development programs emphasizing women's material gains situate economic achievement as an individual act connected with the formal economic structure. Development discourse markets a version of modernity that resonates with the interests of global capital. As targets of development, women unwittingly serve as ideological conduits toward the selling of global modernity.

Overall, women are constructed in mostly passive roles, apart from their connections to the marketplace as entrepreneurs or as consumers, or to the formal political governance structure as candidates or as voters. When project discourse portrays women in more active roles, it does so in relation to women's projected connection to a capitalist economic or democratic political structure.

Moreover, women are articulated as individuals within a pluralist society, rather than as members of a shared collective with the power to mobilize, act, and resist.

The material structure of visibility

Women and gender become visible through the material allocation of resources toward programs as well as the articulation of policies and concepts. This visibility then is manifest through the institutional processes engaged within the development industry. In this section, I explore institutional contexts of funding, organizational structure, gendered composition of development professionals and the politics of language used within organizations.

In response to low funding levels, many development programs have begun to increase their collaboration with private-sector organizations. This commercialization of the development process has been engaged by many of the programs designed to benefit women and girls, with educational strategies being no exception. To illustrate, a current version of the Strategies for Advancing Girls Education Program (SAGE) attempts to mobilize private sectors in support of their efforts. The stated rationale explains that the business community might offer financial support for the educational infrastructure, such as buildings and textbooks (USAID, 1999a).

"Partnering" with private industry allows projects to expand their work while expending fewer resources. The implications of this decision, in the face of economic constraints, are profound. Instead of working with the most needy and marginalized of communities, projects are more likely to target groups of individuals with the ability to consume. In addition, subscribing to a more corporate perspective entails focusing on more short-term tangible results, at the expense of more long-term, nebulous goals, such as improving women's status and human rights (Whelan, 1998).

In addition to issues of funding, development organizations structure their attention to women or gender through the naming of particular divisions, or perhaps through "mainstreaming" or "integrating" these concerns into a variety of divisional sectors. As explained by USAID:

> In development programs, gender matters. Traditions, customs, and laws
> define gender relations within societies, but they often impose costs that
> inhibit sustainable development. ... Every USAID Bureau and mission
> shares the goal of improving the status of women in developing economies
> and emerging democracies (USAID, 2000).

On the positive side, this approach has the potential to legitimize feminist issues within institutional discourse. Given an identifiable budget and reporting structure, this strategy has the capacity to benefit women, recognizing gender as a relationship of power enacted in social and political communities. However, some organizations find it difficult to track how women benefit in these "mainstreamed" or "integrated" programs. A structure of accountability is needed to evaluate both the processes and the outcomes of these projects. This move toward integration may in effect reflect a political response to those interested in eclipsing feminist issues, and those concerned with reducing budgets. Thus, in practice, by incorporating women's issues into other development concerns, gender issues lose visibility. Gender integration thereby implies a potential disintegration of feminist interests.

Next, I consider the composition of organizational staff, particularly in terms of gendered divisions of labor. Feminist concerns suggest that we recognize the importance of hiring women in senior positions of authority within development institutions, and not just focus on women as recipients and targets of aid. While one should not assume that women uniformly approach development in similar ways, some research suggests that women and men within the same organization do justify and understand their work differently (Wilkins, 1991).

In recent research exploring how development professionals in the Japanese International Cooperation Agency (JICA) justified work on women and gender issues, clear differences between male and females staff were discerned (about half of the 39 informants were female). First, the women interviewed were much more likely to engage in discussion of women and gender issues –almost all of the women (83%) compared with only 24% of the men. Among those who did discuss these issues as part of their overall development work, men were more likely to articulate concerns with efficiency, seeing the inclusion of women or gender as a means toward achieving other development goals. In contrast, the women interviewed were more likely to emphasize these approaches as justified in and of themselves, in terms of human rights. The difference here is striking: almost all of the women responding to this question appealed to issues of rights, status, and participation, compared to only one of the men.

Within organizations, issues become visible through the language used to define their terms, as a way of channeling resources and determining accountability. With these sets of issues, attention to "women", "gender", and "feminist" concerns denote different understandings of development issues, while also signaling particular political approaches.

The most dominant approach in larger development institutions still falls within a more women-directed framework, although the term "gender" has been incorporated into published documentation more steadily since the 1995 Beijing conference. For example, the World Bank lists the third Millennium Development goal, "to promote gender equality and empower women –as a central component to its overall mission to reduce poverty and stimulate economic growth" (World Bank, 2004). The Danish International Development Agency and some bilateral institutions describe "gender" (DANIDA, 2000), while USAID describes "women in development" (USAID, 2004a, 2004b) as central cross-cutting issues, along with other central development concerns.

Being more male dominated, these organizations tend to justify their attention to women more often in terms of "efficiency" of programs and as "technical" solutions than in terms of human rights. Terms such as "feminism" are avoided, along with others such as "abortion", in favor of subjects that are seen as less controversial such as "violence against women". Even women working in prominent bilateral development institutions explain that they work within this technical framework in order to depoliticize these issues, thereby establishing credibility and avoiding resistance.

While many development organizations created WID divisions or offices in the 1970s and 1980s (Wilkins, 1999), JICA did not do so until the early 1990s. The year 1995 marked a critical difference in JICA's commitment to WID concerns: attention in annual reports doubled, and the amount of funding specifically devoted to women's issues increased by about 27% from the previous year. But as global attention subsided in the late 1990s, so did JICA's formal recognition of these as central development concerns.

While "gender" became more prominently displayed in the vocabulary used to describe development concerns since 1995, the projects implemented remained entrenched in the domain of WID. More recently, informants across development organizations report that it was politically more expedient to subsume the potentially contentious issues of gender within the relatively innocuous consideration of "poverty". Female development professionals across organizations also describe how difficult it has been to use the vocabulary or framework of "feminism". JICA informants describe how some male staff had been put off by what they considered to be ardent feminist arguments made by women from Nordic countries during international meetings, or akin to feminist movements toward contraceptive rights within Japan during the late 1960s and early 1970s. Several female informants independently made reference to what they termed male staff's "allergic" reaction to "gender" issues, perceived as emanating from feminist, western liberation movements. As issues of poverty gain focus in development work, feminist and gender concerns lose visibility, thus depoliticizing central concerns with power and structure in development processes.

Future focus

Gender needs to be understood not as a monolithic condition with universal characteristics, but as aligned with other markers of difference, such as class, race, and religious identity, within broader power dynamics. Regardless of institutional base, development practice engages in this problematic hierarchical process, reducing women to narrowly caricatured roles. Without a more respectful approach to women and to social change, development strategies will continue to fail.

Moreover, the structural conditions that foster the hierarchical nature of help, along with the process of "othering" that encapsulates women's roles in passive and sexual terms, are difficult to shift. Supporting the work of non-governmental organizations (NGOs) may help to facilitate a process of disengagement from the dominant development approaches, but this strategy itself risks marginalizing issues that need to become more central to our work in the area of social change. If women's conditions are to improve on a global scale, not only the discourse but also the structure of development work need to change.

Although development and other government institutions may exploit women's issues to pursue their own agendas, there is potential for resistance. We need to consider how to engage respectful strategies that recognise the complexity of gender as well as of the processes of social change. We tend to polarise development processes as either hierarchical or participatory, either dominating communities of passive individuals or engaging active participants in key decisions. Critiques of the dominant approach to development as well as the history of the field do justice in recognising the patriarchal assumptions embedded in creating interventions within powerful institutions that are then imposed on groups with less power. Advocates of participation also offer an important contribution by arguing for contexts of implementation that are respectful and informed, on grounds of ethics and effectiveness. In many ways our attempts to understand women's roles in the development process resonate with these broader interpretations of the field. In some approaches, women serve as passive targets for campaigns, while in others women are sought as active participants, though usually as members of recipient communities rather than engaged as paid, authoritative officials in development organisations.

However, all too often this discussion becomes polarised, simplifying complicated dynamics into the very types of dichotomies that have been the subject of critique: modernity vs. tradition; active vs. passive; top-down vs. bottom-up; dominant vs. participatory approach to development. The processes of creating, implementing, and evaluating development policies and programmes are much more complex than these simplified categories allow. Yet, understanding the broader power dynamics is still a critical component of this process. In this regard, feminist theory offers insight into the structures of power that operate in transnational, institutional, as well as social contexts.

While more attention to gender dynamics, as opposed to targeting of individual women as responsible for development failures, holds great potential, there is still the risk that this perspective may become co-opted and thus lose its critical edge. Feminist critiques offer a way of envisioning gender issues that not only brings broader dynamics of power and markers of difference into focus, but also offers an opportunity for new voices to join the chorus.

Chapter 16

The information society: visions and realities in developing countries
Madanmohan Rao

The vision of an information-enabled globally-connected knowledge-based society is driven in large part by the smooth integration of new media (information and communication technologies or ICTs) with traditional media, coupled with technical skillsets, forward-looking government policies, an attitude of life-long learning, and a desire to improve efficiencies and harness innovation in a humanely and environmentally sustainable manner.

This chapter explores dimensions of "breadth and depth" of the information society vision, by presenting a framework for comparing the maturity of different information societies as well as the progress that an individual country has made in its various national ICT initiatives. This framework is used to strengthen existing analyses of the information society and present new roadmaps for researchers and policymakers.

It charts the instrument and industry aspects of ICTs in developing nations, using a comparative framework developed over the years by the author called the "8 Cs" of the digital economy (parameters beginning with the letter C): connectivity, content, community, commerce, culture, capacity, cooperation and capital.

There are two ways of looking at ICT: as an instrument, and as an industry. As an instrument, affordable and usable ICTs can indeed transform the way societies work, entertain, study, govern and live –at the individual, organizational, sector, vocational and national levels. As an industry, ICTs represent a major growing economic sector covering hardware, software, telecom/datacom and consulting services.

Coupled with these two aspects of ICTs (usage and creation), the "8 Cs" framework is used to tease apart some of the key challenges in implementing the vision of knowledge societies, such as increasing ICT diffusion and adoption, scaling up ICT pilot projects, ensuring sustainability and viability of ICT initiatives, creating ICT industries, and systematically analysing research on the global information society. The role of local stakeholders, multilateral agencies, donor institutions and the development community is highlighted. Based on a combination of the "instrument" and "industry" aspects of parameters like connectivity, content, capacity and culture, the information societies of the world can be divided into eight categories: restrictive, embryonic, emerging, negotiating, intermediate, mature, advanced, and agenda-setting.

Through both lenses –instrument and industry– the performance of developing nations lags that of developed nations, but interesting patterns of variation and pockets of excellence are emerging. For instance, India has a thriving content sector and IT industry –but it also has a looming digital divide where ICTs are not accessible or affordable as instruments for a majority of the population. Countries like China have emerged as IT powerhouses –but are still nervous about the impacts that unfettered flows of Internet information can have on their political system.

ICT impacts: a sector-wise analysis

According to ITU findings, 80% of the 500 million Internet users worldwide are in the developed world, and two out of every five people in developed countries are online while only one in 50 has access to the net in developing countries. The Internet in the developed countries is approaching the status of a mainstream medium, but has a long way to go in attaining similar levels of penetration in developing countries. Still, some of the applications and benefits of the information society are becoming evident in developing countries as well.

Despite the yawning digital divide, numerous success stories have emerged of ICT practices in developing countries, even spurring studies on the potential of ICT for poverty alleviation. As these anecdotal reports and project successes began to gather steam, numerous studies and frameworks emerged to provide a more solid theoretical foundation to the nature, evolution and impacts of the information society. These can be classified into the following types of studies: infrastructural, market-oriented, political, cultural, policy-oriented, comparative, regional and strategic. It would be useful to survey some of the relevant literature to arrive at contextualised perspectives on the information society.

For example, Thurow (1999) adopts an international approach (with specific regional and national case studies around the world) to the growth of the new economy. Challenges to accelerating global Internet diffusion and overcoming the digital divide are well charted in the annual reports of the UNDP and World Bank, as well as in special reports of UNCTAD, the Markle Foundation and the Digital Opportunity Task Force.

Ramanathan and Becker (2001) offer a wide-ranging set of essays covering the early stages of the Internet growth in Asia. Tan, Corbett and Wong (1999) offer an academic treatment of developments in IT education, infrastructure and e-commerce in the Asia-Pacific region; much of the data is drawn from the early and mid-1990s. Funk (2001) offers an excellent case study of the growth of the mobile Internet in Japan, innovative content models and consumer utilities for wireless users, and the experience in transferring these models to other markets like Europe.

The importance of the Internet as a component of national infocomm, media and infrastructural policies has been acknowledged by a growing number of countries around the world, and books have been recently published about the information society strategies of for example Britain (Barnett, 2000) and India (Manzar, Rao and Ahmed; 2001). Naroola (2001) covers the growing success of Indian entrepreneurs in Silicon Valley's Internet economy; Singhal and Rogers (2001) touch on the domestic potential of the Internet in India, and Rajora (2002) provides a detailed case study in India of the community-centre model of Internet access and local e-commerce.

Focusing more on the infrastructural and capacity constraints of developing nations, systematic attempts to characterize and categorize instances of ICT application in developing nations have emerged, as in the recent reports of the UNDP, Digital Opportunity Task Force, Markle Foundation, Regency Foundation and Bridges.org.

These typically involve a sector-wise or activity-based approach to ICT impacts on society, such as public health, disaster relief, education, media, civil society, agriculture, industry, services, trade, banking/finance, hospitality, transportation, law enforcement, commerce, government services, politics, cultural identity, workforce and diaspora populations.

ICTs can indeed bring benefits to each of these spheres of activity, via a whole host of applications. Numerous such initiatives have been launched by the cooperative efforts of local and international stakeholders, as summarised in Table 1.

Table 1: ICTs in developing countries: applications, benefits and active organisations

	Applications	Benefits	Organisations
Healthcare	1. Telemedicine (audio/image transmission, collaboration eg. for radiology) 2. Digital publication of medical research 3. Outsourcing of services	1. Increased productivity, reduced travel costs 2. Broader service reach for experts 3. More responsive healthcare services for citizens	World Health Organisation, Medline (NLM), MaterCare
Agriculture	1. GIS systems for planning 2. Tele-education, scientific databases 3. Telecentres, information services for pricing	1. More awareness of innovative approaches 2. Improved food production 3. Seasonal planning, risk mitigation	FAO, WFP, CGIAR, Developing Countries Farm Radio Network, MAYAnet, FarmNet, Famine Early Warning System, GAINS, AgriWatch

Table 1 (cont.)

	Applications	Benefits	Organisations
Education	1. Distance education 2. Teacher training 3. Indigenous education	1. Improved visualisation skills 2. Up-to-date course materials accessible from remote areas 3. Cost savings, on-demand education	OLSET program (South Africa), TeleSecundaria (Mexico), African Virtual University, Orbicom, SchoolNet, RCP
Business	1. e-Banking, e-stockbroking 2. Logistics management 3. Global trading platforms	1. Efficiency, less delays 2. Lower costs of marketing 3. Global exposure	UNCTAD, UNTPDC, WTO, TradeCompass
Media/cultural industries	1. Digital newsrooms 2. Archival technology, methodologies, standards 3. New media formats	1. More responsive news cycles 2. Preservation of local cultural forms via archives, interactive CD-ROMs and web sites 3. Global projection of local media, culture	UNESCO, OneWorld, DigitalPartners, WorldSpace, Drik
Environment	1. GIS mapping 2. Networking of environmental activists 3. Databases of crop patterns	1. Better management of resources 2. Planning for disaster aversion 3. Improved awareness among activists	World Bank GIS Laboratory, OneWorld, IntelSAT, ESRI, ICLEI, WorldWatch, VITA, APC, SDNP, ICLEI
Governance	1. Online information for citizens, businesses, NGOs 2. Planning and management of transportation 3. Simplified procedures for international business	1. Less wastage of citizens' time, better access to crucial information 2. Improved accountability of government officials 3. Simplified tax procedures for business	USAID, ActionAID, Transparency International, APC, CDT
Urban development	1. Urban planning, service delivery 2. Public telecom, Internet facilities 3. Urban telecentres	1. Shared infrastructure for multiple sectors 2. Better coordination of digging up roads 3. Urban telecentres	International Healthy Cities Foundation, SDNP, ICLEI, ADB
Rural development	1. Rural community networks, public call office 2. Rural tourism 3. Healthcare	1. Rural community networks become economic drivers 2. New employment opportunities 3. Access to government services from remote locations	APDIP, SDNP, ITU, Grameen Bank, CIDA

With inputs from "Telecommunications in Action" (Regency Foundation, 1999).

Multilateral organisations ranging from the UN to the World Bank and non-profit foundations ranging from Bridges.org to the Markle Foundation generally make the same overall recommendation: that ICTs can cost-effectively create and unleash the developmental force of human socio-economic and political networks. For emerging economies –and particularly least developed countries– the key challenge will be to align the interests and strengths of various constituents of society and find their appropriate niches in the global information society. Unless adequate steps are taken to increase local ICT capacities, the "digital divide" may exacerbate the existing social and economic inequalities between countries and communities; the potential costs of inaction are greater than ever before.

The "8 Cs" framework

While analysing the impact and potential of ICTs by economic sector is a useful first step (as illustrated in Table 1), it misses a crucial factor: ICTs like the Internet cannot be interpreted merely as digital forms of telecommunications, or as mere computers, or as media outlets. Many early well-intentioned ICT projects in developing countries failed because they were too technology-centric or stopped merely at the installation phase of computers. The information society is not just about connectivity to the global information infrastructure, but about the content that is accessible, the communities that congregate online and offline, the embedded and emerging cultural attitudes, the commercial and other motives behind such activities, an attitude of cooperation and lifelong learning, and a capacity for creating and governing such information spaces. The information society is not just about passively using "black box" technologies, but about actively creating and shaping the underlying technical, information and service infrastructure. Thus, a more powerful framework is needed which can contextualise ICT diffusion, usage and creation with respect to these attributes.

Accordingly, this author has evolved an approach over the years for analysing information societies in the digital age, called the "8 Cs" framework: connectivity, content, community, commerce, culture, capacity, cooperation and capital. This applies both to the instrument (usage) and industry (creation) aspects of ICTs, as outlined in Table 2.

Connectivity

The digital divide in developing countries is most evident at the phase of connectivity, i.e. lack of affordable access to PCs, Internet devices, modems, telephone lines, and Internet connections. Steps to reduce this digital gap include devising cheaper access devices (such as publicly accessible kiosks), lowering tariffs on import of computers and modems, creating Internet community access centres (with leased lines and shared devices), and bringing access rates down by creating a favourable climate of competition between Internet Server Providers (ISPs).

The regulatory climate in many emerging economies has only recently welcomed private sector ISPs, and a key challenge lies in creating a level playing field between government-owned and private sector ISPs (in terms of operating licenses, tariffs, cross-subsidies, and setting up international gateways). A government ISP player with a monopoly in one area (eg. VSAT links, last mile connectivity, international telecoms) should not use this monopoly power to wipe out an entire industry in another sector.

Work has begun on initiatives to increase Internet diffusion via kiosks (in Bangladesh), community centres (in Peru), cybercafes (in Ecuador), wireless delivery and non-PC devices (in India), but much innovation and investment is still called for here.

Costs of dialup and leased lines are dropping, but could become more affordable. Organisational adoption of Intranets and Extranets (and hence VPN services by ISPs) is only slowly emerging in developing countries. Universal access issues and peering agreements will continue to dominate the ISP scenario in many emerging economies for the coming years.

Special concerns arise in cross-country wiring for regions with mountainous terrain, large arid tracts, or with a high density of island space.

No peering agreements for forming national (let alone regional) Internet exchanges exist in most emerging economies; most inter-ISP traffic is routed via the U.S., Europe or East Asia. Much potential lies in the hands of the public sector units, such as the power grid and railway authorities who have existing secure cable connections across the region. National ISP organisations also need to form to create greater collective bargaining power and to pool assets.

Content

The digital divide between nations arises not just in number and density of ISPs, hosts connected to the Net, proportion of individual users online, Internet diffusion ratios, and number of organisations with leased line connections. This imbalance also extends to content, in terms of number of web sites in developing countries, amount of local language content, and use of online content by key sectors.

There are at least seven measures of market maturity for online content in a country (Rao, 2002):

»   total number of web sites about (and published in) the country
»   local relevance and usefulness of this content
»   local language standardisation and usage on the web
»   amount of sub-national content (about states, provinces, cities)
»   presence of meta-content like directories and search engines
»   amount of ad revenues targeted at online audiences via these sites
»   the presence of third-party services from online traffic auditors, ad revenue auditors and market research groups.

Emerging economies need to increase activity along each of these seven dimensions in order to help reduce the content gap. News media, public health services, government-citizen resources, NGOs, SMEs, and emergency relief organisations need to make more content and services available online.

World-class hosting infrastructure must be created in emerging economies so that locally generated content will be predominantly hosted in the region and not outside, this saving lucrative foreign exchange revenues and safeguarding information sovereignty.

Community

Online and offline fora need to be actively promoted to bring in larger and more diverse sections of community to discuss issues of common interest, especially with regard to creatively tackling the digital divide.

While much attention is focused on web publishing, email fora for content distribution and discussion can still play a useful role –especially in areas where bandwidth is low and the quality of phone connections is poor. In that sense, email-based discussion lists are an under-utilised channel in online communications for many emerging economies.

Commerce

Advanced Internet economies have moved beyond basic Internet infrastructure to dynamic e-commerce infrastructure: payment gateways, secure channels, digital certification authorities, overnight courier services, third party audit services, and online tracking capabilities.

To move beyond being mere destinations for e-commerce sales from U.S. and European sites, emerging economies need to close the "e-commerce gap" by effectively building a domestic Internet economy and promoting online transactional capabilities for the consumer, business and government sectors.

This includes updating existing business and intellectual property rights laws to accommodate electronic contracts, online funds transfer, and stronger consumer fraud protection laws. Malaysia's cyberbill and India's IT Act 2000 fall in this category.

Capacity

To close the "digital skills gap", emerging economies need to improve the capacity of their workforces for Internet age roles. This includes improving Internet access and educational offerings in schools and colleges, creating digital libraries for universities, and promoting professional training institutes.

The Internet should also be strongly promoted among sectors which already have the capacity to harness it. Key priority areas for such Internet growth include the software and web solutions/services sectors, whereby an emerging economy can harness the net not just as a tool but as a market in its own right.

Challenges also arise in closing the "techno-legal gap" in crucial capacity areas like cyberlaw. Legal developments concerning content classification, regulation and enforcement in countries around the world must be tracked. Regional representatives from the industry, academia and government should try to be present in forums of the UN, WTO, OECD, G-7, ASEAN, and APEC, dealing with cyberspace content issues like intellectual property rights, copyright protection, online privacy, online crimes, and digital watermarks.

Culture

This is probably the biggest challenge in closing the digital gap, and involves overcoming cultural inhibitions and insecurities about developing competence for surviving in the break-neck speed of the Internet age.

It includes getting governments in emerging economies to stop treating their telecom monopolies like cash cows, and instead getting government telecom players to invest in areas like R&D on Internet telephony, so that the technology is seen as a market opportunity on a global scale and not a threat on a local scale.

It also includes getting career-track diplomats, bureaucrats, academics and public sector employees to take up Internet training and harness the opportunities as well as the plentiful challenges that accompany Internet diffusion.

In areas like making government procedures transparent, a lot of political will and muscle will be needed. For instance, in areas like land records and getting power connections, some unscrupulous middlemen tend to get involved; openness and transparency will threaten them, but the government must display the political to clean up these processes via open content publishing.

Most importantly, it entails the creation of a risk-taking culture, where accepting some initial failures by entrepreneurs should not be treated as sign of weakness or loss of face; high mobility between jobs should also be accepted as a reflection of a high pace of skill acquisition.

Table 2: the "8 Cs" of the information society

	ICTs as an instrument	ICTs as an industry
Connectivity	How affordable and widespread are ICTs (eg. PCs, Internet access, software) for the common citizen?	Does the country have ICT manufacturing industries for hardware, software, datacom solutions and services?
Content	Is there useful content (foreign and local) for citizens to use in their daily lives?	Is content being generated in local languages and localised interfaces? Is this being accessed/used abroad?
Community	Are there online/offline forums where citizens can discuss ICT and other issues of concern?	Is the country a hub of discussion and forums for the worldwide ICT industry?
Commerce	Is there infrastructure (tech, legal) for e-commerce for citizens, businesses and government? How much commerce is transacted electronically?	Does the country have indigenous e-commerce technology and services? Are these being exported?
Capacity	Do citizens and organisations have the human resources capacity (tech, managerial, policy, legal) to effectively harness ICTs for daily use?	Does the country have the human resources capacity (tech, managerial, policy, legal) to create and export ICTs, and set standards?

Table 2 (cont.)

	ICTs as an instrument	ICTs as an industry
Culture	Is there a forward-looking, open, progressive culture at the level of policymakers, businesses, educators, citizens and the media in opening up access to ICTs and harnessing them? Or is there nervousness and phobia about the cultural and political impacts of ICTs?	Are there techies, entrepreneurs and managers pro-active and savvy enough to create local companies and take them global?
Cooperation	Is there adequate cooperation between citizens, businesses, academics, NGOs and policymakers to create a favourable climate for using ICTs?	Is there a favourable regulatory environment in the country for creating ICT companies, M&A activity, and links with the diaspora population?
Capital	Are there enough financial resources to invest in ICT infrastructure and education? What is the level of FDI?	Is there a domestic venture capital industry? Are they investing abroad as well? How many international players are active in the local private equity market? Are there stock markets for public listing?

Cooperation

No single sector can take on the Internet economy by itself; much cooperation at the national level is needed to overcome the sectoral gaps between government, academia, private sector, civil society, and international organisations. This should happen at the state/provincial, national and regional levels; it can also extend to groupings based on culture (eg. Latin America) or language (eg. between the five countries where Tamil is an official language).

A better characterisation would perhaps be the term "coopetition", where traditional competitors team up to a certain degree to grow the entire Internet pie instead of fighting over small slices. Activities like forming Internet advertising bureaus, national Internet industry associations, and chapters of the Internet Society fall in this category.

Capital

The highly volatile Internet economy is making it all too evident that the best chances for an Internet initiative to survive are if it is at least economically self-sustaining.

Thus, the role of government should focus on creating open investment climates for incubation, launch, acceleration and IPO phases of an Internet start-up. The government need not spend excessive funds on incubation projects of its own; it should create conditions and safeguards conducive for the movement of domestic and international capital into the new economy.

Domestic venture capital funds and skills must be promoted, otherwise the "capital gap" in many emerging economies may lead to an excessive and unhealthy dependence on the umbilical cord of high-technology exchanges like NASDAQ in the U.S.

As for capital for software investments, use of freeware and share-ware packages and tools should be encouraged where possible, instead of relying on costly proprietary software solutions, such as in the use of the Linux operating system and Apache Web server for digital publishing.

Based on this "8 Cs" framework, a more sophisticated analysis of the evolution of the information society is possible, for developed and developing nations. The framework allows for a detailed sector-wise SWOT (strength-weak-ness-opportunity-threat) analysis along these 8 parameters which are all neces-sary conditions for success, thus enabling the identification of potential obstacles and strengths in the growth of the information society in developing nations.

Unless care is taken to adequately address all the 8 Cs for each of the sectoral ICT projects or policies, the initiatives will not be sustainable or scaleable across the entire country. For instance, telecentres may not be a financially sus-tainable access option ("connectivity") unless fee-based services ("commerce") are blended with free services for marginalised communities; this will typically require the joint efforts ("cooperation") between development activists and IT-savvy ("capacity") local entrepreneurs. Linguistic and cultural diversity ("con-tent") will not be feasible in the online medium unless local language tools are made affordable and easy to use for content generation and archival; this also calls for standardisation (via "cooperation") of local language representation codes (eg. Unicode) and keyboard layouts, which has been problematic for some Asian languages like Tamil and Khmer.

For the purpose of this chapter, Table 3 teases apart the ICT scenario in developing nations only, focusing largely on innovative responses to the chal-lenges of ICT diffusion and adoption.

Table 3: Innovative responses to the challenges of harnessing ICTs in developing countries: the "8 Cs" framework of necessary conditions

	Education	Business	Government	Civil Society	Healthcare	ICT Industries
Connectivity	Low cost or free access to higher education institutes, followed by schools. *Examples: KENET, IRANET*	Cybercafes for SMEs. *Examples: iWay cybercafe chain in India*	Special ISPs for government agencies. *Examples: National Informatics Centre*	Telecentres, low-cost devices. *Examples: PubliNets in Tunisia, RCP (Peru), Internet Bus (Malaysia), WLL/CorDECT, InfoCentros (El Salvador)*	Handheld devices, health centres, low cost ISPs. *Examples: HealthNet*	Low cost high-bandwidth Internet access. *Examples: STPI*

Table 3 (cont.)

	Education	Business	Government	Civil Society	Healthcare	ICT Industries
Content	Digital libraries. Examples: African Digital Library, African Journals Online	Directories of exporters, MP3 files for music. Examples: HoneyBee Network	Publishing of government content online, interactive services. Examples: e-Census (Philippines)	Content support for rural constituencies, open source tools and open content. Examples; MahilaWeb (Nepal), Centre for Education and Documentation	Tele-radiology, medical journals. Examples: OpthoNews, HELINA-L, MEDINET	Low-cost IT books in India, Webzines about IT industry
Community	Forums for teachers, administrators. Examples: Community learning centres in Ghana, Kenya	Forums for tourism operators. Examples: MarketWatch (Mongolia)	e-Government forums	Rural community networks. Examples: e-Bario (Malaysia), Mountain Forum, VOICES (India), SIDSNet	Forums for AIDS workers. Examples: InfoDev	Lobbying organisations, open source initiatives. Examples: Computer Association of Nepal, NASSCOM in India.
Commerce	Online courses. Examples: African Virtual University	Hybrid payment options. Examples: AfricaOnline, PeopLink, Central Asia Craft Support Association, PAN-Asia	Interactive services for filing taxes online, tenders. Examples: e-Dirham (UAE)	Services for finding prices in urban markets. Examples: Gyandoot	Pricing of e-Health services. Examples: medical transcription in Philippines	Outsourced tech support
Capacity	Workshops for course developers. Examples: Distance education centres in Mauritius	Workshops in cybercafes, dedicated centres. Examples: Metrocomia, Cisco's Networking Academies	Workshops for government officials. Examples: Leland Initiative	Workshops for rural communities. Examples: Nairobits, "Internet clubs" in Egypt, Global Forest Watch	Workshops for healthcare professionals.	Conferences, private sector educational institutes
Culture	Academic networks. Examples: Egyptian Universities Network	Formation of cyberlaws	National policy bodies. Examples: ICT Task Force of Tanzania	Freedom of Information Act	Launching teleconsultation services	Global outlook. Example: The Indus Entrepreneurs

Table 3 (cont.)

	Education	Business	Government	Civil Society	Healthcare	ICT Industries
Cooperation	Formation of consortia, partnerships with ISPs. *Examples: AfricaOnline*	Support from diaspora networks	Regional caucuses *Examples:* e-ASEAN	Governance of Internet infrastructure. *Examples: APNIC, IPEF*	Worldspace, HealthNet, GIPI Project	Joining standards organisations. *Examples: AfNOG*
Capital	Spinning off academic networks as private ISPs. *Examples: Centre for Informatics (Mondlane University)*	Investments by entrepreneurs, formation of regional ISPs. *Examples: DOT Force Entrepreneur Network*	Removal of taxes from computers	Pilot projects by UN, World Bank	Fee-based services for tele-cardiology in Jordan	Intellectual property rights, licensing, venture capital funding. *Examples: FONTEC fund (Chile)*

Source: Madanmohan Rao (2003), "Visions of the Information Society"
<http://www.itu.int/osg/spu/visions/Conference/index.html>.

The information society: visions, realities and positioning

Despite recent turbulence in the so-called "new economy", it is undeniable that new ICTs like the Internet can, under appropriate conditions, transform business-es and markets, change learning and knowledge-sharing, generate global infor-mation flows, empower citizens and communities in new ways that redefine gov-ernance, and create significant wealth and economic growth in many countries.

The "8 Cs" framework can be used not only to analyse ICT initiatives within a sector, community or country, but also to compare and categorise differ-ent information societies. Based on a combination of the "instrument" and "industry" aspects of parameters like connectivity, content, capacity and culture, the countries of the world can be divided into eight categories: restrictive, embry-onic, emerging, negotiating, intermediate, mature, advanced, and agenda-set-ting. ICT diffusion for the populace, strength of online content and cultural sec-tors, and the projection of domestic ICT industries progressively increase along the spectrum, as does openness of political expression (see Table 4).

Developing nations in the "restrictive" phase include countries like North Korea, where an authoritarian regime and foreign policy pressures have cramped the ICT benefits that the citizens could have otherwise enjoyed. Developing countries like Afghanistan and East Timor have moved on into the next phase: "embryonic", where information infrastructure was not well estab-lished or was largely destroyed, and ICT initiatives are now largely being driven by donor agencies.

Large digital divides and extensive donor activities still persist in the next class of information society –"emerging"– but local ICT capacities have emerged and formal ICT policies have been formed (eg. Nepal, Bolivia). Infrastructure and production for Internet and wireless communication are much more widespread and robust in the next category –"negotiating"– but the government is concerned over the political dissent and cultural changes that can be ushered in by unfettered Internet access. Such countries (eg. China) actively promote ICT infrastructure and deployment, but wish to exercise strong control over online content and search engines.

Staying away from political and cultural censorship of new media is a defining characteristic of the next phase of information society –"intermediate"– while also having local ICT capacities and some international ICT or outsourcing players co-existing with large digital divides and active donor presence (eg. India, Brazil, South Africa).

Donor agencies need not play as active a role in the next category of information society –"mature"– where funding for ICT initiatives comes mostly from government agencies or from public-private partnerships. These countries –like Australia and much of Europe– also have large-scale penetration of Internet and wireless, and mature business models for online content and commerce.

Table 4: Classification of information societies based on the "8 Cs" framework

Type	Characteristics	Examples
Restrictive	1. ICT infrastructure is very limited 2. ICT usage is tightly controlled by government 3. Awareness of ICT among general population is very low	North Korea, Myanmar
Embryonic	1. ICT infrastructure is just being rolled out 2. Donor agencies are active in funding and providing human resources 3. Most ICT activity is driven by diaspora, NGOs	Afghanistan, East Timor, Iraq
Emerging	1. Internet infrastructure exists in urban areas 2. Local capacities exist for ICTs, policy bodies are being formed 3. Widespread digital divide exists, e-commerce is not yet widely prevalent	Nepal, Bangladesh, Bolivia, Nigeria
Negotiating	1. Widespread Internet/wireless infrastructure exists 2. Local capacities and markets exist for ICTs, e-commerce 3. Government is "negotiating" benefits and challenges of new media; authorities exercise strong control over online content, search engines; political and cultural censorship of Internet is practised	China
Intermediate	1. Sizeable markets for Internet, e-commerce, wireless exist 2. Digital divide is still an issue, donor agencies are active 3. Political climate is generally free of censorship for traditional and online media	India, Philippines, Brazil, South Africa
Mature	1. Large-scale penetration of Internet, wireless 2. Mature business models for online content 3. Political climate is generally free of censorship for traditional and online media	Australia, New Zealand, Italy
Advanced	1. Large-scale penetration of broadband and wireless Internet (including 2.5G, 3G) 2. Political climate is generally free of censorship for traditional and online media 3. Some ICT companies are major players in global markets; wireless content models are being exported	Japan, South Korea, Sweden

Table 4 (cont.)

Type	Characteristics	Examples
Agenda-setting	1. Large-scale penetration of ICTs, global powerhouses in ICT 2. Political climate is generally free of government censorship 3. National policies on ICTs in these countries are generally followed by other countries, their ICT media and academic journals are dominant on an international scale, donor agencies of these countries drive many ICT initiatives in developing countries	US

Countries in the "advanced" phase have gone a step further –their ICT industries have become global giants (eg. Japan, South Korea, Sweden), in addition to providing cutting-edge infrastructure like broadband Internet and 2.5G/3G wireless. But "agenda-setting" information societies are key players not only in the ICT industry sector but also in formulating regulations and policies regarding convergent media and cyberlaws, publishing academic literature on the information society, thought leadership in news media of the ICT sector, and creating donor programs for ICT initiatives in developing countries.

The challenge for developing nations is to move at least to the "mature" stage on this spectrum. The goal should be to not just be able to tap the world's pool of collective knowledge, but contribute actively in increasing the pool in the information age.

This classification of countries into eight categories is more sophisticated than a mere binary classification of countries into "developed" and "developing" –the spectrum actually allows for five categories of developing countries and three categories of the developed.

This framework for classifying information societies is also much broader and comprehensive than that of the UNDP, which categorises countries into one of only four groups based on ICT performance: leaders (eg. U.S., Sweden, Japan, Korea, Singapore, Australia), potential leaders (Spain, Italy, Hong Kong, Malaysia), dynamic adopters (Thailand, Philippines, China, Indonesia, Sri Lanka, India), and marginalized (Pakistan, Senegal, Nepal). Potential leaders have diffused old technologies widely but innovate little; dynamic adopters have important hi-tech hubs but the diffusion of old technologies is incomplete. Developing countries typically have four choices of policy stances towards new technological innovation: promotional, permissive, precautionary and preventive. This calls for a balance between the freedom to innovate and the desire to mitigate risks.

Chapter 17

Assessing ICT in development: a critical perspective

Manne Granqvist

This chapter suggests some directions for a critical social approach to the assess- | 285
ment of ICT efforts in marginalized regions. It is argued that the dominant way of
understanding ICT in the development context, as represented by mainstream
assessment models, lacks a critical perspective and neglects aspects of fundamental social relevance. A critical perspective needs to recognize the political nature of
technological development and design and in this chapter the notion of the social
embeddedness of technologies and the experience of emancipatory design traditions are put forward as ways for critical assessment initiatives to approach this
task. The chapter finishes with some observations from a case study of an actual
ICT-for-development experience –the Lincos Project in the Dominican Republic–
wherein the relevance of the theoretical discussion is illustrated briefly.

Introduction

Information and communication technologies have become major players on the
development arena. ICT strategies are now incorporated into the programs of
most foreign aid agencies and many NGOs are focusing on the issue of information technology. Governments of economically weak countries which do not wish
to appear as backward are readily joining in and so, with the help of development
banks and multinational companies on the lookout for new markets, the new
technologies are spreading to all corners of the world.

   Significant of what may be defined as the dominant approach to ICT in
the development context is its priority concern for access. Access to information

technologies is regarded as the road to a better life for the inhabitants of economically weak regions. Not only is the advent of these technologies claimed to increase the 'competitiveness' of a society and its people (which in turn is regarded as the key to a prosperous life), but the technologies are argued to possess in themselves qualities that will enhance the well-being of their users, through amazing communication opportunities and a never before experienced access to information and knowledge (between which a distinction is seldom made). This approach is closely related to the information society discourse, whose underlying beliefs are that "a total social transformation is predicted and that this transformation is generally a good and progressive movement" (Uimonen, 2001).

The single most important myth of the ICT-for-development discourse is the 'digital divide' –a metaphor for the uneven global distribution of new technologies, conceived as a major obstacle for the progress of societies regarded as less developed. Academics, report-writers, journalists, and businesspersons are seemingly competing to present the most striking example or figure of how this great rift reveals itself. "Manhattan has got more computers than the whole of Latin America", "Luxemburg has more Internet hosts than Africa" and so the talk goes. Unfortunately, 'progressive' forces have in many cases not hesitated to embrace this concept. Not only are these accounts most tiresome to read but, in stressing them, authors act as if uneven global distribution of material wealth were a new phenomenon, and one isolated from the economic system that may be argued to perpetuate such inequalities (i.e. Smith, 1993). Further, in the words of Uimonen (2001), "by framing this divide in a technocratic terminology according to which progress is inseparable from access to technology, the concept of the digital divide serves to conceal the political nature of technical systems".

The mere highlighting of this so-called divide does not only indicate technological determinism. It also reflects a modernist worldview and development approach, implying that what most urgently needs to be done is to fortify the deployment of ICT in marginalized countries, thus adapting them to the socioeconomic model of the economically powerful regions. Even among those forces eager to actually reach out a helping human hand, to 'guide' marginalized people with tenderness into the golden era, the basic presupposition remains intact: there is a digital divide, we are on the good side, they are on the bad side –we must help them across. This is the underlying assumption that is never questioned. And so Western culture constitutes an opposite, in which its own splendor is reflected and its 'progress' justified.

Assessment models springing out of this perspective generally seek to appreciate the extent to which a community has "bridged the gap", adapted to the "network economy", and how its ICT efforts are being carried out in line with such aspirations (e.g. Harvard Readinessguide, 2001). They typically focus on the dissemination of access, and secondly, on how this access is utilized in economically rational ways. As commented by Menou (2001), "most of these instruments are fraught with an excessive, when not exclusive, focus on ICT infrastructure".

Typically, in these types of assessment guides, different stages of adaptation or "readiness" are presented, against which a community can check itself. The lower stages relate well to the status of many marginalized regions, whereas the upper ones correspond with the circumstances in economically powerful countries. The idea of development as a series of stages, where Western society is the ideal, is thus explicit.

Absent, unsurprisingly, in mainstream discourse is the process of strengthening marginalized groups in the regions that are now beginning to enter the so-called information age. Neglected is the creation of tools and agendas for these people to critically evaluate and respond to the current development, and build a concept of what it means to them. From a social viewpoint, access or infrastructure as such can hardly be regarded as categorically beneficial. Whatever it is that is to be 'accessed', and in what ways, must be subject to sophisticated scrutiny by the people affected. Indeed, socially minded grassroots organizations and pro-active NGOs have long criticized the simplicity of the digital-divide discourse and its exaggerated focus on access, stressing social issues rather than economic and technical ones, and seeking to elaborate assessment models accordingly. Efforts underway by grassroots groups, social movements, and such actors as the Olistica network[1] appear as promising attempts to approach this task.

For such measures to form part of a cogent critical approach, however, there is reason to further elaborate a framework that is capable of dealing with development, as well as technology, and not least the relationship between the two, as conflictual social processes. When approaching ICT in the development context, alternative forces often hesitate to recognize the historical and continuing role of economically dominant societies in perpetuating the conditions of marginalization, stressed by post-development, world-system, and dependency theorists. Further, as regards technology, it is commonly understood by most groups as a tool, ready to be used in different ways and for different purposes, while in itself free from values. There is alarmingly scarce recognition, even among socially minded activists, of the social dimensions of technological development and design. A critical social approach, as proposed in this chapter, builds on a profound critique of traditional development thinking and seriously questions the ICT-for-development discourse. It attempts to rely on the headway made by alternative forces, while extending concerns to include overlooked social dimensions of technology.

A critical stance

The critical social tradition could be associated with Critical Theory and the works of the Frankfurt School, but also with the feminist movement, foucauldian theory,

1 The Latin American Observatory of the Social Impact of ICTs. An action research network dedicated to the assessment of social implications of ICTs in development context. www.funredes.org/olistica.

and post-colonial studies, among other academic lines of thought. Researchers working within the critical tradition typically aim to unmask hidden conflicts, oppressive practices and power structures in the conventional. The critical perspective is often driven by a transformative social vision and an ambition to explore alternative societal practices, based on notions of autonomy, solidarity, self-determination, and emancipation. "The intellectual role [...] of the critical researcher consists in creating the conditions that allow an open discourse between different social actors and not in establishing a superior insight or an authoritarian truth" (Alvesson and Deetz, 2000, original in Swedish). In such discourse, the critical approach aims to give recognition to issues and voices that are typically neglected or hidden and seeks to reveal practices that perpetuate such suppression.

In the development studies context, the critical perspective is today primarily represented by post-development and feminist scholars and activists. The post-development approach has confronted the 'development discourse' (Escobar, 1995), arguing not only that marginalization is the effect of Western dominance but also that development theory and practice has done little else than to reinforce both Western supremacy and 'Third World' marginalization[2]. Feminist development theorists, many adopting the post-development perspective, have put forward the role of women in marginalized regions and the effect on women caused by development[3].

In technology studies, critical theories are abundant and were launched to a certain extent already in the early days of critical theory (e.g. Marcuse, 1999 [1941]). For critical researchers, the task is to analyze the political character of technology and the ways in which technologies form part of societal power structures and political struggles. One contemporary attempt to build a critical theory of technology based on the legacy of the Frankfurt School is Feenberg (1995, 1999, 2002), who through the analysis of technology's role in the distribution of power aims to "enlarge democratic concerns to encompass the technical dimension of our lives" (1999). A similar, but less philosophical, attempt in this direction is Sclove (1995). Feminist scholars have contributed here with different critical understandings of technology that take as their starting point the experiences of women and the reproduction of gender systems through technology development and use[4]. Feminists have also approached the field of technology assessment, arguing for the introduction of gender analysis into all assessment of technologies (i.e. Morgall, 1993). When it comes to design studies and information systems design, the emancipatory or "political" branch of the participatory design tradition[5] has been proposed as a way for both critical theory and feminism to approach technology (Asaro 2000, Dahms and Rahmos, 2002).

---

2 For an introduction to post-development thinking see Rahnema & Bawtree (1997), Sachs (1992) and Escobar (1995).

3 For comprehensive introductions, see Visvanathan et al (1997) and Saunders (2003).

4 Wajcman (1991) and Grint and Gill (1995) are good entry points.

5 Key works here include Ehn (1988) and Bjerknes et al (1987).

In the context of this study, the critical approach serves to direct atten- | 289
tion to issues that are of relevance to the alleged beneficiaries of ICT-for-development projects, and to open up discursive spaces where such issues can be discussed and reflected upon. Drawing from the critical traditions accounted for
above, the ambition here is to link the post-development perspective with critical
understandings of technology in an attempt to contribute to a framework for the
assessment of ICT efforts in marginalized regions from a critical social viewpoint.

The social nature of technological design

Striving towards analyses that are capable of capturing the social and political
implications of information technology, critically minded assessors must be able
to examine issues that are typically neglected or concealed in mainstream discourse. Their analyses must have the capacity to put forward dimensions of technology that, if they are overlooked, help perpetuate specific power relations and
social conditions. It is necessary, therefore, to delve deeper into the social dimensions of technology, focusing on "key aspects of technology that are rarely, if
ever, voiced by computer manufacturers and political pundits" (Armitage, 1999).
As an entry point for this discussion, I will make use of a time/space graph. The
purpose here, rather than to picture 'reality' in an orderly fashion, is to stimulate
discussion. To be sure, social dimensions of technology could be arranged graph-
ically in many other fashions –or not at all, since they could be argued to be
inevitably intertwined. The present model should thus be regarded as nothing but
a source for reflection.

Figure 1: Social dimensions of technology through time/space axis

An initial explanation of this figure, before moving on, is appropriate. Starting out
with the horizontal axis representing the flow of time, area A represents the
processes directly leading up to the implementation of the artifact or system; the
design process. Area B, then, illustrates the activities that follow the introduction

of the artifact; its usage. Along the space axis, field C should be interpreted as the social values expressed in, and the behaviors implied or suggested by, the design of the artifact or system. Thus, although the figure might imply that this process is in some way or another outside of the actual artifact or system, it should rather be interpreted as lying 'beneath its surface'. The field D, finally, represents the social and political context, categorically surrounding and interacting with the technology. Neither of these categories, of course, can have a meaning without the others. They mutually reinforce and entwine each other and can be separated only as abstractions. The purpose of the model is to stress that a social assessment of technologies must encompass all of these dimensions.

As noted above, however, the development and design of technologies has been blatantly neglected as a social issue in the ICT-for-development discourse. This fact should not be blamed solely on ignorance. Investigators, users, and average citizens do not typically have the power (the finances, knowledge, and societal positions) to alter the circumstances of ownership, design processes, and technological outcomes. It is therefore somewhat natural to focus on how best to use technologies. And indeed, the actual utilization of a technology naturally remains a vital social ingredient in any ICT experience. For a critically minded investigator, some issues are of more concern than others. How is access to technologies distributed in terms of gender, age, and societal positions, for instance? Are users and community members in marginalized regions dependent on external forces? Are they fostered into compelling technology consumers or critical technology creators? Are ICTs used within broader strategies for social change or does the "new technology travel on old social relations"? (Vandana Shiva, quoted in Rydhagen and Trojer, 1998).

In order to achieve a thorough understanding of the social aspects of ICT activities, however, I argue that such analysis needs to be interwoven with evaluations of technological design, i.e. the process as well as the outcome. Further, the assessments must be capable of relating these issues to the political context within which they are given a social meaning. In the following, the notion of the social embeddedness of technologies, and the experience of emancipatory design perspectives, will be proposed as ways for a critical assessment approach to deal with the challenges of such a task.

The social embeddedness of technologies

"Technology", claimed Marcuse (1999: 39), "is a social process in which technics proper [...] is but a partial factor". A technological system or artifact could be likened to a written text. Much like an article, a technology can carry and reproduce varying social values through its choice and use of language, its informational content, and its undeclared presumptions. Through its design, it may convey ideological messages and prompt specific social behavior. "In this sense", declares Pfaffenberger (1992), "one may speak legitimately of the political dimension of technological design". Each given technological innovation can be thought of as carrying with it a conjunction of ideas, "any technology represents a cultural invention, in the sense that it brings forth a world; it emerges out of particular cultural conditions and in turn helps create new ones"(Escobar, 1994). A critical theory of technology, as proposed by Feenberg (2002), is thus "suspicious of the advantages the beneficiaries of technological advance derive from the claim that, like justice, technology is socially blind" (66).

Informed by this understanding of technology as a social and political institution, social constructivist and feminist scholars have engaged in exploring the actual political properties of specific technologies, such as workplace machinery and domestic appliances. For those interested in assessing the social aspects of ICTs in economically weak regions, the space opened up by these academics is particularly relevant. There is reason to put greater effort into analyses of the design of chosen technologies and its meaning for users and society in general, and further, to recognize the prospect of alternatives. A critical perspective asserts that technological artifacts come to life through conflicting social processes, and that the realized design of a technology becomes the platform for continuing struggle, where the design as such supports or suppresses different, essentially political, objectives. Thus, as argued by Ehn, "emancipatory practice must not only aim at changing the use of artifacts but also their technical design [...]" (1988: 100). An emancipatory assessment approach must also be informed by this insight, and seek to reveal the ways in which different designs are predisposed towards certain social and political directions.

The corollary of this conception when it comes to the assessment of ICT efforts in marginalized regions is that all technologies, envisioned and implemented, ought to be examined according to the kind of usage they allow, the behaviors they prompt, and the social values they uphold or confront. And not only should the actual information technologies be susceptible to investigation of social embeddedness. One electricity solution may be more sustainable from an ecological point of view than another one, thus affecting the world of citizens and signaling an environmental concern. Manuals and other types of information and instruction accompanying the technology also assist in articulating the values of the technology. Sites chosen for ICT projects, buildings and architecture, organization of user environments such as compilation, placement, and setting out of equipment, all carry with them social meanings and cause reactions with their users. Even the human organization surrounding the ICT practice should be taken into account when assessing embeddedness. Work hierarchies in ICT projects, 'rules of conduct', opening hours, etc., all help constituting the meaning of the technology in the social world.

Of particular concern for the critically minded assessor might be in what ways technologies promote, for instance, activity or passivity; creativity or monotony; autonomy or dependence; critical thought or compliance; collaboration or competition; democracy or hierarchy. In the development context, the findings of such evaluations should be measured against the aspirations of the people that are supposed to benefit from the technologies. In what ways is the design and the visions it is meant to promote interfering with the values, traditions, and interests of community members and marginalized people in general? It must also be acknowledged that one and the same technology may be interpreted and treated differently by different groups. For instance, women may experience difficulties with technologies that were designed by men and with male users in mind. The promoters, owners, or managers of an ICT project may have a thoroughly different perspective of the ICTs than users (and non-users) who may subsequently be susceptible to other experiences than the ones intended by their design. The critical investigator should pay specific attention to how marginalized groups are affected socially by the design of technologies, but also compare this evaluation with the meaning of the same technology for people in more dominant positions.

The design process as politics

Users are of course not always helpless victims of a technology's social embeddedness and, as pointed out by Pfaffenberger (1992): "the ideologies crafted in the course of technological innovation are inherently ambiguous and susceptible to multiple interpretations [...]. But while "there is always a margin of flexibility in how existing technologies may be used or operated, or in what activities may occur in conjunction with them", Sclove (1999) stresses that "a technology's greatest flexibility exists before its final deployment, when artifacts and their accompanying social organization are being conceived and designed". One of the most potent strategies to bias technological outcome towards the interest of its future users, therefore, is to involve them in its design phase. But while the notion of 'participation' has lately appeared as ubiquitous in the development world, it is seldom more than an empty word, adopted by development agencies that in spite of a new vocabulary remain essentially modernist (Heeks, 1999). In development projects related to ICT, the superficiality of the concept is evident in the general incapacity of such projects to build upon specific community interest and knowledge, and also in a failure to learn from the extensive experience of the participatory design tradition, which provides both a theoretical and a practical framework for democratization of the design process.

In the typical ICT-for-development case, non-Western communities are conceived as "know-nots", underdeveloped, and in need of Western structures and infrastructure. Computers and Internet access are provided not as a means to strengthen traditional livelihood and local knowledge, but as an important and very symbolic step on the road to 'modernity', along which non-dominant truths and knowledge are discarded. The information society discourse reinforces this practice in launching categories like 'information-rich' and 'information-poor', which, correlated with technology, deny "the validity of the different types of knowledge that people possess, much of which is transmitted by other means than those of advanced digital technologies" (Uimonen, 2001).

In marginalized regions, the case for using participatory design methods might be particularly strong, especially from a post-development point of view that promotes the emancipation of marginalized regions from the dependence upon Western economic forces and acknowledges the right of the inhabitants of these regions to define their own solutions (and problems for that matter) instead of having ready-made models and accompanying technologies forced upon them. The political branch of participatory design evolved as computer scientists made common cause with industrial workers instead of management when designing workplace information systems (Asaro, 2000). In the development context, similar conflicts of interest prevail, making the design process a thoroughly political process. The expertise of external project members, representing authorities or foreign aid agencies, who 'know about development', is seldom questioned. Sadly, few designers recognize the political agency of their work and few projects in marginalized regions adopt the principles of participatory design[6].

Socially minded actors ought to look closely at participation in the design process. To what extent is a project building upon local knowledge and tradition? Are users taking part in the planning of the project? Are they involved at all in the design work? If they are, how is their participation assisted? Are efforts made to facilitate users' understanding of project plans and requirements specifications? Do community members have the right to turn down suggested technological implementations? If participation in the creation of a society's basic structures is conceived as a fundamental social right, these and more questions must be investigated.

It should further be acknowledged that participation is most often cosmetic. As Heeks points out, "membership is often skewed towards the powerful and away from the marginalized". Even when community members are invited to take part in the realization of a development project, the persons who tend to be selected already share the perspectives of the (normally alien) project initiators, or are willing to adapt to them. And whether formal discrimination is practiced or not, groups of people whose knowledge and interests are culturally and historically suppressed often underestimate their own capacities. A critical evaluation, therefore, cannot be content with participation as such, but must explore the social organization that surrounds it and analyze the power relations that set its foundation. In assessing ICT efforts, critical investigators should strive to reveal whether and how participation, given that it exists at all, actually enforces those voices that are commonly suppressed, in specific situations as well as in society in general.

Observations from the Lincos project

The remainder of this chapter presents a glimpse into the Lincos experience in the Dominican Republic, by presenting a few concluding comments based on a study carried out in late 2002 (Granqvist, 2003). These excerpts make no claim

6 For one exception, see Ramos et al (2002).

to give a thorough account of the Lincos project, but are recounted here only to briefly illustrate the applicability and relevance of the previous discussion in an actual ICT-for-development situation. For an extended report, the original study should be consulted[7].

Lincos (an acronym for "Little Intelligent Communities") is a project initiated by the Costa Rican business-oriented NGO Entebbe in cooperation with an array of commercial and academic institutions (among them Microsoft, HP, MIT, and Harvard University). The idea is to distribute multi-application ICT centers to marginalized regions, and the specific concept is to accommodate the centers in industrial containers. Each center is equipped with a host of technologies: computers, cameras, telephones, a fax machine, a radio transmitter, a telemedicine kit, a tool for water and soil analysis, television sets, plus more. Lincos centers have so far been set up in Costa Rica and the Dominican Republic, and according to the Lincos webpage[8] the project is not only pioneering but also highly successful. A critical social assessment might reach other conclusions, however.

The Lincos container is the obvious example of how a design solution imposes certain social behavior on its users. The limited space offered by these containers prevents people from accessing them, and in some cases causes the technology to be left entirely unused. Its material and its lack of a/c and ventilation have similar effects (producing an unbearable heat), and the same goes for the inadequate electricity solution. Further, the container concept as such signals temporariness, and invigorates the (in this case very well-founded) feeling that the project has been developed externally and brought to the community in a top-down manner as a wrapped-up 'development package'.

For the people of the communities, the design is more or less disastrous. For other persons, the same design may be conceived as successful –particularly for the Lincos officials who view it as a valuable marketing concept, signifying modernity and innovativeness. "They have their reality, we have ours", as one of the staff members currently on strike (protesting the conditions of their workplace) aptly commented, referring to those responsible of the design of the container. The design of the container and its consequent social implications for users may be interpreted in political terms. One understanding is that the interest of the Lincos officials, eager to accomplish a marketable product, has taken precedence over the interest of the community members. As the dominant force in the development of the project and its technologies, the visions of Entebbe and the government have been favored, at the cost of the interests of the community.

The organization of the Lincos project did not only exclude users from participating on any level of the design process, it also kept them from taking part in the planning and introduction of the project, failed to provide a structure for evaluation and totally neglected the local knowledge and situation. To the limited

7 The full text is available at the combined webmag/archive Globala Tider, <www.globalatider.nu>.
8 <www.lincos.net>.

extent that community members were involved, membership was biased towards the already powerful and users were not included. The design team, practicing in another country –not paying visits to the communities at all, let alone sharing their everyday life– had the sole right in both defining the problems and working out the solutions, which were of similar appearance and subsequently applied in an equal fashion in all of the communities. The social consequences of these conditions are at the same time both obvious and serious. Out of a host of expensive technologies, only a handful are used to a reasonable extent. Moreover, since the development of the technology has not formed part of strategies in line with community members' own visions, and since decision making has taken place above their heads, people in general do not feel affiliated with the project and express indifference or, as in the case of some staff members, even frustration towards the project.

The experience might be best summarized by a community member in one of the Lincos villages, in an interview made during the above mentioned study (translated from Spanish):

> "In the case of the Lincos project... there was no real introduction. They didn't tell the people first, before bringing the project, instead they came with the project first and then they spoke to the people. The first thing should be to speak to the people, 'we're bringing a project, and we're bringing it to show you', speaking to different sectors...that way they will know what the people think, 'well, we're going to modify this, we'll drop this thing that the people are not interested in'".
>
> *"That's what they call 'participatory design'..."*
>
> "Exactly, participatory design was never practiced [...]. The obvious consequence of this is that the people didn't give their support, they didn't attach importance to it, and with time the project diminishes, it won't be growing, because the people don't regard it as useful, because it doesn't have any importance for them, it doesn't have any value [...]. The consequence is fatal, very negative, and then the project is lost."

Summary

The main ambition of this chapter has been to highlight the importance of a critical understanding of technological design to form part of a critical social assessment framework and to subsequently provide some practical examples of why such an understanding is relevant. Emphasizing these issues is not enough of course. Elaborating a critical assessment framework is a thorough task that requires further exertions, not least involving those directly concerned. The purpose here has merely been to point out that design issues should be taken seriously in such efforts.

What need is there for a critical assessment framework, then? Can we really ask projects such as Lincos to live up to the radical demands posed by a critical approach to technology and development? Perhaps not, but the point of creating such tools, in my opinion, is not so much to enable simple conclusions on the appropriateness of specific ICT efforts, as it is to guide people into a way of looking at such efforts that does not exclude fundamental social and political issues, thus allowing them to better judge whether the introduction of technologies into their communities is in their interest. If and how citizens of marginalized communities should use ICTs are decisions that have to be made by these people themselves. Today, however, the dominant discourse informing such decision-making is so biased towards the idea of 'progress' and the excellence of Western technology –even to the degree that marginalized people commonly understand their own culture as inferior and equate computers with prosperity– that one important task of critical activists and investigators is to direct attention to alternative understandings and strategies.

Chapter 18

'We were nobody, we were nothing': art, communications and memories of underdevelopment

Sarat Maharaj & Gilane Tawadros

What are the ways in which contemporary art practices and communications |
shape up and interact in the development context today? This chapter takes off
from a discussion about *Faultlines*, a show Gilane Tawadros curated for the Africa
Pavilion, Venice Biennale (2003). With globalization, sectors of the 'developing
world' are increasingly drawn into the orbit of 'advanced world' institutions –into
the art-culture industry, the gallery-museum-biennale system and the communica-
tion-information economy. These entanglements are probed through a range of
art works, films, performances and projects from across the world. Intensified
interconnections brought on by globalization, migration, cultural mix and translation and new technologies mean re-mapping the classic North/South,
developed/developing divide. It does remain the grim, principal fault. But new
problems also crop up 'after development' in the advanced world –new 'zones of
morbidity and backwardness'– putting into question notions of development as
linear progress. Alongside, we have criticisms of the drift of development and
modernity from inside the developing world itself. Contemporary art-communica-
tive activities and strategies explore and embody the dilemmas thrown up under
the circumstances –sometimes also intimating alternative models and other values.

Sarat Maharaj: In *Popular Music from Vittula*, Mikael Niemi gives us a deadpan
rendering of 'everyday backwardness' at the Arctic rim of Sweden. It is a pocket
of murky life left behind in the forward march of the model social democratic
state and its success story. What he touches on strikes a chord across the develop-

ing world: how to take the sound of 'backwardness', how to forge a lingo that both voices it and goes beyond the gag it imposes:

> We gradually caught on to the fact that where we lived wasn't really a part of Sweden. We'd just been sort of tagged on by accident. A northern appendage, a few barren bogs where a few people happened to live, but could only partly be Swedes. We were different, a bit inferior, a bit unedu- cated, a bit simple-minded. We didn't have any deer or hedgehogs or nightingales. We didn't have any celebrities. We didn't have any theme parks. No traffic lights, no mansions, no country squires. All we had was masses and masses of mosquitoes, Torndalen-Finnish swearwords, and Communists.
>
> Ours was a childhood of deprivation. Not material deprivation –we had enough to get by on– but a lack of identity. We were nobody. Our parents were nobody. Our forefathers had made no mark on Swedish history. Our last names were unspellable, not to mention being unpronounceable for the few substitute teachers who found their way up north from the real Sweden. None of us dared write in to Children's Family Favourites because Swedish Radio would think we were Finns. Our home villages were too small to appear on maps. We could barely support ourselves, but had to depend on state handouts. We watched family farms die, and fields give way to undergrowth ... our school exam results were the worst in the whole country. We had no table manners. We wore woolly hats indoors. We never picked mushrooms, avoided vegetables, never held crayfish par- ties. We were useless at conversation, reciting poems, wrapping presents, and giving speeches. We walked with our toes turned out. We spoke with a Finnish accent without being Finnish, and we spoke with a Swedish accent without being Swedish.
>
> We were nothing.

The 'indices of underdevelopment' Niemi chalks up have a quasi-sociological air, a parody of some sober, cumulative table of facts. He gauges 'developmental shortfall' through a stream of impressions, quirky, personal markers, subjective scraps of association –a far cry from hard-nosed statistics or 'scientific method'. The mode is introspective, in the shape of 'first person consciousness'. We are plunged into the lived experience of 'nonentity status', into the thick of 'zones of morbidity'. It adds up to a feel-think-know probe –an epistemic mode for unpack- ing elements of the world, mulling over its stickiness, sensations and intensities that gives us a concrete feel of how things tick 'from the inside'.

Why is this significant for communication in the developmental con- text? For Amartya Sen (1999) analytical approaches have tended to treat develop- ment in narrow, quantitative, 'GNP terms'. Against this, he has proposed we should see rates of material improvement and progress, rising living standards, better conditions and resources as closely tied to the endeavour to engender and expand freedoms and rights. This is a key link if we are to grasp the drift of development 'from the inside', as self-understanding of the process on the part of those who are 'in the thick of it'. In today's interconnecting, globalizing world, the business of tackling unfreedoms and exclusions cannot be put off to some time 'after basic development has taken place'. The communications sphere becomes an essential medium through which individual participants and players identify, interpret and represent their social and cultural wants and needs. In doing this, they begin to shape development itself –orchestrating the process as opposed to having it simply thrust upon them. But what communicative structures and art activities can contribute to this shaping process –to opening up new self-reflexive mental, emotional, semantic dimensions– both for voicing 'backwardness' and for stepping out of it? I wonder, Gilane, whether we might look at this a little bit in the light of your research as curator of *Faultlines*?

Gilane Tawadros: In addressing the keywords communication and development in a global context, we need to distinguish between communications for and on behalf of a globalized capital economy and other types. The former tends to be homogenous, emerging principally from the centres of financial and political power. Its forms are largely unilateral. Although they might be inflected with different accents –capital enterprises have been ingenious with inflecting communications so they can apparently speak to and 'fit in' with different spaces and places– they are nonetheless particular messages with predetermined outcomes within the context of the global economy. Some art practices, on the other hand, create possibilities for another kind of communication –a space, in my view, about dialogue and exchange rather than something one-way. Contemporary art is not always clear-cut or transparent, nor is it homogenous or unilateral. For example, in Moataz Nasr's installation *One Ear of Dough, One Ear of Clay* (2001), the video piece depicts ordinary Egyptians in the street, hunching their shoulders. The gesture is repeated over and over by individuals of various ages, genders and social class –a colloquial physical gesture, a shrug that suggests: "So what can I do about it? That's just the way it is". The work comments on political apathy questioning why people with a history of political engagement at every level of the social order, in direct and instrumental ways, are not as involved politically at this juncture.

In his installation *Tabla* (Venice, 2003), a huge video screen depicting a drummer playing on a traditional Egyptian drum, or tabla, dominates the space. We don't see his face or head, just the tabla clutched between his legs and his hands beating out a powerful, continuous rhythm. The noise ricochets through the exhibition scattered with tablas of varying sizes, like a geographical map of the Nile Delta.

The sound is deafening, relentless. You register the work acoustically before you read it visually, as the sound of difference. Arab music is very much about atonality and dissonance. But it's also a sound that takes over the space and overwhelms the viewer. Furthermore, there is a disparity between the single tabla with a sound that is distinctive and powerful and the reverberations from others that are connected to the main screen and which create sounds in response. The piece works on a number of levels such as the question of political agency, of how individuals are implicated in the political situations in which they find themselves.

SM: Your example is arresting not least because Nasr's Tabla parallels a wider involvement of today's visual artists with 'high-decibel sound saturation'. How to make sense of this? One way is to press the distinction you imply between types and terrains of communication –to look at their archaeologies. From the 1960s, the spread communications and consumerist culture –TV, radio, cinema, advertising, fashion, sport, transport, popular culture, commodity design– saw an increased grooming and styling of the 'look' of the everyday right down to its micro-texture. This 'aestheticization' was summed up pointedly by the situationists as 'the production of the spectacle'. Later, the stakes were raised as reality came to be seen as processed by the artistry of digital simulation technologies. Had this rather stolen the thunder of artists if not upstaged the 'creativity' once associated with 'fine art'? What kind of art was possible that did not simply mirror 'the spectacle' or become ensnared by it? But let us also ask right away whether this was an issue at all for practitioners outside 'the developed world', outside mainstream, advanced consumerist art-culture circuits?

By 2000, electronic systems –satellite, cable, digital terrestrial TV and radio, dial-up Internet and broadband services, mobiles, SMS texting, cashpoints, video, nintendo games, iPods– set on course an intensified 'visualization' of everyday info-data flows. These signifying systems and image economies amount to 'retinal regimes' –a term that connotes, amongst other things, a sense of sheer overload and glut of images, signs, visual representations. Could sound scan the visual, supplement it, if not short-circuit it in the face of its 'retinal condition'? Sonic constructions, multiple frequencies, noise, sonic dirt vibes, inundations and interference become the stuff with which to probe, if not shatter, the 'spectacle', to dispel its ambient muzak. They serve as 'antidotes' that blank out info-spin-jabber in order to allude to other communicative wavelengths, alternative acoustic awareness. In *Popular Music from Vittula*, this sense of difference and of other possibilities is symbolized by the jarring, raw rockunrol awkwardly eked out by stubby-fingered, speechless Niila or by the farm worker turned music teacher who had lost his fingers in an accident and now strummed the guitar with a thick, penile thumb. The sound they manage to croak out are painful spasms of release, of coming to voice, of prising open a chink in the numb silence of 'backwardness'.

By the 1980s the term 'spectacle' takes on an almost entirely pejorative connotation. In the cross-tongued, global Babel of today's image-info-data circulation, it seems better to speak of 'retinal regimes', a term with an oscil-lating positive-negative charge. It signals the pervasive syntax or 'visual esperanto' of the contemporary 'knowledge economy'. Although the latter is billed as cutting across the developed/developing barrier, outside advanced centres its infrastructures are still sparse with patchy access. This is roughly comparable to the lack in the developing world of modern gallery-museum systems and art education-communications structures of the sort that are the staples of the developed world's art-culture industry. Nevertheless, practitioners have invented diverse strategies in Internet-new media domains. Sites and networks devised by Raqs Media Collective (India), Open Circle (India), or Trinity (South Africa) are engaged in 'adisciplinary' manoeuvres –almost ad-lib assemblages of info-images and discourses, experimental inquiry tools interacting with social action, performance, learn-ing sessions, investigative tours of urban spaces that have a feel of the ran-dom walkabout and happening. The 'transborder pants' with multiple-use pockets designed by Torolab (Tijuana, Mexico) can switch over for immigrant or American usage according to how citizenship status embodies and inspects the politics of belonging in the 'laboratory conditions' of the US/Mexico border. These projects are think-know-act contraptions that may not look like 'art' but count as art in their open-ended semantic fission. To pigeonhole them as 'developing world artwork' rather misses the point. As emerging art-communication ploys, they question the norm of the airtight modern gallery-museum system whether inside the developed world or out.

GT: This goes back to whether by communication we mean a one-way conver-sation or a dialogue. Too often, both in the arena of development and the art world, the developed world is seen as having opportunities and goods to offer, and the developing world as the consumer who is potentially avail-able in fantastic numbers. It's more complicated than this because the prod-uct, in terms of the artworks being made in the developing world, are pack-aged, taken back and presented to consumers in the developed world. Here, the artworks are framed in particular ways, which define and pre-scribe how they're read. This is often in the narrow terms, either as part of a national or ethnographic discourse, or as illustrations of preconceived ideas of what the 'developing other's' creative discourse is about.

But the critical point for me is that the work of contemporary artists within the African continent I did get to see –even if my range of evidence was somewhat limited– offered up many ideas, possibilities and points of engagement that I hadn't seen in the developed world. I came back to London, having travelled in Johannesburg and Cairo, for example, thinking, "Here I am in this capital of the developed world where all this infrastruc-ture exists, where there are all these opportunities but the work I'm looking at appears so empty". It was decidedly lacking in the substance we are talking about. What is considered to be at the top of the hierarchy of communication worlds actually seemed empty of knowledge –however full it might be with information. They seemed more akin to global, commercial communications products. I found in Johannesburg and Cairo artists working without infrastructure, in extremely difficult circumstances, without wider cultural or, in some cases, moral support, working in quite isolated spaces. Yet I found work that challenged me, that was not in any way aping Western practice but opening up new forms of artistic practice in making and communication. There are artists in both cities dealing with specific, local questions: they are by no means turning their back on the rest of the world. Nor indeed are they ignorant of the realities of being part of a globalized economy. They are making work that focuses on particular issues but they undoubtedly have a relevance and resonance beyond these particular contexts. If anything, one's sense of being in a globalized economy (and the awareness from artists of its implications) is more heightened in Johannesburg and Cairo than in London or Helsinki.

SM: The global/local imbrications you touch on highlight why we should not pit the local as somehow 'primordial' against the global –the 'either/or' trap. At the end of Apartheid, the focus was either on coaxing the local gallery-museum system out of received racial designations, on encouraging development beyond these barriers or on plugging South Africa into global art-culture circulation through events such as the Biennale. Thinking in official circles gravitated towards the former. After the second Johannesburg Biennale (1997) the 'global option' was scrapped. Under the 'local' umbrella, *Serafina II* (1999) –a musical centred on HIV/AIDs awareness, backed by the Health Minister Nkosazane Zuma, but mired in controversy– was promoted. It was a 'follow up' to the original *Serafina* (1989) –a documentary look at Apartheid around the time of the1976 Soweto uprisings. Today this approach to creativity and development is perhaps sustained in Henning Mankell's story projects –mix of art-communication-education– where those affected by AIDS/HIV are encouraged to write about themselves, their families, their kith, kin and clan, their histories –an 'archive of the everyday' for the orphans left behind (Uganda Child Aid Project, Haus der Kulturen der Welt, Berlin, 28.09.04)

In the meantime, the 'global option' of the Biennale has begun to proliferate across the developing world taking the edge off what artists felt was a 'legitimation test' they had to pass in the heyday of singular Euro-events such as the Venice Biennale. It has steadily come to be seen less as an 'importation', potentially a global/local transaction site for devolving art activities to regional idioms –as with Sharjah, United Arab Emirates or Kwanju, South Korea– if also a mechanism for kick starting local urban regeneration and development.

GT: Clifford Charles's work relates to this inside/outside reach. He deals with how one creates abstract art in the post-apartheid moment, how one addresses the historical facts and experiences of apartheid in a new way that isn't circumscribed or prescribed by the local remit of the anti-apartheid struggle. This had created a requirement for a certain kind of practice that was politically contingent and contingent on the political. Now there is opportunity to link this to the wider theme of what Frantz Fanon called 'the fact of blackness' –possibilities for investigating this signifier in graphic terms of pure black ink on a white page. Charles' ink paintings explore what that might mean in pictorial, aesthetic terms, in the broader context of the history of art and also in the specific locale of post-apartheid South Africa.

SM: You lead us onto an exceptional communications event in the tricky exit from Apartheid –the South Africa Truth and Reconciliation Commission (1996-1998). The cross-examining it staged saw 'perpetrators, beneficiaries and victims' tussling to find a common wavelength. The 'due process' of trial became episodes of theatre, performance and spectacle as the 'silenced' sought to voice unspeakables of the Apartheid years (Krog, 2000; TRC Tapes). At times, it looked like 'communications' itself was in the dock. The relevance of the event straddles the developing/developed fence: it applies to the search for truth and reconciliation in the aftermath of the Central African genocide no less than to the Balkans, to the Chile persecutions, the Northern Ireland sectarian deadlock and to diverse 'zones of Artic unspeakables' across the globe.

But reservations have also been expressed –not least during the course of the Tribunal through the merciless satirical revue Truth Omissions (Pieter-Dirk Uys, 1996) or through the more intimate musings of poetry, in a lyric such as "Maybe you don't have to know why" (Adam Schwartzman, *Book of Stones*, 2004). For Albie Sachs, one of the Commission's originators, its limitations lay in its inability to square the four truth-telling modes he was to identify: forensic, legal, dialogic, phenomenological. Could a juridical framework take on board the self-reflexive intensities of the last two? The Commission's legalistic drive –keen to wrap up matters in the interests of the overall political settlement– functioned with a readymade lingo that some used simply to 'perform' their way through the ritual of 'asking forgiveness and receiving it'.

The Commission's proceedings were riddled with a tension between the timescale of juridical 'due processes' and the durations of truth-telling, the stretched-out temporal cycles of art processes. The latter come into their own as legal procedures reach an impasse or dead end because of lack of hard facts or reliable witness. They carry on the scrutiny by other means –through the immersive, fictive mode– as we see in Walid Ra'ad's project

Missing Lebanese Wars (Atlas Group, 2002, Documenta, Kassel). He ponders how to do justice to the devastated Lebanon when there are the barest scraps to go by, scant sources, no data bank at hand. What methodology is up to it? To map individual lives caught up in the strife, he has to grapple with both the absence of an archive and the likelihood that if one did exist all it might have authorized is an 'official' version. How to voice unutterable, 'missing' and 'disappeared' historical experience? The question parallels dilemmas around representing the Holocaust that Lyotard sees as the impossibility of meeting Robert Faurisson's kind of demand for 'facts'. The 'first hand evidence' Holocaust-deniers tauntingly ask for can only be verified by witnesses who are unavailable precisely because they had been wiped out (Lyotard, 1983).

Beyond such dead-end absolutism of the fact, we have Ra'ad's startling fact-fiction constructs. He launches off from the handy myth of stumbling over a hoard of 226 notebooks belonging to Dr. Fadl Fakhami and a treasure trove of videotapes. The ruse helps him to plumb unthinkable bits of the narrative. He cites, with mock-scholarly referencing, two 'found' videos, Tape 17 and Tape 31. They refer to real life events, to named British and American hostages. To this he adds a make-believe Arab hostage, Souheil Bachar. The situation is staged as a glimpse into captivity, its edgy atmospherics and paranoia. In this fantasy-fact scenario, Bachar grapples with the Lebanon's unimaginables: how to know the other, how to communicate beyond barriers of tribe, religion, nation?

In *A Passage to India* (1924), EM Foster had flagged up this yearning with the catchphrase 'Only connect' –the desire for oneness with the other, 'empathy' as the means to scaling the walls separating colonizer/colonized, self/other. Whether it could be literally fleshed out through body contact is a thought that fleetingly crosses Souheil Bachar's mind as he imagines, in a torrid interior monologue, fumbling around with and fondling his fellow hostages:

> pressed myself against his ass...punched me in the groin. Why they wanted me to fuck them then to fuck me ...

Could the momentary desire to break the taboo of male same-sex contact, to cuddle his cell mates, amount to that authentic embrace in which self/other antagonisms melt away? The thought is banished in a mix of revulsion, loathing, fear of rejection. Do we also sense a glimmer of an ethics of difference here?

In another stab at the 'Missing Wars', Ra'ad zooms in on a bundle of 'found papers' that testify to a professor's passion for horse racing. Each horse represents one or another methodological stance: positivist, empiricist, historical materialist amongst others. All have had their day in the Lebanese battlefields. Is there a winner or are they all deadbeat? Can any

deliver a way of filling in the 'Missing Wars' sagas? His sift through the 'liq-
uidity of solid facts' puts existing approaches into question. Is it at all likely
he could have broached any of this through means other than the concrete,
cross-hatched thinking of art processes?

GT: The capacity for some kinds of art to create such spaces for reflection, for
'indirect' communication is vital –though 'indirect' might not be the correct
word. Perhaps I should say art is not so much 'roundabout or circuitous' as
not completely transparent, not immediately legible, simply because the
problems themselves, the issues and questions are not fully known, and the
answers are also not known. What one needs is precisely that opportunity
to reflect, to take time to pose questions without necessarily answering
them. As you say, the judicial process, the agenda of political, social and
economic requirements for communication completely militate against that
kind of space and time. From this viewpoint, in the exigencies of executing
change and of transforming society, art can often be seen as little more
than an indulgence. When there are pressing issues facing the developing
world, why should one spend time, energy and resources on something
that appears unimportant, which is not necessary in the way food, education, sanitation and water are self-evidently critical in people's lives? The
implication is that this 'indulgence' should only be afforded to society at a
more advanced stage in its development. It assumes a strictly linear progression to social and cultural development and, secondly, a hierarchical organization of priorities. However, the question remains: can social, political and
economic transformation be delivered without knowing what kind of
changes one wants to achieve and to what end, without addressing the full
lexicon of human needs beyond the physical and material?

SM: With globalization in full spate, we cannot shy away from re-conceptualiz-
ing issues of development and modernity from a 21st century perspective
–of re-mapping them, as you mention, in more non-linear fashion. This
means adopting something like a 'recursive model' where we get constant
feedback on how development 'upstream' affects matters 'further down'.
Such a model springs up from present-day factors –from the sheer volatility
of interconnections in today's world system. Its drift is different from earlier
'vertical' top/down approaches such as Walter Rodney's classic *How Europe
Underdeveloped Africa* (1972) that is centred on unpacking lopsided,
exploitative colonial legacies.

This should by no means imply that the North/South divide is no longer
the principal fault line: it persists with its grave disparities and inequalities.
Development has yet to kick off in swathes of the South where some
economies have been thrown of joint by IMF/World Bank 'structural adjustments' while others have been buffeted by WTO rulings. But their actual

desperation is also paralleled by an incipient dynamic, another global picture, where as some zones 'catch up', others 'fall behind' sometimes in the heart of the developed world itself. We have 'upcoming' quality of life alongside 'stagnating, laggard' ones or non-starters. Niemi graphs this as 'backwardness' at the Nordic tip of the globe turning the classic North/South binary upside down: it's the 'relative' South that is flourishing. Not dissimilarly, Tony Cragg's sculpture *Britain as seen from the North* (1981) –a map of the UK made up of consumerist detritus– had shown the fattening effect of the burgeoning Thatcherite boom on the English home counties to the detriment of the North.

The effect of such symbolic inversions is to thicken the plot of the development story. They show how globalization jumbles together developed/developing zones engendering topsy-turvy, though increasingly enmeshed and interdependent relations between different parts of the North/South. It is now less easy to think of 'development problems' as if they were happening 'elsewhere': we are implicated, 'in it' wherever we are. Perhaps this is also why we are left somewhat uneasy by the 'cost-benefit' treatment of development as a malady 'out there' to be tackled briskly by setting up a shopping list of development priorities (Lomberg, 2004; Copenhagen Consensus)[1].

Sen captures the 'thickening of the development plot' in empirical terms by citing certain surprising anomalies: for example, male longevity rates in South India and parts of Bangladesh turn out to be higher than those for African Americans at the core of the developed world, in Washington and Manhattan. We may be inclined to brush these figures aside as isolated glitches rather than symptoms of systemic disorder. But a pattern begins to build up once we correlate such discrepancies with other trends in the developed world: increasing obesity levels as shown up in 'Body Mass Index' distribution research (WHO & International Obesity Task Force, 2004) and its potential impact on reversing what were rising longevity figures; ageing outstripping birth and fertility rates; pervasive mental distress and depression or new forms of morbidity; substance dependency, often triggered by new, taxing work-play-performance expectations; job loss in advanced sectors through outsourcing; environment damage. An array of sticky problems seems to crop up 'after development has taken place'. We face a double-scenario: on the one hand, dire circumstances of want in the developing world: on the other, in the developed world, a rising sense of 'post-development blues'. For in the wake of advanced development we now see new forms of 'malaise and backwardness'. In this uneasy space of 'development and its discontents' –the 'indices of over-development' have yet to be fully collated– art and communications seem to

---

1 <http://www.copenhagenconsensus.com/>.

become more indispensable for the struggle to interpret and shape ideals |
and objectives not only for 'development' but also for life 'after it'.

GT: What you say about the globalizing, later phases of the developed world are
not so much described as a 'crisis'. They are raised as a question about what
we mean by 'development' and its ends when developed societies are beginning to face new, huge problems of the mental health of their population,
increasing rates of obesity and so on. You suggest these might be indications
that something is not quite right in the developed world or in any event with
a flatline, progessivist mapping of development. This seems to parallel the
question one can also pose about whether art in the developed world is
actually adequate to the task of creating spaces other than the commercial.
Can it generate spaces and other dimensions, as you say, of the temporal,
the reflexive and critical, the non-utilitarian? In other words, spaces beyond
those of the culture-consumption industry. Why are these so diminished? It
seems to me it's not only in the domain of the developing world where the
question of the relationship of artistic practice and social needs has to be
looked at and interrogated but also in the developed world.

SM: With globalization, the developing world implicitly poses tough long-term
questions to its advanced counterpart on all the fronts we are looking at:
how to develop modern gallery-museum infrastructures without getting
bogged down in the self-sealing art-culture industry; how to extend 'communications' without becoming simply passive consumers of pre-packed
communications commodities: how to 'do development' without ending
up with 'development blues' –in a 'culture of over-development'. The
empirical issue of how to deliver actual development seems to open up to
queries of a normative kind.

The developed/developing 'entanglements' that show up with globalization amount to a ceaseless process of translation across their lines. With
high-speed communications, migrations, dispersals and movements of people, translation becomes an everyday affair –a process of churning out difference, divergence, teeming diversity. This flies in the face of globalization's overall standardizing drive that breaks down 'the difference of the
other' so as to render the 'foreign and alien' culturally digestible. This kind
of filtering –a logic of assimilation, of making the 'other' into the 'same'–
can also tip over into forms of xenophobia as we may observe from trends
across the North European social democracies once known for their 'tolerance'. With today's translation-migratory drifts, the contemporary appears
as a criss-crossing of heterogeneous, ever-mutating identities, multiple
tongues, disjunctive ways of knowing and living. This suggests we have to
move beyond Jurgen Habermas's sphere of 'communicative action' where
everyday transaction seems to be ultimately between relatively similar cul-

tural subjects and social actors. Though he supplements this by pointing to the 'inclusion of the other', his underlying conceptual scheme is made up of discursive agents with comparatively fixed identities tuned into the same cultural wavelength. They interact on a readymade ground from which they set about shaping a shared living space through ideals they thrash out between themselves in steady 'dialogic' exchange. The ground is one of transparent, rational deliberation: interlocuters think and speak within much the same cognitive parameters. But is today's translation-migration-globalizing scene on as even a keel as this? It is rather more riddled with untranslatable elements, riven with the sense of epistemic non-fit and unsquarable cultural difference, more cacophonic Babel than dialogic swap. It is shot through with a feeling of the 'radical other in our midst' who is neither 'visible nor audible' except perhaps in whittled-down, pre-given terms. The symptomatic figures of this space are its 'deterritorialized' cases –those classified 'sans papiers, non-citizens, clandestini, illegals, deportees, infiltrators'. But it is the black-hole of non-communicating communication represented by the 'suicide bomber' that seems definitive. How to piece together a 'commons' out of this Babelian space, an ever-changing ground where self/other can forge a 'lingo to parley' and to live in and through difference and multiplicity?

Under these conditions, communications genres such as documentary, reportage, bulletins, news round-ups interact and fuse with those of art to spawn new visual-discursive forms. An example is Multiplicity's installation project *Journey Through a Solid Sea* (Stefano Boerri et al, 2002, Documenta, Kassel). It tracks the tragic events of 26.12.96 when a shipload of over 300 'illegals' went down off the Sicily coast –right under the eye, as it were, of the pan-opticon satellite-retinal apparatuses scanning the region. Rumours of the disaster circulating the Mediterranean had been denied all round. Were the developing world families deceivers when they insisted their relatives had drowned? The real calamity came to light when the ID card of one of the 'clandestini' –Anagopalan Ganesu– was fished out of the sea in the pocket of his denims. *La Reppublica*'s dogged reporting, the power of investigative journalism and the media's drive to get to the bottom of things also had the effect of turning events into a somewhat black and white tale. Representations of the various players tended towards 'hyper-indentification' –cold-hearted locals, unscrupulous traffickers, inept police, indifferent authorities were matched by stereotypes of 'illegals, refugees, dodgers'. The installation counters the effect by putting into play a spread of contradictory accounts and individual reactions. Immersed in this clamour of versions and clashing modes of truth-telling, we get a feel 'from the inside' of the anguish and dilemmas, rights and wrongs thrown up by the tragedy.

GT: Salem Mekuria and Zarina Bhimji translate historical events not in a literal but in an experiential sense. Their work hones in on a particular historical episode but then pulls away and extrapolates the implications of that situation for a wider humanity and understanding. In her triptych film installation *Ruptures: A Many-Sided Story* (2003), Mekuria explores the turbulent events that have erupted periodically in the lives of Ethiopian people in recent decades. She offers up neither a linear history nor a seamless narrative but rather a series of fragments which rotate around and interweave with one another reflecting her understanding of time as a circular rather than progressive and chronological, translations of 'how things happened'. Sabah Naim's work addresses the mistranslation of lived experience implicating the global media and communications industry in the consistent misrepresentation of the Arab world. Her photographs of ordinary Egyptians going about their business are drawn upon, painted, scratched and decorated. They are paired with three-dimensional sculptures moulded from newspapers and magazines which are methodically rolled up and squeezed into a sculptural frame, forcing them into a grid in a sense to account for themselves. The work is a critique of the widening gap between two seemingly incommensurate worlds: on the one hand, that of global communications; on the other, the everyday world of Egyptians and their daily effort to survive. In this instance, the artwork operates somewhere in that gap. The artist becomes translator or mediator of critical awareness between these two worlds.

SM: I should like to end by glancing back from today's vantage point at two representations of modernity and the development saga. The first is an early work, *Memories of Underdevelopment* (Gutiérrez Alea, Cuba, 1968). It had spelled out some crucial propositions on the subject. How have these fared? The film had floated the idea that instead of the distinction 'developed/underdeveloped' we would be better off speaking more forthrightly about 'capitalism/socialism'. Though this reverberates with Cold War polemics, it takes on another hue for our time as a reminder to keep open the possibility of alternative approaches to development, other solutions and models at odds with those installed by an apparently all-sweeping corporate globalization. Not least, we can now read the film's proposition against Mrs Thatcher's monetarist policies –accompanied by her monotonous chant 'There is No Alternative' (TINA)– that had reduced the North English mining communities and villages to 'zones of underdevelopment'. Her TINA attitude was forged during protracted strife between workers and bosses in the 1970s when the ailing economy led to Britain being dubbed 'the first developed nation to have slid back into a developing one'. A current curatorial event, Olivier Resseler's *There Must be an Alternative* (Forum Stadpark,

Vienna, 2004[2]) recalls her one-track views in a riposte to versions of similar blinkeredness today. It is the affirmation of 'other possibilities', of a 'plurality of models of advancement' that is the drift of Jeremy Deller's re-enactment –through a battery of techniques and stagings– of the crippling blow Mrs. Thatcher inflicted on the South Yorkshire miners in Orgreave on 18.06.84 (*Battle of Orgreave*, video, 2001).

Memories of Underdevelopment was an unexpected melange of documentary, real footage clips, censors cuts, Hollywood-style excerpts. Though it seems to bear the stamp of 1960s assemblage, it prefigured the sorts of converging of factual-fictional genres we see today –techniques that have enhanced attempts to give more multi-dimensional coverage and analysis of development. The film put into critical spotlight the lead figure Sergio's deep-freeze inaction, his inability to throw in his lot with the 'struggle of the proletariat', his disdain at glimpses of what he saw as their crude manners and taste, their 'lack of culture', 'rottenness' and 'backwardness'. But Elena, the working class woman, sizes him up fairly quickly: "You are neither reactionary nor revolutionary: you are nothing". It is as if Niemi's musings at the Arctic edge of the world forty years later echo her words. Much of Sergio's lassitude, his sense of inertia is attributed to wallowing in 'bourgeois subjectivism and introspection'. Today, however, elements of such 'first person consciousness' appear in more favourable light: 'the view from within' is also about elaborating mental and emotional capacities for scrutinizing values, for taking decisions for oneself –ways of thinking and feeling indispensable to 'development as freedom through self-critical awareness'.

My second example is *The Long March: A Walking Visual Display* (Lu Jie et al, 1998 onwards)[3]. The project explicitly takes a prolonged look back on China's development saga from today's viewpoint to check how things have turned out. It goes down the 'memory lane of underdevelopment' by retracing the route taken by Mao's Red Army, the Long March (1934-1936). The arduous trek had been in the name of stepping out of the oppressive past towards a 'socialism adapted to local conditions', what was later to evolve into a series of five-year plans for modernization spurred on by the slogan 'the great leap forward'. A participant of the original march, Deng Xiaoping, further recast it as a symbol of the 'socialist market economy with Chinese features' in which he saw 'development as the hardcore principle' (The Long March Foundation, NY, 2003: 4). The string of Western intellectuals who 'visited' China –amongst them Parisian post-structuralist stars such as Julia Kristeva, Roland Barthes, Philippe Sollers, Louis Althusser, Gilles Deleuze– added to mythologizing the Long March by teasing out its 'lessons' for the

2 <http://forum.mur.at>.
3 <www.longmarchfoundation.org>.

developed world. Liu Jie's retracing is therefore not only about touching base with actual spots on the original route but also about its various 'ideological appropriations and re-routings'. At any particular site en route, project participants join in with the locals' daily activities or their special crafts as, during one sojourn, with the paperwork skills of villagers (*The Great Survey of Paper-Cutting in Yanchuan County*, Beijing, 2004). The encounter becomes a collective knowledge production and performance, with the potential for sifting through history, personal lives, vagaries of political regimes, issues of human rights, armed struggle, censorship. This is sometimes further relayed through installations, shows and debates through the Internet, mobiles, videos. Everyone becomes a participant-observer analysing both their immediate situation and the heroic march that symbolized an approach to modernization and development which had now lost its appeal. These 'consultation exercises' can sometimes faintly echo the 'correction sessions' of the original bands of Maoist cadres and activists working the countryside with fervour to raise political awareness. The project also resembles a tableau –not unlike Stations of the Cross– where each stopover is occasion for soul-searching, for delving into the current state of material and spiritual affairs. As the certitudes of older models of development crumble, we begin to see them in the light of China's present swing towards free enterprise in step with corporate globalization –something shot through with its own uncertainties. In enacting the original trek, The Long March probes it both as an epic vision of development and as an event of violence, intolerance and repression. It is about taking stock of what had happened in the name of enlightenment and development against the consumerist frenzy of 'post-communist development' in China today.

The two examples above underline why we should heed critiques mounted from within the developing world, by those in the 'thick of the development process' and who face the brunt of it. The landmark film *Mother India* (Mehboob Khan, 1950) had captivated audiences across the developing world –from the Soviet Union through the Arab countries to West Africa– because it had stirringly dramatized classic development issues: the loosening of centuries-old relationships and identities based on tribe and clan, the turbulent exit from traditional society, the painful induction into modern living and values, contradictions of the colonial legacy, bonded labour, 'backwardness'. Mother India tracks the long hard road to independence and improving conditions –as if alluding to both Brecht's *Mother Courage* (1941) and Katherine Mayo's book *Mother India* (1921) that had indicted British colonial authorities for the lack of medical care for 'native women' in her depiction of India as an unremitting 'zone of backwardness'. The film's opening shot is of the lead character, Radha, 'inaugurating' an irrigation dam. From this triumphant moment onwards, the rest of the film is a flashback to 'memories of underdevelopment' –to her struggles against hunger, natural disasters, feudal landlords, debt. The irony is that what the film portrayed as the glorious symbol of development and modernity –the construction of the dam– has today become an ambivalent image of progress. As if speaking back to the North India classic, a film from South India *Thaneer, Thaneer* (Water, Water) (Ramachandran, 2002) confronts its 1950s optimism with a litany of complaints about development 'gone awry', core problems that persist 60 years on. This time, a village stricken by drought has its self-help scheme to channel in water frustrated by redtape, obstructive bureaucracy and corrupt politicians. The new element is the untrusting eye the film casts on the 'rhetorics of development' even asking whether the honest journalist's decision to throw in his job as reporter for a corrupt news editor to become a 'doctoral candidate researching rural development' can contribute to any change at all.

This self-reflexive, knowing stance welling up from within the development process itself is summed up in Zakes Mda's quizzical look at the certitudes of modernity and advancement 'after Apartheid'. His novel *Madonna of Excelsior* (2002) charts the career of a band of diehard nationalists, 'respectable', small town white 'volk' and their black women servants caught up in a sex scandal of the 1970s. They had been charged for contravening the infamous Immorality Act that forbade cross-colour sex. With such god-fearing pillars of the establishment involved, the government was forced to drop the case hurriedly to save face. At the end of Apartheid, the men soon enough learn to mouth the Truth and Reconciliation catchphrases of 'change and forgiveness'. They even join the ANC realizing the benefits of being on the 'winning side'. Here Mda almost prefigures the actual merger of the New National Party with the ANC sealed this year (01.09.04). The talk is of futures, capital ventures, how to plug into global exchange opportunities. One of the Black women victims, Niki, had found a kind of solace spending her days tending bees in hives she set up at the town's edge. She would often simply hand over honey she collected to passers-by who took her fancy. An old diehard, who had been one of the sex abuse ring, now 'reformed' mayor of Excelsior heading the town's new ANC administration, tries to talk her into setting up a honey business. Would it not be smarter actually to sell jars of the sticky stuff than to dish it out free? She holds back quietly from his entrepreneurial zeal –not to mention the 'aspirational' PR of the development agency that had set up shop in the town. She continues to hand over honey to whomever she pleases. Her actions evoke fleetingly the sense of a 'wild economy untouched by development' where perhaps the only rule is spontaneous giving without expectation of return. Something of a non-exploitative, ancestral mode of living and sharing is intimated –'memories of a prehistoric state of underdevelopment'. An image both of sheer 'backwardness' and of critical utopian thinking –it questions the consumerist frenzy and capitalist accumulation, greed and graft in the scramble for development after Apartheid.

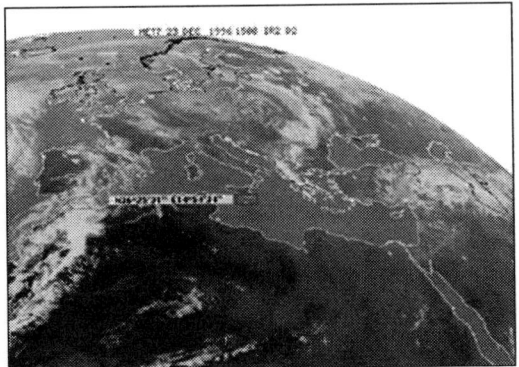

1. 'Multiplicity's' installation project Journey Through a Solid Sea
(Stefano Boerri et al, 2002, Documenta, Kassel).

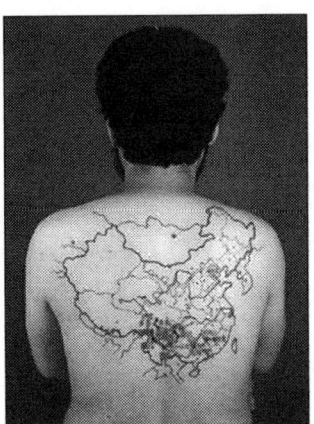

2. The Long March: A Walking Visual Display
(Lu Jie et al, 1998 onwards)

Part III

Case studies

Chapter 19

Miners' radio stations
A unique communication experience from Bolivia
Alfonso Gumucio-Dagron

Very little has been written about the Bolivian miners' community radio stations, and very late, at least in comparison to more recent experiences of participatory communication in other regions of the world[1]. The radio stations have been largely ignored, and I believe the main reason is that they had no institutional 'owner'. These days, we find that an institution or a program lies behind every single new project in the area of development communication and communication for social change, be this an international NGO, a UN development organization or a government agency. I do not question the authenticity or independence of communication experiences that are protected and nourished within institutional frameworks, but it is definitely not the same thing to emerge genuinely from the grassroots as to be a project created with backup helping it to survive

---

1 Very little was published during most of the first 30 years of development of the miners' radio stations, the decades that cover their most vital phase. A few articles were published in the late '70s and early '80s, written by Bolivians in Spanish (Lozada and Kuncar, 1983, and Gumucio, 1982) or, even earlier, in French (Gumucio, 1979). In 1983, Alfonso Gumucio-Dagron and Eduardo Barrios co-directed the first documentary film on the miners' radio stations, with support from UNESCO. The first book, in Spanish, came out only in 1989: *Las radios mineras de Bolivia*, edited by Alfonso Gumucio-Dagron and Lupe Cajías. The book was one of the outcomes of the first international conference on the Bolivian miners' radio stations, "Realidad y Futuro de las Radios Mineras en Bolivia", organised by the Centro de Integración de Medios de Comunicación Alternativa (CIMCA), with support from UNESCO, in the emblematic and historic city of Potosí, in November 1988. This conference gathered both practitioners and academics. Alan O'Connor, who was among the first in the United States to write about this subject, attended the meeting. It took more than a decade for O'Connor to translate and edit his own book *Community Radio in Bolivia - The Miners' Radio Stations* (Mellen, 2004), currently the only work in English on this seminal participatory communication experience originating in the highlands of Bolivia.

and become widely known. The miners' radio stations did not have that backup, nor did they benefit from any publicity orchestrated by an institutional parent. That is one of the reasons why they are, or were, so unique.

I cannot think of many other experiences that synthesize so well the most significant characteristics of participatory communication for social change: born out of the community itself, financed and managed by the community, genuinely participatory on a daily basis, well integrated into the social movement, with a wider than local impact without losing its local priorities.

A snapshot of history

The history of the Bolivian miners' radio stations has been described elsewhere and a mere description would take up most of the space available for this text. For the purpose of this essay it may be enough to say that the origin of the stations goes back as far as 1949, or even 1947, if we include *Radio Sucre*, which was founded in the mining districts of Catavi and Siglo XX by high school teachers in Llallagua, the local town close to the two mining centers[2]. Second came *La Voz del Minero* (1949), this station set up by the miners themselves, which was founded in 1946 by the powerful *Federación Sindical de Trabajadores Mineros de Bolivia* (FSTMB).

The first two radio stations were created amid considerable repression from autocratic and military governments struggling to retain power for a small 'rosca' (rich class), in a country where elections were decided by 10,000 voters, since the large majority of the population was excluded using the argument that only those who could read and write were qualified to vote. It was only after the triumph of the social uprising of April 1952[3] that the miners' radio stations mushroomed at the heart of the most important mining centers. When the *Movimiento Nacionalista Revolucionario* (MNR) came to power and nationalized the mining industry, miners felt the new ownership was an important step toward economic independence. As the years went by, and even though their social situation remained basically the same, mine workers became important political actors and the indisputable leaders of the social movement in Bolivia. Although the country's roughly 30,000 miners represented less than 10% of the working class during the 1960s, their significance for the Bolivian economy was and had always been enormous, since mining products represented as much as 60% of total exports.

At some point in the 1960s, every miners' union in the highlands of Bolivia wanted to have its own radio station. During the 1950s, '60s and '70s, nearly thirty were created, managed and sustained by the workers themselves, who would donate a portion of their monthly wages to cover the operating costs. With few exceptions, all the staff were selected locally. Some of the announcers

2 Lozada, Fernando and Gridvia Kuncar refer to this short-lived station in "An historic experience of self-managed communication", in Fernando Reyes Matta (ed.) *Comunicación Alternativa y Búsquedas Democráticas* (1983), Santiago, Chile: ILET/Friedrich Ebert Stiftung.

3 This resulted in the abolition of the army, the nationalization of private mining, the establishment of universal voting rights and agrarian reform.

who started very young at the microphone of a miners' radio station later migrated to the cities and became well-known journalists. Usually, the union would choose the local Secretary of Culture as director of the station. As Jorge Mansilla Torres recalls: "Who do the miners choose as Secretary of Culture? The most well-read person in the place, the most lettered. To put it in another way: the teacher"[4]. Sometimes, the announcers became as popular as the union leaders.

Radio stations started airing community messages, or calling miners to union meetings, or airing those meetings in full length. People living in the mining camps knew they could use the microphone of the radio not only to request the music they wanted or to announce a sporting activity, but also to complain about the state-owned mining company's abuses and denounce the precariousness of their living conditions. The stations quickly became the cultural, social and political center. Rather than going to the police with a complaint, people would go straight to the radio, even for matters involving family issues, such as "My husband is drinking too much and beats me", or "My neighbor took my chickens".

Although in normal times the radio stations were important for the role they played in education, culture and community service, in times of political turmoil their importance extended beyond Bolivia's borders. During the military coup of 1981, foreign correspondents stranded in Peru or Chile updated their news using the short-wave broadcasts of the miners' radio stations, at a time when all the commercial media in the main cities had been shut down by the military. In case of a national emergency, the first thing workers and their families, and nearby peasants, would do, was rush to the radio station to protect it, because they knew that the first thing the army would attempt to do was to close the stations down. In those critical times, every housewife, student or worker would take turns at the constantly live microphone to tell listeners about how they were resisting. Eventually, all the radio stations were destroyed and closed down, but as soon as the first signs of democracy were in sight, the unions would place the reinstatement of their radio stations among their main demands.

In terms of their historical context, of the development of local capacity and of the solidarity drive that animated all of them, of the use of appropriate technology, of the sense of ownership that was developed, of the generation of local content, of the strengthening of capacities of local staff, of their long history of 50 years, and of their impressive number at peak, for instance, these stations have no parallel with any other community radio story in the world.

A unique example of participatory media

Since most of the alternative media grassroots communication experiences that we know of originated under the tutorship of a formal institution (NGO, church,

---

4 Interviewed by Héctor Schmucler and Orlando Encinas, in *Comunicación y Cultura* No. 8, México, 1982. Jorge Mansilla Torres, born in Llallagua, started as a young announcer and later became director-founder of *Radio Vanguardia* in Colquiri, and a well-known journalist and poet in Bolivia and Mexico, where he lived in exile.

government, international development agency), the miners' radio stations stand as a unique example of a truly participatory process right from its inception. Too often in development media, the participatory process is something that is 'added' to the original scheme by improving 'access' for the surrounding community. This is not so in the case of the miners' radio stations, where the community lay at the origin of the experience.

One could write a case study on each of the almost 30 miners' radio stations that came to life since then, and the result would be thirty different stories in terms of the way they operated, the power of their equipment, or the staff structure. Their equipment, for example, was anything but standard. Some operated in AM, others in FM, or in short wave. The transmitters could be as small as 200 KW or as big as 2,000 KW. This often depended on the population in the mining district, but also changed during the individual history of each station. Some were so poor that they had little to offer in terms of programming; others were proud of their collections of music records and tapes that put their stock at the same level as the national networks. Some had small improvised booths within a union building, and some, such as *Radio Vanguardia* (of Colquiri), had a huge auditorium.

At least five times in their history, in 1965, 1967, 1971, 1978 and 1981, they suffered attacks from the army and destruction of their premises and collections. Even today, some show the scars in the walls.

However different in their individual stories, certain elements make all of them part of the same family in terms of the process of participatory communication, and they are all united by history. A brief description of the main essentials that characterize them all follows.

Participation and ownership

Most of what qualifies today as 'participatory' in communication experiences is actually 'access'. The miners' radio stations were truly participatory, in terms of people knowing that no one could at any point prevent them from expressing themselves through the microphone. But even more important than this individual type of approach to freedom of speech is the fact that the miners' radio stations were the voice of the collective, represented in some of most democratic unions that Latin America has ever known.

In spite of Bolivia's being such a highly politicized country, and the mining districts' specifically being places where all political tendencies would meet (nationalists, communists, Trotskyites, etc.), one important characteristic that was preserved over the years was that the union leader was above all a leader of the union, and only secondly a political party militant. This aspect is personified by the highest of all the leaders in the history of the Bolivian labor movement: Juan Lechín. While he had his own political party, the PRIN, which he used basically in order to gain some parliamentary representation, in the daily struggle he never allowed his party to cast any shadows over his main role as a union leader. A typical mining union in Bolivia would seat side by side leaders that came from such diverse political parties as the POR, the MIR, the MNR, the PCB, the PCML, the PRIN, etc.[5]

The social and political sustainability of the miners' radio stations was guaranteed by the sense of ownership that every single miner and housewife had over the radio station. The fact that such a historically poor segment of the population would voluntarily give one day of its monthly wages for the radio stations is significant. Self-financing and self-management came hand in hand.

Language and cultural pertinence

Miners' radio stations had their own style, creating a style for community radio fitted to the cultural needs of the miners and their families, but also to the surrounding peasant communities. For that reason, language was important. Programming in Quechua and Aymara, the two main languages, was often aired. Peasants and miners would express themselves at the microphone in either of the two languages. Social sustainability benefited from this approach.

But apart from this cultural approach to daily life, there was also a well laid out policy, recognizable in many documents approved by national congresses of the FSTMB, which considered the radio stations not only as instruments for communicating demands for higher pay and better living conditions, but also for enhancing local culture and education. The cultural plans that Libert Forti[6], as Cultural Advisor of the FSTMB, coordinated included everything from theatre, super 8 film production, dance, music, poetry, and photography[7]). The radio stations were instrumental in shaping the cultural platform of the miners' federation.

The amount of culture involved in the process was no doubt a result of the miners' own past as indigenous Aymara and Quechua population. The strength of the cultural baggage they brought into the mining districts fed into the labor movement key values and principles of solidarity, collective work, community decision-making, and communal justice, among other concepts that originated in the pre-Hispanic rural community (known as the Ayllu). These values prevented the miners from building typical trade unions that were only concerned with pay issues.

Local content and networking

Even if the miners' radio stations were too poor to have correspondents in La Paz or other Bolivian cities, they managed to produce their own newscasts. Local

---

5 *Partido Obrero Revolucionario* (POR), the main Trotskyist party; *Movimiento Nacionalista Revolucionario* (MNR), which led the social revolution of 1952; *Partido Comunista de Bolivia* (PCB), the communists aligned with Moscow; *Movimiento de Izquierda Revolucionaria* (MIR), which evolved towards rightist positions; *Partido Comunista Marxista Leninista* (PCML), the Maoists; *Partido Revolucionario de Izquierda Nacionalista* (PRIN), Lechín's own party.

6 Liber Forti is a theatre director and an anarchist with a long tradition of struggling side by side with the Bolivian workers.

7 I happened to be in charge of drafting the film and photography proposal, at Liber Forti's request.

items were, of course, most important but the stations also provided a different view and perspective on national news. Sometimes they would pick up news from the national networks, but if they did, they would often add their own perspective on the issues, i.e. the social and political perspective of miners.

The stations' microphones often traveled out of the studio. Young reporters with small cassette recorders would constantly talk about local problems to workers, housewives, and peasants coming into town. Some of the stations were certainly more open and participatory than others, but in general the local population was instrumental in the creation of local content, and this constituted important feedback for the union itself.

One important aspect that contributed to the institutional sustainability of miners' radio stations was their sense of being part of a larger body. Although they were not formally a network, but merely a series of independent stations guided by similar principles, they often acted as such when common interests were at the top of the agenda. This could occur, for example, when a sporting event such as a car or bicycle race happened to involve several mining districts, or in times of political turmoil when the stations became important as national and international sources of information, as noted above.

The decline

By 1988, only 16 of the 26 radio stations set up since 1949 remained on the air[8]. The main cause was that the mines were closing as the international price of tin collapsed. The United States' strategy was successful in killing the International Tin Council[9]. The Bolivian government tried to halt the highest-ever inflation in history, and dictated economic measures that were radical and painful. As a result, thousands of miners lost their jobs and migrated to the cities.

Although the mining industry decreased drastically, some mining districts where a large population had developed continue to struggle for survival. The weakening of the miners' federation (FSTMB) meant that the leaders fought each other to impose the views of their political parties, thus permanently damaging what the unions had treasured for so long: their political independence. On top of it all, a wave of privatization affected the legislation that protected community radio stations, and opened up a new front for struggle[10].

In spite of the above constraints, there was a late attempt to revive the miners' radio stations by setting up new ones strategically situated to serve both miners' and peasant communities and nearby cities. *Radio Matilde* in the mining

8 These were: *Cumbre, Chichas, Pío XII, La Voz del Cobre, Animas, La Voz del Minero del Sur, Sumaj Orko, San José, La Voz del Minero, Vanguardia, 21 de Diciembre, Radio Nacional de Huanuni* and *Viloco*.

9 During the Second World War the United States forced Bolivia to sell its tin 'for peanuts', way below the international level, as a contribution to the 'war expenses'. Decades later, the US was still able to manipulate the international price using its stocks of Bolivian tin.

10 It was 2004 before a new decree issued by President Carlos Mesa recognized community radio stations, and their importance for education, culture and social development.

district of the same name, north of La Paz, was the result of such an attempt, actually being the only station to last for about 18 months after coming to life early in 1985. By that time it had been transferred into the hands of peasants in the Chaguaya community.

Bolivian miners' radio stations today cannot claim the importance they held during forty years from the early 1950s onward. However, they are a unique example of participatory communication for social change. Their history is only now being studied and recognized. Compared with other participatory communication and freedom of speech movements in the world, these stations stand as an example of political consciousness and perseverance in the social struggle.

In the words of Alan O'Connor: "The so-called 'black bloc' of anti-globalization protestors demonized by mainstream media fifty years later seem positively polite and fun-loving when measured against the history of armed resistance and strikes of the Bolivian miners"[11].

The dynamic between the miners' unions and miners' radio stations acquired the power of dynamite in the context of Bolivia's struggle for a participatory society.

---

11 In his introduction of "*Community Radio in Bolivia - The Miners' Radio Stations*".

Chapter 20

The citizen, media and social change in Namibia

Ullamaija Kivikuru

According to a fairly recent survey[1], South Africans and Namibians exhibit the greatest awareness of the concept of democracy in Southern Africa, and they have a largely positive understanding of the concept. However, South Africans and Namibians are more likely to emphasize the realization of socio-economic outcomes as more crucial to democracy than key procedural components, such as elections, multi-party competition or freedom of speech. They seem to be becoming pessimistic. They put significantly less trust in elected institutions, seeing them as less responsive to public opinion, and are dissatisfied with the performance of these bodies (Mattes et al, 1998). Respondents give more positive evaluations to the present democratic system than to *apartheid*, but there are also signs of a certain 'nostalgia' for the ways these countries were governed under *apartheid*.

These intriguing results could perhaps be interpreted as follows: Africans who have lived under an indigenous authoritarian government (e.g. Banda, Mugabe) have learned to attach an independent value to democracy that has not yet widely evolved in Namibia and in South Africa. Rather, ordinary people in these two countries are distressed about the slowness of change, and per-

1 Afrobarometer Series, based on a sample of 2,200 South Africans, carried out from July 6 to August 6, 2000. A similar survey was carried out in late 1999 and early 2000 in Namibia, Zimbabwe, Botswana, Zambia and Lesotho. The results are reported in Mattes et al, *Views of Democracy in South Africa and the Region: Trends and Comparisons, The Southern African Democracy Barometer*, Number 2, October 2000. According to this, South Africans score 60% and Namibians 58% in a question on respect for democracy, while the figures for most others are around 70-80%.

haps even the direction their governments have chosen to take. Accordingly, they rank quite poorly in terms of interest and participation in democratic politics.

In attempts to motivate people into political activity in these two countries, attention has been focused on the media, especially radio. Unlike many other African countries, the media in both South Africa and Namibia do reach large audiences, and many studies have explicitly identified the special ability of radio to "mediate the popular word" (Martín-Barbero, 1993: 235). Radio speaks the language known by the majority of the population, for an oral language is not simply the product of illiteracy. The oral language of the radio is a bridge between symbolic-expressive rationality and instrumental informative rationality. Radio is a medium that, for the general audience, fills the vacuum left by the disappearance or weakening of the role played by traditional institutions in the construction of meaning, such as oral tradition or inherited community rules (e.g. Martín-Barbero, 1993: 234-236). In South Africa, there are more than 80 community radio stations, aiming to 'give voice to the voiceless'. Not all community radio stations have operated that well, but South Africa's community radio sector is still referred to in neighbouring countries as an example to follow.

South Africa is a large country, and no doubt one of the most confusing in the world today. Although class differences may be even greater in a number of other countries, the contradictions are striking: a small number of the population lead a post-industrial life, while the majority lack even the basic necessities of life. This contradiction is reflected in the position of the media. In Namibia, which is far smaller, a similar contradiction is also visible. Since independence, political power has been dominated by one party, SWAPO, and this party is predominantly led by blacks, but it is only political power which has changed hands. The wealth is still concentrated in large farms owned predominantly by the German-speaking white minority, while industries are predominantly controlled by Afrikaans-speaking whites.

Namibia only gained independence in 1990, a latecomer on the African continent, but with a constitution that became one of the most democratic in Africa. But it is not constitutions that make countries democratic, it is the implementation of official texts. Thus, one of the most urgent tasks for the national broadcaster, the NBC (Namibia Broadcasting Company), was to develop a genuine profile for the institution. On the one hand, it had to make a clear departure from the *apartheid* past and encourage nation-building; on the other, it also had to promote reconciliation and freedom of expression. The main mouthpiece for such endeavours was radio, still the most important medium in the country, covering some 98% of the population.

A clear-cut division between public and community media similar to that made in South African media policies has not been carried out in Namibia. Media policies strongly support national-level mass communication. Broadcasting channels have usually acted more or less as vehicles for those in power, although today there are also private local radio stations, some educational or religious, but most only play popular music. The total number of community radio stations is barely half a dozen and they are scattered, offering no realistic comparison with South Africa. The strongest government influence is today perhaps felt at NBC Television, but the largest audience is gathered by NBC Radio. Some commercial satellite/terrestrial television services, such as M-Net, are available but are only taken up by hotels and bars, plus the urban well-to-do. The situation is made even more complex by the fact that the dominant party, SWAPO, has part-ownership in several private media institutions, including local radio as well as television services.

Occasionally, the government or individual ministers try to regulate the media, but due to the complex structure of the mediascape[2], a big fuss is made and after a while the efforts to exert pressure tend to get forgotten. As in most countries, Namibian media structures are not very flexible and are apt to change. Even such a radical change as the independence struggle did not result in great structural transformations, although content was gradually changed. The rigidity of media structures is also a security mechanism, because if the infrastructure is continuously on the move, multiplicity of media content tends to get lost among the rapid changes.

The target of most control attempts has been *The Namibian* newspaper, which offered a consistently dissident voice in Namibian society during *apartheid* rule. During the last few years, the government has declined to use *The Namibian* as its advertising channel, although the paper has the highest readership figures in the country.

Thus, the Namibian public is fairly sophisticated in its relationship to the media, and the public is more used to contradictory approaches in the mediascape than in many other countries on the continent. However, the number of people using the media regularly remains limited, and they are mainly located in towns. If the public are able to express sophistication in media matters, official media policies are quite vague and lack consistency. However, it could be claimed that both the public and the private media no doubt see it as one of their basic functions to inform citizens about their rights and responsibilities. Independence is quite new and unanimously valued in the dominant ideoscape, the ideological atmosphere (see Appadurai, 1989). 'Purely' entertainment media meant to bring in money for their publishers are imported from South Africa, especially popular magazines in great numbers. The target audience of these media is predominantly the white and coloured middle class.

---

2 The concept "mediascape" was introduced to research literature by Arjun Appadurai (e.g. 1989). It means the whole media scenery, i.e. media content as well as structures, but viewed from the recipient's perspective. Appadurai explains the social life of an individual as filled with changing values and disjunctures caused by changes in five 'scapes': mediascape, ideoscape (ideological 'scenery' in the community), ethnoscape (people on the move), technoscape (technology on the move) and moneyscape (money on the move). In this article, mediascape is used in a somewhat more concrete way, meaning of the totality of all media and their content in a society.

Accordingly, it can be claimed that the structure of the mediascape has not changed much with the new line of politics followed since independence. The content has naturally changed, but perhaps not radically. The wider public has long been used to a public/private mix in media matters and, even more, to a media mix which disagrees both internally and with the power elites. Even during *apartheid* there were private media –though in those days only newspapers– criticizing those in power, while certain other private media more or less openly recognized the authority of *apartheid* rule.

This legacy of multiplicity continues. For a small and relatively poor African country, even now Namibia offers its southern urban population a numerous and many-voiced media mix. In the poorer, totally black northern regions, media distribution is weak, although it has improved in recent years. Today, most newspapers arrange for distribution in the north and offer pages in northern languages.

Undoubtedly, one legacy of the *apartheid* period is the extremely weak status of community media. Thus, it can be said that in Namibia the media have remained in the hands of the power elites, and the multiplicity of the mediascape in fact only confirms that the power elites are multiple and their interests contradictory. The elite orientation of the media is reflected especially strongly in the weakness of local media. Local radio stations are few and not very local in their broadcasting, and community papers are almost non-existent. Practically all the private radio stations in the country are commercial and broadcast to central and southern towns. Further, plans to focus parts of the media system at the grassroots level via libraries have proved unsuccessful. For a while, library services managers cherished a plan to re-focus all HIV/AIDS information distribution on computers placed at existing village libraries. The idea behind this was that people were already accustomed to using local libraries. Instead of establishing separate local media centres, as in Mozambique[3], the existing structures could be used. This plan for turning the libraries into a kind of public service channel did not succeed, however, again mainly due to rigid structures and organizational ideologies. Libraries and the media were considered to be two separate institutional systems which could not be merged together. Instead, a large project for strengthening local government was launched with foreign assistance, involving the extensive training of local government employers in the use of computers.

What is interesting is the fact that, despite the rhetoric regarding the strengthening of decentralized political power, no serious plans have been made either to establish new community media or to adopt community-oriented information as part of the existing media system. The few attempts made by the

3 Mozambique has an extensive regional media centre project going on with support from the UNDP, UNESCO, and several Nordic countries. The aim is to decentralize both media use and media content-gathering by establishing media centres with newspapers, radio and television sets, computers and modest printing equipment in all the regions.

Polytechnic of Namibia to establish and strengthen community media are in fact | **329** the only consistent arrangements operating in the country so far[4].

There are probably several reasons why new forms of citizens' media have met with difficulties. One is no doubt simply the fact that the population is so small and scattered that only very small and very local media might work as a balancing factor in the Windhoek-dominated mediascape today; even regional media would face an extensive and expensive task in coping with distribution (Spitulnik, 2002). They would also probably meet political resistance, because the nation-building ideology is still running high. To some extent, the media appearing in several languages also cater for specific population groups. The national radio operates in seven languages, the national television predominantly in English, but four minority languages are used regularly in news and current affairs programmes. Newspapers appear in three languages.

Top/down or bottom/up - does it really matter?

But would a top/down or a bottom/up ideology be best in promoting democracy via the media? Does it really matter? The following provides a short description of a case which started as top/down but which in fact has become a mediation of the 'popular word'.

The programme concerned has many detailed elements, usually linked to community media. Community media have been popular since the 1960s, mainly taking the form of literacy papers linked to massive literacy campaigns and of community radio stations, advocating improvements in health and agriculture. These have experienced a renaissance during the past 10-15 years. In particular, community radio has become highly popular among foreign donors in Africa. Grassroots-oriented community media, produced and controlled by local people, sound like an ideal tool for the promotion of democracy: these media are able to 'give a voice to the voiceless', to discuss matters important to 'ordinary people' and to exert pressure on decision-makers. Today, there are community radio stations in most African countries. The best-organized system is found in South Africa, where even the Constitution recognises the role of grassroots media. The country has more than 80 community radio stations which have been given a licence and basic equipment by either the government or foreign donors, but which are meant to be operated independently by volunteers. This fine idea has not always been easy to implement: even modest production demands resources and professional competence, and quite often local decision-makers have contradictory ideas about programming policies. All community radio stations have eco-

---

4 Namibia Polytechnic has had a community paper project in a small town, including local training and support for the monthly paper *Sunflower*. The Polytechnic's community journalism projects, which include field trips to rural areas, have also yielded locally oriented supplements, named *Echoes*, which have been inserted into the newspaper *The Namibian*. Certain development projects have produced publications on ecology, water and health issues, and one community radio, UNAM Radio, has been a stronghold of HIV/AIDS information.

nomic difficulties, and fairly many of them are actually mouthpieces of either local politicians or projects financed by foreign donors. Thus, their local character and bottom/up policy could be questioned (Teer-Tomaselli, 2001).

The Namibian grassroots-oriented radio scheme was originally a top/down exercise. Right from the beginning, NBC Radio had quite a challenging task in Namibia, because it was supposed to operate both in the form of a national channel (National Radio) in English, but also in six other languages through what was called the Language Service. Only a small proportion of the population were fluent in the new official language, English. In Namibia English was considered 'neutral', unlike, say, German and Afrikaans which carried bitter memories from the past.. Hence, one of the roles of the National Radio channel was to promote nation-building, also via the new national language. Even so, it proved impossible to do away with the Language Service, which operates even today in Afrikaans, Damara-Nama, German, Oshiwambo, Otjiherero and Rukavango.

In August 1991, the NBC Board decided to introduce in a 9-10 a.m. time slot a 'national window', broadcasting in English via National Radio but also being sent out on the whole spectrum of the Language Service channels. While planning the programme, the then Manager of National Radio recalled a visit he had made to London and his strange experience in Hyde Park, where speakers freely took the podium and spoke on an incredible variety of topics. What if the time slot could be developed into a similar platform for Namibians? The top management were hesitant but allowed the programme, called *Chatshow*, to be launched. To begin with, the presenter mostly played music on the live morning programme, but gradually people found the courage to phone in.

Afterwards, certain Namibians have seen the programme format as an immediate answer to the demands laid down in the Windhoek Declaration (1991)[5], underlining the significance of freedom of expression and the need for a multiplicity of mediascapes in Africa. However, according to the individuals who put the programme on air, the two were parallel but separate processes, taking place independently of each other[6]. No doubt *Chatshow* –soon unofficially renamed *People's Parliament* by its listeners– might have been cut more easily during its initial difficulties without the somewhat euphoric atmosphere following the Windhoek Conference.

The objectives of the programme were elaborated during the first months of operation, although the basic line was clear right from the beginning. The programme was set up to give people a platform for venting the anger they felt because of the bitter past. *Chatshow* was meant to become a platform for

5 The Windhoek Declaration was formulated at a UNESCO-organized seminar in Windhoek by media practitioners and researchers from African countries recently converted to multiparty democracies. It emphasizes the crucial role independent media play in the promotion of democracy.

6 Both the then Radio Manager Rector Mutelo and the first presenter Robin Tyson point out that the emergence of *Chatshow* was an internal affair within the NBC, defining its new profile according to the needs of the new nation.

healing, for promoting peace, unity and nation-building, and for creating a culture of tolerance. The idea was not to bury differences but to develop a meaningful debate between the government and the opposition. Another of *Chatshow's* roles was to promote use of the English language among the general public.

The *Chatshow* platform is free for people to express themselves on politics, on the economy, on military issues, on abortion, on local government, on bad roads, on poor service in public and private institutions, or on world politics. Roughly two-thirds of the contributions include a question, while most others offer comments or broader views. Over the years, both National Radio and the Language Services have acquired some true friends who contribute to the programmes on a continuous basis, but there are also occasional callers who are regular listeners but who do not contribute actively very often. Further, most regular callers have their own 'networks' which provide them with questions and enquiries. Thus, instead of phoning themselves, people approach a person known for his/her ability to express him/herself well.

It could be claimed that, of the two main objectives, nation-building and reconciliation, nation-building seems to have been more strongly promoted over the years. This was partly the result of the overall set-up: each large language group was approached separately, as during *apartheid*. Further, the prohibition on racially-related statements perhaps led to the fact that all callers were rather careful about referring to people's skin colour or tribal background, because these were the primary reasons for discrimination during *apartheid* times. A devil's advocate might in fact claim that the structure of the programme family –the same programme in various languages– and the deliberate avoidance of tribalism in content are slightly contradictory. In practice, however, these flaws are not conspicuous. The National Radio programmes *Chatshow* and its feedback programme, *Open Line,* are no doubt the main mouthpieces of *People's Parliament.* The six other programmes in other languages have been used mainly for localizing problems and activating people who are not fluent in English.

Can a single radio programme format have national significance?

The *People's Parliament* programme family receives some 11,000 calls annually, and it is one of the top three most listened-to programmes. Issues brought up on *People's Parliament* are referred to in homes, at workplaces and in Parliament, because the scope of issues discussed ranges from clean water problems in a particular village to the President's speeches, and the participants genuinely disagree. Sometimes the debate becomes quite animated. An interesting detail, especially concerning the English-language service, is that several people phoning in to the programmes are actually representatives of wider concerns. The grassroots –whether organized or not– have found their representatives in individuals who are known to be good at presenting their case efficiently. Individuals come to these people with their concerns and ask them to mediate the issue to *People's*

Parliament. In a large country with what is still a strongly centralized administrative system, *People's Parliament* offers a channel where village folk can express their concerns, and the programme has credibility because it also allows those in power to defend themselves in feedback sessions. Members of Parliament often refer to issues brought up in the programmes.

No exact listener surveys have been carried out on *People's Parliament*, to say nothing of 'softer' monitoring and reception surveys. But the presenters assume that their basic audience is composed of people from all strata of the social spectrum, while comprising more middle-aged and older groups. Occasionally, younger people also get interested in some of the debates on the air, and might then form the majority of the callers on a particular programme. Still, it can be claimed that while the Namibian population is relatively young, more than half the total population being under 20, *People's Parliament* mostly attracts middle-aged and elderly citizens. Several surveys have documented that the young tend to prefer the commercial radio stations that exist in abundance, especially in the capital Windhoek and some bigger towns. In the countryside, the NBC stations are the only ones available (65% of the population still live in rural areas, although the city of Windhoek is growing fast).

Just over two-thirds of the callers are men, although the proportion of women is somewhat larger, at 35-40%, on the German and Afrikaans programmes. On the other hand, a few of the most frequent participants are women, quite often advocates speaking for some 10-15 'back-up' individuals who have chosen an articulate woman to express their mutual concerns. It is more typical for women participants to network frequently. Another feature typical of women callers is that they seem to be more concerned about concrete, practical issues, while men often widely discuss political matters and religion, for example. Certain frequent contributors create a profile for themselves, and they are known all over the country. Probably the best-known national figure is a blind liberation struggle veteran called Uncle Paul in Windhoek, who contributes to both the National Radio and the Oshiwambo service. But there are quite a few frequent regional callers as well. Quite often these are either people with a 'known past' (e.g. freedom fighters) or present-day activists (members of NGOs).

Although television is gradually also making its way to the masses in African societies, radio is still the medium which seems to respond most flexibly to social change. Television production is expensive and television is nowhere near as mobile as radio. Further, radio has long traditions in the transmission of essential information. Death announcements and workplace programmes have been important channels not only for distributing topical information but for keeping the urban and the rural in continuous contact. In Zimbabwe, the *Chakafukidza* programme combines modernity and customary tradition.

During the struggle against *apartheid* in Southern Africa, radio programmes, legitimate and illegitimate, maintained contact between members of liberation movements. *People's Parliament* continues these traditions, but it also carries a hint of the now so popular American-origin public journalism[7], because it encourages people to become active. However, it does not talk about grassroots-level organization and joint action, and hence its political power can be questioned. Is *People's Parliament* a tension-relief mechanism rather than a genuine tool of democracy? On the other hand, in a society based on mass action and on a liberation movement that became the dominant party with a variety of mass organizations supporting it, a programme talking about joint problems, but on the individual level, might be credible precisely because it remains at that level. Popular it certainly is in any case –so popular that not even censorship has ever tried to touch it. Another issue is whether it is able to reach the country's urban youth.

7 Public journalism is a trend which emphasizes the fact that journalists should be advocates of recipients' interests, not those favoured by power-holders and other elites. In public journalism, journalists should monitor the public's concerns via surveys, citizens' meetings and the like, should open up the media so that ordinary people can express themselves in the public arena, and should work with members of the public to find solutions to people's concerns. "We should not only inform the public but form publics", says Jay Rosen, one of the advocates of this trend, which is currently favoured by hundreds of local and regional media in the US.

Chapter 21

Missed opportunities in post-war Bosnia

Kemal Kurspahic

The post-Dayton media landscape in the Balkans could not have been more
unfavorable for the development of free and pluralistic media. This chapter analyses the short comings and offers a list of recommendations that might contribute
to setting priorities and achieving better results in the next stages of "media intervention", not only in the Balkans but also in countries experiencing a less traumatic transition to democracy[1].

The American-brokered Dayton Peace Agreement, initialed on
November 21, 1995, in Dayton, Ohio, and signed on December 14 in Paris, ended
the three-and-a-half-year war in Bosnia, which left more than 200,000 people
dead and more than one and a half million driven from their homes. Focused on
the main task at Dayton, "to end a war"–as the main negotiator, American
ambassador Richard Holbrooke's book (1998) is entitled– international mediators
almost completely neglected the role of the media in the peace process. The
media were mentioned only briefly, in Annex 3 of the agreement, giving the
Organization for Security and Cooperation in Europe (OSCE) a mandate for media
issues as part of its role in organizing and supervising elections. The signatories
are obliged by that Annex to "ensure that conditions exist for the organization of
free and fair elections, in particular a politically neutral environment... [and] shall
ensure freedom of expression and of the press"[2].

---

1 The chapter is based on the author's book *Prime Time Crime: Balkan Media in War and Peace* (2003).
2 Dayton Peace Agreement, Annex 3, the Agreement on Elections.

Thus Dayton left the Balkan media in the hands of those who had used them to stir ethnic intolerance in the first place. Yugoslav media remained in Slobodan Milosevic's hands; Croatian in Franjo Tudjman's; and Bosnian in the hands of the three nationalist parties.

The post-Dayton media landscape in the Balkans could not have been more unfavorable for the development of free and pluralistic media. On the one hand, the international institutions fully realized that the media had played an instrumental role in creating and maintaining the war mentality, a fact that had been established in reports, memoirs, and debates on the Balkans in the 1990s. On the other hand, the agreement left the "bad guys" in control not only of their by now "ethnically pure" territories but also of the media in all three states as well as Bosnia's two entities and ten cantons.

There was a built-in obstacle to the stated goal of the international intervention in the post-Dayton years: while supporting the Dayton agreement might have been the price to end the war, leaving control of the area in the hands of those most responsible for the war made it extremely difficult to develop the institutions of a functioning civil society, including the media. Following the Dayton script, most of the international post-war media efforts in Bosnia con-tributed to the apartheid-like partition of the country. In the process the few inde-pendent media voices that supported a multiethnic Bosnia remained not only under attack by the nationalist parties that had an interest in fostering ethnic sep-aration, but also marginalized by many in the international donor community who chose to work with the ethnic separatists in support of Dayton.

The initial results were, predictably, tragic. For example, the president of the council controlling the most influential media organization in Republika Srpska –Serb Radio and Television (SRT)– was Momcilo Krajisnik, the closest asso-ciate of war-time Bosnian Serb leader, Radovan Karadzic. Krajisnik himself was later indicted and arrested for war crimes. Under his direct supervision, Serb TV treated Republika Srpska as a separate state, actively undermining any effort to reintegrate the country. The station reported on events in the Federation only in its "From Abroad" news program. Everything the SRT did following the signing of the Dayton agreement was aimed at proving that there was no possibility of coex-istence among the three Bosnian ethnic groups. The international community's first High Representative in Bosnia, Carl Bildt, was quoted as saying: "They put out propaganda that even Stalin would be ashamed of"[3].

Bosnia's post-war media landscape mirrored the image of that devas-tated country. In Serb and Croat-controlled territories, all media –newspapers, radio, and television alike– preached ethnic apartheid. In the Bosniak-controlled areas, the pre-war mainstream multiethnic media such as the daily *Oslobodjenje* (Libreration) and Radio and TV of Bosnia Herzegovina, continued to exist under a

3 International Crisis Group Report: *Media in Bosnia and Herzegovina - How International Support Can be More Effective*, March 17, 1997, page 5.

double burden. They had suffered heavy losses in their struggle to operate under the siege –with their facilities and assets bombed and looted, dozens of the most experienced journalists gone, and millions of German marks in debt– all of which would be difficult to recover under even the most favorable conditions. But there was an additional burden: the international community's acceptance of Bosnia's "new realities" of partition. While internationals still paid lip service to the media that maintained the spirit of inter-ethnic tolerance under the most adverse conditions, they didn't see a role for them in a country organized strictly along Bosniak-Croat-Serb lines.

"Daytonized" media

By early 1996, on the heels of a 60,000-strong NATO-led peacekeeping force, dozens of international NGOs and hundreds of mostly well-intentioned enthusiasts –journalists, media practitioners, and trainers– converged on Bosnia with a mission and, in some cases, a respectable amount of money to help establish free media in the country. Unfortunately, they made some strategic misjudgments as well as some regrettable mistakes. Strategically, they were instructed to operate within the Dayton framework, making the Bosnian media a party to all compromises with the ultranationalists instead of encouraging and supporting them to break free and become independent observers and critics of nationalist manipulation of the past and present.

Why was it necessary to "daytonize" the Bosnian media, making them a part of the "deal with the devil", when that issue had not been regulated by the peace agreement? Carl Bildt told me that when he came to Bosnia he found the media as divided as the country. There was never any decision on the part of the international community to "daytonize" the media, Bildt said. He explained that

> there was great international reluctance to do anything that could be seen as interference in the media. SDA had a very strong constituency in Washington, and I remember that any slight move that might be interpreted as undermining BH TV had to be handled very carefully in light of this. With [the Serb] Pale TV the problem was different. I argued for us to use our military instruments to force it to behave less virulently, but this came up against the fears of "mission creep" in NATO, and it was not until General Wesley Clark took over European command that NATO agreed to take direct action against the Pale transmitters. Although I had argued vigorously for that action, it happened only after I had left[4].

Regardless of their intentions, the international organizations legitimized the nationalists' control over the media by accepting that they had to deal exclusively with the ultranationalists. The newly-established OSCE's Media Experts Commission, for example, in addition to international representatives, included

4 Carl Bildt: e-mail to the author, March 16, 2002.

the designated representatives of the three Bosnian governments (Joint, Federal, and Serb) as well as "qualified media specialists appointed by each of the parties". Of course, these "parties", the same ones that presided over the war, were not likely to appoint independent-minded, tolerant, anti-nationalist individuals to the body controlling the media. This need among international mediators always to have clear ethnic representation with people appointed by the "the parties" or "acceptable to all three sides" favored either solid nationalists or mediocre journalists with no name or reputation. It was a criterium that sidelined, in media rebuilding efforts, those who belonged to "the fourth party": the party of professional journalism.

One notable exception in supporting early efforts to establish free media in Bosnia was George Soros's Open Society Fund. Open Society had, after all, two distinct advantages over all other media donors: first, the organization had extended its helping hand to the struggling Bosnian media even during the siege of Sarajevo, well aware of what Bosnia used to be; and second, it relied on Bosnian media professionals with a deep understanding of local values and priorities.

The country's media scene presented both Bosnian journalism and international "media interventionists" with a variety of challenges. For example, Bosnian Radio and TV, which compromised its pre-war reputation for independence by accepting Muslim SDA-led government control during the war, was still the best equipped, most professional and to some extent multiethnic broadcast outlet, with the best prospect of being rebuilt as a state-wide public broadcasting station. But instead of cutting off the instruments of SDA control and restoring its country-wide outreach, complemented by the development of regional electronic media, the international community practically legalized the war-time looting of its assets, transmitters, and equipment, leaving them in the hands of "Serb TV" and "Croat TV", and accepting hard-line Serbs' and Croats' claim that anything coming from Sarajevo was "unacceptable". No wonder then that, in the months leading up to the first post-war elections held in September 1996, nationalist Serb and Croat TV continued to insist on war-time partition, treating the territories under the control of nationalist parties as states completely separate from Bosnia-Herzegovina.

"Carl Bildt TV"

Looking for alternatives, the international community opted for a TV and radio program of its own. Just before the elections, it launched TV-IN, later renamed OBN (Open Broadcast Network), and FERN (Free Elections Radio Network) Radio. OBN started on September 7, 1996, with a credibility problem. It was called "Carl Bildt TV", suggesting it was under the control of the Office of the High Representative (OHR), and was dismissed by all three nationalist parties. SDS and HDZ dismissed it for being established in Sarajevo and being carried predominantly through the Bosniak TV network; the SDA labeled it "unpatriotic", a competition to "our Bosnian TV".

OBN faced both technological and professional limitations. Technologically, it needed a network of local TV stations to carry its signal to the Bosnian audience. Initially, there were five stations: NTV 99 and Hayat in Sarajevo, TV Mostar, the Zenica-based Zetel, and TV Tuzla, with NTV 99 withdrawing from the project as soon as it received its share of the internationally-supplied equipment. OBN was largely understaffed in its central studio, while member-stations were not able to contribute news programming at a level expected in the country-wide network. Affiliation with local partners, some of which were clearly Muslim-only, hurt credibility. For example, throughout the month of Ramadan, Hayat TV broadcast long hours of religious programming produced in Iran, playing into the hands of both Serb and Croat nationalists who wanted to undermine anything all-Bosnian.

The international community proved, once again, that it had the ability to raise money for its Bosnian democratic experiment –investing some $20 million over a period of five years in this new network– but not a clear understanding of the best ways to achieve its stated goals. A fraction of the money invested in the project would have been enough to bring together some of the best Bosnian journalists to produce a high-quality prime time news journal and an issue-oriented weekly political magazine instead of relying heavily on imported foreign programming. With all of its generous investment, OBN was never given the most precious asset: an "A" team of editors who would shape a program focused on priorities in the peace process. After all, that focus was missing in international policy toward Bosnia as well.

Post-war Bosnia saw an explosion of new media outlets. According to a study by Zoran Udovicic, president of the Media Plan Institute, in mid-1991 there were 377 newspapers and other publications in Bosnia, 54 local radio stations, 4 TV stations, one wire service, and state Radio-Television with 3 channels. At the end of the war in 1995 there were 272 active media outlets: 203 in the Federation and 69 in Republika Srpska. In March 1997, there were 490: 270 in the Federation and 220 in Republika Srpska[5]. The problem was that –with the war-time exodus of hundreds of journalists, the absence of educated young professionals in both newsrooms and management, and the lack of a functional economy– most of the newly-started media depended either on international donors or on local war profiteers with dubious political agendas. In the absence of a strategy, which could have included the creation of a high-quality national public broadcast system and support for the establishment of a respectable daily, much of the donors' money was wasted on media projects of no relevance. "A cost-benefit analysis of media investment in 1996 indicates a poor return. The problem is lack of overall strategy and absence of expertise", an International Crisis Group report of March 18, 1997, stated.

5 Zoran Udovicic: taped interview by the author in Sarajevo, February 2, 2000.

The fate of *Oslobodjenje*

In a country deeply divided into three nationalist-controlled territories, there was little room left for media still advocating inter-ethnic tolerance. A case in point was the fate of *Oslobodjenje*. Internationally praised as "the paper that refused to die", and awarded all of the most prestigious prizes in world journalism –Paper of the Year, The Consciousness and Integrity in Journalism Award, The Sakharov Award for Freedom of Thought, The Freedom Award, and The Golden Pen of Freedom, to mention just a few –*Oslobodjenje* faced the challenge of surviving the peace. With almost all pre-war assets destroyed and looted, with a huge wartime debt, and more and more senior journalists leaving after years of heroic unpaid work, the paper was also exposed to constant attacks in the newly-established nationalist Bosniak media. The Muslim SDA, unable to control *Oslobodjenje*, backed a new daily –*Dnevni avaz* (Daily Avaz)– giving it generous financial support, exclusive access to information, and even police and army support in distribution.

Oslobodjenje, while anti-nationalist and independent of the ruling parties, was losing the battle for readers. The paper lost some of its best journalists, partly because it was unable to pay them, partly because of an increasing divide between the management and editorial board over how to survive. In that struggle for day-to-day survival, the paper failed to re-energize and to develop a clear long-term strategy for regaining its central place in Bosnian journalism.

Nevertheless, the lively and somewhat chaotic media scene in Bosniak-majority territories proved to be the most pluralistic in Bosnia with the battle between "the most read" and "the most respected" dailies (*Avaz* and *Oslobodjenje*, respectively), as well as the rivalry between the two independent weeklies (*Dani* and *Slobodna Bosna*), plus the continuous campaign in the nationalist weekly (*Ljiljan*) against all of the independent-minded journalists and media outlets, and a variety of radio and television stations to boot. Bosniak leader Alija Izetbegovic prided his party on "allowing the greatest media freedom in the region". The fact is that it was not the party that "allowed" the freedom, but Bosnian journalists who won and preserved it in spite of their government. Izetbegovic himself, irritated by the criticism of his party in the independent media, attacked some of the Bosnian magazines as "media prostitutes", allegedly selling their services for a handful of dollars to the international donors. In that, he was just replaying the same old song used by Milosevic and Tudjman in efforts to silence the opposition in Serbia and Croatia. He thought it was perfectly fine if the donor was, for example, his party but not the international organizations.

Izetbegovic –together with Muslim religious community leader Mustafa Ceric– was instrumental in trying to impose further Islamization of public life in the territories under his control. In 1996, on the occasion of the first post-war New Year celebration, he openly criticized Bosnian TV for projecting images of public drinking, singing, and Santa Claus appearances, "which are not our tradition". The fact is that Bosniaks not only traditionally celebrated the New

Year but also shared in the religious holidays of their Catholic, Orthodox, and Jewish neighbors. Santa Claus bringing gifts to children was part of this in schools, communities, and companies. Ceric also attacked Bosnian TV for using terms such as "the Holy Father" and "his Holiness" in reporting about Pope John Paul II's activities, accusing it of "Catholization of Bosniaks". That was just part of the systematic campaign against secularism, conducted through Dzemaludin Latic's Muslim weekly *Ljiljan*. Latic was a close associate of Izetbegovic, who led *Ljiljan*'s attack against mixed marriages, as well as a campaign against prominent Sarajevo poet Marko Vesovic and a number of secular Bosniak intellectuals.

Editors of the two best political weeklies in Bosnia, Senad Pecanin of *Dani* and Senad Avdic of *Slobodna Bosna*, were a constant target of radical Bosnian Islamists' attacks. Pecanin said that:

> There is an extremely high price attached to practicing independent jour-
> nalism here. And very few people are ready to pay it. That includes threat-
> ening phone calls at 2 or 3 a.m. with the caller telling me where my car is
> parked or the exact route my child takes to a day care center. Latic's *Ljiljan*
> once ran a doctored photo of me with Salman Rushdie depicting me as an
> 'enemy of Islam'. President Izetbegovic himself, after we ran a dossier on
> crimes committed against Serb and Croat civilians by renegade command-
> ers of the Bosnian Army, accused us publicly of causing $200-300 million in
> damage for international assistance denied to Bosnia. Then Ceric repeats
> these accusations. And as a consequence, the printing company increases
> the price of printing us; some distributors refuse to sell us; and some adver-
> tisers cancel their contracts. Not to mention one of Sarajevo's notorious
> warlord's entry into my office pointing, fortunately, only a toy gun to my
> head, or a bomb exploding in front of *Dani's* office[6].

Avdic was physically attacked and beaten in a downtown Sarajevo hotel on December 24, 1995. After that, he ran an open letter in *Slobodna Bosna* addressed to Izetbegovic, claiming that the police and military intelligence "enable the state to have information on every single politician, officer, or jour- nalist", and concluding that the attack was an attempt "to settle accounts" with him. "I do not know how much of this you can control", Avdic wrote to Izetbegovic. "If you cannot, it is horrible, and one should flee this country. If you can but do not do it, it is no less dangerous and horrible"[7]. Prominent Bosnian writer Miljenko Jergovic, reporting on the Bosnian media in *Nedjeljna Dalmacija*, concluded, "If you judge it by *Slobodna Bosna*, there are Western European stan- dards of freedom of the press in Sarajevo"[8]. But the price tag for Avdic's editorial independence included some fifteen court cases, two suspended sentences, and

6 Senad Pecanin: taped interview by the author in Sarajevo, February 2, 2000.

7 Sanja Despot and Snjezana Pavic, "Wait Until the State Starts Thinking", *Novi list*, Jan 7, 1996.

8 Miljenko Jergovic, *Ljiljan* Carries the SDA Banner, *Nedjeljna Dalmacija*, June 14, 1996.

even an arrest at his office to take him to court. His case prompted High Representative Karlos Vestendorp to intervene in Bosnia's judicial system by moving the alleged libel cases from the criminal to the civil courts, thus taking the threat to prosecute away from nationalist authorities, since in civil courts charges can be brought only by individuals.

Victims of violence - and silence

The state of the media was less satisfactory in Republika Srpska and even worse in the Croat-controlled territories of Bosnia. An international presence in the election process forced the ruling SDS to allow the existence of some alternative newspapers. The International Crisis Group reported that

> of these, Nezavisne novine was by far the most influential, evolving from a fortnightly newspaper into a weekly in June and a daily in August [of 1996] with financial assistance from the UK's Overseas Development Agency, the U.S. Agency for International Development (USAID), and George Soros' Open Society Fund. Moreover, the daily boasted a circulation of 4,000 and the weekly a circulation of 9,000, which though objectively low was nevertheless far greater than any other publication in Republika Srpska[9].

On August 25, 1999, Nezavisne novine ran an exclusive, entitled "Renegade group of Prijedor policemen massacred more than 200 Bosniaks; Republika Srpska Army saved survivors, murderers escaped prosecution". That report –on a crime that had happened seven years before, on August 22, 1992– was the first ever in the Republika Srpska media on war crimes perpetrated by Serbs. The paper published a thorough investigative report on how some 200 Bosniaks from the Prijedor area, former inmates of the notorious Omarska concentration camp, were bused to the Koricani cliffs on Vlasic mountain in Central Bosnia and summarily executed. Seven of them survived the massacre, and Nezavisne novine ran their testimony. The report prompted an avalanche of threats to the paper's staff, accusing them of "betraying the nation", but the paper continued to print new revelations of the crimes committed by the Serb paramilitary.

The price of such reporting proved to be high. On October 22, 1999, Reuters reported that a Bosnian Serb editor had lost his legs in blast. Zeljko Kopanja, 45, founder, publisher, and editor of Nezavisne novine, was on his way to his office at 7:15 a.m. when an explosive device planted under his car went off. The blast severed one of Kopanja's legs, and he was brought to Banjaluka Clinical Center in critical condition. Surgeons amputated what was left of both of his legs. Two weeks later, fighting both physical and emotional pain, Kopanja asked his friends and family to put him in a wheelchair so he could "take a walk" down Banjaluka's main pedestrian street, he said in an interview. "Seeing people in the

9 "The Media in Bosnia and Herzegovina: How International Support Can be More Effective", International Crises Group Report, March 18, 1997.

[Gospodska] street, some of them just shaking my hand, some sobbing, I knew I had done the right thing. And I knew I had to persevere (in exposing the war crimes) since I had sacrificed so much. I don't think that any nation is criminal. It's individuals and certain policies, not a whole nation", Kopanja said of his motives to continue publishing[10]. "After all, what would my life be like if I confined myself to a wheelchair and my home only!" He agreed that he was a victim not only of the Serb war criminals, who wanted to silence him, but also indirectly of the silence in other Serb media about the war crimes. "The silence of the others has left us too lonely, exposed to accusations and vulnerable to attack. No one else [in the Republika Srpska media] has joined us. But I don't think it was politically or ideologically motivated silence. It was fear", Kopanja said.

Future priorities and recommendations

The experience of the 1990s offers lessons for "media intervention" in the Balkans and in other countries and regions undergoing transitions to democracy. Most important among these, international peace agreements and international institutions that newly independent countries wish to join should lay out clear, explicit guidelines and criteria concerning the independence of the media. The Dayton agreement omitted this critical piece, leaving the media in all three states –Serbia, Croatia, and Bosnia– in the hands of those most responsible for the wars in the first place. No wonder the media continued to promote nationalist agendas and images, supporting their own leaders' and ruling parties' wartime goals, condemning neighbors, and resisting international efforts to bring about democratic reform and reconciliation.

What could or should have been done better? Following is a list of recommendations that might contribute to setting priorities and achieving better results in the next stages of "media intervention", not only in the Balkans but also in countries experiencing a less traumatic transition to democracy.

Ownership of the media

Ownership proved to be the single most decisive tool in the decade of nationalist media manipulation throughout the former Yugoslavia. The tragedy of the Serbian, Croatian, and Bosnian media –and this is equally true for the whole public sector in those countries– was that their transition in the 1990s was not a real step from one-party monopoly to multiparty democracy. In all three cases, the Communist Party monopoly was replaced by a nationalist party monopoly, using the same totalitarian instruments of control. Milosevic in Serbia and Tudjman in Croatia –both products of hard-line communist ideology– established immediate and absolute control over all state media. They took over state radio and television stations and the national dailies, *Politika* and *Vjesnik* respectively, and they

10 Zeljko Kopanja: interview by the author in Washington, D.C., November 16, 2000.

expanded their parties' media empires by taking control of a number of independent and regional media outlets. The method was the same: the Milosevic and Tudjman governments took over almost all Serbian and Croatian newspapers, declaring that their privatization during the late 1980s under Yugoslav reformist Ante Markovic was illegal, and making them a part of their propaganda machinery. This was the fate of *Borba*, *Vecernje novosti*, and *Ekonomska politika* in Serbia, and of *Slobodna Dalmacija* and *Danas* in Croatia, among others.

The winning coalition of nationalist parties in Bosnia after the first multiparty elections in 1990 tried to use the Milosevic–Tudjman recipe to subjugate the media in the republic, but Bosnian journalists challenged the law adopted in the nationalist-controlled parliament in spring 1991. They rejected the nationalist claim of "the right of the democratically elected parliament to appoint media editors and managers". By the end of that year, journalists had won a Constitutional Court case, arguing that even if the Bosnian media, as elsewhere in the former Yugoslavia, enjoyed some state support, the money belonged to the Bosnian public and not to the ruling parties. At *Oslobodjenje*, we went so far as to reject publicly any further state subsidy if it would be used as blackmail over our editorial policy. The Bosnian media victory was soon overshadowed, however, by the media war drums over the rivers separating Bosnia from Serbia and Croatia. Milosevic's radio and television signals were imposed over all the Serb-occupied territories of Bosnia, and Tudjman's over the Croat-controlled territories. The Bosnian voices of tolerance were replaced by voices of hate. Their dominance in all three states continued long after the Dayton Peace Agreement was initialed on November 21, 1995. Until the year 2000, the media remained in the hands of warmongers, creating obstacles to reconciliation.

Lesson learned: make the independence of the media an important part of future peace agreements and one of the must-do requirements for international acceptance of states in transition. These requirements must include the overhaul of laws regulating the media and the acceptance of international standards of freedom of expression. In Serbia, Croatia, and Bosnia, the still-prevailing concept of state media needs to be replaced with the concept of truly public media.

Representative managing and advisory boards

While state and regional government support of public media may still have a role until there is a functioning economy, it is necessary to develop a legal framework to protect independent media from political, party, and parliamentary control. One way to do this in postwar and transitional societies is through the internationally supervised establishment of representative managing and advisory boards comprising a broad civil society spectrum. These boards might include representatives of independent associations of journalists and their labor unions; scholars and writers; artists and athletes; human rights and other NGO activists; prominent public figures and religious community leaders; international organizations

concerned with press freedom; and other international institutions engaged in
democracy building. Their role should be to oversee and assist in the development of internationally acceptable standards and practices, providing protection
for, rather than control of, the newly independent media.

Professional associations of journalists

Throughout the region, professional associations of journalists have an important
role to play in efforts to restore the credibility and raise the standards of journalism. Except for the Croatian Society of Journalists (HND), which remained active
in its efforts to protect and educate its members throughout a decade of oppressive HDZ rule, most other regional associations have disintegrated along ideological or ethnic lines. In Bosnia, there was not only a divide between associations of
professional and not-so-professional journalists, but also between associations
based on ethnic exclusivity. In the highly politicized, nationalistic environment of
the 1990s, supposedly professional associations of journalists rallied behind
"patriotic causes". They neglected their primary responsibilities: to establish,
uphold, and develop standards and ethics of journalism; to organize and represent journalists in their search for decent pay, job security, benefits, and better
work conditions; to protect their membership –regardless of ethnic backgrounds–
against political and economic pressures from governments and political parties.
If they were to shift their focus away from the nationalist policies of the past
toward real-life issues and challenges, Balkan journalists would soon find that
their common interests and concerns are more numerous and more vital than
their differences.

Watchdog journalism

A crucial missing link in rebuilding media credibility in the postwar Balkans is the
absence of a tradition of watchdog journalism. In post-communist societies, the
media did not have experience in critically examining and reporting on the work
of state and party institutions, and no institutions were responsive to public interests. The nationalist parties of the 1990s –like the communists in the post-World
War II period– did not have to answer questions about what they were doing or
why. It took almost five years after Dayton for the first major breakthrough in this
area, when the international High Representative in Bosnia introduced the
Freedom of Information Act providing citizens' access to most information possessed by the government and other public institutions. While the Act creates a
legal framework for greater media access to the secretive world of power, there is
a need to develop a wide public information network: public affairs offices within major governmental and public institutions; a communications culture in which
individuals and institutions are more responsive and available for legitimate public concerns, interviews, and press conferences; and access to records and databases of government and other public institutions. To help create that culture of

transparency and public accountability, much more needs to be done to oblige public institutions to have their own public relations officers, to train communications specialists for these positions, and, more than anything else, to train journalists to ask questions of the greatest public relevance.

Education for journalism

Postwar Balkan journalism has a desperate need for creative educational initiatives. While there are some positive experiences –including the BBC School of Journalism within the Media Center and the High College of Journalism within the Media Plan Institute, both in Sarajevo, the region needs a thorough overhaul of its formal schools of journalism. For the most part, these schools are based in former socialist schools of political science that have no tradition of educating modern media professionals. During the decade of war and propagandist manipulation, the newsrooms in Serbia, Croatia, and Bosnia were devastated. Some of the best professionals have left or been forced to leave; they have been replaced with young, often uneducated and inexperienced reporters and editors who have practiced more party propaganda than real journalism ever since. To meet both the short-term demand for qualified journalists and long-term development needs, the postwar Balkan media must pursue innovative educational approaches. These could include on-the-job training within the newsrooms of major media outlets such as national radio, TV, and dailies, conducted by experienced regional and international "editors-in-residence". Working with journalists on their major daily assignments, leading them through story development –from the initial idea, to finding proper sources and documents, to shaping the story and providing adequate photos and graphs– would help establish some basic standards in regional journalism. Even some simple rules, such as consulting multiple sources for each story and always looking for "the other side" of an argument, would greatly improve the quality and credibility of the media.

Another innovative approach might include cooperative efforts in developing and executing coverage of major ongoing issues and events, such as election campaigns, truth and reconciliation processes, economic reforms, and international integration processes. A local–regional–international team of editors and journalists working together to shape major media coverage of critical issues would provide valuable learning experience for working journalists and help set standards for future coverage of these issues. For example, media development institutions operating in the Balkans could sponsor election campaign coverage by selected media outlets –statewide radio and TV and leading dailies and weeklies– including hands-on participation by competent regional and international advisers. Since Balkan media are more preoccupied with day-to-day survival than with long-term educational or development concerns, international donors could help by offering comprehensive educational projects, soliciting applications, and offering professional and material support to those who qualify. Working on such projects, with the full participation of regional and international advisers, would provide local editors and journalists with the skills for future coverage of political campaigns in their countries.

International exchange

Expanded international exchange should be an integral part of journalism education. There should be a more systematic effort to provide talented Balkan journalists who work for relevant national media with an opportunity to spend some time –three months, a semester, or an academic year– in an international newsroom environment interacting and working with scholars and practitioners. The combination of research, newsroom exposure, and internships at major international media organizations would offer a valuable learning experience for work in the region.

Education of media managers

Of equal importance for a long-term media development strategy is education for media management. Training managers to develop a sound business strategy –with the proper balance of news and advertising; the optimum balance between full-time staff and freelancers; and the best methods for increasing circulation, classified advertisement, subscriptions, and other income-generating initiatives– is key to the gradual move from media dependency on donors to self-sustainability.

Refocusing donor strategies

International media donors still have a valuable role to play in the development of independent Balkan media, but they, too, need to refocus their strategies. Instead of sometimes indiscriminate spending on projects of dubious quality or relevance, they might identify –on the basis of their performance in the 1990s and their creative and business potential– media outlets deserving support in their search for higher professional standards and profitability. These outlets should be offered a comprehensive aid package including financial support, investment, and lines of credit to achieve their goals.

Developing the media market

A competitive media market is needed to reduce media dependence on public funds. In the Balkan experience of the 1990s, even internationally supervised privatization left nationalist governments in charge of the instruments of economic harassment against independent media. The governments could silence the media at will by controlling –through networks of their cronies– printing presses, distribution networks, newsprint supply, discriminative taxes, allocation of radio frequencies, and manipulation of advertising. Prospects for the development of independent media would be substantially improved through lower taxes, equal access to basic supplies and frequencies, nondiscriminatory sales networks and advertising, and the development of smaller, less expensive, and more competitive printing facilities. Once a competitive media market exists in conjunction with long-term support for the most relevant media outlets, the market will decide, for example, which of the approximately 80 television and 200 radio stations currently operating in Bosnia Herzegovina should continue as economically viable businesses.

Truth and reconciliation

Just as the Balkan media participated in the ultranationalist crusades of the 1990s, preparing the ground for war and justifying the worst atrocities in Europe since the end of World War II, they now have a crucial role to play in truth and reconciliation efforts. Five years after Dayton, the public in Serbia and Croatia still has not been told the truth about the Bosnian war of 1992-1995. As long as this is so, not only the history but also the future of the region will be vulnerable to nationalist distortions and the accumulation of hatreds for new tensions and conflicts. Experience tells us that acknowledging and honoring the victims on all sides, examining the record of atrocities, and neither denying crimes nor blaming everyone equally, provide the best bases for reconciliation and coexistence in the Balkans. Documenting and making public the atrocities and sufferings on all sides would help the people of the region understand the complexities of the conflict and the pain of the innocent: presenting to the Serbs the full extent of the siege and killings of Vukovar and Sarajevo, the concentration camps in the Prijedor area, and the Srebrenica massacre; educating the Croats about atrocities committed in their name against Bosniaks in Herzegovina and Central Bosnia and against Serbs in Operation Storm in Croatia; and telling Bosniaks about the crimes committed against the Serbs during the siege of Sarajevo and against the Croats in the Konjic and Bugojno areas.

Once confronted with documents and pictures of these crimes, presented to them during the previous decade as part of a heroic and even sacred fight for survival, people will be better able to understand and support bringing war criminals to trial. Such efforts to uncover the truth and mete out justice are a precondition for the children of this tragic region, in which every generation of the twentieth century has experienced war –my grandparents' generation in 1914, my parents' in 1941, my children's and mine in the 1990s– to finally join a peaceful and prosperous Europe.

Chapter 22

Radio in Afghanistan: socially useful communications in wartime

Gordon Adam

This case study examines the experience of radio broadcasting aimed at bring- |
ing about developmental change in Afghanistan over the past twenty-five years.
One particular project is examined –the radio soap opera *New Home New Life*
which has been broadcasting since 1994. Alongside other examples of radio, it is
analysed in terms of methodology and the constraints involved in broadcasting to
a conflict area. It examines *New Home New Life*'s impact and pulls together some
lessons learned for future media interventions of this kind.

Preamble: the social communication process

In 1930, the German writer Bertolt Brecht suggested that:

> radio could be the most wonderful public communication system imagina-
> ble, a gigantic system of channels –could be, that is, if it were capable not
> only of transmitting but of receiving, of making listeners hear but also
> speak, not of isolating them but connecting them (Lewis and Booth, 1989).

What Brecht did not understand –because radio at that time was a top-down
medium– was how in later decades technological advances have worked with programme innovation to transform radio into an interactive medium which can connect people and enable communication between governments and populations
and vice versa. The phone-in programme, for example, and the increasing use of
text messaging, have both allowed listeners to have their say. This inclusiveness has
created a degree of "ownership" by listeners over programmes. In many countries,

this helps programme producers broadcast on issues relevant to the audience, who then listen with greater interest and loyalty. Developing countries are catching up, as mobile telephony and deregulation of the media lead to new programming initiatives. Where there is no easy access to phones, this "feedback loop" requires more pro-active work by the broadcasters –going to villages, consulting listeners on priority issues, recording their reactions to programmes etc. In conflict areas this process of "socially useful" programming is often driven by broadcasters, as the government either does not exist, is very weak, or preoccupied with pressing military issues. Afghanistan is a particularly interesting example because of the size and loyalty of its radio audience, which gave credible broadcasters a remarkable opportunity to influence social and behaviour change over the past twenty-five years. In this case study, I am avoiding the academic debate over "social" or "behaviour" change by taking the view that one cannot happen without the other. Thus, when an Afghan decides to allow his wife to be vaccinated because of hearing a radio programme, he does so after consulting his peers and after social norms have adjusted, making this an acceptable action. His behaviour change is an integral part of a wider social change.

From news to "intended outcomes" programmes

In the mid 1980s, BBC broadcasters were faced with a set of opportunities, as well as a number of difficulties, in developing "socially useful" radio programs in Afghanistan –in other words, programs that are designed to have an "intended outcome". It should be stressed that in wartime, impartial radio news programmes from respected broadcasters are "socially useful" in that they are often the only reliable means for people to learn about security and political issues on which their lives may depend. The respected American broadcaster and correspondent during the Second World War, Ed Murrow, explained this succinctly: "To be persuasive we must be believable; to be believable we must be credible; to be credible we must be truthful".

In the context of this case study, "socially useful" is interpreted to cover programmes aimed at some kind of social or behaviour change in the fields of health, awareness of landmines, social issues relating to the family and gender relationships, drug addiction and a host of other topics. On the positive side, the BBC had an unrivalled reputation for fair reporting and analysis of a vicious and largely secret war between the Soviet occupiers with their Afghan government allies against the various bands of *mujahedin* (holy warriors) and their supporters during the 1980s. In wartime, travel is difficult and dangerous, people are isolated and often afraid, and the radio is all-important as a source of reliable news and comment[1]. Evidence from the time indicates that Afghans were voracious radio listeners to every station broadcasting in Pashto and Persian, particularly the BBC, VOA (Voice of America), Deutschewelle, Radio Iran, Radio Pakistan and All India

1 For more discussion see Skuse (2002).

Radio. They listened to Radio Afghanistan as well, most of them with deep scepticism, though there were some socially useful programmes, particularly a daily
one on family life. In Pakistan, 82% of male Afghan Pashto speakers and 42% of
women listened to the BBC Pashto Service in 1988[2]. Many made real sacrifices to
buy batteries, and those without radios often listened with their neighbours.

In the 1980s, the BBC had a large, loyal audience both inside
Afghanistan and amongst the five to six million Afghan refugees in Pakistan, Iran,
the Gulf States and further a field. This was fertile ground for extending programmes to socially useful issues, and for providing advice on everyday survival
from health to mines-awareness. The rationale was compelling: in rural areas of
Afghanistan people's lives had been turned upside down; most schools and
health centres had been destroyed and they had to face the hazards from millions
of anti-personnel mines sprayed from aircraft. Farmers faced new challenges in
cultivating crops and keeping their animals alive. There was a need for basic services supplied by NGOs to be supported by information about coping with the
burning issues of everyday life. Radio Afghanistan was not fulfilling these information needs, particularly those related to rural areas and the refugee camps
where most people lived.

The biggest problem for the BBC Pashto and Persian services was that
they broadcast from London, some 5,000 kms away. Programmes which set out
to provide useful advice on health, farming and social issues had to research the
specific issues with great care –difficult at such a distance. The BBC's Audience
Research department was geared almost exclusively to finding out how many
people were listening, not what their broadcasting needs were. Another problem
was that effective social communication is participatory and interactive, again
made very difficult by distances and dangers of travel inside the country. There
were hardly any phones available to listeners, and cell and satellite phones had
yet to be invented. Also, programmes aimed at social change were very new to
the BBC, and many people within the corporation were hostile to the concept. It
was, they believed, akin to propaganda.

Then there was cost: programmes aimed at social or behaviour
change are comparatively expensive to research and produce. Even BBC foreign
news was poorly resourced twenty years ago: there was a single international
news reporter in Pakistan tasked with covering the Afghan war as well as
Pakistan, and a couple of London based analysts who wrote on political and military developments. Donors were slow to understand the potential impact of
broadcasting socially useful programmes despite the well-known popularity of
the BBC amongst Afghans. The British Overseas Development Administration
(now Department for International Development, DFID), quickly rejected a funding query on the grounds that this would be "double funding" the BBC World
Service (which is funded by a government grant-in-aid). Despite increased suffer-

2 International Broadcasting and Audience Research Report, Pashto Service listening, BBC, 1988.

ing by the population in the face of an increasingly destructive civil war, it took eighteen months to find funds from United Nations agencies (UNDP and UNICEF) and the International Committee of the Red Cross to launch *New Home New Life,* the BBC radio soap opera which went on the air in April 1994 and has been broadcast three times weekly in Pashto and Dari (Persian) ever since.

New Home New Life

Although there had been several educational series beforehand, including a drama called *Good Health, New Home New Life* was the most significant BBC radio pro-gramme aimed at bringing about social change in Afghanistan. It was produced in the region –Peshawar in Pakistan– as Afghan cities were either unsafe or too remote. This allowed participative research with listeners, and recruitment of some of the finest Afghan writers and broadcasters who had fled war-torn Kabul. A total of about one hundred and fifty staff were eventually involved –writers, radio pro-ducers, educationalists, an evaluation team and some fifty part-time actors. For the first time, a soap opera was broadcast in Dari as well as Pashto –the two major lan-guages of the country. Evaluations of the previous radio soap *Good Health*[3] had confirmed that soap opera was a popular and effective genre amongst Afghans, especially women, whose numbers listening regularly to the Pashto Service dou-bled following its broadcast[4]. The audience soon became used to the multiple sto-rylines, which could focus on specific themes for months on end without boring the audience or appearing to preach at them. This repetition is often essential if key issues are to become accepted and acted on by listeners.

The over-arching reason for *New Home New Life's* popularity was its mix of fast moving, well-written topical storylines and fine acting. It was also the only topical radio drama available to a population which was isolated and starved of entertainment. The skills of Afghanistan's most talented writers and actors were rapidly honed into the genre of soap-opera. Major storylines ranged from the gently romantic saga of the heroine Gulalai, whose health worker activities were a role model for female listeners, to the escapades of the village chief Jabbar Khan and his clowning servant Nazir. The comic scenes struck a chord with the black humour that Afghans have found so popular throughout their dark years of conflict and oppression. The drama also tackled serious issues familiar to listeners –living with lawlessness, international humanitarian law, infant and child health, abuse of drugs, protecting livestock from disease, rural livelihoods, deforestation, mines awareness, education for girls, marrying young girls to much older men, and the practice of trading unmarried women in order to end family or tribal feuds. Despite the strong pro-women agenda, even the Taliban were avid listeners, caught up in the suspense of what would happen next to their favourite characters. There were popular outcries from listeners on

3 Unpublished focus group survey, 1990 (in possession of the author).
4 IBAR, 1984 and 1988, BBC, London.

a number of occasions, for instance when one popular character was 'killed' by a stray bullet in a feud, and when another tried to commit suicide rather than be married against her will.

There was no preconceived theoretical basis to this approach, but it approximated to the example of the long running radio soap in the UK, *The Archers,* and to the Mexican TV producer Manuel Sabido's use of *telenovela,* broadcast initially in support of a government literacy campaign. This use of soap opera or serial drama characters to promote social and behaviour change was later summed up by the American social psychologist, Albert Bandura:

> The format was creatively founded on the basic social cognitive principles in which efficacious modelling serves as the principle means to inform, motivate and enable people to make a better life for themselves (1997: 506).

However, Bandura warns:

> Social persuasion alone is not enough to promote adoptive behaviour. To increase receptivity one must also create optimal conditions for learning the new ways, provide the resources and positive incentives for adopting them, and build supports into the social system to sustain them (514).

In a war zone, this creates some difficulties: how can mass media interventions be supported by government programmes and incorporated into a social system when there is no meaningful government and little security? The response of the *New Home New Life* team, or BBC Afghan Education Projects (AEP) as it became known, was to make maximum use of radio –two repeats within a week, as well as other channels available to reinforce the key issues of the soap opera: series of radio educational feature programmes were produced, and a cartoon magazine in Dari and Pashto language versions, colourfully produced and using simple language, was distributed through the NGOs. These aid organisations working inside Afghanistan and in the refugee camps of Pakistan provided additional information, goods and services that formed the basis of the drama's educational content.

The absence of government was a mixed blessing: the major down side was the lack of nationwide service delivery and of Bandura's "positive incentives", but on the other hand there was a refreshing lack of bureaucracy and a "can-do" attitude from Pakistan based NGOs involved in health, education, farming, de-mining and other activities. Close collaboration with the NGOs was central to *New Home New Life:* they were invited to monthly consultative meetings so they could comment on draft storylines and ensure they were culturally appropriate and technically accurate. The listeners were also consulted through regular needs assessment surveys inside Afghanistan and amongst Afghan refugees.

At the same time, listeners were often quick to comment on the authenticity of the plots: in the case of one dramatised spot on the dangers of people returning to houses which had been booby-trapped, one listener wrote to the BBC that the dialogue between family members delighting in seeing all their possessions again was wholly unrealistic. "If soldiers had been in the house, it would have been looted" was his comment. There were other instances where the advice given was not appropriate –inevitably so bearing in mind the size of the country and the diversity of the audience. Indeed, in order to be entertaining, *New Home New Life* had to portray a happier existence than was typical for most listeners. There is evidence that the audience realised this, but nevertheless they continued to listen and learn from the storylines, and even to internalise some of the more dramatic moments, such as holding condolence services in mosques for characters who had "died" (Skuse, 2002). This degree of identification with the drama led to a gradual assumption by many listeners that *New Home New Life* was "owned" by them rather than being imposed on them.

Editorial challenges

New Home New Life was high profile: the scheduling of the programme was prime time. The editorial stance was daring but not reckless. It was not overtly political, but many of its storylines were controversial in these volatile times of civil war, Taliban rule and social upheaval. Girls' education has been consistently championed by the drama, as have women working outside the home. Repressive customs such as forced marriages to end disputes were dramatised. Sterility amongst males –commonly blamed on women and used as an excuse for taking a second wife– was tackled. Despite the sensitivity of the topics, research conducted at the time concluded that *New Home New Life* successfully created a fictional "space" which allowed hitherto taboo social issues to be discussed and questioned within the family, the first stage of shifting social norms:

> the production does not mount a particularly vigorous challenge to patriar-
> chal authority, since it is recognised that this would alienate more of the
> audience than it would win over; rather, it seeks to work within normative
> culture, eking out small spaces for manoeuvre in which change can be
> advanced from within the relative safety of soap opera gossip (Skuse,
> forthcoming)

The danger of landmines is a constant hazard to the inhabitants of Upper and Lower villages, the two fictional communities of the drama. Celebratory gun firing, and the use of weapons to settle disputes, the targeting of civilians in warfare, the extortion of money at roadblocks, were all subjected to scrutiny in *New Home New Life* storylines. These, and many others, all represented a challenge to common practices in Afghanistan during these unstable times. As the increasingly lawless mujahedin or Taliban were often the worst offenders, the potential for creating offence was there. Political assassination was common in Peshawar, and the BBC AEP staff were possible targets of violence, although there was nothing disgruntled Afghan authorities could do to disrupt the actual transmissions which were international and outside their control. This is one major advantage of recruiting a major international broadcaster to focus on socially useful pro- grammes in wartime or in a post-conflict situation. They have the transmission networks to reach populations through short and medium wave broadcasts that are beyond the control of hostile governments. As the current popularity of Radio Free Afghanistan –funded by the US Congress– shows, listeners in Afghanistan are able to make a distinction between the quality of programmes and the possi- ble political agendas of those who fund the station.

In the event, there have been no serious threats against the BBC AEP, despite the controversial nature of many storylines. The main reason for this was the popularity of the programme. The quality of writing and acting was high, the issues which were raised were topical, relevant and well researched. Critically, they were also presented within the broad cultural parameters of Islam and Afghan society, and not imposed on Afghan listeners from a western standpoint, as some aid organisations tended to do with, for instance, issues involving women's rights[5].

Obtaining a successful balance was the prime responsibility of the first BBC AEP Project Manager, John Butt, an Englishman with incisive editorial judge- ment, but also a convert to Islam and fluent in Pashto and Dari. With his knowl- edge of the languages, Afghan culture and religion, he was personally able to edit the final scripts, avoid indiscretions and unintended ambiguities. He oversaw the use of simple Pashto and Dari in dialogue –a language which listeners could identify with as colloquial language in everyday use. This was not easy, as both languages are normally written in a more formal style. He also established the edi- torial standards for his Afghan successors, but his great achievement was steering AEP a steady course in the uncertain early days before success was assured, and when the whole project was vulnerable to pressure from the Afghan authorities, donors and even an initially sceptical BBC management.

When the Taliban came to power in 1995, they reportedly debated whether or not to ban radio listening at the same time as banning TV viewing. However, moderate voices prevailed, realizing the enormous resentment such an edict was to cause a people so devoted to their radios for news and –thanks to New Home New Life– entertainment and education. On a number of issues, the Taliban even issued edicts prohibiting practices that had been highlighted by the drama; one example was the story of Asghar, a student at a madrassah (religious school) who was sent to battle. Following the broadcast, the Taliban swiftly banned the practice of sending young students to the front, and providing madrassahs to accommodate them[6]. Whether this edict was always respected is another matter.

5 For an interesting analysis of NGOs and gender issues see "Afghanistan: Pride and Principle" in Vaux (2001).
6 Butt, John: personal communication to the author.

Impact

Despite the evidence of its popularity, the central test of *New Home New Life*'s usefulness –as that of any media intervention in any war zone where interpersonal support and reinforcement is very limited– is whether people are influenced in their behaviour through listening to it. This was monitored by quarterly missions carried out by the AEP evaluation team in different regions of Afghanistan. From the "before and after" surveys (see below), it is clear that people learned from the drama, and that they remembered what they learned. But there are two central problems to any evaluation of this kind: the first is separating what people *say* they do with this information from assessing what they *actually do*, and secondly, isolating the impact of the chosen media intervention from those of other media or interpersonal interventions. Regarding the latter constraint, Afghanistan at war presented an opportunity: there was so little development communication work going on, and BBC's popularity was so well documented, that it was possible to attribute impact on key issues to the soap opera. It was, however, more difficult to isolate *actual* from *reported* behaviour or social change.

However, the project benefited from expert assistance from two quarters: training from Dr. Astier Almedom, an expert in participatory rural appraisal from the London School of Hygiene and Tropical Medicine, for the AEP Evaluation Team in techniques of participatory rural appraisal, and the work of Andrew Skuse, then an anthropology doctoral candidate from University College London. They both added qualitative anthropological data to help understand the communication process between broadcaster and listener and hence the true impact of the soap opera[7]. Finally, a large-scale survey conducted by CIET International gave some remarkable quantitative results on impact.

Examples of reported behaviour and social change

From the many unsolicited examples of behaviour and social change recorded since 1988, several stand out. One is a letter from a health worker in Kunar province from 1991 where he was undertaking a vaccination campaign. He wrote

> ...unfortunately the women of the area were not prepared to be vaccinated by us. The next day, while sitting with elders of the area, we heard a BBC (health) message about the tetanus bacteria ... and how important the vaccination programme was ... we were happy and surprised to see that the next day the men of the area who had obviously listened to the BBC brought 300 of their women to be vaccinated[8].

Significantly, this re-think was probably prompted by the interpersonal reinforcement of the healthworkers –support for the Bandura thesis that mass media are

---

7 Both contributed to subsequent publications: Almedom, 1996 and Skuse, 2002 and forthcoming.
8 BBC World Service Press Release, 15th August 1991.

most effective if backed up by 'incentives'– in this case vaccinations, and health workers on hand to answer questions. This extract from a diary kept by a village woman in a different part of Afghanistan indicates a similar impact five years later:

> 28/11/96: A team of vaccinators came to our village [...] I asked them if the elders of the families tried to stop them vaccinating people. They replied that a few years back there were some people in families who were against vaccination; they allowed the children to come but not the ladies. Now that they have listened to the drama most people know that they should be vaccinated and they let women go too[9].

The diary writer went on to describe a conversation with a woman at a wedding ceremony who confided that she feared for the health of her children because:

> I heard from the drama that the disease is caused by mosquitoes. I will try and get nets for the windows and doors and I am sure the children won't get this disease if I can find nets.

The BBC AEP's evaluation team uncovered a similar story some 500 km north in the city of Mazar-e-Sharif, though significantly there was no reinforcement by health workers:

> In Mrs Wazir's house in Mazar-e-Sharif, the first thing we noticed was a bright white mosquito net covering the bed ... showing us the mosquito net, she said she made it herself with netting cloth because nets are not available in Mazar. She laughed and said the BBC told her to do it[10].

And another anecdote from the BBC AEP team on the impact of one of the soap opera's strongest themes –the dangers of dealing in scrap metal, particularly to the children who forage for it on old battlefields:

> I have a friend named Abdul Ghani. He used to have a scrap metal shop. When an explosion took place in Painda's [character from New Home New Life] scrap shop, killing some and wounding others, Abdul Ghani gave up his scrap business and opened a cloth shop instead[11].

And this was recorded by a journalist during Taliban rule in 1998:

> One woman, who gave her name as Imam Jam's wife said that the example of Gulalai [female healthworker from New Home New Life] had persuaded her to let her daughters work outside the house. Her daughter, cradling a 10 days old baby, said she had even taken off her burqa (veil) once or twice. Her mother clicked her tongue in disapproval[12].

9 "Three Day Diary", Skuse, Andrew, BBC AED Evaluation Newsletter Vol. 1 No. 1, 1997.
10 Project Report for WHO 1996-7, BBC AEP, Peshawar.
11 Annual Report for DFID 1997-8, BBC AEP, Peshawar.
12 "The BBC sends a Message" in Soap, Independent, 25 July 1998, p. 16.

These few extracts indicate the power of credible radio drama characters to model behaviour which listeners can later recall. The next section examines the more difficult question as to whether they act on what they have heard.

Examples of actual change

From the earliest BBC educational broadcasts, it was clear that Afghans were quick to learn and remember facts from radio programmes. In other words, their knowledge improved through radio listening. With *New Home New Life* the BBC AEP introduced a more systematic evaluation process, asking specific questions related to important issues before and after the relevant episodes of the drama, and then returning two years later to ask the same questions to test recall. A sample of 300 respondents was used, taken from a town, a village on the road and a village off the road. The results are indicative only, and not representative of the entire population as the samples were small and not strictly random. But the trends are revealing. The percentages are those who answered correctly.

Mines Awareness

Q1: What are the warning signs of mines? (A: red paint).
Q2: What do you do when an unfamiliar object is found (A: inform the mine-clearance team).

	Before (April 1995)		After (October 1995)		Later (Feb 1997)	
	Men	Women	Men	Women	Men	Women
Q1:	67%	19%	89%	56%	91%	76%
Q2:	19%	14%	43%	52%	89%	59%

Q1: When should weaning be introduced? (A: between 3 and 6 months after birth).
Q2: What should a lactating mother who has TB do when feeding her child? (A: cover her mouth).
Q3: What is the best protection against malaria? (A: mosquito nets).

	Before (April 1995)		After (October 1995)		Later (Feb 1997)	
Q1:	38%	43%	72%	73%	56%	50%
Q2:	31%	30%	73%	96%	45%	91%
Q3:	73%	54%	90%	96%	84%	93%[13]

The data show variable results –perhaps influenced by the duration and attractiveness of the different storylines– but the general trend is an increase in knowledge and an ability to remember the key points (without reinforcement), and considerable knowledge retention two years later.

Unlike the surveys above, which indicate knowledge acquisition or reported behaviour change, the example below is a rare example of actual behaviour or social change.

13 "Long Term Memory and *New Home New Life*", in Evaluation Newsletter, Vol. 1 No. 1, BBC AEP, Peshawar (undated).

This is a survey commissioned by the United Nations Office for the Coordination of Humanitarian Aid to Afghanistan (UNOCHA) and undertaken by CIET International –*The 1997 Mine Awareness Evaluation*. From a large sample taken from 86 sentinel sites representing some 57,000 people from over 9,000 households inside Afghanistan, and including 86 male, 86 child and 7 female focus groups as well as interviews with 471 mine victims, the survey was required to assess the most effective way of informing Afghans about the dangers of land-mines. Fieldwork was focused on a random sample of sentinel communities selected to represent four United Nations administered regions –Herat, Kandahar, Jalalabad and Kabul. Along with *New Home New Life*, the efforts of three other organisations involved in community-based training were assessed. The results showed that the BBC was not only effective in getting the key messages across, but in fact had a strikingly positive impact on mines casualties:

> Considering only those in mine affected areas, a non-listener was twice as likely to be a mine victim after 1994 [when *New Home New Life* started], in comparison with a *New Home* listener (odds ratio 2.01, $p < 0.05$). This encouraging indicator contrasts with the notable absence of evidence of impact on mine events by the three direct [face-to-face] training pro-grammes[14].

This survey –which was as close to a scientific nationwide sampling as it was pos-sible to have at that time– also found that BBC listeners were more likely to report mines incidents than non-listeners; 23% of respondents said they would not enter a marked minefield or mined building, and 27% recalled the long run-ning *New Home New Life* story of Jandad who lost a leg in a mine incident, had depression during his months of recovery, but finally found a job, got married and had children. There were distortions in the survey, particularly in terms of the small number of female respondents. However, 50% of household heads replied they listened to the BBC, of whom 93% listened to *New Home New Life,* 73% of them with their wives and children. Almost all reported that their wives listened to the programme. These encouraging findings are in line with the BBC's own surveys on mines awareness, and that of Handicap International, one of the other mines training programmes evaluated by CIET. According to a HI report from 1996, of the 31 respondents, 26 could remember specific drama stories on mines awareness[15].

What these examples –and particularly the CIET survey– indicate is that listeners *can* change behaviour through exposure to the mass media *alone,* contrary to the claims of many researchers, including Bandura. But to achieve this level of impact, programmes have to be well researched, produced and struc-tured, and broadcast at times convenient for the target listeners.

---

14 "The 1997 National Mine Awareness Evaluation: final report to UNOCHA", CIET International, 1998.
15 Quoted in "Radio for Meeting Learning Needs in Emergencies", paper delivered by John Butt at a workshop on Multi-Channel learning organised by UNICEF in Cairo in October 1996.

Alliances for peace-building between media and aid organisations

Another significant influence of radio in Afghanistan was recorded in November 1994, when a combination of special announcements and features broadcast on a number of BBC programmes including the soap opera, gave the widest possible publicity to the biggest immunisation campaign in Afghanistan for 17 years. Thanks to this, along with painstaking efforts of WHO (World Health Organisation), UNICEF and local NGOs who set up the infrastructure for the campaign and negotiated with government and warlords, there was a nationwide ceasefire for one week –the first in Afghanistan for 16 years. Not only were one million children and 300,000 women vaccinated, but hostilities were suspended– a revealing example of what can be achieved when an issue benefiting all sides is effectively negotiated during a period of conflict. It was also a lesson on what can be achieved when the mass media and aid workers collaborate closely. The BBC's role in this first groundbreaking campaign led to discussion in the correspondence columns of the London *Times* on the importance of mass media collaborating with aid organisations in ventures of this kind[16].

This set a precedent, and a number of subsequent ceasefire NIDs (national immunisation days) were subsequently negotiated in Afghanistan, one of them due to take place just as coalition forces were about to invade Afghanistan in October 2001. The aid agencies had pulled out of Afghanistan, there was near panic in Kabul because the American bombing campaign was expected at any time, yet the NID was scheduled to continue. The BBC broadcast a series of announcements after *New Home New Life* along the lines of "despite the current difficulties, the national immunisation day is taking place as scheduled", and "even if you are on the move, please get your children vaccinated: emergencies will pass, but if a child catches polio, the child may have to live with paralysis throughout life"[17]. The NID happened, and a large number of children were vaccinated. Later, one woman in Kabul spoke to the BBC and said:

> With a lot of people leaving Kabul, one thought the Americans were coming to wipe Afghanistan off the face of the earth. But when we heard in *New Home New Life* that vaccination was being carried out and when we saw it happening, I suddenly thought 'there is still hope'. That is how I got my children vaccinated and I decided to stay put for which I am happy. Many other people who ran, suffered a lot[18].

16 Letters column, 31.1.95 and 3.3.95, *The Times* of London.
17 Siddiqi, Shirazuddin - personal communication to the author (May 2004).
18 Siddiqi, op cit.

Immediate post-conflict challenges

The current simmering conflict in Afghanistan is posing new challenges for BBC AEP and other broadcasters of "socially useful" programs. There is increased competition from international and national radio stations. And while it was possible in wartime to set the social and educational broadcasting agenda in consultation with aid organisations, in the post-conflict era close collaboration with government is needed. This is particularly true in Afghanistan where the transitional government headed by President Karzai is sensitive over the presence of western coalition forces and is keen to show it is in charge over non-security matters. There are multiple problems, one being that the Afghan civil service, decimated by 25 years of conflict and emigration, has a huge shortfall of skills and resources with which to run the country.

Education is an interesting example of this: the Afghan Ministry of Education has largely reverted to a traditional centralised model of service delivery and teacher training based on 1970s learning psychology. There is little understanding of "child centred" educational methods, of modern cognitive approaches or how modern media programmes and technology can help fulfil the urgent need for education at all levels. This has proven to be a challenge for *It's Great to Learn*, part of the Afghan Primary Education Project (APEP), funded by USAID since February 2003 and implemented by Media Support Solutions, which provides tailor-made radio programmes aimed at improving primary teachers' skills. *It's Great to Learn* is based on the proposition –tested through *New Home New Life*– that Afghans are capable of learning from radio listening alone, and putting what they learn into action. Programmes feature a combination of learning themes from the primary school curricula in Pashto, Dari, Maths, Science and Health, Social Studies and Life Skills, along with General Teaching Methodologies focusing on child centred learning. Teachers –who number about 85,000 in total– have the opportunity to be tested on their knowledge after a year, and be awarded a course certificate.

In the Afghan situation, this programme is an obvious short-to-medium term measure bearing in mind the destruction of the educational infrastructure including teacher-training institutions, and the continuing insecurity in the country. Radio's ability to deliver programmes quickly is also responding to the population's urgent desire for education. Girls were banned from going to school under the Taliban, and female teachers –80% of the total– were not allowed to work. Lack of trained teachers is now a major constraint, and if radio can be used to help raise standards, it will be fulfilling an important role in the country's reconstruction.

Despite all this, the Afghan Ministry of Education has been ambivalent over these radio programmes. Education has traditionally been a core function of the state, and it is hard for civil servants brought up in this tradition to accept an outside initiative in teacher training. Also, radio has traditionally been seen as very much a junior partner to traditional teacher training. There is a reluctance to accept that extraordinary situations require unconventional approaches, including examining teachers in what they have learned from the radio programmes. Teachers are often educated only to 8th or 9th grade, and many in remote areas have no immediate prospect of improving their skills through conventional further training. *It's Great to Learn* also aims to appeal to parents and older siblings who are supporting the educational process, so programmes have to be of general as well as specific interest. This raises another challenge –how to persuade professional educators that the programmes are sufficiently "serious" to be truly useful as a teacher training tool. Much advocacy effort is required so the Ministry assumes ownership of the new approaches. Ultimately it is likely that the strength of the programmes' impact on listeners will win or lose hearts and minds in Kabul's corridors of power.

Freedom of the airwaves

Along with using the media for specific educational or development related purposes, the other major trend in Afghanistan's post-war reconstruction is the freeing of the media from government control. Under the influence of the international community, the embryonic Afghan government was prevailed on to pass a liberal media law in 2002 that allows freedom of expression and the proliferation of private media. This is in sharp contrast to most other Asian countries where the government have been very slow to deregulate the media. One exception is Cambodia, which was influenced by the international community in a similar direction after the UN supervised the elections of 1993.

This process has, in Afghanistan, been oiled by generous aid money for independent radio stations, including a network run by women. Whether they will thrive after the short-term funds dry up, remains to be seen. Lack of donor funds to train people in production skills –a long-term process– can ultimately lead to failure in encouraging media diversity.

Potentially, community based radio stations can have a very positive impact on development –indeed, some twenty of them are broadcasting the daily *It's Great to Learn* programmes. Through their close contact with listeners they are in a good position to enable communication rather than simply provide information. On the other hand, in the politically fragile situation of Afghanistan, they can also become mouthpieces for regionally based warlords who have not been supportive of the government, or even of peace. And while the independent radio sector has been generously funded, Radio Afghanistan has received much less help in restructuring itself, though it has benefited from new transmission and television equipment. As with many state broadcasting organisations, it has too many staff who are badly paid and weakly led. For foreign donors, reforming Radio Afghanistan is not a tempting project –it will be a very long term process, and will almost certainly lead to conflict between donors and government. Whether the current proliferation of independent radio stations is of lasting help to Afghanistan will depend on international donors and local broadcasters working together to make the stations serve the needs of its listeners rather than being the voice-pieces of powerful local vested interests.

Conclusion

New Home New Life shows that Afghan listeners can absorb key information from the radio drama, and in some instances act on it, without reinforcement from the state or other sources. This is a challenge to Bandura's proposition that "social persuasion" by itself will not succeed in bringing about adoptive behaviour, and this challenge will need to be sustained if *It's Great to Learn* is to work successfully as a teacher training tool. But other examples –for instance the cease-fires to facilitate immunisation campaigns– have also provided support to Bandura's thesis that mass media are more effective when backed by complementary activities on the ground. In a country as large, as remote and as dangerous as Afghanistan, this support can only be delivered sparingly. So the role of radio, which reaches into the homes of most Afghans, remains essential.

Ultimately, the question remains as to whether the Afghan broadcasting experience is relevant in other conflict and post-conflict areas. All situations are unique, and the Afghan trust of the BBC is not replicated everywhere though it is, for instance, in Somalia where listening figures to the BBC are also very high. But a convincing case can be made that people with access to radios do respond to solutions-oriented entertaining programmes, particularly those in their own vernacular languages, which reflect their lives and with which they can identify. In Botswana, a country facing HIV/AIDS prevalence rates of between 30% and 40%, a new radio soap opera attracted two thirds of the country's young people as regular listeners within 18 months of starting, despite there being no history of soap operas in the Setswana language. The evidence is that the show is positively influencing attitudes and behaviour on HIV/AIDS[19]. Organisations such as Search for Common Ground can point to the positive impact of radio drama on national broadcasters in places such as Burundi and Sierra Leone. Radio-based social education projects have mushroomed over the past decade, with the BBC World Service establishing a trust to promote and implement new projects of this kind[20]. With the help of improved satellite delivery systems, deregulation of broadcasting and new digital technology, it seems that the humble transistor radio receiver still has an important part to play in "socially useful" communication with the poor, the remote and those afflicted by war.

Lessons learned

What lessons, then, can be learned from the experiences of broadcasting to Afghanistan during wartime and in the immediate post-conflict period?

19 Makgabaneng Quantitative Survey, CDC, Atlanta, 2002.
20 For a fuller analysis of radio soap operas see Myers (2002).

1   International broadcasters can have considerable influence during wartime, if they are credible and produce relevant socially useful programmes that are entertaining as well as informative. It is important to be close enough to the situation to undertake the necessary rolling research and consultation so the listening audience's social needs are constantly reflected.

2   If they are well produced and transmitted in good quality at prime time, radio programmes can change perceptions and behaviour *on their own* without the "the resources and positive incentives" supporting them which Bandura discusses. The evidence from Afghanistan is that having interpersonal contact to reinforce the issues is a great help, for instance in the anecdote from the healthworker and the national immunisation days cited above. But the impact of radio alone is striking in the case of the mines awareness campaign evaluated by CIET international, and from the BBC AEP's own monitoring reports.

3   Partnerships with aid organisations and/or government are important in terms of verifying the accuracy of programmes, and in service delivery –such as school or teacher education, immunisation or mines clearance.

4   The media being based close to the conflict is important for many reasons: keeping abreast of events which can be fast changing; choosing the appropriate aid organisation with whom to collaborate –some are better informed and more professional than others; having access to listeners for monitoring and needs assessment; and for recruiting staff who have a close understanding of what most concerns the population.

5   Drama –and especially soap opera– is an effective means through which to provide socially useful information. Role modelling through carefully researched characters can be a powerful influence on listeners. But it is comparatively expensive to produce, and there is a danger that it can be misused, hence the need for thorough prior research and continuous monitoring of impact.

6   Use of everyday language is all-important –people identify with not only what is said but *how* it is said. This may mean arbitrating between different dialects, and teaching actors how to read colloquial rather than formal texts. In radio social communications, it is vital to write for the voice in an accessible way.

7   The structuring of information –key messages– in drama or a long running series like *It's Great to Learn,* and then monitoring whether the listeners are absorbing it, is vital to a successful outcome. Careful planning is needed to sequence information and issues for each audience.

8   Priority target audiences have to be identified in advance and the impact of programming on them has to be monitored regularly, and

passed on to the production team so they can adjust the programmes if required. The monitoring team should also identify the specific needs of the target audiences which the programmes can address.

9   Broadcasters have to ensure, as far as possible, that the target audiences have access to the programmes This implies determining in advance when the best time for radio listening is, and whether the target groups have ready access to radios. Also providing audible radio frequencies at the appropriate time on radio stations that are seen as being credible –something which again has to be researched in advance

10 In deregulating the media, it is important to provide sustained, long-term help in production to independent community-based radio stations, etc., so they can enable communication and work with listeners to provide socially useful programming, rather than be simply mouthpieces for local vested interests

In the immediate post-conflict period, providers of socially useful radio programming need to establish links with government broadcasters and other relevant ministries –for instance health or education– in addition to links with aid organisations. Often, government ideas will be traditional, and capacity building activities are needed to update old ideas. Difficulties can result from territorial jealousies, bureaucracy and corruption, and the process is likely to take time. But it is important that new governments should assume a degree of ownership if the initiative is to endure beyond the end of the project. And it is important that domestic broadcasters are helped to assume greater responsibility for socially useful radio programming.

Chapter 23

From the Sandinista revolution to telenovelas: the case of *Puntos de Encuentro*

Clemencia Rodríguez

Every two months María Castillo and Esperancita Núñez cover the long distance between their cities and Managua, the national capital. María travels south,
from Chinandega near the Honduran border; her journey begins when she rides
a bus for 120 kilometers to the capital. Esperancita travels north, from Rivas, near
the border with Costa Rica; although only 100 kilometers, her trek can take much
longer, due to the frequent impassable conditions of the road.

The city's busy streets welcome María and Esperancita with the swel-
tering, sticky noise of a million Nicas trying to navigate buses, bicycles, and horse-
pulled carts. The two women find their way to *Puntos de Encuentro* (*Puntos*), a
feminist non-governmental organization (NGO) where *La Boletina*[1] is published
four times a year since 1991 (*Puntos de Encuentro* 1997b, 4). Their journey's
objective is to pick up bundles of the recently published new issue of *La Boletina*,
a magazine designed to support and strengthen Nicaragua's women's movements. María packs her bundles into a taxi and heads for the station where, with
some help from the driver, she loads them in the bus for their return to
Chinandega. Once there, *La Boletina* will be distributed for free to dozens of
other NGOs, women's organizations, and collectives. Esperancita will do the same
in the southern region. These two women are part of a network of twenty
women who come to Managua from the departmental capitals throughout the

1 *La Boletina* is a play of words on the Spanish word for "newsletter", which is "boletín", always in the
masculine.

national territory to collect twenty-six thousand issues of *La Boletina* to be distributed to 500 organizations in the country.

Each issue of *La Boletina* contains numerous sections, articles, and announcements by women's organizations and collectives different from *Puntos*. More than *Puntos'* organizational newsletter, *La Boletina* is a magazine made available to Nicaragua's progressive social movements by *Puntos*. Using *La Boletina* as their communication vehicle, social movements can move various issues into public arenas, from gender roles and homophobia to hierarchical relationships between adults and youth. *La Boletina* illustrates well the communication for social change style of *Puntos de Encuentro*. Like *La Boletina*, *Puntos de Encuentro*'s communication initiatives are deeply connected with Nicaraguan progressive social movements. Also, like *La Boletina*, the goal of *Puntos de Encuentro* is to break into Nicaraguan contemporary cultural fabric with alternative proposals. In the following pages I intend to document the exceptional work of *Puntos de Encuentro* in the area of communication for social change.

Puntos de Encuentro can easily be classified as an entertainment-education (E-E) NGO. *Puntos* is a non-profit organization that produces entertainment media to effect change in Nicaragua's society; *Puntos* conducts fomative and summative research and evaluation in order to design and assess communication processes; *Puntos* carefully designs fictional characters and plots that address problematic health and lifestyle issues. Thus, at first sight, *Puntos* follows step by step the procedures generally described as essential to the communication strategy labeled entertainment-education (Singhal et al, 2004; Papa et al, 2000; Singhal and Rogers, 2002; Singhal and Rogers, 1999; Nariman, 1993). However, in the following pages I intend to demonstrate how, at the level of its communication approach, *Puntos de Encuentro* differs from traditional E-E. I want to propose that if we limit the analysis to the description of communication strategies and research methodologies, the work of an organization such as *Puntos* will fit the formulas of traditional E-E. However, if we delve into philosophical foundations around issues of communication, culture, and social change, *Puntos'* project comes into view with all its distinctiveness.

The goal of this chapter is twofold: first, to document the history of *Puntos de Encuentro* as a communication for social change non-governmental organization of the global south; and, second, to analyze *Puntos de Encuentro*'s philosophical approach to communication, culture, and social change.

Puntos is born out of a sense of malaise

In 1979 the Sandinista revolution swept through Nicaragua and transformed the social, political, and cultural fabric of this nation with the force of a hurricane. The revolution, led by the FSLN (Frente Sandinista de Liberación Nacional), was itself a hybrid of socialist agendas, progressive Catholicism, popular culture, and fascinating class alliances. After the triumph of the Sandinistas in 1979, Nicaraguans, together with thousands of foreigners[2] who had converged in the country to be a part of this utopian society still to be designed, rolled up their sleeves and proceeded to re-invent the entire social fabric, from a half socialized, half capitalist mixed economy, to a Ministry of Culture led by a Jesuit priest whose main goal was to make a poet of every Nicaraguan[3].

Finding themselves the center of this turmoil, three women, Ana Criquillion, Vilma Castillo, and Olga María Espinoza, experienced the complexity of implementing a utopia in reality. As with many other Nicaraguans, they found that the progressive, egalitarian agendas of Sandinista ideology clashed with the oppressive, authoritarian, and even dictatorial everyday practices embodied by Sandinistas themselves in their interpersonal relations. These women found that one thing was to believe in an abstract utopia, but that the challenge to implement it in the quotidian was a much more difficult task. While many Nicaraguans succumbed to the sense of malaise provoked by a revolution that had been unable to dissolve oppressive everyday cultural practices, these three women decided to re-direct their work toward the transformation of everyday life: "Our interest in transforming power relations in daily life arose of not wanting [the revolution] to remain an abstract idea but to be embodied in the ways we interact" (quoted in Hernández and Campanile, 2000: 2).

From these personal herstories rose the need to create an institution able to crystallize the utopia of a quotidian practice free of hierarchical and oppressive power relationships. This is the origin, in 1991, of *Puntos de Encuentro* (literally Meeting Points and figuratively Common Ground). *Puntos'* slogan is "para transformar la vida cotidiana", or "to transform daily life". *Puntos de Encuentro* was created as "a feminist social change organization dedicated to promote individual and collective autonomy and empowerment of young people and women" (*Puntos de Encuentro*, 1997b: 1). *Puntos* defines its mission in the following terms: "to promote equal rights and opportunities for everyone regardless of age, sex, class, race, sexual orientation, physical or mental disability and any other social condition. We believe that no condition should be the source of discrimination or oppression, and that the different oppressions are interrelated and must be addressed as such in order to combat the structural injustices and violence in our society" (*Puntos de Encuentro*, 1997b: 1).

2 According to Minter (2002), "hundreds of U.S. citizens worked in Nicaragua as internacionalistas for extended periods, and tens of thousands more visited on short-term solidarity visits. Church networks and sister city programs proliferated, with many being sustained into the 1990s and the current era, long after the FSLN's electoral defeat" (18). This is an important piece of data since Amy Bank, one of the earliest members of *Puntos* and current co-director, came from her native California to help build revolutionary Nicaragua.

3 From 1979 to 1988 a Roman Catholic priest –Ernesto Cardenal– became Nicaragua's minister of Culture. Cardenal believed that, given the opportunity, every human being could produce art. During his ministry, hundreds of poetry workshops were offered even in the most isolated provinces; the result was an exceptional movement of popular poetry written by peasants, farmers, children, the elderly. Cardenal's office at the time was a bathroom in the mansion of former dictator Anastasio Somoza's mistress, (for more on the Sandinista revolution see Walker, 1985. For more on Cardenal's approach to culture see Ministerio de Cultura, 1982 and Dore, 1985).

Puntos de Encuentro: not just another NGO

Puntos de Encuentro emerges from the realization that, in Foucault's words, power is capillary (Foucault, 1972, 1978). According to Foucault, power, or the force to shape the environment according to one's desire, operates not only at the levels of authorities, public arenas, and politicians, but more importantly at the level of everyday life. That is, hierarchies determining inclusions and exclusions are created and maintained by thousands of human interactions performed in everyday life. The hierarchy man/woman, for example, is maintained by minute "common sense" interactions, such as a man opening the door for the woman, deciding when they're going to have sex, or hitting her when she doesn't "behave."

From its origin, *Puntos de Encuentro* assumed an approach to social change based on the need to question and to transform everyday life interaction that legitimizes oppressive power hierarchies. The everyday, the quotidian, became *Puntos'* arena of struggle.

One of the features that makes *Puntos de Encuentro* unique is its founders' goal to create an institution that attempts to practice what it preaches. In other words, *Puntos'* institutional design embodies the aspiration for an everyday life in which women, men, the young and not-so-young meet as equals to join forces toward common goals. *Puntos'* janitors, driver, secretaries, professionals, and directors come from a world where title, class, gender, race, and age predetermine their place in a social hierarchy. However, once they cross the threshold dividing *Puntos* from the outside world, they come into an environment that purposefully attempts to challenge traditional hierarchies while developing clear and transparent criteria and procedures for decision-making and accountability to the collective. For example, a recent meeting to deal with a financial crisis involved Miguel, a man hired in 1993 as *Puntos'* driver, and Ana, a founding member and executive director. At *Puntos*, while hierarchies are not entirely absent, authority is established on the basis of skills, experience, and level of commitment with the institution, and not necessarily by title or position (Arostegui and Carrión, 1997: 7)[4]. In the words of Ana Criquillion, founder of *Puntos*: "this means denying oneself privileges at the personal level… being the director does not mean you need a bigger office, a company car… or to have the last word" (quoted in Hernandez and Campanile, 2000: 8).

Puntos de Encuentro emerged as a feminist NGO not only on account of its effort toward gender equity in Nicaragua, but also in its attempt to infuse the organization itself with feminist characteristics; thus, *Puntos'* feminist stand becomes apparent in its nurturing work environment; in terms of its first director Ana Criquillion: "I believe that what we have done in these years of crisis, the fact

4 In general, in Latin America, there is a difference between "mixed" organizations that may or may not have a "gender perspective" and "feminist" organizations, which are usually all women. *Puntos* wanted to create a new kind of institution, an explicitly feminist organization that would be mixed from the beginning, so that men could be part of a feminist project and culture, meaning that traditional gender hierarchies would be challenged explicitly from the beginning.

that we managed to maintain an institution with such a level of solidarity, of caring, of being able to count on one another is a real accomplishment" (*Puntos de Encuentro*, 2002: 24).

Puntos' success in creating an alternative everyday life within its institutional walls is due to its ability to produce a counter-culture; that is, a culture that questions established meanings, and "common sense truths". *Puntos'* organizational culture cultivates the notion that there are not fixed truths, and that the same phenomenon can be interpreted as good or bad, depending on the context: "one of the things we learned was to appreciate and to value each and every one of us, including the defects [...] that is, we learned to take advantage of everything we are in order to meet our goals; we learned to see that even our limitations can be of value in certain situations..." (*Puntos de Encuentro*, 2002: 23).

Puntos' approach to communication for social change

In 1991 *Puntos* embarked in the task of transforming everyday life among Nicaraguan women, men, adults, children, and youth. *Puntos* defines its goal as dismantling oppressive, unequal power relationships in which men dominate women, or adults rule the lives and decisions of younger ones. *Puntos de Encuentro* assumes that oppressive power relationships are legitimized by local cultures transmitted from one generation to another via collective and individual memory. For example, a father hits his child because his individual memory and the collective imagination of Nicaraguans associate hitting a child with disciplining a child. That is, the meaning associated with the behavior of hitting a child is legitimized as something not only normal, but desirable. *Puntos'* role is to question the connection between the behavior (hitting) and the meaning of the behavior (disciplining), and to propose a new connection, for example that hitting –even for "well-intentioned" reasons, is oppressive, disrespectful, and counterproductive parenting.

Puntos operates at the level of symbolic meanings that traditional Nicaraguan cultures have assigned to different human interactions, and attempts to question such meanings. Puntos, in other words, is an organization dedicated to the transformation of everyday life's oppressive cultural practices. Because *Puntos* does not define its target as the transformation of behaviors, but the transformation of cultural norms, its approach to social change is collective and not individual-based (Gumucio-Dagron, 2001). Cultural meanings are defined collectively and therefore have to be deconstructed and reconfigured by the collective. *Puntos* shares the Freirean assumption that each individual should participate fully in shaping her/his own destiny; thus *Puntos* works toward the concientization and empowerment of individuals who will in turn collectively dismantle dominating cultures and re-invent new forms of more equitable interaction.

Traditional approaches to E-E emerge from an understanding of communication for social change as one-directional persuasive communication directed to an individual and intended to effect behavioral or attitudinal change in that individual (Singhal and Rogers, 1989, 1999; Nariman, 1993; Kincaid, 2002; Slater and Rouner, 2002; Piotrow and de Fossard, 2004). The goal of traditional E-E is to persuade target audiences to adopt prosocial behaviors or attitudes; Singhal and Rogers (1999), for example, defined the role of communication for social change in the following terms: "to influence audience awareness, attitudes, and behaviors toward a socially desirable end" (9), or "to promote *good* behavior and to dissuade *bad* behaviors"(Sabido, quoted in Singhal and Rogers, 1999· 53, my emphasis). Within this framework, interventions are designed to promote certain attitudes and behaviors pre-defined as socially desirable or good.

The design of traditional E-E revolves around a formula in which a prosocial behavior is predefined by the producers; characters and storylines are developed around the adoption of the desirable "good" behavior; characters are divided between those who accept to adopt the prosocial behavor, those who reject it, and those who are uncertain (Sabido, 2004: 70). Then "[during] the course of the soap opera, each of these three basic groups of characters will interact and create circumstances that will result in their moving closer to or farther away from the proposed social behavior. When characters move closer to the proposed social behavior, they are visibly rewarded. Likewise, when they move away from the proposed behavior, they are visibly punished" (Nariman, 1993: 63). Some examples of traditional E-E include "a wise father who spaced his family and prospered versus the foolish father with many children who could not pay for food" (Piotrow and de Fossard, 2004: 44); or a man who dies from AIDS while his brother, who decides to adopt the prosocial behavior, is rewarded with a good family life (Kincaid, 2002).

The theoretical foundation of traditional E-E is Bandura's social cognitive theory of individual and social change (Bandura, 2004). Built on an understanding of human change as cause/effect, unidirectional, and fairly controlable processes, Bandura's theory is entirely absent from *Puntos de Encuentro*'s conceptual foundations.

Puntos de Encuentro takes a very different approach to social change. According to *Puntos* "societies have to decide for themselves how to change"; therefore, more than prescribing certain behaviors, *Puntos* intervenes by encouraging "a coherent critique of traditional and official discourses" (Bradshaw and *Puntos de Encuentro*, 2001: 1) and a dialogue around alternative proposals. Instead of zeroing in on a specific "good" behavior, *Puntos* sees its role as a facilitator of a communication space where taken-for-granted traditional practices can be questioned and where alternative cultural practices can be presented, considered, and discussed. *Puntos* generates a communication space where excluded or marginalized alternatives have a chance to become central, to be incorporated into social fabric, to become "common sense". *Puntos* is proud to "remove taboo subjects from 'the closet' onto the public agenda and mainstream consciousness" (Bradshaw and *Puntos de Encuentro*, 2001: 1). Issues such as rape, homosexuality, and abortion, considered taboo in Nicaragua, have been boldly tackled by *Puntos*. Instead of targeting individuals with prescriptions, *Puntos'* goal is to disrupt Nicaragua's cultural fabric and everyday life world.

Puntos de Encuentro generates communication processes that do not reify the hierarchy between the active producers of messages pre-defined as socially desirable, and the passive receivers of those messages. The goal of *Puntos* is not that Nicaraguan audiences adopt its messages, but instead that alternative interpretations of reality have a chance to be a part of a national conversation. Thus, instead of prescribing specific behaviors to be adopted by individuals[5], *Puntos'* communication processes propose new cultural articulations and symbolic codifications. *Puntos* messages tend to be open ended, intended to be considered and discussed collectively according to each community's social, economic, and cultural context.

Equally important, alternative interpretations pushed forward by *Puntos* communication processes emerge from Nicaragua's progressive social movements, not just from a small group of "expert" decision-makers. In other words, *Puntos* sees its role as a communicator who takes –otherwise marginal– alternative cultural options from Nicaragua's progressive social movements and situates them at the center of the public arena. Thus, these options can be openly discussed, considered, deliberated, and contemplated by Nicaraguans.

Puntos pursues the goal of transforming everyday life oppressive practices on two fronts: first, questioning mainstream traditional meanings and encouraging the discussion of alternative options; and second, strengthening collective struggles toward social and cultural change. Because it understands social and cultural change as collective processes, not as individual behavioral change, *Puntos* is deeply anchored in Nicaragua's progressive social movements. Humberto Abaunza (2001) defines one of *Puntos'* main strategies as: "to strengthen the capacity of social movements to shape public policy" (1).

Recent proposals in the field of development communication scholarship posit the rich potential of social movements' theory to move the field away from early modernization theories (Huesca, 2001). According to Huesca (2001), new social movements are "heterogenous groups forming outside of formal institutions and operating in discontinous cycles to forge collective meanings and identities that direct action" (421); new social movements emerge from the discontent of citizens who distrust traditional institutions (such as labor organizations and political parties) to bring about social, political, and cultural change. New social movements (i.e., women's movements, ethnic minority movements, human rights, environmentalists, etc.) emerge as citizens form groups that allow them to re-define collective identities and visions for the future. These identities and visions serve as forces that drive collective action and collective social change.

5 Behaviors defined as socially desirable by traditional E-E include spacing/limiting family, breastfeeding, avoiding risky sexual behavior, washing hands before eating, keeping fingernails short, valuing girls education, or using certain parental skills (Piotrow and de Fossard, 2004: 41).

It is at the level of meanings that can be fed into these identities and visions that *Puntos de Encuentro* understands its intervention.

Puntos produces new meanings that, carried by campaigns, media, and other forms of interpersonal and mass communication, become the raw material of collective dialogues among Nicaraguans. These communication processes are in turn supported with *Puntos'* initiatives that connect social movements, build alliances among different social movements (for example gay, women's, and youth social movements), confront a conservative status quo[6], and connect local social movements with global movements for social justice.

Working within this framework, *Puntos de Encuentro* maintains a mix of different communication strategies that work in a well integrated manner: research and communication, movement building, advocacy, and education.

Research and campaigns

In 1999 *Puntos* embarked on one of its most innovative campaigns: a campaign targeting Nicaraguan men against masculine violence in the family. For a Latin American feminist NGO to channel significant resources and energy toward men was as exceptional as it was controversial (Rivera, 2000: 25). The campaign emerged from a research study about the connection between masculine identity and male violence against women in Nicaragua completed by *Puntos* (*Puntos de Encuentro*, 1998a: 9)[7]. Here again, *Puntos'* participation in social movements proved essential. Since its early days, *Puntos* had cultivated the formation of The Men-Against-Violence Group. Thanks to this alliance with the Men's Group, *Puntos* had access to over 200 local grassroots organizations and 700 volunteers to conduct the study (*Puntos de Encuentro*, 1999: 6).

At the end of October 1998 Hurricane Mitch devastated Nicaragua with a series of floods, mud slides, loss of crops, houses, animals, roads, and bridges. Several thousand Nicaraguans lost their lives, and tens of thousands more lost their homes. Knowing well that masculine violent behavior intensifies in post-natural disaster phases, *Puntos* decided to connect its 1999 campaign to Hurricane Mitch. The campaign built on several main ideas: first, that violence against women constitutes a "disaster" in terms of damage to people and society; that unlike a hurricane, which is a natural phenomenon, male violence is not "natural" or unavoidable, it is totally within men's control to avoid. And finally, that a family free of violence would contribute to the social and economic reconstruction of the country[8]. With this campaign *Puntos* offered an alternative articulation of Nicaraguan masculinity, away from the interpretation of "man" as a

---

6 What *Puntos* called "the ideological counter-offensive."

7 The reseach report was published as "Nadando contra la corriente: buscando pistas para prevenir la violencia masculina en las relaciones de pareja" [Swimming Upstream: seeking clues to prevent masculine violence in couples].

8 The campaign slogan was "La violencia contra las mujeres: un desastre que los hombres SÍ podemos evitar" [Violence against women: a disaster that as men we CAN prevent].

creature of violent nature and closer to "man" as a person who needs to decide if abussive behavior in the family will be or not part of his repertoire.

Enlisting once more the talent of McCann Erickson, *Puntos* designed a multimedia strategy that included television, radio, and printed materials[9]. In order to capitalize the lesson learned during the previous campaign, *Puntos* designed communication materials to be used at the local level by hundreds of grassroots organizations and collectives that form Nicaragua's gender social movements; the materials were to be used as part of these groups' conscientization and mobilization activities, therefore they became central to hundreds of interpersonal and group communication activities. The materials included a booklet to facilitate workshops on masculine violence in the family, 3,000 caps and 5,000 calendars to be distributed among workshop participants.

Puntos succeeded in forming alliances with 250 local grassroots organizations, NGOs, local governments, local media, and local journalists to participate in the "masculine violence as disaster" campaign. However, instead of using these organizations as instruments to implement its campaign, *Puntos* encouraged them to develop their own communication initiatives around the theme of masculine abussive behavior and to connect with the campaign without losing their own identities. As a result, a myriad of other communication processes, including different campaign materials, songs, theatre, banners, cultural events, and workshops were implemented in each regional and cultural context (*Puntos de Encuentro*, 2000: 9).

Reflecting on this experience, *Puntos* notes how this type of work empowers local civil society and its social movements by building bridges among local organizations, linking local organizations to a national social movement, and legitimizing grassroots organizations as they become more visible among their local constituencies when associated with a national and high profile campaign (*Puntos de Encuentro*, 2000: 36). In addition, *Puntos* came to understand the enormous demand for well designed and produced communication materials that local groups could use in their own creative ways but lacked the know-how or the resources to produce their own.

The campaign was evaluated using pre- and post-campaign surveys with samples of 2,000 men each, and a post-campaign survey among 660 women; also a series of pre and post in-depth interviews was conducted. According to the quantitative data, men exposed to the campaign said the messages helped them self-reflect (40%), improved life with their spouse (29%), and provided new information (18%). Eighty-five percent of the men exposed to the campaign said men changed as a result of exposure; 76% of the women surveyed agreed (*Puntos de Encuentro*, 2000: 32).

9 The campaign included two 35' TV spots, four radio 30' spots, 76,000 posters, 75,000 stickers, 75,000 educational brochures, and eleven billboards displayed on the main cross-roads throughout the country. Radio and TV spots ammounted to approximately 500 TV transmissions and 17,200 radio transmissions (*Puntos de Encuentro*, 2000: 7).

Television E-E

Since the mid 1990s, feeling the limitation of short-lived campaigns to maintain its presence in an on going national dialogue, *Puntos* began exploring the possibility of using the media to maintain an uninterrupted conversation with national audiences. Knowing that Nicaraguans "have a TV set before they have running water or a floor" (Amy Bank as quoted in Miller 2002), and that telenovelas are the preferred media genre in the country, *Puntos* decided to explore the possibility of producing a television drama. The idea was to use a legitimate medium such as television to maintain an "ideological counter-offensive" in the form of proposed alternatives to the conservative status quo. To many, the idea of producing a weekly series in a country with almost no domestic television industry, no studios, no editing facilities, no script writers, no directors or producers, seemed unattainable.

For the next three years *Puntos* embarked on the Herculean task of developing the necessary human and technological resources to produce a weekly television series. Given the incipient state of Nicaragua's television industry, *Puntos* had to build everything from the ground up: from a team of scriptwriters to shooting and editing facilities. *Puntos* brought in a North American television writer to develop a team of young Nicaraguan scriptwriters; next, *Puntos* identified a team of youngsters without any acting experience and began intensive weekly training routines in different acting techniques, stage movement, and acting for the camera (*Puntos de Encuentro*, 1998b: 10).

In February of 2001, produced by Amy Bank and directed by Virginia Lacayo, the first episode of *Sexto Sentido* aired on Sunday at 4 pm. In half-hour episodes, *Sexto Sentido* develops parallel story lines about six young Nicaraguans dealing with issues of gender, sexuality, and oppressive interpersonal relationships. Maintaining an ongoing tension between oppressive relationships and individual and collective actions toward liberation and equality, the characters of *Sexto Sentido* find different ways out of traditional ideologies. In the words of Amy Bank: "essentially what we are trying to do as an organization is to take radical social and political ideas about human rights, about democracy, about respect and differences, about the right to live without violence, about discrimination... quite radical ideas, and put them out into the mainstream, totally flying in the face of traditional conservative values and what most of the media continue to promote. We want to say 'listen! you may think that these are alternative ideas, but they are not marginal', and we are going to have them all over the place, so that they become mainstream ideas" (Amy Bank as quoted in Miller, 2002).

In its first season, *Sexto Sentido*'s three young women and three young men dealt with a controlling boyfriend, teen pregnancy, homophobia, a violent father, conflicts with parents, rape, abortion, alcoholism, first-time sex, and a host of other issues. In what follows I present three elements that make *Sexto Sentido* an exceptional case of entertainment-education: first, how the work of progressive social movements and grassroots organizations informs story lines and character development; second, how each episode of *Sexto Sentido* is well grounded in Nicaragua's popular culture; and third, the use of a communication strategy that integrates mass communication with group communication and interpersonal communication.

A series of consecutive episodes of *Sexto Sentido* developed the story of Elena, a young woman living with her mother, her abusive father, and her younger siblings. As the story develops Elena experiences different phases of the cycle of domestic violence: from thinking that getting hit is "normal", and blaming herself for "provoking" her father's violent behavior, to finally deciding that she and her family deserve a life free of violence. Thus, Elena strives to make alliances with her mother in order to bring about change. At one point, a friend informs Elena of a law that defends victims of intra-family violence (Miller, 2002).

To understand the strong connection between the storyline and Nicaragua's movement against violence against women we have to go back to 1992 when the *Red de Mujeres contra la Violencia* [Women's Network Against Violence] emerged out of a newly formed national autonomous women's movement[10]. *Puntos* was an active member of this network from its origin; several *Puntos* staff helped develop the network's projects, including campaigns against family violence, and in 1994, the network had its first office in *Puntos'* building.

It is no coincidence then that two of *Sexto Sentido*'s script writers as well as the producer of the series are active members of the Women's Network Against Violence. The strong connection between *Puntos*, the network, and Nicaragua's women's movement facilitates an easy flow between grassroots initiatives and *Puntos'* media programming. Thus, when *Sexto Sentido*'s writer Erika Castillo put the last touches on a script about Elena, her character comes to life with the empathy of a writer who knows firsthand the experiences of hundreds of Nicaraguan women who survive or succumb to abussive relationships. Clearly, the legacy of organized civil society feeds the storylines of *Sexto Sentido*.

By the late 1990s the Women's Network against Violence had become a leader of the women's movement in Nicaragua. Thanks to intense and continuous efforts of advocacy, lobbying, social mobilization, and communication, the network has been able to move domestic violence from invisibility and silence into the public agenda. In 1996, the network drafted and promoted what would become Law 230, designed to protect victims of domestic violence. Still, many Nicaraguans were unaware of the law or how to use it to protect themselves. In 2001, *Puntos* and the network joined hands once again, to produce 50,000 booklets explaining Law 230, using a photo of "Elena" on the cover. At the same

10 In 1991, in a collective decision to separate the women's movement from the Sandinista women's organization (AMNLAE), Nicaraguan women leaders convened the "Fifty-two percent Festival". In a clear act of rejection of Sandinista's exclusionary party politics, the leaders held the Festival at the same time as the AMNLAE national convention. During the Festival the movement decided to call for an autonomous movement embracing different struggles for genger equity and not only Sandinista agendas. One of the first collective projects of the autonomous movement was the Red de Mujeres contra la Violencia. (CITAR CAPITULO DE ANA SOBRE HISTORIA MOVIMIENTO DE MUJERES).

time that Elena, in *Sexto Sentido*, was learning about Law 230, Nicaragua was blanketed with free booklets (Miller, 2002).

In the same manner in which *Puntos* is an active member of the Network of Women Against Violence, it participates in national networks of the AIDS movement, the youth movement, the gay and lesbian movement, the men-against-violence movement, and the women with disabilities movement, among others.

Each episode of *Sexto Sentido* is carefully crafted to connect with Nicaragua's popular imaginary. Recent scholarship on race and media reveals the extent to which Latin American media contents carry colonial messages that conceal racial hierarchies behind race myths (Wade, 2000), or reify whiteness as more desirable. In contrast, *Sexto Sentido* is produced from a profound respect for the culture and the historical experience of its audiences; in contrast with most Latin American television series, in which the main characters are white, blonde, and blue-eyed, *Sexto Sentido*'s actors and actresses reflect well Nicaragua's mestizo ethnic fabric. While *Sexto Sentido*'s sets are more "posh" than the majority of Nicaraguans' milieu, they are designed to capture the everyday life of the working class majority.

According to Miguel Sabido, the founding father of E-E soap operas, "[t]he major problems of mankind can only be solved if the large masses of population in developing countries behave in a socially useful manner" (Sabido, 2004: 73)[11]. Far from this patronizing attitude, so common in traditional E-E, *Sexto Sentido* embraces the popular, in the sense that Jesús Martin Barbero (1993) gives to the term, and proposes new directions in which local cultures can grow. While it is common for E-E projects to conduct formative research into the everyday lives of target communities as "merely a tool for pretesting preconceived concepts and images with the target audience" (McKee et al, 2004: 339), *Puntos* assumes Nicaragua's popular cultures as its own historical context and therefore its own battle-ground. Instead of positioning itself as an outsider sender of finished truths, with *Sexto Sentido Puntos* joins the national conversation as an equal participant with radical proposals.

In its efforts to move the boundaries of what is considered legitimate within Nicaraguan cultures, *Puntos* has made great strides in different areas of the everyday world. Using television drama to express the legitimacy, beauty, and dignity of the experience of the mestizo working and lower middle classes, *Puntos* has sent messages that question hierarchies established around class and race. With characters that subvert traditional gender and age relationships, *Puntos* proposes a different option to establish relationships among different genders and age groups. *Sexto Sentido* portrays the first non-caricatured gay character in the histo-

---

11 It is beyond the scope of this analysis to cuestion the validity of this statement with factual information; however, the ease with which Sabido blames people from the global south for "the problems of mankind" while exonerating the north's corporate sector and lifestyles based on never-ending consumption, is worrisome.

ry of Nicaragua's popular cultures, a character that allows audiences to visualize a social fabric devoid of homophobia. With the character of Elena, *Sexto Sentido* introduces an alternative interpretation of domestic abuse not as a necessary evil that women and children have to accept because "that's the way men are" but as an oppressive practice, and the target of Nicaragua's women's movement. Through Elena's exploits, audiences learn that hundreds of Nicaraguans with a different vision for their society have organized around a women's movement that strives for harsher laws against abussive men, better resources for survivors of domestic violence, and a different cultural codification of masculinity.

I believe one of *Puntos'* future challenges is to move these boundaries still further in the area of race, by addressing issues of blackness and indigenous cultures and their integration (or not) into a multicultural nation. *Puntos* has begun moving in this direction by introducing Johnson, a young Afro-Nicaraguan, and Shevony, a young half Creole and half Miskito woman from Puerto Cabezas as *Sexto Sentido's* main characters.

Capitalizing from past lessons on the virtues of an integral communication strategy that combines E-E and mass communication with social mobilization through group and interpersonal communication, *Puntos* implemented a complex series of communication processes to broaden and intensify the dialogue incited by *Sexto Sentido*. This strategy, called *Somos Diferentes, Somos Iguales* [We are Different, We are Equal], includes a radio talk-show, published materials (such as the Law 230 booklet), workshops, and discussion groups.

Radio Sexto Sentido[12], *Puntos'* radio call-in show, produced by youth for youth, planned its programming to parallel *Sexto Sentido's* story lines; by calling in, young Nicaraguans can discuss the characters' experiences and decisions with *Sexto Sentido's* actors and actresses and with other callers.

Moreover, the entire cast of *Sexto Sentido* travels throughout the country to facilitate discussions, workshops organized by social movements in hundreds of localities. Here, in small groups, young Nicaraguans have access to communication spaces where they can question traditional discourses on gender, sexual identity, and oppressive interpersonal relationships. Thanks to these newly found communication spaces, many youth are able to break out of isolation; they find other youth asking the same questions, experiencing the same feelings; ultimately, they find community.

Interpersonal communication as social mobilization

Perhaps one of the features that makes *Puntos* an exceptional communication for social change NGO is its ability to maintain a line of work in social mobilization and interpersonal/group communication parallel to, and integrated with, its

12 *Radio Sexto Sentido* transmits Monday through Friday on *Radio Universidad* (national coverage) and nine local radio stations throughout the country. *Radio Sexto Sentido* has a fan club with 143 members as of 2000. The target audience of *Radio Sexto Sentido* is Nicaraguans between the ages of 13 and 25.

campaigns and media programming. Grounded in the profound belief that social change is brought about collectively and not via individual change exclusively, *Puntos* believes that movement building and advocacy are important aspects of its mission.

La Universidad de las Mujeres [The Women's University] was developed by *Puntos* as a way to create a space where leaders of the women's movements, as well as non-organized women[13], could learn and grow. Constantly offering short courses on themes such as "Gender and Development", "Power relationships: Sexism and adultism", or "Introduction to electronic mail", the university draws hundreds of women (and men) into this space of analysis and reflection. An important aspect of the university is its program on masculinity, a space for men to discuss, reflect, and question traditional notions of masculinity. *Puntos'* leadership youth camps are part of this same line of action. The camps convene hundreds of youth leaders for workshops, discussions, and panels frequently tied into *Puntos'* media messages[14].

Maintaining these communication spaces where small groups interact, discuss, reflect, and question has made *Puntos* into an organization that understands change as a multifaceted process involving not only interaction with the media, but also a complex mesh of interactions between an individual and his/her community, with his/her self image, and with his/her community's image of him/herself. Elsewhere, E-E scholars have emphasized the role of interpersonal communication in processes of social change (Papa et al, 2000; Piotrow and de Fossard, 2004; La Pastina, Patel, Schiavo, 2004). Still, we need to maintain clear distinctions between E-E projects that use interpersonal communication to further the influence of pre-defined socially desirable behaviors (Abdulla, 2004) and E-E projects that include social mobilization via interpersonal and group communication as part of their agenda. Soul City in South Africa (Usdin et al, 2004), *Puntos de Encuentro* in Nicaragua, and *Meena* in South India (McKee et al, 2004) are clear cases of E-E that take on advocacy and social mobilization as part of their agenda to strengthen progressive social movements. In these cases, interpersonal and group communication are implemented to foster discussion of alternative articulations of social reality, not as vehicles to move prosocial media messages deeper into community and intimate spheres.

Conclusion: theory from smart practice

Traditionally communication scholars think development communication theory as the product of academics. According to this traditional formula, a scholar affiliated with a university (generally located in the global North) conducts research about processes of communication for social change, E-E, or development com-

---

13 Non-organized women refers to women who do not participate in any social movement, grassroot initiative, or collective.

14 Due to shrinking funding by international donors, *Puntos* has had to reduce many of these projects.

munication (generally located in the global South); novel theoretical approaches emerge from data analysis, which are, in turn, applied by governmental or non-governmental organizations in their development communication projects. In these pages I have tried to show how, as development communication scholars and practitioners, we need to look outside of the formula in order to appreciate how theory can emerge from the practice of a smart and creative Central American NGO.

Indeed, *Puntos* has developed substantial theoretical insights into communication for social change. Grounded on complex epistemological reflection on how change happens in communities, *Puntos* articulates local cultures as the product of constantly evolving discourses-in-interaction. As they interact, social discourses engage in processes of domination, resistance, and negotiation; in each of these processes, cultural meanings are produced, circulated, and consumed (Geertz, 1973). It is these cultural meanings that make social reality intelligible, therefore alternative visions of society presuppose alternative cultural meanings. It is through the processes of production and circulation of meaning that behaviors, attitudes, and beliefs are either sanctioned or de-legitimized. From this perspective, *Puntos* perceives its role as an outspoken participant of a national conversation in which meanings circulate, gain legitimacy, or become marginal. *Puntos*' counter-cultural or alternative proposals circulate into the national dialogue via the mass media (radio, television, print, billboards, posters, etc.), interpersonal and small group communication (*Universidad de las Mujeres*, youth leadership training, participation in social movements), and even public relations (lobbying). *Puntos*' proposals resonate then from one realm of national life to another, including public forums (social movements' street demonstrations, rallies, marches, etc.), public spaces (billboards), public arenas (lobbying), family media spheres (radio listening, television viewing), small groups (camps, workshops), and even intra-personal communication (reading and reflecting).

Puntos feeds not only the national conversation, but also innumerable other parallel conversations at the local level, the community level, and the family level. *Puntos*' strong connections with local NGOs and collectives allow the organization to bring its messages to local forums and, at the same time, to stay in touch with regional differences. *Puntos* is very aware of strong regional and local differences, and participates in each of these conversations, paying attention to each distinct interlocutor. Although *Puntos* generates messages of national coverage, this NGO does not adopt the one-message-fits-all approach, which blankets national audiences with a single message and discounts ensuing distinct local dialogues. As local NGOs and collectives appropriate its materials, *Puntos*' national messages trigger countless local and distinct communication processes as important as the process of national diffusion, if not more so. *Puntos* devotes much energy, time, and resources to its active participation in these local processes.

Finally, *Puntos* integrates two dimensions of social change traditionally operating separate from each other: E-E and mobilization. Historically, E-E has been in the hands of development communication organizations, governmental institutions, and communication scholars. Mobilization has been the forte of organized civil society, social movements, grassroots organizations, and political science scholars. In *Puntos*, these two spheres operate in an integral manner, assuming a dialectical relationship between communication and mobilization[15]. In fact, one of *Puntos'* present and future challenges rests in navigating people's expectations as it cannot easily be labeled as a social movement, a development communication organization, or an NGO (Rivera, 2000).

As a participant of national dialogues on gender, youth, and sexual identities, *Puntos* contributes to this conversation in several different ways. *Puntos* produces counter-cultural messages that otherwise would not have a chance to be considered, discussed, and reflected on by most Nicaraguans. In an attempt to build bridges and to find common ground with others, *Puntos* maintains its cultural counter-offensive as a way to drive a wedge into the status quo by deconstructing conservative discourse and analyzing its implications for people and their well-being, and then offering alternatives. And finally, *Puntos* serves as a catalyst of personal, intra-family, local, regional, and national conversations that would not exist otherwise.

Looking into the future, *Puntos* faces several serious challenges. First, maintaining its idiosyncratic organizational culture was easier as a small NGO. Today, *Puntos* has grown to include a whole television production team, a research team, and the staff necessary to support all other projects, hence preserving its egalitarian spirit becomes more difficult. Second, as I mentioned before, *Puntos* will need to confront at some point the fact that many Nicaraguan communities have been historically excluded from most national, regional, and local conversations. Nicaragua has paid lip service to the notion of being a multi-ethnic, multi-lingual nation, but in reality Miskito, Mayangna (Sumu), Garifuna, Rama, and Afro-Nicaraguan communities have been "erased" from the national imaginary. The challenge, for *Puntos*, will be how to reverse this erasure without losing its national audiences; that is, how to integrate languages, ethnicities, and cultures that mestizo Nicaraguans deem "uninteresting" without losing its appeal[16].

Finally, I am left perplexed by how the changing winds of international development aid has made it hard for even the most enthusiastic of international donors to support *Puntos de Encuentro*. In 2002, precisely at the time when it had matured into an exceptional communication for social change NGO at the global level, able to integrate research and practice, capable of articulating the local with the national and the global, and skillful enough to produce some of

---

15 One of *Puntos* internal documents reads: "we need to always remember that television is not a medium that mobilizes" (*Puntos de Encuentro*, 1997a: 28).

16 In words of Amy Bank: "This is definitely a challenge: for example, now that we have main characters from the Coast in Sexto Sentido, there will be some dialogue in Creole English and possibly eventually in Miskito as well. We'll have to put sub-titles in Spanish. But not all our viewers are literate... so we're going to have access issues no matter what" (Bank, 2003).

the most innovative communication for social change strategies in the region, *Puntos* found itself in a financial crisis that almost resulted in having to close its doors. Some of *Puntos'* stable donors have a policy that after ten years of continuous funding, it is time for a change. Other donors have had reductions in their Latin American budgets, turning their attention to other parts of the world. Nicaraguan NGOs in general have also suffered donor pullouts due to lack of confidence in a government known for its corruption. The changing trends in aid programs mean that even enthusiastic donors can not find the right "pocket" of funds from which to support *Puntos*, since its work defies easy categorization. And finally, many donors are under pressure to invest in projects that apply replicable formulas to obtain immediate and measurable impact. The challenge is then, as is too frequently the case, how to overcome the contradiction among first world donors and third world processes. My hope is that scholarship such as this text can help international donors to develop more empathic relationships with third world grantees.

To build the wisdom and expertise of *Puntos* requires a long-term process. Successful communication for social change processes do not emerge from applying formulas. They originate from careful and respectful relationships built between an organization and a community. Such relationships require that organizations operate at many different levels, such as forming alliances, understanding local cultures, and maintaining close connections with local social movements. *Puntos* has managed to succeed in all these fronts, partly because of its great organizational flexibility. *Puntos'* ability to grow into a hybrid that operates well in very different areas, such as mobilization, E-E, research, education and training, and advocacy has made it into an organization deeply connected with the people it wants to communicate with. However, as in any other case of human communication, building these strong connections takes a long-term commitment and on-going support. And this is what donors need to understand.

As the field of entertainment education grows and expands, new categories and forms of classification will be needed to articulate differences and nuances that emerge from further analyses. Indeed, Tufte has already begun this trend toward more nuanced E-E categories by refering to first, second, and third E-E generations. In this light, I propose the term "activist E-E" to refer to the work of organizations such as *Puntos de Encuentro*, which use E-E strategies to intervene in the cultural fabric and to strenghten progressive local social movements; this term can serve to differentiate this type of E-E from more traditional "behavior change E-E".

Recent academic publications suggest that E-E scholars are trying to move E-E conceptualizations away from clear-cut binary theoretical frameworks. Issues addressed in these recent works include the limitations of traditional E-E theories (Singhal and Rogers, 2002), the non-linearity of social change processes (Papa et al, 2000), the narrowness of individual-centered theories of social change (Singhal and Rogers, 2002, 2004), and the need for more complex methodological approaches (Singhal and Rogers, 2004). A few E-E scholars have already begun these novel and exciting explorations, such as Arvind Sighal (2004) with his analysis of Augusto Boals and Paulo Freire's theories of participation and empowerment, Thomas Tufte's (2004) application of Martin Barbero's theory of mediations to E-E, Thomas Jacobson and Douglas Storey (2004) and their work on Habermas' communicative theory and E-E, and Papa et al (2000) with their use of Gramsci's theory of hegemony to analyze E-E in India.

In my view, it is urgent that E-E scholarship addresses two "black holes" that remain in its theoretical universe: bodies of theory that articulate culture understood as the circulation of meaning (such as cultural studies, semiotics, symbolic anthropology, and postcolonial theory) and theoretical frameworks that articulate power (such as feminist scholarship, Marxist and post-Marxist theories, Foucault and Bourdieu's elaboration of power, and queer theory). Combined with more interpretative and long term evaluation studies, the field of E-E scholarship could be starting a fascinating journey.

Chapter 24

SiMchezo! magazine
Community media making a difference
Minou Fuglesang

Introduction

> *Even those who cannot read the magazine contribute to the discussion when we talk about issues from the (SiMchezo!) magazine. Doing this they also receive the right health messages. I remember one day we spent two hours discussing 'What are STIs'. There came out many real life examples from different people.*
>
> Woman, *Njombe*

SiMchezo! **magazine** represents an innovation in community media. It aims to saturate private and public fora of society with open talk about sensitive issues surrounding sexuality and HIV/AIDS through edutainment. Engaging people emotionally, spurring open discussion and interpersonal exchange about issues that are conventionally considered taboo by using examples from their own real lives, has proved to be one of the huge assets of *SiMchezo!* magazine. This is a prerequisite for creating supportive environments, fundamental for any behavior and wider social changes to occur in lifestyles.

SiMchezo! reaches out to the rural areas of Tanzania to target the semi-literate, out of school youth and their communities. The magazine is published bi-monthly and has thereby become a recurring molder of lifestyles which communicates about a set of issues in-depth and from many angles. Now a popular vehicle for information, the copies are consumed intensely –with up to 15 people reading each copy– and there is high demand for more.

SiMchezo! is part of the Health Information Project (HIP), a multimedia 'edutainment' initiative targeting young people with information about a range of 'cool' and healthy lifestyle issues. Sexuality, reproduction, HIV/AIDS, life skills, career opportunities, violence and drugs are all topics communicated by using real life stories and testimonials, photonovels, advice columns, and other formats that engage audiences emotionally. All HIP products, whether print or electronic, outreach events, or promotion campaigns, complement and reinforce each other. They communicate similar content and messages in different ways to different segments of the audience. FEMINA magazine has been the centre piece of the HIP since the start, with distribution focusing on secondary schools. Spin-off products and activities like *SiMchezo!* have evolved rapidly to form a comprehensive HIP multimedia package.

The HIP communication strategy develops culturally sensitive and appropriate content through interactivity with the audience and participatory production methods. HIP strives to move away from simplified messages and slogans to give young people and their guardians guidance and advice on how to apply their knowledge of HIV to their daily lives but without preaching or prescribing a single response. HIP advocates for individual decision making and personal responsibility.

Feedback studies show that HIP products like *SiMchezo!* and FEMINA have succeeded in creating an empowering 'lifestyle brand' for young Tanzanians with clearly documented change effects. Not only have the different media products created forums for open talk about sensitive issues, stirring engagement and debate, they have with their long-term recurring presence in the audiences' lives, become trendsetters, sources of comfort, critical thinking, knowledge and fun as young people grow up and have to deal with a range of serious lifestyle issues. The edutainment methodology HIP has created and put to use is working.

Background

HIV/AIDS still represents a huge communication challenge throughout Tanzania. The issues of sexuality and HIV/AIDS continue to be surrounded by denial, silence and shame. The number of HIV positive people is increasing (currently estimated at more than 12% of the population in the age group 15-49), and there is no sign of a prevalence decline in Tanzania. Therefore there is more than ever an urgent need to promote and scale-up information and prevention activities that aim to reduce the spread of HIV through social and behavior change interventions, especially for young people while at the same time advocating for the importance of living positively, care and treatment, and stigma reduction (Richey, 2004). Yet appropriate information about the disease and related issues remains hard to access. Outdated, simple messages about A for abstention, B for being faithful and C for condom use are still dominating, even though it is clear that these have so far failed to achieve behaviour change. People require more than just awareness and basic education, they need advice on how to deal with these issues and make decisions in their relationships and in their social settings. Many have lost interest in understanding the virus and risk behaviour, and HIV infection is still on the increase. People continuously need to be alerted on the dangers involved, so that they internalize a way of dealing with the threat of the virus.

In Tanzania, the traditional initiation rites, *unyago na jando*, constituted modes of guided communication on sexuality and responsible behaviour for young people in most tribal contexts. These have gradually disappeared or lost their significant function as in many other African countries (Fuglesang, 1997). Parent-child communication about sexuality has always been considered inappropriate. Although extended family members –aunts, uncles and grandparents– have played this role in the past, this is breaking down as urbanization results in families that are more fragmented. Furthermore, the school system has not been able to assume the important role as a transmitter of lifeskills around sensitive sexuality issues. Implementation of sexuality education and HIV/AIDS curricula in schools has been met with reluctance and resistance on moral grounds for many years. The fear is that this type of education will encourage promiscuity. Young people are therefore still largely left to deal with the increasing influx of media images, myths and peer pressure on their own and it is difficult for them to access adequate, appropriate information or services that accommodate their unique needs. Teenage pregnancies and the high rates of new HIV infections, drug and alcohol abuse are the result.

In Tanzania, the political commitment to help fight the HIV epidemic was slow to emerge. Yet such committement is vital as HIV is not just a biomedical and health problem but a political and cultural problem as well as a socioeconomic problem. Since 2001 the Tanzania AIDS Commission (TACAIDS) has been operating under the Office of the Prime Minister. This has enhanced prominence of the issue on the government agenda, but huge challenges still lie ahead to mobilize society for prevention of new infections and support of those children, youth and adults who are affected and infected. Serious efforts need to be made to reduce stigma, denial, and discrimination. People have to understand that there is a difference between HIV and AIDS and that people can live positively with HIV for many years without getting AIDS. People are still reluctant to test voluntarily to find out their HIV status, and testing facilities are not widely available. Many cases are therefore not reported, and statistics are inconsistent. The provision of life-prolonging drugs, ARVs, on a wider scale in 2004 as part of the government's new care and treatment plan, is a further challenge. In Tanzania, as in so many other countries on the continent, civil society organisations have played a very important role in spearheading and pioneering prevention work as well as HIV care and treatment, and will have a crucial role to play also in the coming years. Many so called behaviour change, care and support interventions are now in place in the country. However, more synergy between initiatives is needed. There has to be a more concerted effort to encourage partnerships and collaboration between organizations, between the government and the civil society. Interventions have to be taken to scale, and more people have to be reached, particularly in the poor under-resourced rural areas.

With globalization and a growing market economy in Tanzania, media and information technology has become more accessible, and dissemination and distribution facilities have improved. This has made it possible to increasingly work through and develop new media vehicles for HIV communication. If content is culturally relevant, linked and rooted in the face-to-face encounters of everyday life, reinforcing and creating legitimacy around these, media communication has vast potential to reach large audiences and effect positive social change. The HIP multimedia lifestyle initiative is a prominent example.

HIP products and strategy

HIP produces four regular, recurring media vehicles as well as other supportive activities and materials:

1 *FEMINA Magazine* 60 pages, English/Swahili language, full-color, quarterly. Targets youth, particularly in secondary school settings. 2004 reached 92,000 copies. Distributed to over 1,200 schools which compose most of the secondary schools in Tanzania, 120 like minded NGOs and at commercial outlets in urban areas. Covers a broad range of lifestyle issues.

2 *FEMINA TV Talk Show*. 30 minute, Swahili language, weekly talk show, with in-studio, out-of-studio and comedy segments. Young hostess invites guests –youth, celebrities, topic experts, politicians to the studio. At other times the show is shot out in the field. The first for and by youth. The audience is youth and their families across Tanzania, particularly in urban areas. Aired on the private TV channels (Channel 10 and CTN). Interactive through SMS responses and contributions.

3 *Si Mchezo! Magazine*. 32 pages, bi-monthly Swahili language, full-colour. Targeted audience is rural, out–of-school, semi-literate youth aged 15-30 and their communities. Print run in 2004 reached 76,000 with an estimated reader of 15 persons per copy. Most distributed free of charge through large scale employers, NGOs and local government, paid subscriptions to workplaces and large organizations. The 5 southern regions of Tanzania have been in focus up till 2004, but distribution and editorial collection is gradually expanding to other regions as demand continues to grow.

4 *<www.chezasalama.com>* Interactive, bilingual (English and Swahili), regularly updated (weekly) website. Mirrors the content of

other HIP products. The targeted audience is Swahili and English speaking youth that can be reached over the World Wide Web.

5   *FEMINA User Guide.* A one-off publication to help facilitate the use of FEMINA magazine as a teaching and learning tool in schools, communities and clubs. Contains ideas for activities, exercises and reflections.

6   *Booklets.* Short, less than 50 pages, one-off publications covering specific themes. The audience is the general public, or depending on the nature of the publication. So far, four booklets: AIDS in our community, Living Positively with HIV/AIDS, 26 testimonials of PLHA, and a popularized version of the national HIV/AIDS policy.

7   *Community Mobilization.* Road shows, school visits and clubs. The HIP team travels out to the regions to meet the audience in communities and schools all over the country. This promotes the HIP lifestyle further. The road shows include drama, music, ques-tion-and-answer sessions about sexuality and living positively with HIV, and offers opportunities for exchange but also helps the HIP team monitor use of the magazine in the community and school settings. HIP also encourages the formation of clubs, vol-untary reading and discussion fora in and out of school where community action is also encouraged.

8   *Public relation and promotion.* Media campaigns, billboards, posters, postcards, as well as more traditional media such as wall murals, are also being used.

The Health Information Project (HIP) was set up in 1999 in order to find new creative and strategic ways of communicating about the issues at the core of the HIV/AIDS epidemic in Tanzania[1]. HIP sought to develop youth-friendly and culturally sensitive formats and content for communication where interactivity with the audience, con-tinuous, long-term presence, access and scale were to be the main concerns.

Strategic communication to enhance social and behaviour change is very important as it has the potential to slow down if not stop the epidemic. We know however, that changing social and behaviour patterns is very difficult. Engaging people and communities in adopting and adapting new ideas about their social relations, to help them internalize these ideas and then express them in new practices/changed behaviour, is a huge challenge.

1 The HIP is implemented by East African Development Communication Foundation (EADCF), also known as the Ngoma Foundation. The core HIP project is funded by SIDA, with funding for expansion and spin-off activities from NORAD, GTZ, USAID, and UNAIDS, AYA, FHI, RFE, Foundation for Civil Society.

HIP believes in the power of entertainment, hence it builds on an entertainment-education strategy. The initiative aims to entertain, educate and empower youth in appealing, high quality formats that mirror contemporary youth culture and language, lifestyle and aspirations. Entertainment-education appeals to the emotions and makes people open and receptive to the facts that are communicated. While most initiatives that use the entertainment-education methodology use the fictional drama to communicate, HIP uses docudrama which is rooted in journalistic tradition, real life testimonials and human interest stories. Anyone who has a story to tell, whether celebrity or street vendor, will be heard through interviews, testimonials, letters and short essays from readers. Research shows that this narrative approach is not experienced as didactic or preachy by young audiences, as it mirrors people and language like themselves. The magazine's visual presentation and photography follow the same principles. HIP does not use professional models but ordinary youth to model or simply portray themselves. HIP products engage the audience further because consumption is a pleasurable activity. They appreciate the quality paper and print, the playful design and decoration, the colour and visual images, and they appreciate the sensation of the open talk about normally secret issues. The approach developed by HIP has a broad popular appeal.

Common to all the HIP products is an *interactive and participatory production process* which ensures that young people's 'voices' and concerns become the sounding board. HIP is constantly learning from its audience, young people contribute with their ideas and experiences and pose for the photographs. Constant interaction with young people through editorial collection in the field, 'formative research' in focused groups at the HIP offices or in their own settings like schools, youth centres or rural communities, is important. This provides opportunity for texts, story lines, interpretation of articles, images to use, etc., to be discussed. Outreach activities including 'roadshows' in selected communities with large scale public question-and-answer sessions about living positively with HIV, sexuality and risk is another forum for interaction. The *constant feedback* generated in such interaction enables the editorial team to refine messages, explore new angles to topics, sharpen the design and identify gaps in knowledge. The process also has a strong empowering function for those involved and enhances their own understanding of the issues at hand. Conducting this kind of on-going research is one of the core elements of the HIP and is essential to the edutainment approach.

Theoretical grounding

HIV prevention programmes have to be guided by communication strategies and be *grounded in theory* and the local socio-cultural context. Furthermore, they need to be based on a multidisciplinary approach. The complexity of the issues involved entails that a holistic approach is necessary for understanding.

HIP and its entertainment-education strategy are grounded in the classic theories of behaviour change communication. At the heart of understanding this process is Bandura's social learning theory, which states that human learning can occur through observing media role models. This type of learning can be as effective as experiential learning. *Role modelling* is core to the HIP approach. Identifying with role models is an emotional process, and the significance of emotions in HIV prevention can not be underestimated. The epidemic spreads mainly through sexual relationships, which implies that feelings of romance and desire are usually involved. Transmission of the virus is not just a rational process in which an individual's knowledge of consequences guides that individual's actions. Entertainment-education appeals to the emotions and makes people open and receptive to the facts as well as to the emotional dilemmas that are communicated. For this reason entertainment-education interventions seem to be particularly appropriate for behaviour change communication, and they have proved to be very effective in motivating preventive action (Singhal and Rogers, 2003).

However, social learning theory is primarily concerned with individually oriented behaviour change. HIP finds this limiting and is concerned as well with context and agency. The theories of participation and action by Paulo Freire have therefore also inspired the HIP approach. The principles of dialogue, interaction, problem posing, reflection and conscientalization are fundamental to empowerment and social change. The HIP vehicles are designed to activate readers, individually but also collectively to think critically, to take control of their lives and find solutions rather than passively allowing action to happen to them. As Freire argued, people have to be empowered to imagine change, and to practice it. They have to learn to analyze social problems and transform reality through direct action. HIP strives to understand the social and cultural context of behaviours and has therefore a larger social change agenda.

Insights particularly from anthropology are consequently fundamental to the HIP philosophy. The initiative is concerned with people's whole lifestyle and how gender and power is culturally constructed (Caplan, 1987). Understanding traditional rituals and symbolic meanings is fundamental; the traditional initiation rites have always been the mode of transmitting knowledge about sexuality to youth in transition to adulthood in tribal societies. An understanding of how young people search for identity and meaning in a rapidly changing world and their creation of and participation in local and global 'youth cultures' is also important. Furthermore, an understanding of their engagement with and interpretation of the mass media is key (Fuglesang, 1994). Whether living in rural or urban areas of Tanzania young people today acquire a lot of their knowledge of issues relating to sexuality from their peers, and increasingly from the mass media (Fuglesang, 1997; Rwebangira and Liljeström et al, 1998). Sex is still a taboo topic for parent/child communication. However, the flow of media messages is saturated with contradictory and sensational images of sex, love and relationships. Young people's fascination with the media and with the entertainment industry can therefore bee seen as a resource that can effectively be used to communicate more pro-social messages.

HIP is also inspired by theories of visual literacy, an understanding of how audiences interpret visual images; photos, photo-novels and cartoons are key to the development of appropriate, effective content form (Fuglesang, 1982).

Strategic partnerships

Creating *strategic partnerships* that can reinforce the HIP media-based messages in interpersonal communication is important. Agreements are set up with like-minded NGOs, secondary schools, district government and large scale employers working on the ground. In order for the print products, especially, to reach the intended audience, it is essential to have such entry points to local communities. The strategy is to encourage products such as FEMINA magazine and *SiMchezo!* magazine, even video tapes of the TV Talk Show, to be used by these local organizations in the context of their work through peer educators, community based distributors, and workplace programs. Distribution and dissemination of the HIP products is a huge challenge, and partners like the ones mentioned are a key to the distribution system that HIP has built up to ensure that the magazines reach all targeted destination. A commercially based distribution system that builds on newspaper vendors around the country has also been built up to ensure that the products are transported to the many organizations and schools that are on our distribution list in every region of Tanzania.

The HIP products all highlight the work of its partner organizations in *content*. They are the topic experts on specialized issues that HIP editors and producers draw on when doing research and interviewing experts. Advertising their activities and their services is also key. This ensures a 'link to services', essential in any sexual and reproductive health and HIV/AIDS prevention program. HIP has made efforts to empower PHLAs and their interest organizations by employing individuals to work with the HIP team. An HIV positive woman has her own column in the FEMINA magazine where she openly shares her thoughts and fears about living positively, death, stigma, love and hope. She and other HIV positive also travel with the HIP road-show team around the country and speak to the public face to face. HIP has made the HIV positive community in Tanzania visible, by integrating them systematically into media products and other activities.

The *corporate sector* is valuable for the HIP initiative, both in terms of image and lessons to be learnt from marketing, distribution, publishing, but also for extra income generation. HIP products are used in corporate as well as government workplaces. A program component which has grown substantially during the past years, generating sponsorship and income through sales of advertisements but also more printed copies, has become a key element, generating a 'cost-sharing' on win win principles and fostering social responsibility in the business community.

Without *political leadership*, the fight against HIV/AIDS will fail. HIP systematically seeks out top political leaders for interviews. FEMINA TV Talk Show has collaborated with Prime Minister Fredrick Sumaye in producing a show for the World AIDS Day about children affected or infected by HIV. Mama Karume, and

Makamba, the Regional Commissioner of Dar es Salaam, have both featured in the FEMINA magazine. All parliamentarians regularly receive copies of the FEMINA HIP magazine in Parliament (Bunge) in Dodoma, and we have made efforts to engage them in the fight against HIV. HIP is also collaborating with the Ministry of Education, Institute of Curriculum Development, in helping them train teachers and introduce the Family Life Education curriculum in secondary schools. HIP is also involved in editing students' books for this curriculum. District and regional government officials are partners in that they are key in the distribution and dissemination of the HIP products all over Tanzania. TACAIDS has been a partner on recent projects, and HIP recently made a popular version of the national HIV strategy with support from them.

SiMchezo! magazine production activities

The rural areas of Tanzania are vast, and still largely underserved; there is little information material available and the rural way of life is seldom reflected in the media. The challenge is to reach out to these areas with the ambition to educate and mobilize people to start talking openly and to take on a healthy lifestyle agenda in the context of HIV/AIDS. *SiMchezo!* magazine was designed and set up as a spin-off to FEMINA magazine in 2002, to do just this. The entry point is youth, but the magazine also engages other 'gatekeepers' like parents, local leaders and consequently the broader community. The idea was to develop a community media vehicle that has a distinct rural identity and which mirrors the rural way of life in Tanzania and how people in such setting think and deal with issues relating to sexuality, their lifestyles and the HIV epidemic. The media vehicle is for and by the rural community.

Since its launch in 2002 the *SiMchezo!* magazine has grown steadily in popularity and in numbers, began with 10,000 copies in three districts in southern Tanzania. HIP has been able to sustain this enthusiasm by increasing the printrun. Beginning December 2004 HIP is printing 76,500 copies of the magazine. Distribution has been focused in the five southernmost regions of Tanzania.

An innovative community based method of editorial collection has been developed for *SiMchezo!* The two editors travel out to selected rural areas with a laptop and digital camera to collect stories. The production builds on such modern production technology, which has simplified and transformed editorial work. Editors meet with various youth groups, partner organizations and community members and get ideas for story lines. Scripts for photo-novels are chiselled out with the help of the community members, who also act and pose as models for the photographs. The script and photos are written, shot, edited and basically completed within a day for one article or photo-novel. The language is 100% simple, direct, straightforward Swahili, vernacular is even used. Local NGOs, CBOs, and key individuals also help to recommend issues and persons to contact, and generally help to facilitate constant feedback and dialogue with *SiMchezo!*'s audiences.

A variety of topics on sexuality, general health and lifestyles are covered in each *SiMchezo!* issue, i.e. pregnancy prevention, STIs, and HIV/AIDS; gender; girls education; human rights; alcohol/drug abuse; violence; religion/spirituality; living with HIV/AIDS; care and support for those infected and affected by HIV/AIDS; peer pressure; stigma and discrimination; and communication between parents and youth. Content is shaped using formats such as personal testimonial, news from the regions, income generation and money management, photonovel, music top-ten, peer and expert advice, case studies of community change, health services available, letters from readers, 'your voice', and cartoon story.

Importantly, *SiMchezo!* has a 'Chezasalama' page. The slogan 'play/dance it safe, which HIP used for one of its information and promotion campaigns is about a holistic healthy lifestyle. The page provides information on safer sex practices and activities youth can do when abstaining from sexual intercourse. Furthermore, *SiMchezo!* and HIP has launched the Beyond ABC campaign. For years the key HIV prevention slogans has been the ABC; A for abstention, B for being faithful and C for using condoms. HIP believes it is high time we go beyond this and learn the other letters of the sexual health alphabet. We need to become fully literate. We need to learn the H for hugging, the K for kissing, the M for masturbation, the O for oral sex. The campaign was launched through all HIP products, and has created waves of support and engaged young as well as old *SiMchezo!* readers. In spite of the fact that some of the topics such as masturbation are sensitive, people agree that it is a safer sex practice that needs to be talked about and even encouraged in the context of abstention from sex and a search for safer sex options. Parents have stated they would rather have HIP promote masturbation than condoms when addressing young people.

The last time content format of *SiMchezo!* was reviewed, some significant changes were made. Eight new pages were added to the magazine (24>32) to give room for expansion of columns like 'your voice' from one to two pages, due to enthusiasm and demand. Introduction of money management and income generation page was also due to demand. Even more important than HIV/AIDS in many people's opinion is poverty. Links between poverty and spread of HIV/AIDS are well documented. Introduction of the '*Tulichovuna*' ('that which we have harvested') page was the experience with the cover story. Since the start, the cover story has featured profiles of ordinary youth who have made a change in their life, role modeling individual behaviour change. '*Tulichovuna*' does the same for the community level –it gives examples of people in communities working together to achieve change. This offers inspiration to others.

Introduction of '*Pasipo na Daktari*', general health topics such as clean water, malaria, fever and dehydration, was also done after requests from readers.

In order for *SiMchezo!* magazine to reach its intended audience in the best possible way, it is essential to have an entry point into the local communities. This point has varied according to the situation, but the magazine always works in the spirit of partnership. For example in Iringa Region, which has been one of the focal regions for *SiMchezo!* distribution since the beginning of the magazine. Large-scale employers at tea and wattle estates introduced the magazine to their workforces and the surrounding communities. In other areas, district and regional officials have been instrumental in linking *SiMchezo!* with the efforts of non-governmental organizations (NGOs) and community-based organizations (CBOs) including faith-based organizations. The magazine has also been distributed at local clinics, hospitals and HIV testing facilities.

HIP encourages local organizations to use the magazine as part of peer education and community outreach efforts, e.g., workshops, festivals and sports programs. Experience shows that acceptance of *SiMchezo!* magazine is very positive when readers receive 'backup' from local peer educators or health staff who can help explain and discuss content, and respond to questions that may arise. The magazine in turn reports on partner activities and, for instance, their peer education work. The magazine focuses also on documenting and highlighting in a positive way different community actions, i.e. steps that communities are taking to safeguard young people, such as changing behaviors/customs that put them at risk of pregnancy, STIs and HIV, as we shall see below.

Every quarter, *SiMchezo!* and the HIP team organize community outreach events in collaboration with local organizations. The two editors plus other HIP team members travel to the regions, with stand up comedians or drama groups, and a HIV positive woman who does question-and-answer sessions, to conduct four hour 'roadshows'. Such events serve to strengthen the magazine's relationship with its readers in many ways. Here HIP speaks not only to the youth but to the whole community. The outreach events also directly inform content development for the magazine. They also stimulate the magazine's participatory production process and monitoring and evaluation efforts. It is easier to rally people to participate when they have had a big public presentation of the magazine and the production team behind it. They appreciate to see the editors and feel that they are part of the production process.

SiMchezo! results

Monitoring, evaluation and documentation is key to the HIP communication strategy. HIP engages in extensive formative and process oriented research, and knowledge about the magazine's effect and impact is of vital importance for the overall project and funders, but also for the continued relevance of the editorial content. HIP has monitored the previous two phases of *SiMchezo!* closely using a triangulation of methods, including quantitative surveys, focus groups discussions, analysis of letters and interviews with key people in the field. As part of its second phase, a quantitative survey is underway using Ruvuma Region as the study site. Focus group discussions were conducted at the same site, as well as from Iringa and Mtwara Regions. Below we shall explore some of the findings from these focus group discussions.

Trust in *SiMchezo!*

Readers express that they place a high level of trust in *SiMchezo!* magazine; they are confident that the information contained in the magazine is true and accurate. This is significant because people are often confused, even paralyzed by the myths and conflicting messages they hear elsewhere. Why do they trust *SiMchezo!*? HIP attributes the strong confidence in and 'ownership' of the magazine to the production approach, the regular interaction between the readers and the editorial team –the readers are involved in the production, they see the editors and they meet the team. It reflects their reality, speaks their language, they are given a voice and *SiMchezo!* doesn't preach, it respects the readers' need for information and capacity to be responsible and make their own decisions. The fact that people believe that the magazine provides 'facts' and 'evidence' enables us to say that it has been effective in correcting misconceptions about the difference between HIV and AIDS, and other related myths around modes of transmission, the efficacy of the condom, and masturbation. The magazine's clear and direct language and appealing way of presenting issues help accentuate this impression in feedback.

Open talk and conducive atmosphere

A key objective of *SiMchezo!* is to encourage open talk and exchange among people, e.g between partners, parents and adolescents. Discussion is fundamental to prevention work; through such exchanges people revisit their views, learn new things and are encouraged to act to create an open environment where individual behaviour change is possible. The *SiMchezo!* magazine has been very effective in stimulating discussion about HIV and breaking the silence around the issue. It has contributed to a conducive atmosphere for change at the community level. As we shall see, there are many examples of how the magazine has initiated both individual and collective change processes in communities where the magazine has been distributed.

Some of the testimonial cover stories on *SiMchezo!* come from youth who have been so inspired and informed by the magazine that they have changed habits of behavior to the better and now want to share their story with other readers to talk about their experiences and what triggered them to change and to sustain that behaviour change. Such sharing of experiences is very powerful and other youth tell us that they again have been inspired to change by reading the stories of others, i.e. role modeling. The following letter is revealing:

'*SiMchezo!* has changed my thinking'.

I am glad to appear in *SiMchezo!* testifying how the magazine has completely changed my thinking in as far as secondary abstinence is concerned. Educators have always been preaching on the importance of secondary abstinence and I have read a number of publications on that particular subject. However, I never thought it was possible for one to stop sex after he/she has been 'addicted to it' until when I read a true story by

Nehemia Sanga, of Makete, in *SiMchezo!* issue 15. The true story convinced me to believe that it was possible to practice secondary abstinence and it gave me confidence that I can also do it!

The minute I read the testimony, I decided that I am also going to change and I am glad I did! I used to have sex at least thrice a week but I have now managed to remain abstinent for almost two months and a half now! This is fantastic and I am sure I will make it. I commend *SiMchezo!* for this strategy of giving us real life stories because they work more than mere words. *SiMchezo!* has also been publishing articles on policies affecting youths and the rights of youths, something that has not only informed me about my rights but also empowered me to demand them.

I commend you for the fantastic job.

Young man, *Tunduru*

Because issues are openly discussed in the magazine by people from their own community who are the models, people are particularly interested. They talk about what they have read in the magazine. The magazine is clearly an ice breaker; it brings sensitive issues out into the open and reduces the shame of talking about sexuality and the underlying causes of HIV/AIDS. The magazine triggers open discussion in workplaces, among groups of people as well as among partners.

Before the magazine it was difficult to communicate with your friend on issues of sexuality and STIs, but you give someone the magazine and then you inquire what he/she has grasped from it, they talk openly without hiding anything. In this way you realize that he/she gets a lot of useful information.

Young man, *Madoda tea estate, Njombe*

During the discussion at work, in the Ushauri Wangu (my advice page), people agree that it is not always necessary to have sex when you erect. There are other ways like masturbation. I like this comment, and people now say that the magazine addresses innermost issues which were not possible to be talked openly about in the past.

Man, *Njombe*

HIP staff has also experienced that communities where *SiMchezo!* is accessible discuss issues raised in *SiMchezo!* and are taking collective action in different ways. In Tandahimba district in Mtwara region, the community made, after the topic was discussed in *SiMchezo!*, a collective decision to ban dance rituals at night as there was a tendency for couples to pair off and engage in risky sex after the dance. The dances are still performed, but only during the day! This is one example of how *SiMchezo!* content influences community cooperation and collective problem solving and stimulates collective initiatives to fight HIV/AIDS.

People engage intensely, the magazine appeals to all ages, demand is high

People express that they can talk with confidence for they have the facts from the magazine get answers to some of their problems and queries about STIs, condom use or menstrual cycle, the evidence as they say. Talk becomes empowering, as they have the evidence from the magazine.

Not all readers of course feel comfortable in the beginning with the open, straight forward way the topics are presented in *SiMchezo!* They are simply not used to it and this has created intense discussion between people with different views. A few stated that they used to think it 'crazy' to talk too openly about STIs in front of other people in public, but after reading about it in the magazine they realized that it may not be so bad to do it. Because the magazine is trusted, a legitimacy is therefore created when it comes to talking openly in a certain way.

> After you have brought the *SiMchezo!* magazine here it is now easy for people to communicate on STIs easily. You know there were these health messages for quite long time now with low impact. Now I can say people can discuss openly about STIs. Other people cannot talk to their friends even if they have problems, but after reading the magazine you see them discuss about the magazine content.
>
> Young man, *Tanwat Factory, Njombe*

Among couples or sexual partners, many are taking the courage to speak up with their partners after reading articles in *SiMchezo!* that encourage couples to do just that.

> The magazine has helped us discuss things with our sexual partners. At first it was difficult to convince my partner to use condom, because I was afraid to talk to him. But now I can buy condoms and I have at home. I tell my fellow friends to speak out to their sexual partners.
>
> Woman, *Maganga Tea Estate, Mafinga*

The qualitative data clearly shows that people of all ages enjoy *SiMchezo!* and benefit from its messages. The magazine appeals to adults as well as youth because it tackles real life issues in their own rural areas. People engage intensively with *SiMchezo!* contents. Workers at the plantation estates of Mufindi and Tanwat in Iringa Region and people in the surrounding communities have since the start of the magazine project engaged in intense discussions about the contents. The demand for the magazine has increased steadily. People come early in the month to request copies from the local health centers from where the magazine is distributed, and come with an increased repertoire of questions. There is according to Betty Liduke, the matron of the Tanwat company hospital, a renewed interest in voluntary HIV testing and STI treatment since *SiMchezo!* magazine has been distributed in that district.

We stay at a far village, almost 20km from here (Idetero Tea Estate). We usually carry copies of the magazine to our families and friends on the weekends. Many people in our village can access the magazine now. We discuss contents of the magazine. They really love it.

Man, Idetero Tea Estate

Parent/child communication

The communication gap between adolescents and their parents greatly benefits from the presence of *SiMchezo!* magazine as well. Usually adults find it difficult to respond to adolescents' questions and concerns, due to the sensitivity of the issues, and other socio-cultural barriers. This hinders open and frank discussions between elders and youth. Often adolescents are met with distrust, suspicion, anger, hostility or just silence when they approach adults for information and guidance, regardless of whether they are sexually active.

The magazine has become a Tool for parents. By giving the *SiMchezo!* magazine to them they have communicated even if they are not yet ready to discuss sex with their children. But feedback shows that parents feel that information and guidance important and see the magazine as helping them in that role. According to feedback *SiMchezo!* is the only way many parents can communicate with their daughters and sons. Some say that they realize that the young people need the information and that they are not to blame for getting into trouble because they themselves as parents have left it to the government and the schools to teach them and it's not being done. Furthermore, some admit they don't stay close to their children and listen to their problems. They agree that they should try to, as it is encouraged in the magazine.

I have my daughter of 11 years old, she is in Standard Five. At first, I was not ready for her to read the magazine. I left the magazine in my bedroom. To my surprise I met her reading the magazine, I didn't say anything to her. Later she discovered that I had received a new issue of the magazine and she asked for it. I was puzzled, but I knew that the information in the magazine is useful to her.

Father, Tanwat estate, Njombe

The magazine increases communication among people here in Njombe. According to African culture, men cannot talk to their daughters on issues relating to sexuality and STI. Some of the parents have the courage to talk to their daughters and sons; it is good, but for those who cannot talk it then they should use the magazine to communicate.

Man, Kibena Tea Estate, Njombe

Use by peer educators

At Tanwat estate, HIV workplace peer educators use *SiMchezo!* as part of their education program. For them the magazine becomes a reference material and something they can use as an entrypoint to discussion. They highly appreciate the magazine and say that it creates status and legitimacy for them in their job to use and be associated with *SiMchezo!*

Conclusion

In more ways than one *SiMchezo!* has become one of the most significant vehicles of the HIP multimedia initiative. With it, HIP is reaching out to the rural youth, in underserved communities around Tanzania where information and support are desperately needed. The magazine clearly has effect in the communities where it is distributed. It creates trust and open talk and engagement with sense-making of sensitive issues. This all contributes to creating a supportive environment which is fundamental for any behaviour and wider social changes to occur. Interpersonal communication is clearly spurred among partners, but even between parents and children. It is further used as an education tool by the HIV peer educators of many organizations. The ever growing demand for copies is also an indicator of effect.

The HIP multimedia intervention has gone beyond the boundaries of its main information agenda, HIV/AIDS, to include a whole array of health lifestyles issues, including those of democracy, voluntarism, and civil rights. The *SiMchezo!* greatly contributes to the notion of HIP becoming an empowering lifestyle brand, a source of friendship and support for young people growing up in Tanzania today. The long-term, recurring feature of the media vehicles greatly contributes to make this happen. A letter from a young girl, Morogoro, sums it up:

> Dear Editor, I would like to congratulate you on what you're doing, surely it is so fantastic... Truly, *SiMchezo!* has increased my awareness about life and how to face it. I face so many difficulties but *SiMchezo!* has made it simpler. Thanks again and God Bless you.

The HIP approach stands on the shoulders of what other initiatives have done in the field of entertainment-education worldwide, having adopted and adapted ideas. HIP has developed its own distinct approach. The pioneering participatory production process of *SiMchezo!* with modern digital technology, which mostly takes place in the 'field' in the rural areas with the participation of local youth groups, is helping HIP refine and fine tune its overall methodology and approach. The docudrama approach used in the magazine is setting a trend for other youth media in the region. HIP receives many requests for information about how it works when producing the edutainment vehicles. As HIP scales up and expands during the coming years as a response to its popular reception, the project will also increasingly share its experiences by organizing regular regional training courses in the HIP edutainment methodology and document the communication strategy used. HIP is a an example of an initiative rooted in the tradition of com- munication for development. The HIP products model new culturally appropriate realities and challenges oppressive power structures in society. HIP believes that for people to take prevention seriously and internalize protective ways of dealing with HIV, you have to engage them in discussion and sense making about their whole lifestyle and that of their communities.

Chapter 25

Young voices travel far: a case study of *Scenarios* from Africa

Kate Winskell & Daniel Enger

One night as twenty-year-old Olga Kiswendsida Ouédraogo from Burkina Faso was leaving the office building in Ouagadougou where she was working as an intern, she heard the security guards, stationed at the entrance to the compound, laughing uproariously. As she approached their guard post, she saw they were watching a tiny television set perched precariously on a shelf. The door guards were not known for their sense of humour and Olga's curiosity was piqued, so she stopped in the shadows to observe. "I was astounded to see that they were watching my film"[1].

Olga's film is a short fiction film, a little over two minutes in length, called "The Shop" ("La Boutique"). It started life as an idea she thought up for a scriptwriting competition, which had served as a pretext for her to take some time off revision for her final school-leaving exams. The film is about a young man whose girlfriend, at a moment of nascent passion, discovers that he's forgotten to buy condoms and sends him to the corner shop to buy some. Intimidated by the other customers, he buys packet after packet of biscuits until, finally, other customers show him the way, including an old man who comes in asking for condoms for his fourth wife. The last scene shows the young man running home, laden with condoms and biscuits, just in time to see his girlfriend ride off on her moped yelling "It's too late!"[2].

1 Olga Kiswendsida Ouédraogo, personal conversation, January 2004.
2 The *Scenarios* films can be viewed in English online with a high speed Internet connection at <http://www.globaldialogues.org/Films.htm>.

Olga says that hearing the laughter of the "stoic" security guards as they watched her film was the "greatest reward I could have had". People react to "The Shop" with similar hilarity all around the world. It seems that the young man's embarrassment strikes a universal human chord. The film is available in at least nineteen languages and has been broadcast in almost every country in sub-Saharan Africa and others far beyond –in Fiji, Cyprus, Sri Lanka, Haiti... A colleague from Senegal[3] overheard a conversation outside a shop in a poor district of the Madagascan capital, Antananarivo. A young man had just bought biscuits and his friend was teasing him, saying that he knew he had really been trying to buy condoms. They were joking about Olga's film.

Olga's idea for the "The Shop" was one of 4,000 stories contributed by 13,000 young people from Senegal, Mali and Burkina Faso for a 1997 contest. Over a three-month period, scores of local organisations in the three West African countries had mobilised young people up to the age of 24 to come up with an idea for a short fiction film that would educate their communities about HIV/AIDS. The winning ideas were selected by a succession of juries at national and then at international level, before being transformed into short films by leading African directors. These were then dubbed into a range of languages, donated to broadcasters, and distributed at community level on VHS cassette and CD-Rom.

Olga's film, "The Shop", was directed by fellow Burkinabè Idrissa Ouédraogo[4], whose latest feature film had been in contention for the Palme d'Or, the most coveted prize at the Cannes Film Festival, earlier that year. Olga had the pleasure of acting as his on-set adviser for "The Shop". Having grown up in Ouagadougou, the capital of African cinema and home to FESPACO, the bi-annual Pan-African Film Festival, she had long nurtured the dream of becoming a film director herself. In January 2004, her ambition was fulfilled as she co-directed two *Scenarios* films with young Senegalese director Hamet Fall Diagne.

Since 1997, when Olga thought up the idea for "The Shop", more than 42,000 young people from 25 African countries have participated in three *Scenarios from Africa* contests, and twenty-eight films have been produced. Available in up to twenty languages, the first 13 films have been broadcast in almost every country in sub-Saharan Africa, often intensively, and are widely used as a discussion tool at community level. In addition to her directorial debut, Olga has attended international film festivals, sat on juries to select winning *Scenarios* scripts, featured in *Scenarios* films, adapted the films for use on radio, and co-ordinated the most successful national *Scenarios* contest in Burkina Faso to date, encouraging a new generation of young Africans to follow her lead.

3 The late and sadly missed Abasse Kâ.
4 Olga and Idrissa are not related. Ouédraogo is a very common last name in Burkina Faso.

Background

Scenarios from Africa[5] is a community mobilisation, education, research and media process with the goal of improving the lives of those infected and affected by HIV/AIDS, reducing the vulnerability of populations at risk of infection, and helping local a organisations develop their capacity for effective HIV/AIDS education. It is also highly diverse collection of individuals and their organisations committed to fighting the HIV/AIDS epidemic.

 Scenarios from Africa grew out of a 1995-1996 cross-cultural research project exploring innovative methods of HIV communication for young people. In several West African countries visited in the course of the research, the present authors witnessed a disproportionate emphasis being placed in HIV/AIDS education on biomedical aspects of the epidemic, to the neglect of behavioural and contextual factors. This was leaving young people thinking of HIV as a spiky red virus that attacks people's white blood cells, rather than as a social phenomenon of urgent relevance to their day-to-day lives and behaviour. It was also evident that there was a real shortage of audio-visual tools that were adapted to HIV education needs and culturally appropriate and linguistically accessible to local communities. Drawing inspiration from a French model[6], *Scenarios from Africa* was designed with local partner organisations[7] to address these concerns: to encourage young people to situate the epidemic in potentially real-life narratives, and to produce a collection of short fiction films to generate dialogue and reflection at community level. Over the course of the past eight years the process has evolved significantly and grown in richness.

 The bedrock of *Scenarios from Africa* is partnership. The process is founded on the collaboration of literally hundreds of diverse partners, large and small, from a wide range of sectors, civil society, private and governmental. Despite its high media profile, evident in the distribution of Olga's film "The Shop", its centre of gravity is firmly rooted at community level. Many of the members of the *Scenarios from Africa* team are community-based organisations (CBOs) living and working in their own urban, peri-urban or rural milieux in direct contact with local people. They work in a variety of fields of development. Many are dedicated to HIV/AIDS prevention, support, treatment and care, some are run by people living with HIV/AIDS (PLWHA), and some address the needs of specific groups (street kids, women, the disabled…). Add to this foundation leading African film directors, actors and production teams, music celebrities, broadcasters, government ministers, international non-governmental organisations

5 *Scenarios from Africa* exists thanks to the primary support of Comic Relief (UK), the UK Department for International Development (DFID), the Pfizer Foundation, the Community Fund, and UNFPA.

6 "3,000 Scénarios contre un virus", carried out by CRIPS and its partners in France in the early 1990s. We are indebted to CRIPS for their friendship, support and ongoing collaboration.

7 A key partner in the conceptualisation phase and since, Africa Consultants International (ACI), Dakar, had laid the foundation for *Scenarios from Africa* in Senegal by helping to build a remarkable CBO network through a series of training courses.

(NGOs), schools and tens of thousands of young people, and you get an idea of the diverse human core of *Scenarios from Africa*.

Methodology

Although the *Scenarios from Africa* process follows a basic methodology, team members incorporate its activities and resources into their programmes in the manner of their choosing, so as best to complement and enhance their own ongoing work. The Scenarios process involves three basic steps, which can be broken down into additional components as follows:

Contest

» An international contest is held in which hundreds of partners work together to mobilise young Africans up to the age of 24 to develop creative ideas for short films on HIV/AIDS.

Selection and Analysis

» Selection: in a dialogue-based process, contest winners are selected by juries made up of: PLWHA and other specialists in HIV prevention, treatment and care; former contest winners and other young people; and communication specialists, including the internationally acclaimed filmmakers who go on to transform the winning ideas into short films.

» Analysis: the creative works submitted in the contest are analysed with a view to gaining a deeper understanding of young Africans' communication needs. Findings are fed into script adaptation and film production and circulated to the wider AIDS community.

Production and Distribution

» Adaptation: selected winning scenarios undergo a lengthy and rigorous adaptation and pre-testing process at the hands of local and international specialists, particularly PLWHA, and local communities.

» Production: leading African directors and their production teams transform the adapted scripts into short fiction films between 2 and 15 minutes long. The films are also adapted for use on radio.

» Users' guide: drawing on community-level and partner feedback, along with input provided through the selection and adaptation processes, a discussion guide is formulated to facilitate effective use of the films.

» Dubbing: the films and radio shows are dubbed into a range of African and European (English, French, Portuguese) languages.

» Distribution: the films and radio shows are donated to broadcasters on a rights-free basis and distributed at no cost to CBOs, NGOs and schools.

Figure 1 summarises the *Scenarios* process and its intended outcomes

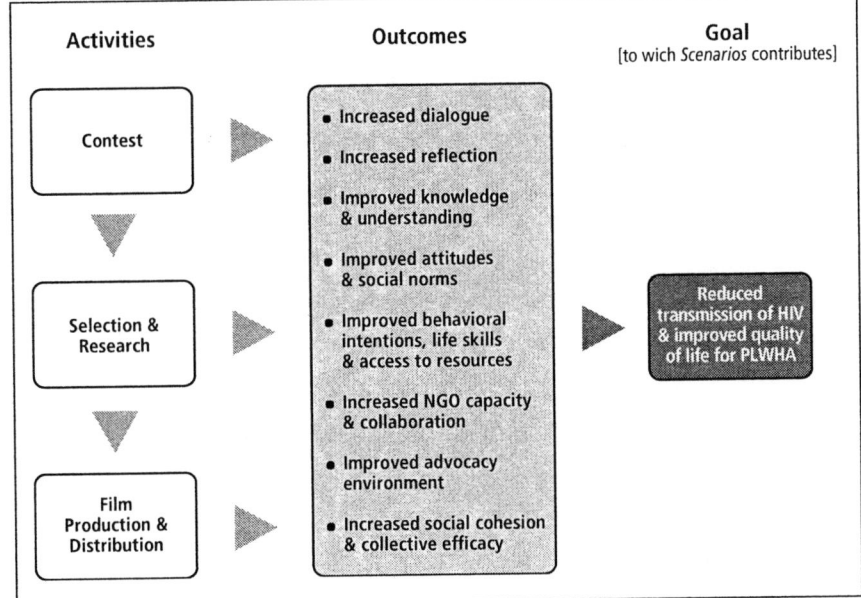

Activities	Outcomes	Goal [to wich *Scenarios* contributes]
Contest	• Increased dialogue • Increased reflection • Improved knowledge & understanding • Improved attitudes & social norms	
Selection & Research	• Improved behavioral intentions, life skills & access to resources • Increased NGO capacity & collaboration	Reduced transmission of HIV & improved quality of life for PLWHA
Film Production & Distribution	• Improved advocacy environment • Increased social cohesion & collective efficacy	

Activities

Contest

Originally held only in three countries in the Western Sahel, under the name "Scenarios from the Sahel", the contest is progressively scaling up to cover all of sub-Saharan Africa. The vast majority of young participants are mobilised at community level. However, the contest is also publicised on television, radio and in the press on a national and international level, with partners like the French-language satellite television station TV5 and the youth magazine *Planète Jeunes* playing a key role in providing international publicity. Young people can also take part by post or via the Internet.

They are encouraged to work in teams to promote dialogue and information-sharing and to facilitate the participation of those who have not had the advantage of formal schooling. Emphasis is increasingly being placed on providing the participants with access to mentors, especially PLWHA (who are under no pressure to disclose their serological status), who are a source of guidance, advice and help with writing. Priority is also being placed on maximising opportunities for the young participants to develop life skills by encouraging them to develop their stories through role play, improvisation, and other forms of experiential learning.

The contest leaflet provides a list of suggested situations which they can, if they choose, use as a starting point for their stories. This list is developed through a consensus survey of *Scenarios from Africa* team members. Suggested situations cover a wide gamut of themes, for example:

> *The boss is worried about AIDS, but he's also very creative. He comes up with lots of ideas, some of them very amusing, to inform his staff about HIV/AIDS.*

Or

> *Buying condoms isn't always easy* (the theme which Olga used as inspiration for "The Shop").

Colleagues have created "scenarios" with literacy classes, nomadic populations, theatre troupes, street kids, maids, sex workers, refugees, orphans, taxi drivers, metalworkers, gardeners, entire school classes (with over 100 children) and children as young as five…

Selection and analysis

The winning ideas are selected by a succession of juries. Each scenario is read by at least two jurors at the national level (and by many more at the international level). Wherever jurors disagree on the merits of an individual scenario, they debate until they reach a consensus.

Members of the first contest juries were quick to recognise that the stories provide unanticipated rich insight into the attitudes, language, and perspectives of the young authors. They came to see the selection of winning ideas as an innovative means of assessing the participants' current communication needs and of identifying some of the strengths and weaknesses of the communication activities around HIV/AIDS conducted in their region to date. Sometimes misunderstandings are manifest in the plot of a story. For example, a character has unprotected sex on a Saturday night (where he is presumed to contract HIV), only to visit the doctor the following Monday morning, where he or she is diagnosed as having AIDS. The considerable number of stories like this indicate that efforts to communicate the speed of progression or the asymptomatic phase of HIV infection to young people have not always met with success.

The stories also tell us about the young participants' attitudes towards PLWHA, and their perceptions of gender norms and HIV/AIDS-related social norms. Jurors are often pleasantly surprised by what they read. On the basis of their reading, they make comments and recommendations for improved practice. These are discussed in plenary and compiled into a report for wider circulation. A research project is planned in collaboration with Emory University in Atlanta and other international partners to conduct an in-depth analysis of the stories, comparing them by geographic region and tracking changes over time, since the first contest in 1997.

Production

The first step in adapting winning scripts is incorporating the comments and recommendations of jurors. These first drafts are then revised in line with feedback from local specialists, and the young author and the director, where possible, and tested at community level. Feedback leads to further adaptations, further consultations with key stakeholders, and further pre-testing in a rigorous process that can take many months.

The films cover a wide range of themes, for example: the basic facts of transmission; the pain of stigmatisation; non-medicinal ways of helping those living with HIV; disclosure within a serodiscordant couple; wife inheritance; a child's experience of losing his parents to AIDS; the advantages of getting tested; seduction and intergenerational sex in the school context; parent-child dialogue… As the subjects addressed are based on current local needs, the themes treated evolve with the epidemic. The first collection (thirteen films made between 1997 and 2001) tended to focus on prevention issues, whereas the latest collection (produced in 2003-2004) places increasing emphasis on the perspectives and needs of PLWHA. The compilation cassette is designed to be a flexible educational resource, allowing facilitators to select the films that best meet the needs of a specific audience.

Varying in tone from very funny to profoundly touching, the films aim to be optimistic and hopeful, to approach their subject matter in a fresh and novel way, and to generate a powerful emotional response. One of the most popular –and funniest– films from the first collection, "Iron Will", directed by Fanta Régina Nacro and based on an original idea by Malick Diop Yade, aged 18, and his team from Senegal, tells the story of Moussah, a young man who has a hard time keeping his interest in women in check. With a friend already ill with HIV/AIDS, he is well aware of the dangers he faces. His male friends tell him about the prevention strategy they've chosen as an alternative to condoms. They feel it corresponds well to where they are in their lives right now. But poor Moussah doesn't realise that the expression they are using –"iron underpants"– is their way of talking about "mind over matter" in the face of sexual temptations… and he takes their advice literally, with hilarious results!

In addition to tremendous amusement (one colleague reported witnessing a group of nuns howling with laughter!), the film also sparks dialogue about male abstinence, a behavioural option with a significant image problem, and other prevention strategies. Like Olga's film, "Iron Will" certainly captures people's imagination. It has, for example, led to the expression "iron underpants" entering Malian youth culture, in the local Bambara language, as a code for talking about abstinence and prevention more generally. The influence of "Iron Will" is also evident in a number of scenarios written for the 2002 *Scenarios* contest, following distribution of the film, and it even spawned an "Iron Underpants" film festival in Jamaica the same year.

Although often used with groups, the films can also be used very effectively in individual counselling sessions. A colleague in Burkina Faso recounts one instance where he did everything he could to calm down a man who had just received a positive test result, but without success. It was not until he showed the man the *Scenarios* film "Shared Hope", in which a young woman confides her positive test result to a friend, that he calmed down and became receptive to counselling.

Distribution

Broadcasters appreciate receiving the high quality programming for free and value the films' short format, which allows them to use them as fillers between programmes. In several countries, including Benin, Mali, Côte d'Ivoire, Guinea, Haiti and the Democratic Republic of Congo, national television stations have taken the initiative to produce special programmes on HIV/AIDS in which the *Scenarios* films are broadcast and then discussed by local specialists. In Nigeria, individual films have been broadcast during the prime-time news, and in several countries they have been broadcast immediately before, during or after Cup of African Nations and World Cup football matches.

A compilation VHS cassette of the films is distributed on a non-profit basis to NGOs, schools and other community organisations. The films have been used in training courses and local prevention activities; as the foundation for counselling and for lifeskills training modules; by mobile cinema units (often on white walls or on a sheet strung between two trees in rural areas); on long-distance bus services and in neighbourhood video clubs; on closed-circuit television in hotels; and in waiting rooms of clinics and counselling and testing centres. They are also used by and for migrant Africans within Africa and on other continents, and in foreign language teaching.

In addition to VHS cassettes, the films are also distributed on CD-Rom. This format is proving to be a surprisingly valuable way to reach small groups in rural communities, allowing a handful of people to watch the films on a laptop computer under a tree in a village, with no need for an external power source or cumbersome equipment[8].

Philosophy

Scenarios from Africa is coordinated by the British NGO Global Dialogues, of which the present authors are founding members. As our name suggests, we are committed to dialogue as a guiding philosophical principle, a *modus operandi*, and a primary outcome of our activities.

For us, the term *dialogue* encapsulates principles of partnership, empowerment, and efficacy. It echoes Paulo Freire's principle of dialogical educa-

8 In an innovative application of modern information technologies for development purposes, DynaEntreprises/Senegal, which produced the CD-Rom, has also set up interactive, touch-sensitive kiosks in the waiting area of a popular credit union in Senegal allowing people to select and watch a film in French or three local languages while they are waiting to be served.

tion, in which existing power relations are undermined, and the teacher is simultaneously learner and the learner is simultaneously teacher. We also believe that dialogue should be one of the primary goals of HIV communication in line with the conclusions of a recent report assessing twenty years of HIV communication:

> Communication strategies need to be redirected so that they give prominence to the creation of communication environments which encourage interpersonal communication, dialogue and debate, and which focus as much on providing a voice to those most affected by HIV as they do on educating them through messages. The evidence increasingly suggests that only when people become truly engaged in discussions and talking about HIV, does real individual and social change come about (Scalway, 2003).

Through its various component activities, the *Scenarios* process is designed to operate at multiple, mutually reinforcing levels –at the level of the individual, community, society and civil society– in pursuit of long-term social change objectives.

Empowerment and capacity development

In the *Scenarios* process, community mobilisation is the foundation for a high profile media campaign. This is empowering and motivating for the young participants, the teams of local organisations who implement the contest process, and the creative teams that transform the winning ideas into short films. This empowerment is a crucial way of building social cohesion and individual and collective efficacy, preserving one of the most precious weapons in the fight against AIDS: the belief that we, as individuals and as communities, can make a difference. As PLWHA partners in Burkina Faso have commented: "*Scenarios from Africa* is reaching every corner of the continent, changing attitudes towards those of us who live with the virus –and WE are at the heart of it all! You can't imagine what that means to us. It makes us feel so useful, so strong"[9].

Scenarios from Africa is an ongoing cyclical process, with a long term perspective. One of its primary aims is to increase the effectiveness of HIV communication in a sustainable way. To this end, the process seeks to operate in a culture of learning. This is especially fostered by the selection sessions, at which communication, HIV and youth specialists learn from one another and from the young authors of the scenarios. As one juror at the 2003 selection session commented: "Taking part in this jury has allowed us to gauge the impact of messages that have been directed at young people and to evaluate the possible interpretations of the messages and images. It's very useful feedback that will help shape future trends" (Global Dialogues, 2003c). The culture of learning also extends to the film set. Senegalese director Hamet Fall Diagne remembers how the entire crew became involved in the topic when they were making a film. "The sound

9 Personal conversation, March 2004.

man would stop working and correct someone who said something wrong [about HIV]. It was like a training session"[10].

The process is designed to increase exchange, collaboration and synergies. One of the ways it seeks to reinforce partner structures is by heightening their visibility and helping local communities and other organisations become aware of the resources and services they offer. This is often particularly valuable to recently established organisations or projects. Before the 2002 contest, the *Scenarios* coordinator in northern Togo noted that the HIV community in that neglected part of the country had not established any collaborative fabric to speak of. Today, she reports, collaboration revolves around the "*Scenarios* network"[11]. Association with the *Scenarios* process also often serves to accentuate the credibility of local organisations at community level. One CBO representative in Senegal has commented that "the contest gives our organisation a kind of aura" (Global Dialogues, 2003c).

Mass media and community reinforcement

It is generally agreed that health communication through the mass media has greatest impact when it is reinforced through interpersonal channels. The *Scenarios* films are extremely effective at generating dialogue. In addition, they have the advantage of multiple distribution platforms –via broadcasts on television and radio and through diverse kinds of screenings by NGOs and CBOs, followed by discussion, at community level. Given the involvement of CBOs in the entire *Scenarios* process, their level of ownership of the final products is correspondingly high. They are therefore in a particularly strong position to advocate for and reinforce the message of the films.

The criteria for selecting the winning scenarios that will be turned into films and radio shows are debated at the start of each selection session. The films are intended to be short enough for effective and efficient use as dialogue triggers in time-limited educational sessions, but long enough to contextualise behaviour, generate real emotional engagement, and thereby increase identification and risk perception. A script does not need to be polished or factually accurate at this stage, but it does need to display the creativity and originality that will allow it –through the skills of top directors, actors and production teams– to attract and retain attention and give rise to constructive debate.

Thought-provoking narratives, behavioural models

The limitations of didactical and "top-down" approaches when addressing complex behaviours related to sexuality, particularly in resource-poor environments, are evident. If long term social change is to occur, it is crucial to promote critical

10 Personal conversation, August 2001.
11 Personal conversation, March 2003.

thinking throughout society about existing social and gender inequities, which often stymie efforts at individual behaviour change. Both the contest and the films seek to provoke reflection on the root causes of HIV, not least the vulnerability of women, while at the same time promoting strong female role models. The contest provides a particularly powerful forum for discussion as more than half of all participants work in mixed-gender teams.

Male and female members of audiences respond very positively to the strong female characters in the films. In pre-testing of some of the first films in Mali, young men and women in urban and rural contexts said this was one of the things they liked best. "A Ring on her Finger", in which Nancy resists the stratagems her boyfriend uses to try and get her into bed, often provokes applause from the audience. According to a partner in northern Mozambique, "Nancy and Kady [the girlfriend in "The Shop"] inspire our women to contemplate what they want out of relationships. The men in our groups also appreciate these strong women: as one male seminar participant recently noted, 'I want a woman like that, because then I'll know that when she says yes, she really *wants* to be with me'"[12].

Other films model family support for a person with AIDS ("Uncle Ali", 2000; "African Solidarity", 2004); marital fidelity –in the person of a newly-elected African president! ("Safe Journey", 2004); a couple getting tested for HIV ("Good Reasons", 2004); business-owners helping to protect their workforce from HIV ("The Champions", 2004); or a schoolgirl calling for increased access to antiretrovirals ("A Call to Action", 2004).

Outcomes

Over 42,000 young people from 25 African countries have taken part in the three *Scenarios from Africa* contests held to date. Evaluations, both external and internal, indicate that the number of people influenced by the contest and associated debate is likely to be considerably higher than the actual number of participants. As one contest participant told an external evaluator, "AIDS is replacing football as the most talked about subject. Before we were not interested, but now we are" (Global Dialogues, 2001).

The contests have proved extremely effective at encouraging young people to seek out information, at generating dialogue with a wide range of people, and at encouraging reflection about HIV/AIDS. As one teacher in Senegal commented: "The marked improvement in knowledge levels became evident when we [teachers] asked specific questions at the end of the contest about topics that had been the source of confusion among students when the contest began". Another teacher in Togo explained that "Before the contest it was shocking, embarrassing to talk about AIDS. Now *Scenarios from the Sahel* has become the way in to talking about AIDS in the school" (Global Dialogues, 2003a).

12 Personal correspondence, September 2004.

Over half of all participants to date were members of a mixed-gender team, and over 40% were female. In addition to increasingly reaching young people across the continent, the contests have been very successful at reaching young people throughout individual countries. More than a quarter of all participants in the 2002 contest came from a small or medium-sized town, and 13% came from a village. When asked why they decided to take part in the contest, young people state that their main reason was a desire to raise awareness and to speak out. As one contest participant told an external evaluator: "Nobody ever listens to us. We participated in the contest because it finally gave us a chance to say what we think and what we feel" (Global Dialogues, 2001).

The 2002 *Scenarios from Africa* contest team was composed of hundreds (at least 400) of partner organisations or individual outreach workers. In several project countries in 2002, people living with HIV/AIDS served as contest outreach workers and actively engaged participants in dialogue as they went about creating their scenarios. Contest team members made themselves available to respond to questions on the contest and on HIV/AIDS in general –questions asked not only by potential participants, but also by parents, teachers, and traditional and religious leaders. This approach dramatically enhanced community participation in the implementation of the project.

An external evaluation assessing the 2002 contest in Burkina Faso and Togo concluded:

> The contest was a wonderful opportunity for synergies and for the mobilisation around the fight against HIV/AIDS of hundreds of associations.... The diversity of the organisations involved was also a source of richness and a factor in its success: neighbourhood youth associations, school youth groups, information centres, support centres of people living with HIV/AIDS, representatives of educational establishments, the communal authorities... (Global Dialogues, 2003a).

The contest reinforces the existing work of partners "by providing a concrete activity to implement, and complementing their on-going activities" (Global Dialogues, 2001). The *Scenarios* process increases links between participants and partners and facilitates contacts between partner organisations, "which is leading to better collaboration now and most likely in the future" (ibid.).

In the 2002/2003 selection process, a total of 113 people from 95 organisations served as jurors at the national or international level. Jury members say that the selection process is "instructive and stimulating, aiding them to rethink current strategies and activities in order to achieve greater impact" (ibid.).

Between 1997 and 2001, thirteen films were produced based on ideas thought up by young people in the original three *Scenarios* countries. All thirteen films are available in at least 12 languages. By September 2004, almost 17,000 video cassettes or CD-Roms of the films had been distributed at community level in Africa in a range of languages. In addition, over 600 audio cassettes or CDs of the audio versions of the films (for use on radio) had been distributed. By March 2004, broadcast of the films had been confirmed on over 75 television stations in or serving Africa. The films have been broadcast on locally-based stations in at least 35 countries of continental Africa. Distribution of the 2004 *Scenarios from Africa* films in a range of languages will commence in January 2005.

It is impossible to estimate how many people have been reached by the compilation video, but it is likely that it runs into at least hundreds of thousands. Television broadcasts of the films are likely to have reached tens of millions of Africans. As the representative of one Senegalese NGO told an external evaluator, "We personally have touched hundreds, no thousands of people with these tapes directly, without even attempting to calculate how many millions have been touched through the mass media" (Global Dialogues, 2003b).

External evaluators assessed the reception of the films in Senegal and in Burkina Faso and Togo respectively in spring 2003, and concluded:

> The films are widely distributed and their success is real, as they have become the primary awareness-raising resource used by the actors in the field of prevention and care whom I met. Young people say they are moved by the stories recounted in the films and many of them say that their behaviour has changed or is going to change after seeing *Scenarios from the Sahel*. They have contributed to raising the awareness of the general public and particularly young people –while entertaining them– about the modes of prevention linked to realistic and feasible behaviour change. (Global Dialogues, 2003a)

External evaluators are understandably cautious about attributing changes in behaviour to the *Scenarios* process. However, they record repeated instances of young people and NGO representatives doing exactly this, such as girls saying they will abstain from pre-marital sex, facilitators being approached by women for male and female condoms, or the number of young people coming for HIV testing increasing following awareness-raising with the films. In quantitative surveys respondents report that the films make them more inclined to practice a range of risk reduction strategies.

Local partners attribute the appeal of the films to a range of factors, but the consensus is clearly that the process is key to the success of the product:

> ...the *Scenarios from the Sahel* films are a vision of young people, they present things as young people recount them... In other IEC films, the audience is told this is what you have to do. Here, the *Scenarios from the Sahel* films show the reality. This is the behavior that has the most favourable consequences. This is behaviour at its worst. For example, in "The Shop", they are shown a model. There is no judgement, no condemnation of the action. Behaviours are simply presented with their advantages and disadvantages, without judgement, leaving the viewer to decide

what's best for him (representative of national youth organisation in Burkina Faso, cited in Global Dialogues, 2003b).

A colleague working for a community-based organisation in northern Mozambique writes that participants in their HIV training seminars often ask to watch the *Scenarios* films a second, third or fourth time: "The characters embody our own –often hidden– struggles and emotions, and give an example of how we too may respond. They portray a very real world –an African world, where HIV is raging and heroes are learning to fight back"[13].

Conclusions

The *Scenarios* process works in an integrated way, drawing on existing local infra-structure and resources. It operates at multiple mutually-reinforcing levels, with a view to challenging stigma and the root causes of HIV infection and fostering the kind of social cohesiveness that can lead to long-term change. We believe that this is only possible through concerted, coordinated, multi-sectoral efforts that build the capacity of local organisations and help local people to talk about, identify and address their needs and priorities. This action is facilitated and reinforced through the mass dissemination of communication resources that are scripted and produced locally and that model behaviour and advocate for change.

The active community involvement in the production of the *Scenarios* media products ensures their relevance and appeal. In turn, the mass distribution of these products is a powerful motivator for community mobilisation. This methodology is empowering for the young participants, the organisations involved and the creative teams that transform the winning ideas into short films.

The films themselves are high quality, fictional, non-didactic, emotionally powerful, and long enough to contextualise behaviour and promote emotional engagement. Their availability in African languages makes them accessible to the communities that need them most. Their objective is to promote dialogue, reflection, and hope, helping to generate collective efficacy.

Without doubt, young people are key beneficiaries of the *Scenarios* process. However, that process also serves to put young people in a position such that society in general becomes the beneficiary of their knowledge, creativity, and energy.

13 Ibid.

Chapter 26

Communication functions in an evolving context of rural development
Ricardo Ramírez

While rural development today is understood as a broad field that encompasses |
multiple livelihoods and sectors, during the 1970s and '80s it was closely associated
with a 'transfer of technology' approach in support of agriculture and forestry
(Röling, 1988). The underlying model was the diffusion of innovations that placed
emphasis on the adoption of new technology as a way of enabling farmers to
become more productive (Rogers, 1983). Many government organizations and
development agencies were structured along these lines, with agricultural, livestock,
forestry and fishery departments. Extension and information were usually made separate departments. In communication, most of these organizations functioned within a 'transmission world-view'. This was certainly the case with the agricultural extension organizations that for many years were designed under the World Bank 'training and visit' (T&V) system, which sought to spread agricultural innovation through
contact farmers as a way of improving production and –ideally– rural incomes. While
today's debates on extension are firmly rooted in how they may actually reduce
poverty, poverty reduction was at the time presumed to be a consequence of the
T&V approach (Farrington et al, 2002). Critics of this approach in the late 1970s and
the '80s were concerned that rural poverty was a more complex matter. Rural development called for an approach that supported multiple livelihoods, not just productive ones. Moreover, the communication dimension referred not only to the transfer
of new ideas; it also embraced the acknowledgment of what people already knew.
In the example from Peru, outlined below, modern audiovisual media were used to
capture and share these traditional insights in unprecedented ways.

Case study: Peru

In Peru, a project supported by the Food and Agriculture Organization of the United Nations (FAO) during the mid to late 1970s experimented with the use of video to help document traditional knowledge and share it among other groups in the highlands. The approach was termed *pedagogía audiovisual* (audiovisual pedagogy), suggesting an adult education approach to video. The model developed by Manuel Calvelo Rios and colleagues centered on reviving traditional wisdom in the form of agricultural know-how that was well adapted to specific agro-ecologies and deserved to be documented, analyzed and shared. The model differed from the conventional 'message-channel-receiver' model and was rather one of 'interpreter-medium-interpreter'[1] where each person involved in the communication process was perceived as an active receiver and sender of messages (Calvelo Ríos, 2003). The approach centered on producing training materials on existing techniques, and producing educational modules on video, with accompanying workbooks for facilitators and farmer trainees. The videos would be used together with hands-on training events. The approach also focused on celebrating traditional knowledge, which was noteworthy at a time dominated by the modernist approach to agricultural development, where expert advise from scientists was perceived as being superior.

The process centered on the notion that training meant helping people take action and modify their reality (Fraser, 1987). It fitted the notion advanced in Brazil by Paulo Freire, who in the early 1970s wrote about education and communication as the basis for conscientization and criticized agricultural extension as a top-down process (Freire, 1973). The development of audiovisual pedagogy in Peru took place in opposition to conventional agricultural extension, which as we shall see later, was predominantly rooted in the 'transmission' world-view and therefore shared little with the participatory or 'symmetric' world-view. This meant that within organizations, the promotion of Communication for Development met with opposition by units or partner organizations or agencies that worked in the 'transmission' world-view[2].

---

1 'Interpreter' is used as a translation for the Spanish term 'interlocutor'; another possible term would be 'intermediary', though the term 'locutor' refers to the action of talking.

2 The term 'communication' has been understood in many ways by practitioners and planners, with most if not all interpretations falling into two basic perspectives: the 'transmission' world-view that centers on a one-way process of information transfer, vs. the 'symmetric' world-view that emphasizes shared perceptions in the context of interaction (Windahl et al, 1992). These two interpretations have been at the heart of the evolution of communication for rural development and debate among its practitioners. Those comfortable with the transmission world-view have tended to work under modernist assumptions about development, focused on the notion that the diffusion of innovations would help solve basic problems of underdevelopment. This school of thought suggested that lack of knowledge was the key issue needing attention; and so found the transmission focus appropriate. In contrast, those who understood the challenge of rural development in the context of unequal distribution of resources found meaning in a dependency theory that pointed to social change and structural transformation as necessary steps toward improving rural livelihoods (Waisbord, 2001). The two perspectives embodied different world-views that incorporated contrasting perspectives (elaborated further in other chapters of this book).

Another development | 419

In the mid 1970s, the Dag Hammarskjöld Foundation published a groundbreaking report entitled "What now? Another Development" that called for attention to the satisfaction of needs, beginning with the eradication of poverty. It advocated self-reliant and endogenous development that relied on societies' own strengths, and called for development in harmony with the environment. The report underlined that development required structural transformation and that immediate action was both necessary and possible (Dag Hammarskjöld Foundation, 1975). The communication work done by the FAO in Peru was certainly in line with this thrust. Essentially it was based on principles of adult education, very much along a Freirian line of thinking, and was entirely compatible with Another Development. The momentum for a trend in favor of more participatory perspectives was being set in motion.

A few years later, a voice from the field was heard when the Dag Hammarskjöld Foundation published a book by Andreas Fuglesang, a seasoned practitioner. *About Understanding –Ideas and Observations on Cross-Cultural Communication* (1982) has become a classic for communication practitioners in many fields. It builds on the way oral culture processes information and shares it. It is rich with examples that show how we all perceive the world differently. It emphasizes communication as a process of sharing concepts. A quote from a Zambian woman says it all:

> Why do you Mzungu [white people] not try to understand the minds of Africans more than their ability to work? You people do not understand, your words do not belong to our minds (Fuglesang, 1982).

During the 1980s the term *participatory communication* began to emerge. In Latin America this perspective was rooted in several decades of work –*Radio Sutatenza* experience in Colombia and the miners' radios in Bolivia, to name just a couple. The term sought to emphasize collective meaning-making (as the Latin root of communication *communis facere* emphasizes). However, it did not actually represent a unified model and was therefore not easy to define, though all agreed that it represented a very different approach compared with the transmission model (Gumucio-Dagron, 2001; White et al, 1994; Bessette, 1996).

During the late 1980s and early '90s, the thrust toward human and sustainable development caused a shift in thinking, and rural development thinking began to encompass a broader picture. This is especially true with regard to focus on poverty alleviation, which meant that attention also had to be given to other sectoral issues: food security, employment, rural industry, policy, migration, and land tenure issues, to name just a few.

During the 1990s the way communication for development was promoted shifted along with the development trends of the day. At the FAO we emphasized its contribution to 'sustainable development' building on "Our Common Future", the report of the World Commission on Environment and

Development (1987); and to 'human development' following the UNDP Human Development Report of 1991. The 1991 Roundtable on Development Communication in Rome concluded that a major effort was needed in order to reach decision-makers and drive home the contribution of communication for development in this field (FAO, 1991a). One concrete product was the 1991 video "Sharing Knowledge", which emphasized the role of communication in sustainable development. The video includes an opening statement by Gro Brundtland, then Prime Minister of Norway and Chairperson of the World Commission on Environment and Development, in which she said:

> Sustainable development is a major challenge for the next century. People are central to that task. The only way we can work for a common cause, for common interest, to improve our condition, is really through communication. Basically, it has to do with democracy, with participation, with spreading of knowledge and insight and ability to take care of our future. (FAO, 1991b).

In other words, over a period of two decades a shift took place from an emphasis on the transmission of agricultural information, to an acknowledgement that rural development is a multi-sectoral, complex context. During the 1990s, FAO pioneered communication projects in Asia, Latin America and the Caribbean and Africa, and produced a significant number of case studies documenting innovative approaches. Whether this meant rural radio in west Africa, where people at the grassroots were directly involved in producing programs, or a farmer-centered approach to communication campaign design in the Philippines, the emphasis was on participation.

By the start of the new century, the FAO had consolidated its experience with participatory communication and had produced case studies, evaluations and manuals, and specialized publications on gender and communication (Coldevin & FAO, 2000; Mefalopulos and Kamlongera, 2002; Balit, 1999). While this is not the place to review each of these in detail, the overall collection of publications is indicative of the coming-of-age of an applied discipline[3].

Case study: Philippines[4]

Rural communities exchange information with multiple sources including other farmers, traders, input suppliers, non-governmental organizations, outreach workers, and research institutions. These different actors constitute agricultural communication networks and interact regularly in multiple ways to form new relationships for innovation. At times, they lobby and influence policy-makers in search of improved access to markets, technology or incentive programs. The

3 For a complete list of publications refer to <http://www.fao.org/sd/KN1_en.htm> and to the CD prepared in 2000 <http://www.fao.org/sd/CDdirect/CDre0052.htm>.

4 Some of the material presented here is based on Ramírez, R. (1997) *Understanding Farmers' Communication Networks: Combining PRA with Agricultural Knowledge Systems Analysis*, London: IIED.

best extension systems in the world develop where farmers are organized and able to lobby for the technical assistance that they consider the top priority –not the other way around (Röling, 1988). It is the demand capacity of farmers that dictates the quality and effectiveness of the extension support. The opposite process, whereby extension systems conceivably strengthen farmers' production systems through technology, is more a myth about the transfer of technology model than an observable reality.

The notion of agricultural knowledge and information systems (AKIS) was developed in the late 1980s by researchers at Wageningen Agricultural University in the Netherlands. The AKIS model describes the two-way flow of information and knowledge among researchers, extension organizations and farmers. In other words, the model is a concept that runs against the linear information dissemination systems which were developed in most national agricultural research systems under the transfer of technology model. It is a perspective that emphasizes multiple actors and focuses on the description and analysis of linkages with a view to improving them. In this approach, communication is seen as a central component.

In the AKIS perspective, a two-way exchange of information is crucial for innovation. As a consequence, the role of extension has been reformulated from a one-way persuasive channel into a two-way channel for requests and answers that facilitates the learning process for farmers, extension staff and researchers. But the change from disseminating to facilitating requires staff with fundamentally different attitudes, skills and knowledge. From the point of view of the AKIS, and of participatory research, the facilitator can be described as a broker of information demands and supplies.

Following the growing trend in participatory analyses where information is visualized, and borrowing from the AKIS notion, an approach was developed to map the knowledge networks. This research was first developed through an FAO project in the Philippines and then further tested in Ethiopia and Peru. Since then, the mapping of networks of stakeholders has been used in communication planning in other parts of the world and in other sectors, such as rural water planning (Ramírez and Quarry, 2004a, 2004b).

This approach allows researchers, field workers and rural communities to identify the networks of information exchange jointly, bringing these actors together in a closer learning and planning process. It has three stages:

1 mapping of actors and linkages;

2 analysis of linkage performance; and

3 an action plan for modifying roles and improving linkages.

Figure 1. Linkage map prepared with the farmers of Barangay Mamala, Region IV, the Philippines

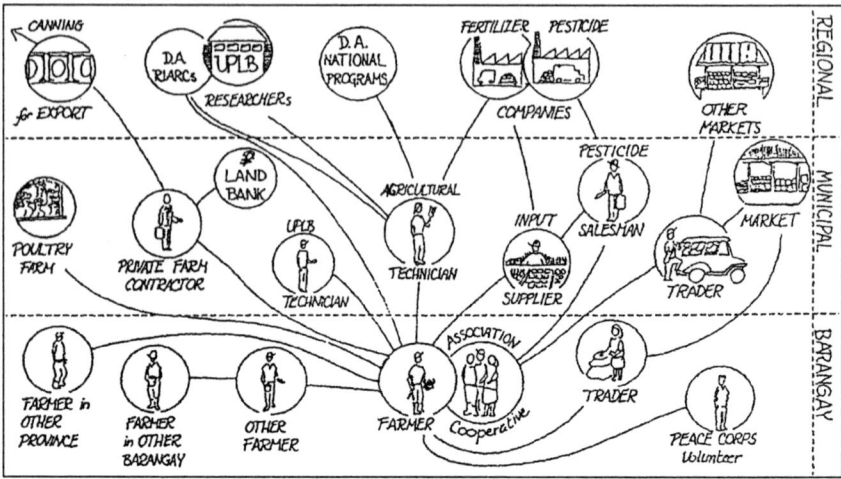

The linkage map (Figure 1) shows stakeholders by their location (barangay or village, municipal, and regional/national) and indicates their linkages. It captures what people 'know' in a tacit manner about their networks but have not had a chance to organize or analyze. Once key linkages have been identified, they can be analyzed using a simple matrix (Figure 2). The criteria for analysis can be developed in each context, yet the key criteria tend to focus on who controls the linkage (the power dimension).

Figure 2

Site: Barangay Mamala	Criteria for assessing performance						
Linkage	Awareness of other actor's service	Relevance of other actor's service	Timeliness of other actor's service	Accessibility of other actor's service	Communication medium through which link is mediated	Linkage control	Remarks
Farmer — Farmer [linkage outcome: seed variety exchange]	Empathy; sharing same predicament	High	Regular contact	Fully accessible	Oral; demonstration	Equally shared by both actors	Effective link between two actors who share same reality; a linkage with unexplicited potential
Farmer — AT: Agricultural Technician [Extension worker]	F aware that AT's function is not open to his influence; aware that AT lacks expertise in most topics	F has experimented but rejected the recommendation; the service is therefore considered to be of limited relevance	F receives information/advise without timely supply of technology or inputs. At times these become available one year later	Irregular	F describes AT's message delivery as traditional and top-down [black-board lecturer] without printed materials	F has no control	Very little impact in terms of technology transfer. Sometimes useful impact in enhancing F's organization
[linkage outcome: limited dissemination of technology; some support to F organization]	AT only partially aware of F's strengths and needs	AT does not perceive F's knowledge as worthy; AT has no training to diagnose/assess needs with the participation of F	AT plans visits as per instruction and schedules agreed with the M.A.O. AT has 6-7 barangays to visit and lacks funds for travel	AT's access to farmer is irregular	AT lectures but does not diagnose or learn from F	AT controls, although under directives handed down from M.A.O. [institutional control]	[as above]

In the case of the Philippines, the major linkages identified were analyzed using | **423**
the following six criteria:

1 actors' *awareness* of other actors' functions in a linkage;

2 *relevance* of other actors' services;

3 *timeliness* of other actors' services: if the information input is pro-
   grammed to coincide with the availability of other inputs, then the
   service is timely;

4 *accessibility* to other actors' services: if an extension worker is able to
   visit farmers regularly this can enhance the relevance and timeliness of
   the service;

5 *communication media* through which a link is mediated;

6 *control* over the initiation and management of a linkage: when farmers have demand capacity over the services in their area, the other criteria listed here can be better ensured.

The matrix provides the foundation for improved communication and an action
plan can be derived on the basis of this data. Other work also from the Philippines
used indicators to describe change in the information systems used by different
stakeholders (Lawrence, 1995). These included: amount of information, diversity
of sources, relevance, satisfied demand, credibility, complementarity of information sources, linkages between information sources, access by users, direction of
information flow, democratic control, and use of indigenous knowledge. While
there is no quantitative indicator of linkage performance, in essence an effective
link contributes to the actors' learning process while also responding to the
immediate needs of their job or economic activity.

A major advantage of this approach is the new perspectives that it can
bring to field workers who have been trained in conventional, one-way approaches to communication. This approach highlights the amount of know-how farmers
already have, noting that they tend to be each other's major sources of information; it shows the potential new roles for extension workers as brokers of information across multiple disciplines; it demonstrates the importance of horizontal
exchange of information as opposed to vertical; and it sheds light on the importance of shared power as a foundation for effective, trustful linkages among
stakeholders. The methodology on its own does not give any final answers, but it
does provide entry points. It calls for a process whereby extension workers along
with other municipal actors become facilitators in identifying and assessing problems and exploring solutions through networks.

Communication functions in an evolving context of rural development

A review of communication functions is a useful way of locating the above case
study in the context of this chapter about rural development. Communication for

rural development encompasses several complementary communication functions. The three major functions are: the communication of new policies, making things known (or educational communication), and facilitative communication. The original emphasis on transmission is highly compatible with the first two functions. By contrast, the case study emphasizes a participatory function that fits in well with the notion of social or facilitative communication. Table 1 explores the three functions in some detail.

Table 1. Communication functions and their attributes (adapted from Röling, 1994)

Communication function	Purposes	Initiator	Evidence of success
Policy communication	Making policies, programs, and the evolving procedures known	Government agency	Stakeholders demonstrate awareness by applying procedures or suggesting modifications to them
Educational communication: making things known, sharing knowledge	Making technical know-how accessible to increase knowledge about the production, transformation, organization and marketing dimensions of agriculture; including price information. Worldwide, there is a trend toward a closer engagement by farmers in technology development and adaptation in contrast to the conventional role of passive receiver of extension messages.	Service providers and farmers (with training on accessing content and transforming it)	Service providers are able to seek and find information sources and repackage materials for farmer learning. Farmers adopt practices or reject them knowledgeably; utilizing communication methods and media to enhance farmer-to-farmer linkages
Social or facilitative communication: platforms for participation and debate	Providing platforms for stakeholders to exchange perspectives, explore new ideas and programs, appreciate differences of opinions, negotiate common goals, develop partnerships, propose changes to programs and become confident participants able to articulate needs and opinions	Farmers' groups, district authorities, service providers, and local groups/organizations with support from a facilitator and a neutral convener	Stakeholders participate, become empowered, take action, and take over ownership of the program

The Philippines case study constitutes a means of bringing different parties together to visualize and understand their linkages. While this process could be started by many of the initiators listed, it often requires a neutral convener. International projects in the past have played this role and it is increasingly important to have organizations that can play this convening role and bring different parties to the table to negotiate common interests.

This notion of communication as a platform for negotiation is coherent with the notion of another sevelopment in that it is an example of participatory communication. It is an action-oriented tool that can be applied to project planning involving multiple stakeholders. It embodies the 'symmetric' world-view (Waisbord, 2001). In my experience, this approach has influenced practitioners in many fields of rural development, including water and sanitation, health, fisheries, and forestry. It has been instrumental in negotiation workshops arranged to review agricultural services in the context of privatization and decentralization (Lightfoot et al, 2001).

Communication for rural development requires attention to every function of communication (Table 1 only highlights three); it is not a matter of one versus another. Communication strategies, be they in agriculture or water and sanitation, need to embrace a combination of these functions (Ramírez and Quarry, 2004a; 2004b). Rural development approaches today give much attention to stakeholder interaction, in what is often referred to as 'actor-oriented approaches' (Biggs and Matsaert, 2004). Communication is well suited to supporting these emerging world-views. This has been so for several decades, but now we also have evidence and methods to share.

Rural development has evolved in the last few decades. Today, it is a field of applied research and action that is quite complex. There is an acknowledgement that many stakeholders need to be involved and that their perspectives are bound to be different. This suggests a need for processes of negotiation, not only about strategies, but more importantly about common understanding. The following definition of communication for development encapsulates these complementary dimensions:

> Communication for development is the use of communication processes, techniques and media to help people towards a full awareness of their situation and their options for change, to resolve conflicts, to work towards consensus, to help people plan actions for change and sustainable development, to help people acquire the knowledge and skills they need to improve their condition and that of society, and to improve the effectiveness of institutions (Fraser and Restrepo-Estrada, 1998).

Chapter 27

Bridging digital divides
Lessons learned from the IT initiatives of the Grameen Bank in Bangladesh

Arvind Singhal, Peer J. Svenkerud, Prashant Malaviya, Everett M. Rogers & Vijay Krishna

The mobile phone is like a cow. It gives me "milk" several times a day. And all I need to do is to keep its battery charged. It does not need to be fed, cleaned, and milked. It has now connected our village with the world.

Parveen Begum, owner and sole dispenser of mobile telephony services in Village Chakalgram, Savar Thana, Bangladesh, in a personal interview (May 2, 2001)

I want my fellow Americans to know that the people of Bangladesh are a good investment. With loans to buy cell phones, entire villages are brought into the information age. I want people throughout the world to know this story

U.S. President Bill Clinton in an address during his meeting with members of the Village Phone Project in Dhaka, Bangladesh in March, 2000

As a great social leveler, information technology ranks second only to death. It can raze cultural barriers, overwhelm economic inequalities, even compensate for intellectual disparities. In short, high technology can put unequal human beings on an equal footing, and that makes it the most potent democratizing tool ever devised.

Sam Pitroda (1993), the visionary technologist who spearheaded India's telecommunications revolution

A third of the world's population has never made a phone call. This fact emphasizes what has become known as the digital divide –the tremendous gap between people with access to information technology (IT) and those without (Martínez-Frías, 2003). The present chapter discusses the experience of the Grameen Bank in Bangladesh in harnessing information technologies for social change. We especially focus on the Grameen's mobile telephony operations, including how the organization integrates mobile telephony services with solar power and Internet services to overcome the digital divide.

Grameen Bank, mobile telephony, and social dividends

How can information technologies be harnessed in rural areas, where there is no dedicated electrical power, and where the cost of installing, maintaining, and purchasing such services is cumbersome? One answer to this problem is provided by the Grameen (rural) Bank in Bangladesh. Founded in 1983 by Professor Muhammad Yunus, the Grameen Bank is a system of lending small amounts of money to poor women so that they can earn a living through self-employment. No collateral is needed, as the poor do not have any. Instead, the women borrowers are organized in a group of five friends. Each group member must repay their loan on time, while ensuring that other group members do the same, or else their opportunity for a future loan is jeopardized. This delicate dynamic between "peer-pressure" and "peer-support" among Grameen borrowers is at the heart of its widespread success (Auwal and Singhal, 1992; Papa, Auwal and Singhal, 1995; Papa, Auwal and Singhal, 1997; Yunus, 1999).

By 2004, the Grameen Bank had loaned the equivalent of $ 4.3 billion (US dollars) to 3.5 million poor borrowers (of which 95% are women borrowers), and had an enviable loan recovery rate of 98%. The idea of microlending, based on the Grameen Bank experience, has spread throughout the world, and has everywhere proven effective in gaining a high rate of repayment of the loans. In short, interpersonal networks are effective collateral for poor women.

In 1997, Professor Yunus established a non-profit organization called Grameen Telecom with the vision of placing one mobile phone in each of the 68,000 villages of Bangladesh. At that time, there was one telephone in Bangladesh for every 400 people, representing one of the lowest telephone densities in the world[1]. There was virtually no access to telephony services in rural areas. Professor Yunus realized that while it was not possible for each rural household to own a telephone, it is possible through mobile telephone technology to provide access to each villager.

Thus the Grameen Telecom's Village Phone Project (VPP) was born. In 1997, Grameen Telecom formed a joint venture company called GrameenPhone Ltd. (GP) in partnership with Telenor of Norway, Marubeni of Japan, and

1 In 2004, there exists one telephone in Bangladesh for every 175 people.

Gonofone Development Corporation of the US[2]. The company, GP, was awarded license to operate nation-wide GSM-900 cellular network on 11 November, 1996. GP started its operation on March 26, 1997.

Creating win-win synergies

The business model of the VPP was deceptively simple and a potential win-win for everyone involved, including the service providers and the end users (Singhal, Svenkerud and Flydal, 2002). Four business entities were involved in the VPP: GrameenPhone (the for-profit business), Grameen Telecom (the not-for-profit business), Grameen Bank (the not-for-profit micro-credit bank), and the mobile handset owner in the village, commonly referred to as the Village Phone Lady (who was a member of Grameen Bank) (Malaviya, Singhal, Svenkerud and Srivastava, 2004a, 2004b).

GrameenPhone sold bulk airtime to Grameen Telecom at half the regular rate that was levied in the urban areas. The handsets were made available to villagers through Grameen Bank loans. Grameen Telecom was responsible for the sales, marketing, servicing and administration of the village phones. This arrangement meant that GrameenPhone avoided the costs of billing and bill collection from the village phone users, and had a steady revenue stream from Grameen Telecom. Grameen Bank benefited by cross-selling to villagers (who were existing Grameen Bank borrowers) the opportunity to start an additional business of providing mobile phone services in their village. Because the initial loan for a mobile phone set was about USD 390, an amount few villagers could invest on their own, these Grameen Bank members took loans to lease or purchase the mobile telephone sets, thus generating additional income for Grameen Bank (Malaviya, Singhal, Svenkerud and Srivastava, 2004b). In addition, villagers settled their monthly telephone bills while repaying their loan amounts. For Grameen Telecom, the VPP set-up meant that it could be optimistic about fulfilling its promise of providing mobile telephony in villages for the rural poor of Bangladesh. While most telephone companies targeted only the rich living in the cities, Grameen Telecom's VPP targeted the rural poor, particularly women, because 95% of Grameen Bank borrowers are women. The Village Phone Ladies benefited because they now had an independent source of revenue. The villagers who used the mobile phones to make and receive calls benefited because they were now "connected" to the rest of the world, using one of the most modern cellular technologies of the world, while paying one of the cheapest cellular rates in the world. And from the perspective of the Government of Bangladesh, with the 'mobile' presence of the village telephone lady, rural residents could receive and make telephone calls, obviating the need to install expensive large-scale telephone exchanges and digital switching systems.

2 Telenor Corporation is the majority owner of Grameen Phone's equity (over 50%); Grameen Telecom owns about 35% of the equity, and the other partners own the balance.

Rising profits

Since its inception in 1997, Grameen Phone's subscription has doubled each year to reach over a million subscribers by December 2003 (Malaviya, Singhal, Svenkerud and Srivastava, 2004b), which represents the biggest subscriber base and coverage of any mobile telephony operator in Bangladesh, and in South Asia. The company turned a profit in 2000 of $14 million, which steeply climbed to over $110 million in 2002 (Malaviya, Singhal, Svenkerud and Srivastava, 2004b). Many believe that even brighter business prospects lie ahead: demand for mobile telephony services in Bangladesh is estimated at about 5 to 6 million subscribers (out of a population of 130 million people). Grameen Phone's growing mobile telephony network in the country and its financial viability help the Grameen Telecom's Village Phone Project to piggyback on it.

Social dividends

By April 2004, some 54,000 village phones were operating (about 5% of all GrameenPhone's subscribers) in about 36,000 Bangladeshi villages. These 54,000 village phones were serving an estimated 65 million rural inhabitants, more than 60% of Bangladesh's rural population. The village phones, on average, generated 2-3 times more revenues for GrameenPhone than a personal use city subscription, although the total revenue from these village phones was a relatively small percent of total GrameenPhone revenues (6%) (<www.telecommons.com/villagephone>, 2000).

Although the village phones contributed a small percent toward GrameenPhone revenues, they yielded a very high social impact in terms of reaching 65 million rural Bangladeshis who previously did not have access to telephony services. Studies indicated that the VPP had a very positive economic impact in rural areas, creating a substantial consumer surplus, and immeasurable quality-of-life enhancements[3]. For instance, the village phone obviated the need for a rural farmer to make a trip to the city to find out the market price of produce. The village phone accomplished this task at about one-fourth the cost of taking the trip to the city and almost instantaneously (as compared to the hours of time it can take to make the trip to Dhaka). Further, the village phone helped families keep in touch with relatives overseas, to know about remittances sent to them from migrant workers overseas, and patients to arrange appointments with the doctors in the cities. Also, people living in the villages were thinking and doing things somewhat differently after the mobile phone arrived. For instance, many villagers started maintaining livestock and poultry stocks as it now became possible to contact experts if there was ever an outbreak of a poultry or livestock disease (Malaviya, Singhal, Svenkerud and Srivastava, 2004b). They could also learn of the current market prices of their poultry products achieving higher returns on

3 See Richardson et al (2000) and Bayes et al (1999).

sales. The supply of agricultural inputs like diesel and fertilizer become more stable in the villages because dealers could monitor the supply situation throughout the year and guard against any unforeseen contingencies.

Rural women in Bangladesh also became increasingly empowered through the Village Phone Project. Usually, technological "toys" (such as cameras, radios, cassette players and others) are appropriated by rural men. However, through the VPP the mobile phone was placed in the hands of rural women. Now even a rich landowner had to come to their home to access the telephone service. He had to wait in line for his turn if another villager was using the phone at that time. The home of the village phone lady became an important location on the village map, often being referred to as the *Phone Bari* (or "home of the phone"). The VPP thus conferred status and prestige on rural Bangladeshi women.

So what have been the overall effects of the Village Phone Project in rural Bangladesh? The Village Phone Project makes telephony services accessible and affordable to poor, rural Bangladeshis, spurs employment, increases the social status of the village telephone ladies, provides access to market information and to medical services, and represents a tool to communicate with family and friends within Bangladesh and outside (Richardson et al, 2000; Bayes et al, 1999; Quadir, 2003).

Integrating telephony with solar power and Internet services

Another information technology venture of the Grameen Bank is the Village Internet Program (VIP), a pilot project in which borrowers obtain loans to purchase and operate "cyber kiosks" for profit. The purpose behind the "cyber kiosks" is for Grameen borrowers to have increased access to agricultural and market information for business use, to provide distance and virtual education through remote classroom facilities, and to provide computer-based employment (such as data-entry, transcription services, etc.) in rural areas, as an alternative to massive migration to the cities (Yunus, 1998).

The VIP is supported by established infrastructures and technologies within the Grameen family of companies. For instance, Grameen Shakti ("Energy") has developed photovoltaic solar systems to provide electricity to villages that lie beyond the national grid of central station electricity. The plan of VIP is to have cyber kiosks that run on solar power and connect to the Internet by mobile wireless, microwave, and laser connections. Each cyber kiosk will be run as an independently-owned and operated franchise of Grameen Communications, in which the borrower will earn money by selling Internet, telephony, and other computer-related services (Yunus, 1998).

Lessons learned

The key lessons of the Grameen Bank approach to the use of mobile telephony and Internet services are the following.

1. *Poor people should not just be the passive consumers of communication technology, but rather its owners.* When poor people own communication technology in ways to provide increased access to information to the resource-poor and, in so doing, create a viable business proposition for themselves, they help bridge the digital and economic divide in society.

2. *Low-income emerging markets for information technology products can be profitable.* Reaching out to rural customer segments in emerging markets should not always be equated with charity and benevolence; rather it is possible to create models of social entrepreneurship which subscribe to multiple, co-existing, and mutually-reinforcing (win-win) bottom-lines (Prahalad, 2004; Quadir, 2003; Singhal, Svenkerud and Flydal, 2002). In low-income markets, such as in Bangladesh and other developing countries, companies must view the consumers as actively engaged in seeking a good life, not as passive consumers who merely want satisfaction (Letelier, 2003). The GrameenPhone was able to identify culturally relevant opportunities by making the link between culture and the purchase motive of the consumers.

Grameen's venture (in cooperation with Telenor of Norway and others) shows that multiple bottom-lines, such as the following, can be met.

>> *Commercial interests* in terms of revenues, profits, and growth.

>> *Social cause-related interests* in terms of serving unserved and underserved markets nationally, and also serving poor, rural, illiterate inhabitants who are traditionally excluded from traditional markets –thus overcoming the digital divide.

However, Telenor's forays into Bangladesh were not free of problems, pointing to the complexities in forging long-term win-win partnerships. The bureaucratic and regulatory hurdles under the state-owned telecommunications monopoly Bangladesh Telegraph and Telephone Board (BTTB), as well as Bangladesh's unstable political regime, is problematic for GrameenPhone's business operations (Malaviya, Singhal, Svenkerud and Srivastava, 2004b). For instance, the uncertain political support and the fear of heavy taxation have forced Telenor to re-invest all its profits into the Bangladeshi venture rather than attempt to take these profits out of country as dividend for its shareholders (Telenor's shareholders, understandably, were clamoring to receive dividends).

3. *Development organizations that have a good "brand" value and wide rural reach in a developing country, are uniquely positioned to partner with corporations to extend the benefits of information technology in rural areas.* Here Grameen's collaboration with Telenor Corporation of Norway is instructive. Clearly, in Bangladesh, "Grameen" has tremendous brand equity by virtue of its widespread success in poverty alleviation, empowerment of rural women, and its well-known credo that "good development is good business" (which is also the slogan of the Village Phone Project). Many in Bangladesh feel that the "Grameen" brand is far more recognized in Bangladesh than even Coca Cola! So

branding the new venture Grameen Phone brought instant credibility to Telenor's | **433**
business venture in Bangladesh. Also, Telenor's partnering with Grameen Telecom
made possible the Village Phone Project, whereby Grameen Bank borrowers who
take loans to lease or purchase the mobile telephone sets now settle their monthly telephone bills through the bank workers. The already existing village-based
loan disbursement and repayment infrastructure of the Grameen Bank allows for
handling the logistics of the Village Phone Project at a very small, additional marginal cost.

That said, Grameen Bank's involvement in the Village Phone Project is
perceived by some as problematic. Critics argue that the selection process of village telephone ladies propagates inequity by disallowing the most disadvantaged
rural women to participate (Singhal and Rogers, 2001). At the present time, the
"selected" village phone lady should have (a) a solid record of borrowing and
repaying Grameen Bank loans, (b) a successful existing business, for example, a
village grocery store, (c) a residence that is centrally located on the village map,
and (d) a family member who knows English letters and numbers. Few village
women in Bangladesh fulfill these criteria. Further, such a 'self-selection' of village
telephone ladies propagates a monopolistic control of telephony services at the
village level.

Conclusions

Despite the aforementioned problems and constraints, the Grameen Bank's integrated initiatives in harnessing information technologies for development are
exemplary and laudatory. That is one reason why the GrameenPhone project
directly inspired, in 2003, the MTN villagePhone project in Uganda to bring
telephony to underserved areas. This project –representing a unique collaboration
between Grameen Foundation USA, MTN Uganda (the country's largest telecommunications service provider), and five local microfinance institutions– was operational in 350 Ugandan villages by mid-2004, serving close to one million rural
inhabitants. By 2008, the MTN villagePhone project is estimated to place 5,000
village phones in rural Uganda, serving 10 million poor inhabitants who previously had no access to telephony.

In conclusion, the Grameen information technology operations in
Bangladesh, and its emerging replication in Uganda, demonstrate how "penny"
capitalism can operate creatively to bridge the digital divide and serve the under-
dogs of society.

Chapter 28

Theatre for Development in Africa
Christopher Kamlongera

Various terms are (and can be) used for Theatre for Development (TFD), for |
example: popular theatre, propaganda theatre, case drama, developmental theatre forum, or sometimes, political theatre. Each of these terms indicates to some
extent what this theatre tries to achieve. Theatre for Development is being developed as one way of helping the masses in the developing world to come to terms
with their environment and the onus of improving their lot culturally, education-
ally, politically, economically and socially.

It is a cliche to say indigenous performances in Africa contain within
them some functional element. In most cases this takes the form of a didactic
statement. While performers might engage in doing spectacular movements
and dances, they also carry within the performances special messages or lessons to some members of their audience. Some work in Theatre for
Development is a direct result of recognizing this characteristic in indigenous
Africa performances.

Western, "conventional" theatre activities in Africa, initiated by the
colonial education systems in a bid to develop the cultural life of the natives in
Africa, is another source of theatre for development. While 'straight drama' was
being taught and encouraged among the natives particularly through schools and
colleges, its development was very much pegged to missionary intentions of
eradicating pagan behaviour and any uncivil habits evident in their lives. So we
find that even the plays that were being developed from folk tales placed heavy
emphasis on the moral qualities of the stories.

Drama was not being pursued simply for its own sake, but also as a tool for inculcating behavioural patterns amongst Africans. In other words, drama was being used as a tool for teaching something other than drama itself. The didactic possibilities inherent in the dramatic art form were thus being exploited to the full. It is also from this background that work in Theatre for Development derives its origins. We can therefore say that the development of this theatre is due to three factors:

» colonial attempts to improve Africans through drama,

» a recognition on the part of colonialists that some positive aspects of behaviour could be extruded from indigenous performances, and

» the Africans' own reaction to these colonial attempts at developing their culture.

In 1930 G. A. Stevens reported British attempts to boost 'the aesthetic education of the negro' (Stevens, 1930: 92-93). Developing theatre skills was part of this education. One method employed in order to create this theatre was 'to take a native legend or story with a moral, split up the action into as many as eight or nine different scenes, each dealing with one dramatic moment, and interspersed with considerable knock-about dancing and singing'. It is interesting to note how close this technique is to theatre for development work going on today.

In 1931, Mary Kelly wrote about some experimental work being carried out by missionaries at the Holy Cross Mission, Pondoland (South Africa) (Kelly, 1931: 109-113). Here, these people 'were concerned with the fact that the christianizing of the natives seemed to mean the removal of much of their lowest instincts rather than of any ideal, and they felt that something should be suggested to take their place'. In other words the process of 'Christianizing' was one of deculturizing the African which needed checking without losing the 'civilizing' mission. One way of doing this was to adopt and dramatize local folklore, giving it an obvious Christian story bias.

Earlier at a conference on African Drama held by the 'Village Drama section of the British Drama league' in September 1932, this sort of work was endorsed as one positive way towards developing African drama[1]. At this conference "it was decided: (a) That a collection of themes should be made available for the use of native teachers (b) That a report of his conference should be sent to all educationalists in Africa, with a letter asking for their experience in the work, and for any conclusions that they had formed on it". The result of such a resolution was to push theatre work in Africa more directly under the wing of educationalists rather than mere missionaries. It also extended the areas of interest in terms of themes beyond the Bible story.

It should therefore be no wonder to see a report from Kenya in 1933 having nothing to do with 'religious drama', but community development. W. H.

1 "Notes", *Oversea Education*, Volume IV, No. 3, April 1933, pp. 160-161.

Taylor reporting his "observations on the dramatic talent of Africans" spoke of the work which was being carried out at the Jeans School of Kabete (in Kenya) whose task was the harnessing of "the natural dramatic talent of Africans and utilizing it for educational purposes and, finally, developing it in so far as it was amenable to conscious development for purely artistic ends" (Taylor, 1933: 17-20). Here was the first evidence of direct use of a theatre art for purposes other than aesthetic education. For although the religious drama mentioned earlier on seemed to do the same, its exponents talked more in aesthetic language than anything else. The moral tone of their work was always taken for granted. The work at Kabete had nothing to do with morality –in the Christian sense. Taylor continued to say that:

> In our first task we were actuated by utilitarian motives, our aim being to use the stage for propaganda purposes. The Jeans teacher, it must be remembered, is more than a supervisor of village schools; he is a man with a new faith and a new ideal centred round 'Better Homes', 'Cleaner Gardens and Plantations'. Various ways of instilling these tenets into the pagan population have been tried by Jeans teachers, but no one way has proved so successful in its practical outcome as the lecture combined with the propaganda play.

In this work technique was 'crudely' propagandist. There was no attempt to be subtle about the message. Continuing to describe his work Taylor said:

> The moral or points to be emphasized were always placed in a favourable position by the use of characters personifying animals from native lore. If the object of the play was to teach the value of grainstores, it was the clever Hare who profited by its use and Hyena who regretted clinging to the old methods; if we were trying to show the value of good management of a village school, the poor type of teacher was generally represented by the Monkey or Hyena and the better type by the Hare or the Bee. The acting was burlesque in the extreme and often overdone, but the point or points to be stressed were much discussed afterwards and taken to heart.

This work was highly recommended by specialists outside the teaching profession too. Taylor reported that even medical officers and sanitary inspectors in the area commented favourably on the work that his school was doing (ibid.: 18). One point that can easily be ignored in all this work is the emphasis that was being placed upon coaching the native teacher how to handle the drama work among his compatriots. At another conference on native drama held by the British Drama League again in 1933, it was popularly felt amongst those who attended (teachers, missionaries and administrators) that having introduced drama among the natives the next step was:

> To ask African teachers to make a selection of the native themes, so that a large amount of African folk-tales should be ready for dramatic use: from which, and simultaneously with which, [...] the African teachers should be

encouraged to make plays with their pupils and the adults of the villages, and that the highly educated African should, wherever possible, see these plays and note the methods and growth[2].

In another context, and much later, in Northern Rhodesia (now Zambia) H. H. Ferreira talked about "The Use of Social Case Drama in Training African Social Workers" by the colonial government (Ferreira, 1953: 35-40). Here he spelt out how in Northern Rhodesia they were using the so called 'social case drama' to combat "the problem (…) of conveying technical knowledge and subtleties of "case work" technique to a student body whose education and grasp of English, the language of instruction, was limited; the problem of students failing to grasp abstract ideas".

This work, like that of Taylor, was supplementing lectures and field work. He said that the basis of the work was role play. The technique here was simply to leave the role playing in the hands of the student who played case worker- after he had devised the whole situation together with the various characters he was to be involved with. The playing of the roles was gone into without any rehearsal. The students were just left to play their parts as best as they could. Following this would be a session of criticism from the students on how well the whole case had been handled by the case worker. For Ferreira, this allowed two things: maximum consideration of 'cultural' issues in social work as well as maximum participation from students in the process of learning.

So far we can see how the earlier part of the last century shows a clear emphasis upon propaganda theatre rather than theatre for art's sake that dominated the later half of the century. All educational endeavours during the earlier part of the century were motivated by utilitarian aims. The emphasis in missionary schools was on moral teaching. As time went on and as the idea of developing drama caught on, moves towards using drama for educational purposes became more pronounced. The concept of the Jeans school played a leading role in this development. The areas tackled through this drama ranged from hygiene to modern methods of agriculture. These are areas that still occupy the minds of present day practitioners. There is a re-emergence of this drama on the continent. Why is this so? Let us look at this new phenomenon closely to answer this question.

Rationale

It has been a common view among African (nationalist) intellectuals and politicians that performing arts have always been fulfilling a utilitarian role in the community and that to encourage this serves to forestall nearly lost African heritage:

> There are many reasons why our forefathers chose to use songs, dance drums and masks to educate their young, to comment on the socio-politi-

2 *Oversea Education*, Volume V, No. 2, January 1934, pp. 125-128. It would be interesting to see what the British Drama League Archives has, particularly in relation to African responses to this call.

cal conditions in their societies and to preserve their historical legends. One
of the reasons is that our forefathers realized that one of the most effective methods of education is through audio-visual aids of what was familiar. In other words our forefathers subscribed to the modern education axiom that if he sees and hears he remembers. They also realized that by presenting ideas through a variety of media such as songs, dance, mime, poetic recitals, ordinary narrative and masquerades, one is able to capture the imagination of the people. It was the function of our traditional theatre, not merely to entertain, but also to instruct[3].

Talking about the sudden resurgence of this theatre in the third world today, Ross Kidd explains the interest in it as

> an outgrowth of uses of rural theatre in the fundamental education campaigns of the '40s and '50s and the search for ways of supplementing the mass media which have been shown to be incapable of affecting change on their own without some intermediary process[4].

This view is partly supported by David Kerr, who says that popular theatre is being encouraged as a tool for adult education

> because of deficiencies in existing educational institutions and communications media which stem from elitism of colonial education and its irrelevancy to the goals of national development (Kerr, 1981: 145-155).

Both Ross Kidd and David Kerr relate theatre for development to non-formal education. They also share one philosophical basis in their discussion of this education: a philosophy deriving from the ideas of Paulo Freire. Of his work in Botswana (called *Laedza Batanai*) Kidd says it was "a non-formal education project [...] which attempted to follow a Freirean model" (Kidd and Byram, 1981). He goes on to say that "one of the key features of this programme was the use of popular theatre as the medium for encouraging participation, raising issues, fostering discussion and promoting collective action". From Nigeria, in West Africa, Michael Etherton, talking about his work with students of drama at Ahmadu Bello University, Zaria, among local farmers in a project called *Wason Manoma*, said their intentions in this were to communicate "to rural communities specific development objectives"[5]. The basis of this work was

> the realization that the real media for disseminating scientific information helpful to rural African communities are the so-called folk media: masquerades, drumming and dancing, story-telling and the songs of the wandering

3 Mudenda, Hon. E.H.K., Speech at the Oficial Opening of the *Theatre for Development* Workshop held at Chalimbana In-Service Training Institute on 19 August 1979 (in *Theatre for Development* by Chifunyise, Kerr and Dall), published by I.T.I. (Z) (1978), pp. 4-7.
4 Kidd, R. "Liberation for Domestication" in *Educational Broadcasting International*, p. 3.
5 Etherton, Michael, "Drama for Farmers", *The Times*, London, December 1, 1977.

praises-singers… which make the community development message so immediate and pertinent emphasizing the basic goals of participation and self-reliance.

On a slightly different premise, later on, Etherton and Ngugi wa Thiong'o embarked on developing a theatre which was more directly political in its texture although within the mode of this Theatre for Development. Talking about "Street Theatre in Northern Nigeria", Abah and Etherton lament the dearth of "radical street theatre in contemporary African towns" (Abah and Etherton, 1982: 121). And in trying to meet this need at Ahmadu Bello University, they tried to produce plays relevant to the needs of a neighbouring squalid suburb (ibid.: 5). The idea here was to first awaken the minds of the residents of this place to the need for knowing their rights and demanding fair attention from the government. Etherton says that for this theatre to succeed,

> the plays must take the part of the local people. They should reflect life from the viewpoint of the villagers themselves; and they should not avoid articulating criticism of government policy which is inadequate. Thus, although they may initially set out to be less than political in their aims, these plays may end up as the most politically active of all African theatre (Etherton ,1980: 57-85).

Believing that "crisis is the condition of social action in the Third World today", Etherton justifies this theatre by saying it is

> a legitimate political objective to discover strategies and organisation skills for functioning politically and creatively within the context of the crisis (Abah and Etherton, 1982: 20).

Ngugu wa Thiong'o talks of the need for bridging the gap between the bourgeoisie and the proletariat. His work in Limuru demonstrates this (ibid.: 16). Working in a voluntary 'adult literacy' project with Ngugi wa Mirri, Ngugi wa Thiong'o saw the need for educating his people beyond the alphabet, to include 'culture'. This way, his people could be made ready for a true 'homecoming' which they still have to achieve when neo-colonialism is out of the way. He argued that colonialism still existed in Kenya in spite of independence. Its life depended on cultural control. Language, being central to culture, any vernacular in Kenya, fell victim to colonial or neo-colonial exploitation. It got suppressed in a variety of ways by the exploiter. He argued that independence in Africa had failed to recognize this fact and consequently it had not achieved its true meaning. Until 'flag' independence was accompanied by cultural independence there would be no 'homecoming' for Africans. African writers could play a part in bringing this about. They could do so by addressing themselves to the majority in a language and style the majority of their people can understand.

This is how his theatre work in Gikuyu came into being. While he shares the ultimate goal of his work with other practitioners of Theatre for

Development, he differs from them in his emphasis on artistry. He insists that whatever he does with his people should be well done, polished and profession-al. Other practitioners tend to de-emphasize this aspect. The message is all they really care about. However, the goal of both Etherton and Ngugi wa Thiong'o here still remains non-formal education.

The nature of Theatre for Development

In almost all cases where this theatre is in existence, it is led by a team of experts who work with various types of extension workers or 'village level workers' assist-ing them "to get their health, nutrition, and agricultural messages across to rural villagers using entertainment and fun"[6]. We might add adult literacy campaigns to this list, too. Throughout the continent, we find projects of one type or anoth-er engaged in Theatre for Development.

Areas that come under this headline vary from straight drama to songs which are employed in any way as media for communicating ideas related to rural development. The government of Sierra Leone/Care project used 'dramatizations, music and visual aids to bring new information and ideas to the villagers to help them keep healthy and improve their agricultural practices'. *Laedza Batanani* Popular Theatre in Botswana, like Chikwakwa Travelling Theatre of Zambia and the Extension Services Department in Malawi, included puppetry and dance in their work. So we can say that broadly speaking Theatre for Development involves a wide range of resources. Here we are going to isolate a few elements of this theatre in order to illustrate how it is created.

Songs

Usually these are campaign songs, composed and sung by teams of extension workers either alone or together with the people among whom they work. In some cases the songs are recorded on tapes and distributed all over the country for playing through the radio or portable tape recorders during working sessions. Where the latter is the case, the help of properly trained musicians is sought. This was the case in Sierra Leone's project LEARN whose theme song was sung by Big Fayia and the Military Jazz Band. The songs are sung in vernacular languages and usually their tunes are well known adaptations of popular music styles. The guid-ing principles in composing such songs are:

- » simple catchy tune,
- » simple words and lots of repetition,
- » clear message[7].

---

6 Project LEARN, *Instructor's Guide*, Government of Sierra Leone/Care Publication, March 1982, Freetown.

7 Youngman, Frank (1976), *Report on Bosele Tshwarayanang*. Bosele Tshwarayanang Publications, No. 6, University College of Botswana, Institute of Adult Education, 1979, initially published by Kgatleng District Extension Team U.B.S., Botswana Extension College, 1977: 3.

Dance

Dances employed in this theatre are those that already possess within themselves abundant mimetic potential, for what actually takes place here is what should properly be termed dance-drama. An example of such dances is Malipenga or *Mganda* found in Tanzania and Zambia[8]. Although it is danced to the accompaniment of songs, the dominant part of the music comes from drums, whistles and gourds that are specially designed to play like some form of trumpet. To the beat of such instruments, dancers mime several scenes in which they can depict whatever message they choose to show. In theatre for development, these messages fall within the total intentions of the project. We have watched school children in Malawi use this dance to give audiences a lesson on childcare.

Puppetry

This usually forms part of mobile information campaigns. Between 1962 and 1990 the Malawi Ministry of Agriculture employed puppetry in its campaigns. The Extension Services section of the Ministry serviced not just Agriculture, but Forestry and Game sections also. They prepared and performed puppet shows up and down the country. The idea in such campaigns usually was to teach modern methods of agriculture as well as forest and game conservation to farmers and villagers in general. In spite of its popularity amongst practitioners, puppetry lost its grip on its adult audiences. It was found to be too childish in some cases, whereas in some places it was found to be culturally not admissible[9].

The puppetry show took on a simple story line that the audience was supposed to follow without problems. Usually it built on stock characters that could easily be identified. The puppetry employed popular recorded music to go with the show. Very often the show was interspersed with such music and commentary other than the puppets' own dialogue[10]. The problems these shows tried to tackle were usually a common phenomenon amongst the audiences, so that no questions about the clarity of the message arose. The setting too was always a direct take-off of everyday life. The drama in these was almost always sustained by quarrels between characters who stood for opposing points of view in the story. The stories were mostly built around imagery from local folklore sources.

Drama

This is the most extensively used of the art forms of the lot said to come under Theatre for Development. The work in drama varies from plays performed for vil-

---

8 Ibid.: p. 17. Also see T.O. Ranger's *Dance and Society in East Africa*.

9 Personal communication with the Chief Extension Officer, Ministry of Agriculture and Natural Resources, Malawi, 1981.

10 Youngman, op. cit., p. 15.

lagers by outside groups to those created and performed by the villagers themselves. As the Sierra Leone experience shows:

> These dramas feature the adventures of a typical village farm family. In
> each story a situation is presented that a villager might encounter. Some of
> the dramas show that the problem might be solved, while others are left
> unresolved to encourage the listeners or audience to work out their own
> solutions. Each drama is in the vernacular languages of the people in which
> the project is presently being implemented[11].

This work is presented as radio drama as well as stage presentation. The aspect of
how 'the problem presented might be solved' in work, like that of *Laedza Batanai*
Popular Theatre in Botswana, sometimes becomes the king pin of all work in
Theatre for Development. This is particularly so where it is felt, by the organizers,
that there is "low community participation and indifference to government development efforts in the area" (Kidd and Byram, 1981: 1). In such a situation, rather
than solve problems, the drama is supposed to be thought provoking.

All this work is improvised. Teams of extension workers and sometimes students collect problems prevalent in particular areas of campaigns. Using
these as themes they develop improvised dramas that are rehearsed very briefly
and quickly before presentation. This technique has its own flaws, especially
where aesthetics are concerned. There is not enough time and thought given to
the format of the presentation and styles of acting. The idea in most projects is to
minimize theatricality as much as possible, so that everybody attending the project can participate without feeling inferior to another person. The over-all aim is,
as we have said already, "to increase participation of community members in
development projects by involving them in the planning and running of the theatre programme" (ibid.: 11). But to limit this theatre to such intentions also suggests that it has no future. More important are perhaps the implications such a
fast growing and widely used theatre has for theatre *per se*.

Ngugi wa Thiong'o's work, which seems to be the only one of its type,
to care about proper theatrics, started from a script written by one author who
presented it to the masses to re-write and direct *en masse*[12]. Talking about how *I
will marry when I want* (1981) was a product of his work in Limuru, he says, he
was commissioned by the adult literacy organizers to script a play as a supplement to the straight teaching that was going on at the centre. What they had in
mind, was a script for 'modern' theatre, but in the vernacular. Artistic intentions
were to be primary. When he presented the script to the centre and was made to
produce it, the students (adult literacy classes) at the centre were more than willing to participate. Rehearsals were open to the whole group of students there
—even if they were not participating in the play. Directing was helped by a good

---

11 Project LEARN, op. cit.
12 Ngugi wa Thiong'o, talk on "Modern Writing in Africa" at the College of Adult Education, All Saints,
Manchester, June 1982.

deal of comments from the entire public watching the rehearsals. A direct result of this was that several criticisms and alterations were made to the script. This was in terms of language as well as plot and theme. What ultimately came out (as claimed by Ngugi wa Thiong'o) was the people's own play.

The success of such work goes beyond mere numbers of people who saw the performance. Ngugi says that after the production he noticed how people came together to share ideas; families that were disintegrating became reconciled and wanted to confer amongst themselves before decisions on projects were made[13]. For the writer, the whole experience revealed a new dimension to the relationship between the writer and his readers or audience.

Returning from detention, Ngugi wa Thiong'o could not resist the temptation of producing another play. This time it was a musical, *Mother, Cry for Me* (1982). The play was banned in rehearsal. Why was Ngugi wa Thiong'o's work thwarted by the Kenyan authorities? They regarded it as political agitation.

In Malawi, Theatre for Development work has been firmly established now as a key tool in the mobilization of communities towards their development. Let us turn to two examples of this work to demonstrate how this works. The two examples are drawn from the work of (a) the German Technical Cooperation (GTZ) and the Malawi Government's Liwonde Agricultural Development Division on primary health care and (b) USAID and the Government of Malawi on Girl's Attainment in Basic literacy and Education (GABLE).

Theatre for Development and community mobilization in practice

Work in community mobilization rests on the premise that the most important element in rural development and poverty reduction is community participation. Community participation here means the involvement of the community in making their own decisions and taking their own actions aimed at improving their lot. Theatre for Development has been enlisted by many development projects in this kind of work. It has been employed as a research tool for getting to know a community before actually settling in with a project. At other times it has been used as a way of creating awareness about development issues and engaging the community in a dialogue. Some times Theatre for Development has been employed as a way of mobilizing communities to rally behind some development activities and carry out related activities. It has also been used in evaluation of projects that has been done in a participatory manner. Let us look at some concrete examples of such work.

Mobilizing rural communities for primary health care in Malawi

In the late 1980s, the Malawi Government, with GTZ assistance, initiated a Primary Health Care (PHC) system in the south-eastern part of the country under one of its agricultural development divisions (Liwonde Agricultural Development

---

13 Ngugi wa Thiong'o., op. cit., talk at Manchester.

Division). This PHC approach was based on the belief that western styled health facilities by themselves may not necessarily result in improved health conditions for the people of the area. The people had to be motivated to help themselves in health matters. This was done through dissemination of health information and education in a culturally accepted manner at the community level.

Ordinarily, provision of health education and information in Malawi is the responsibility of the Ministry of Health. Other non-governmental organisations in the field of health work hand in hand with the Ministry in the provision of these services. Major tools for the health education and information dissemination are publications (booklets, magazines, leaflets, posters and flip-charts) and radio programmes written and presented either in English (the official government language) or Chichewa (the national language). Most of these publications carry information on how to prevent diseases like AIDS, malaria, measles, tuberculosis, leprosy, cholera, diarrhoea and many other common communicable diseases.

To fully utilise these outlets one has to be literate or rich enough to own a radio. Unfortunately, Malawi at the time of this intervention had very high illiteracy rates, and very few people in the country had access to the radio (National Statistical Office, 1991). This implied that health radio broadcasts meant for rural communities were not being accessed by the intended audiences. Being aware of these impediments, the Primary Health Care team of Liwonde Agricultural Development Division worked out an alternative method for reaching and mobilizing the community.

The guiding priciples for introducing primary health care in this area were:

» starting with people's concerns and priorities;

» recognising people's motivation and participation as the basis of all work;

» avoiding imposition of ideas from the top and strengthening grass-roots involvement;

» involvement of people from other ministries.

Recognising that most primary health care activities suffer from lack of involvement of communities in the early stages of planning, the PHC team chose to work with the Chancellor College Theatre for Development team (University of Malawi) as a tool for engaging the communities as early as possible through theatre activities. Theatre for Development (TFD) was used to probe, stimulate and tease out ideas from the community (Kalipeni and Kamlongera, 1996).

The organisational structure of the PHC team comprised three groups, namely; the community; Liwonde ADD Primary Health Care team; the Theatre for Development team.

These teams interacted as equals and could work independent of each other. The community was made up of people from villages that were neighbours and coming under one traditional authority. They also shared cultural values and language(s). The community's task was to provide reports on health issues and to seek advice from the PHC team. At the same time, they were to provide feedback to the TFD team after conducting self evaluation. The PHC team was made up of a medical doctor and some public health workers. These people were supported by colleagues from other ministries in the Liwonde Agricultural Development Division. The role of the PHC team was to provide technical manpower to train and motivate local PHC workers as well as give PHC support services. The team also liaised with the TFD team on how best to motivate the communities. The TFD's primary task was to motivate the community to identify their own health and organisational problems through open and participatory plays.

The structure just described fitted into an already existing national development tradition of self-help projects. This tradition thrived on the ability of the one party regime (at the time) to bring together traditional leaders and party authorities to create Area Action Committees. These served as a tool for generating community resources, mobilising labour and materials for development projects and a channel of communication on official, political and developmental issues.

Utilising this already wellknown organisational structure, the PHC team advised communities to elect their own village health committees. In some villages, communities already had committees. Most of these were dominated by men. Even where elections were just being held, the tendency was to elect men into key offices. However, through TFD, open and candid discussions were held –on who really played a critical role when it came to matters of primary health care. In most cases where men had been elected into key positions, they offered to step down as they admitted they would not be able to fulfil the task as they were likely to be away from the village most of the time. They also admitted that most of the concerns being addressed at the time related to young children who would still be in the direct care of mothers. So, they felt it would not be fair to dominate the village health committees when their role was marginal.

The starting point for the community mobilisation work was collection of health data for the communities and their area from various sources, like hospital records, national statistics, research reports and journal articles, by the PHC team. Information so gathered provided a synopsis of the situation of health care in the area. This information was shared with the TFD team before it set out for the villages. The information also provided some benchmark for future assessment of the impact of the mobilization work.

Entry into the villages was spearheaded by the Theatre for Development team. The team entered a village through the local authority structures in place. Once in the village, the TFD joined in the daily life of the community. They participated in their joys and sorrows as would be done by any member of that community. This is the way they gathered information for their dramas. The first activity undertaken by the theatre team was to find out from the community what it thought about its primary health care status. Information gathered earlier by the PHC team provided a spring board for the TFD team's investigations. The team gathered as much as possible information about the culture of the community. They also got information on preferred and used communication networks. This information was put alongside that gathered by the PHC team.

The TFD team created plays and songs based on this combined information. The team then rehearsed and performed the plays at venues that were traditionally used by the community itself whenever they were holding ceremonies or festivals of one kind or another in the village.

Acting in the performance encouraged participation of audiences in the dialogue going on between actors. This was factored into the performance through a technique referred to as "opening up the play". This was a way of asking direct questions to the audience at critical points of the story line in the play and then incorporating responses as the actors returned to the plot. Through this theatre activity a bigger picture of the community's health status emerged. Dialogue about this picture involved everybody in the community. Because of the "play" nature of drama, anybody present at performances felt free to comment and contribute to the dialogue that was developing about primary health care in the community. This dialogue continued even after performances to become everyday conversation on everybody's lips. These dialogues led to communities seeking ways through which they could solve their primary health care problems. Much as the concept had been mooted at the Liwonde Agricultural Development Division, the communities took over the process of solving their problems. They owned the problem and started looking for ways of improving the situation. This included reorganising themselves and creating village health committees.

After one year of reorganising and setting up Village Health Committes in the selected villages, evidence of self-propelled activity could be seen. As a matter of fact, some of them won a WHO sponsored "Clean Village" award for two years running. Records on water and sanitation for the area showed an increase in numbers of hand-dug wells and latrines. On maternal care, some traditional birth attendants were selected by the villages to be trained to provide basic antenatal care including iron supplementation, malaria treatment and high risk screening. Some "community doctors" were selected and trained to diagnose common conditions and administer basic medication. The "community doctors" started to collaborate with the traditional attendants on certain issues such as immunisation of children. All these were working on a voluntary basis (Kalipeni and Kamlongera, 1996).

Neighbouring villages were requesting the PHC team to start similar activities in their own villages. The village-based service providers were attending to more than just their villages. Their services were in demand in other villages too. One could argue that this community had been successfully mobilized to set up a primary health care system. A lesson or two might be learnt from this experience.

Community mobilization work just described was well within government attempts to improve health services in the country. It was within policies of the Ministry of Health, otherwise approval for the approach would not have been granted. The macro-policy environment was also right for the exercise to be fulfilled. This was an environment that encouraged an integrated approach to rural development. Government ministries worked together and supported each other in their work.

The PHC team respected the communities they worked with. They did not temper with the socio-cultural set up of the community. Where there was a need to change ways of doing things, it was left to the community to come to such a conclusion. Even with TFD facilitation, the community's communication networks were not disturbed. What were strengthened were links between the community and the other two components, i.e. TFD and PHC teams. The PHC mobilization work can be describes as follows (Kalipeni and Kamlongera, 1996).

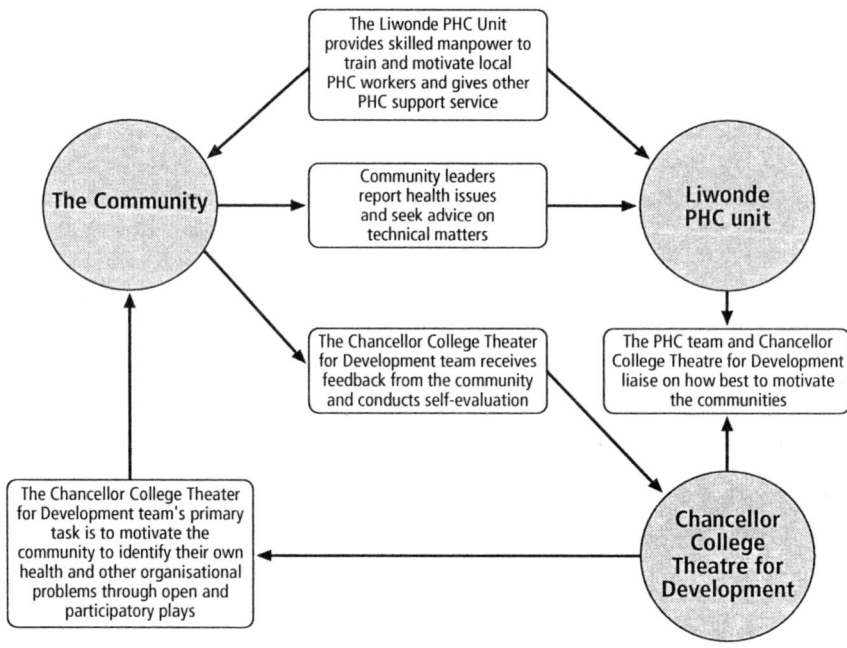

Experiences of the Primary Health Care initiative in Liwonde spurred the Theatre for Development team on to lending their skills to other initiatives. One such initiative was a social mobilisation campaign on girls education in Malawi. An examination of this campaign shows another dimension of what community mobilisation can be.

GABLE SMC

The GABLE Social Mobilization Campaign (GABLE SMC) was a Government of Malawi Project, funded by USAID and contracted to Creative Associates International Inc. (CAII, Rehani). The main objective of the project was to "increase peoples' awareness of the positive effects of girls' education on individuals, families, communities, and nations" and in so doing, change attitudes about the importance of girls' primary education.

To achieve this objective, the project employed what it referred to as "a grassroots outreach approach to message dissemination and community mobilisation" (CAII, Rihani). The GABLE project involved (a) project personnel, (b) University of Malawi's Chancellor College (TFD) students, (c) Ministry of Women's and Children's Affairs, Community Development and Social Welfare, and (d) Ministry of Education and Culture. Since the project aimed to work with communities directly, field officers from the two ministries involved were seen as the gateway to the communities. It was therefore necessary to make sure that everybody understood what the project was all about and how it was to work. This work won the FAWE award for coming up with an innovative way in encouraging girls' education in Africa (CAII, Rihani).

The process being described here was first piloted in one district whose statistics on girl child enrolment in primary school were among the lowest in the country. Experiences of this pilot social mobilization campaign convinced the GABLE team that they could go full throttle throughout the country albeit piecemeal. After the pilot, the team understood what worked and what did not. Initial furrows into distant districts from the pilot one showed how different cultures responded to sending the girl child to school, and so prepared the GABLE SMC team on how to deal with different situations. The process being described below was streamlined after some experiences of working up and down the country.

Stage one: situation analysis

The GABLE SMC covered the entire country of Malawi. It attempted to reach all corners of the country. In each district the GABLE team started by contacting district commissioners (who are in essence government heads in a district), a district education officer, a district community development officer and all traditional authorities. This contact was through a meeting during which the GABLE team collected information with which to develop a situation analysis of girls education. Apart from this, the meeting also served to familiarize the district authorities with the goals of the project.

Stage two: site selection

While getting a situation analysis of girls education (through socio-cultural, economic and the general educational make-up of the district) from government officials, the GABLE SMC staff also gathered data from other sources. The information helped the GABLE team to select sites for their intervention. The criteria for selecting a site were:

» balanced scattering of site in a district;
» targeting site with diverse cultural, religious and economic conditions;
» populations with unique feature like sparsity or density;
» areas with particular difficulties in getting and retaining girls in school up to end of primary education.

Stage three: participatory research

After selecting sites to work in, in a district, the GABLE team, comprising some GABLE field officers and TFD members, went out to start work in the field. The TFD team members formed the core of the research team. GABLE SMC says that

> The team of researchers/performers was made up of fifty students; twenty-five men and twenty-five women (representing) nearly every district and language group in the country and were studying a variety of subject areas at the college (CAII, Rihani).

Prior notice would have been given to the traditional authority of a particular site of the forthcoming visit (lasting 5 to 10 days), through government extension/development workers in the area. So, before doing anything in the village, the team went to the traditional authority to announce their arrival. The chief welcomed them and organised accommodation for them wherever he could. Otherwise, the team arranged their own accommodation within the site. The idea was for the team to become part of the village community as much as possible. The purpose of the visit was to triangulate the situation analysis developed out of prior meetings with government officials and traditional authorities at the beginning.

Stage four: field worker training

Field workers from the two ministries involved were to become facilitators of activities in the villages selected for the campaign. GABLE felt it was necessary to train and prepare them for this task. So, special field worker training was organised. The objective was to create a cadre of knowledgeable, skilled, action-oriented facilitators.

The training included a look at the GABLE SMC field methodology and the role the field workers were going to play in the project implementation. To come up with a workable curriculum, GABLE SMC carried out a training needs assessment. The findings from this assessment suggested that field workers needed more exposure to participatory methods and communication skills ideal for development work.

Stage five: community-based sensitisation

While at the beginning communities were brought into the GABLE project through the TFD and GABLE SMC staff, field workers from the two ministries taking part in the project took over working with communities as soon as they were trained. A key element in the community-based sensitization was the way field workers involved communities by identifying some key members (people who held positions of respect and authority) and training them on GABLE SMC goals and activities, and preparing them to take over the sensitization activities in the villages.

The training workshops culminated in the production of action plans that informed further activities to be carried out by the villagers themselves at village level. Monitoring was factored into the community-based sensitization through the field workers and the leaders of the community. Once an action plan had been agreed on, field workers from the area monitored progress. Leaders of the community did the same at the community level. This transfer of responsibilities to the villagers helped to establish ownership of the project among them and set the stage for more of their involvement in the GABLE SMC activities.

Stage six: village-based initiatives

Village-based initiatives grew out of action plans drawn during the community-based sensitization workshops. During the training of community leaders, it was agreed that all of them from a particular area meet to revisit their action plans and make sure that they were not overlapping, or unrealistic in terms of what they expected from the communities. A key product of these meetings was a schedule of meetings with the community during which the community would be informed about the GABLE SMC project and asked to discuss the issue of girls' education. While field workers and school teachers would be invited to attend these meetings, they were not there to participate. The meetings were being facilitated by the community leaders. The idea was to allow maximum freedom to the community to identify and discuss local constraints to girls' education and to brainstorm possible solutions to the constraints. It was during these meetings that concrete action was being suggested and workable schedules of activities agreed upon.

From the GABLE SMC work we suggest a slightly more elaborate model than the one developed out of the PHC work in the Liwonde ADD.

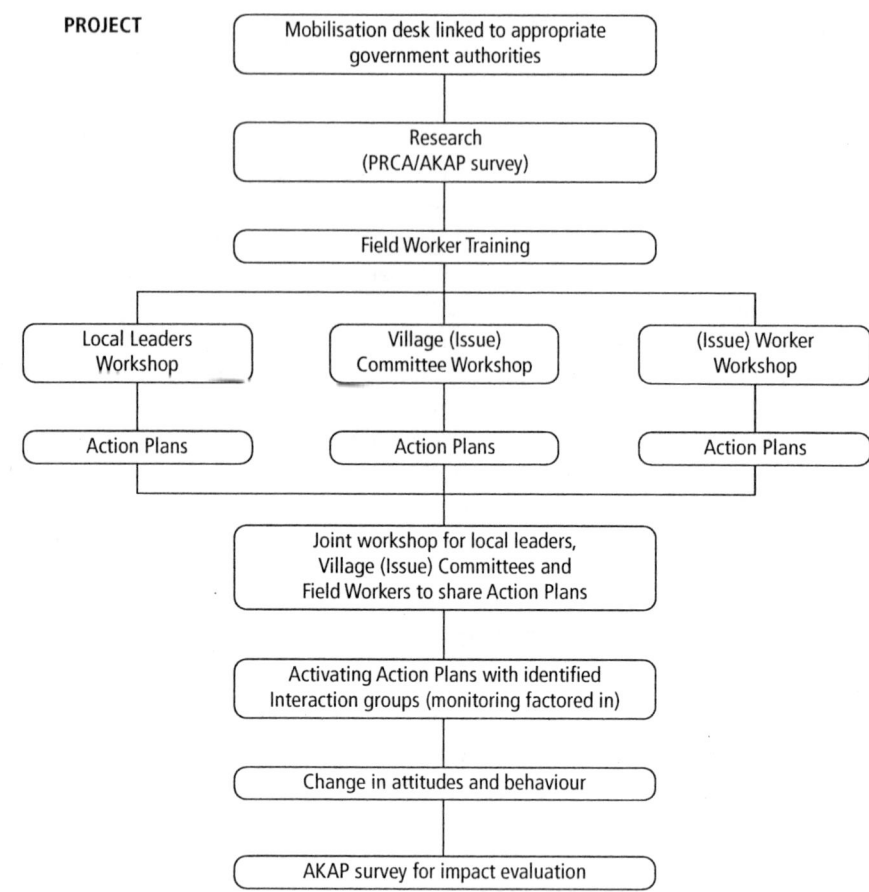

In this model, the PRCA stands for Participatory Rural Communication Appraisal, while AKAP survey stands for a survey of levels of awareness, knowledge, attitude and practices. The instrument for the survey is to be developed out of the PRCA findings (Anyaebgunam, Mefalopulos and Moetsabi, 1998). The results of this survey are to add a quantitative aspect to the qualitative PRCA findings as well as provide a benchmark for the final impact evaluation. The PRCA is supposed to involve communities in identifying possible problems and solutions as well as local communication networks that should inform any communication strategy to be developed in mobilizing the community. This work is to be carried out by the TFD team and the community. The final AKAP survey is to be based on the instrument used during the first survey. The workshops for community members and field workers are stages 4 and 5 in the description above. The impact evaluation should combine PRCA and a final survey based on the benchmark set at the beginning.

Notes on the authors

Oscar Hemer is Senior Lecturer in journalistic and literary creation at Malmö University, School of Arts and Communication, the initiator and coordinator of the international Master course in Communication for Development (ComDev) <www.k3.mah.se/comdev> and executive editor of the ComDev webmag *Globala Tider* <www.globalatider.nu>. He has written several works of fiction and non-fiction. His last published book is the essay *Äventyraren vid världens ände* (The Adventurer at the World's End), 2003. Contact: <oscar.hemer@k3.mah.se>.

Thomas Tufte is Professor of Communication at Roskilde University. He has also taught at the Malmö ComDev Master course since its inception. Tufte was the UNESCO Chair of Communication at UAB, Barcelona (2003), member of DANIDA's international HIV/AIDS think-tank (2001-2002), and has worked as a consultant in international health and development for many international agencies. Publications include *Living with the Rubbish Queen-telenovelas, culture and modernity in Brazil* (2000), *Media, Minorities and the Multicultural Society - Scandinavian Perspectives* (2003), *Global Encounters-Media and Cultural Transformation* (2002). Forthcoming is: *Communication for Social Change Anthology: Historical and Contemporary Readings* (co-editor with Alfonso Gumucio-Dagron). Contact: <ttufte@ruc.dk>.

Thomas Hylland Eriksen is Professor of Social Anthropology at the University of Oslo and holds a Special Chair in Human Security at the Free University of

Amsterdam. His research has focused on cultural and local aspects of globalisation, and he has written extensively about identity politics. He has also published textbooks and critical essays. He is currently directing a strategic research programme on "Cultural complexity in the new Norway" (2004-2009). His latest books in English are *Tyranny of the Moment* (2001), *Globalisation-Studies in anthropology* (2003) and *What is anthropology?* (2004).
<http://folk.uio.no/geirthe/> Contact: <t.h.eriksen@sai.uio.no>.

Kevin Robins is Professor of Sociology, City University, London. He is presently involved in an EU Framework project, "Changing City Spaces: New Challenges to Cultural Policy in Europe", dealing with migrant cultures and transnationalism. His books include *Into the Image: Culture and Politics in the Field of Vision* (1996), *Times of the Technoculture* (1999, with Frank Webster), and *British Cultural Studies* (2001, with David Morley). Contact: <cos01kr@gold.ac.uk>.

Asu Aksoy is a Research fellow at Goldsmiths College, University of London. She has been doing research on the changing cultural identities of new migrant groups in Europe. At present she is working on the EU Framework programme's "Changing City Spaces" project, where she is looking at the extent to which cultural diversity policies and urban metropolitan contexts in Europe contribute to the opening up of present societies to diversity, complexity and cultural tolerance. Contact: <a.aksoy@gold.ac.uk>.

Silvio Waisbord is Senior Program Manager at the Academy for Educational Development in Washington. He is currently working on capacity building and communication in various health areas. Previously, he was Associate Profesor of Journalism and Media Studies at Rutgers University and Director of the Journalism Resources Institute. He has published in development communication, journalism, and media globalization. He holds a PhD in sociology from the University of California, San Diego. Contact: <swaisbord@smtp.aed.org>.

Jan Servaes is Professor and Head of the School of Journalism and Communication at the University of Queensland in Brisbane, Australia, Editor-in-Chief of *Communicating for Social Change: A Global Journal*, Associate Editor of *Telematics and Informatics: An international journal on telecommunications and Internet technology* and Editor of the Hampton Book Series "Communication, Globalization and Cultural Identity". He has been President of the European Consortium For Communications Research (ECCR) and Vice-President of the International Association of Media and Communication Research (IAMCR), in charge of Academic Publications and Research, from 2000 to 2004. Contact: <j.servaes@uq.edu.au>.

Patchanee Malikhao is Lecturer in the Business School at the University of Queensland, Australia. She has undertaken research, lecturing, and advisory work around the world on international and development communication, printing technology and pre-press systems. She is currently doing PhD research on Western versus Buddhist HIV/AIDS communication campaigns in Thailand. Contact: <p.malikhao@uq.edu.au>.

Nancy Morris is Associate Professor in the Department of Broadcasting, Telecommunications and Mass Media at Temple University in Philadelphia, Pennsylvania, USA. She is the author of *Puerto Rico: Culture, Politics and Identity* (1995) and co-editor of *Media and Globalization: Why the State Matters* (2001). Contact: <nancy.morris@temple.edu>.

Maria Celeste H. Cadiz is Dean and Associate Professor, College of Development Communication, University of the Philippines, Los Baños. She has written extensively on participatory aspects of communication for development. Contact: <mchc@mudspring.uplb.edu.ph>.

James Deane is Managing Director of the Communication for Social Change Consortium <www.communicationforsocialchange.org>. He was formerly Executive Director and a founding member of the Panos Institute, London. He has written extensively on communication issues, particularly on the role of media and communication technologies in development, on communication for social change and on the HIV/AIDS pandemic over the last two decades. Key publications include: *The other information revolution: media and empowerment in developing countries* (2003) and *Missing the message: 20 years of learning from HIV/AIDS* (commissioning editor, 2003). Contact: <jdeane@communicationforsocialchange.org>.

Ulla Carlsson is Director of Nordicom (Nordic Information Centre for Media and Communication Research) at Göteborg University. She is a founding and continuing editor of the *Nordicom Review* and she has edited several Nordicom publications on media development, media concentration, media statistics, media history, popular culture, media theory and children and media. She is also Director of the UNESCO International Clearinghouse on Children, Youth and Media. Most of her research focuses on international communication and the globalization of media. Contact: <ulla.carlsson@nordicom.gu.se>.

Tim Allen is Reader in Development Studies, Development Studies Institute, London School of Economics. He has expertise in the fields of complex emergencies, ethnic conflict, forced migration, local conception of health and healing, East Africa (especially Sudan, Uganda and Kenya), development aid and agencies and ethics of aid. Key publications include: *Culture and global change* (with Tracey Skelton, 1999), *The media of conflict: war reporting and representations of ethnic violence* (with Jean Seaton, 1999) and "The right to interfere?: Bernard

Kouchner and the new humanitarianism" (with David Styan), in *Journal of International Development*, August 2000. Contact: <T.Allen@lse.ac.uk>.

Nicole Stremlau is a PhD student at the London School of Economics, researching the role of the media in post-war situations with a focus on East Africa. She is also Director of the Africa Media Programme at the Stanhope Centre for Comparative Communications Policy Research in London. Contact: <n.a.stremlau@lse.ac.uk>.

Rafael Obregón is Associate Professor and Director of the Communication for Development Research Programme at Ohio University. He has been Regional Communication Advisor in the Child and Adolescent Health Unit, Pan American Health Organization/World Health Organization, and Assistant Professor in the Program of Social Communication, Universidad del Norte, Colombia. Obregón has worked and published extensively in health and development communication. His most recent publication is "The Role of Communication in the Integrated Management of Childhood Illness: Progress, Lessons Learned, and Challenges in Latin America" in Haider, Muhiuddin (2005). He is a member of the Review Board of the *Journal of Health Communication*. Contact: <robregon@communicationforsocialchange.org>.

Mario Mosquera is a temporary consultant for the Pan American Health Organisation and lecturer and researcher at the University of El Norte, Barranquilla, Colombia. He has worked extensively in Latin America on a variety of research and action projects in health promotion, mostly focused on communication and people's participation as key components of primary health care programmes. Mosquera is currently a leading researcher in community-based programs in sexual reproductive health and dengue prevention. He has published in international public health journals such as *Health Policy & Planning* and *Cadernos de Saude*. Contact: <mmosquera@uninorte.edu.co>.

Paolo Mefalopulos is currently employed as Senior Communications Officer in the Division of Development Communication of the World Bank. He had extensive media experience before starting to work with some of the major international organizations (among them UNESCO, FAO, and the European Union) in the field of communication for development. He has published several articles on the theory and practices of development communication and he is co-author of *Participatory Rural Communication Appraisal: Starting with the people* (1998), and main author of *Participatory Communication Strategy Design* (2002) and *Introducción a la Comunicación Participativa*. Contact: <pmefalopulos@worldbank.org>.

Karin Gwinn Wilkins is Graduate Advisor and Associate Professor with the Department of Radio-TV-Film at the University of Texas in Austin. Her research interests include international and development communication, as well as media and social change. Wilkins serves as the Chair of the Intercultural/Development Division of the International Communication Association. Her latest book is *ReDeveloping Communication for Social Change* (2000). She is also a regular contributor to several journals and anthologies on communication and development. Contact: <kwilkins@mail.utexas.edu>.

Madanmohan Rao is Research Director at the Asian Media Information and Communication centre (AMIC) and adjunct faculty at IIIT, Bangalore. He is the editor of three book series: "The Asia Pacific Internet Handbook", "The Knowledge Management Chronicles" and "AfricaDotEdu". Madan was formerly the communications director at the United Nations Inter Press Service bureau in New York, and has spoken at conferences and workshops all over the world. Contact: <madan@techsparks.com>.

Manne Granqvist graduated from the Master course in Communication for Development at Malmö University in 2003. He currently works as a bookstore clerk and freelance journalist while thinking about applying for doctoral studies. Contact: <mne01@tiscali.se>.

Sarat Maharaj became Professor of History and Theory of Art at Goldsmiths College, London, in 1997. He is currently Professor of Visual Art and Knowledge Systems, Lund University. He was the first Rudolf Arnheim Professor at Humboldt University, Berlin, and co-curator of Documenta X1 2002. His recent research and publications cover cultural translation and difference and visual art as knowledge production. Contact: <s.maharaj@virgin.net>.

Gilane Tawadros was appointed Director of the Institute of International Arts, London, in 1994. She has published and lectured widely on contemporary art and criticism. She has edited books, catalogues and talks around issues of cultural diversity, globalization and new media. Her curatorial projects have been notable not least for showing artists and art practices from outside the cultural mainstream. She was curator of the Africa Pavilion, Venice Biennale, 2003. Contact: <institute@iniva.org>.

Alfonso Gumucio-Dagron is currently Managing Director for Programmes at the Communication for Social Change Consortium, with experience from Africa, Asia, South Pacific, Latin America and The Caribbean. He is the author of various studies on communication, and has also published several books of poetry and narrative and directed documentary films on cultural and social issues. His most famous book on communication is *Making Waves, participatory development for social change* (2001). Contact: <gumucio@communicationforsocialchange.org>.

Ullamaija Kivikuru is professor of journalism at the Swedish School of Social Science, University of Helsinki, Finland. She has been working with eastern and southern African media questions for more than 25 years, most recently with community-based media in South Africa and Namibia. Her doctoral thesis *Tinned Novelties or Creative Culture* (1990) focused on Tanzania, and she also developed another study, *Changing mediascapes?* (1996), on community media on the slopes of Mount Kilimanjaro. In the home sphere, she has been especially interested in media and democracy. Contact: <ullamaija.kivikuru@helsinki.fi>.

Kemal Kurspahic was the editor-in-chief of the Bosnian daily *Oslobodjenje* in Sarajevo, 1988-1994. He has received numerous awards, including the *World Press Review*'s International Editor of the Year; the Bruno Kreisky Award for Human Rights in 1993; the International Press Institute's World Press Freedom Hero in 2000, and the South Eastern Europe Media Organization's Erchard Busek Award for Better Understanding in the Region in 2003. He is the author of four books, most recently *Prime Time Crime: Balkan Media in War and Peace* (2003). Contact: <kurspahic@aol.com>.

Gordon Adam is director of Media Support, a Scottish-based NGO and consultancy working in development communications projects in Southern Africa and Afghanistan, which advises the British Government (DFID) on mass media and development. A BBC trained radio journalist, he wrote extensively on Afghanistan and South Asia, and was Head of the BBC Pashto Section for eight years. His publications include several handbooks on media, development and conflict, and he is a guest lecturer on the Master in Communication for Development course at Malmö University. Contact: <gordonadam@btinternet.com>.

Clemencia Rodríguez is Associate Professor at the University of Oklahoma, USA. She has conducted research since 1984 on communication and social change and citizens' media in different international contexts. Her publications include *Fissures in the Mediascape. An International Study of Citizens' Media* (2001), "Citizens' Media and the Voice of the Angel/Poet" in *Media International Australia* (2002) and "The Bishop and His Star: Citizens' Communication in Southern Chile" (in Couldry and Curran, 2003). Contact: <clemencia@ou.edu>.

Minou Fuglesang is a media anthroplogist and a health promoter. Since 1999 she is working as a project coordinator in a civil society organization, EADCF, in Tanzania, operating the HIP multimedia edutainment initiative. HIP comprises a series of print and electronic media vehicles as well as community outreach events. Fuglesang participated in founding and setting up the initiative. She worked for many years as a researcher and consultant to SIDA and other development and technical agencies from her base at the Division of International Health, Karolinska Institute and Medical University in Stockholm. Her fields of speciality are media, culture, gender, youth, sexual and reproductive health and HIV/AIDS. Contact: <minou.fuglesang@phs.ki.se>.

Kate Winskell and **Daniel Enger** have co-managed *Scenarios from Africa* under
the aegis of the British NGO Global Dialogues since 1996. Kate Winskell is a Visiting Assistant Professor in the Department of Global Health of Rollins School of Public Health at Emory University in Atlanta, and Associate Director of Emory's Center for Health, Culture and Society. Contact: <swinske@sph.emory.edu> <info@globaldialogues.org>.

Ricardo Ramírez teaches in the School of Environmental Design and Rural Development at the University of Guelph, Canada. Before that he was involved in consulting and research efforts in rural communication and resource management projects. He has worked with non-governmental organizations in Latin America and the Caribbean, spent five years working with the Communication for Development unit of the Food and Agriculture Organization of the UN (FAO) in Rome, and has worked in the Netherlands as coordinator of the information and communication unit of a sustainable agriculture project. More recently Ramirez has designed the communication strategy for the new national agricultural advisory services programme in Uganda (NAADS). Contact: <rramirez@uoguelph.ca>.

Arvind Singhal is Professor of Communication Studies and Presidential Research Scholar at Ohio University. He is co-author (with Everett M. Rogers) of *Entertainment-Education: A Communication Strategy for Social Change* (1999), *India's Communication Revolution: From Bullock Carts to Cyber Marts* (2001) and *Combating AIDS: Communication Strategies in Action* (2003). He is also lead editor of *Entertainment-Education and Social Change: History, Research, and Practice* (2004). Contact: <singhal@oak.cats.ohiou.edu>.

Peer J. Svenkerud is Senior Vice President with the Norwegian State Lottery. He was previously director of governmental affairs with Telenor ASA and director with Burson Marsteller. His major research interests are in the areas of corporate social responsibility and corporate governance. Contact: <peer-jacob.svenkerud@norsk-tipping.no>.

Prashant Malaviya is Associate Professor of Marketing at INSEAD (The European Institute of Business Administration), France. His research, teaching and practice interests are in the areas of marketing excellence, consumer psychology, customer orientation, and brand building. His research has appeared in several outlets, including the *Journal of Marketing*, *Journal of Marketing Research*, and *Journal of Consumer Research*. Contact: <prashant.MALAVIYA@insead.edu>.

Everett M. Rogers was until his death in October 2004 Distinguished Professor Emeritus in the Department of Communication and Journalism at the University of New Mexico. He was one of the pioneers in the field of communication for development, publishing his classic, *Diffusion of Innovations*, in 1962, and since having published extensively for almost half a century. Among his last publications are (co-authored with Arvind Singhal) *India's Communication Revolution: From Bullock Carts to Cyber Marts* (2001) and *Combating AIDS: Communication Strategies in Action* (2003).

Vijay Krishna is Associate Professor of Communication at Indiana University Southeast, teaching courses in advertising, public relations, and public communication campaigns. Contact: <vkrishna@psu.edu>.

Chris Kamlongera is Director of the Centre of Communication for Development (CCD), Southern Africa Development Community (SADC). His main fields of interests are: social mobilisation/communication for development; performing arts in communications; drama and English language teaching; arts administration; textbook writing. Kamlongera has worked with several universities in Tanzania, Zambia and Zimbabwe. He has published many articles on various topics related to his fields of interest, case studies, monographs and books. Contact: <ckamlongera@fanr-sadc.co.zw>.

References

A Documentary History of a New World Information and Communication Order | 461
Seen as an Evolving and Continuous Process 1975-1986 (1988) Paris:
UNESCO (Communication and Society 19). Available at <www.unesco.org>.

Abah, O. S. and Etherton, M. (1982) *The Samaru Projects: Street Theatre in
Northern Nigeria*. Zaria: Ahmadu Bello University.

Abaunza, H. (2001) "Somos diferentes somos iguales. La experiencia de *Puntos
de Encuentro* en la promoción de los derechos humanos de las y los
jóvenes de Nicaragua". Paper delivered at the VIII Mesa Redonda sobre
Comunicación y Desarrollo, Managua, Nicaragua, 26-28 November.

Abdulla, R. A. (2004) "Entertainment-education in the Middle East: Lessons
learned from the Egyptian Oral Rehydration Therapy Campaign". In
Singhal et al (2004).

Adam, G. (1999) "The Media and Complex Emergencies", in Brassey's *Defence
Handbook*, London: Centre for Defence Studies.

Adam, G. and Harford, N. (1999) *Radio and HIV/AIDS: making a difference*.
Geneva: UNAIDS. Available at <www.unaids.org>.

Adam, G. and Holguin, L (2003) "The Media's Role in Peace Building: Asset or
Liability?". *Our Media 3 Conference*, Barranquilla, Colombia (May 19-
23, 2003).

"Afghanistan, Crosslines Essential Field Guide" (2004) Geneva: Crosslines
<www.crosslinesguides.com>.

462 | Airhihenbuwa, C., Makinwa, B., and Obregon, R. (2000) "Toward a New Communications Framework for HIV/AIDS", *Journal of Health Communication*, Vol. 5 (supplement), p. 5-15, 101-112.

Aksoy, A. and Robins, K. (1997) "Peripheral vision: cultural industries and cultural identities in Turkey", *Paragraph*, 20(1): 75-99.

Aksoy, A. and Robins, K. (2000) "Thinking across spaces: transnational television from Turkey", *European Journal of Cultural Studies*, 3(3): 345-367.

Aksoy, A. and Robins, K. (2003) "The enlargement of meaning: social demand in a transnational context", *Gazette: The International Journal for Communication Studies*, 65(4-5): 365-388.

Ali, S. M. (2002) "Øst er øst og vest er vest" (East is east and west is west), in Eide, E. and Ottosen, R. (eds.) *Krigens retorikk* (The Rhetorics of War). Oslo: Cappelen.

Allen, R. (ed.) (1995) *To Be Continued... Soap operas around the world*. New York, NY: Routledge.

Allen, T. and Seaton, J. (eds.) (1999) *The Media of Conflict*. London: Zed.

Almedom, A. (1996) "Hygiene Evaluation Procedures: a handbook for water supply and sanitation projects", London: International Nutrition Foundation for Developing Countries.

Altman, Dennis (2001) *Global Sex*. London and Chicago: The University of Chicago Press.

Amin, S. (1997) *Capitalism in the Age of Globalization*. London: Zed.

Anyaebgunam, C., Mefalopulos, P. and Moetsabi, T. (1998) "Participatory Rural Communication Appraisal", SADC Centre of Communication for Development and FAO Regional Project GCP/RAF/297/ITA.

Antunes, M. C., Stall, R. D., Paiva, V., Peres, C. A., Paul, J., Hudes, M. and Hearst, N. (1997) "Evaluating an AIDS Sexual Risk Reduction Program for Young Adults in Public Night Schools in São Paulo, Brazil", *AIDS* 11 (supplement 1), pp. 121-127.

Appadurai, A. (1989) "Disjuncture and Difference in the Global Cultural Economy". In Featherstone, M. (ed.) *Global Culture, Nationalism, Globalisation and Modernity*. London: Sage.

Appadurai, A. (1996) *Modernity at Large. Cultural Dimensions of Globalization*. Minneapolis: University of Minnesota Press.

Appadurai, A. (ed.) (2001) *Globalization*. Durham, N.C.: Duke University Press.

Argyris, C. and Schon, D. A. (1991) "Participatory Action Research and Action Science Compared: A Commentary" in Whyte, William F. (ed.) *Participatory Action Research*. Newbury Park, CA: Sage, p. 85-98.

Armitage, J. (1999) "Resisting the Neoliberal Discourse of Technology: the Politics of Cyberculture in the Age of the Virtual Class". Online article: *ctheory.net* <www.ctheory.net/text_file.asp?pick=111>.

Arostegui, J. and Carrion, L. (1997) "Evaluación Institucional. Managua: Puntos de Encuentro". Institutional evaluation report.

Asaro, P. M. (2000) "Transforming Society by Transforming Technology: the Science and Politics of Participatory Design" in *Accounting, Management and Information Technology*, Vol. 10, pp. 257-290.

Ashcroft, B., Griffiths, G. and Tiffin, H. (2000) *Post-Colonial Studies. The Key Concepts*. London: Routledge.

Auwal, M.A., and Singhal, A. (1992) "The diffusion of Grameen Bank in Bangladesh: Lessons learned about rural poverty alleviation" in *Knowledge: Creation, Diffusion, and Utilization*, 14(1), pp. 7-28.

Avgerou, C. (2002) *Information Systems and Global Diversity*. Oxford: Oxford University Press

Backer, T. E., Rogers, E. M. and Sopory P. (1992) *Designing Health Communication Campaigns: What Works?* Newbury Park, CA: Sage.

Balit, S. (1999) *Voices for Change: Rural Women and Communication*. Rome: FAO.

Bandura, A. (1977) *Social Learning Theory*. Englewood Cliffs, NJ: Prentice-Hall.

Bandura, A. (1997) *Self-efficacy: the exercise of control*. Basingstoke: W. H. Freeman.

Bandura, A. (2004) "Social cognitive theory for personal and social change by enabling media". In Singhal et al (2004), pp. 75-96.

Baran, P. (1957) *The Political Economy of Growth*. New York: Monthly Review Press.

Barnett, S. (2000) *e-Britannia: The Communication Revolution*. Luton: University of Luton Press.

Bartelson, J. and Ringmar, E. (1985) "Två fallstudier: USA lämnar ILO och UNESCO". In Huldt, B. & Falk, M. (eds.) *FN vid 40 – Internationellt samarbete i kris*. Stockholm: Utrikespolitiska Institutet.

Bateson, G. (1972) *Steps to an Ecology of Mind*. New York: Bantam.

Bauman, K. E. (1997) "The Effectiveness of Family Planning Programs Evaluated with True Experimental Designs". In *American Journal of Public Health* 87(4): pp. 666-669.

Baumann, Z. (1998) *Globalisation*. London: Routledge.

Baumann, Z. (2000) *Globalization. The Human Consequences*. Cambridge: Polity Press.

Baumann, Z. (2003) *Liquid Love*. Cambridge: Polity Press.

Bayes, A., von Braun, J. and Akhter, R. (1999) *Village pay phones and poverty reduction*. Bonn, Germany: Center for Development Research.

Beam, S. (1992) "Surveying the Territory: Re-examining MacBride and Theories of Development" *Gazette* 50 (1992) 2-3, pp. 109-146.

464 | Beck, U. (1999) *World Risk Society*. Cambridge: Polity Press.

Becker, J. (2001) "Zwischen Abgrenzung und Integration: Anmerkungen zur Ethnisierung der türkischen Medienkultur" in Becker, J. and Behnisch, R., (eds.) *Zwischen Abgrenzung und Integration: Türkische Medienkultur in Deutschland*. Rehburg-Loccum: Evangelische Akademie, pp. 9-24.

Beltran, L. R. (1976) "Alien Premises, Objects, and Methods in Latin American Communication Research", *Communication Research*, 3, pp. 107-134.

Bertrand, J. T., Santiso, R., Linder, S. H. and Pineda, M. A. (1987) "Evaluation of a Communications Program to Increase Adoption of Vasectomy in Guatemala". *Studies in Family Planning* 18 (6), pp. 361-370.

Bessette, G. a. Rajasunderam, C.V. (eds.) (1996) *Participatory Development Communication: A West African Agenda*. Ottawa and Penang: IDRC and Southbound.

Bessette, G. (2004) *Involving the Community*. Ottawa and Singapore: IDRC and Southbound.

Biagioli, C. (2004) *L'Uso Della Comunicazione Per lo Sviluppo Umano: Il Caso Soul City*. Università per Stranieri di Perugia.

Biggs, S. and Matsaert, H. (2004) "Strengthening poverty reduction programmes using an actor-oriented approach: Examples from natural resources innovation systems". AgREN Network Paper, 134.

Bishop, R. (1975) "How Reuters and AFP Coverage of Independent Africa Compares", *Journalism Quarterly* 52(1975).

Bjerknes, G., Ehn, P. and Kyng, M. (1987) *Computers and Democracy: A Scandinavian Challenge*. Aldershot: Averbury.

Blomström, M. & Hettne, B. (1984) *Development Theory in Transition. The Dependency Debate and Beyond*. London: Zed.

Bloom, A. (1987) *The Closing of the American Mind*. New York: Simon and Schuster.

Boal, A. (1979) *The Theatre of the Oppressed*. New York: Urizen Books.

Boeren, A. (1992) "Getting Involved: Communication for Participatory Development". In Boeren, A. and Epskamp, K. (eds.) *The Empowerment of Culture: Development Communication and Popular Media*. The Hague: Centre for the Study of Education in Developing Countries (CESO), pp. 47-59.

Boserup, E. (1970) *Women's Role in Economic Development*. New York: St. Martin's Press.

Boulay, M., Storey, D. and Sood, S. (2000) *Indirect Exposure to a Family Planning Mass Media Campaign in Nepal*. Center for Communication Programs, The Johns Hopkins University School of Public Health.

Bouman, M. (1999) "The Turtle and the Peacock—the Entertainment-Education Strategy on Television". Haag: Thesis Wageningen Agricultural University/CIP-Data Koninklijke Bibiotheek .

Boyd-Barrett, O. (1980) *The International News Agencies*. London: Sage.

Boyd-Barrett, O. (1997) "Global News Wholesalers as Agents of Globalization", in Sreberny-Mohammadi et al (1997).

Bradshaw, S. and Puntos de Encuentro (2001) "Gendered communication strategies: A case study". Managua: Puntos de Encuentro. Document requested by MS America Central.

Braman, S. and Sreberny-Mohammadi, A. (eds.) (1996) *Globalization, Communication and Transnational Civil Society*. Cresskill: Hampton Press.

Bräutigam, D. (2000) *Aid dependence and governance: What happens when institutions are too weak to handle large amounts of aid?* Stockholm: Sida.

Brown, W. J. and Cody, M. J. (1991) "Effects of a Prosocial Television Soap Opera in Promoting Women's Status", *Human Communication Research* 18 (1), pp. 114-142.

Brune, F. (1993) *'Les médias pensent comme moi!': fragments du discours anonyme*. Paris: L'Harmattan.

Brunt, J. H., Lindsey, E. and Hopkinson, J. (1997) "Health Promotion in the Hutterite Community and the Ethnocentricity of Empowerment", *Canadian Journal of Nursing* 29 (1), pp. 17-28.

Butler, G. (2001) *Where's the Loot? Who really made the money during the high-tech boom, how they did it, and how you can do the same next time*. Australia: Allen and Unwin.

de la Cadena, M. (2001) "Reconstructing race. Racism, culture and mestizaje in Latin America", *NACLA* 34, No. 6, pp. 16-23.

Cadiz, M. C. H. (1999) "Models and Approaches in Communication for Development". In Velasco, M. T. H., Cadiz, M. C. H. and Lumanta, M. F., *DEVC 208: Social Marketing and Social Mobilization for Development*. Los Baños, Laguna, Phil.: University of the Philippines Open University, pp. 15-52.

Cadiz, M. C. H. (1994) *Communication and Participatory Development*. College, Laguna: UPLB College of Agriculture.

Calás, M. B and Smircich, L. (1996) "From "the woman's" point of view: Feminist approaches to organization studies". In Clegg, S. R., Hardy, C. and Nord, W. R. (eds.) *Handbook of Organization Studies*. London: Sage, pp. 218-257.

Calvelo Ríos, M. (2003) *Comunicación para el Cambio Social*. Oficina Regional FAO para América Latina y el Caribe: FAO.

Campbell, V. (2004) *Information Age Journalism*. London: Arnold

Canetti, E. (1991) *The Secret Heart of the Clock*. London: André Deutsch.

Caplan, P. (1987) *The Cultural Construction of Sexuality*. London: Tavistock.

Cardiff, D. and Scannell, P. (1987) "Broadcasting and national unity". In Curran, J., Smith, A. and Wingate, P. (eds.) *Impacts and Influences: Essays on Media and Power in the Twentieth Century*. London: Methuen.

466 | Cardinal, L., Costigan, A., and Heffernan, T. (1994) "Working towards a feminist vision of development". In Dagenais and Piché (1994), pp. 409-428.

Cardoso, F.H. (1979) *Dependency and Development in Latin America*. Berkeley: University of California Press.

Carlsson, U. (1998) *Frågan om en ny internationell informationsordning; en studie i internationell mediepolitik* (The issue of a New World and Information Order; a study in media politics). Göteborg: Göteborg University, Dept. of Journalism and Mass Communication.

Carlsson, U. (2003) "The Rise and Fall of NWICO. From a Vision of International Regulation to a Reality of Multilevel Governance". *Nordicom Review* No. 2, 2003.

Castells, M. (1996, 1997, 1998) *The Information Age*. Oxford: Blackwell.

Castells, M. (2001) *The Internet Galaxy*. Oxford: Blackwell.

Center for International, Health, and Development Communication (1991) "Communication for Child Survival". HEALTHCOM Project Final Report: Part II. Working Paper 1001. Annenberg School for Communication, University of Pennsylvania.

Cerqueira, M. T. and Olson, C. M. (1995) "Nutrition Education in Developing Countries: An Examination of Recent Successful Projects". In Pinstrup-Andersen, P., Pelletier, D. and Alderman, H. (eds.) *Child Growth and Nutrition in Developing Countries: Priorities for Action*. Ithaca, NY: Cornell University Press, pp. 53-77.

Chakrabarty, D. (2000) *Provincializing Europe. Postcolonial Thought and Historical Difference*. Princeton University Press.

Chetley, A. (2001) "Improving health, fighting poverty: the role of information and communication technology (ICT)". London: Exchange. <www.healthcomms.org/pdf/findings1.pdf>.

Chetley, A. (2002) "Communication that works". European Centre for Development Policy Management, 12 December 2002. <www.ecdpm.org>.

Chu, G. (1987) "Development Communication in the Year 2000: Future Trends and Directions". In Jayaweera, N. and Amunugama, S., (eds.) *Rethinking Development Communication*. Singapore: Asian Mass Communication Research and Information Centre (AMIC), pp. 95-107.

Chua, P., Bhavnani, K. and Foran, J. (2000) "Women, culture, development: A new paradigm for development studies?" *Ethnic and Racial Studies*, 23(5), pp. 820-841.

Cloud, D. (2004) "To Veil the Threat of Terror: Afghan Women and the Clash of Civilizations In the Imagery of the U.S. War on Terrorism". *Quarterly Journal of Speech* 90, pp. 285-306.

Cohen, A. P. (1994) *Self Consciousness: An Alternative Anthropology of Identity*. London: Routledge.

Coldevin, G. and FAO (2000) "Participatory communication and adult learning for rural development". *The Journal of International Communication*, 7(2), pp. 51-69.

Coleman, P.L. and Meyer, R.C. (1989) "Entertainment for Social Change". Proceedings from the 1st enter-educate conference, March 29-April 1, 1989. Center for Communication Programs. Johns Hopkins University, the Annenberg School for Communication. University of Southern California, Center for Population Options.

Communication Theory (2002) 12: 2. Special Issue on Entertainment-Education. Oxford University Press.

Cornwall, A. and Jewkes, R. (1995) "What is Participatory Research?". *Social Science and Medicine* 41 (12), pp. 1667-1676.

Cooke, B. and Kothari, U. (eds.) (2001) *Participation: The New Tyranny*. London: Zed Books.

Couldry N. and Curran, J. (eds.) (2003) *Contesting Media Power*. Boulder, CO: Rowman and Littlefield.

Covey, S. (1989) *The Seven Habits of Highly Effective People*. New York, London, Toronto, Sydney, Tokyo, and Singapore: Simon and Schuster, Inc.

Curran, J. and Park, M.J. (eds.) (2000) *De-Westernizing Media Studies*. London: Routledge.

DANIDA (2000) "Gender Equality in Danish Development Co-operation: A Contribution to the Revision of Danish Development Policy". Working Paper 10. Copenhagen: Ministry of Foreign Affairs.

Dagenais, H. and Piché, D. (eds.) (1994) *Women, Feminism and Development*. Montreal: McGill-Queen's University Press.

Dagron, A. G. (2000) *Making Waves, Stories of Participatory Communication for Social Change*. New York: Rockefeller Foundation.

Dahms, M. and Ramos, E. (2002) "Development from within: Community Development, Gender and ICT's" in Floyd, C. et al (eds.) *Feminist Challenges in the Information Age*. Opladen Leske und Budrich.

International Communication for Development Roundtable "Declaration". Managua, November 2001. <www.comminit.com/roundtable2/index.html>.

Department for International Development (2002) *Scaling-up and communication: guidelines for enhancing the developmental impact of natural resources systems research*. London: DFID.

Development Dialogue (1975) "What Now? Another Development" 1/2. Uppsala: Dag Hammarskjöld Foundation.

Development Dialogue (1978)2, (1981)2, (1984)1-2. (1985)1, (1989)1. Available at <www.dhf.uu.se/publications.html>.

Díaz, M., Simmons, R., Díaz, J., González, C., Makuch, M. Y. and Bossmeyer, D (1999) "Expanding Contraceptive Choice: Findings from Brazil", *Studies in Family Planning* 30 (1), pp. 1-16.

468 | Diaz-Bordenave, J. (1976) "Communication of Agricultural Innovations in Latin America: The Need for New Models", *Communications Research*, 3, pp. 43-62.

Dickson, G. (2000) "Aboriginal Grandmothers' Experience with Health Promotion and Participatory Action Research", *Qualitative Health Research* 10 (2), pp. 188-213.

Dore, E. (1985) "Culture". In Walker, T. (ed.) *Nicaragua. The First Five Years*. New York: Praeger, pp. 413-422.

Downing, J. D.H. (2001) *Radical media: rebellious communication and social movements*. Thousand Oaks, CA: Sage.

Edwards, M. (1999) *Future positive: International co-operation in the 21st century*. London: Earthscan.

Edwards, M., Hulme, D. and Wallace, T. (2000) *Increasing leverage for development: challenges for NGOs in a global future*. Bloomfield, CT: Kumarian press.

Eek, H. (1979) "Principles Governing the Use of the Mass Media as Defined by the United Nations and UNESCO". In Nordenstreng, K. and Schiller, H. (eds.) *National Sovereignty and International Communication*. Norwood: Ablex.

Ehn, P. (1988) *Work-oriented Design of Computer Artifacts*. Stockholm: Arbetslivscentrum.

Eisele, T. Macintyre, K., Eckert, E., Beier, J and Killeen, G. (2000) "Evaluating Malaria Interventions in Africa: A Review and Assessment of Recent Research". *MEASURE* Evaluation Working Paper WP-00-19. Chapel Hill, NC: Carolina Population Center.

Eknes, A. and Andresen, L. (1999) *Local Media Support*. Oslo: FAFO. <www.fafo.no>.

Ellingsen Tunold, B.M. (1984) *The UNCLOS III Negotiations and the Deep Sea-bed Regime: The Common Heritage of Mankind for the Benefit of Mankind as a Whole*. Oslo: Fridtjof Nansens Institut.

Elsaesser, T. (1994) "European Television and National Identity, or 'What's there to Touch when the Dust has Settled'". Paper presented to the conference on Turbulent Europe: Conflict, Identity and Culture, London, July.

Eng, E., Briscoe, J. and Cunningham, A. (1990) "Participation Effect from Water Projects on EPI", *Social Science and Medicine* 30 (12), pp. 1349-1358.

Enger, D. and Winskell, K. (1999) *Scenarios from the Sahel: Working Together to Fight AIDS*, New York: UNDP.

Eriksen, T. H. (2001a) "Between universalism and relativism: A critique of the UNESCO concepts of culture". In Cowan, J., Dembour, M.B. and Wilson, R. (eds.) *Culture and Rights: Anthropological Perspectives*. Cambridge: CUP.

Eriksen, T. H. (2001b) "Ethnic identity, national identity and intergroup conflict: The significance of personal experiences", in Ashmore, R.D., Jussim, L. and Wilder, D. (eds.) *Social identity, intergroup conflict, and conflict reduction*. Oxford: Oxford University Press.

Escobar, A. (1994) "Welcome to Cyberia", *Current Anthropology*, Vol. 35, No. 3, pp. 211-235.

Escobar, A. (1995) *Encountering Development. The Making and Unmaking of the Third World*. New Jersey: Princeton University Press.

Estrella, M. (ed.) (2000) *Learning from Change: issues and experiences in participatory monitoring and evaluation*. London: Intermediate Technology Publications.

Etherton, M. (1980) "Trends in African Theatre" in *African Literature Today*, No. 10.

FAO. (1991a) "Report of the Roundtable on Development Communication". Rome: FAO.

FAO. (1991b) *Sharing Knowledge: Communication for Sustainable Development*. Development Support Communication Branch, FAO (17', video).

FAO (2002) "Regional Workshop for Designing and Implementing Multimedia Communication Strategies and National Communication Policies" <http://www.fao.org/sd/2003/KN0403_en.htm>.

Fadul, A. M. (ed.) (1993) *Serial Fiction in TV. The Latin American Telenovelas*. Sao Paulo: USP.

Farrington, J. C., Kidd, A., Beckman, M. and Cromwell, E. (2002) "Creating a Policy Environment for Pro-Poor Agricultural Extension: The Who? What? and How?" *Natural Resources Perspectives*, Vol. 80. London: ODI.

Fascell, D.B. (ed.) (1979) *International News. Freedom under Attack*. Beverly Hills: Sage.

Feenberg, A. (1995) *Alternative Modernity. The Technical Turn in Philosophy and Social Theory*. Berkeley: Univ. of California Press.

Feenberg, A. (1999) *Questioning Technology*. London and New York: Routledge.

Feenberg, A. (2002) *Transforming Technology. A Critical Theory Revisited*. New York: Oxford University Press.

Fejes, F. (1986) "State and Communication Policy in Latin America", *Critical Studies in Mass Communication*, Vol. 3, Number 2.

Fernandez-Armesto, F. (1996) *Millennium: A History of Our Last Thousand Years*. London: Black Swan.

Ferreira, H.H. (1953) "The Use of Social Case Drama in Training African Social Workers". Rhodes-Livingstone Institute Papers No. XIII. Manchester: MUP.

Fetterman, D.M. (2001) *Foundations of Empowerment Evaluation*. Thousand Oaks, CA: SAGE.

Figueroa, M.E., Kincaid, L., Rani, M. and Lewis, G. (2001) "Guidelines for the measurement of process and outcome of social change interventions". Baltimore, MD: CCP/JHU. Prepared for the Rockefeller Foundation.

Figueroa, M.E., Kincaid, L., Rani, M. and Lewis, G. (2002) *Communication for Social Change: An Integrated Model for Measuring the Process and Its Outcomes*. New York: Rockefeller Foundation.

470 | Finkielkraut, A. (1987) *Le défaite de la pensée*. Paris: Gallimard.

Flournoy, S.M. and Stewart, R.K. (1997) *CNN Making News in the Global Market*. Luton: John Libbey Media.

Foster, E.M. (1924, 1998) *A passage to India*. New Brunswick, NJ: Transaction Publishers.

Foster, M. (1972) "An Introduction to the Theory and Practice of Action Research in Work Organizations", *Human Relations* Vol. 15 No. 6, as reproduced in Kemmis, S. and McTaggart, R. (eds.) (1988) *The Action Research Reader*. Geelong, Victoria: Deakin University, pp. 529-556.

Foucault, M. (1972) *The Archaeology of Knowledge*. New York: Pantheon.

Foucault, M. (1978) *History of Sexuality. Volume 1: An Introduction*. New York: Pantheon.

Fox, Elisabeth. "Managing Communication for Development". Notes from a presentation to the IADB Development Communication seminar, July 1, 2003. <www.comminit.com>.

Frank, A. G. (1966) *Capitalism and Underdevelopment in Latin America: Historical Studies of Chile and Brazil*. New York, NY: Monthly Review Press.

Fraser, C. (1987) "Un Nuevo Enfoque para la Comunicación Rural: La Experiencia Peruana en Video para la Capacitación Campesina, Estudio de Caso de Comunicación para el Desarrollo". Rome: FAO

Fraser, C. and Restrepo-Estrada, S. (1998) *Communicating for Development: Human Change for Survival*. London and New York: I.B. Taurus.

Freedman, R. (1997) "Do Family Planning Programs Affect Fertility Preferences? A Literature Review". *Studies in Family Planning* 28 (1), pp. 1-13.

Freimuth, V. S. (1992) "Theoretical Foundations of AIDS Media Campaigns", in Edgar, T., Fitzpatrick, M.A. and Freimuth, V.S. (eds.) *AIDS: A Communication Perspective*. Hillsdale, NJ: Lawrence Erlbaum, pp. 91-110.

Freire, P. (1967) *La educación como práctica de la libertad*. Caracas: Nuevo Orden.

Freire, P. (1972) *Cultural Action for Freedom*. London: Penguin Books.

Freire, P. (1973) *Education: The Practice of Freedom*. London: Writers and Readers Publishing Cooperative.

Freire, P. (1987) *Literacy–Reading the Word and the World*. South Hadley, Mass.: Bergin and Garvey.

Freire P. (1993) *Pedagogy of the Oppressed*. New York: Continuum.

Fuenzalida, V. (1994) *La apropiación educativa de la telenovela*. Santiago: CPU.

Fuenzalida, V. (1997) *Televisión y Cultura Cotidiana. La influencia social de la TV percibida desde la cultura cotidiana de la audiencia*. Santiago: CPU.

Fuglesang, A. (1982) *About Understanding: Ideas and Observations on Cross Cultural Communication*. Uppsala: Dag Hammarskjöld Foundation.

Fuglesang, M. (1994) *Veils and Videos: Female youth culture on the Kenyan coast*. Stockholm: Almqvist and Wiksell.

Fuglesang, M. (1997) "Lessons for Life. Past and present modes of sexuality education in Tanzanian society". In *Social Science and Medicine*, Vol. 44.

Fukuyama, F. (1993) *The End of History and the Last Man*. New York: Avon.

Funk, J. L. (2001) *The mobile Internet: How Japan dialled up and Europe disconnected*. Hong Kong: ISI Publications.

Galtung, J. (1971) "A Structural Theory of Imperialism". *Journal of Peace Research* 8(1971)2, 81-118.

Gao, M. Y. (2005) "Participatory Communication Research and HIV/AIDS Control: A Study among Gay Men and MSM in Chengdu, China". Unpublished PhD thesis. Australia: The University of Newcastle.

Garbo, G. (1983) "The Role of the IPDC in the Implementation of the New World Information and Communication Order". Presentation at Conference of NAMEDIA, New Delhi, India 9-12 December.

García-Canclini, N. (1990) *Culturas Híbridas*. Mexico City: Grijalbo.

García-Canclini, N. (1988) "Culture and Power: The State of Research". In *Media, Culture and Society*, Vol. 10, pp. 467-97.

García-Canclini, N. (1982) *Las Culturas Populares en el Capitalismo*. México: Nueva Imagen.

Gazette (2004) Special issue on the World Summit on the Information Society. No. 3-4.

Geertz, C. (1973) *The Interpretation of Cultures: Selected Essays by Clifford Geertz*. New York: Basic Books.

Geertz, C. (1983) *Local Knowledge. Further Essays in Interpretive Anthropology*. New York: Basic Books.

Geertz, C. (1995) *After the Fact: Two Countries, Four Decades, One Anthropologist*. Cambridge: Harvard University Press.

Gerbner, G. (1993) "UNESCO in the US Press". In Gerbner et al (1993).

Gerbner, G.; Mowlana, H. and Nordenstreng, K. (eds.) (1993) *The Global Media Debate: It's Rise, Fall, and Renewal*. Norwood: Ablex.

Giddens, A. (1991) *Modernity and Self-Identity. Self and society in the late modern age*. Cambridge: Polity Press.

Global Dialogues (2001) "External Evaluation Report, Senegal" (unpublished).

Global Dialogues (2003a) "External Evaluation Report, Burkina Faso/Togo" (unpublished).

Global Dialogues (2003b) "External Evaluation Report, Senegal" (unpublished).

Global Dialogues (2003c) 2002/3 "Contest and Selection of Winners: Final Report" available at <www.globaldialogues.org>.

472 | Goddard-Power, S. (1981) 'The U.S. View of Belgrade', in *Journal of Communication* 3(1981)4.

Goddard-Power, S. (1984) "UNESCO at Belgrade: The U.S. View". In Gerbner, G. and Siefert, M. (eds.) *World Communications*. New York/London: Longman.

Granqvist, M. (2003) "Assessing ICT Efforts in Marginalized Regions from a Critical Social Viewpoint. Learning from the Case of Lincos". Malmö: Malmö University. Master thesis available at <www.globalatider.nu>.

Grint, K. and Gill, R. (1995) *The Gender-Technology Relation: Contemporary Theory and Research*. Bristol: Taylor and Francis.

Gripsrud, J. (ed.) (1999) *Television and Common Knowledge*. London: Routledge.

Gumucio-Dagron, A. (2001a) *Making waves*. New York: Rockefeller Foundation.

Gumucio-Dagron, A. (2001b) "Myths and paradigms of participatory communication". Paper presented at Our Media, Not Theirs, ICA Pre-Conference on Alternative Media, Washington, 24 May 2001.

Gumucio-Dagron, A. (2001c) "Comunicación para la salud: El reto de la participación", in *Agujero Negro*, 1-6. Available at <www.agujeronegro.org/uno.htm>.

Habermas, J. (1962) *Strukturwandel der Offentlichkeit*. Neuwied and Berlin: Luchterhand.

Habermas, J. (1989) *Structural Transformation of the Public Sphere*. Cambridge, Mass: MIT Press.

Haider, M. (ed.) (2005) *Global Public Health Communication: Challenges, Perspectives and Strategies*. Boston: Jones and Bartlett Publishers.

Hamelink, C. (1979) *The New International Economic Order and the New International Information Order*. Paris: UNESCO (International Commission for the Study of Communication Problems 34).

Hamelink, C. (1980) *Communication in the Eighties: A Reader on the MacBride Report*. Rome: IDOC.

Hamelink, C. (1997) *The Politics of World Communication*. London: Sage.

Hancock, L., Sanson-Fisher, R. W., Redman, S., Burton, R., Burton, L., Butler, J, Girgis, A., Gibberd, R., Hensley, M., McClintock, A., Reid, A., Schofield, M., Tripodi, T., and Walsh, R. (1997) "Community Action for Health Promotion: A Review of Methods and Outcomes 1990-1995". In *American Journal of Preventive Medicine* 13 (4), pp. 229-239.

Harley, W.G. (1984) "UNESCO and the International Programme for the Development of Communications". In Gerbner, G. and Siefert, M. (eds.) *World Communications*. New York/London: Longman.

Harris, P. (1976) "Selective Images: An Analysis of the West African Wire Service of an International News Agency". Paper prepared for the 4th session of the IAMCR 10th General Assembly and Scientific Conference, University of Leicester, 1976.

Harvard Readinessguide (2001) "Readiness for the networked world: a Guide for | **473** Developing Countries". Harvard: Center for International Development at Harvard University.

HealthCom (1992) "Results and realities: A decade of experience in communication for child survival". Washington, DC: AED.

Hedebro, G. (1982) "Communication and Social Change in Developing Nations: A Critical View". Ames: Iowa State University Press.

Heeks, R. (1999) "The Tyranny of Participation in Information Systems. Learning from Development Projects". Working Paper. Manchester: Institute for Development Policy and Management.

Hegde, R. S. (1996) "Narratives of silence: Rethinking gender, agency, and power from the communication experiences of battered women in South India". In *Communication Studies*, 47, pp. 303-317.

Hegde. R. S. (1998) "A view from elsewhere: Locating difference and the politics of representation from a transnational feminist perspective". In *Communication Theory*, 8(3), pp. 271-297.

Hemer, O. (1989) *Peninsula*. Stockholm: Agora.

Hemer, O. (1994) "El Boom Revisited", in *Marginal* No. 3. Oslo.

Hernandez, T. and Campanile, V. (2000) "Feminists at work. A case study of transforming power relationships in everyday life: Puntos de Encuentro". In *Institutionalizing gender equality: Commitment, policy and practice. A global source book*. Amsterdam: Royal Tropical Institute.

Hildebrandt, E. (1994) "A Model for Community Involvement in Health (CIH) Program Development". In *Social Science and Medicine* 39 (2), pp. 247-254.

Hinden, M. J.; Kincaid, D. L., Kumah, O. M., Morgan, W. and Kim, Y.M. (1994) "Gender Differences in Media Exposure and Action during a Family Planning Campaign in Ghana". In *Health Communication* 6 (2), pp. 117-135.

Hjarvard, S. (1995) *Internationale TV-nyheder. En historisk analyse af det europæiske system for udveksling af TV-nyheder*. Århus: Akademisk forlag.

Hjarvard, S. (ed.) (2001) *News in a Globalized Society*. Göteborg: Nordicom

Hogle, J., Edward, E., Green, E., Nantulya, V., Stoneburner, R. and Stover, J. (2002) "What happened in Uganda? Declining HIV prevalence, behaviour change, and the national response". Washington: USAID.

Holbrooke, R. (1998) *To End a War*. New York: Random House.

Hornik, R. (1988) *Development Communication: Information, Agriculture, and Nutrition in the Third World*. NY: Longman Inc.

Hornik, R. (1989) "The Knowledge-Behavior Gap in Public Information Campaigns: A Development Communication View". In Salmon, C. T. (ed.) *Information Campaigns: Balancing Social Values and Social Change*. Newbury Park, CA: Sage, pp. 113-138.

Hornik, R. (1990) "Alternative Models of Behavior Change", Working Paper 131. Philadelphia: Annenberg School for Communication.

Hornik, R. (1997) "Public Health Education and Communication as Policy Instruments for Bringing About Changes in Behavior". In Goldberg, M. E., Fishbein, M. and Middlestadt, S. E. (eds.) *Social Marketing: Theoretical and Practical Perspectives*. Mahwah, NJ: Lawrence Erlbaum, pp. 45-58.

Hornik, R., Contreras-Budge, E., Ferencic, N., Koepke, C. and Morris, N. (1991) "Results from the Evaluation of the PREMI/HEALTHCOM Project in Ecuador 1985-1988". Center for International, Health, and Development Communication, Annenberg School for Communication, University of Pennsylvania: Pennsylvania. Working Paper 1003.

Hornik, R. (ed.) (2002) *Public health communication: Evidence for behaviour change*. Mahwah, N.J.: L. Erlbaum.

Hoskins, C., McFayden, S. and Finn, A. (1997) *Global Television and Film: An Introduction to the Economics of the Business*. Oxford: Clarendon Press.

Huesca, R. (2000) "Communication for Social Change among Mexican Factory Workers on the Mexico-United States Border". In Wilkins, K. G. (ed.) *ReDeveloping Communication for Social Change: Theory, Practice, and Power*. Lanham, MD: Rowman and Littlefield, pp. 73-87.

Huesca, R. (2001) "Conceptual contributions of new social movements to development communication research". In *Communication Theory* 11(4), pp. 415-433.

Huntington, S. (1996) *The Clash of Civilizations and the Remaking of a World Order*. New York: Simon and Schuster.

Hussain, A, Aarø, L. E. and Kvåle, G. (1997) "Impact of a Health Education Program to Promote Consumption of Vitamin A Rich Foods in Bangladesh". In *Health Promotion International* 12(2), pp. 103-9.

Höhne, H. (1977) "Report über Nachrichtenagenturen. 1. Die Situation auf den Nachrichtenmärkten der Welt". Baden-Baden: Nomos Verlagsgesellschaft.

Jankélévitch, V. (1974) *L'Irréversible et la nostalgie*. Paris: Flammarion.

Japhet, G (1999) *Edutainment. How to make Edutainment work for you: a step by step guide to designing and managing an edutainment project for social development*. Johannesburg: Soul City.

Jato, M. N., Simbakalia, C., Tarasevich, J. M., Awasum, D. N., Kihinga, C. N. B. and Ngirwamungu, E. (1999) "The Impact of Multimedia Family Planning Promotion on the Contraceptive Behaviour of Women in Tanzania". In *International Family Planning Perspectives* 25(2), pp. 60-67.

Kalipeni, E. and Kamlongera, C. (1996) "The Role of Theatre for Development in Mobilising Rural Communities for Primary Health Care: The Case of Liwonde PHC Unit in Southern Malawi". In *Journal of Social Development in Africa* 11, 1.

Kane, T. T., Gueye, M., Speizer, I., Pacque-Margolis, S., and Baron, D. (1998) "The Impact of a Family Planning Multimedia Campaign in Bamako, Mali". In *Studies in Family Planning* 29 (3), pp. 309-323.

Kelly, M. (1931) "African Drama". In *Oversea Education*, Vol. II, No. 3.

Kepel, G. (2002) *Chronique d'une guerre d'Orient (automne 2001): suivi de Brève chronique d'Israël et de Palestine (avril-mai 2001)*. Paris: Gallimard.

Kerr, D. (1981) "Didactic Theatre in Africa". In *Harvard Education Review*, 51, Vol. I

Kidd, R. et al (1978) *Laedza Batanani: Organizing Popular Theatre*. The Laedza Batanani Experience. Institute of Adult Education. University of Botswana.

Kidd, R. and Byram, Martin (1981) *Demystifying Pseudo-Freirian non-formal Education: A case description and analysis of Laedza Batanani*. Toronto: International Council for Adult Education.

Kincaid, D. L. (1979) "The Convergence of Communication". Papers of the East-West Communication Institute No. 18. Honolulu, Hawaii: East-West Center.

Kincaid, D. L., Payne Merritt, A., Nickerson, L., de Castro Buffington, S., de Castro, M. P. P. and de Castro, B. M. (1996) "Impact of a Mass Media Vasectomy Promotion Campaign in Brazil". In *International Family Planning Perspectives* 22(4), pp. 169-75.

Kincaid, D. L. (2000) "Mass Media, Ideation, and Behavior: A Longitudinal Analysis of Contraceptive Change in the Philippines". Paper presented at the International Communication Association's 50th annual meeting.

Kincaid, D. L. (2002) "Drama, emotion, and cultural convergence". In *Communication Theory*, 12(2), pp. 136-152.

Kothari, R. (1984) "Communication for Alternative Development: Towards a Paradigm". In *Development Dialogue*, 1984: 1:2. Available at <www.dhf.uu.se>.

Kotler, P. and Roberto, E. L. (1989) "The Social Marketing Approach to Social Change". In *Social Marketing: Strategies for Changing Public Behavior.* NY: The Free Press.

Krishnatray, P. K. and Melkote, S. R. (1998) "Public Communication Campaigns in the Destigmatization of Leprosy: A Comparative Analysis of Diffusion and Participatory Approaches. A Case Study of Gwalior, India". In *Journal of Health Communication* 3, pp. 327-344.

Krog, A. (1999) *Country of My Skull*. London: Jonathan Cape.

Kumar, K. (1994) "Communication Approaches to Participation and Development: Challenging the Assumptions and Perspectives". In White, Nair and Ascroft (1994), pp. 76-94.

Kurspahic, K. (2003) *Prime Time Crime: Balkan Media in War and Peace*. Washington, D.C.: United States Institute of Peace Press.

La Pastina, A., Dhaval, P. and Schiavo, M. (2004) "Social merchandizing in Brazilian telenovelas". In Singhal et al (2004), pp. 261-279.

Laverack, G., Sakyi, B. E. and Hubley, J. (1997) "Participatory Learning Materials for Health Promotion in Ghana-a case study". In *Health Promotion International* 12 (1), pp. 21-26.

476 | Lawrence, A. (1995) "The neglected uplands: Innovation and environmental change in Matalom, Philippines". Agricultural Extension and Rural Development Department, AERDD, University of Reading. Working paper 95/11.

Lazarsfeld, P. F., Berelson, B. and Gaudet, H. (1944) *The People's Choice*. NY: Columbia University Press.

Letelier, M. F, Flores, F., and Spinosa, C. (2003) "Developing productive customers in emerging markets". In *California Management Review*, 45(4).

Lettenmaier, C., Krenn, S., Morgan, W., Kols, A.and Piotrow, P. (1993) "Africa: Using Radio Soap Operas to Promote Family Planning". In *Hygie* 12 (1), pp. 5-10.

Levin, H.J. (1984) "U.S. Communication Policies at Home and Abroad: Are they Consistent?". In Gerbner and Siefert (1984).

Lewis, P. and Booth, J. (1989) *The invisible Medium: Public, Commercial and Community Radio*. London: Macmillan.

Lightfoot, C., Ramírez, R., Groot, A. N., R., Alders, C., Shao, F., Kisauzi, D. and Bekalo, I. (2001) "Learning Our Way Ahead: Navigating Institutional Change and Agricultural Decentralisation". *Gatekeeper Series*, Vol. 98. London: IIED.

Lins Da Silva, C. E. (1985) *Muito alem do Jardim Botánico: Um estudo sobre a audiencia do Journal Nacional da Globo entre trabalhadores*. Sao Paulo: Summus Editorial.

Lomberg, B. (2004) *Global Crises, Global Solutions*. Cambridge: Cambridge University Press.

Lucas, F. (1991) "Strategies on People Empowerment". Lecture delivered to the Institute of Development Communication staff, 29 October 1991, UPLB, College, Laguna.

Luthra, R. (1996) "International communications instruction with a focus on women". In *Journalism and Mass Communication Educator*, winter, pp. 42-51.

Lynch, J. (2002) "Reporting the World. A practical check-list for the ethical reporting of conflicts in the 21st Century". <http://www.transnational.org/features/2002/Lynch_ReportingBook.html>.

Lyotard, J-L (1983) *Le Différend*. Paris: Ed. De Minuit (1988: *The Differend: Phrases in Dispute*. Transl. by G Van der Abbeele. Minneapolis: University of Minnesota Press).

McAnany, E. (1993) "The Telenovela and Social Change". In Fadul (1993).

MacBride, S. and Roach, C. (1993) "The New International Information Order". In Gerbner, Mowlana and Nordenstreng (1993).

McChesney, R. (1999) *Rich Media, Poor Democracy: Communication Politics in Dubious Times*. Chicago: University of Illinois Press.

McCombie, S. and Hornik, R. (1992) "Evaluation of a Workplace-based Peer Education Program Designed to Prevent AIDS in Uganda". Center for

International, Health, and Development Communication Working Paper 1011. Annenberg School for Communication, University of Pennsylvania.

McDivitt, J. A. (1991) "The Healthcom Project in Jordan: Final Case Study Evaluation Project". Center for International, Health, and Development Communication Working Paper 1004. Annenberg School for Communication, University of Pennsylvania.

McDivitt, J. A. and McDowell, J. (1991) "Results from the Evaluation of the Healthcom Project in Central Java". Center for International, Health, and Development Communication Working Paper 1002. Annenberg School for Communication, University of Pennsylvania.

McDivitt, J. A., Zimicki, S. and Hornik, R. (1997) "Explaining the Impact of a Communication Campaign to Change Vaccination Knowledge and Coverage in the Philippines". In *Health Communication* 9(2), pp. 95-118.

McDivitt, J. A., Zimicki, S., Hornik, R. and Abulaban, A. (1993) "The Impact of the Healthcom Mass Media Campaign on Timely Initiation of Breastfeeding in Jordan". In *Studies in Family Planning* 24(5), pp. 295-309.

Macdonald J. J. (1992) *Primary Health Care: Medicine in its place*. London: Earthscan.

McKee, N. (1992) *Social Mobilization and Social Marketing in Developing Communities: Lessons for Communicators*. Penang, Malaysia: Southbound.

McKee, N. (1994) "A community-based learning approach: Beyond social marketing". In White, Nair, and Ascroft (1994).

McKee, N. et al (eds.) (2000) *Involving People, Evolving Behaviour*. Southbound Penang/UNICEF.

McKee et al. (2004) "Cartoons and comic books for changing social norms: Meena, the South Asian girl". In Sighal et al (2004), pp. 331-350.

McKillip, J. (1989) "Evaluation of Health Promotion Media Campaigns". *Evaluating Health Promotion Programs* 43, pp. 89-100.

Malaviya, P., Singhal, A., Svenekrud, P.J., and Srivastava, S. (2004a) "Telenor in Bangladesh (A): The prospect of doing well and doing good". Fontainebleau, France: INSEAD Business School.

Malaviya, P., Singhal, A., and Svenekrud, P.J., and Srivastava, S. (2004b). "Telenor in Bangladesh (B): Achieving multiple bottom lines at GrameenPhone". Fontainebleau, France: INSEAD Business School.

Manderson, L. (1992) "Community Participation and Malaria Control in Southeast Asia: Defining the Principles of Involvement". In *Southeast Asian Journal of Tropical Medicine and Public Health* 23 (supplement 1), pp. 9-17.

Manzar, O., Rao, M. and Ahmed, T. (2001) *The Internet Economy of India 2001*. New Delhi: INOMY Media Limited.

Marcuse, H. (1999) [1941] "Some Social Implications of Modern Technology". In Kellner, D. (ed.) *Technology, War and Fascism. Collected Papers of Herbert Marcuse*, Vol. I. London: Routledge.

478 | Marmo da Silva, J. and Chagas Guimarães, M. A. (2000) "Odô-Yá Project: HIV/AIDS Prevention in the Context of Afro-Brazilian Religion". In *Journal of Health Communication* 5 (Supplement), pp. 119-122.

Martin-Barbero, J. (1993) *Communication, Culture and Hegemony. From Media to Mediations*. London: Sage.

Martin-Barbero, J. (2002a) "Desencuentros de la sociabilidad y reencantamientos de la identidad". *Analisi*, No. 29. Bellaterra: Universidad Autónoma de Barcelona/Server de Publicaciones, p. 45-62.

Martin-Barbero, J. (2002b) *La Educación Desde la Comunicación*. Buenos Aires: Grupo Editorial Norma.

Martínez-Frías, J. (2003) "The importance of ICTs for developing countries". *Interdisciplinary Science Reviews*, 28(1), pp. 10-15.

Maslog, C. C. et al (eds.) (1997) *Communication for People Power: An Introduction to Community Communication*. UNESCO- Project TAMBULI. Institute of Development Communication, UPLB, College of Mass Communication, UP Diliman and UNESCO National Commission, Philippines.

Mattes, J. et al (1998) *Commitment to Democracy: Pulse: A Barometer of South African Democracy*. Cape Town: Idasa.

Mattes, J. et al (2000) "Views of Democracy in South Africa and the Region: Trends and Comparisons". In *The Southern African Democracy Barometer*, No. 2.

Maxwell, R. (1997) "Internationalizing Communication: The Control of Difference and the Global Market". In Mohammadi, A. (ed.) *International Communication and Globalization*. London: Sage, pp. 191-209.

Mda, Z. (2002) *Madonna of Excelsior*. New York: Farrar, Straus, Giroux.

Mefalopulos, P. and Kamlongera, C. (2002) *Participatory Communication Strategy Design*. Harare and Rome: SADC Centre for Communication for Development and FAO.

Melkote, S. and Steeves, H. L. (2001) *Communication for Development in the Third World: Theory and Practice for Empowerment*. New Delhi: Sage.

Menou, M. (2001) "IsICTometrics: Toward an alternative vision and process". Working paper presented at RICYT and Observatório das Ciências e das Tecnologias Seminar on Indicators of the Information Society and Scientific Culture, Lisbon.

Meyer, M. K. and Prugl, E. (1999) *Gender Politics in Global Governance*. Lanham: Rowman and Littlefield.

Milikowski, M. (2000) "Exploring a model of de-ethnicisation the case of Turkish television in the Netherlands". In *European Journal of Communication*, 15(4), pp. 443-468.

Miller, L. (2002) *Novela Novela*. Video.

Mimouni, R. (1992) *De la barbarie en général et de l'intégrisme en particulier*. Paris: Le pré aux clercs.

Ministerio de Cultura (1982) *Hacia Una Política Cultural de la Revolución Popular Sandinista*. Managua: Ministerio de Cultura.

Minkler, M. (ed.) (1997) *Community Organizing and Community Building for Health*. New Brunswick, NJ: Rutgers University Press.

Minter, W. (2002) "Global and regional configurations of late Cold War conflict: Comparing Angola, Mozambique and Nicaragua". Paper prepared for workshop on 'Civil War and Cold War: 1975-1990: Comparative Perspectives on Southern Africa, Central America and Central Asia', Columbia University, 14-15 November.

Mody, B. (1991) *Designing messages for development communication: An audience participation-based approach*. New Delhi: Sage.

Mohanty, C. T. (1991a) "Cartographies of struggle: Third world women and the politics of feminism". In Mohanty, C. T., Russo, A., and Torres, L. (eds.) *Third world women and the politics of feminism*. Bloomington: Indiana University Press, pp. 1-50.

Mohanty, C. T. (1991b) "Under western eyes: Feminist scholarship and colonial discourses". In Mohanty et al (1991).

Morgall, J. M. (1993) *Technology Assessment. A Feminist Perspective*. Philadelphia: Temple University Press.

Morley, D. (2000) *Home Territories: Media, Mobility and Identity*. London: Routledge.

Morris, N. (2003) "A Comparative Analysis of the Diffusion and Participatory Models in Development Communication". In *Communication Theory*, Vol. 13, No. 2, p. 225-248.

Morris, N. and Waisbord, S. (2001) *Why states matter*. Landham, MD: Rowman and Littefield.

Moyana, T. T. (1988*) Education, Liberation and the Creative Act*. Harare: Zimbabwe Publishing House.

Myers, M. (2002) *Institutional Review of Educational Radio Dramas*. Atlanta: CDC.

Myhre, S. L. and Flora, J. A. (2000) "HIV/AIDS Communication Campaigns: Progress and Prospects". In *Journal of Health Communication* 5 (Supplement), pp. 29-45.

Nair, K. and White, S. (eds.) (1993) *Perspectives on development communication*. New Delhi: Sage.

Nariman, H. N. (1993) *Soap operas for social change. Toward a methodology for entertainment-education television*. Westport, Connecticut: Praeger.

Naroola, G. (2001) *Entrepreneurial Connection: East Meets West in the Silicon Valley*. New Delhi: Tata McGraw-Hill.

Navarro, V. (1986) *Crisis, Health and Medicine. A social critique*. New York, London: Tavistock publication.

480 |

Nederveen Pieterse, J. (2001) *Development Theory. Deconstructions/Reconstructions*. London: Sage.

Neft, N. and Levine, A. D. (1997) *Where Women Stand: An International Report on the Status of Women in 140 Countries*. NY: Random House.

Ngugi wa Thiong'o (1981) "Kenyan Culture: The National Struggle for Survival". In *Writers in Politics. Essays*. London: Heinemann.

Ngugi wa Thiong'o (1981b) *I Will Marry When I Want*. Nairobi: Heinemann.

Ngugi wa Thiong'o (1982) *Mother, City for Me*. Nairobi: Heinemann.

Niemi, Mikael (2000) *Populärmusik från Vittula*. Stockholm: Norstedts (Popular Music from Vittula, 2003. New York: Seven Stories Press).

Nordenstreng, K. (1984) *The Mass Media Declaration of UNESCO*. Norwood: Ablex.

Nordenstreng, K. (1984) "Defining the New International Information Order". In Gerbner and Siefert (1984).

Nordenstreng, K. and Varis, T. (1974) "Television Traffic–A One-Way Street. A Survey and Analysis of the International Flow of Television Programme Material". Paris: UNESCO (Reports and Papers on Mass Communication 70).

O'Connor, A., (1991) "Emergence of Cultural Studies in Latin America". In *Critical Studies in Mass Communications*, 8, pp. 60-73.

Oakley, P. and Clayton, A. (2000) *Monitoring and Evaluation of Empowerment: A resource document*. Oxford: INTRAC.

Ogundimu, F. (1994) "Communicating Knowledge of Immunization for Development: A Case Study from Nigeria". In Moemeka, A. A. (ed.) *Communicating for Development: A New Pan-Disciplinary Perspective*. New York: State University of New York Press, pp. 219-243.

Oliveira, M. C. B. (1993) "Communication Strategies for Agricultural Development in the Third World". In *Media Asia* Vol. 20 No. 2, Singapore: AMIC, pp. 102-108.

Panos (2001) "Background Document to the International Communication for Development Roundtable". Managua, November. <www.comminit.com/roundtable2/indez.html>.

Papa, M. J., Auwal, M. A., and Singhal, A. (1995) "Dialectic of control and emancipation in organizing for social change: A multitheoretic study of the Grameen Bank in Bangladesh". In *Communication Theory*, 5, pp. 189-223.

Papa, M. J., Auwal, M. A., and Singhal, A. (1997) "Organizing for social change within concertive control systems: Member identification, empowerment, and the masking of discipline". In *Communication Monographs*, 64, pp. 1-31.

Papa et al (2004) "Entertainment-Education and social change: An analysis of parasocial interaction, social learning, collective efficacy, and paradoxical communication". In *Journal of Communication* 50 (4), pp. 31-55.

Parker, W. (2005) "Ideology, Hegemony and HIV/AIDS: The Appropriation of Indigenous and Global Spheres". Unpublished PhD thesis. University of Kwazulu-Natal, South Africa.

Parpart, J. (1995) "Post-modernism, gender and development". In Crush, J. (ed.) *Power of development*. New York: Routledge, pp. 253-265.

Patil, P. G. and Kincaid, D. L. (2000) "AIDS Prevention among Men in the Philippines: Path Models of the Effects of a Mass Media Communication Campaign on Condom Intention and Use". Paper presented at the International Communication Association's 50th annual meeting.

Patron, M. C. (ed.) (1987) *The Community Organizing Process (illustrated)*. Diliman, Quezon City: UP College of Social Work and Community Development.

Pedalini, L. M., Dallari, S. G. and Barber-Madden, R. (1993) "Public Health Advocacy on Behalf of Women in São Paulo: Learning to Participate in the Planning Process". In *Journal of Public Health Policy* 14 (2), pp. 183-197.

Pfaffenberger, B. (1992) "Technological Dramas". In *Science, Technology and Human Values*, Vol. 17, Issue 3, pp. 282-312.

Pfeffer, N. and Coote, A. (1991) "Is quality good for you? A critical review of quality assurance in welfare services". Social Policy Paper No. 5. London: Institute for Public Policy Research.

Phillips, C. (2000) *The Atlantic Sound*. London: Secker and Warburg.

Phillips, C. (2001) *A New World Order*. London: Secker and Warburg.

Piotrow, P. T., Kincaid, D. L., Hindin, M. J., Lettenmaier, C. L., Kuseka, I., Silberman, T., Zinanga, A., Chikara, F., Adamchak, D. J., Mbizvo, M. T., Lynn, W., Kumah, O. M. and Kim, Y.-M. (1992) "Changing Men's Attitudes and Behavior: The Zimbabwe Male Motivation Project". *Studies in Family Planning* 23 (6), pp. 365-375.

Piotrow, P. T., Rimon II, J. G., Winnard, K, Kincaid, D. L., Huntington, D and Convisser, J. (1990) "Mass Media Family Planning Promotion in Three Nigerian Cities". *Studies in Family Planning* 21 (5), pp. 265-274.

Piotrow, P.T., Kincaid, D.L., Rimon II, J.G. and Rinehart, W. (1997) *Health Communication: Lessons from Family Planning and Reproductive Health*. Westport, CT: Praeger.

Piotrow, P. T. and de Fossard, E. (2004) "Entertainment-education as a public health intervention". In Singhal et al (2004).

Pitroda, S. (1993) "Development, democracy, and the village telephone". In *Harvard Business Review* 71(6), pp. 66-77.

Population Reference Bureau (2001) "Abandoning female genital cutting". Washington, DC: PRB.

Portes, A., Guarnizo, L. E. and Landolt, P. (1999) "The study of transnationalism: pitfalls and promise of an emergent research field". In *Ethnic and Racial Studies*, 22(2), pp. 217-237.

482 | Prahalad, C. K. (2004) *The fortune at the bottom of the pyramid: Eradicating poverty through profits*. Philadelphia, PA: Wharton School Publishing.

Pribadi, W., Muzaham, F., Santoso, T., Rasidi, R., Rukmono, B. and Soeharto (1986) "The Implementation of Community Participation in the Control of Malaria in Rural Tanjung Pinang, Indonesia". *Southeast Asian Journal of Tropical Medicine and Public Health* 17 (3), pp. 371-378. Available at <www.ncbi.nlm.nih.gov/entrez/>.

Puntos de Encuentro (1995) "Informe Anual de Actividades" (preliminary version). Managua: Puntos de Encuentro.

Puntos de Encuentro (1997a) "Evaluación de la campaña 'La próxima vez...'". Managua: Puntos de Encuentro.

Puntos de Encuentro (1997b) "Communication strategies for the empowerment of women and young people in Nicaragua. Some lessons learned". Paper presented at the Health Development Policy Project on Communication Strategies Working Group Meeting, Washington DC.

Puntos de Encuentro (1998a) "Campaña contra la violencia masculina en la familia". Managua: Puntos de Encuentro. Proyecto presentado a la Agencia Interamericana de Desarrollo.

Puntos de Encuentro (1998b) "Plan institucional 96-98". Managua: Puntos de Encuentro.

Puntos de Encuentro (1999) "Informe Global 1999". Managua: Puntos de Encuentro.

Puntos de Encuentro (2000) "Evaluación de la campaña 'La violencia contra las mujeres es un desastre que los hombres SÍ podemos evitar'". Managua: Puntos de Encuentro.

Puntos de Encuentro (2002) "La historia, los logros, anécdotas de Puntos de Encuentro desde 1990 al 2002". Managua: Puntos de Encuentro. Transcript of staff meeting.

Purdey, A. F., Adhikari, G. B., Robinson, S. A. and Cox, P. W. (1994) "Participatory Health Development in Rural Nepal: Clarifying the Process of Community Empowerment". In *Health Education Quarterly* 21 (3), pp. 329-343.

Quadir, I. (2003) "Bottom-up economics". *Harvard Business Review*, 81(8), pp. 18-20.

Quebral, N. C. (2002) *Reflections on Development Communication (25 years after)*. College, Laguna: College of Development Communication, University of the Philippines, Los Baños.

Rahnema, M. and Bawtree, V. (eds.) (1997) *The Post-Development Reader*. London: Zed Books.

Rajora, R. (2002) *Bridging the Digital Divide: Gyandoot, the Model for Community Networks*. New Delhi: Tata McGraw-Hill.

Ramanathan, S. and Becker, J. (2001) *Internet in Asia*. Singapore: Asian Media and Information Communication Centre.

Ramírez, R. (1997) *Understanding Farmers' Communication Networks: Combining PRA with Agricultural Knowledge Systems Analysis*. London: IIED.

Ramírez, R. and Quarry, W. (2004a) *Communication for Development: A Medium for Innovation in Natural Resource Management*. Ottawa and Rome: IDRC and FAO.

Ramírez, R. and Quarry, W. (2004b) "Communication strategies in the age of decentralisation and privatisation of rural services: Lessons from two African experiences". AgREN Network Paper, 136.

Ramos E., Santos S, Mariani A., Rossal M., Oliveira R., Cord D. and Timmerman J. (2002) "Designing for an Ecological Agricultural Association: A PD Case Study". In Binder, T., Gregory, J., and Wagner, I. (eds.) *Participation and Design: Inquiring Into the Politics, Contexts and Practices of Collaborative Design Work*. PDC 2002 Proceedings of the Participatory Design Conference, Malmö, Sweden.

Rao, M. (ed.) (2002) *The Asia-Pacific Internet Handbook, Episode IV: Emerging Powerhouses*. New Delhi: Tata McGraw-Hill.

Reardon, K. K. and Rogers, E. M. (1988) "Interpersonal Versus Mass Media Communication: A False Dichotomy". In *Human Communication Research* 15(2), pp. 284-303.

Richards, M., Thomas, P. and Nain, Z. (2001) *Communication and Development: The Freirean Connection*. Hampton Press, Cresskill: NJ.

Richardson, D., Ramirez, R., and Haq, M. (2000). "Grameen telecom's village phone programme in rural Bangladesh: A multimedia case study". Ottawa, Canada: Canadian International Development Agency.

Richey, L. A. (2004) "From the Policies to the Clinics: the reproductive health paradox in post adjustment health care". In *World Development*, Vol 32.

Rifkin, S. B. (1996) "Paradigms Lost: Toward a New Understanding of Community Participation in Health Programmes". *Acta Tropica* 61, pp. 79-92.

Rivera, L. M. (2000) "Evaluación de cuatro ejes de trabajo de la Fundacion Puntos de Encuentro". Managua: Puntos de Encuentro. Evaluation of the organization.

Rivero, Y. M. (2002) "Erasing blackness: The media construction of 'race' in Mi Familia, the first Puerto Rican situation comedy with a black family". In *Media, Culture, and Society* 24, 4, pp. 481-497.

Robertson, R. (1992) *Globalization – Social Theory and Global Culture*. London: Sage.

Robins, K. and Aksoy, A. (2004) "Parting from phantoms: what is at issue in the development of transnational television from Turkey". In Friedman, J. and Randeria, S. (eds.) *Worlds on the Move: Globalisation, Migration and Cultural Security*. London: I.B. Tauris, pp. 179-206.

Robins, K. and Aksoy, A. (2001) "From spaces of identity to mental spaces: lessons from Turkish-Cypriot cultural experience in Britain". In *Journal of Ethnic and Migration Studies*, 27(4), pp. 685-711.

484 | Roche, C. (2000) "Impact Assessment for Development Agencies: Learning to Value Change". London: Oxfam.

Rockefeller Foundation (1999) "Communication for Social Change: A Position Paper and Conference Report". New York: Rockefeller Foundation.

Rodney, W. (1972) *How Europe underdeveloped Africa*. London: Bogle-L'Ouverture; Tanzania Publishing House.

Rodriguez, C. (2001a) *Fissures in the Mediascape: An International Study of Citizens' Media*. Cresskill, NJ: Hampton Press.

Rodriguez, C. (2001b) "Shattering butterflies and amazons: Symbolic constructions of women in Colombian development discourse". In *Communication Theory*, 11(4), pp. 472-494.

Rodríguez, C. (2001c) "Race, Class, and Gender in Yo Soy Betty La Fea: The National and the Transnational". A paper delivered at the Global Fusion 2001: Mass Media, Free Trade, and Alternative Responses, Saint Louis, MO, October.

Roe, K. M., Berenstein, C., Goette, C. and Roe, K. (1997) "Community Building through Empowering Evaluation: A Case Study of HIV Prevention Community Planning". In Minkler (1997), pp. 308-322.

Rogers, E. M. (1962, 1965) *Diffusion of Innovations*. NY: Free Press of Glencoe.

Rogers, E. M. (1976) "Communication and Development: The Passing of the Dominant Paradigm". In Rogers, E. M. (ed.) *Communication and Development: Critical perspectives*. Newbury Park, CA: Sage.

Rogers E. M (1987) "Communication and development today". Paper presented at the Seminar on Communication and Change 'An agenda for the new age of communication'. Honolulu, August.

Rogers, E. M. and Kincaid. D. L. (1981) *Communication networks: A paradigm for new research*. New York: Free Press.

Rogers, E. M., Vaughn, P. W., Swalehe, R. M. A., Rao, N., Svenkerud, P., and Sood, S. (1999) "Effects of an Entertainment-education Radio Soap Opera on Family Planning Behavior in Tanzania". *Studies in Family Planning* 30 (3), pp. 193-211.

Rola, A. C. and Foronda, C. A. (eds.) (2003) *New Frontiers in Research for Sustainable Development*. College, Laguna, Phil.: Institute of Strategic Planning and Policy Studies, College of Public Affairs, University of the Philippines, Los Baños.

Rouse, R. (1995) "Questions of identity: personhood and collectivity in transnational migration to the United States". In *Critique of Anthropology*, 15(4), pp. 351-380.

Rowley, K. C., Daniel, M., Skinner, K., Skinner, M., White, G. A., and O'Dea, K. (2000) "Effectiveness of a Community-directed 'Healthy Lifestyle' Program in a Remote Australian Aboriginal Community". In *Australian and New Zealand Journal of Public Health* 24 (2), pp. 136-144.

Rwebangira, M and Liljeström, R. (1998) *Haraka haraka–look before you leap. Youth at the crossroad of customs and modernity.* Uppsala: Nordic Africa Institute.

Rydhagen, B. and Trojer, L. (1998) "ICT and the role of universities-a technopolitical and post-colonial challenge". Paper presented at the International conference 'Information Technology, Transnational Democracy and Gender'. Luleå: Luleå University of Technology.

Røgilds, F. (2001) *Charlie Nielsens Rejse.* Copenhagen: Politisk Revy.

Röling, N. (1994) "Communication support for sustainable natural resource management. Knowledge is power? The use and abuse of information in development". *IDS Bulletin* 25 (2), pp. 125-133.

Röling, N. (1988) *Extension Science.* Cambridge: Cambridge University Press.

Sabido, M. (2004) "The origins of entertáinment-education". In Singhal et al (2004), pp. 61-74.

Sanchez, M., García, R., and Campos, M. (1994) "La Actitud Participativa en Salud: Entre la teoría y la práctica". Secretariado de publicaciones, Universidad de Murcia, Spain.

Sarri, R. C. and Sarri, C. M. (1992) "Organizational and Community Change through Participatory Action Research". *Administration in Social Work* 16 (3), pp. 99-122.

Scalway, T. (2002) *Critical challenges in HIV communication.* London: Panos.

Scalway. T (2003) *Missing the Message: 20 years of learning of HIV/AIDS.* London: Panos.

Sachs, W. (ed.) (1992) *The Development Dictionary. A Guide to Knowledge as Power.* London: Zed Books.

Said, E. (1978) *Orientalism.* New York: Pantheon Books.

Saunders, K. (ed.) (2003) *Feminist Post-Development Thought. Rethinking Modernity, Post-Colonialism and Representation.* London: Zed Books.

Scannell, P. (1989) "Public service broadcasting and modern public life". In *Media, Culture and Society,* 11(2), pp. 135-166.

Scannell, P. (1996) *Radio, Television and Modern Life.* Oxford: Blackwell.

Scannell, P. (2000) "For-anyone-as-someone structures". In *Media, Culture and Society,* 22(1), pp. 5-24.

Schlesinger, P. (1993) "Introduction", in Martín-Barbero (1993).

Schramm, W. (1964) *Mass Media and National Development. The Role of Information in the Developing Countries.* Stanford: Stanford University Press.

Schwarz, C., and Jaramillo, O. (1986) "Hispanic American Critical Communication Research in Its Historical Context". In Atwood, R. and McAnany, E. (eds.) *Communication and Latin American Society.* Madison, WI: The University of Wisconsin Press, pp. 48-75.

486 | Sclove, R. (1995) *Democracy and Technology.* New York: Guilford.

Sen, A. (1999) *Development as Freedom.* Oxford: Oxford University Press.

Servaes J. (1985) "Toward an alternative concepts of communication and development". In *Media and Development.* Vol. 32, No. 42-5.

Servaes, J. (1999) *Communication for Development. One world, multiple cultures.* Cresskill, N.J.: Hampton Press.

Servaes, J., Jacobson, T. L. and White, S. A. (eds.) (1996) *Participatory Communication for Social Change.* London: Sage.

Servaes, J. (ed.) (2002) *Approaches to Development: Studies on Communication for Development.* New York: UNESCO.

Sherry, J. (1997) "Prosocial Soap Operas for Development: A Review of Research and Theory". In *Journal of International Communication* 4 (2), pp. 75-101.

Shome, R. (1996) "Postcolonial interventions in the rhetorical canon: An "other" view". In *Communication Theory,* 6(1), pp. 40-59.

Singh, K. and Gross, B. (1981) "MacBride: The Report and the Response". *Journal of Communication* 31(1981) 4.

Singhal, A. and Rogers, E. M. (1989) "Educating Through Television". *Populi* 16 (2), pp. 38-47.

Singhal, A. and Rogers, E. M. (1999) *Entertainment-education: A Communication Strategy for Social Change.* Mahwah, NJ: Lawrence Earlbaum.

Singhal, A., and Svenkerud, P.J. (2001) "Harnessing information technologies for rural development: Lessons learned from the Grameen Bank in Bangladesh". Paper presented to the International Conference on Communication in a Democratic Society, Bangkok, Thailand.

Singhal, A., Svenkerud, P.J., and Flydal, E. (2002) "Multiple bottom lines: Telenor's mobile telephony operations in Bangladesh". In *Telektronikk,* 98(1), pp. 153-160.

Singhal, A. and Rogers, E. M. (2001) *India's Communication Revolution. From bullock carts to cyber marts.* New Delhi: Sage.

Singhal, A. and Rogers, E. M. (2002) "A Theoretical Agenda for Entertainment-Education". In *Communication Theory,* 12:2, pp. 117-135.

Singhal, A. and Rogers, E. M. (2003) *Combating AIDS – Communication strategies in action.* London: Sage Publications.

Singhal, A, Cody, M. J., Rogers, E. M. and Sabido, M. (eds.) (2004) *Entertainment-Education and Social Change.* Mahwah, N.J.: Lawrence Erlbaum

Singhal, A. (2004) "Entertainment-education through participatory theater: Freirean strategies for empowering the oppressed". In Singhal et al (2004).

Skare Orgeret, K. and Rönning, H. (2002) "IPDC–at a Watershed. An Evaluation of the International Programme for the Development of Communication IPDC's Structure, Organisation and Implementation". Oslo: NORAD.

Skeie, S. S. (2003) "Learning Through Entertainment. A Study of the Usage of the Entertainment-Education Strategy among Ethnic Minorities in Vietnam". Master Thesis, Faculty of Education, Institute for Educational Research, University of Oslo.

Skeie, S. S. (2005) "Entertainment-Education: Communication Strategies for Promoting a Culture of Piece". Unpublished paper.

Skelton, T. and Allen, T. (eds.) (1999) *Culture and Global Change*. London: Routledge.

Skuse, A. (2002) "Vagueness, familiarity and social realism: making meaning of radio soap opera in south eastern Afghanistan". In *Media, Culture and Society*, Vol. 24. London: Sage.

Skuse, A. (2003) "Communication, Education and HIV/AIDS. A Guidance Note". Prepared for DFID (Department for International Development, UK).

Skuse, A. (forthcoming) "Radio soap opera, gossip and social change in Afghanistan". Unpublished draft.

Slater, M. D. and Rouner, D. (2002) "Entertainment-Education and elaboration likelihood: Understanding the processing of narrative persuasion". In *Communication Theory* 12(2), pp. 173-191.

Smitasiri, S. and Dhanamitta, S. (1999) "Sustaining Behavior Change to Enhance Micronutrient Status: Community- and Women-based Interventions in Thailand". Washington, DC: ICRW.

Smith, D. (1993) "Technology and the Modern World-System: Some Reflections". In *Science, Technology and Human Values*, Vol. 18, Issue 2, pp. 186-195.

Smith, W. A. and Elder, J. (1998) *Applied behavior change*. Washington, DC: Academy for Educational Development.

Snyder, J. and Ballentine, K. (1996) "Nationalism and the Marketplace of Ideas". In *International Security*, Vol. 21, No. 2.

Sood, S., Menard, K. and Witte, K. (2004) "The Theory behind Entertainment-Education", in Singhal et al (2004), p. 118-145.

Soul City (2000) "Thoughts on Behaviour Change". Johannesburg: Soul City.

Speller V., Learmonth A. and Harrison D. (1997) "Education and debate. The search for evidence of effective health promotion". *British Medical Journal*, 9 August, pp. 315 and 361-363.

Spitulnik, D. (2002) "Alternative Small Media and Communication Spaces". In Melber, H. (ed.) *Re-examining Liberation in Namibia. Political Culture since Independence*. Stockholm: Nordiska Afrikainstitutet.

Sreberny-Mohammadi, A. (1996) "International feminism(s): Engendering debate in international communications". In *The Journal of International Communication*, 3(1), pp. 1-3.

Sreberny-Mohammadi, A. et al (eds.) (1997) *Media in Global Context. A Reader*. London: Arnold

Stald, G. and Tufte, T. (eds.) (2002) *Global Encounters: Media and Cultural Transformation*. Luton: University of Luton Press.

Starosta, W. J. (1994) "Communication and Family Planning Campaign: An Indian Experience". In Moemeka, A. A. (ed.) *Communicating for Development: A New Pan-Disciplinary. Perspective*. New York: State University of New York Press, pp. 244-260.

Staudt, K. (1985) *Women, Foreign Assistance and Advocacy Administration*. New York: Praeger.

Steeves, H. L. (2000) "Gendered Agendas: Dialogue and Impasse in Creating Social Change". In Wilkins (2000), pp. 7-26.

Stevens, G. A. (1930) "The Aesthetic Education of the Negro". In *Oversea Education*, Vol. I, No. 3.

Storey, D. J., Boulay, M., Karki, Y., Heckert, K. and Karmacharya, D. M. (1999) "Impact of the Integrated Radio Communication Project in Nepal, 1994-1997". In *Journal of Health Communication* 4, pp. 271-294.

Storey, D. J. and Jacobson, T. L. (2004) "Entertainment-education and participation: Applying Habermas to a population program in Nepal". In Singhal et al (2004), pp. 417-434.

Straubhaar, J. (1991) "Beyond Media Imperialism: Asymmetrical Interdependence and Cultural Proximity". In *Critical Studies in Mass Communication* 8, pp. 39-59.

Suarez, L., Mendivil, C. and Vega, J. (2004) "Joven habla joven: Una experiencia de comunicación y salud en una población del Caribe colombiano: Los y las jóvenes urbano/rurales, sus culturas y sus identidades alrededor de la sexualidad". *Investigación y Desarrollo*, Vol. 12, No. 1, pp. 44-77.

Svenkerud, P. J. and Singhal, A. (1998) "Enhancing the Effectiveness of HIV/AIDS Prevention Programs Targeted to Unique Population Groups in Thailand: Lessons Learned from Applying Concepts of Diffusion of Innovation and Social Marketing". In *Journal of Health Communication* 3, pp. 193-216.

Tan, F., Corbett, S. and Wong, Y. Y. (1999) *Information Technology Diffusion in the Asia Pacific: Perspectives on Policy, Electronic Commerce and Education*. London: Idea Group Publishing.

Taylor, W.H. (1933) "Observations on the Dramatic Talent of Africans". In *Oversea Education*, Vol. V, No. 1.

Teer-Tomaselli, R. (2001) "Who is the "Community" in Community Radio? A case study of community radio stations in Durban, Kwa-Zulu Natal". In Tomaselli, K.G. and Dunn, H. (eds.) *Media, Democracy and Renewal in Southern Africa*. Colorado Springs: International Academic Publishers.

Thomas, P. (1994) "Participatory development communication: Philosophical premises". In White, Nair, and Ashcroft (1994).

Thompson, J. B. (1995) *The Media and Modernity. A Social Theory of the Media*. Cambridge: Polity Press.

Thompson, M. (1999) *Forging War. The Media in Serbia, Croatia, Bosnia and Herzegovina*. Luton: University of Luton Press.

Thompson, M. and Price, M. (eds.) (2002) *Forging Peace. Intervention, human rights and the management of media space*. Edinburgh: Edinburgh University Press.

Thurow, L. (1999) *Building Wealth: The New Rules for Individuals, Companies and Nations in a Knowledge-Based Economy*. New York: Harper Collins.

Transnational Communities <http://www.transcomm.ox.ac.uk>.

Tufte, T. (1990) "Interview with Paulo Freire". Unpublished. Sao Paulo, Brazil.

Tufte, T. (1995) "How do telenovelas serve to articulate hybrid cultures in contemporary Brazil?" In *Nordicom Review*, 2, pp. 29-35.

Tufte, T. (2000) *Living with the Rubbish Queen. Telenovelas, Culture and Modernity in Brazil*. Luton: University of Luton Press.

Tufte, T. (2001) "Entertainment-Education and Participation - Assessing the Communication Strategy of Soul City". In *Journal of International Communication*. IAMCR/Macquarie University, Sydney, Vol. 7:2, pp. 25-51.

Tufte, T. (2002) "Femina Health Information Project. September 1999–January 2002. An Evaluation". Stockholm: Sida.

Tufte, T. (2003a) "Edutainment in HIV/AIDS Prevention. Building on the Soul City Experience in South Africa". In Servaes, J. (ed.) *Approaches to Development. Studies on Communication for Development*. Paris: UNESCO, Communication Development Division.

Tufte, T. (2003b) "HIV/AIDS, Globalisation and Ontological Insecurity–Key Communication Challenges in HIV/AIDS Prevention". Paper Presented at the 11th FELAFACS Conference, Puerto Rico, 4-8 October.

Tufte, T. (2004a) "Soap operas and sense making: mediations and audience ethnography". In Singhal et al (2004).

Tufte, T. (2004b) "Happy marriage or fatal attraction? Bridging paradigms, rethinking theory and improving practice: The case of HIV/AIDS Communication". Inaugural public lecture as full professor given at Roskilde University, 26 November.

Tufte, T. et al (1987) "Interview with Paulo Freire". Unpublished. Sao Paulo, Brazil.

Tunstall, J. (1977) *The Media are American. Anglo-American Media in the World*. London: Constable.

Usdin et al (2004) "No short cuts in entertainment-education: Designing Soul City step-by-step". In Singhal et al (2004), pp. 153-176.

Uimonen, P. (2001) *Transnational.dynamics@development.net: Internet, Modernization and Globalization*. Stockholm: Almqvist and Wiksell International.

Ume-Nwagbo, E. N. E. (1986) "'Cock Crow at Dawn': A Nigerian Experiment with Television Drama in Development-communication". In *Gazette* 37 (4), pp. 155-167.

490 | United Nations (2002) "Global challenge, global opportunity: Trends in sustainable development". New York: UN.

UNAIDS. Airhihenbuwa, C.O., Makina, B. Frith, M & Obregon, R. (eds.) (1999) *Communications Framework for HIV/AIDS: A new direction*. Geneva: UNAIDS.

UNESCO (2003) "Statistical Yearbook". Paris: UNESCO.

UNESCO (2003) "Basic Texts on the Information Society". Paris: UNESCO, WSIS Publications Series.

USAID (1999a) "Impact Evaluation: Promoting Primary Education for Girls in Pakistan". Washington, DC: USAIDS.

USAID (1999b) "Gender Matters: From the Ashes of War. Women and Reconstruction". Washington, DC: USAID Office of Women in Development.

USAID (2000) "Polio free by the year 2000". Washington, DC: USAID.

USAID (2004a) "Women in Development". Washington, DC: USAID.

USAID (2004b) "Women, Men, and Development". Washington, DC: USAID.

Uys, P.-D. (1996) *Truth Omissions*. London: Tricycle.

Valente, T. W. and Saba, W. P. (1998) "Mass Media and Interpersonal Influence in a Reproductive Health Communication Campaign in Bolivia". In *Communication Research* 25 (1), pp. 96-124.

Valente, T. W., Watkins, S. C., Jato, M. N., van der Straten, A. and Tsitsol, L. (1997) "Social Network Associations with Contraceptive Use among Cameroonian Women in Voluntary Associations". In *Social Science and Medicine* 45 (5), pp. 677-687.

Valente, T. W., Kim, Y. M, Lettenmaier, C., Glass, W. and Dibba, Y. (1994) "Radio Promotion of Family Planning in the Gambia". In *International Family Planning Perspectives* 20 (3), pp. 96-100.

Vaughan, P. W., Rogers, E. M., Singhal, A. and Swalehe, R. M. (2000) "Entertainment-Education and HIV/AIDS Prevention: A Field Experiment in Tanzania". In *Journal of Health Communication* 5 (Supplement), pp. 81-100.

Vaux, T. (2001) *The Selfish Altruist*. London: Earthscan.

Vega, J. and Suarez, L. (2003) "Jóvenes y Sexualidad: La experiencia de Joven Habla Joven". Paper presented at the IV International Communication Conference, Universidad del Norte, Colombia.

Visvanathan, N., Duggan, L. and Nisonoff, L. (eds.) (1997) *The Women, Gender and Development Reader*. London: Zed Books

Wade, P. (2000) *Music, Race and Nation. Música tropical en Colombia*. Chicago: The University of Chicago Press.

Waisbord, S. (2000) "Family tree of theories, methodologies, and strategies in development communication". New York: Rockefeller Foundation. Available at The Communication Initiative, <www.comminit.com/pdf/familytree.pdf>.

Waisbord, S. (2002) "State, Development, and Communication". In Gudykunst, W. and Mody, B. (eds.) *Handbook of Intercultural and International Communication*. Newbury Park, CA: Sage, pp. 437-455.

Wajcman, J. (1991) *Feminism Confronts Technology*. Cambridge: Polity Press.

Walker, T. (ed.) (1985) "Nicaragua. The First Five Years". New York: Praeger.

Wallerstein, I. (1991) *Unthinking Social Science*. Cambridge: Polity Press.

Wallerstein, N. and Sanchez-Merki, V. (1994) "Freirian Praxis in Health Education: Research Results from an Adolescent Prevention Program". In *Health Education Research* 9 (1), pp. 105-118.

Wallerstein, N., Sanchez-Merki, V. and Dow, L. (1997) "Freirian Praxis in Health Education and Community Organizing: A Case Study of an Adolescent Prevention Program". In Minkler (1997), pp. 195-211.

Wang, C. and Burris, M. A. (1994) "Empowerment through Photo Novella: Portraits of Participation". In *Health Education Quarterly* 21(2), pp. 171-86.

Warnock, K. (2002) "Reducing Poverty: is the World Bank's strategy working?" London: Panos.

Weiss, E. and Gupta, G. R. (1998) "Bridging the Gap: Addressing Gender and Sexuality in HIV Prevention". Washington DC: ICRW.

Westoff, C. F. and Rodríguez, G. (1995) "Mass Media and Family Planning in Kenya". In *International Family Planning Perspectives* 21 (1), pp 26-31, 36.

Whelan, D. (1998) *Recasting WID: A Human Rights Approach*. Washington DC: ICRW.

White, S. A., Nair, K. S. and Ascroft, J. (1994) *Participatory Communication: Working for Change and Development*. New Delhi, Thousand Oaks, London: Sage.

White, S. A. (ed.) (1999) *The art of facilitating participation: releasing the power of grassroots communication*. New Delhi: Sage.

Wilkins, K. G. (1991) "Development Communication Interpretations in Organizational Contexts". Unpublished Dissertation. University of Pennsylvania.

Wilkins, K. G. (1997) "Gender, Power and Development". In *The Journal of International Communication* 4(2), pp 102-120.

Wilkins, K. G. (1999) "Development Discourse on Gender and Communication in Strategies for Social Change". In *Journal of Communication* 49(1), pp. 44-64.

Wilkins, K. G. (2000) "Accounting for Power in Development Communication". In Wilkins (2000), pp. 197-210.

Wilkins, K. G. (ed.) (2000) *Redeveloping Communication for Social Change: Theory, Practice and Power*. Boulder: Rowman and Littlefield.

492 | Wilkins, K. G. and Mody, B. (2001) "Reshaping development communication: Developing communication and communicating development". In *Communication Theory*, 11(4), pp. 1-11.

"Working with the Media in Conflicts and Other Emergencies" (2000) London: DFID. Available under publications on <www.dfid.gov.uk/>.

World Commission on Environment and Development (1987) "Our Common Future". Oxford and New York: Oxford University Press.

WHO (1978) "Declaration of Alma-Ata". International Conference on Primary Health Care, Alma-Ata, USSR, 6-12 September.
<http://www.who.int/hpr/NPH/docs/declaration_almaata.pdf>.

WHO/UNICEF (1978) "Primary Health Care". Alma Ata 1978. Health for All Series No.1.

WHO (1989) "Call for Action. Promoting Health for Developing Countries". Geneva: WHO.

WHO (1999) TB Advocacy. <www.who.int/gtb/publications/TBAdvocacy/>.

WHO (2002) "Scaling up the response to infectious diseases".
<www.who.int/infectious-disease-report/2002/goingtoscale.html>.

WSIS (2003) "Civil Society Declaration to the World Summit on the Information Society, 'Shaping Information Societies for Human Needs'". Adopted by the WSIS Civil Society Plenary on 8 December.

Wright, A. L., Naylor, A. Wester, R., Bauer, M. and Sutcliffe, E. (1997) "Using Cultural Knowledge in Health Promotion: Breastfeeding among the Navajo". In *Health Education and Behavior* 24 (5), pp. 625-639.

Xin, R. (2003) *Hidden Voices: the good women of China*. New York: Vintage.

Yoder, P. S., Hornik, R. and Chirwa, B. C. (1996) "Evaluating the Program Effects of a Radio Drama about AIDS in Zambia". In *Studies in Family Planning* 27 (4), pp 188-203.

Yoder, P. S., Zheng, Z. and Zhou, F. (1991) "Results of the HEALTHCOM Evaluation in Zaire Lubumbashi, 1988-1990". Center for International, Health, and Development Communication Working Paper 1010. Annenberg School for Communication, University of Pennsylvania.

Yoon, C.S. (1996) "Participatory Communication for Development". In Bessette and Rajasunderam (1996).

Yunus, M. (1999) *Banker to the poor: Micro-lending and the battle against world poverty*. New York: Public Affairs.

Yunus, M. (1998) "Alleviating poverty through technology". In *Science*, 282, pp. 409-410.

de Zalduondo, B.O. (2001) "Second Generation HIV/AIDS Communication: Applying Lessons Learned". Presentation to USAID, Washington.

Zimicki, S., Hornik, R., Verzosa, C. C., Hernandez, J. R., de Guzman, E., Dayrit, M., Fausto, A., Lee, M. B. and Abad, M. (1994) "Improving Vaccination

Coverage in Urban Areas through a Health Communication Campaign: The 1990 Philippine Experience". In *Bulletin of the World Health Organization* 72 (3), pp 409-422.

Este libro se terminó de imprimir en el
taller de Gráficas y Servicios S.R.L.
Santa María del Buen Aire 347
en el mes de septiembre de 2005.
Primera impresión, 1.500 ejemplares.

Printed in Argentina